WORLD TRAVEL ATLAS

ISBN: 1–902221–56–7

© 2002 Columbus Publishing, except where marked*

* Information for the Skiing & Snowboarding maps on pages 61 and 146 © 2001 Snow24 plc.
* Information for the Human Rights map on page 17 © 1999 The Observer.

Columbus Publishing, Jordan House, 47 Brunswick Place, London N1 6EB, United Kingdom
Tel: +44 (0)20 7608 6666 • Fax: +44 (0)20 7608 6569 • E-mail: booksales@columbus-group.co.uk

Cartographic Editor: David Burles.

Production Editor: Brian Quinn of Space Design & Production Services Ltd, London EC2.

Additional Cartography: James Anderson, Jane Voss, Iorwerth Watkins & Pam Alford of Anderson Geographics, Amersham.

Contributors: Patrick Fitzgerald, Tony Peisley, Patrick Thorne, Graham Lowing, Jon Gillaspie, Ruth Blakeborough, Ned Middleton, Dave Richardson, Lynda Anderson, Alan Mais, Sachiko Burles.

Continental Introductions: Graham Lowing & Brian Quinn.

Cover Design: Warren Evans of Space Design & Production Services Ltd, London EC2.

Colour Proofing: Kingswood Steele, London EC2.

Distribution Managers: Emma Charge, Helen Argent, David Bonner (Columbus Publishing, London); Michael Knopp (Columbus Publishing, Germany); David Frank, Amanda Schaal (SF Travel Publications, USA).

Printed by: Excelprint, Hadleigh, Suffolk.

Founding Editor: Mike Taylor of the University of Brighton.

Publisher: Pete Korniczky.

This publication has been created from a wide range of sources, and where appropriate these have been credited on the relevant maps, charts or articles. The publishers would like to thank all the organisations and individuals who have helped in the preparation of this edition, with particular thanks to Greenpeace International's Political and Science Department in Amsterdam; Karen Davies of UNEP; Andrea Stueve of TIA; The Observer; The Travel Industry World Yearbook; Snow24 plc; IATA; Eileen Hook of California Tourism; UNESCO; Justin Percival; Jonathan Vernon-Powell of Nomadic Thoughts; Chris Clack; Dan Josty; Penny Locke; Kate Meere; Charlotte Evans; Andy Steele, Oliver Bowdridge and Simon Jones of Kingswood Steele; Alan Horsfield of EMG; John Doyle and Lisa Wellesley of Resolution.

The publishers welcome comments as to how future editions could be improved still further. Many of the changes made to this edition have been suggested by users of the book: your response will, therefore, be influential.

For more information on • ordering additional copies • bulk purchase rates • overseas rates and distributors • overbranded editions • content licensing • cartographic commissions • please contact the publishers at the above address.

Contents

KEY TO TOPOGRAPHIC MAPS

Communications

✈ Airport *main international gateways and domestic hubs*

—— ----- Main road, motorway • Road in tunnel

—o— ----- Main passenger railway, with station • Railway in tunnel

—— Dedicated high-speed rail line *focus maps only*

------------ Ferry route *selected passenger routes: focus maps only*

Boundaries & boxes

—·—·— International boundary

---------- Disputed international boundary

— — — Internal administrative boundary

—— National park, game reserve

▭ Area featured in a focus map

Settlement

● ● ○ ○ ○ Towns and cities *size of dot is determined by population; largest symbol indicates a city with over one million inhabitants*

■ ■ □ □ National capital *named in CAPITAL LETTERS*

Built-up area *larger scale focus maps only*

∴ ⌂ Archaeological site, ancient ruins • Important building/s (e.g castle, temple)

◆ Other place of interest (e.g. park, reserve, natural feature, small settlement)

Physical features (see individual map pages for elevation tints)

△ ▽ Mountain peak • Land depression *with altitude in metres*

= Pass, canyon *with altitude in metres*

River, with waterfall, with dam • Seasonal river

Lake • Seasonal lake

—— Canal

Coral reef

World

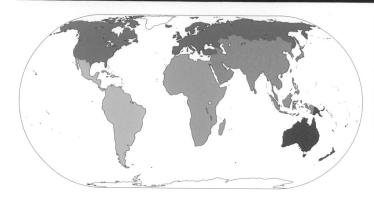

GNI figures relate to 1999. Population figures are taken from the most recent census or reliable estimate. Travel figures (from the WTO) are generally for 1999, but where these are unavailable or unreliable, figures from earlier years have been used. All travel figures are based on overnight stays, not same-day visitors. Where data for certain countries was not available, this has been regarded as zero. Global totals for Visitor Arrivals/Travel Departures and Visitor Receipts/Travel Expenditure do not equal each other due to differing methods of reporting inbound and outbound data. For more information on what is regarded as a country for the purposes of this book, and for more detailed statistical information, please see the Countries A-Z section from page 184.

Key facts

Number of Countries	226
Area ('000 sq km)	135,463
Population ('000)	5,973,801
Population Density (/sq km)	44
Gross Nat. Income (US$m)	29,986,364
Visitor Arrivals ('000)	649,223
Visitor Receipts (US$m)	456,402
Travel Departures ('000)	594,797
Travel Expenditure (US$m)	397,040

Information on the six continents into which, for the purposes of this book, the world has been divided may be found on the following pages:

- Europe: 46-47
- Africa: 102-103
- Asia: 114-115
- Australasia & Oceania: 132-133
- USA & Canada: 140-141
- Latin America & the Carribbean: 162-163

I N 1999, international travel and tourism receipts (not including international air fares) were over US$450 billion, roughly 1.5% of the world's GNI of US$30 trillion. According to many estimates (which include the indirect economic benefits) the figure is far larger. The number of jobs directly or indirectly supported by this activity in incalculable. Yet despite its importance, it is a fragile industry, depending crucially on economic prosperity and political stability. It has the advantages of being a global product, but all the manifest disadvantages – particularly in times of uncertainty – of being both non-essential and expensive. Yet the travel business has weathered every storm to date. Since 1950, international visitor arrivals have risen some 26-fold, with every year except 1982 setting a new record. The appetite for foreign travel, the means to pay for it and the choice of destinations all appeared to be capable of ever-increasing and ever-profitable expansion. Warnings of the dangers of over-development and unsustainability have led to what might be termed a more ethical approach in some parts of the industry, but have done little to halt the upward trend. Even wars, terrorism and recession – all regional in scope and limited in time – have caused little more than blips. The events of 11 September 2001 and the threat of global recession present the international travel trade with its sternest test yet. The question is not whether the industry will survive in its present form, but rather what its new form will be. Its delicate economics, and all its traditional assumptions, strategies and alliances, have now come sharply into focus.

That said, there are several points of optimism. Many previous challenges – the Oil Crisis, Lockerbie and the Gulf War, to pick but three – have been overcome. Despite new communication technology, the need for business travel remains strong. Many (but by no means all) countries attract a large number of visitors from neighbouring states, an 'inter-domestic' market that is often less volatile than a long-haul one. Crises often produce as many winners as losers, as the respective fortunes of EasyJet and BA in late 2001 have shown. Above all, the habit of travel has become widespread and ingrained. It remains the only business where customers are happy to travel thousands of miles to buy a product, sight unseen. Hundreds of millions of people will continue to do so. Yet many uncertainties remain. Of these, perhaps the two most acute concern the futures of the aviation industry and of the US outbound travel market.

Of all the uncomfortable truths that face the airline business, two of the more obvious perhaps bear repetition. Firstly, there are few cost savings in flying an empty plane as opposed to a full one; secondly, an empty seat on a particular flight can never subsequently be sold. As a result, the pursuit of volume and market share here assume greater importance than in many other industries. On this level, 2000 was successful. IATA's figures for international flights show passengers up by 9% on 1999, the biggest rise since 1992: passenger loads also increased, by 2.2%. Key regions performed strongly, including Europe (9.5%) and the North Atlantic (4.9%), while Latin America rose by a remarkable 18%, reversing 1999's 7% decline. The world economy was booming, and further growth seemed assured.

Yet there is a gloomier side to the picture, for neither revenues nor profits could match this increase in passengers. 2000 corporate results showed airline profits falling to US$4 billion against 1999's US$6.2 billion: still a vast sum, but one that represents a margin of only 1.3%. Since 1998, the growth in airline passengers has tended to be between 1.5 and 2.5 times greater than the growth in world GDP, with the exception of the period of the Gulf War. After this conflict, passenger numbers soon revived; but significantly, profitability did not return to 1989 levels until 1995. Yields (operating revenue per km) have also been declining steadily since 1992. Cost-cutting, an obvious solution to all this, proved ineffective in 2000 (a fall of just 0.1%): partly because the increase in operating revenue had by now dropped below that of inflation; partly because of rising fuel prices in 1999/2000. Delay congestion costs also took their toll. Overstaffing seemed not to be the problem, for 2000 saw the lowest increase in employee numbers since 1994. Nor were the staff shirking: by IATA's measure of revenue-km/employee, productivity increased by 6.9% in 2000 over 1999.

■ Visitor arrivals

The world's 25 most visited countries in 1999 (millions)
Source: WTO

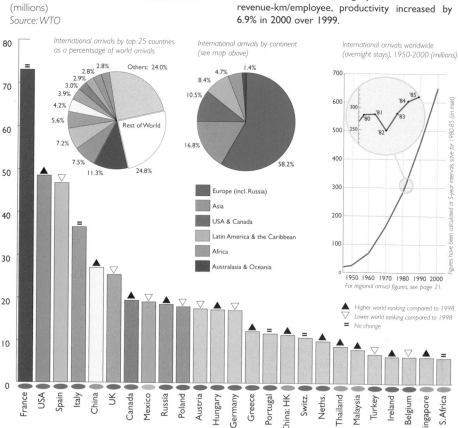

International arrivals by top 25 countries as a percentsage of world arrivals

International arrivals by continent (see map above)

International arrivals worldwide (overnight stays), 1950-2000 (millions)

- ■ Europe (incl. Russia)
- ■ Asia
- ■ USA & Canada
- ■ Latin America & the Caribbean
- ■ Africa
- ■ Australasia & Oceania

▲ Higher world ranking compared to 1998
▽ Lower world ranking compared to 1998
= No change

For regional arrival figures, see page 21.

Figures have been calculated at 5-year intervals, save for 1980-85 (on inset)

- In economic terms, international travel and tourism receipts are classified as exports, and international tourism expenditure as imports. According to the World Tourism Organisation's (WTO's) Tourism Economic Report (1998), travel and tourism is one of the top five export categories for 83% of countries and the main source of foreign currency for 38% of them.
- In 1998, according to figures produced by the WTO in conjunction with the World Trade Organisation and the International Monetary Fund, international travel and tourism and international transport costs accounted for US$532billion, around 8% of all export earnings on goods and services worldwide and more than any other trade category.
- According to Air Transport World (July 2001), in 2000 the world's 523 airlines flew a total of 1.8 billion passengers and a total of 3.25 trillion Revenue Passenger Kms (RPKs). Over 38% of passengers and over 35% of RPKs were on US-registered airlines: Europe's respective figures were 29.6% and 31%.
- IATA's league table of the world's largest airlines by passenger numbers in 2000 contains the same carriers in the top 25 as in 1999 and 1998.
- With the exception of 1982, international visitor receipts and international departures have grown in every year since 1950.
- 17 countries received over 10 million international visitors in 1999. 53 others received over 1 million.
- 16 countries supplied more than 10 million international travellers in 1999. 39 others supplied more than 1 million.
- 9 countries received in excess of US$10billion from international travel in 1999. 48 others received in excess of US$1billion.
- 10 countries spent in excess of US$10billion on international travel in 1999. 36 others spent in excess of US$1billion.
- Every continent saw visitor numbers rise in 1999 compared to 1998.
- The biggest travellers, the Germans, have, on average, 35 vacation days a year: nationals of the USA, second place in the travellers' league, have only 13.
- Over 40 countries (including France, Hong Kong (China), Portugal, Greece, Singapore and most of the islands in the Caribbean) receive annually more visitors than their population. In a further 20 cases (including Canada, Italy, Tunisia, the Netherlands and the Czech Republic) the annual visitor total is in excess of 50% of the population.
- More people are killed on the roads of the USA in six months than have been in all commercial aviation accidents since 1960.
- Each day in 1999, some 7,000 pieces of luggage going through the US domestic network were temporarily or (more rarely) permanently lost. Of these 2.5 million bags, some 30,000 were never reunited with their owners and were auctioned off.
- The WTO predicts that international travel arrivals will exceed 1.5 billion by 2020. Of these, 25% will be intraregional and the remainder long-haul. In the period 1995-2020, long-haul travel is predicted to grow at a faster rate than intraregional travel: 5.4% as opposed to 3.8%.
- And finally, a few warnings from some other travellers; against, for example, companions:
  'Ain't no surer way to find out whether you like people of hate them than to travel with them.' (Mark Twain);
  ...luggage:
  'He who would travel happily must travel light.' (Antoine de Saint-Exupéry);
  ...cameras:
  'Travel is a strategy for accumulating photographs.' (Susan Sontag);
  ...and ignorance:
  'In travelling, a man must carry some knowledge with him, if he would bring any home.' (Samuel Johnson).
  Let the final word come from Sa'di, the 13th century Persian poet: *'Roam abroad in the world and take your fill of its enjoyments, before the day comes when you must leave it for good...'*

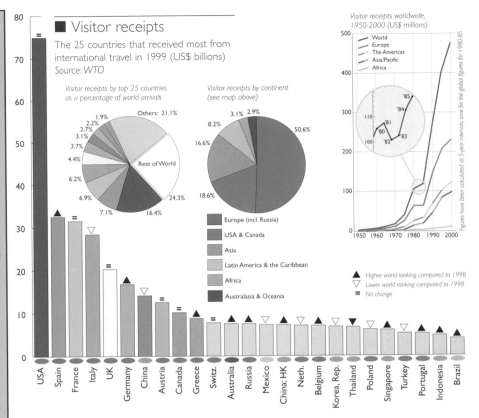

■ Visitor receipts

The 25 countries that received most from international travel in 1999 (US$ billions)
Source: WTO

Visitor receipts by top 25 countries as a percentage of world arrivals

Others: 21.1%
1.9%
2.2%
2.7%
3.1%
3.7%
4.4%
6.2%
6.9%
7.1%
16.4%
24.3%
Rest of World

Visitor receipts by continent (see map above)

3.1% 2.9%
8.2%
16.6%
18.6%
50.6%

Europe (incl. Russia)
USA & Canada
Asia
Latin America & the Caribbean
Africa
Australasia & Oceania

Visitor receipts worldwide, 1950-2000 (US$ millions)
World
Europe
The Americas
Asia/Pacific
Africa

Figures have been calculated at 5-year intervals, save for the global figures for 1980-85

▲ Higher world ranking compared to 1998
▽ Lower world ranking compared to 1998
= No change

(Bar chart countries:) USA, Spain, France, Italy, UK, Germany, China, Austria, Canada, Greece, Switz., Australia, Russia, Mexico, China: HK, Neth., Belgium, Korea. Rep., Thailand, Poland, Singapore, Turkey, Portugal, Indonesia, Brazil

And then, in 2001, even the volume came under threat, particularly for the majors; and particularly transatlantic routes, which have often suffered from an over-capacity. With their key markets in danger, many large airlines made further attempts to slash jobs and rationalise their fleets. For Swissair and Sabena, even this was not enough. With many previously profitable regional markets already lost to the low-cost airlines, and with the added challenge in Europe of the burgeoning high-speed rail services eating into their still-lucrative short-break and business travel sales, the future for many long-established big players is uncertain. The pointers are for a period of rationalisation, with global mergers creating a smaller number of super-carriers.

Even before the terrorist attacks, the industry's situation was thus one of having more passengers, serviced by proportionately fewer staff, but producing less profit; of inflationary pressure thwarting cost-cutting; of falling yields and margins; of fierce competition in key sectors; and of the darkening threat of a slowdown in global GDP. In retrospect, the crisis of confidence which followed the events of 11 September may not prove the biggest problem the industry has to face.

Of the world's travellers, none are such inveterate flyers as the North Americans. With distances so great and the long-distance rail network so poor, air travel has become a linchpin of American society. The USA has over 18,000 airports. Seven out of the eight largest domestic IATA airlines in the world are US-registered; these seven carried over 400 million passengers between them in 2000. Tighter security procedures may deter some internal flyers, and will also be a constant reminder that air travel is more hazardous, more irksome and (almost certainly) more expensive than previously. This will do little to help overseas destinations in their efforts to woo North American visitors, on whose regular presence so many of their businesses and, in some cases,

national economies, depend. A mixture of prudence and patriotism may encourage more Americans to spend their vacations enjoying the diverse attractions offered by their own country.

Despite such challenges, the global travel industry showed many signs of resilience from Autumn 2001. Times of change encourage the questioning of old assumptions and habits, and offer opportunities for those offering new and exciting travel options. Above all, it must be borne in mind that the underlying trend towards growth is very strong.

Underlying trends
Since 1950, the annual average growth rate of international visitor arrivals has dropped below 4% in only one five-year period (1980-85). For several years, including 2000, every region of the world has shown a growth in international visitor arrivals. In 2000, the World Tourism Organisation (WTO) predicted a more moderate pace of growth for 2001, reflecting the view that 2000's strong global economic performance was unlikely to be bettered. Despite this, and recent events, many forecasts indicate that total visitor arrival figures for 2001 will still see an increase over 2000 and be comfortably in excess of 700 million.

Europe and North America remain the most popular regions. What is encouraging for the global health of the industry is that, while these are still increasing, arrivals to other regions – notably East Asia – are growing at a far faster pace. The WTO's *Tourism 2020 Vision* forecasts that global international arrivals are likely to exceed 1.5 billion by 2020. Under this model, Europe and America will remain the most visited regions, but with a diminished market share.

The world leaders in the travel numbers league seem to have their positions assured. By some margin, the French receive the most visitors, the Germans travel the most and the Americans spend

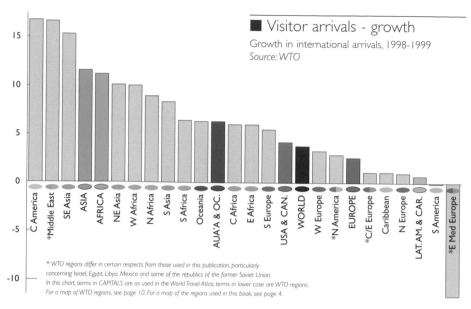

■ Visitor arrivals - growth

Growth in international arrivals, 1998-1999
Source: WTO

*: WTO regions differ in certain respects from those used in this publication, particularly concerning Israel, Egypt, Libya, Mexico and some of the republics of the former Soviet Union. In this chart, terms in CAPITALS are as used in the World Travel Atlas; terms in lower case are WTO regions. For a map of WTO regions, see page 10. For a map of the regions used in this book, see page 4.

and receive the most money; this despite their having only around one third of the annual vacation days of many European countries. The most significant medium-term development is likely to be the emergence of China, not only as a destination but also as a source of travellers.

Travel remains something of an exclusive club: the 10 most visited countries accounted for over 50% of all tourist arrivals in 1999. It is also something of a crowded one: in nearly one-fifth of the world's countries the annual visiting population exceeds the native one, on occasions by a factor of more than 10.

Future trends
For those willing to travel, there will be many bargains to be had. From theme parks to business hotel rooms, supply has recently outstripped demand. Package holidays remain a mainstay of the global market but an increasingly aware clientele is looking for deals. Europeans in particular are masters in searching for sunshine and ski holiday bargains through TV, newspapers ads – and, of course, the internet.

Changing lifestyles are also continuing to have their effects on travel patterns. A healthier outlook to fitness and the ever-younger early retirement opportunities in Europe and the US in particular have bred a customer base that is far more active than many previous generations. This has already worked to the advantage of many parts of the world with less developed traditional tourism infrastructures, particularly in Central America and in parts of Africa and South East Asia.

Partly because of this, activity and special-interest holidays also seem set to increase yet further in popularity. The rain forests of South and Central America, the jungles of Asia, the mountains of Europe and the deserts of Australia and North Africa all have their dangers, both natural and man-made: yet this has not deterred the hikers, bikers, trekkers, campers, skiers and snowboarders that now span the widest possible generations gaps. Traditional beach holidays, though still popular, are increasingly being replaced or augmented by trips which contain at least an element of something more intellectually or physically stimulating. The recent growth in city breaks (particularly in Europe) and theme park visits (particularly in North America) are examples of this.

It is worth briefly considering two established – and highly successful – special-interest holiday types: cruising and winter sports. Despite in neither case being cheap holiday options, with growths of around 500% and around 300% respectively since 1980, both have performed very well in attracting new customers; both are also well able to retain existing ones. It is, however, perhaps, winter sports – with its larger, younger, more active and more geographically dispersed market – that chimes the better with the mood of the times. Both sectors seem well set for future growth, but in both cases more choice is being demanded by consumers as part of a package. A recent survey conducted by

Snow24 indicated that increasing emphasis is being placed on the quality of accommodation (particularly in Europe) and on the range of other activities available. In this regard, it is worth noting the growth of tailor-made holidays generally: still something of a niche market for those prepared to spend the time and money on creating an ideal holiday, but indicative of growing consumer discrimination. Success is likely to go to those companies that react best to this.

The world is filling up: will space be the next frontier? Some companies are predicting a viable industry by 2020. The key question for the travel trade, as the *Travel Industry World Yearbook* dryly observes, will be 'is it commissionable?'

Environmental issues
One issue that has affected all parts of the travel industry is that of the environment. All forms of travel have an impact on the planet, as do the creation and maintenance of what visitors expect on arrival: while travellers' impact on the societies with which they come into contact with has not always been beneficial. All sectors have been forced to become more aware of the effects of their transient presence. Sustainable tourism has long been a goal for the travel industry yet, despite many and various attempts, it has never quite come off. Eventually, the benefits will be felt by all; but in the short-term, there has been much squabbling as to what regulations there should be, who should enforce them and – most pressingly – who should pay for it all. From the Balearics to the Seychelles, recent attempts to pass on often fairly minor 'eco-taxes' have collapsed in the face of opposition from tour operators already operating on very tight margins.

■ Visitor expenditure

The 25 countries whose residents spent the most on international travel in 1999 (US$ billions)
Source: WTO

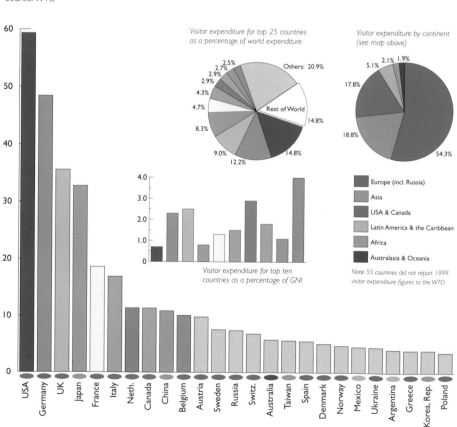

Visitor expenditure for top 25 countries as a percentage of world expenditure

Others: 20.9%
Rest of World
2.5%
2.7%
2.9%
2.9%
4.3%
4.7%
8.3%
9.0%
12.2%
14.8%
14.8%

Visitor expenditure by continent (see map above)

2.1% 1.9%
5.1%
17.8%
18.8%
54.3%

Visitor expenditure for top ten countries as a percentage of GNI

Europe (incl. Russia)
Asia
USA & Canada
Latin America & the Caribbean
Africa
Australasia & Oceania

Note: 55 countries did not report 1999 visitor expenditure figures to the WTO

World: Introduction

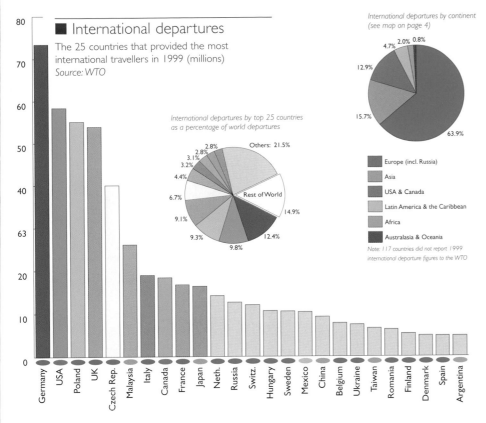

International departures
The 25 countries that provided the most international travellers in 1999 (millions)
Source: WTO

International departures by top 25 countries as a percentage of world departures

Others: 21.5%
2.8%
2.8%
3.1%
3.2%
4.4%
6.7%
9.1%
9.3%
9.8%
12.4%
14.9%

Rest of World

International departures by continent (see map on page 4)

0.8%
2.0%
4.7%
12.9%
15.7%
63.9%

- Europe (incl. Russia)
- Asia
- USA & Canada
- Latin America & the Caribbean
- Africa
- Australasia & Oceania

Note: 117 countries did not report 1999 international departure figures to the WTO

Countries (bar chart): Germany, USA, Poland, UK, Czech Rep., Malaysia, Italy, Canada, France, Japan, Neth., Russia, Switz., Hungary, Sweden, Mexico, China, Belgium, Ukraine, Taiwan, Romania, Finland, Denmark, Spain, Argentina

much some may deplore this development, it evinces English's powerful flexibility which no other major language can match.

Conclusion
Without doubt the travel industry is in a time of transposition, from the confident major key of recent years to one of a more uncertain character. The strong growth of the late 1990s appears to be slowing (although slower growth is, of course, still growth). Many long established names are under threat. Traditional travel patterns, while not being swept away, are being reappraised. Environmental concerns are looming larger in travellers' priorities. New technology is providing new expectations, new solutions and new problems. Travellers are becoming more discriminating and more demanding. The events of 11 September served to bring many of these already-present trends into sharp focus. The industry is vast, well-established and truly global, and most signs indicate that the process of adaptation has already begun. The results will be a travel business that is fitter and stronger. In the short-term at least, it will probably be somewhat leaner as well.

In view of its dominance of the global travel economy, perhaps the last words should come from a citizen of the United States. 'Change is the law of life,' President John F Kennedy observed, speaking in Frankfurt in June 1963. 'Those who look only to the past or the present are certain to miss the future.' Indeed.

Maps, charts and statistics on general global themes follow on pages 8 to 45. See also the *Countries A-Z* section from page 184, and the *Index* from page 193.

Thanks to: Patrick Thorne; Tony Peisley; Dave Richardson; Patrick Fitzgerald; IATA.

The challenge for each company in the travel industry is whether it is prepared to not only go 'green' but also to promote it, with any extra costs as a necessary evil; while, at the same time, ensuring that it does not as a result lose more customers – and revenue – than it gains.

Worldwide, hotels are washing towels less frequently and switching to low-wattage bulbs. Car hire firms are investigating alternative fuel sources as well as buying low-emission vehicles and even battery-powered versions for city use. Sports clubs are watering their golf courses twice a week rather than once a day. Every little helps. The World Wide Fund for Nature has posed the question to the industry: 'Other companies have to pay for what they pollute; why should tourism be different?'

E-commerce
A survey conducted by Energis in June 2001 among 250 European e-commerce strategists concluded that travel is the sector most likely to show the biggest growth in on-line sales. The WTO agreed, predicting in November 2001 that by 2006 more than 25% of travel bookings would be electronic. Particularly since the advent of CRS systems in the 1980s, the travel trade has been used to accessing electronic booking and availability data itself: the reverse trend, that of providing its own information to clients, has developed rather more fitfully. A survey carried out by Equinus in association with ABTA in May 2001 (as reported by Paul Richer of Genesys, writing in *TTG*) concluded that while two thirds of UK travel companies have websites, 'very few have price information, let alone product availability or on-line booking capability.' Without such facilities, many expensively constructed sites are thus little more than free information services.

The Internet is an unrivalled source of immediate (though often confusing) information. According to the Travel Industry Association of America, around

one third of Americans get their holiday ideas from electronic sources. From this, it is a short step to making bookings directly. As public confidence in on-line payment grows, the travel trade runs the risk of being cut out of the loop altogether.

Finally, it is worth mentioning that the growth of on-line sales and information is likely to be good news for English and the 420 million or so people who speak it as a mother tongue. 'e-mail English' is, according to some purists, already moving towards being a written dialect of the language. However

Leading airlines
The 25 world's top 25 airlines by passengers flown in 2000 (millions)
Source: IATA, World Air Transport Statistics

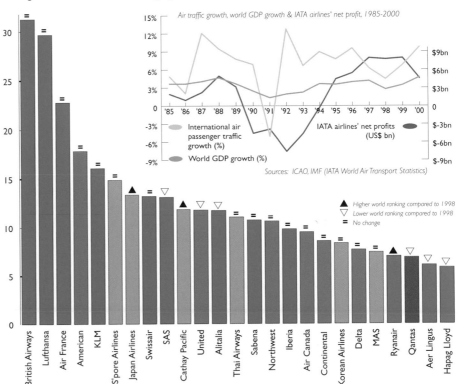

Air traffic growth, world GDP growth & IATA airlines' net profit, 1985-2000

International air passenger traffic growth (%)
World GDP growth (%)
IATA airlines' net profits (US$ bn)

Sources: ICAO, IMF (IATA World Air Transport Statistics)

▲ Higher world ranking compared to 1998
▽ Lower world ranking compared to 1998
= No change

Airlines: British Airways, Lufthansa, Air France, American, KLM, S'pore Airlines, Japan Airlines, Swissair, SAS, Cathay Pacific, United, Alitalia, Thai Airways, Sabena, Northwest, Iberia, Air Canada, Continental, Korean Airlines, Delta, MAS, Ryanair, Qantas, Aer Lingus, Hapag Lloyd

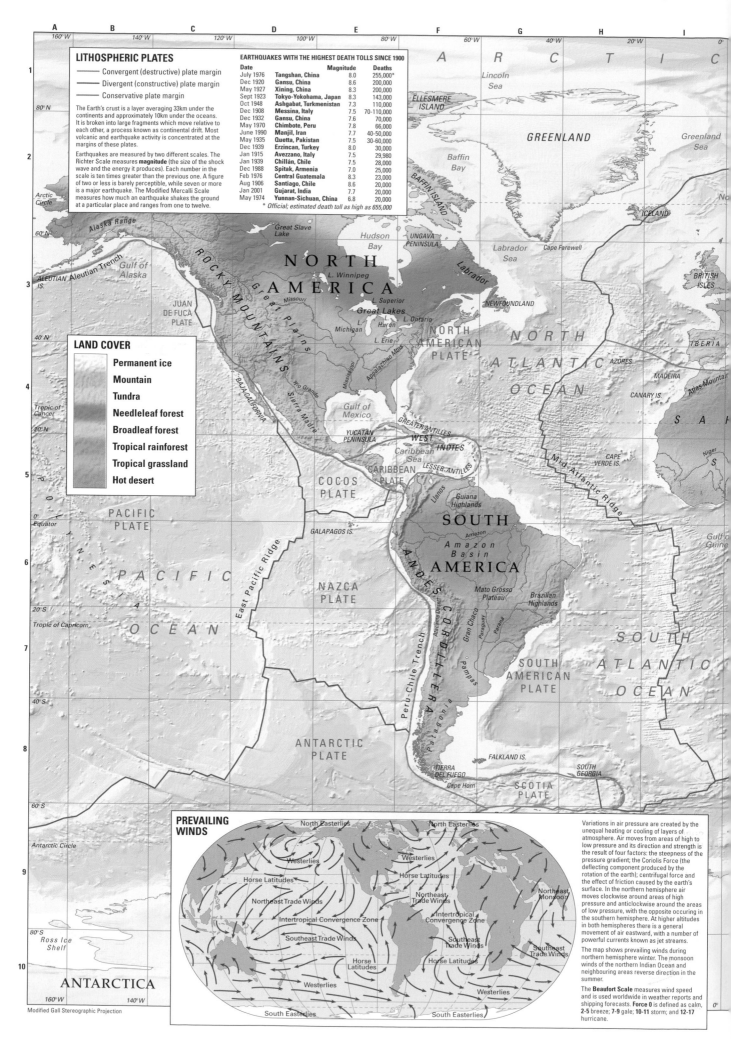

LITHOSPHERIC PLATES

— Convergent (destructive) plate margin
— Divergent (constructive) plate margin
— Conservative plate margin

The Earth's crust is a layer averaging 33km under the continents and approximately 10km under the oceans. It is broken into large fragments which move relative to each other, a process known as continental drift. Most volcanic and earthquake activity is concentrated at the margins of these plates.

Earthquakes are measured by two different scales. The Richter Scale measures **magnitude** (the size of the shock wave and the energy it produces). Each number in the scale is ten times greater than the previous one. A figure of two or less is barely perceptible, while seven or more is a major earthquake. The Modified Mercalli Scale measures how much an earthquake shakes the ground at a particular place and ranges from one to twelve.

EARTHQUAKES WITH THE HIGHEST DEATH TOLLS SINCE 1900

Date		Magnitude	Deaths
July 1976	Tangshan, China	8.0	255,000*
Dec 1920	Gansu, China	8.6	200,000
May 1927	Xining, China	8.3	200,000
Sept 1923	Tokyo-Yokohama, Japan	8.3	143,000
Oct 1948	Ashgabat, Turkmenistan	7.3	110,000
Dec 1908	Messina, Italy	7.5	70-110,000
Dec 1932	Gansu, China	7.6	70,000
May 1970	Chimbote, Peru	7.8	66,000
June 1990	Manjil, Iran	7.7	40-50,000
May 1935	Quetta, Pakistan	7.5	30-60,000
Dec 1939	Erzincan, Turkey	8.0	30,000
Jan 1915	Avezzano, Italy	7.5	29,980
Jan 1939	Chillán, Chile	7.5	28,000
Dec 1988	Spitak, Armenia	7.0	25,000
Feb 1976	Central Guatemala	7.5	23,000
Aug 1906	Santiago, Chile	8.6	20,000
Jan 2001	Gujarat, India	7.7	20,000
May 1974	Yunnan-Sichuan, China	6.8	20,000

* Official; estimated death toll as high as 655,000

LAND COVER

- Permanent ice
- Mountain
- Tundra
- Needleleaf forest
- Broadleaf forest
- Tropical rainforest
- Tropical grassland
- Hot desert

PREVAILING WINDS

Variations in air pressure are created by the unequal heating or cooling of layers of atmosphere. Air moves from areas of high to low pressure and its direction and strength is the result of four factors: the steepness of the pressure gradient; the Coriolis Force (the deflecting component produced by the rotation of the earth); centrifugal force and the effect of friction caused by the earth's surface. In the northern hemisphere air moves clockwise around areas of high pressure and anticlockwise around the areas of low pressure, with the opposite occuring in the southern hemisphere. At higher altitudes in both hemispheres there is a general movement of air eastward, with a number of powerful currents known as jet streams.

The map shows prevailing winds during northern hemisphere winter. The monsoon winds of the northern Indian Ocean and neighbouring areas reverse direction in the summer.

The **Beaufort Scale** measures wind speed and is used worldwide in weather reports and shipping forecasts. **Force 0** is defined as calm, **2-5** breeze; **7-9** gale; **10-11** storm; and **12-17** hurricane.

Modified Gall Stereographic Projection

Physical

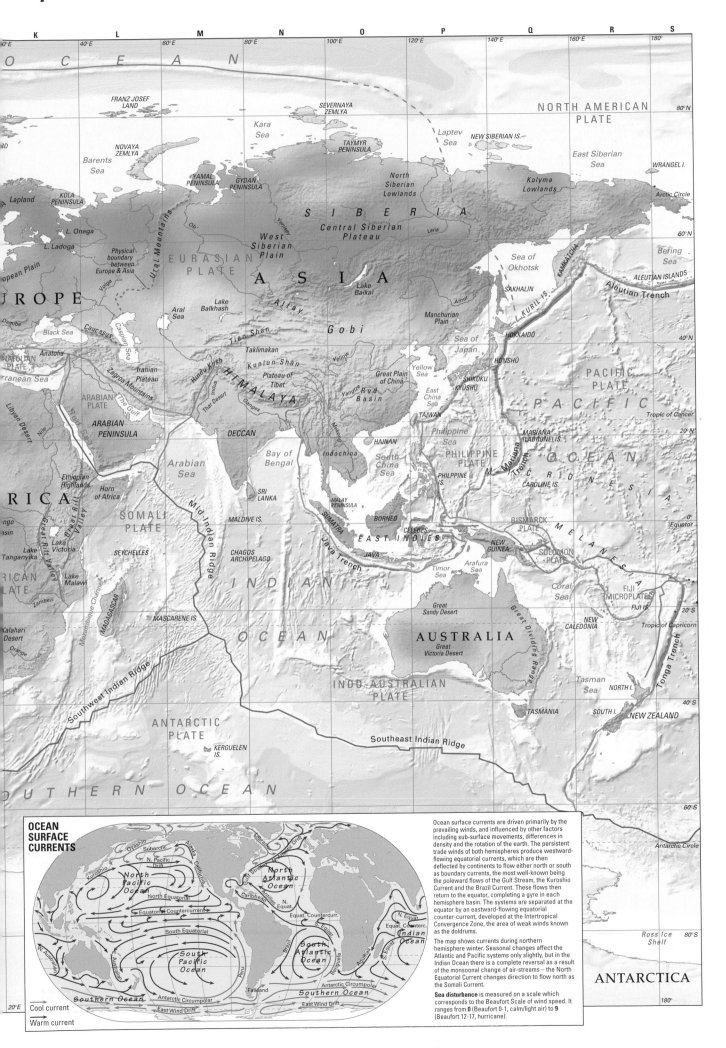

K   L   M   N   O   P   Q   R   S

40°E   60°E   80°E   100°E   120°E   140°E   160°E   180°

O C E A N

FRANZ JOSEF LAND

NORTH AMERICAN PLATE

80°N

Kara Sea

Laptev Sea

NEW SIBERIAN IS.

NOVAYA ZEMLYA

TAYMYR PENINSULA

SEVERNAYA ZEMLYA

East Siberian Sea

WRANGEL I.

Barents Sea

KOLA PENINSULA

Lapland

YAMAL PENINSULA

GYDAN PENINSULA

North Siberian Lowlands

Kolyma Lowlands

Arctic Circle

L. Onega

L. Ladoga

Physical boundary between Europe & Asia

Ural Mountains

Ob.

Yenisey

S I B E R I A

Central Siberian Plateau

Lena

60°N

Bering Sea

European Plain

EURASIAN PLATE

West Siberian Plain

A S I A

Sea of Okhotsk

KAMCHATKA

ALEUTIAN ISLANDS

EUROPE

Volga

Aral Sea

Lake Balkhash

Altay

Lake Baikal

Amur

SAKHALIN

KURIL IS.

Aleutian Trench

Danube

Black Sea

Caucasus

Caspian Sea

Tien Shan

Gobi

Manchurian Plain

HOKKAIDŌ

40°N

ANATOLIAN PLATE

Anatolia

Iranian Plateau

Zagros Mountains

The Gulf

Taklimakan

Kunlun Shan

Yellow

Sea of Japan

HONSHŪ

Mediterranean Sea

Libyan Desert

Nile

Red Sea

ARABIAN PLATE

Hindu Kush

HIMALAYA

Plateau of Tibet

Yangtze

Great Plain of China

Red Basin

Yellow Sea

East China Sea

SHIKOKU

KYŪSHŪ

PACIFIC PLATE

Tropic of Cancer

AFRICA

Ethiopian Highlands

Horn of Africa

ARABIAN PENINSULA

Thar Desert

Ganges

Indus

DECCAN

Mekong

HAINAN

Indochina

TAIWAN

Philippine Sea

MARIANA (LADRONE) IS.

P A C I F I C   O C E A N

20°N

Congo Basin

Great Rift Valley

Lake Victoria

Lake Tanganyika

SOMALI PLATE

Arabian Sea

SRI LANKA

Bay of Bengal

South China Sea

PHILIPPINE PLATE

PHILIPPINE IS.

Mariana Trench

CAROLINE IS.

M I C R O N E S I A

Lake Malawi

Zambezi

Mid-Indian Ridge

MALDIVE IS.

MALAY PENINSULA

SUMATRA

BORNEO

CELEBES

BISMARCK PLATE

M E L A N E S I A

Equator

AFRICAN PLATE

SEYCHELLES

CHAGOS ARCHIPELAGO

Java Trench

JAVA

E A S T   I N D I E S

NEW GUINEA

SOLOMON PLATE

FIJI MICROPLATES

FIJI IS.

20°S

Kalahari Desert

Orange

Mozambique Channel

MADAGASCAR

MASCARENE IS.

I N D I A N

Timor Sea

Arafura Sea

Great Sandy Desert

Great Dividing Range

Coral Sea

NEW CALEDONIA

Tropic of Capricorn

O C E A N

AUSTRALIA

Great Victoria Desert

NEW

Tasman Sea

NORTH I.

Tonga Trench

INDO-AUSTRALIAN PLATE

TASMANIA

SOUTH I.

NEW ZEALAND

40°S

Southwest Indian Ridge

ANTARCTIC PLATE

KERGUELEN IS.

Southeast Indian Ridge

S O U T H E R N   O C E A N

60°S

Antarctic Circle

OCEAN SURFACE CURRENTS

Ovashio

Subarctic

Alaska

California

Labrador

N. Atlantic Drift

Kuroshio

N. Pacific Drift

North Pacific Ocean

Gulf Stream

North Atlantic Ocean

North Equatorial

Antilles

Caribbean

N. Equat.

Equatorial Countercurrent

Equat. Countercurr.

N. Equat.

Equat. Counterc.

Indian Ocean

South Equatorial

Brazil

South Atlantic Ocean

Agulhas

Equat.

South Pacific Ocean

W. Australian

Peru

Benguela

Falkland

Antarctic Circumpolar

N. Equat.

Equat. Counterc.

Southern Ocean

Antarctic Circumpolar

East Wind Drift

Southern Ocean

East Wind Drift

20°E

→ Cool current

→ Warm current

Ocean surface currents are driven primarily by the prevailing winds, and influenced by other factors including sub-surface movements, differences in density and the rotation of the earth. The persistent trade winds of both hemispheres produce westward-flowing equatorial currents, which are then deflected by continents to flow either north or south as boundary currents, the most well-known being the poleward flows of the Gulf Stream, the Kuroshio Current and the Brazil Current. These flows then return to the equator, completing a gyre in each hemisphere basin. The systems are separated at the equator by an eastward-flowing equatorial counter-current, developed at the Intertropical Convergence Zone, the area of weak winds known as the doldrums.

The map shows currents during northern hemisphere winter. Seasonal changes affect the Atlantic and Pacific systems only slightly, but in the Indian Ocean there is a complete reversal as a result of the monsoonal change of air-streams – the North Equatorial Current changes direction to flow north as the Somali Current.

Sea disturbance is measured on a scale which corresponds to the Beaufort Scale of wind speed. It ranges from **0** (Beaufort 0-1, calm/light air) to **9** (Beaufort 12-17, hurricane).

Ross Ice Shelf

80°S

ANTARCTICA

180°

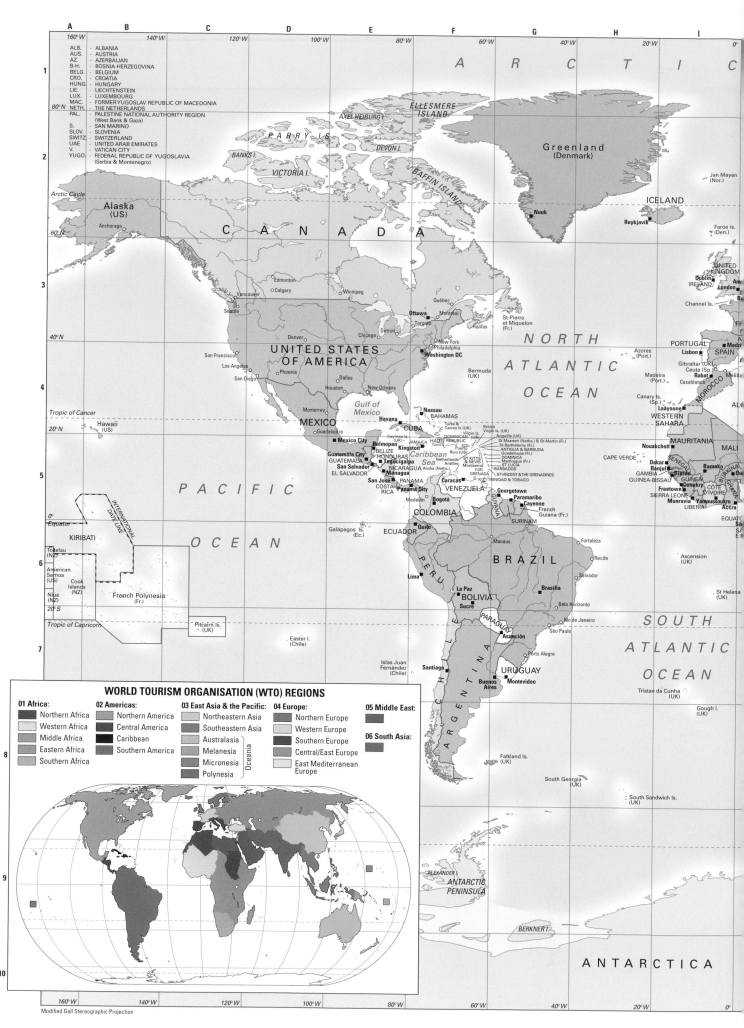

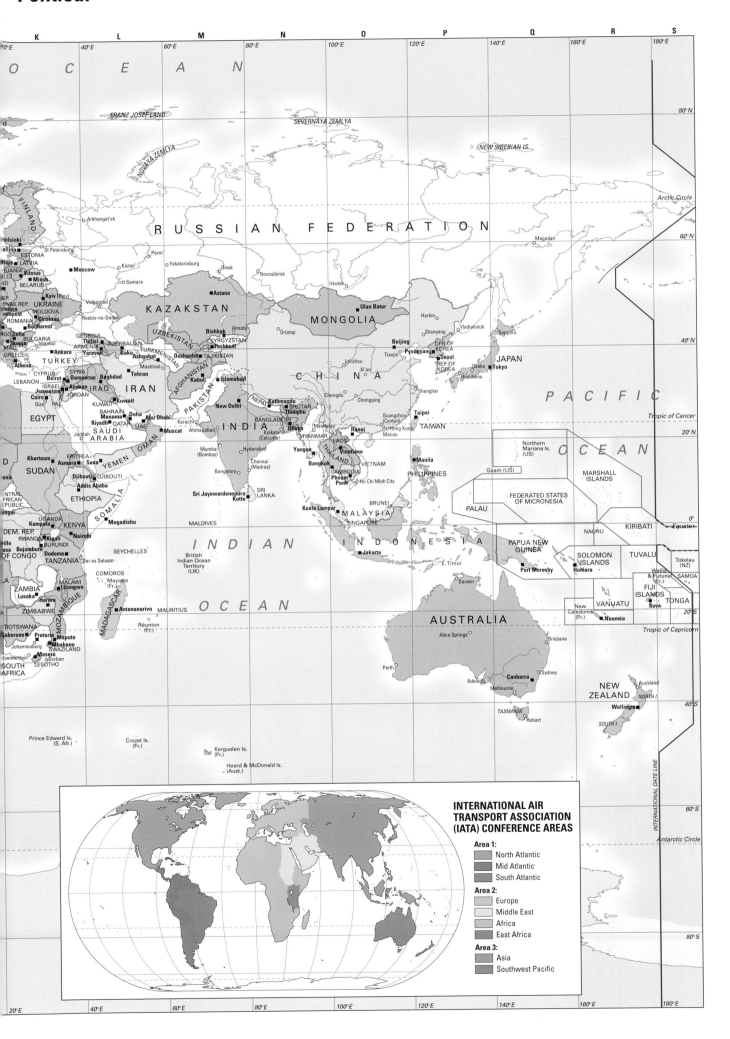

O C E A N

FRANZ JOSEF LAND

SEVERNAYA ZEMLYA

NEW SIBERIAN IS.

80° N

Arctic Circle

60° N

FINLAND

Helsinki
Tallinn
Riga   ESTONIA
St Petersburg
LATVIA
UANIA   Vilnius
ND   BELARUS   Minsk
EP.   Kyiv (Kiev)
VAK REP. UKRAINE
islava MOLDOVA
apest   Chisinau
ROMANIA
GO Sofia Bucharest
BULGARIA
Skopje   Istanbul
GREECE
Athens   TURKEY
CYPRUS
LEBANON SYRIA   Beirut
ISRAEL Damascus
Jerusalem Amman
JORDAN
Cairo   JORDAN
Giza
PAL.   EGYPT
KUWAIT   Kuwait
BAHRAIN Manama
Riyadh   QATAR Doha   Abu Dhabi
SAUDI   UAE
Jeddah   ARABIA

Moscow

Arkhangel'sk

Perm
Yekaterinburg
Kazan'
Samara
Volgograd
Rostov-na-Donu
GEORGIA Tbilisi
ARMENIA Baku
Yerevan AZERBAIJAN
Ankara

R U S S I A N   F E D E R A T I O N

60° N

Magadan

Omsk
Novosibirsk

Irkutsk

KAZAKSTAN

Astana

Bishkek Almaty
KYRGYZSTAN
Tashkent
UZBEKISTAN
TURKMENISTAN Dushanbe TAJIKISTAN
Ashgabat
Mashhad
Tehran
IRAN
AFGHANISTAN Kabul Islamabad
PAKISTAN
New Delhi
Karachi
Ahmadabad
Mumbai (Bombay)
Hyderabad
Bangalore
Chennai (Madras)
SRI LANKA

Sri Jayewardenepura Kotte

Ürümqi

MONGOLIA

Ulan Bator

Lanzhou

C H I N A

Chengdu

Chongqing

Xi'an

Beijing
Tianjin

Harbin

Shenyang

Vladivostok

DPR OF KOREA
Pyongyang
Seoul
REP. OF KOREA

Sapporo

JAPAN
Osaka Tokyo
Hiroshima

P A C I F I C

Shanghai

NEPAL Kathmandu
BHUTAN Thimphu
BANGLADESH
Kolkata (Calcutta) Dhaka
I N D I A
MYANMAR
Mandalay
Yangon
Bangkok
THAILAND
CAMBODIA
Phnom Penh
LAOS Vientiane
VIETNAM
Hanoi
Ho Chi Minh City

Guangzhou (Canton) Taipei
Hong Kong TAIWAN
Macau

Manila
PHILIPPINES

Northern Mariana Is. (US)

Guam (US)

MARSHALL ISLANDS

FEDERATED STATES OF MICRONESIA

PALAU

O C E A N

Tropic of Cancer
20° N

40° N

20° N

Khartoum
SUDAN
ERITREA Asmara
Sana
YEMEN OMAN
DJIBOUTI Djibouti
Addis Ababa
ETHIOPIA
SOMALIA
Mogadishu

UGANDA Kampala
KENYA Nairobi
RWANDA Kigali
BURUNDI Bujumbura
Dodoma
TANZANIA Dar es Salaam

CENTRAL AFRICAN REPUBLIC
angui
DEM. REP. OF CONGO

MALDIVES

British Indian Ocean Territory (UK)

SEYCHELLES

I N D I A N

BRUNEI

MALAYSIA

Kuala Lumpur
SINGAPORE

I N D O N E S I A

Jakarta

E. Timor

PAPUA NEW GUINEA
Port Moresby

SOLOMON ISLANDS
Honiara

NAURU

TUVALU

KIRIBATI

Equator
0°

COMOROS
Mayotte (Fr.)

ZAMBIA Lusaka
Harare
ZIMBABWE
MOZAMBIQUE
BOTSWANA
Gaborone Pretoria Maputo
Johannesburg Mbabane
SWAZILAND
SOUTH AFRICA Maseru Durban
loemfontein LESOTHO

MALAWI Lilongwe

Antananarivo
MADAGASCAR MAURITIUS

Réunion (Fr.)

O C E A N

Darwin

AUSTRALIA

Alice Springs

Perth

Adelaide

Brisbane

Sydney
Canberra
Melbourne

New Caledonia (Fr.) VANUATU

Nouméa

Wallis & Futuna (Fr.) SAMOA
FIJI ISLANDS Suva TONGA

Tokelau (NZ)

NEW ZEALAND
NORTH I.
Wellington

Auckland

Tropic of Capricorn
20° S

TASMANIA Hobart

SOUTH I.

40° S

Prince Edward Is. (S. Afr.)

Crozet Is. (Fr.)

Kerguelen Is. (Fr.)

Heard & McDonald Is. (Aust.)

INTERNATIONAL DATE LINE

60° S

Antarctic Circle

80° S

INTERNATIONAL AIR TRANSPORT ASSOCIATION (IATA) CONFERENCE AREAS

Area 1:
- North Atlantic
- Mid Atlantic
- South Atlantic

Area 2:
- Europe
- Middle East
- Africa
- East Africa

Area 3:
- Asia
- Southwest Pacific

Climate

Climate classification legend

Polar: no warm season (warmest month below 10°C)
Ice cap (perpetual frost: all months below 0°C) and Tundra (warmest month between 0°C and 10°C)

Cooler humid: rainy climates with severe winters (coldest month below 0°C, warmest month above 10°C)
Subarctic (less than four months over 10°C), Continental cool summer (warmest month below 22°C) and Continental warm summer (warmest month above 22°C)

Warmer humid: rainy climates with mild winters (coolest month between 0°C and 18°C, warmest month above 10°C)
Temperate (warmest month below 22°C), Humid Subtropical (warmest month above 22°C) and Mediterranean (dry season in summer)

Dry Steppe/semi-arid and Desert/arid

Tropical humid: rainy climates with no winter (coolest month above 18°C)
Savannah (with a dry season, either in summer or winter) and Rainforest (constantly moist or monsoon rain with only a short dry season)

WEATHER EXTREMES

Highest temperature in the shade: Al 'Azīzīyah, Libya
57.8°C (136.0°F) on 13th Sept 1922

Hottest place: Dalol, Ethiopia
average annual temperature of 34.4°C (94.0°F)

Lowest temperature: Vostok Base, Antarctica
-89.2°C (-128.6°F) on 21st July 1983

Coldest place: Plateau Base, Antarctica
average annual temperature of -56.6°C (-69.9°F)

Coldest inhabited place: Noril'sk, Russian Federation
average annual temperature of -10.9°C (12.4°F)

Greatest snowfall: Mt Rainier, Washington, USA
31,102 mm (1,224.5 inches) over a 12-month period, 1972-73

Most sunshine: Yuma, Arizona, USA
averages 4,127 hours of sunshine per year

Least sunshine: South Pole
no sunshine for 182 days a year

Highest surface wind speed
• Tornado: Oklahoma City, Oklahoma, USA
512 km per hour (318 miles per hour) on 3rd May 1999
• High altitude: Mt Washington, New Hampshire, USA
372 km per hour (231 miles per hour) on 12th Apr 1934
• Low altitude: Qaanaaq (Thule), Greenland
333 km per hour (207 miles per hour) on 8th Mar 1972

Windiest place: Commonwealth Bay, Antarctica
322 km per hour (200 miles per hour) in gales

Heaviest hailstones: Gopalganj, Bangladesh
weighing up to one kilogram (2.2 lb) on 14th Apr 1986

Driest place: Atacama Desert, Chile
virtually no rain throughout the year

Wettest place: Mawsynram, Meghalaya, India
11,873 mm (467.4 inches) during a 12-month period

Most rainy days: Mt Waialeale, Hawaii
up to 350 rainy days per year

Most thunder days: Tororo, Uganda
up to 251 days per year

TEMPERATURE CONVERSION

Celsius	-10	0	10	20	30	40
Fahrenheit	14	32	50	68	86	104

RAINFALL CONVERSION

Millimetres	102	203	305	406	508	610
Inches	4	8	12	16	20	24

The Arctic Circle marks the northernmost point at which the sun can be seen during the northern hemisphere's winter solstice. Positioned at 66° 30' N.

The Tropics of Cancer and Capricorn are lines of latitude, 23° 28' N and S, where the sun appears directly overhead at noon during the summer solstice in the respective northern and southern hemispheres.

The Antarctic Circle marks the southernmost point at which the sun can be seen during the southern hemisphere's winter solstice. Positioned at 66° 30' S.

Map labels

ARCTIC OCEAN
PACIFIC OCEAN
INDIAN OCEAN
SOUTHERN OCEAN
NORTH ATLANTIC OCEAN
SOUTH ATLANTIC OCEAN

WRANGEL I.
EAST SIBERIAN SEA
LAPTEV SEA
SEVERNAYA ZEMLYA
KARA SEA
NOVAYA ZEMLYA
FRANZ JOSEF LAND
BARENTS SEA
SVALBARD
GREENLAND SEA
NORWEGIAN SEA
LINCOLN SEA
ELLESMERE I.
AXEL HEIBERG I.
DEVON I.
BAFFIN I.
BAFFIN BAY
LABRADOR SEA
NEWFOUNDLAND
LABRADOR
HUDSON BAY
SOUTHAMPTON I.
VICTORIA I.
BANKS I.
PARRY IS.
BEAUFORT SEA
ALASKA
GULF OF ALASKA
QUEEN CHARLOTTE IS.
VANCOUVER I.
BERING SEA
ALEUTIAN IS.
HAWAIIAN IS.
KAMCHATKA
SEA OF OKHOTSK
SAKHALIN
KURIL ISLANDS
NEW SIBERIAN IS.
CENTRAL SIBERIAN PLATEAU
WEST SIBERIAN PLAIN
URAL MOUNTAINS
L. Baikal
ALTAI
TIEN SHAN
TAKLIMAKAN
GOBI
PLATEAU OF TIBET
HIMALAYA
THAR DESERT
DECCAN
BAY OF BENGAL
SRI LANKA
ARABIAN SEA
ARABIAN PENINSULA
THE GULF
CASPIAN SEA
Aral Sea
L. Balkhash
STEPPE
RED BASIN
MANCHURIAN PLAIN
SEA OF JAPAN
HOKKAIDŌ
HONSHŪ
SHIKOKU
KYŪSHŪ
EAST CHINA SEA
YELLOW SEA
TAIWAN
SOUTH CHINA SEA
HAINAN
INDOCHINA
MALAY PENINSULA
PHILIPPINE SEA
PHILIPPINE IS.
SULU SEA
BORNEO
SUMATRA
JAVA
MALDIVE IS.
CHAGOS ARCHIPELAGO
SEYCHELLES
MASCARENE IS.
MADAGASCAR
East Indies
PACIFIC OCEAN
MICRONESIA
Melanesia
MARIANA IS. (LADRONE IS.)
CAROLINE IS.
SOLOMON IS.
NEW GUINEA
NEW BRITAIN
CELEBES
FIJI IS.
NEW CALEDONIA
CORAL SEA
TASMAN SEA
NEW ZEALAND
TASMANIA
AUSTRALIA
GREAT DIVIDING RANGE
GREAT VICTORIA DESERT
GREAT SANDY DESERT
Polynesia

NORTH EUROPEAN PLAIN
SCANDINAVIA
LAPLAND
L. Ladoga
L. Onega
CARPATHIANS
ALPS
BLACK SEA
CAUCASUS
ANATOLIA
MEDITERRANEAN SEA
IBERIA
BRITISH ISLES
NORTH SEA
ICELAND
MADEIRA
AZORES
CANARY IS.
CAPE VERDE IS.
ATLAS MOUNTAINS
SAHARA
LIBYAN DESERT
RED SEA
SAHEL
ETHIOPIAN HIGHLANDS
HORN OF AFRICA
CONGO BASIN
GULF OF GUINEA
KALAHARI DESERT
Cape of Good Hope
L. Victoria
Tororo
Dalol
Al 'Azīzīyah
Mawsynram
Gopalganj
Noril'sk

GREENLAND
Qaanaaq (Thule)
Cape Farewell
Mt Washington
L. Superior
L. Huron
L. Michigan
L. Erie
L. Ontario
L. Winnipeg
Great Bear Lake
Great Slave Lake
ROCKY MOUNTAINS
GREAT PLAINS
SIERRA MADRE
APPALACHIANS
Oklahoma City
Yuma
Mt Rainier
BAJA CALIFORNIA
GULF OF MEXICO
LONG I.
BAHAMA IS.
CUBA
HISPANIOLA
West Indies
CARIBBEAN SEA
TRINIDAD
GALÁPAGOS IS.
EASTER I.
AMAZON BASIN
SELVAS
LLANOS
BRAZILIAN HIGHLANDS
MATO GROSSO PLATEAU
GRAN CHACO
PAMPAS
ANDES
CORDILLERA
Atacama Desert
PATAGONIA
TIERRA DEL FUEGO
Cape Horn
FALKLAND IS.
SOUTH GEORGIA
SCOTIA SEA
DRAKE PASSAGE
Mt Waialeale

Tropic of Cancer
Equator
Tropic of Capricorn
Arctic Circle
60°N
40°N
20°N
20°S
40°S

Time

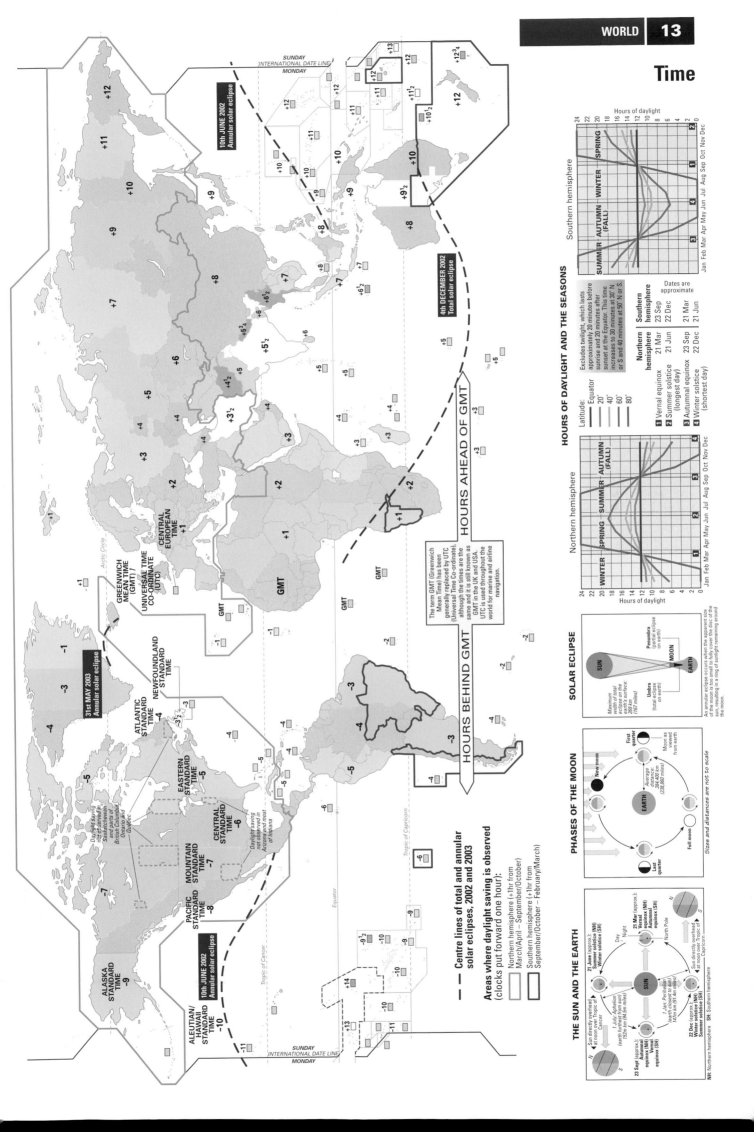

Environment: Land Use & Greenhouse Gases

AGRICULTURAL LAND AND FORESTS

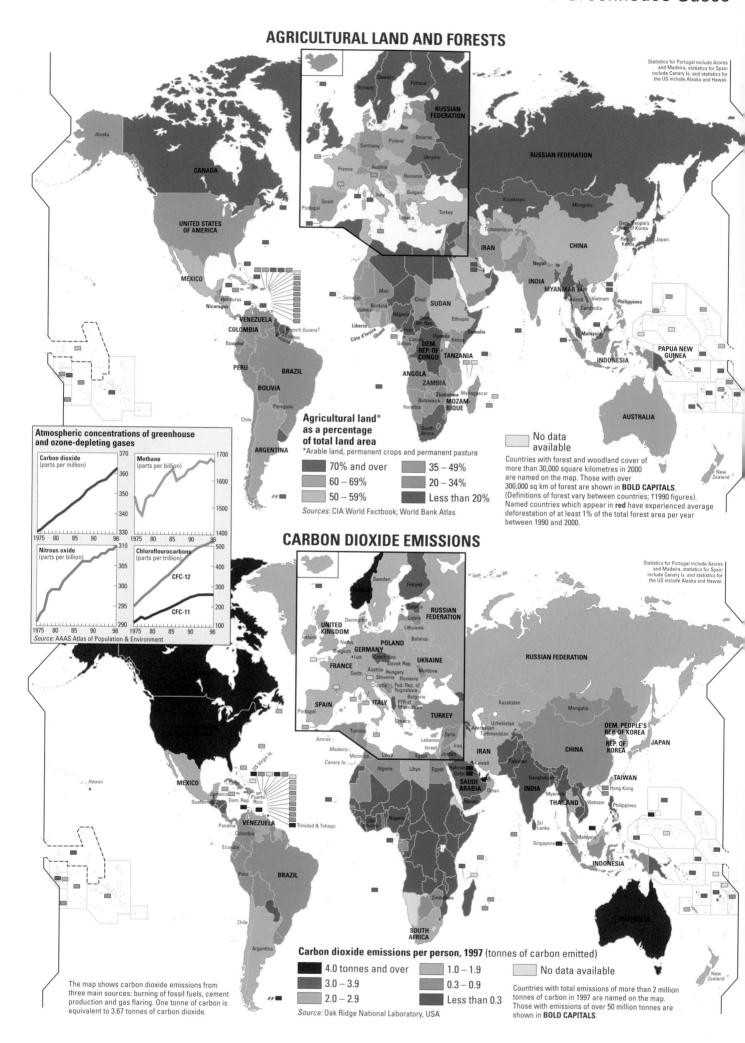

Statistics for Portugal include Azores and Madeira, statistics for Spain include Canary Is. and statistics for the US include Alaska and Hawaii.

Agricultural land*
**as a percentage
of total land area**
*Arable land, permanent crops and permanent pasture

- 70% and over
- 60 – 69%
- 50 – 59%
- 35 – 49%
- 20 – 34%
- Less than 20%

Sources: CIA World Factbook; World Bank Atlas

No data available

Countries with forest and woodland cover of more than 30,000 square kilometres in 2000 are named on the map. Those with over 300,000 sq km of forest are shown in **BOLD CAPITALS**. (Definitions of forest vary between countries; †1990 figures). Named countries which appear in **red** have experienced average deforestation of at least 1% of the total forest area per year between 1990 and 2000.

Atmospheric concentrations of greenhouse and ozone-depleting gases

Carbon dioxide (parts per million)

Methane (parts per billion)

Nitrous oxide (parts per billion)

Chloroflourocarbons (parts per trillion)

CFC-12

CFC-11

Source: AAAS Atlas of Population & Environment

CARBON DIOXIDE EMISSIONS

Statistics for Portugal include Azores and Madeira, statistics for Spain include Canary Is. and statistics for the US include Alaska and Hawaii.

Carbon dioxide emissions per person, 1997 (tonnes of carbon emitted)

- 4.0 tonnes and over
- 3.0 – 3.9
- 2.0 – 2.9
- 1.0 – 1.9
- 0.3 – 0.9
- Less than 0.3
- No data available

Countries with total emissions of more than 2 million tonnes of carbon in 1997 are named on the map. Those with emissions of over 50 million tonnes are shown in **BOLD CAPITALS**.

The map shows carbon dioxide emissions from three main sources: burning of fossil fuels, cement production and gas flaring. One tonne of carbon is equivalent to 3.67 tonnes of carbon dioxide.

Source: Oak Ridge National Laboratory, USA

Environment

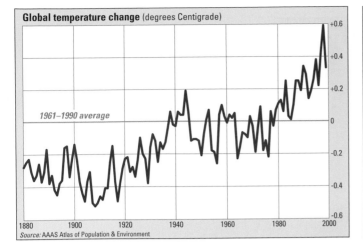

Global temperature change (degrees Centigrade)

1961–1990 average

Source: AAAS Atlas of Population & Environment

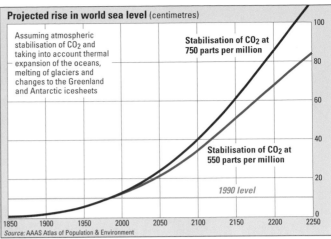

Projected rise in world sea level (centimetres)

Assuming atmospheric stabilisation of CO_2 and taking into account thermal expansion of the oceans, melting of glaciers and changes to the Greenland and Antarctic icesheets

Stabilisation of CO_2 at 750 parts per million

Stabilisation of CO_2 at 550 parts per million

1990 level

Source: AAAS Atlas of Population & Environment

PRINCIPAL ENVIRONMENTAL TREATIES

All the themes addressed on these pages, and many others besides, are the subject of a range of international conventions and treaties. Within some of these, various protocols also exist to provide action plans in specific areas. The list below is a selection of the most important of these various agreements. In their various ways, they all seek to encourage environmental awareness and protection, thereby addressing the effects of mankind's impact on the planet.
This information was compiled largely by Greenpeace. For more information on the work Greenpeace is doing in these areas, visit www.greenpeace.org. For more information on the various treaties, conventions and protocols themselves, see the website address within each entry.

23/6/61 Date treaty in force   **44** Ratifications (at Nov '01)

Principal Areas of Responsibility

🐦 Wildlife protection   ✪ Pollution control
≈ Marine protection   ✿ Bio-diversity
✗ Ozone depletion/climate change

Antarctic Treaty 🐦✿✪ 23/6/61 44
The treaty is designed to protect the Antarctic continent from the exploitation of its raw materials and to ensure the use of its territory for peaceful purpose only, such as scientific research. In addition to several other objectives, the treaty also prescribes the preservation and conservation of Antarctic living resources.

ASCOBANS 🐦≈✪ 29/3/94 8
Agreement on the Conservation of Small Cetaceans of the Baltic and North Seas
www.ascobans.org
With the establishment of this environmental treaty, Northern European countries such as Denmark, Germany and the UK sought to secure long-term protection of small cetaceans in the Baltic and North Seas from hazards such as high bycatch rates and habitat deterioration.

Barcelona Convention 🐦≈✪ Adopted '95, but not in force 11
The Barcelona Convention for the Protection of the Mediterranean Sea
www.unepmap.gr
Established in 1976 for the protection of the Mediterranean as part of the UNEP Regional Seas Programme. Its objective is to achieve international co-operation for a co-ordinated and comprehensive approach to the protection and enhancement of the Mediterranean marine environment.

Basel Convention ✪ 5/5/92 149
Basel Convention on the Control of Transboundary Movements of Hazardous Wastes and their Disposal
www.unep.ch/basel
The Basel Convention provides targets for the reduction of hazardous wastes and the creation of adequate disposal facilities; since 1998, it has also instituted a ban on waste exports from OECD to non-OECD countries.

CBD 🐦✿ 29/12/93 182
Convention on Biological Diversity
www.biodiv.org
29 December 1993 • 182
The Convention's objectives are 'the conservation of biological diversity, the sustainable use of its components and the fair and equitable sharing of the benefits arising out of the utilization of genetic resources.' It is the first comprehensive agreement to address all aspects of biological diversity. Its objectives have led to a broad work plan, involving all primary sectors (forests, oceans, and agriculture) and cross-cutting issues such as genetic engineering, indigenous peoples, technology transfer and intellectual property rights.

CCAMLR 🐦≈✿✪ 7/4/92 31
Convention on the Conservation of Antarctic Marine Living Resources
www.ccamlr.org
The convention focuses on the conservation of Antarctic marine living resources by attempting to minimise the risk of irreversible changes to the Antarctic marine ecosystem and ensuring an increase in the populations of exploited species.

CITES 🐦 1/7/75 155
Convention on International Trade in Endangered Species of Wild Fauna and Flora
www.cites.org
This is the only treaty whose focus is the global protection of plant and animal species from unregulated international trade. A classification of endangered species is constantly monitored and updated to co-ordinate protection measures.

HELCOM 🐦≈✿✪ 17/1/00 10
Convention on the Protection of the Marine Environment of the Baltic Sea Area, 1992
www.helcom.fi
This is the first convention to take into account all aspects of the Baltic marine environment and its protection. It deals with all aspects of pollution, including land-based, from ships, from dumping, and resulting from the exploration and exploitation of the sea-bed and its subsoil. The convention also regulates co-operation in combating marine pollution by oil and other harmful substances.

London Convention ≈✪ 30/8/75 78
London Convention on the Prevention of Marine Pollution by Dumping of Wastes and Other Matter
www.marine.gov.uk/london_convention.htm
This Convention is the principal international instrument to limit marine pollution and ocean contamination by dumping of wastes and other harmful matter.

OSPAR ≈✪ 25/3/98 16
Convention for the Protection of the Marine Environment of the North-East Atlantic
www.ospar.org
In 1992, this Commission replaced, and combined the aims of, the Oslo Convention on the Prevention of Marine Pollution by Dumping of Ships & Aircraft (1972) and the Paris Convention for the Prevention of Marine Pollution from Land-Based Sources (1974).

Ramsar 🐦≈
Ramsar Convention on Wetlands
www.ramsar.org
2 February 1971 • 130
This convention, signed in Ramsar, Iran, in 1971, is an intergovernmental treaty which provides the framework for international cooperation for the conservation and prudent use of wetlands and their resources. There are presently over 1,100 wetland sites, totaling 87.25 million hectares, designated for inclusion in the Ramsar List of Wetlands of International Importance.

Stockholm Convention ✪ Adopted '01, but not in force 2
Stockholm Convention on Persistent Organic Pollutants
www.irptc.unep.ch/pops/default.html
This Convention focuses on the elimination of a priority list of 12 of the most hazardous persistent organic pollutants (POPs), the elimination of other existing POPs and the prevention of the marketing of new chemicals with POP's characteristics.

UNCLOS ≈✪ 16/11/94 137
United Nations Convention on the Law of the Sea
www.un.org/depts/los
This Convention addresses protection and preservation of the marine environment to reflect customary international law with respect to maritime navigation. In addition, it provides basic obligations to prevent and reduce pollution from land-based sources, from sea-bed activities subject to national jurisdiction and from ocean dumping.

UNFCCC & Kyoto Protocol ✗ 21/3/94 186
United Nations Framework Convention on Climate Change
www.unfccc.org
The objective of the Convention is to achieve stabilisation of greenhouse gas concentrations in the atmosphere at a level that would prevent dangerous anthropogenic interference with the climate system. Such a level should be achieved within a time frame sufficient to allow ecosystems to adapt naturally to climate change, to ensure that food production is not threatened and to enable economic development to proceed in a sustainable manner. As part of the UNFCCC, the widely discussed Kyoto Protocol commits its signatories to targets in the reduction and limitation of their national greenhouse gas emission. To date, the Protocol has yet to receive the 55 national ratifications necessary for it to come into force.

Vienna Convention & Montréal Protocol ✗ 1/1/89 183
Montreal Protocol on Substances that Deplete the Ozone Layer
www.unep.org/unep/secretar/ozone
The Montréal Protocol operates within the framework of the 1985 Vienna Convention, which seeks to protect human health and the environment against adverse effects resulting from depletion of the ozone layer. The Montréal Protocol is specifically concerned with the protection of the ozone layer by taking precautionary measures to control global emissions of substances that deplete it, such as CFCs and Halons. It also seeks to promote the exchange of appropriate technological research.

People: Population & Urbanization

POPULATION

The **population density** of the states, provinces and territories of Canada, the USA and Australia are shown individually. The Azores and Madeira are treated separately from mainland Portugal, the Canary Islands separately from mainland Spain.

Population density, 1999
(people per square kilometre)

- 250 and over
- 100 – 249
- 50 – 99
- 20 – 49
- 5 – 19
- Less than 5

Sources: World Bank; Statesman's Yearbook; United Nations

Population growth rate,
1995 – 2000 *(annual average)*

- ◆ 3.0% and over
- ◆ Population decrease
- No data available

Countries with a total population of more th[an] two million in 1999 are named on the map. Those with an population of over 50 million are shown in **BOLD CAPITALS**.

Total world population since 1910 (millions)

People living in urban areas (% of world total)

29.7	37.8	47.4	58.9
1950	1975	2000	2025

High projection
Medium projection
Low projection

Sources: AAAS Atlas of Population & Environment; United Nations

URBANIZATION

Statistics for Portugal include Azores and Madeira, statistics for Spain include Canary Is. and statistics for the US include Alaska and Hawaii.

The UN defines the term 'urban agglomeration' as a contiguous area inhabited at a density regarded as urban, ignoring administrative boundaries.

Where the agglomeration extends beyond the principal city's metropolitan area to include significant neighbouring towns and cities, these are indicated on the map.

Proportion of population living in urban areas, 2000

- 80% and over
- 65% – 79%
- 50% – 64%
- 35% – 49%
- 20% – 34%
- Less than 20%
- No data available

Source: United Nations

Urban agglomerations estimated to contain more than four million inhabitants in 2000 are shown on the map. Those with over ten million inhabitants are indicated in **RED**.

People: Development & Rights

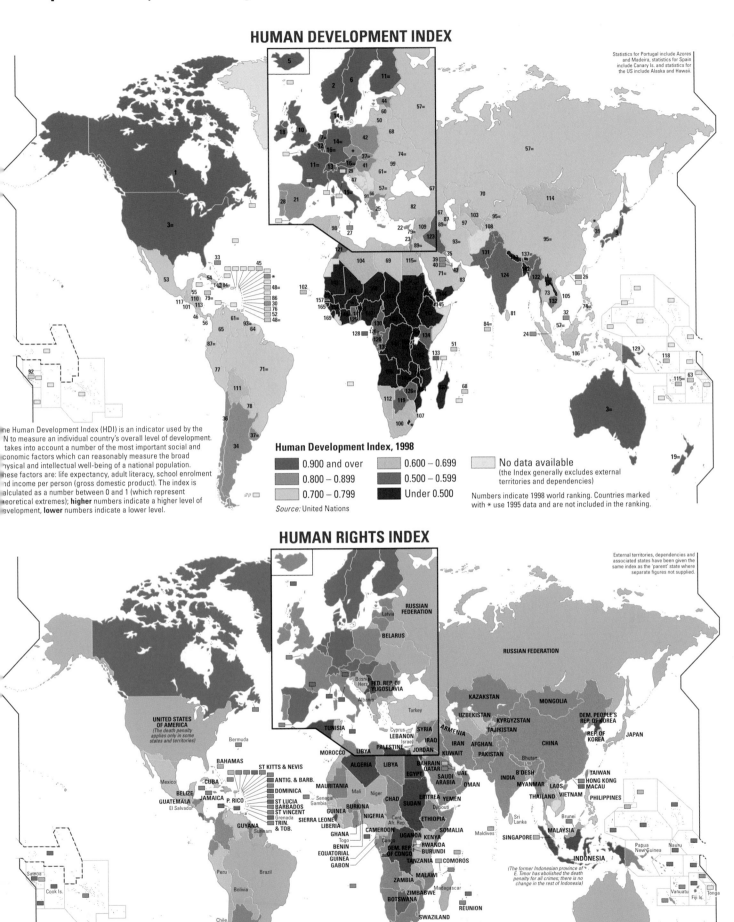

HUMAN DEVELOPMENT INDEX

Statistics for Portugal include Azores and Madeira, statistics for Spain include Canary Is. and statistics for the US include Alaska and Hawaii.

The Human Development Index (HDI) is an indicator used by the UN to measure an individual country's overall level of development. It takes into account a number of the most important social and economic factors which can reasonably measure the broad physical and intellectual well-being of a national population. These factors are: life expectancy, adult literacy, school enrolment and income per person (gross domestic product). The index is calculated as a number between 0 and 1 (which represent theoretical extremes); **higher** numbers indicate a higher level of development, **lower** numbers indicate a lower level.

Human Development Index, 1998

0.900 and over	0.600 – 0.699
0.800 – 0.899	0.500 – 0.599
0.700 – 0.799	Under 0.500

No data available
(the Index generally excludes external territories and dependencies)

Source: United Nations

Numbers indicate 1998 world ranking. Countries marked with * use 1995 data and are not included in the ranking.

HUMAN RIGHTS INDEX

External territories, dependencies and associated states have been given the same index as the 'parent' state where separate figures not supplied.

The Human Rights Index is compiled from ten different indicators: for each one, a country is given a mark between 0 (best) and 3 (worst). The **higher** the total, the worse the country's human rights performance by this measure.
The ten indicators are: judicial death sentences, judicial executions, extra-judicial executions, 'disappearances', deaths in custody, torture or inhumane treatment in custody, 'prisoners of conscience', unfair trials, detention without trial or charge within a reasonable time and abuses by opposition groups (as a reflection of a government's failure to protect its citizens).

Human Rights Index

20.0 and over	5.0 – 8.5
14.0 – 19.5	2.0 – 4.5
9.0 – 13.5	Under 2.0

No data available

Compiled by the Observer Newspaper in association with Amnesty International. All data 1999.

Countries which retain and use the death penalty for some offences are named in **BOLD CAPITALS** on the map. Countries shown in thin type have either abolished the death penalty except for 'exceptional' offences, *or* the penalty remains on statute but either a) has not been used for at least ten years, b) is the subject of a formal commitment not to carry out executions.

Wealth: Income & Growth

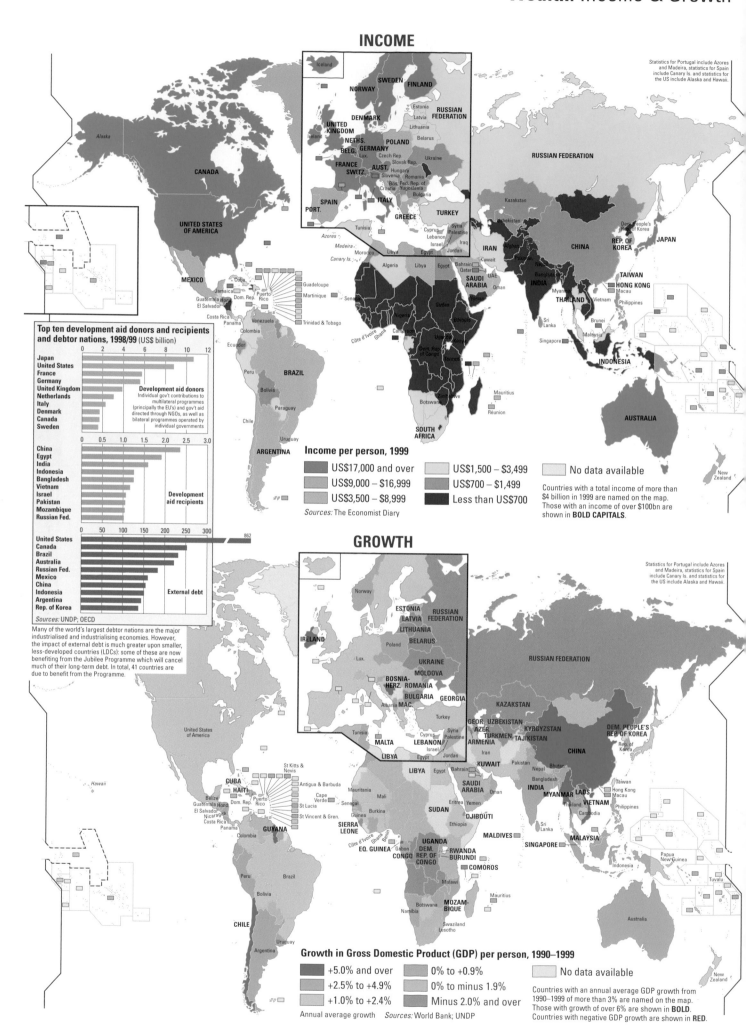

INCOME

Statistics for Portugal include Azores and Madeira, statistics for Spain include Canary Is. and statistics for the US include Alaska and Hawaii.

Top ten development aid donors and recipients and debtor nations, 1998/99 (US$ billion)

Development aid donors
(0 – 12)
Japan
United States
France
Germany
United Kingdom
Netherlands
Italy
Denmark
Canada
Sweden

Development aid donors: Individual gov't contributions to multilateral programmes (principally the EU's) and gov't aid directed through NGOs, as well as bilateral programmes operated by individual governments

Development aid recipients
(0 – 3.0)
China
Egypt
India
Indonesia
Bangladesh
Vietnam
Israel
Pakistan
Mozambique
Russian Fed.

External debt
(0 – 300)
United States — 862
Canada
Brazil
Australia
Russian Fed.
Mexico
China
Indonesia
Argentina
Rep. of Korea

Sources: UNDP; OECD

Many of the world's largest debtor nations are the major industrialised and industrialising economies. However, the impact of external debt is much greater upon smaller, less-developed countries (LDCs): some of these are now benefiting from the Jubilee Programme which will cancel much of their long-term debt. In total, 41 countries are due to benefit from the Programme.

Income per person, 1999

- US$17,000 and over
- US$9,000 – 16,999
- US$3,500 – 8,999
- US$1,500 – $3,499
- US$700 – $1,499
- Less than US$700
- No data available

Sources: The Economist Diary

Countries with a total income of more than $4 billion in 1999 are named on the map. Those with an income of over $100bn are shown in **BOLD CAPITALS**.

GROWTH

Statistics for Portugal include Azores and Madeira, statistics for Spain include Canary Is. and statistics for the US include Alaska and Hawaii.

Growth in Gross Domestic Product (GDP) per person, 1990–1999

- +5.0% and over
- +2.5% to +4.9%
- +1.0% to +2.4%
- 0% to +0.9%
- 0% to minus 1.9%
- Minus 2.0% and over
- No data available

Annual average growth   *Sources:* World Bank; UNDP

Countries with an annual average GDP growth from 1990–1999 of more than 3% are named on the map. Those with growth of over 6% are shown in **BOLD**. Countries with negative GDP growth are shown in **RED**.

Wealth: Economic Activity

Income from each sector as a percentage of GDP, 1998/99

Legend:
- 60% and over
- 45% – 59%
- 30% – 44%
- 20% – 29%
- 10% – 19%
- 5% – 9%
- Less than 5%
- No data

Source: CIA

AGRICULTURE

Agriculture (the **primary** sector of the economy) comprises farming, fishing and forestry

INDUSTRY

Industry (the **secondary** sector of the economy) comprises construction, manufacturing, mining (including oil and gas extraction) and power generation

SERVICES

Services (the **tertiary** sector of the economy) comprises administration and public services (including those provided by central and local government), media, retail, tourism and transport

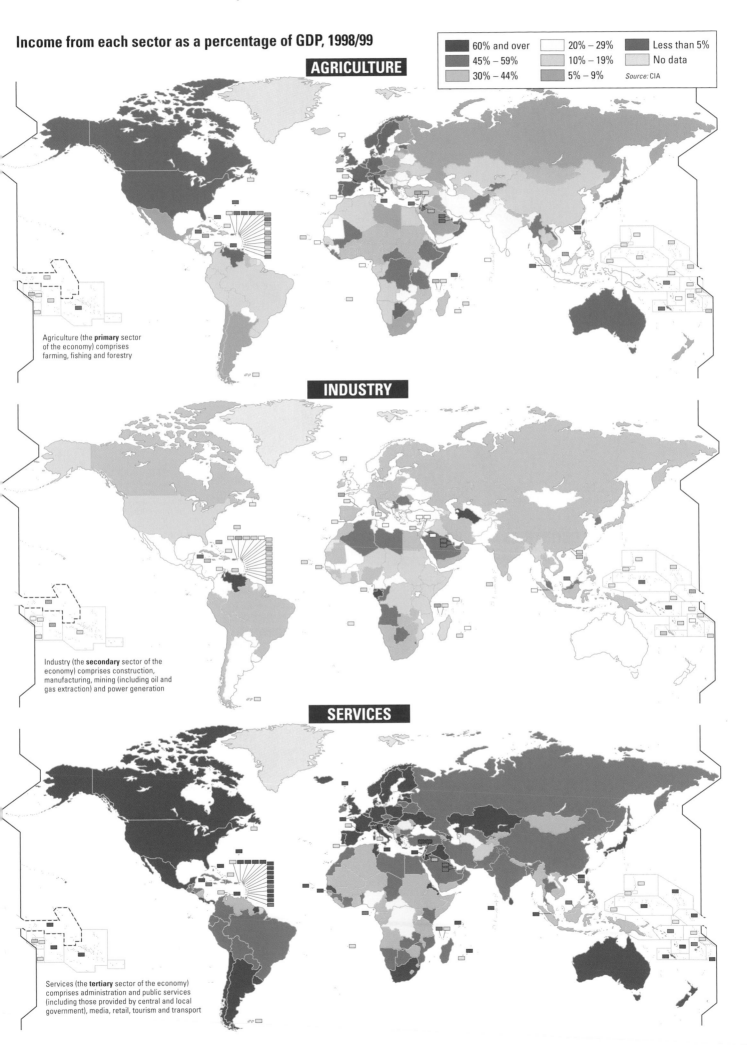

VISITOR RECEIPTS

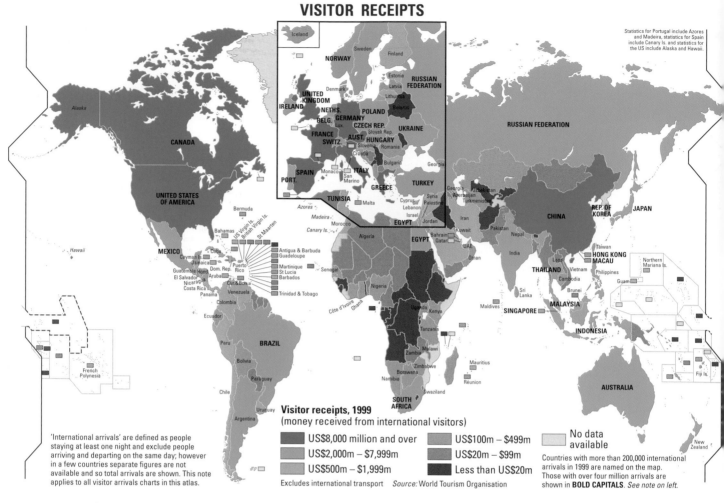

Statistics for Portugal include Azores and Madeira, statistics for Spain include Canary Is. and statistics for the US include Alaska and Hawaii.

Visitor receipts, 1999
(money received from international visitors)

- US$8,000 million and over
- US$2,000m – $7,999m
- US$500m – $1,999m
- US$100m – $499m
- US$20m – $99m
- Less than US$20m
- No data available

'International arrivals' are defined as people staying at least one night and exclude people arriving and departing on the same day; however in a few countries separate figures are not available and so total arrivals are shown. This note applies to all visitor arrivals charts in this atlas.

Countries with more than 200,000 international arrivals in 1999 are named on the map. Those with over four million arrivals are shown in **BOLD CAPITALS**. *See note on left.*

Excludes international transport   *Source:* World Tourism Organisation

TOP TEN COUNTRIES (ARRIVALS)

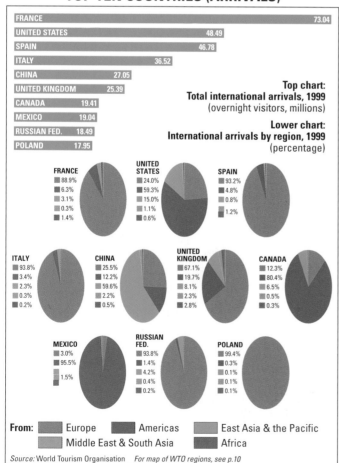

FRANCE	73.04
UNITED STATES	48.49
SPAIN	46.78
ITALY	36.52
CHINA	27.05
UNITED KINGDOM	25.39
CANADA	19.41
MEXICO	19.04
RUSSIAN FED.	18.49
POLAND	17.95

Top chart:
Total international arrivals, 1999
(overnight visitors, millions)

Lower chart:
International arrivals by region, 1999
(percentage)

FRANCE
- 88.9%
- 6.3%
- 3.1%
- 0.3%
- 1.4%

UNITED STATES
- 24.0%
- 59.3%
- 15.0%
- 1.1%
- 0.6%

SPAIN
- 93.2%
- 4.8%
- 0.8%
- 1.2%

ITALY
- 93.8%
- 3.4%
- 2.3%
- 0.3%
- 0.2%

CHINA
- 25.5%
- 12.2%
- 59.6%
- 2.2%
- 0.5%

UNITED KINGDOM
- 67.1%
- 19.7%
- 8.1%
- 2.3%
- 2.8%

CANADA
- 12.3%
- 80.4%
- 6.5%
- 0.5%
- 0.3%

MEXICO
- 3.0%
- 95.5%
- 1.5%

RUSSIAN FED.
- 93.8%
- 1.4%
- 4.2%
- 0.4%
- 0.2%

POLAND
- 99.4%
- 0.3%
- 0.1%
- 0.1%
- 0.1%

From:
- Europe
- Americas
- East Asia & the Pacific
- Middle East & South Asia
- Africa

Source: World Tourism Organisation   *For map of WTO regions, see p.10*

TOP TEN COUNTRIES (DEPARTURES)

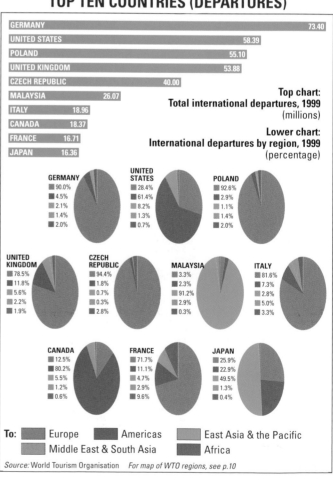

GERMANY	73.40
UNITED STATES	58.39
POLAND	55.10
UNITED KINGDOM	53.88
CZECH REPUBLIC	40.00
MALAYSIA	26.07
ITALY	18.96
CANADA	18.37
FRANCE	16.71
JAPAN	16.36

Top chart:
Total international departures, 1999
(millions)

Lower chart:
International departures by region, 1999
(percentage)

GERMANY
- 90.0%
- 4.5%
- 2.1%
- 1.4%
- 2.0%

UNITED STATES
- 28.4%
- 61.4%
- 8.2%
- 1.3%
- 0.7%

POLAND
- 92.6%
- 2.9%
- 1.1%
- 1.4%
- 2.0%

UNITED KINGDOM
- 78.5%
- 11.8%
- 5.6%
- 2.2%
- 1.9%

CZECH REPUBLIC
- 94.4%
- 1.8%
- 0.7%
- 0.3%
- 2.8%

MALAYSIA
- 3.3%
- 2.3%
- 91.2%
- 2.9%
- 0.3%

ITALY
- 81.6%
- 7.3%
- 2.8%
- 5.0%
- 3.3%

CANADA
- 12.5%
- 80.2%
- 5.5%
- 1.2%
- 0.6%

FRANCE
- 71.7%
- 11.1%
- 4.7%
- 2.9%
- 9.6%

JAPAN
- 25.9%
- 22.9%
- 49.5%
- 1.3%
- 0.4%

To:
- Europe
- Americas
- East Asia & the Pacific
- Middle East & South Asia
- Africa

Source: World Tourism Organisation   *For map of WTO regions, see p.10*

Travel Indicators

VISITOR EXPENDITURE

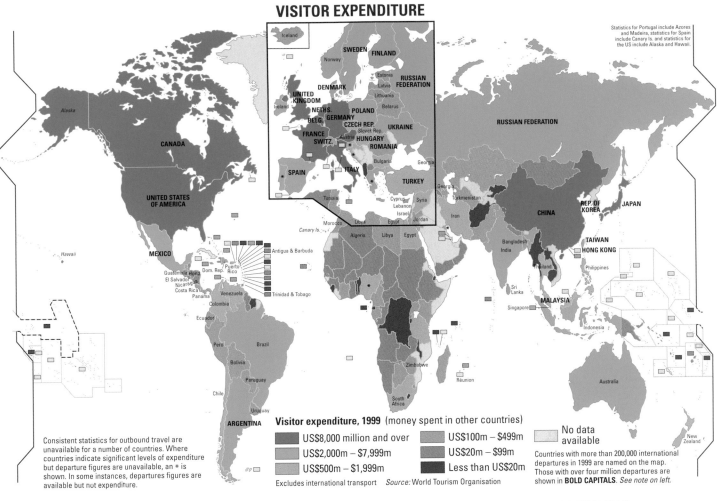

Statistics for Portugal include Azores and Madeira, statistics for Spain include Canary Is. and statistics for the US include Alaska and Hawaii.

Visitor expenditure, 1999 (money spent in other countries)

- US$8,000 million and over
- US$2,000m – $7,999m
- US$500m – $1,999m
- US$100m – $499m
- US$20m – $99m
- Less than US$20m
- No data available

Excludes international transport *Source:* World Tourism Organisation

Consistent statistics for outbound travel are unavailable for a number of countries. Where countries indicate significant levels of expenditure but departure figures are unavailable, an * is shown. In some instances, departures figures are available but not expenditure.

Countries with more than 200,000 international departures in 1999 are named on the map. Those with over four million departures are shown in **BOLD CAPITALS**. *See note on left.*

ARRIVALS, 1960–1999

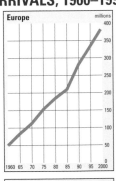
Europe (millions)

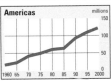
Americas (millions)

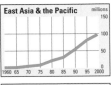
East Asia & the Pacific (millions)

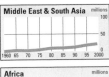
Middle East & South Asia (millions)

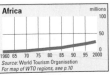
Africa (millions)

Source: World Tourism Organisation
For map of WTO regions, see p.10

TOP FIVE EARNERS

UNITED STATES
Visitor receipts in 1998: US$71.3bn; 1999: US$74.9bn
Arrivals at frontiers, 1998 (thousands of visitors) from:

Canada	13,422	Brazil	909
Mexico	9,276	Italy	611
Japan	4,885	Venezuela	541
United Kingdom	3,975	Argentina	524
Germany	1,902	Netherlands	490
France	1,013	Australia	461

SPAIN
Visitor receipts in 1998: US$29.8bn; 1999: US$32.5bn
Arrivals at frontiers, 1998 (thousands of visitors) from:

United Kingdom	11,372	Switzerland	1,251
Germany	10,781	Portugal	1,175
France	5,235	United States	899
Italy	1,797	Japan	388
Belgium	1,745		
Netherlands	1,678		

FRANCE
Visitor receipts in 1998: US$29.9bn; 1999: US$31.5bn
Arrivals at frontiers, 1998 (thousands of visitors) from:

Germany	14,770	United States	2,911
UK & Ireland	11,359	Spain	2,875
Netherlands	10,203	Poland	659
Belgium & Lux.	8,364	Portugal	636
Italy	5,806	Japan	604
Switzerland	3,682	Canada	543

ITALY
Visitor receipts in 1998: US$29.9bn; 1999: US$28.4bn
Arrivals at frontiers, 1998 (thousands of visitors) from:

Germany	8,644	Switzerland	1,338
United States	3,586	Netherlands	913
France	2,253	Spain	875
Japan	2,018	Belgium	646
United Kingdom	1,969	Poland	457
Austria	1,628	Australia	405

UNITED KINGDOM
Visitor receipts in 1998: US$21.0bn; 1999: US$20.2bn
Arrivals at frontiers, 1998 (thousands of visitors) from:

United States	3,880	Italy	1,090
France	3,274	Spain	879
Germany	2,830	Sweden	676
Ireland	2,310	Canada	673
Netherlands	1,718	Australia	603
Belgium	1,183	Switzerland	583

TOP FIVE SPENDERS

UNITED STATES
Visitor spending in 1998: US$56.5bn; 1999: US$59.4bn
Principal destinations, 1998 (thousands of tourists):

Mexico	17,735	Germany	1,964
Canada	14,893	Bahamas	1,250
United Kingdom	3,880	Spain	899
Italy	3,586	Netherlands	865
France	2,911	Switzerland	861
Puerto Rico	2,544	Jamaica	829

GERMANY
Visitor spending in 1998: US$48.9bn; 1999: US$48.5bn
Principal destinations, 1998 (thousands of tourists):

France	14,770	Netherlands	2,668
Spain	10,781	Switzerland	2,169
Austria	9,697	Turkey	2,145
Italy	8,644	Greece	2,137
Poland	6,700	United States	1,902
United Kingdom	2,830	Czech Republic	1,731

UNITED KINGDOM
Visitor spending in 1998: US$32.3bn; 1999: US$35.6bn
Principal destinations, 1998 (thousands of tourists):

Spain	11,372	Portugal	1,723
France*	11,359	Netherlands	1,599
United States	3,975	Germany	1,582
Ireland	3,729	Belgium	1,023
Greece	2,044	Cyprus	1,015
Italy	1,969	Turkey	902

JAPAN
Visitor spending in 1998: US$28.8bn; 1999: US$32.8bn
Principal destinations, 1998 (thousands of tourists):

USA (ex. Hawaii)	2,877	Thailand	986
Italy	2,018	Guam	975
Hawaii	2,008	Singapore	844
Republic of Korea	1,954	Taiwan	827
China (ex. HK)	1,572	Germany	815
Hong Kong	1,101	Australia	751

FRANCE
Visitor spending in 1998: US$17.8bn; 1999: US$18.6bn
Principal destinations, 1998 (thousands of tourists):

Spain	5,235	Tunisia	709
United Kingdom	3,274	Portugal	697
Italy	2,253	Morocco	633
United States	1,013	Austria	512
Germany	835	Greece	486
Belgium	835	Netherlands	457

Source: World Tourism Organisation

*Combined UK & Irish tourists to France

Energy: Deposits & Production

MAJOR FOSSIL FUEL DEPOSITS & HYDROELECTRIC SCHEMES

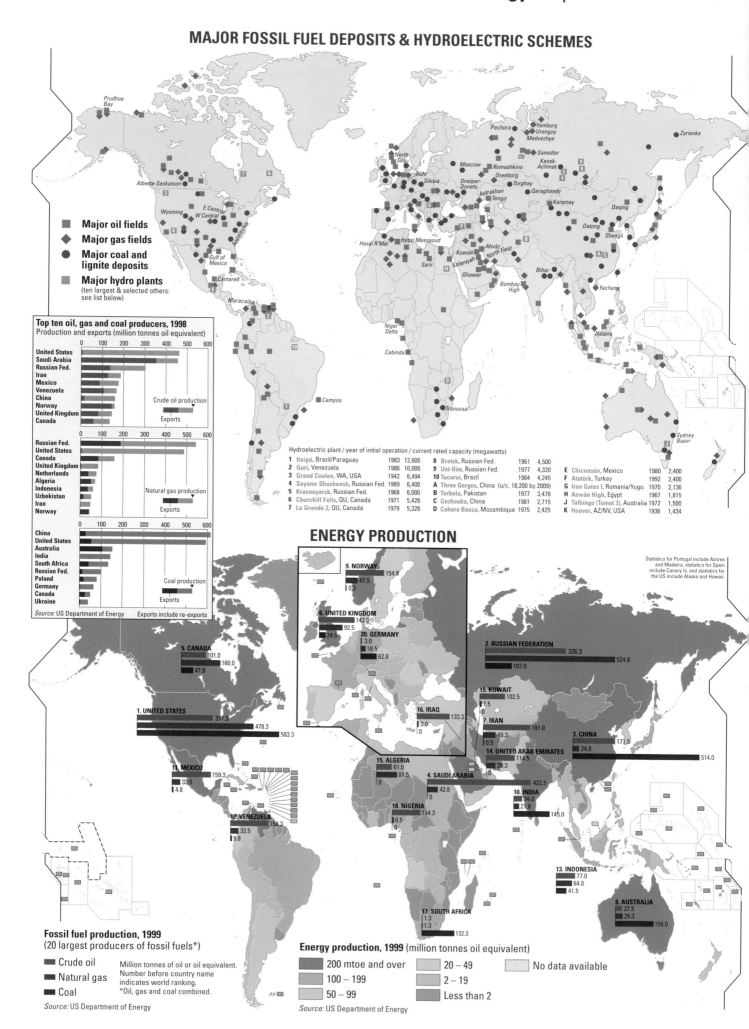

■ **Major oil fields**

◆ **Major gas fields**

● **Major coal and lignite deposits**

■ **Major hydro plants**
(ten largest & selected others: see list below)

Top ten oil, gas and coal producers, 1998
Production and exports (million tonnes oil equivalent)

Crude oil production / Exports

United States
Saudi Arabia
Russian Fed.
Iran
Mexico
Venezuela
China
Norway
United Kingdom
Canada

Natural gas production / Exports

Russian Fed.
United States
Canada
United Kingdom
Netherlands
Algeria
Indonesia
Uzbekistan
Iran
Norway

Coal production / Exports

China
United States
Australia
India
South Africa
Russian Fed.
Poland
Germany
Canada
Ukraine

Source: US Department of Energy   Exports include re-exports

Hydroelectric plant / year of initial operation / current rated capacity (megawatts)

1 Itaipú, Brazil/Paraguay	1983	12,600	
2 Guri, Venezuela	1986	10,000	
3 Grand Coulee, WA, USA	1942	6,494	
4 Sayano-Shushensk, Russian Fed.	1989	6,400	
5 Krasnoyarsk, Russian Fed.	1968	6,000	
6 Churchill Falls, QU, Canada	1971	5,428	
7 La Grande 2, QU, Canada	1979	5,328	
8 Bratsk, Russian Fed.	1961	4,500	
9 Ust-Ilim, Russian Fed.	1977	4,320	
10 Tucurui, Brazil	1984	4,245	
A Three Gorges, China (u/c, 18,200 by 2009)			
B Tarbela, Pakistan	1977	3,478	
C Gezhouba, China	1981	2,715	
D Cahora Bassa, Mozambique	1975	2,425	
E Chicoasén, Mexico	1980	2,400	
F Atatürk, Turkey	1992	2,400	
G Iron Gates I, Romania/Yugo.	1970	2,136	
H Aswān High, Egypt	1967	1,815	
J Talbingo (Tumut 3), Australia	1972	1,500	
K Hoover, AZ/NV, USA	1936	1,434	

ENERGY PRODUCTION

Statistics for Portugal include Azores and Madeira, statistics for Spain include Canary Is. and statistics for the US include Alaska and Hawaii.

9. NORWAY 154.8 / 47.5 / 0.3

6. UNITED KINGDOM 142.0 / 92.5 / 24.0

20. GERMANY 3.0 / 18.5 / 62.8

2. RUSSIAN FEDERATION 326.3 / 524.8 / 107.0

5. CANADA 101.0 / 160.0 / 47.8

1. UNITED STATES 311.3 / 478.3 / 583.3

19. KUWAIT 102.5 / 7.5 / 0

7. IRAN 191.0 / 49.3 / 0.5

3. CHINA 171.5 / 24.8 / 514.0

16. IRAQ 133.3 / 3.0 / 0

14. UNITED ARAB EMIRATES 114.5 / 35.3 / 0

11. MEXICO 159.3 / 33.5 / 4.8

15. ALGERIA 61.0 / 81.5 / 0

4. SAUDI ARABIA 422.5 / 42.8 / 0

10. INDIA 34.0 / 21.8 / 145.0

12. VENEZUELA 158.3 / 32.5 / 5.8

18. NIGERIA 114.3 / 6.5 / 0

13. INDONESIA 77.0 / 64.0 / 41.5

17. SOUTH AFRICA 1.3 / 1.3 / 132.3

8. AUSTRALIA 27.5 / 29.3 / 155.0

Fossil fuel production, 1999
(20 largest producers of fossil fuels*)

■ Crude oil
■ Natural gas
■ Coal

Million tonnes of oil or oil equivalent. Number before country name indicates world ranking. *Oil, gas and coal combined.

Source: US Department of Energy

Energy production, 1999 (million tonnes oil equivalent)

- 200 mtoe and over
- 100 – 199
- 50 – 99
- 20 – 49
- 2 – 19
- Less than 2
- No data available

Source: US Department of Energy

Energy: Consumption & Renewables

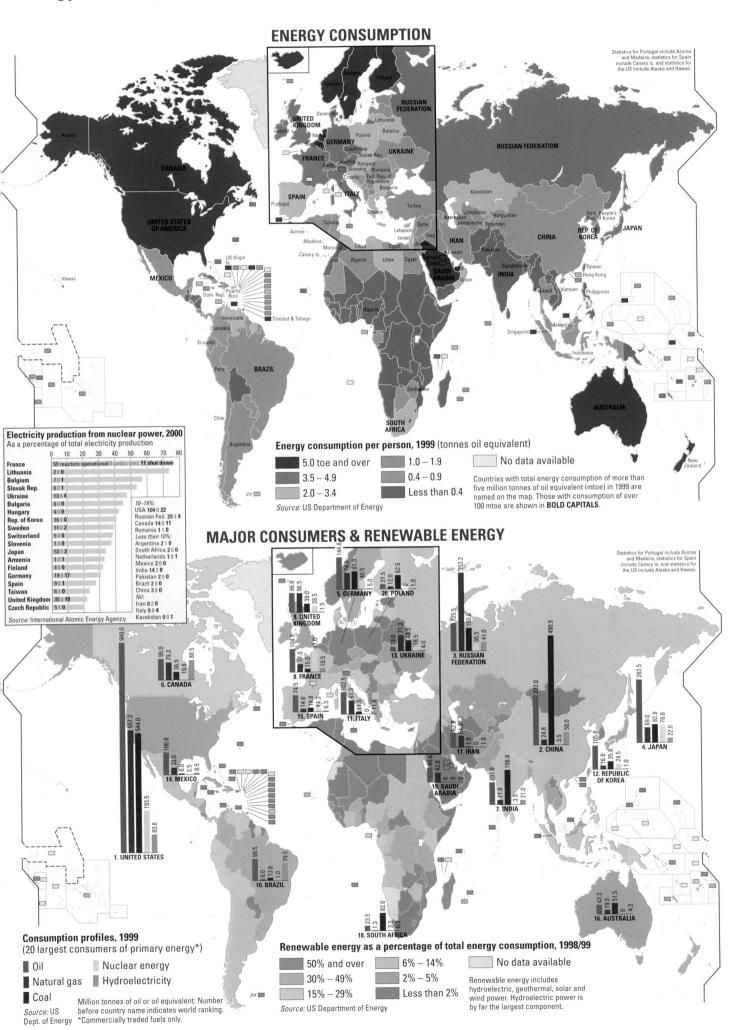

ENERGY CONSUMPTION

Statistics for Portugal include Azores and Madeira, statistics for Spain include Canary Is. and statistics for the US include Alaska and Hawaii.

Energy consumption per person, 1999 (tonnes oil equivalent)

- 5.0 toe and over
- 3.5 – 4.9
- 2.0 – 3.4
- 1.0 – 1.9
- 0.4 – 0.9
- Less than 0.4
- No data available

Countries with total energy consumption of more than five million tonnes of oil equivalent (mtoe) in 1999 are named on the map. Those with consumption of over 100 mtoe are shown in **BOLD CAPITALS**.

Source: US Department of Energy

Electricity production from nuclear power, 2000
As a percentage of total electricity production

	0	10	20	30	40	50	60	70	80

France — 59 reactors operational 0 under con. 11 shut down
Lithuania — 2 0 0
Belgium — 7 0 1
Slovak Rep. — 6 2 1
Ukraine — 13 4 4
Bulgaria — 6 0 0
Hungary — 4 0 0
Rep. of Korea — 16 4 0
Sweden — 11 0 2
Switzerland — 5 0 0
Slovenia — 1 0 0
Japan — 53 3 2
Armenia — 1 0 1
Finland — 4 0 0
Germany — 19 0 17
Spain — 9 0 1
Taiwan — 6 2 0
United Kingdom — 35 0 10
Czech Republic — 5 1 0

10–19%:
USA 104 0 22
Russian Fed. 29 3 4
Canada 14 0 11
Romania 1 1 0
Less than 10%:
Argentina 2 1 0
South Africa 2 0 0
Netherlands 1 0 1
Mexico 2 0 0
India 14 2 0
Pakistan 2 0 0
Brazil 2 0 0
China 3 8 0
Nil:
Iran 0 2 0
Italy 0 0 4
Kazakstan 0 0 1

Source: International Atomic Energy Agency

MAJOR CONSUMERS & RENEWABLE ENERGY

Statistics for Portugal include Azores and Madeira, statistics for Spain include Canary Is. and statistics for the US include Alaska and Hawaii.

Consumption profiles, 1999
(20 largest consumers of primary energy*)

- Oil
- Natural gas
- Coal
- Nuclear energy
- Hydroelectricity

Million tonnes of oil or oil equivalent. Number before country name indicates world ranking.
*Commercially traded fuels only.

Source: US Dept. of Energy

1. UNITED STATES 949.0 557.3 544.0 193.5 83.8
2. CHINA 222.0 24.8 490.5 3.5 58.0
3. RUSSIAN FEDERATION 225.5 353.3 103.8 30.5 41.0
4. JAPAN 282.5 69.0 82.8 78.8 22.0
5. GERMANY 144.8 74.3 81.3 40.5 15.0
6. CANADA 95.0 79.3 36.5 19.8 88.5
7. INDIA 101.0 21.8 156.8 3.5 21.0
8. FRANCE 104.5 37.0 15.0 97.0 18.5
9. UNITED KINGDOM 86.8 86.5 39.0 28.5 1.5
10. BRAZIL 99.5 6.0 13.8 1.0 79.5
11. ITALY 102.5 61.3 11.5 1.8
12. REPUBLIC OF KOREA 105.8 16.8 35.8 24.5 1.0
13. UKRAINE 19.0 71.3 48.3 18.5 4.0
14. MEXICO 100.8 33.0 6.0 2.5 8.5
15. SPAIN 74.5 14.8 18.8 44.3 6.3
16. AUSTRALIA 42.3 19.5 51.5 0 4.3
17. IRAN 62.8 51.3 1.0 1.8
18. SOUTH AFRICA 23.5 1.3 82.0 3.3 0.3
19. SAUDI ARABIA 65.8 42.8 0 0
20. POLAND 21.5 62.5 1.0

Renewable energy as a percentage of total energy consumption, 1998/99

- 50% and over
- 30% – 49%
- 15% – 29%
- 6% – 14%
- 2% – 5%
- Less than 2%
- No data available

Renewable energy includes hydroelectric, geothermal, solar and wind power. Hydroelectric power is by far the largest component.

Source: US Department of Energy

International Organisations

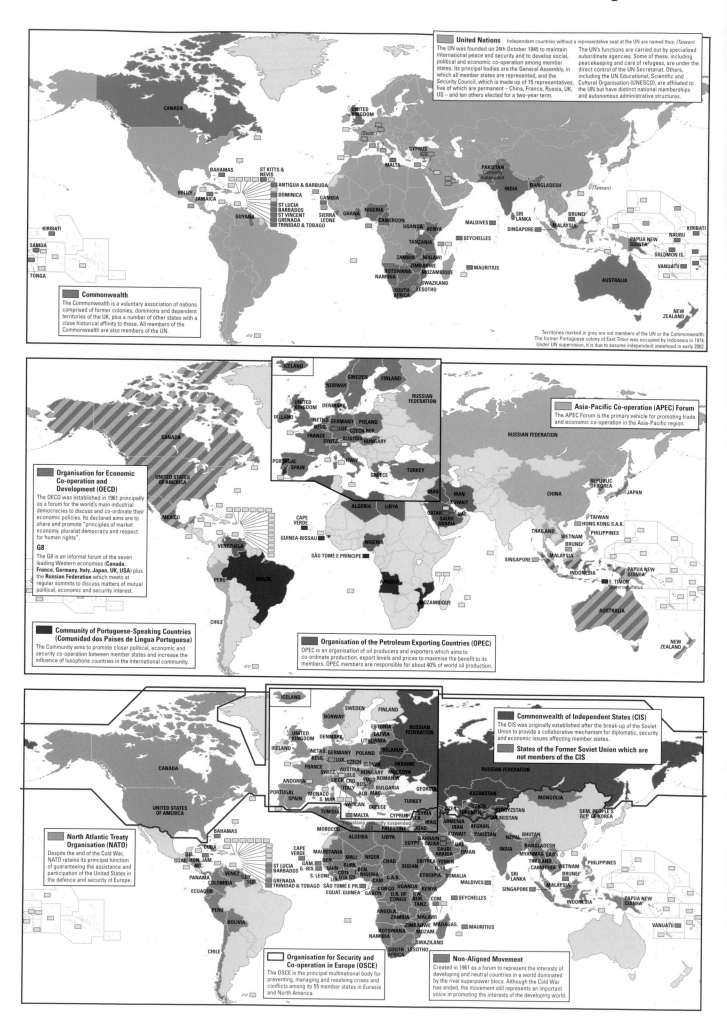

United Nations Independent countries without a representative seat at the UN are named thus: *(Taiwan)*

The UN was founded on 24th October 1945 to maintain international peace and security and to develop social, political and economic co-operation among member states. Its principal bodies are the General Assembly, in which all member states are represented, and the Security Council, which is made up of 15 representatives, five of which are permanent – China, France, Russia, UK, US – and ten others elected for a two-year term.

The UN's functions are carried out by specialised subordinate agencies. Some of these, including peacekeeping and care of refugees, are under the direct control of the UN Secretariat. Others, including the UN Educational, Scientific and Cultural Organisation (UNESCO), are affiliated to the UN but have distinct national memberships and autonomous administrative structures.

Commonwealth

The Commonwealth is a voluntary association of nations comprised of former colonies, dominions and dependent territories of the UK, plus a number of other states with a close historical affinity to these. All members of the Commonwealth are also members of the UN.

Territories marked in grey are not members of the UN or the Commonwealth. The former Portuguese colony of East Timor was occupied by Indonesia in 1974. Under UN supervision, it is due to assume independent statehood in early 2002.

Organisation for Economic Co-operation and Development (OECD)

The OECD was established in 1961 principally as a forum for the world's main industrial democracies to discuss and co-ordinate their economic policies. Its declared aims are to share and promote "principles of market economy, pluralist democracy and respect for human rights".

G8

The G8 is an informal forum of the seven leading Western economies (**Canada, France, Germany, Italy, Japan, UK, USA**) plus the **Russian Federation** which meets at regular summits to discuss matters of mutual political, economic and security interest.

Community of Portuguese-Speaking Countries (Comunidad dos Paises de Lingua Portuguesa)

The Community aims to promote closer political, economic and security co-operation between member states and increase the influence of lusophone countries in the international community.

Asia-Pacific Co-operation (APEC) Forum

The APEC Forum is the primary vehicle for promoting trade and economic co-operation in the Asia-Pacific region.

Organisation of the Petroleum Exporting Countries (OPEC)

OPEC is an organisation of oil producers and exporters which aims to co-ordinate production, export levels and prices to maximise the benefit to its members. OPEC members are responsible for about 40% of world oil production.

North Atlantic Treaty Organisation (NATO)

Despite the end of the Cold War, NATO retains its principal function of guaranteeing the assistance and participation of the United States in the defence and security of Europe.

Commonwealth of Independent States (CIS)

The CIS was originally established after the break-up of the Soviet Union to provide a collaborative mechanism for diplomatic, security and economic issues affecting member states.

States of the Former Soviet Union which are not members of the CIS

Organisation for Security and Co-operation in Europe (OSCE)

The OSCE is the principal multinational body for preventing, managing and resolving crises and conflicts among its 55 member states in Eurasia and North America.

Non-Aligned Movement

Created in 1961 as a forum to represent the interests of developing and neutral countries in a world dominated by the rival superpower blocs. Although the Cold War has ended, the movement still represents an important voice in promoting the interests of the developing world.

International Organisations

North American Free Trade Agreement (NAFTA)
NAFTA provides for a free trade zone and customs union among its members. Signed in 1994, it aims to remove all previous restrictions on trade and investment by 2009.

Organisation of American States (OAS)
Established in 1948, the OAS is the principal diplomatic and security forum for the nations of South and Central America and the Caribbean. It has become especially involved in efforts to promote human rights in the region and in the struggles against corruption and drug trafficking.

*Cuba was suspended from the OAS in 1962 and is barred from any participation in the Organisation. However, it remains a formal member.

Rio Group
Set up in 1987 as a forum for joint political action among the nations of South and Central America, especially with regard to US policy. Its remit also includes promotion of free trade and joint action against drug trafficking and corruption.

Andean Community of Nations
The Andean Group was formed in 1969 to promote economic and political integration among member states. Its present incarnation, which followed revisions to the original charter, dates from 1996.

BLUE ITALICS Latin American Integration Association (ALADI)
ALADI's ultimate objective is the creation of a common market throughout South America. A system of preferential tariffs is designed to help individual states and further economic harmonisation.

Southern Common Market (MERCOSUR)
MERCOSUR is a customs union and free trade zone for the southern part of Latin America. Currently its main objective is economic harmonisation. The Associated States (Bolivia & Chile) participate in the free trade zone only.

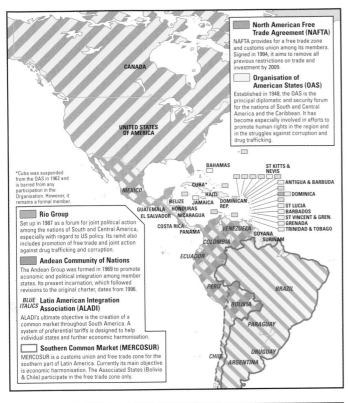

European Union (EU)
Originally created as a customs union and free trade zone, the EU has developed into an organisation in which almost all aspects of economic policy and, increasingly, foreign and security policies are harmonised among its 15 member states. See also pp 92-93.

European Free Trade Association (EFTA)
EFTA was established in 1959 as an alternative to the body which became the European Union. EFTA is very largely concerned with trade liberalisation.

European Economic Area (EEA)
The EEA was set up in 1994 as an institutional structure to promote free trade and co-operation between EFTA and EU. All EFTA and EU members (with the exception of Switzerland) belong to the EEA.

Western European Union (WEU)
The WEU was created to bolster the European arm of NATO. Since then, however, it has acquired a new role as an embryonic structure for a future European Union defence organisation. Members are shown thus: ITALY associate members: POLAND observers: AUSTRIA associate partners: ROMANIA

Council of Europe
Created in 1949 to strengthen a common European commitment to parliamentary democracy, the rule of law and respect for human rights. Its original ten signatories have now grown to 43, including a number of former Soviet and Yugoslav republics.

*The autonomous territories of Åland, Faroe Is. and Greenland have distinct representation on the Nordic Council as part of their national delegations.

Nordic Council
Formed in 1952 as a forum for co-operation among the Nordic countries and works to develop common Nordic policies.

Baltic Council
Established in 1993 to co-ordinate policy in the areas of foreign policy, justice, environment and education between these former Soviet republics.

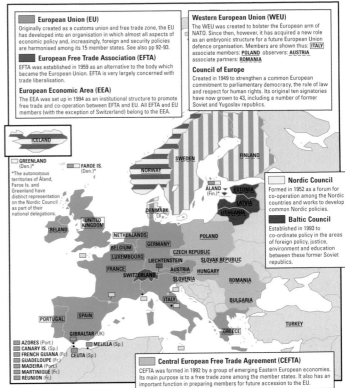

Central European Free Trade Agreement (CEFTA)
CEFTA was formed in 1992 by a group of emerging Eastern European economies. Its main purpose is to a free trade zone among the member states. It also has an important function in preparing members for future accession to the EU.

Central American Common Market (CACM)
The CACM was formed in 1960 with the objective of creating a customs union and free trade zone in Central America.

Caribbean Community and Common Market (CARICOM)
CARICOM was established in 1973, replacing the former Caribbean Free Trade Association. In doing so, it took over the Association's role in promoting free trade (eventually leading to a common market), but also assumed new co-ordinating responsibilities in the fields of foreign policy and regional security.

Organisation of Eastern Caribbean States (OECS)
The OECS was created in 1981 with the objectives of harmonising economic, foreign and security policies among member states.

*The Bahamas is a member of the Community but not of the Common Market (i.e. it subscribes to CARICOM's diplomatic and security functions but not to the trade elements).
†Haiti has failed to lodge a formal instrument of accession. Its membership is thus in abeyance.

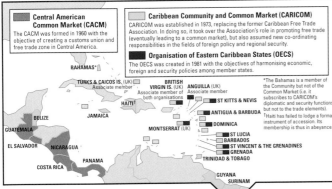

Black Sea Economic Co-operation Pact (BSEC)
Based in Turkey, the BSEC is a forum for economic co-operation among the Black Sea littoral states and others in the region.

Economic Co-operation Organisation (ECO)
The ECO was set up in 1985 to promote regional co-operation among the non-Arab states of Western and Central Asia. Following the break-up of the Soviet Union, a number of former Soviet republics joined.

South Asian Association for Regional Co-operation (SAARC)
Formed in 1985 to improve co-operation among member countries, the SAARC focuses mainly on economic development and technical issues.

League of Arab States
Formed in 1945, the function of the organisation is primarily diplomatic and designed to support and co-ordinate matters of common concern among Arab states. Historically, it has played a major role in the Israeli-Palestinian conflict.

Gulf Co-operation Council (GCC)
The GCC was established in 1981 as a forum for the conservative states of the Gulf to co-ordinate and develop their economic, political, cultural and security policies.

Indian Ocean Commission (IOC)
The IOC was created in 1982 to promote trade and economic co-operation in the region. The EU is the major donor, with most of the money allocated to a series of projects supporting fisheries, maritime transport, tourism and the environment.

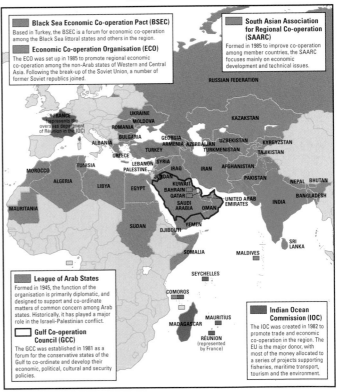

BOLD CAPITALS Organisation of African Unity (OAU)
Formed in 1963, the OAU's aims are the promotion of African unity and solidarity, co-ordination of national policies in a variety of areas, and the defence of national sovereignty. Starting in 2002, the OAU will undergo a major overhaul of its institutions with the ultimate objective of establishing a political and economic union along the lines of the European Union. It will be renamed the African Union.

Union of the Arab Maghreb
The main political and economic bloc in Arab North Africa was created in 1989 as a vehicle to promote economic and political co-operation. Since 1994, the foundations of a free trade zone have been put in place.

CFA Franc Zone
The Communauté Financière de l'Afrique (CFA) is a group of 14 African countries, mostly former French colonies, which use the CFA Franc as currency and have adopted other fiscal and monetary measures under agreements with the French government. The CFA Franc is fixed in value to the French Franc (100 CFA = 1 FF) and the Euro (665.96 CFA = 1 Euro).

Common Market for Eastern and Southern Africa (COMESA)
Set up in 1994 with the aims of establishing a free trade area and customs union by eliminating barriers to intra-COMESA trade.

Economic Community of West African States (ECOWAS)
Originally established to create a common market and free trade zone in West Africa, ECOWAS has since assumed important diplomatic and security functions, most prominently in the area of conflict resolution.

Southern African Development Community (SADC)
The SADC was created in 1992 by southern African states concerned to limit and counter the dominant political and economic influence of South Africa in the region. Since the end of apartheid, South Africa has joined the SADC which is now the principal forum for regional co-operation and trade promotion.

*The Comoros, a former member of the CFA, continues to peg its currency to the CFA Franc.

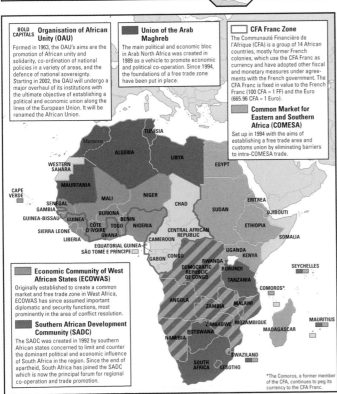

South Pacific Forum (SPF)
The Forum was created primarily to promote economic and social co-operation amongst member states. However, it has also become the Pacific islands' principal voice in the context of a number of vital regional issues such as nuclear testing and global warming.

Association of South-East Asian Nations (ASEAN)
Although its founding charter envisaged economic and social functions for the organisation, ASEAN was primarily an anti-communist strategic body from its establishment in 1967 to the end of the Cold War. During the 1990s, however, its wider role has come into play.

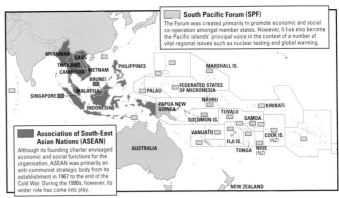

Business

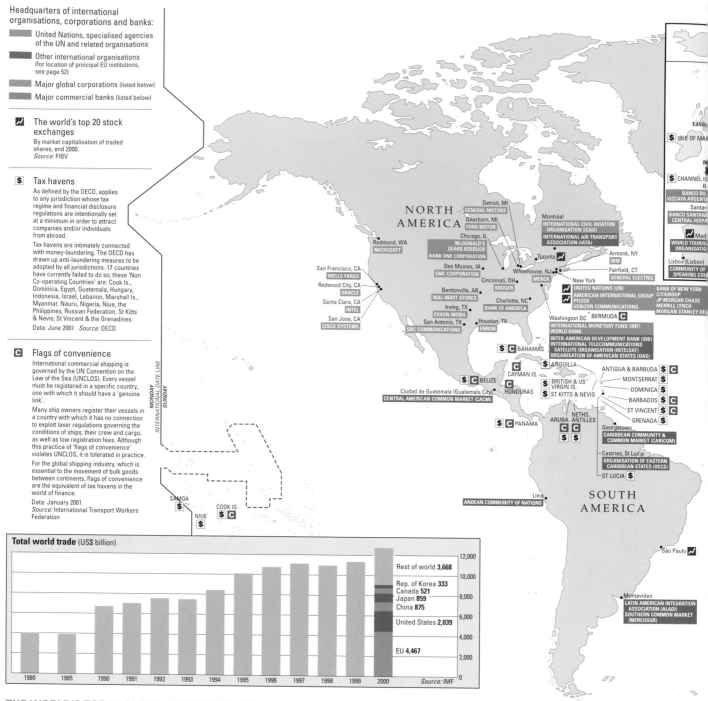

Headquarters of international organisations, corporations and banks:

- United Nations, specialised agencies of the UN and related organisations
- Other international organisations (for location of principal EU institutions, see page 52)
- Major global corporations (listed below)
- Major commercial banks (listed below)

The world's top 20 stock exchanges
By market capitalisation of traded shares, end 2000.
Source: FIBV

$ Tax havens
As defined by the OECD, applies to any jurisdiction whose tax regime and financial disclosure regulations are intentionally set at a minimum in order to attract companies and/or individuals from abroad.

Tax havens are intimately connected with money-laundering. The OECD has drawn up anti-laundering meaures to be adopted by all jurisdictions. 17 countries have currently failed to do so; these 'Non Co-operating Countries' are: Cook Is., Dominica, Egypt, Guatemala, Hungary, Indonesia, Israel, Lebanon, Marshall Is., Myanmar, Nauru, Nigeria, Niue, the Philippines, Russian Federation, St Kitts & Nevis; St Vincent & the Grenadines.
Data: June 2001 *Source:* OECD

C Flags of convenience
International commercial shipping is governed by the UN Convention on the Law of the Sea (UNCLOS). Every vessel must be registered in a specific country, one with which it should have a 'genuine link'.

Many ship owners register their vessels in a country with which it has no connection to exploit laxer regulations governing the conditions of ships, their crew and cargo, as well as low registration fees. Although this practice of 'flags of convenience' violates UNCLOS, it is tolerated in practice.

For the global shipping industry, which is essential to the movement of bulk goods between continents, flags of convenience are the equivalent of tax havens in the world of finance.
Data: January 2001
Source: International Transport Workers Federation

Total world trade (US$ billion)

Rest of world	3,668	
Rep. of Korea	333	
Canada	521	
Japan	859	
China	875	
United States	2,039	
EU	4,467	

Years: 1980, 1985, 1990, 1991, 1992, 1993, 1994, 1995, 1996, 1997, 1998, 1999, 2000. *Source:* IMF

THE WORLD'S TOP 20 GLOBAL CORPORATIONS (excluding banks)

By annual turnover (US$ million):		By number of employees (thousands):		By market capitalisation (US$ million):	
Exxon-Mobil	210,392	Wal-Mart Stores	1,244	General Electric	477,406
Wal-Mart Stores	193,295	Daimler/Chrysler	450	Cisco Systems	304,699
General Motors	184,632	Siemens	447	Exxon Mobil	286,367
Ford Motor	180,598	General Motors	386	Pfizer	263,996
Daimler/Chrysler	150,070	McDonald's	364	Microsoft	258,436
Royal Dutch/Shell	149,146	Ford Motor	346	Wal-Mart Stores	250,955
BP	148,062	Deutsche Post	324	Vodafone Group	227,175
General Electric	129,853	Hitachi	324	Intel	227,048
Mitsubishi	126,579	Sears Roebuck	323	Royal Dutch/Shell	206,340
Toyota Motor	121,416	IBM	316	American Internat.	206,084
Mitsui	118,013	General Electric	313	Nokia	197,497
Itochu	109,757	Volkswagen	306	Merck	195,743
Total Fina Elf	105,870	Kroger	305	Oracle	182,270
NTT	103,235	Unilever	295	BP	178,006
Enron	100,789	Matsushita	290	DoCoMo	175,435
AXA	92,782	Vivendi Universal	290	SBC Communications	174,830
IBM	88,396	Philips Electronics	232	IBM	164,086
Marubeni	85,351	NTT	224	GlaxoSmithKline	160,406
Volkswagen	78,851	SBC Communications	220	EMC Corporation	155,976
Hitachi	76,127	Toyota Motor	211	Verizon Commun.	147,852

Data: July 2001 *Source:* Fortune 500 | Data: May 2001 *Source:* FT Surveys | Data: May 2001 *Source:* FT Surveys

THE WORLD'S TOP 20 BANKS

By Tier One capital (US$ million):		By assets (US$ million):		By market capitalisation (US$ million):	
Citigroup	54,498	Mizuho Group	1,259,498	Citigroup	250,143
Mizuho Group	50,502	Citigroup	902,210	HSBC Holdings	140,693
Bank of America	40,667	Deutsche Group	874,706	JP Morgan Chase	103,113
JP Morgan Chase	37,581	JP Morgan Chase	715,348	Morgan Stanley DW	99,056
HSBC Holdings	34,620	Bk of Tokyo-Mitsub.	675,640	Wells Fargo	89,251
Crédit Agricole	26,383	HSBC Holdings	673,614	Bank of America	82,745
I & C Bank of China	22,792	HypoVereinsBank	666,707	ING Bank	77,806
Deutsche Bank	20,076	UBS	664,560	UBS	73,673
Bk of Tokyo-Mitsub.	20,050	BNP Paribas	645,793	Royal Bk of Scotland	62,865
Sakura	20,035	Bank of America	642,191	Merrill Lynch	60,883
Bank One Corp.	19,824	Credit Suisse Group	603,381	Lloyds TSB	60,663
HypoVereinsBank	19,806	Sumitomo Bank	540,875	Mizuho Group	58,128
UBS	19,488	ABN-AMRO	506,687	Credit Suisse Group	57,719
BNP Paribas	18,889	Crédit Agricole	498,426	Barclays Bank	53,360
Sumitomo Bank	18,124	I & C Bank of China	482,983	Deutsche Bank	51,048
Royal Bk of Scotland	18,011	Norinchukin Bank	462,593	Banco Santander CH	48,311
ABN-AMRO	17,689	Royal Bk of Scotland	461,511	Bk of Tokyo-Mitsub.	46,986
Bank of China	17,086	Barclays Bank	458,787	Banco Bilbao BVA	46,774
Credit Suisse Group	16,566	Dresdner Bank	449,898	Bank One Corp.	46,395
Wells Fargo	16,096	Commerzbank	427,718	Bank of New York	41,466

Data: July 2001 *Source:* The Banker | Data: July 2001 *Source:* The Banker | Data: May 2001 *Source:* FT Surveys

Business

Headquarters in cities marked in **red** are listed on the right

EUROPE
ASIA
AFRICA
AUSTRALIA

Amsterdam
PHILIPS ELECTRONICS
ABN-AMRO
ING BANK

Basel (Basle)
BANK FOR INTERNATIONAL SETTLEMENTS (BIS)

Bonn
DEUTSCHE POST

Bruxelles/Brussel (Brussels)
EUROPEAN UNION (EU)
NORTH ATLANTIC TREATY ORGANISATION (NATO)
WESTERN EUROPEAN UNION (WEU)
WORLD CUSTOMS ORGANISATION

Cambridge
INTERNATIONAL WHALING COMMISSION (IOC)

Den Haag/'s-Gravenhage (The Hague)
INTERNATIONAL COURT OF JUSTICE
ROYAL DUTCH/SHELL GROUP

Edinburgh
ROYAL BANK OF SCOTLAND

Frankfurt am Main
COMMERZBANK
DEUTSCHE BANK
DRESDNER BANK

Genève (Geneva)
INTERNATIONAL LABOUR ORGANISATION (ILO)
INTERNATIONAL TELECOMMUNICATIONS UNION (ITU)
WORLD HEALTH ORGANISATION (WHO)
EUROPEAN FREE TRADE ASSOCIATION (EFTA)
EUROPEAN BROADCASTING UNION (EBU)
INTERNATIONAL AIR TRANSPORT ASSOCIATION (IATA)
INTERNATIONAL COMMITTEE FOR THE RED CROSS
INTERNATIONAL ORGANISATION FOR STANDARDISATION (ISO)
WORLD COUNCIL OF CHURCHES
WORLD TRADE ORGANISATION

Gland
WORLD-WIDE FUND FOR NATURE /
WORLD WILDLIFE FUND (WWF)

Greenford
GLAXOSMITHKLINE

Lausanne
INTERNATIONAL OLYMPIC COMMITTEE (IOC)

London
INTERNATIONAL MARITIME ORGANISATION (IMO)
AMNESTY INTERNATIONAL
THE COMMONWEALTH
EUROPEAN BANK FOR RECONSTRUCTION & DEVELOPMENT (EBRD)
INTERNATIONAL MARITIME SATELLITE ORGANISATION (INMARSAT)
BP   BARCLAYS BANK   LLOYDS TSB
UNILEVER PLC   HSBC HOLDINGS

Lyon (Lyons)
INTERPOL

Newbury
VODAFONE GROUP

München (Munich)
SIEMENS
HYPOVEREINSBANK

Paris
UN EDUCATIONAL, SCIENTIFIC &
CULTURAL ORGANISATION (UNESCO)
CFA FRANC ZONE
ORGANISATION FOR ECONOMIC
CO-OPERATION & DEVELOPMENT (OECD)
AXA
TOTAL FINA ELF
VIVENDI
BNP PARIBAS
CREDIT AGRICOLE

Rotterdam
UNILEVER NV

Strasbourg
COUNCIL OF EUROPE

Stuttgart
DAIMLER/CHRYSLER

Vernier
INTERNATIONAL ROAD FEDERATION (IRF)

Wolfsburg
VOLKSWAGEN

Zürich
FEDERATION INTERNATIONAL DE
FOOTBALL ASSOCIATION (FIFA)
CREDIT SUISSE GROUP
UBS

Stockholm
Espoo (Esbo) NOKIA
Helsinki (Helsingfors)
København (Copenhagen)
NORDIC COUNCIL
Wolfsburg
GERMANY
Frankfurt aM
Stuttgart
München (Munich)
Basel (Basle)
LIECHTENSTEIN
Milano (Milan)
Minsk
COMMONWEALTH OF
INDEPENDENT STATES (CIS)
Vienna
INTERNATIONAL ATOMIC ENERGY AGENCY (IAEA)
UN INDUSTRIAL DEVELOPMENT ORGANISATION (UNIDO)
ORGANISATION OF THE PETROLEUM EXPORTING COUNTRIES (OPEC)
ORGANISATION FOR SECURITY & CO-OPERATION IN EUROPE (OSCE)
Roma (Rome)
FOOD & AGRICULTURE
ORGANISATION (FAO)
Istanbul
BLACK SEA ECONOMIC
CO-OPERATION PACT (BSEC)
MALTA C
CYPRUS C
LEBANON C
Rabat
Tehrān
ECONOMIC CO-OPERATION
ORGANISATION (ECO)
El Qâhira (Cairo)
LEAGUE OF ARAB STATES
BAHRAIN $
Ar Riyâd (Riyadh)
GULF CO-OPERATION COUNCIL (GCC)
Beijing (Peking)
BANK OF CHINA
INDUSTRIAL & COMMERCIAL BANK OF CHINA
Kathmandu
SOUTH ASIAN ASSOCIATION
FOR REGIONAL CO-OPERATION
MYANMAR C
CAMBODIA C
SRI LANKA C
MALDIVES $
SEYCHELLES $
Abuja
ECONOMIC COMMUNITY OF WEST
AFRICAN STATES (ECOWAS)
Abidjan
AFRICAN DEVELOPMENT BANK
Addis Ababa
ORGANISATION OF
AFRICAN UNITY (OAU)
Lusaka
COMMON MARKET FOR EASTERN
& SOUTHERN AFRICA (COMESA)
Gaborone
SOUTHERN AFRICAN DEVELOPMENT
COMMUNITY (SADC)
Quatre Bornes, Mauritius
INDIAN OCEAN COMMISSION (IOC)
MAURITIUS C
Sôul (Seoul)
Tôkyô
DOCOMO   MITSUBISHI   BANK OF TOKYO-MITSUBISHI
HITACHI   MITSUI   MIZUHO FINANCIAL GROUP
ITOCHU   NIPPON TELEPHONE & NORINCHUKIN BANK
MARUBENI   TELEGRAPH (NTT)   SAKURA
Toyota
TOYOTA MOTOR
Ôsaka
MATSUSHITA ELECTRICAL INDUSTRIES
SUMITOMO BANK
Taipei
Xianggang (Hong Kong)
Manila
ASIAN DEVELOPMENT BANK
Singapore
ASIA-PACIFIC ECONOMIC CO-OPERATION (APEC) FORUM
INTERNATIONAL AIR TRANSPORT ASSOCIATION (IATA)
Jakarta
ASSOCIATION OF SOUTH-EAST
ASIAN NATIONS (ASEAN)
MARSHALL IS. $ C
NAURU $
TUVALU
VANUATU $ C
TONGA $
Suva
SOUTH PACIFIC
FORUM (SPF)
Nouméa
PACIFIC
COMMUNITY (SPC)
AUSTRALIA
Sydney

MONDAY / INTERNATIONAL DATE LINE / SUNDAY

Stock market charts

NEW YORK *Dow Jones Industrial Average*
(values: 0 – 12,000; years 1991 92 93 94 95 96 97 98 99 2000 01)

NASDAQ (New York) *NASDAQ-100*
(values: 0 – 5,000; years 1991 92 93 94 95 96 97 98 99 2000 01)

TOKYO *Nikkei-225*
(values: 0 – 30,000; years 1991 92 93 94 95 96 97 98 99 2000 01)

LONDON *FTSE-100*
(values: 0 – 7,000; years 1991 92 93 94 95 96 97 98 99 2000 01)

PARIS *CAC-40*
(values: 0 – 7,000; years 1991 92 93 94 95 96 97 98 99 2000 01)

FRANKFURT *DAX*
(values: 0 – 8,000; years 1991 92 93 94 95 96 97 98 99 2000 01)

TORONTO *TSE-300*
(values: 0 – 12,000; years 1991 92 93 94 95 96 97 98 99 2000 01)

HONG KONG *Hang Seng*
(values: 0 – 20,000; years 1991 92 93 94 95 96 97 98 99 2000 01)

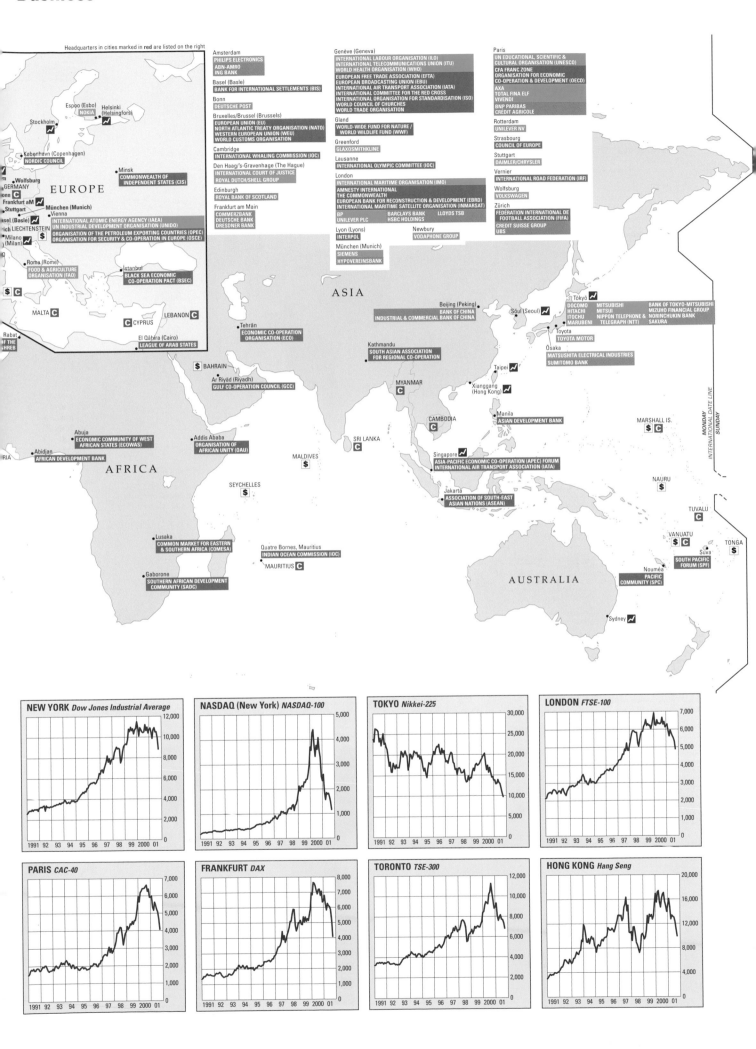

Telecommunications: Land & Cellular Services

FIXED LINE TELECOMMUNICATIONS

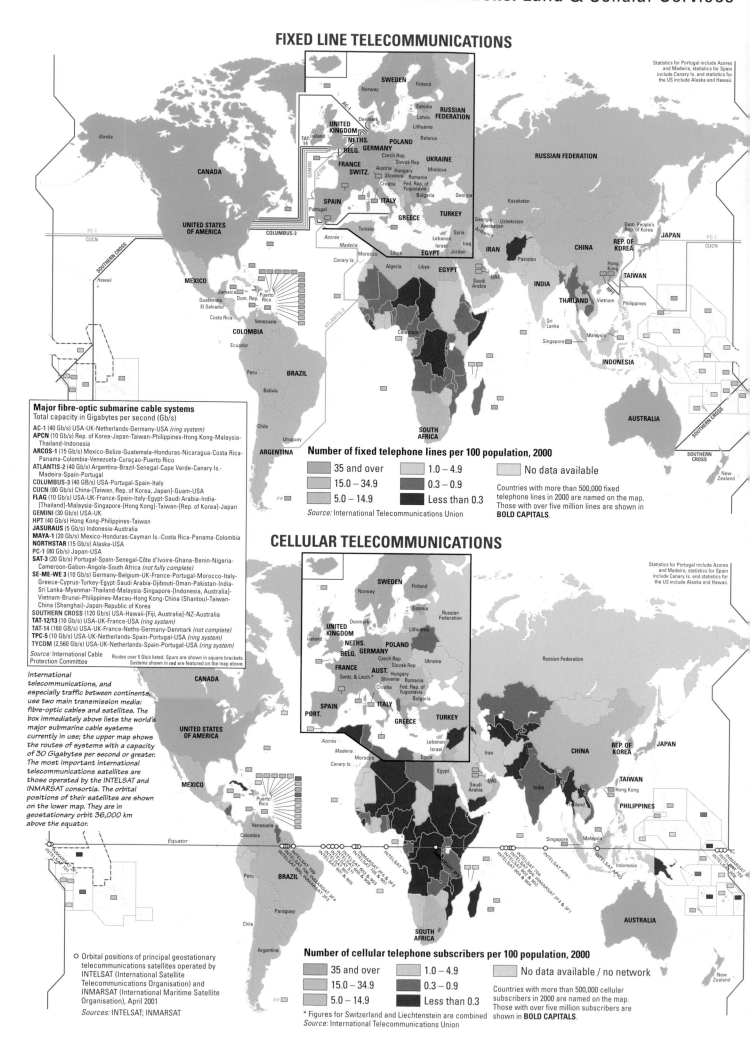

Statistics for Portugal include Azores and Madeira, statistics for Spain include Canary Is. and statistics for the US include Alaska and Hawaii.

Number of fixed telephone lines per 100 population, 2000

- 35 and over
- 15.0 – 34.9
- 5.0 – 14.9
- 1.0 – 4.9
- 0.3 – 0.9
- Less than 0.3
- No data available

Countries with more than 500,000 fixed telephone lines in 2000 are named on the map. Those with over five million lines are shown in **BOLD CAPITALS**.

Source: International Telecommunications Union

Major fibre-optic submarine cable systems
Total capacity in Gigabytes per second (Gb/s)

AC-1 (40 Gb/s) USA-UK-Netherlands-Germany-USA (ring system)
APCN (10 Gb/s) Rep. of Korea-Japan-Taiwan-Philippines-Hong Kong-Malaysia-Thailand-Indonesia
ARCOS-1 (15 Gb/s) Mexico-Belize-Guatemala-Honduras-Nicaragua-Costa Rica-Panama-Colombia-Venezuela-Curaçao-Puerto Rico
ATLANTIS-2 (40 Gb/s) Argentina-Brazil-Senegal-Cape Verde-Canary Is.-Madeira-Spain-Portugal
COLUMBUS-3 (40 GB/s) USA-Portugal-Spain-Italy
CUCN (80 Gb/s) China-[Taiwan, Rep. of Korea, Japan]-Guam-USA
FLAG (10 Gb/s) USA-UK-France-Spain-Italy-Egypt-Saudi Arabia-India-[Thailand]-Malaysia-Singapore-[Hong Kong]-Taiwan-[Rep. of Korea]-Japan
GEMINI (30 Gb/s) USA-UK
HPT (40 Gb/s) Hong Kong-Philippines-Taiwan
JASURAUS (5 Gb/s) Indonesia-Australia
MAYA-1 (20 Gb/s) Mexico-Honduras-Cayman Is.-Costa Rica-Panama-Colombia
NORTHSTAR (15 Gb/s) Alaska-USA
PC-1 (80 Gb/s) Japan-USA
SAT-3 (20 Gb/s) Portugal-Spain-Senegal-Côte d'Ivoire-Ghana-Benin-Nigeria-Cameroon-Gabon-Angola-South Africa (not fully complete)
SE-ME-WE 3 (10 Gb/s) Germany-Belgium-UK-France-Portugal-Morocco-Italy-Greece-Cyprus-Turkey-Egypt-Saudi Arabia-Djibouti-Oman-Pakistan-India-Sri Lanka-Myanmar-Thailand-Malaysia-Singapore-[Indonesia, Australia]-Vietnam-Brunei-Philippines-Macau-Hong Kong-China (Shantou)-Taiwan-China (Shanghai)-Japan-Republic of Korea
SOUTHERN CROSS (120 Gb/s) USA-Hawaii-[Fiji, Australia]-NZ-Australia
TAT-12/13 (10 Gb/s) USA-UK-France-USA (ring system)
TAT-14 (160 GB/s) USA-UK-France-Neths-Germany-Denmark (not complete)
TPC-5 (10 Gb/s) USA-UK-Netherlands-Spain-Portugal-USA (ring system)
TYCOM (2,560 Gb/s) USA-UK-Netherlands-Spain-Portugal-USA (ring system)

Source: International Cable Protection Committee

Routes over 5 Gb/s listed. Spurs are shown in square brackets. Systems shown in red are featured on the map above.

International telecommunications, and especially traffic between continents, use two main transmission media: fibre-optic cables and satellites. The box immediately above lists the world's major submarine cable systems currently in use; the upper map shows the routes of systems with a capacity of 30 Gigabytes per second or greater. The most important international telecommunications satellites are those operated by the INTELSAT and INMARSAT consortia. The orbital positions of their satellites are shown on the lower map. They are in geostationary orbit 36,000 km above the equator.

CELLULAR TELECOMMUNICATIONS

Statistics for Portugal include Azores and Madeira, statistics for Spain include Canary Is. and statistics for the US include Alaska and Hawaii.

○ Orbital positions of principal geostationary telecommunications satellites operated by INTELSAT (International Satellite Telecommunications Organisation) and INMARSAT (International Maritime Satellite Organisation), April 2001

Sources: INTELSAT; INMARSAT

Number of cellular telephone subscribers per 100 population, 2000

- 35 and over
- 15.0 – 34.9
- 5.0 – 14.9
- 1.0 – 4.9
- 0.3 – 0.9
- Less than 0.3
- No data available / no network

Countries with more than 500,000 cellular subscribers in 2000 are named on the map. Those with over five million subscribers are shown in **BOLD CAPITALS**.

* Figures for Switzerland and Liechtenstein are combined
Source: International Telecommunications Union

Telecommunications: Internet & Media

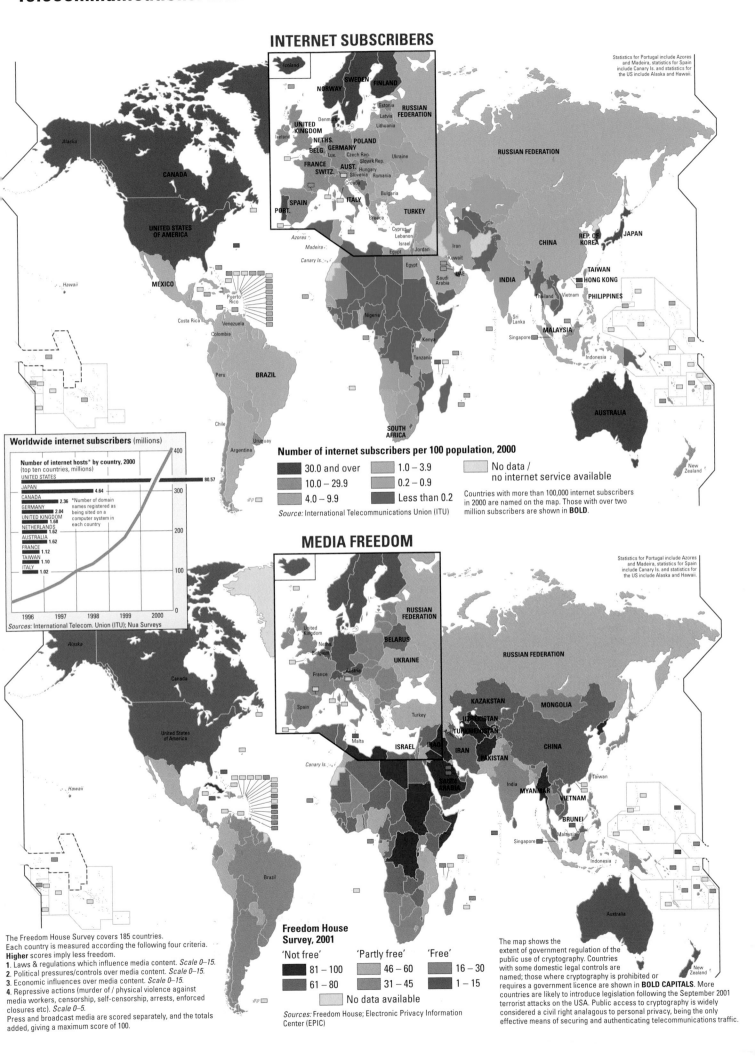

INTERNET SUBSCRIBERS

Statistics for Portugal include Azores and Madeira, statistics for Spain include Canary Is. and statistics for the US include Alaska and Hawaii.

Worldwide internet subscribers (millions)

Number of internet hosts* by country, 2000
(top ten countries, millions)

Country	
UNITED STATES	80.57
JAPAN	4.64
CANADA	2.36
GERMANY	2.04
UNITED KINGDOM	1.68
NETHERLANDS	1.62
AUSTRALIA	1.62
FRANCE	1.12
TAIWAN	1.10
ITALY	1.02

*Number of domain names registered as being sited on a computer system in each country

1996 1997 1998 1999 2000

Sources: International Telecom. Union (ITU); Nua Surveys

Number of internet subscribers per 100 population, 2000

- 30.0 and over
- 10.0 – 29.9
- 4.0 – 9.9
- 1.0 – 3.9
- 0.2 – 0.9
- Less than 0.2
- No data / no internet service available

Source: International Telecommunications Union (ITU)

Countries with more than 100,000 internet subscribers in 2000 are named on the map. Those with over two million subscribers are shown in **BOLD**.

MEDIA FREEDOM

Statistics for Portugal include Azores and Madeira, statistics for Spain include Canary Is. and statistics for the US include Alaska and Hawaii.

The Freedom House Survey covers 185 countries. Each country is measured according the following four criteria. **Higher** scores imply less freedom.
1. Laws & regulations which influence media content. *Scale 0–15.*
2. Political pressures/controls over media content. *Scale 0–15.*
3. Economic influences over media content. *Scale 0–15.*
4. Repressive actions (murder of / physical violence against media workers, censorship, self-censorship, arrests, enforced closures etc). *Scale 0–5.*
Press and broadcast media are scored separately, and the totals added, giving a maximum score of 100.

Freedom House Survey, 2001

'Not free'
- 81 – 100
- 61 – 80

'Partly free'
- 46 – 60
- 31 – 45

'Free'
- 16 – 30
- 1 – 15

- No data available

Sources: Freedom House; Electronic Privacy Information Center (EPIC)

The map shows the extent of government regulation of the public use of cryptography. Countries with some domestic legal controls are named; those where cryptography is prohibited or requires a government licence are shown in **BOLD CAPITALS**. More countries are likely to introduce legislation following the September 2001 terrorist attacks on the USA. Public access to cryptography is widely considered a civil right analagous to personal privacy, being the only effective means of securing and authenticating telecommunications traffic.

SPENDING ON HEALTH

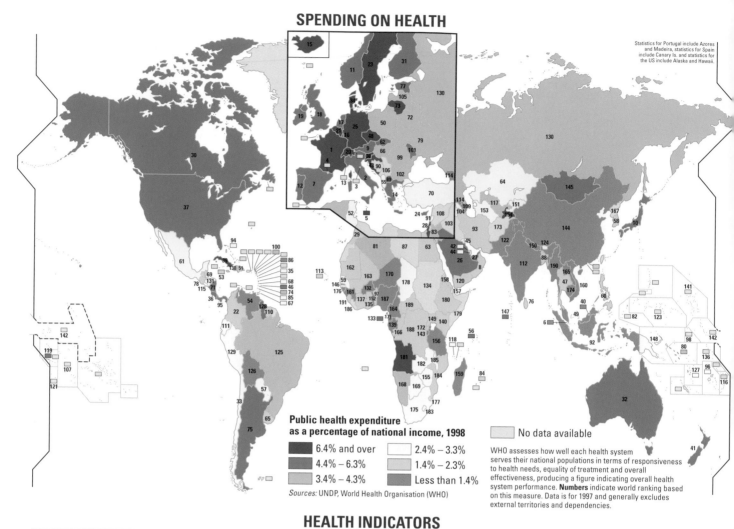

Statistics for Portugal include Azores and Madeira, statistics for Spain include Canary Is. and statistics for the US include Alaska and Hawaii.

Public health expenditure as a percentage of national income, 1998

- 6.4% and over
- 4.4% – 6.3%
- 3.4% – 4.3%
- 2.4% – 3.3%
- 1.4% – 2.3%
- Less than 1.4%
- No data available

Sources: UNDP, World Health Organisation (WHO)

WHO assesses how well each health system serves their national populations in terms of responsiveness to health needs, equality of treatment and overall effectiveness, producing a figure indicating overall health system performance. **Numbers** indicate world ranking based on this measure. Data is for 1997 and generally excludes external territories and dependencies.

HEALTH INDICATORS

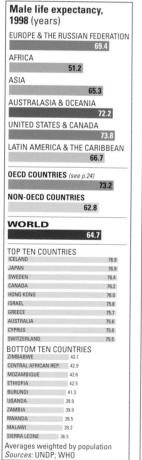

Male life expectancy, 1998 (years)

EUROPE & THE RUSSIAN FEDERATION	69.4
AFRICA	51.2
ASIA	65.3
AUSTRALASIA & OCEANIA	72.2
UNITED STATES & CANADA	73.8
LATIN AMERICA & THE CARIBBEAN	66.7
OECD COUNTRIES (see p.24)	73.2
NON-OECD COUNTRIES	62.8
WORLD	**64.7**

TOP TEN COUNTRIES
ICELAND	76.9
JAPAN	76.9
SWEDEN	76.4
CANADA	76.2
HONG KONG	76.0
ISRAEL	75.8
GREECE	75.7
AUSTRALIA	75.6
CYPRUS	75.6
SWITZERLAND	75.5

BOTTOM TEN COUNTRIES
ZIMBABWE	43.1
CENTRAL AFRICAN REP.	42.9
MOZAMBIQUE	42.6
ETHIOPIA	42.5
BURUNDI	41.3
UGANDA	39.9
ZAMBIA	39.9
RWANDA	39.5
MALAWI	39.2
SIERRA LEONE	36.5

Averages weighted by population
Sources: UNDP; WHO

Female life expectancy, 1998 (years)

EUROPE & THE RUSSIAN FEDERATION	77.3
AFRICA	54.0
ASIA	68.4
AUSTRALASIA & OCEANIA	77.1
UNITED STATES & CANADA	80.4
LATIN AMERICA & THE CARIBBEAN	72.5
OECD COUNTRIES (see p.24)	79.6
NON-OECD COUNTRIES	66.4
WORLD	**68.9**

TOP TEN COUNTRIES
JAPAN	83.0
FRANCE	82.1
CANADA	81.9
SWITZERLAND	81.9
SPAIN	81.6
HONG KONG	81.5
ICELAND	81.4
ITALY	81.3
NORWAY	81.3
AUSTRALIA	81.2

BOTTOM TEN COUNTRIES
BURKINA	45.5
MOZAMBIQUE	45.0
ETHIOPIA	44.4
BURUNDI	44.0
ZIMBABWE	44.0
RWANDA	41.7
UGANDA	41.5
ZAMBIA	41.0
MALAWI	39.8
SIERRA LEONE	39.4

Averages weighted by population
Sources: UNDP; WHO

Mortality* in childbirth, 1998 (per 10,000 births)

EUROPE & THE RUSSIAN FEDERATION	2.9
AFRICA	68.5
ASIA	23.2
AUSTRALASIA & OCEANIA	7.9
UNITED STATES & CANADA	0.8
LATIN AMERICA & THE CARIBBEAN	13.3
OECD COUNTRIES (see p.24)	1.9
NON-OECD COUNTRIES	29.1
WORLD	**24.0**

Averages weighted by population
Source: UNDP
*Death of mother during childbirth

Infant* mortality, 1998 (per 1,000 live births)

EUROPE & THE RUSSIAN FEDERATION	15.3
AFRICA	145.5
ASIA	70.5
AUSTRALASIA & OCEANIA	23.6
UNITED STATES & CANADA	7.8
LATIN AMERICA & THE CARIBBEAN	37.8
OECD COUNTRIES (see p.24)	10.8
NON-OECD COUNTRIES	78.7
WORLD	**66.0**

Averages weighted by population
Source: UNDP
*Child under five years old

Number of people per doctor, 1998

EUROPE & THE RUSSIAN FEDERATION	337
AFRICA	2,404
ASIA	1,205
AUSTRALASIA & OCEANIA	993
UNITED STATES & CANADA	412
LATIN AMERICA & THE CARIBBEAN	775
OECD COUNTRIES (see p.24)	449
NON-OECD COUNTRIES	1,037
WORLD	**920**

Averages weighted by population
Source: UNDP

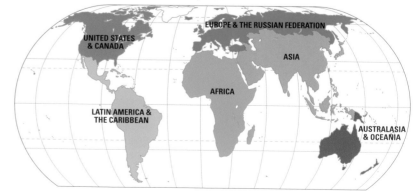

Health: Areas of Risk

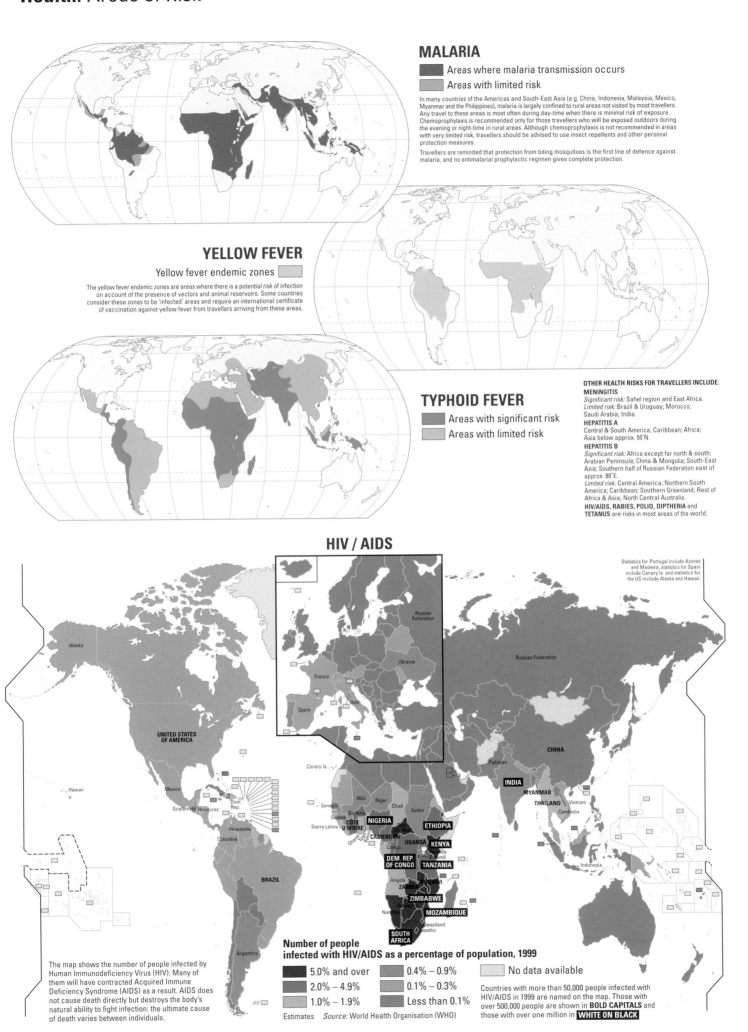

MALARIA

■ Areas where malaria transmission occurs

■ Areas with limited risk

In many countries of the Americas and South-East Asia (e.g. China, Indonesia, Malaysia, Mexico, Myanmar and the Philippines), malaria is largely confined to rural areas not visited by most travellers. Any travel to these areas is most often during day-time when there is minimal risk of exposure. Chemoprophylaxis is recommended only for those travellers who will be exposed outdoors during the evening or night-time in rural areas. Although chemoprophylaxis is not recommended in areas with very limited risk, travellers should be advised to use insect repellents and other personal protection measures.

Travellers are reminded that protection from biting mosquitoes is the first line of defence against malaria, and no antimalarial prophylactic regimen gives complete protection.

YELLOW FEVER

Yellow fever endemic zones ■

The yellow fever endemic zones are areas where there is a potential risk of infection on account of the presence of vectors and animal reservoirs. Some countries consider these zones to be 'infected' areas and require an international certificate of vaccination against yellow fever from travellers arriving from these areas.

TYPHOID FEVER

■ Areas with significant risk

■ Areas with limited risk

OTHER HEALTH RISKS FOR TRAVELLERS INCLUDE:

MENINGITIS
Significant risk: Sahel region and East Africa.
Limited risk: Brazil & Uruguay; Morocco; Saudi Arabia; India.

HEPATITIS A
Central & South America; Caribbean; Africa; Asia below approx. 50°N.

HEPATITIS B
Significant risk: Africa except far north & south; Arabian Peninsula; China & Mongolia; South-East Asia; Southern half of Russian Federation east of approx. 80°E.
Limited risk: Central America; Northern South America; Caribbean; Southern Greenland; Rest of Africa & Asia; North Central Australia.

HIV/AIDS, RABIES, POLIO, DIPTHERIA and **TETANUS** are risks in most areas of the world.

HIV / AIDS

Statistics for Portugal include Azores and Madeira, statistics for Spain include Canary Is. and statistics for the US include Alaska and Hawaii.

The map shows the number of people infected by Human Immunodeficiency Virus (HIV). Many of them will have contracted Acquired Immune Deficiency Syndrome (AIDS) as a result. AIDS does not cause death directly but destroys the body's natural ability to fight infection: the ultimate cause of death varies between individuals.

Number of people infected with HIV/AIDS as a percentage of population, 1999

■ 5.0% and over	■ 0.4% – 0.9%
■ 2.0% – 4.9%	■ 0.1% – 0.3%
■ 1.0% – 1.9%	■ Less than 0.1%

■ No data available

Estimates   *Source:* World Health Organisation (WHO)

Countries with more than 50,000 people infected with HIV/AIDS in 1999 are named on the map. Those with over 500,000 people are shown in **BOLD CAPITALS** and those with over one million in **WHITE ON BLACK**

Sport

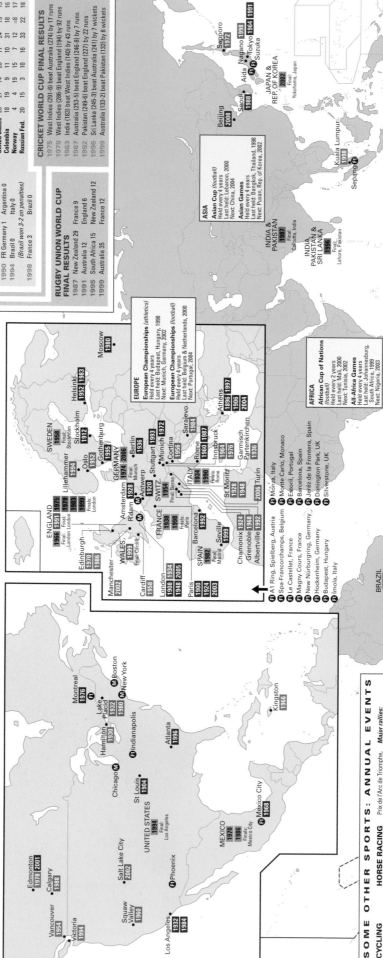
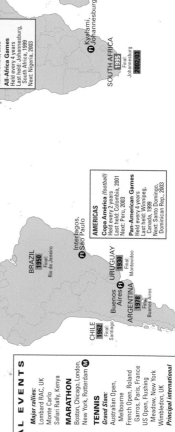

MAJOR INTERNATIONAL SPORTING EVENTS

SUMMER OLYMPICS
The first modern Olympic Games, founded by Frenchman Baron de Coubertin, were held at Athens in 1896. They are held every four years. An extra Olympics were held in 1906 to celebrate the tenth anniversary of the 1896 games. The next Games are due to be held at Athens in 2004 and Beijing in 2008.

WINTER OLYMPICS
The first separate Winter Games took place in 1924 at Chamonix, France. The games originally took place in the same year as the Summer Olympics, but beginning in 1994, are now held in between the Summer Games. The next Winter Olympics are due to be held at Salt Lake City, Utah in 2002 and at Turin in 2006.

COMMONWEALTH GAMES
Originally the British Empire Games and first held in 1930 at Hamilton, Ontario. Renamed the British Empire and Commonwealth Games in 1954, the British Commonwealth Games in 1970 and the Commonwealth Games in 1978. Held every four years, the next Games are due to be held at Manchester in 2002.

WORLD ATHLETICS CHAMPIONSHIPS
The World Athletics Championships were first held in Helsinki in 1983, and at four-year intervals until 1991. They are now held every two years. The next Championships are due to be held at Paris in 2003 and London in 2005.

FOOTBALL WORLD CUP
Association Football's premier event. Brazil kept the Jules Rimet Trophy after winning it for the third time in 1970. The teams now compete for the FIFA World Cup. Held every four years, the next competition is due to be hosted by Germany in 2006.

CRICKET WORLD CUP
The venue of the first Cricket World Cup in 1975 was England. Played every three to five years, it was not until 1987 that the competition was held outside England. The next World Cup is due to be held in South Africa in 2002/03.

RUGBY UNION WORLD CUP
The first Rugby Union World Cup was held in 1987 and is now held every four years, with the next competition in Australia and New Zealand in 2003.

FIFA WORLD RANKINGS

	May 1994	1995	1996	1997	1998	1999	2000	2001
France	17	17	5	4	17	2	3	1
Brazil	–	17	1	1	1	3	1	1
Argentina	6	8	8	21	6	7	5	3
Italy	16	2	7	6	14	4	4	4
Portugal	22	16	18	16	39	15	15	5
Spain	9	3	6	5	15	8	4	6
Czech Rep.	–	22	10	8	5	2	2	7
Netherlands	11	5	13	3	25	9	21	8
Germany	2	5	2	2	2	3	6	9
Paraguay	60	103	62	22	29	20	17	10
Yugoslavia	75	85	73	48	8	16	11	11
Romania	10	11	16	9	22	10	10	12
Mexico	13	9	12	4	12	4	13	13
England	15	21	24	13	5	11	12	14
United States	23	27	19	14	26	11	24	15
Colombia	18	19	9	11	34	15	15	16
Norway	2	4	7	8	10	31	–8	17
Russian Fed.	20	15	3	10	16	33	22	18

FOOTBALL WORLD CUP FINAL RESULTS

1930	Uruguay 4	Argentina 2
1934	Italy 2	Czechoslovakia 1
1938	Italy 4	Hungary 2
1950	Uruguay 2	Brazil 1
1954	FR Germany 3	Hungary 2
1958	Brazil 5	Sweden 2
1962	Brazil 3	Czechoslovakia 1
1966	England 4	FR Germany 2
1970	Brazil 4	Italy 1
1974	FR Germany 2	Netherlands 1
1978	Argentina 3	Netherlands 1
1982	Italy 3	FR Germany 1
1986	Argentina 3	FR Germany 2
1990	FR Germany 1	Argentina 0
1994	Brazil 0	Italy 0 *(Brazil won 3-2 on penalties)*
1998	France 3	Brazil 0

CRICKET WORLD CUP FINAL RESULTS

1975	West Indies (291-8) beat Australia (274) by 17 runs
1979	West Indies (286-9) beat England (194) by 92 runs
1983	India (183) beat West Indies (140) by 43 runs
1987	Australia (253-5) beat England (246-8) by 7 runs
1992	Pakistan (249-6) beat England (227) by 22 runs
1996	Sri Lanka (245-3) beat Australia (241) by 7 wickets
1999	Australia (133-2) beat Pakistan (132) by 8 wickets

RUGBY UNION WORLD CUP FINAL RESULTS

1987	New Zealand 29	France 9
1991	Australia 12	England 6
1995	South Africa 15	New Zealand 12
1999	Australia 35	France 12

EUROPE
European Championships (athletics)
Held every 4 years
Last held: Budapest, Hungary, 1998
Next: Munich, Germany, 2002
European Championships (football)
Held every 4 years
Last held: Belgium & Netherlands, 2000
Next: Portugal, 2004

ASIA
Asian Cup (football)
Held every 4 years
Last held: Lebanon, 2000
Next: China, 2004
Asian Games
Held every 4 years
Last held: Bangkok, Thailand, 1998
Next: Pusan, Rep. of Korea, 2002

AFRICA
African Cup of Nations (football)
Held every 2 years
Last held: Mali, 2000
Next: Tunisia, 2002
All-Africa Games
Held every 4 years
Last held: Johannesburg, South Africa, 1999
Next: Nigeria, 2003

AMERICAS
Copa América (football)
Held every 2 years
Last held: Colombia, 2001
Next: Peru, 2003
Pan-American Games
Held every 4 years
Last held: Winnipeg, Canada, 1999
Next: Santo Domingo, Dominican Rep., 2003

WORLDWIDE
Goodwill Games
Held every 3-4 years
Last held: Brisbane, Australia, 2001
Next: Calgary, Canada, 2005
Pan-Arab Games
Last held: Amman, Jordan, 1999
Next: Algeria, 2003
World Student Games ('Universiade')
Held every 2 years
Last held: Beijing, China, 2001
Next: Taegu, Rep. of Korea, 2003

SOME OTHER SPORTS: ANNUAL EVENTS

CYCLING
Major tours:
Giro d'Italia (Tour of Italy)
Tour de France
Tour DuPont, USA
Vuelta d'España (Tour of Spain)
Classics:
Belgium:
Fléche Wallonne
Liège-Bastogne-Liège,
Tour of Flanders
France:
Grand Prix des Nations
Paris-Nice
Paris-Roubaix
Italy:
Milan-San Remo
Tour of Lombardy
Paris-Brussels

HORSE RACING
English Classics:
1,000 & 2,000 Guineas, Newmarket
St Leger, Doncaster
Derby & Oaks, Epsom
Triple Crown, USA:
Kentucky Derby, Louisville
Belmont Stakes, NY
Preakness Stakes, Baltimore
Other major races:
Cheltenham Gold Cup, UK
Dubai World Cup
Grand National, Aintree, UK
Irish Derby, The Curragh
Melbourne Cup, Australia

Major rallies:
Lombard RAC, UK
Monte Carlo
Safari Rally, Kenya

GOLF
Majors:
British Open
US Open
US Masters
US PGA Championship
Principal international tournament:
Ryder Cup (every 2 yrs)

MOTOR RACING
Circuits which have held a Formula One race since 1990 are marked (F1)
Indianapolis 500, USA
Le Mans 24-hour race, France

MARATHON
Boston, Chicago, London, New York, Rotterdam

TENNIS
Grand Slam:
Australian Open, Melbourne
French Open, Roland Garros, Paris, France
US Open, Flushing Meadow, New York
Wimbledon, UK
Principal international tournament:
Davis Cup

(F1) A1-Ring, Spielberg, Austria
(F1) Spa-Francorchamps, Belgium
(F1) Le Castellet, France
(F1) Magny Cours, France
(F1) New Nurburgring, Germany
(F1) Hockenheim, Germany
(F1) Imola, Italy
(F1) Monza, Italy
(F1) Monte Carlo, Monaco
(F1) Estoril, Portugal
(F1) Barcelona, Spain
(F1) Jeréz de la Frontera, Spain
(F1) Donington Park, UK
(F1) Silverstone, UK

Military

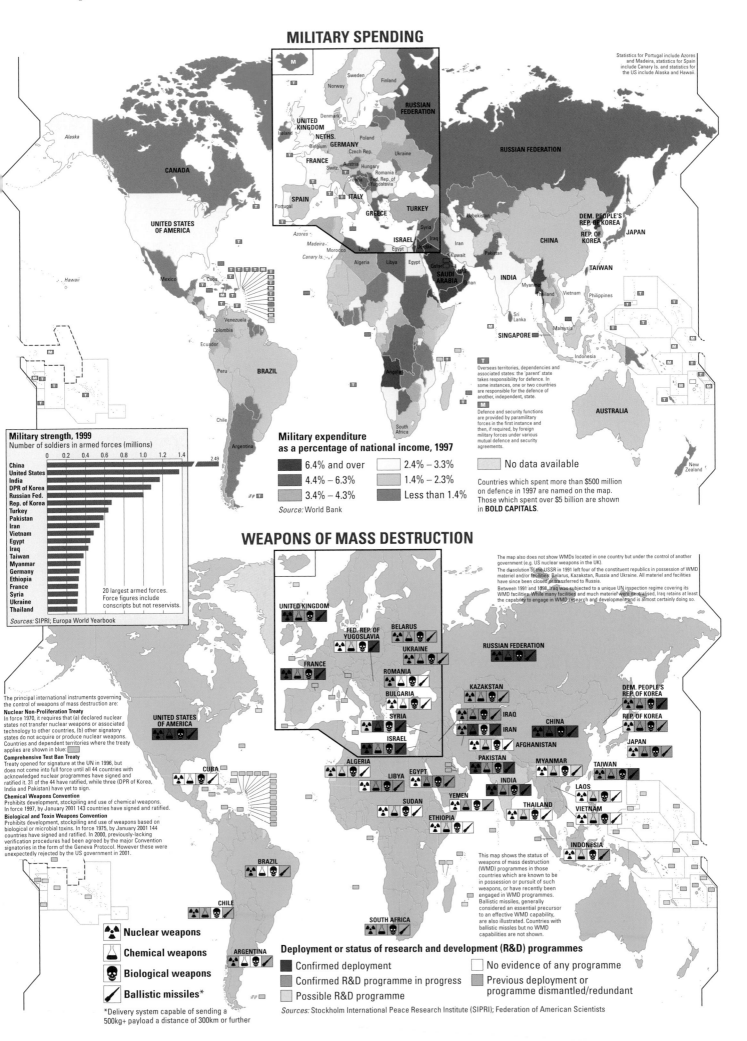

MILITARY SPENDING

Statistics for Portugal include Azores and Madeira, statistics for Spain include Canary Is. and statistics for the US include Alaska and Hawaii.

Military expenditure as a percentage of national income, 1997

- 6.4% and over
- 4.4% – 6.3%
- 3.4% – 4.3%
- 2.4% – 3.3%
- 1.4% – 2.3%
- Less than 1.4%
- No data available

Source: World Bank

Countries which spent more than $500 million on defence in 1997 are named on the map. Those which spent over $5 billion are shown in **BOLD CAPITALS**.

T Overseas territories, dependencies and associated states: the 'parent' state takes responsibility for defence. In some instances, one or two countries are responsible for the defence of another, independent, state.

M Defence and security functions are provided by paramilitary forces in the first instance and then, if required, by foreign military forces under various mutual defence and security agreements.

Military strength, 1999
Number of soldiers in armed forces (millions)

	0	0.2	0.4	0.6	0.8	1.0	1.2	1.4	
China									2.49
United States									
India									
DPR of Korea									
Russian Fed.									
Rep. of Korea									
Turkey									
Pakistan									
Iran									
Vietnam									
Egypt									
Iraq									
Taiwan									
Myanmar									
Germany									
Ethiopia									
France									
Syria									
Ukraine									
Thailand									

20 largest armed forces. Force figures include conscripts but not reservists.

Sources: SIPRI; Europa World Yearbook

WEAPONS OF MASS DESTRUCTION

The map also does not show WMDs located in one country but under the control of another government (e.g. US nuclear weapons in the UK).

The dissolution of the USSR in 1991 left four of the constituent republics in possession of WMD materiel and/or facilities: Belarus, Kazakstan, Russia and Ukraine. All materiel and facilities have since been closed or transferred to Russia.

Between 1991 and 1998, Iraq was subjected to a unique UN inspection regime covering its WMD facilities. While many facilities and much materiel were neutralised, Iraq retains at least the capability to engage in WMD research and development and is almost certainly doing so.

The principal international instruments governing the control of weapons of mass destruction are:

Nuclear Non-Proliferation Treaty
In force 1970, it requires that (a) declared nuclear states not transfer nuclear weapons or associated technology to other countries, (b) other signatory states do not acquire or produce nuclear weapons. Countries and dependent territories where the treaty applies are shown in blue:

Comprehensive Test Ban Treaty
Treaty opened for signature at the UN in 1996, but does not come into full force until all 44 countries with acknowledged nuclear programmes have signed and ratified. 31 of the 44 have ratified, while three (DPR of Korea, India and Pakistan) have yet to sign.

Chemical Weapons Convention
Prohibits development, stockpiling and use of chemical weapons. In force 1997, by January 2001 143 countries have signed and ratified.

Biological and Toxin Weapons Convention
Prohibits development, stockpiling and use of weapons based on biological or microbial toxins. In force 1975, by January 2001 144 countries have signed and ratified. In 2000, previously-lacking verification procedures had been agreed by the major Convention signatories in the form of the Geneva Protocol. However these were unexpectedly rejected by the US government in 2001.

This map shows the status of weapons of mass destruction (WMD) programmes in those countries which are known to be in possession or pursuit of such weapons, or have recently been engaged in WMD programmes. Ballistic missiles, generally considered an essential precursor to an effective WMD capability, are also illustrated. Countries with ballistic missiles but no WMD capabilities are not shown.

☢ **Nuclear weapons**

⚗ **Chemical weapons**

☠ **Biological weapons**

🗡 **Ballistic missiles***

Deployment or status of research and development (R&D) programmes

- Confirmed deployment
- Confirmed R&D programme in progress
- Possible R&D programme
- No evidence of any programme
- Previous deployment or programme dismantled/redundant

*Delivery system capable of sending a 500kg+ payload a distance of 300km or further

Sources: Stockholm International Peace Research Institute (SIPRI); Federation of American Scientists

Airports

The world's main airports are shown here with their international three-letter codes.

Many cities have more than one airport, and a separate code for the city itself. The codes shown here are for each city's principal airport or airports.

International Air Transport Association (IATA) Conference Areas

Area 1:
- North Atlantic
- Mid Atlantic
- South Atlantic

Main office: Montréal

Area 2:
- Europe
- Middle East
- Africa
- East Africa

Main office: Geneva

Area 3:
- Asia
- SW Pacific

Main office: Singapore

World airline traffic

Billion passenger-kilometres (international & domestic passenger services)

Source: International Civil Aviation Authority

1 Puerto Rico (US)
2 Virgin Is. (US, UK)
3 Anguilla (UK)
4 St Maarten (Neths.) & St Martin
5 ST KITTS & NEVIS
6 Montserrat (UK)
7 ANTIGUA & BARBUDA
8 Guadeloupe (Fr.)
9 DOMINICA
10 Martinique (Fr.)
11 ST LUCIA
12 ST VINCENT & THE GRENADINES
13 Bonaire (Neths.)
14 Curaçao (Neths.)
15 Aruba (Neths.)

AREA 1, NORTH ATLANTIC

ACA Acapulco, Mexico
ALB Albany, NY, USA
ANC Anchorage, AK, USA
ATL Atlanta, GA, USA
BDL Hartford, CT, USA
BIL Billings, MT, USA
BNA Nashville, TN, USA
BOI Boise, ID, USA
BOS Boston, MA, USA
BUF Buffalo, NY, USA
BWI Baltimore-Washington International, MD, USA
CLE Cleveland, OH, USA
CLT Charlotte, NC, USA
CVG Cincinnati, OH, USA
CUU Chihuahua, Mexico
DCA Washington Ronald Reagan, VA, USA
DEN Denver, CO, USA
DFW Dallas-Fort Worth, TX, USA
DTW Detroit, MI, USA
EWR New York Newark, NJ, USA
FLL Fort Lauderdale-Hollywood, FL, USA
GDL Guadalajara, Mexico
GEG Spokane, WA, USA
GOH Nuuk (Godthåb), Greenland
HNL Honolulu, HI, USA
IAD Washington Dulles, VA, USA
IAH Houston, TX, USA
IND Indianapolis, IN, USA
JAX Jacksonville, FL, USA
JFK New York John F. Kennedy, NY, USA
LAS Las Vegas, NV, USA
LAX Los Angeles, CA, USA
LGA New York LaGuardia, NY, USA
MCI Kansas City, MO, USA
MCO Orlando, FL, USA
MEM Memphis, TN, USA
MEX Ciudad de México (Mexico City), Mexico
MIA Miami, FL, USA
MKE Milwaukee, WI, USA
MSP Minneapolis-St Paul, MN, USA
MSY New Orleans, LA, USA
MTY Monterrey, Mexico
ORD Chicago, IL, USA
PDX Portland, OR, USA
PHL Philadelphia, PA, USA
PHX Phoenix, AZ, USA
PIT Pittsburgh, PA, USA
PWM Portland, ME, USA
RDU Raleigh-Durham, NC, USA
RSW Southwest Florida, FL, USA
SAN San Diego, CA, USA
SEA Seattle, WA, USA
SFJ Kangerlussuaq, Greenland
SFO San Francisco, CA, USA
SJD San José del Cabo, Mexico
SLC Salt Lake City, UT, USA
STL St Louis, MO, USA
SYR Syracuse, NY, USA
TPA Tampa, FL, USA
UAK Narsarsuaq, Greenland
YEG Edmonton, AL, Canada
YFB Iqaluit, NU, Canada
YHM Hamilton, OT, Canada
YHZ Halifax, NS, Canada
YMX Montréal Mirabel, QU, Canada
YOW Ottawa, OT, Canada
YQB Québec, QU, Canada
YQX Gander, NF, Canada
YUL Montréal Dorval, QU, Canada
YVR Vancouver, BC, Canada
YXE Saskatoon, SA, Canada
YYC Calgary, AL, Canada
YYT St John's, NF, Canada
YYZ Toronto, OT, Canada
YZF Yellowknife, NT, Canada

AREA 1, MID ATLANTIC

ANU Antigua
BAQ Barranquilla, Colombia
BDA Bermuda
BGI Barbados
BOG Bogotá, Colombia
BZE Belize City, Belize
CAY Cayenne, French Guiana
CCS Caracas, Venezuela
FPO Freeport, Bahamas
GEO Georgetown, Guyana
GND Grenada
GUA Ciudad de Guatemala (Guatemala City), Guatemala
GYE Guayaquil, Ecuador
HAV La Habana (Havana), Cuba
KIN Kingston, Jamaica
LIM Lima, Peru
LPB La Paz, Bolivia
MGA Managua, Nicaragua
NAS Nassau, Bahamas
PAP Port-au-Prince, Haiti
PBM Paramaribo, Surinam
POP Puerto Plata, Dominican Republic
POS Port of Spain, Trinidad
PTY Ciudad de Panamá (Panama City), Panama
SAL San Salvador, El Salvador
SDQ Santo Domingo, Dominican Republic
SJO San José, Costa Rica
SJU San Juan, Puerto Rico
SKB St Kitts
SRZ Santa Cruz, Bolivia
SVD St Vincent
TGU Tegucigalpa, Honduras
UIO Quito, Ecuador
UVF Hewanorra, St Lucia

AREA 1, SOUTH ATLANTIC

ARI Arica, Chile
ASU Asunción, Paraguay
BSB Brasília, Brazil
EZE Buenos Aires, Argentina
GIG Rio de Janeiro, Brazil
GRU São Paulo-Guarulhos, Brazil
IPC Easter Island
MAO Manaus, Brazil
MVD Montevideo, Uruguay
REC Recife, Brazil
SCL Santiago, Chile
SSA Salvador, Brazil

AREA 2, EUROPE*

BAK Baki (Baku), Azerbaijan
EVN Yerevan, Armenia
FNC Funchal, Madeira
KEF Reykjavík, Iceland
KUF Samara, Russian Federation
LPA Las Palmas de Gran Canaria, Canary Is.
MMK Murmansk, Russian Federation
OUL Oulu, Finland
PDL Ponta Delgada, São Miguel, Azores
PXO Porto Santo, Madeira
SMA Vila do Porto, Santa Maria, Azores
TBS T'bilisi, Georgia
TER Terceira, Azores
TFN Tenerife North, Canary Is.
TFS Tenerife South, Canary Is.
TOS Tromsø, Norway
VOG Volgograd, Russian Federation

AREA 2, MIDDLE EAST*

ADE Adan (Aden), Yemen
AUH Abu Zaby (Abu Dhabi), UAE
BAH Bahrain
BGW Baghdad, Iraq
DHA Dhahran, Saudi Arabia
DOH Ad Dawhah (Doha), Qatar
DXB Dubayy (Dubai), UAE
JED Jiddah (Jeddah), Saudi Arabia
KRT Khartoum, Sudan
KWI Al Kuwayt (Kuwait)
LXR Luxor, Egypt
MCT Masqat (Muscat), Oman
RUH Ar Riyad (Riyadh), Saudi Arabia
SAH Sana'a, Yemen
THR Tehran, Iran

AREA 2, AFRICA*

ABJ Abidjan, Côte d'Ivoire
ABV Abuja, Nigeria
ACC Accra, Ghana
ADD Adis Abeba (Addis Ababa), Ethiopia
ASM Asmara, Eritrea
BEW Beira, Mozambique
BGF Bangui, Central African Republic
BJL Banjul, The Gambia
BJM Bujumbura, Burundi
BKO Bamako, Mali
BZV Brazzaville, Congo
CKY Conakry, Guinea
COO Cotonou, Benin
CPT Cape Town, South Africa
DKR Dakar, Senegal

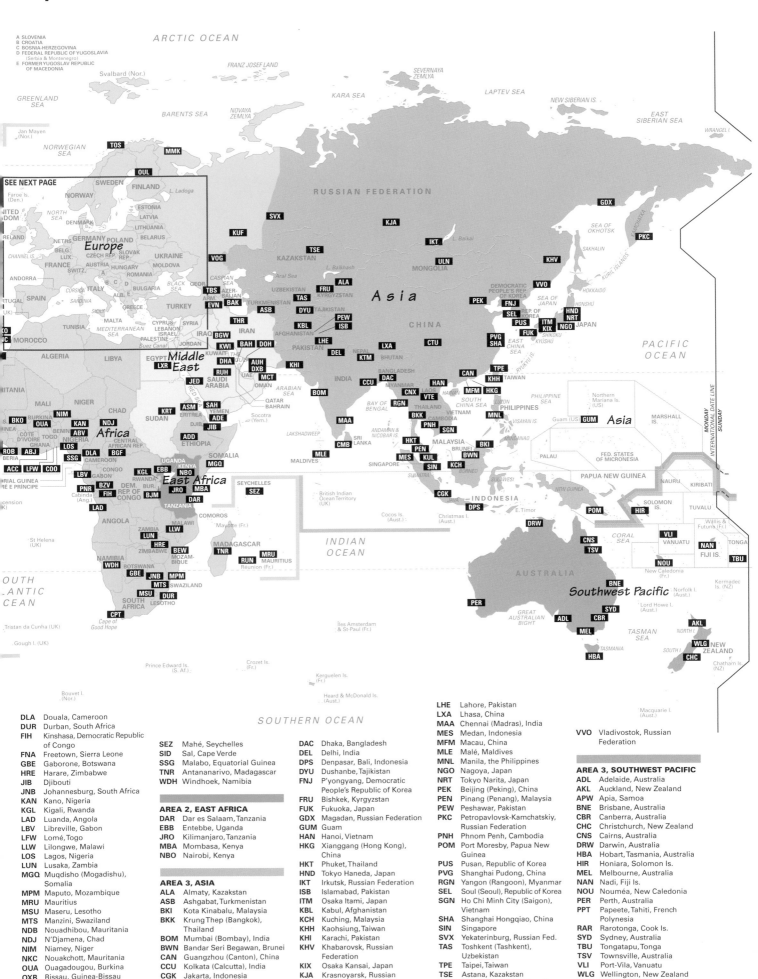

Airports

A SLOVENIA
B CROATIA
C BOSNIA-HERZEGOVINA
D FEDERAL REPUBLIC OF YUGOSLAVIA (Serbia & Montenegro)
E FORMER YUGOSLAV REPUBLIC OF MACEDONIA

DLA Douala, Cameroon
DUR Durban, South Africa
FIH Kinshasa, Democratic Republic of Congo
FNA Freetown, Sierra Leone
GBE Gaborone, Botswana
HRE Harare, Zimbabwe
JIB Djibouti
JNB Johannesburg, South Africa
KAN Kano, Nigeria
KGL Kigali, Rwanda
LAD Luanda, Angola
LBV Libreville, Gabon
LFW Lomé, Togo
LLW Lilongwe, Malawi
LOS Lagos, Nigeria
LUN Lusaka, Zambia
MGQ Muqdisho (Mogadishu), Somalia
MPM Maputo, Mozambique
MRU Mauritius
MSU Maseru, Lesotho
MTS Manzini, Swaziland
NDB Nouadhibou, Mauritania
NDJ N'Djamena, Chad
NIM Niamey, Niger
NKC Nouakchott, Mauritania
OUA Ouagadougou, Burkina
OXB Bissau, Guinea-Bissau
PNR Pointe-Noire, Congo
ROB Monrovia, Liberia
RUN Réunion

SEZ Mahé, Seychelles
SID Sal, Cape Verde
SSG Malabo, Equatorial Guinea
TNR Antananarivo, Madagascar
WDH Windhoek, Namibia

AREA 2, EAST AFRICA
DAR Dar es Salaam, Tanzania
EBB Entebbe, Uganda
JRO Kilimanjaro, Tanzania
MBA Mombasa, Kenya
NBO Nairobi, Kenya

AREA 3, ASIA
ALA Almaty, Kazakstan
ASB Ashgabat, Turkmenistan
BKI Kota Kinabalu, Malaysia
BKK Krung Thep (Bangkok), Thailand
BOM Mumbai (Bombay), India
BWN Bandar Seri Begawan, Brunei
CAN Guangzhou (Canton), China
CCU Kolkata (Calcutta), India
CGK Jakarta, Indonesia
CMB Colombo, Sri Lanka
CNX Chiang Mai, Thailand
CTU Chengdu, China

DAC Dhaka, Bangladesh
DEL Delhi, India
DPS Denpasar, Bali, Indonesia
DYU Dushanbe, Tajikistan
FNJ P'yongyang, Democratic People's Republic of Korea
FRU Bishkek, Kyrgyzstan
FUK Fukuoka, Japan
GDX Magadan, Russian Federation
GUM Guam
HAN Hanoi, Vietnam
HKG Xianggang (Hong Kong), China
HKT Phuket, Thailand
HND Tokyo Haneda, Japan
IKT Irkutsk, Russian Federation
ISB Islamabad, Pakistan
ITM Osaka Itami, Japan
KBL Kabul, Afghanistan
KCH Kuching, Malaysia
KHH Kaohsiung, Taiwan
KHI Karachi, Pakistan
KHV Khabarovsk, Russian Federation
KIX Osaka Kansai, Japan
KJA Krasnoyarsk, Russian Federation
KTM Kathmandu, Nepal
KUL Kuala Lumpur, Malaysia

LHE Lahore, Pakistan
LXA Lhasa, China
MAA Chennai (Madras), India
MES Medan, Indonesia
MFM Macau, China
MLE Malé, Maldives
MNL Manila, the Philippines
NGO Nagoya, Japan
NRT Tokyo Narita, Japan
PEK Beijing (Peking), China
PEN Pinang (Penang), Malaysia
PEW Peshawar, Pakistan
PKC Petropavlovsk-Kamchatskiy, Russian Federation
PNH Phnom Penh, Cambodia
POM Port Moresby, Papua New Guinea
PUS Pusan, Republic of Korea
PVG Shanghai Pudong, China
RGN Yangon (Rangoon), Myanmar
SEL Soul (Seoul), Republic of Korea
SGN Ho Chi Minh City (Saigon), Vietnam
SHA Shanghai Hongqiao, China
SIN Singapore
SVX Yekaterinburg, Russian Fed.
TAS Toshkent (Tashkent), Uzbekistan
TPE Taipei, Taiwan
TSE Astana, Kazakstan
ULN Ulaanbaatar (Ulan Bator), Mongolia
VTE Viangchan (Vientiane), Laos

VVO Vladivostok, Russian Federation

AREA 3, SOUTHWEST PACIFIC
ADL Adelaide, Australia
AKL Auckland, New Zealand
APW Apia, Samoa
BNE Brisbane, Australia
CBR Canberra, Australia
CHC Christchurch, New Zealand
CNS Cairns, Australia
DRW Darwin, Australia
HBA Hobart, Tasmania, Australia
HIR Honiara, Solomon Is.
MEL Melbourne, Australia
NAN Nadi, Fiji Is.
NOU Nouméa, New Caledonia
PER Perth, Australia
PPT Papeete, Tahiti, French Polynesia
RAR Rarotonga, Cook Is.
SYD Sydney, Australia
TBU Tongatapu, Tonga
TSV Townsville, Australia
VLI Port-Vila, Vanuatu
WLG Wellington, New Zealand

* See next page for other airports in these areas

Airports

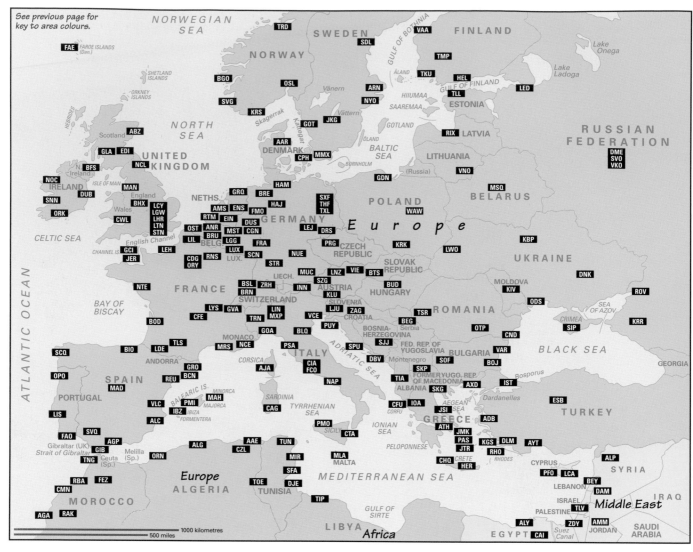

Europe and North Africa's main airports are shown here with their international three-letter code.

Many cities have more than one airport, and a separate code for the city itself. The codes shown here are for each city's principal airport or airports.

AREA 2, EUROPE

AAE	Annaba, Algeria
AAR	Århus, Denmark
ABZ	Aberdeen, Scotland
ADB	Izmir (Smyrna), Turkey
AGA	Agadir, Morocco
AGP	Málaga, Spain
AJA	Ajaccio, France
ALC	Alacant (Alicante), Spain
ALG	Alger (Algiers), Algeria
AMS	Amsterdam, The Netherlands
ANR	Antwerpen (Antwerp), Belgium
ARN	Stockholm Arlanda, Sweden
ATH	Athína (Athens), Greece
AXD	Alexandroúpoli, Greece
AYT	Antalya, Turkey
BCN	Barcelona, Spain
BEG	Beograd (Belgrade), Federal Republic of Yugoslavia
BFS	Belfast, Northern Ireland
BGO	Bergen, Norway
BHX	Birmingham, England
BIO	Bilbao, Spain
BLQ	Bologna, Italy
BOD	Bordeaux, France
BOJ	Burgas, Bulgaria
BRE	Bremen, Germany
BRN	Bern (Berne), Switzerland
BRU	Bruxelles/Brussel (Brussels), Belgium
BSL	Basel (Basle)-Mulhouse-Freiburg, Switzerland
BTS	Bratislava, Slovak Republic
BUD	Budapest, Hungary
CAG	Cágliari, Italy
CDG	Paris Roissy-Charles de Gaulle, France
CFE	Clermont-Ferrand, France
CFU	Kérkira (Corfu), Greece
CGN	Köln (Cologne)-Bonn, Germany
CHQ	Haniá (Canea), Greece
CIA	Roma (Rome) Ciampino, Italy
CMN	Casablanca, Morocco
CND	Constanta, Romania
CPH	København (Copenhagen), Denmark
CTA	Catánia, Italy
CWL	Cardiff, Wales
CZL	Constantine, Algeria
DBV	Dubrovnik, Croatia
DJE	Jerba, Tunisia
DLM	Dalaman, Turkey
DME	Moskva (Moscow) Domodedovo, Russian Federation
DNK	Dnipropetrovs'k, Ukraine
DRS	Dresden, Germany
DUB	Dublin, Ireland
DUS	Düsseldorf, Germany
EDI	Edinburgh, Scotland
EIN	Eindhoven, The Netherlands
ENS	Enschede, The Netherlands
ESB	Ankara, Turkey
FAE	Vágar, Faroe Islands
FAO	Faro, Portugal
FCO	Roma (Rome) Fiumicino/Leonardo da Vinci, Italy
FEZ	Fès, Morocco
FMO	Münster-Osnabrück, Germany
FRA	Frankfurt am Main, Germany
GCI	Guernsey
GDN	Gdansk, Poland
GIB	Gibraltar
GLA	Glasgow, Scotland
GOA	Génova (Genoa), Italy
GOT	Göteborg (Gothenburg), Sweden
GRO	Girona, Spain
GRQ	Groningen, The Netherlands
GVA	Genève (Geneva), Switzerland
HAJ	Hannover (Hanover), Germany
HAM	Hamburg, Germany
HEL	Helsinki (Helsingfors), Finland
HER	Iráklio (Herakleion), Greece
IBZ	Eivissa (Ibiza), Spain
INN	Innsbruck, Austria
IOA	Ioánina, Greece
IST	Istanbul, Turkey
JER	Jersey
JKG	Jönköping, Sweden
JMK	Míkonos, Greece
JSI	Skíathos, Greece
JTR	Thíra, Greece
KBP	Kyiv (Kiev), Ukraine
KGS	Kos (Cos), Greece
KIV	Chisinau (Kishinev), Moldova
KLU	Klagenfurt, Austria
KRK	Kraków (Cracow), Poland
KRR	Krasnodar, Russian Federation
KRS	Kristiansand, Norway
LCY	London City, England
LDE	Lourdes, France
LED	Sankt-Peterburg (St Petersburg), Russian Federation
LEH	Le Havre, France
LEJ	Leipzig-Halle, Germany
LGG	Liège, Belgium
LGW	London Gatwick, England
LHR	London Heathrow, England
LIL	Lille, France
LIN	Milano (Milan) Linate, Italy
LIS	Lisboa (Lisbon), Portugal
LJU	Ljubljana, Slovenia
LNZ	Linz, Austria
LTN	London Luton, England
LUX	Luxembourg
LWO	L'viv (L'vov), Ukraine
LYS	Lyon (Lyons), France
MAD	Madrid, Spain
MAH	Maó (Mahón), Spain
MAN	Manchester, England
MIR	Monastir, Tunisia
MLA	Malta
MMX	Malmö, Sweden
MRS	Marseille (Marseilles), France
MSQ	Minsk, Belarus
MST	Maastricht, The Netherlands
MUC	München (Munich), Germany
MXP	Milano (Milan) Malpensa, Italy
NAP	Nápoli (Naples), Italy
NCE	Nice, France
NCL	Newcastle, England
NOC	Horan (Knock), Ireland
NTE	Nantes, France
NUE	Nürnberg (Nuremberg), Germany
NYO	Stockholm Skavsta, Sweden
ODS	Odesa (Odessa), Ukraine
OPO	Porto (Oporto), Portugal
ORK	Cork, Ireland
ORN	Oran, Algeria
ORY	Paris: Orly, France
OSL	Oslo, Norway
OST	Oostende (Ostend), Belgium
OTP	Bucuresti (Bucharest), Romania
PAS	Páros, Greece
PMI	Palma de Mallorca, Spain
PMO	Palermo, Italy
PRG	Praha (Prague), Czech Republic
PSA	Pisa, Italy
PUY	Pula, Croatia
RAK	Marrakech, Morocco
RBA	Rabat, Morocco
REU	Reus, Spain
RHO	Ródos (Rhodes), Greece
RIX	Riga, Latvia
RNS	Reims, France
ROV	Rostov-na-Donu, Russian Federation
RTM	Rotterdam, The Netherlands
SCN	Saarbrücken, Germany
SCQ	Santiago de Compostela, Spain
SDL	Sundsvall, Sweden
SFA	Sfax, Tunisia
SIP	Simferopol, Ukraine
SJJ	Sarajevo, Bosnia-Herzegovina
SKG	Thessaloníki (Salonika), Greece
SKP	Skopje, FYR of Macedonia
SNN	Shannon, Ireland
SOF	Sofiya (Sofia), Bulgaria
SPU	Split, Croatia
STN	London Stansted, England
STR	Stuttgart, Germany
SVG	Stavanger, Norway
SVO	Moskva (Moscow) Sheremetyevo, Russian Federation
SVQ	Sevilla (Seville), Spain
SXF	Berlin Schönefeld, Germany
SZG	Salzburg, Austria
THF	Berlin Tempelhof, Germany
TIA	Tiranë (Tirana), Albania
TKU	Turku (Åbo), Finland
TLL	Tallinn, Estonia
TLS	Toulouse, France
TMP	Tampere, Finland
TNG	Tanger (Tangier), Morocco
TOE	Tozeur, Tunisia
TRD	Trondheim, Norway
TRN	Torino (Turin), Italy
TSR	Timisoara, Romania
TUN	Tunis, Tunisia
TXL	Berlin Tegel, Germany
VAA	Vaasa (Vasa), Finland
VAR	Varna, Bulgaria
VCE	Venézia (Venice), Italy
VIE	Wien (Vienna), Austria
VKO	Moskva (Moscow) Vnukovo, Russian Federation
VLC	Valencia, Spain
VNO	Vilnius, Lithuania
WAW	Warszawa (Warsaw), Poland
ZAG	Zagreb, Croatia
ZRH	Zürich, Switzerland

AREA 2, MIDDLE EAST

ALP	Halab (Aleppo), Syria
ALY	El Iskandarîya (Alexandria), Egypt
AMM	Amman, Jordan
BEY	Bayrut (Beirut), Lebanon
CAI	El Qâhira (Cairo), Egypt
DAM	Dimashq (Damascus), Syria
LCA	Larnaca, Cyprus
PFO	Pafos (Paphos), Cyprus
TLV	Tel Aviv-Yafo, Israel
ZDY	Gaza, Palestine National Authority Region

AREA 2, AFRICA

TIP	Tarabulus (Tripoli), Libya

Flight Times

Average flight times from London, New York and Singapore to other major destinations. Hours do not include stopover time, when necessary, from one destination to another.

Less than 2 hours
2 hours – 4 hours 59 mins
5 hours – 8 hours 59 mins
9 hours – 14 hours 59 mins
15 hours – 24 hours 59 mins
25 hours and over

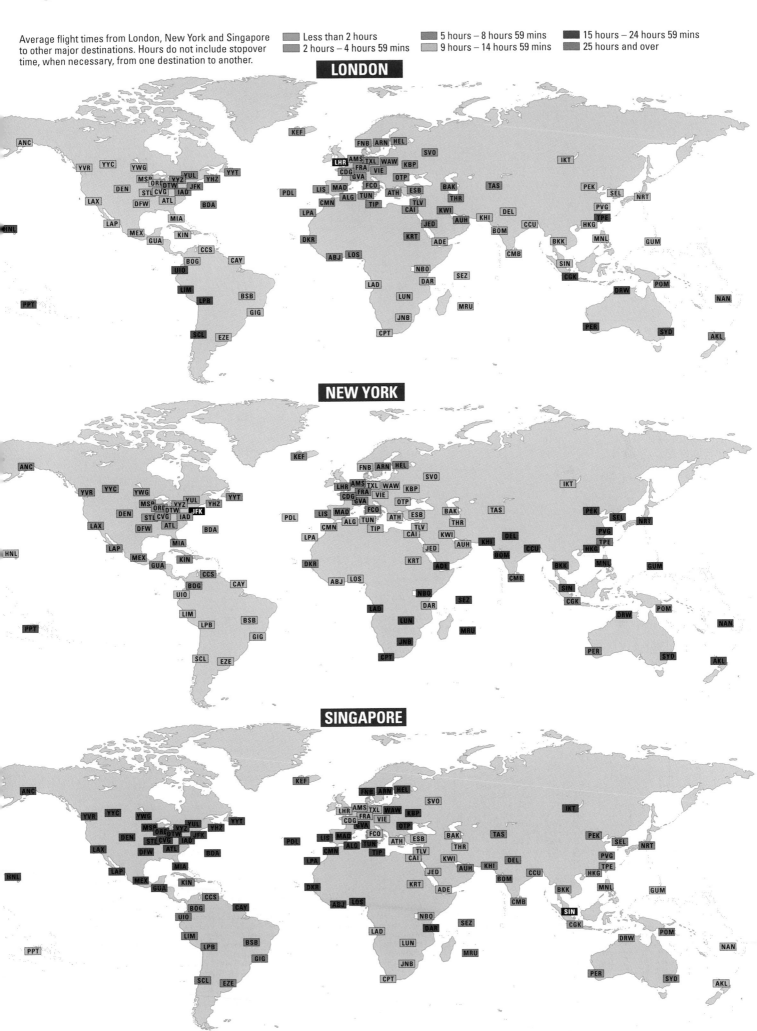

Cruising

The main ocean and river cruise areas are highlighted along with the most visited ports (red dots). Follow the green line for a typical three-month world cruise route. The Mediterranean and the Caribbean, the two most popular cruising regions, are shown in extra detail below.

Not all ships can dock alongside all ports. On these occasions, ship's launches are used to tender passengers ashore. In some remote regions such as Antarctica, passengers can only travel ashore by zodiac boats.

Cruises are year-round except in the following regions, where climate or sea conditions limit the season:
Alaska: cruises scheduled between May and September;
US East Coast May – Sept;
Baltic May – Sept;
South Africa Nov – Mar;
Antarctica & South America (Cape Horn) Nov – Feb.

Cruise passengers, 1980–2000

Total worldwide cruise passengers (millions)

Estimated regional breakdown, 2000 (thousands)

Caribbean/Florida (incl. Panama Canal) **5,080**
Mediterranean Sea/Black Sea/Red Sea **1,200**
Alaska/Canada **760**
Norwegian Fjords/Baltic **700**
Asia **650**
Mexican Riviera **500**
US East Coast **200**
Bermuda **180**
Hawaiian Is. **160**
South America/Antarctica **160**
Other regions **510**

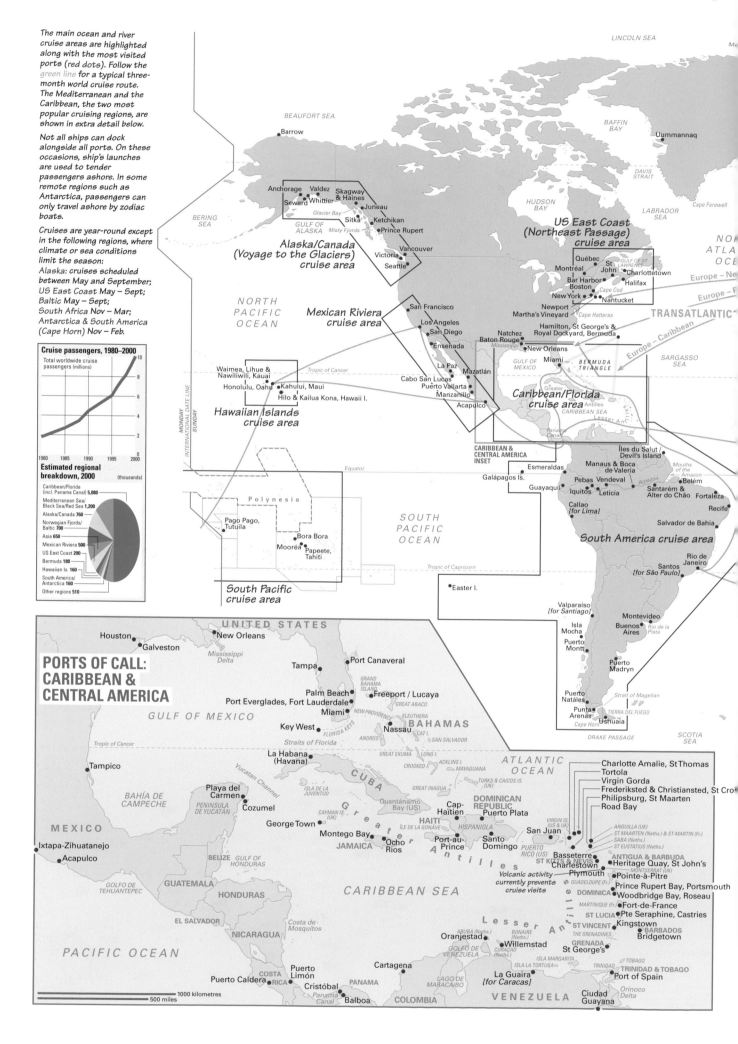

Cruising

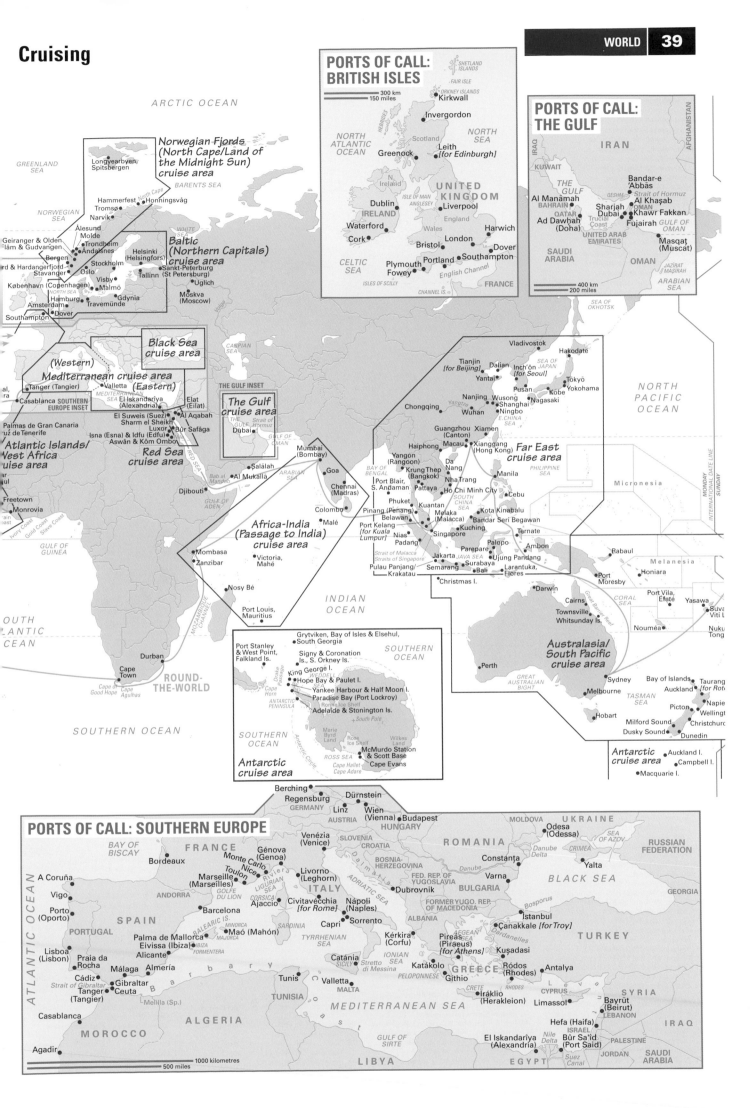

PORTS OF CALL: BRITISH ISLES

300 km
150 miles

SHETLAND ISLANDS
FAIR ISLE
ORKNEY ISLANDS
Kirkwall
Invergordon
HEBRIDES
NORTH ATLANTIC OCEAN
Scotland
NORTH SEA
Greenock
Leith [for Edinburgh]
N. Ireland
Ireland
ISLE OF MAN
ANGLESEY
UNITED KINGDOM
Dublin
IRELAND
Liverpool
Wales
England
Waterford
Harwich
Cork
London
CELTIC SEA
Bristol
Dover
Plymouth
Portland
Southampton
Fowey
English Channel
ISLES OF SCILLY
CHANNEL IS.
FRANCE

PORTS OF CALL: THE GULF

IRAQ
IRAN
AFGHANISTAN
KUWAIT
THE GULF
QESHM
Strait of Hormuz
Bandar-e 'Abbās
Al Manāmah
BAHRAIN
OMAN
QATAR
Sharjah
Al Khaşab
Ad Dawḩah (Doha)
Dubai
Khawr Fakkan
Trucial Coast
Fujairah
GULF OF OMAN
UNITED ARAB EMIRATES
SAUDI ARABIA
OMAN
JAZĪRAT MAṢĪRAH
Masqaţ (Muscat)
ARABIAN SEA
400 miles
200 miles

ARCTIC OCEAN

GREENLAND SEA

Norwegian Fjords (North Cape/Land of the Midnight Sun) cruise area

Longyearbyen, Spitsbergen

BARENTS SEA

NORWEGIAN SEA

Hammerfest
North Cape
Honningsvåg
Tromsø
Narvik
WHITE SEA

Ålesund
Molde
Trondheim
Åndalsnes
Helsinki (Helsingfors)

Baltic (Northern Capitals) cruise area

Geiranger & Olden
Flåm & Gudvangen
Bergen
Stockholm
Sankt-Peterburg (St Petersburg)
...rd & Hardangerfjord
Stavanger
Oslo
Visby
Tallinn
Uglich

København (Copenhagen)
NORTH SEA
Malmö
Moskva (Moscow)
Amsterdam
Hamburg
Gdynia
Southampton
Dover
Travemünde

Black Sea cruise area

CASPIAN SEA

(Western)

Mediterranean cruise area (Eastern)

THE GULF INSET

Tanger (Tangier)
Valletta
Elat (Eilat)
Casablanca SOUTHERN EUROPE INSET
El Iskandarîya (Alexandria)
MEDITERRANEAN SEA
Al Aqabah

The Gulf cruise area

El Suweis (Suez)
Sharm el Sheikh
Bûr Safâga
Dubai

Palmas de Gran Canaria
...ruz de Tenerife
Isna (Esna) & Idfu (Edfu)
Aswân & Kôm Ombo
Luxor
GULF OF OMAN

Atlantic Islands/
West Africa
...uise area

Red Sea cruise area

Mumbai (Bombay)
Bab al Mandab
Al Mukallā
ARABIAN SEA

...ar

Goa

Freetown
Djibouti
Salālah
Chennai (Madras)

Monrovia
GULF OF ADEN

Ivory Coast
Gold Coast
Slave Coast
Colombo

Africa-India (Passage to India) cruise area

Malé

GULF OF GUINEA

Mombasa
Zanzibar
Victoria, Mahé

Nosy Bé

INDIAN OCEAN

Port Louis, Mauritius

Vladivostok
Hakodate

Tianjin [for Beijing]
Dalian
SEA OF JAPAN
Inch'ŏn [for Seoul]
Yantai
Pusan
Tōkyō
NORTH PACIFIC OCEAN
Nanjing
Wusong
Shanghai
Kōbe
Yokohama
Chongqing
Wuhan
Ningbo
Nagasaki
Yangtze
E. CHINA SEA

Guangzhou (Canton)
Xiamen
Haiphong
Macau
Xianggang (Hong Kong)
Far East cruise area

Yangon (Rangoon)
Da Nang
Manila
PHILIPPINE SEA
Micronesia

Krung Thep (Bangkok)
Nha Trang
Port Blair, S. Andaman
Pattaya
Ho Chi Minh City
Cebu

Phuket
Kuantan
SOUTH CHINA SEA

Pinang (Penang)
Melaka (Malacca)
Kota Kinabalu
Belawan
Bandar Seri Begawan
Port Kelang [for Kuala Lumpur]
Nias
Kuching
Ternate
Padang
Singapore
Rabaul
Melanesia
Palopo
Parepare
Ambon
Jakarta
JAVA SEA
Ujung Pandang
Honiara
Strait of Malacca
Straits of Singapore
Semarang
Surabaya
Larantuka, Flores
Port Moresby
Port Vila, Efaté
Pulau Panjang/Krakatau
Bali
Christmas I.
Darwin
Yasawa

MONDAY
INTERNATIONAL DATE LINE
SUNDAY

Suva
Viti L.

Cairns
Nouméa
Nuku...
Tong...

Australasia/
South Pacific cruise area

Townsville
Whitsunday Is.
CORAL SEA

Perth
GREAT AUSTRALIAN BIGHT

Grytviken, Bay of Isles & Elsehul, South Georgia
SOUTHERN OCEAN

Port Stanley & West Point, Falkland Is.
Signy & Coronation Is., S. Orkney Is.

WEDDELL SEA
King George I.
Hope Bay & Paulet I.
Yankee Harbour & Half Moon I.
Paradise Bay (Port Lockroy)
Adelaide & Stonington Is.

Drake Passage
Cape Horn
ANTARCTIC PENINSULA

Sydney
Bay of Islands
Tauranga [for Roto...]
Auckland
Melbourne
TASMAN SEA
Picton
Napier
Wellington
Hobart
Milford Sound
Christchurch
Dusky Sound
Dunedin

ROUND-THE-WORLD

Durban
Cape Town
Cape of Good Hope
Cape Agulhas

SOUTH ATLANTIC OCEAN

SOUTHERN OCEAN

Marie Byrd Land
Ross Ice Shelf
Wilkes Land
Ronne Ice Shelf
South Pole
Antarctic Circle

SOUTHERN OCEAN

Antarctic cruise area

McMurdo Station & Scott Base
Cape Evans
ROSS SEA
Cape Hallet
Cape Adare

Antarctic cruise area
Auckland I.
Campbell I.
Macquarie I.

PORTS OF CALL: SOUTHERN EUROPE

Berching
Dürnstein
Regensburg
GERMANY
Linz
Wien (Vienna)
Budapest
AUSTRIA
HUNGARY
MOLDOVA
UKRAINE

Venézia (Venice)
SLOVENIA
CROATIA
ROMANIA
Odesa (Odessa)
SEA OF AZOV
RUSSIAN FEDERATION

BAY OF BISCAY
FRANCE
Génova (Genoa)
Monte Carlo
Nice
DALMATIA
BOSNIA-HERZEGOVINA
FED. REP. OF YUGOSLAVIA
Danube Delta
CRIMEA
Yalta

Bordeaux
Toulon
Marseille (Marseilles)
RIVIERA
Livorno (Leghorn)
Dubrovnik
Constanţa
Varna
BLACK SEA
GEORGIA

A Coruña
ANDORRA
GOLFE DU LION
LIGURIAN SEA
ITALY
ADRIATIC SEA
FORMER YUGO. REP. OF MACEDONIA
BULGARIA
Bosporus

Vigo
Ajaccio
CORSICA
Civitavecchia [for Rome]
Nápoli (Naples)
ALBANIA
Istanbul

Porto (Oporto)
SPAIN
Barcelona
SARDINIA
Capri
Sorrento
Çanakkale [for Troy]
TURKEY
Dardanelles

PORTUGAL
BALEARIC IS.
MINORCA
TYRRHENIAN SEA
Kérkira (Corfu)
Pireás (Piraeus) [for Athens]
Kuşadası

Lisboa (Lisbon)
Palma de Mallorca
MAJORCA
Maó (Mahón)
AEGEAN SEA

Praia da Rocha
Eivissa (Ibiza)
IBIZA
FORMENTERA
Catánia
SICILY
Stretto di Messina
IONIAN SEA
Katákolo
GREECE
Ródos (Rhodes)
Antalya

Cádiz
Alicante
Málaga
Almería
PELOPONNESE
Githio
CRETE
CYPRUS
L e v a...
SYRIA

Tanger (Tangier)
Gibraltar
Ceuta
Valletta
MALTA
Iráklio (HeraEeleion)
Limassol
Bayrût (Beirut)
LEBANON

Strait of Gibraltar
Tunis
RHODES
IRAQ

Casablanca
B a r b a r y
MEDITERRANEAN SEA
TUNISIA
GULF OF SIRTE
Hefa (Haifa)
ISRAEL
El Iskandarîya (Alexandria)
Bûr Sa'îd (Port Said)
PALESTINE
SAUDI ARABIA

Agadir
MOROCCO
ALGERIA
LIBYA
Nile Delta
EGYPT
JORDAN
Suez Canal

1000 kilometres
500 miles

UNESCO: Natural Heritage

The UNESCO World Heritage List consists of sites considered to be of global importance either because of their natural heritage or their significant man-made contribution to world culture. Countries which are signatories to the World Heritage Convention can submit potential sites to UNESCO, which considers each proposal under strict criteria and lists each site where one or more natural or cultural criteria have been met. Some sites are listed as combined sites; these appear on both maps.

The natural sites shown here are either:

significant natural features, areas which constitute the habitat of threatened species of outstanding value, or areas of outstanding scientific or conservation value or natural beauty.

Sites nominated should:
(i) be outstanding examples representing major stages in earth's history; or
(ii) be outstanding examples representing significant on-going ecological and biological processes; or
(iii) contain superlative natural phenomena or areas of outstanding natural beauty and aesthetic importance; or
(iv) contain the most important habitats for conservation of biological diversity, including significant threatened species.

Properties named in red are included on the list of World Heritage in Danger.

For further information, contact:

UNESCO World Heritage Centre, 7 place de Fontenoy, 75352 Paris 07 SP, France.
Tel: +33 (0)1 45 68 15 71.

www.unesco.org/whc
www.ovpm.org

Sites marked with an asterisk (*) are featured in Columbus Travel Guides' *Tourist Attractions and Events of the World*, 2nd edition.
For more information, call +44 (0)20 7608 6666.

UNITED STATES & CANADA

1 Kluane National Park & Reserve*, Glacier Bay National Park & Preserve, Wrangell-St Elias National Park & Preserve and Tatshenshini-Alsek Provincial Wilderness Park, Alaska/Yukon
2 Nahanni National Park, Northwest Territories
3 Wood Buffalo National Park, Northwest Territories/Alberta
4 Canadian Rocky Mountains Parks (incl. Banff and Jasper National Parks*), British Columbia/Alberta
5 Waterton-Glacier International Peace Park, Alberta/Montana
6 Dinosaur Provincial Park, Alberta
7 Miquasha Park, Québec
8 Gros Morne National Park, Newfoundland
9 Hawaii Volcanoes National Park*, Hawaii
10 Olympic National Park, Washington
11 Redwood National Park, California
12 Yosemite National Park*, California
13 Grand Canyon National Park*, Arizona
14 Carlsbad Caverns National Park, New Mexico
15 **Yellowstone National Park***, Wyoming
16 Mammoth Cave National Park, Kentucky
17 Great Smoky Mountains National Park, Tennessee/North Carolina
18 **Everglades National Park***, Florida

LATIN AMERICA & THE CARIBBEAN

19 El Vizcaíno whale sanctuary, Mexico
20 Reserva Biósfera Sian Ka'an, Mexico
21 Parque Nacional Tikal*, Guatemala
22 Barrier Reef Reserve System, Belize
23 **Reserva Biósfera Río Plátano**, Honduras
24 Area de Conservación Guanacaste, Costa Rica
25 Parque Nacional Isla del Coco, Costa Rica
26 Cordillera de Talamanca and Parque Internacional La Amistad, Costa Rica/Panama
27 Parque Nacional del Darién, Panama
28 Parque Nacional Desembarco del Granma, Cuba
29 Morne Trois Pitons National Park*, Dominica
30 Central Surinam Nature Reserve, Surinam
31 Parque Nacional Canaima, Venezuela
32 Parque Nacional Los Katios, Colombia
33 **Parque Nacional Sangay**, Ecuador
34 Parque Nacional Galápagos*
35 Parque Nacional Río Abiseo, Peru
36 Parque Nacional Huascarán, Peru
37 Santuario histórico Machu Picchu*, Peru
38 Parque Nacional del Manú, Peru*
39 Parque Nacional Noel Kempff Mercado, Bolivia
40 Parque Nacional Jaú, Brazil
41 Parque Nacional Serra da Capivara, Brazil
42 Discovery Coast Atlantic forest reserves, Brazil
43 Southeast Atlantic forest reserves, Brazil
44 Pantanal conservation area, Brazil
45 **Parque Nacional do Iguaçu***, Brazil
46 Parque Nacional de Iguazú*, Argentina
47 Parque Nacional Talampaya & Parque Provincial Ischigualasto, Argentina
48 Península Valdés, Argentina
49 Parque Nacional Los Glaciares*, Argentina

EUROPE (including Atlantic islands and Turkey)

50 High Coast, Sweden
51 Lapponian area, Sweden
52 St Kilda, Scotland
53 Giant's Causeway* and its coast, Northern Ireland
54 Messel Pit fossil site, Germany
55 Paris: banks of the Seine, France
56 Mont St-Michel* and its bay, France
57 Golfe de Girolata, Golfe de Porto, les Calanche and Réserve naturelle Scandola, Corsica, France
58 Mont Perdu/Monte Perdido, France/Spain
59 Ibiza: biodiversity and culture, Spain
60 Parque Nacional Coto de Doñana, Spain
61 Laurisilva of Madeira
62 Parque Nacional de Garajonay, Gomera, Canary Is.
63 Ísole Eólie (Lipari), Italy
64 Bialowieza Forest & Belovezhskaya Pushcha, Poland/Belarus
65 Aggtelek Caves and the Slovak karst, Hungary/Slovak Republic
66 Skocjan Caves, Slovenia
67 Plitvice Lakes National Park*, Croatia
68 Durmitor National Park, Federal Republic of Yugoslavia
69 **Kotor and its gulf**, Federal Republic of Yugoslavia
70 Ohrid Lake and its region, Former Yugoslav Republic of Macedonia
71 Danube Delta, Romania
72 **Srebarna Nature Reserve**, Bulgaria

73 Pirin National Park, Bulgaria
74 Metéora, Greece
75 Áthos, Greece
76 Hierapolis-Pamukkale, Turkey
77 Göreme National Park* and Cappadocia rock sites, Turkey

RUSSIAN FEDERATION

78 Western Caucasus
79 Komi virgin forests
80 Golden Mountains of Altay
81 Lake Baikal
82 Kamchatka volcanoes

AFRICA

83 **Ichkeul National Park**, Tunisia
84 Tassili n'Ajjer, Algeria
85 Bandiagara Cliffs: Land of the Dogon, Mali
86 Banc d'Arguin National Park, Mauritania
87 **Parc national des Oiseaux du Djoudj (Djoudj National Bird Sanctuary)**, Senegal
88 Parc national du Niokolo Koba, Senegal
89 **Mount Nimba Nature Reserve**, Guinea/Côte d'Ivoire
90 Parc national de la Komoé, Côte d'Ivoire

Map labels:
LINCOLN SEA
ELLESMERE I.
AXEL HEIBURG I.
PARRY ISLANDS
DEVON I.
BANKS I.
VICTORIA I.
BAFFIN BAY
QIKIQTALUK (BAFFIN I.)
Greenland (Den.)
BEAUFORT SEA
BAFFIN BAY
DAVIS STRAIT
Cape Farewell
Alaska (US)
Great Bear Lake
Great Slave Lake
HUDSON BAY
LABRADOR SEA
CANADA
BERING SEA
GULF OF ALASKA
L. Winnipeg
L. Superior
SOUTHAMPTON I.
ALEUTIAN ISLANDS
VANCOUVER I.
L. Huron
L. Michigan
L. Ontario
L. Erie
LONG I.
NEWFOUNDLAND
St-Pierre et Miquelon (Fr.)
UNITED STATES OF AMERICA
Bermuda (UK)
NORTH ATLANTIC OCEAN
Tropic of Cancer
BAJA CALIFORNIA
GULF OF MEXICO
BAHAMAS
Hawaiian Is. (US)
MEXICO
Turks & Caicos Is. (UK)
CUBA
DOMINICAN REPUBLIC
HAITI
JAMAICA
Cayman Is. (UK)
CARIBBEAN SEA
GUATEMALA
EL SALVADOR
HONDURAS
NICARAGUA
Panama Canal
BARBADOS
GRENADA
TRINIDAD & TOBAGO
COSTA RICA
PANAMA
VENEZUELA
GUYANA
SURINAM
French Guiana (Fr.)
COLOMBIA
PACIFIC OCEAN
KIRIBATI
Tokelau (NZ)
SAMOA
American Samoa (US)
Cook Is. (NZ)
Niue (NZ)
French Polynesia (Fr.)
Equator
Galápagos Is. (Ec.)
ECUADOR
PERU
BRAZIL
BOLIVIA
PARAGUAY
Tropic of Capricorn
Pitcairn Is. (UK)
Easter I. (Chile)
Islas Juan Fernández (Chile)
CHILE
URUGUAY
ARGENTINA
Falkland Is. (UK)
South Georgia (UK)
TIERRA DEL FUEGO
Cape Horn
DRAKE PASSAGE
SCOTIA SEA

1 Puerto Rico (US)
2 Virgin Is. (US, UK)
3 Anguilla (UK)
4 St Maarten (Neths.) & St-Martin
ST KITTS & NEVIS
6 Montserrat (UK)
7 ANTIGUA & BARBUDA
8 Guadeloupe (Fr.)
9 DOMINICA
10 Martinique (Fr.)
11 ST LUCIA
12 ST VINCENT & THE GRENADINES
13 Bonaire (Neths.)
14 Curaçao (Neths.)
15 Aruba (Neths.)

UNESCO: Natural Heritage

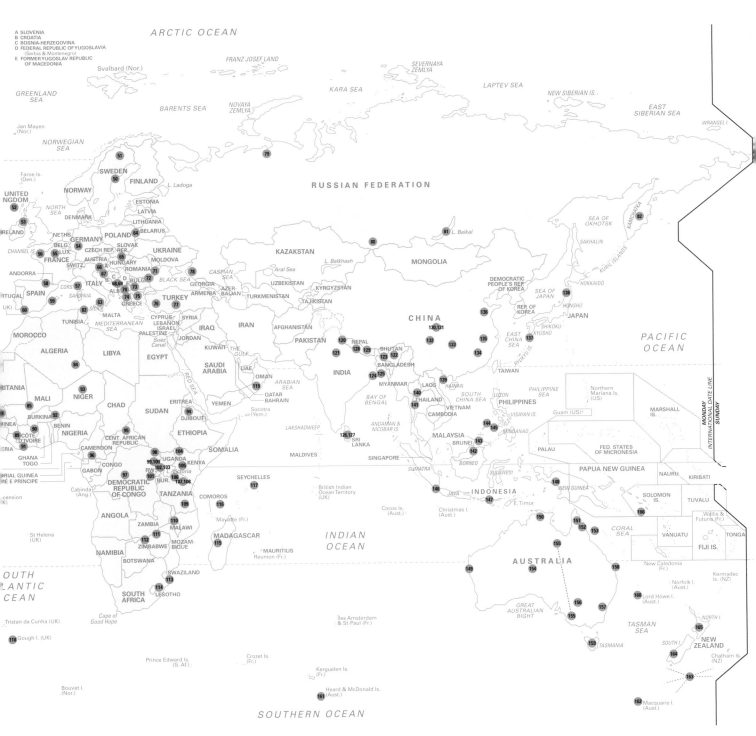

A SLOVENIA
B CROATIA
C BOSNIA-HERZEGOVINA
D FEDERAL REPUBLIC OF YUGOSLAVIA
  (Serbia & Montenegro)
E FORMER YUGOSLAV REPUBLIC
  OF MACEDONIA

91 Parc national de Taï, Côte d'Ivoire
92 Parc national du "W", Niger
93 **Aïr and Ténéré Natural Reserves**, Niger
94 **Simien National Park**, Ethiopia
95 **Parc national de Manovo-Gounda-St Floris**, Central African Republic
96 Réserve du Dja, Cameroon
97 **Parc national de la Salonga**, Dem. Rep. of Congo
98 **Parc national de la Garamba**, Dem. Rep. of Congo
99 **Réserve du Okapi**, Dem. Rep. of Congo
100 **Parc national des Virunga**, Dem. Rep. of Congo
101 **Parc national du Kahuzi-Biega**, Dem. Rep. of Congo
102 **Ruwenzori Mountains National Park**, Uganda
103 Bwindi Impenetrable Forest National Park*, Uganda
104 Sibiloi and Central Island National Parks, Kenya
105 Mount Kenya National Park* and forest, Kenya
106 Serengeti National Park*, Tanzania
107 Ngorongoro Conservation Area, Tanzania
108 Kilimanjaro National Park*, Tanzania

109 Selous Game Reserve, Tanzania
110 Lake Malawi National Park*, Malawi
111 Mana Pools National Park and Sapi & Chewore safari areas, Zimbabwe
112 Victoria Falls (Mosi-oa-Tunya)*, Zambia/Zimbabwe
113 Greater St Lucia Wetland Park, South Africa
114 uKhahlamba-Drakensberg Park, South Africa
115 Réserve du Tsingy Bemaraha, Madagascar
116 Groupe d'Aldabra, Seychelles
117 Vallée de Mai Nature Reserve, Seychelles
118 Gough Island Wildlife Reserve

ASIA
119 Arabian Oryx Sanctuary, Oman
120 Nanda Devi National Park, India
121 Keoladeo National Park, India
122 **Manas Wildlife Sanctuary**, India
123 Kaziranga National Park*, India
124 Sundarbans National Park, India
125 Sundarbans, Bangladesh
126 Dambulla Golden Rock Temple, Sri Lanka
127 Sinharaja Forest Reserve, Sri Lanka

128 Royal Chitwan National Park, Nepal
129 Sagarmatha National Park, Nepal
130 Jiuzhaigou Valley Scenic and Historic Interest Area, Sichuan, China
131 Huanglong Scenic and Historic Interest Area, Sichuan, China
132 Emei Shan and Leshan Giant Buddha, Sichuan, China
133 Wulingyuan Scenic and Historic Interest Area, Hunan, China
134 Wuyi Shan, Fujian, China
135 Huang Shan, Anhui, China
136 Tai Shan, Shandong, China
137 Yaku-shima, Japan
138 Shirakami-Sanchi, Japan
139 Ha Long Bay, Vietnam
140 Sukhothai and its region: historic towns, Thailand
141 Thung Yai-Huai Kha Khaeng Wildlife Sanctuaries, Thailand
142 Gunung Mulu National Park, Malaysia
143 Kinabalu Park, Malaysia
144 Puerto-Princesa Subterranean River National Park, the Philippines
145 Tubbataha Reef Marine Park, the Philippines
146 Ujung Kulon National Park and Krakatau Nature Reserve, Indonesia

147 Komodo National Park, Indonesia
148 Lorentz National Park, Indonesia

AUSTRALASIA & OCEANIA
149 Shark Bay, Australia
150 Kakadu National Park*, Australia
151 Queensland wet tropics, Australia
152 Central eastern rainforest reserves, Australia
153 Great Barrier Reef*, Australia
154 Uluru-Kata Tjuta National Park*, Australia
155 Naracoorte & Riversleigh: fossil mammal sites, Australia
156 Willandra Lakes region, Australia
157 Greater Blue Mountains area, Australia
158 Fraser Island, Australia
159 Tasmanian wilderness, Australia
160 Lord Howe island group, Australia
161 Heard and McDonald Islands
162 Macquarie Island
163 New Zealand Sub-Antarctic islands
164 Southwest New Zealand parks (Fiordland*, Aoraki/Mount Cook* and Westland National Parks)
165 Tongariro National Park*, New Zealand
166 East Rennell, Solomon Islands
167 Henderson Island, Pitcairn Islands

UNESCO: Cultural Heritage

The UNESCO World Heritage List consists of sites considered to be of global importance either because of their natural heritage or their significant man-made contribution to world culture. Countries which are signatories to the World Heritage Convention can submit potential sites to UNESCO, which considers each proposal under strict criteria and lists each site where one or more natural or cultural criteria have been met. Some sites are listed as combined sites; these appear on both maps.

The cultural sites shown here are either:
monuments, architectural works, works of monumental sculpture and painting or archaeological sites.

Sites nominated should:
(i) represent a unique artistic achievement; or
(ii) exhibit an important interchange of human values on developments in architecture or technology, monumental arts, town planning and landscape design; or
(iii) bear exceptional testimony to a cultural tradition or civilisation; or
(iv) be an outstanding example of building or architecture which illustrates (a) significant stage(s) in human history; or
(v) be an outstanding example of traditional human settlement or land-use; or
(vi) be associated with events, traditions, ideas, beliefs or artistic and literary works of outstanding universal significance.

Properties named in red are included on the list of World Heritage in Danger.

The Organisation of World Heritage Cities (OWHC) was established in 1993 with the aim of assisting member cities adapt and improve their management methods in relation to the specific requirements of having a site inscribed on the UNESCO World Heritage List.

World Heritage Cities are named on the map.

For further information on Heritage Sites and Heritage Cities, contact:

UNESCO World Heritage Centre,
7 place de Fontenoy,
75352 Paris 07 SP,
France.
Tel: +33 (0)1 45 68 15 71.

www.unesco.org/whc
www.ovpm.org

Sites marked with an asterisk (*) are featured in Columbus Travel Guides' *Tourist Attractions and Events of the World*, 2nd edition. For more information, call +44 (0)20 7608 6666.

UNITED STATES & CANADA
1 Anthony Island, British Columbia
2 Head-Smashed-In Buffalo Jump, Alberta
3 Québec: historic area*
4 Lunenburg: old city, Nova Scotia
5 L'Anse aux Meadows Historic Park, Newfoundland
6 Mesa Verde National Park, Colorado
7 Chaco Culture National Historical Park, New Mexico
8 Pueblo de Taos, New Mexico
9 Cahokia Mounds State Historic Site, Illinois
10 Charlottesville: Monticello and University of Virginia, Virginia
11 Philadelphia: Independence Hall*, Pennsylvania
12 Statue of Liberty*, New York

LATIN AMERICA & THE CARIBBEAN
13 Sierra de la San Francisco: rock paintings, Mexico
14 Paquimé Casas Grandes: archaeological site, Mexico
15 Zacatecas: historic centre, Mexico
16 Guadalajara: Hospicio Cabañas, Mexico
17 Guanajuato: historic town and adjacent mines, Mexico
18 Querétaro: historic monuments, Mexico
19 Teotihuacán: pre-Hispanic city*, Mexico
20 El Tajín: pre-Hispanic city, Mexico
21 Morelia: historic centre, Mexico
22 Ciudad de México (Mexico City): historic centre and Xochimilco, Mexico
23 Xochicalco: archaeological site, Mexico
24 Popocatépetl: monasteries, Mexico
25 Puebla: historic centre, Mexico

26 Tlacotalpan: historic monuments, Mexico
27 Monte Albán: archaeological site*, and Oaxaca: historic centre, Mexico
28 Palenque: pre-Hispanic city and national park*, Mexico
29 Campeche: historic fortified town, Mexico
30 Uxmal: pre-Hispanic city, Mexico
31 Chichén-Itzá: pre-Hispanic city*, Mexico
32 Parque Nacional Tikal*, Guatemala
33 Quiriguá: archaeological park, Guatemala
34 Antigua, Guatemala
35 Copán: Maya site, Honduras
36 Joya de Cerén: archaeological site, El Salvador
37 León Viejo: ruins, Nicaragua
38 Portobelo and San Lorenzo: fortifications, Panama
39 Ciudad de Panamá (Panama City): historic district and the Salón Bolívar, Panama
40 St George: historic town and related fortifications, Bermuda
41 Viñales valley, Cuba
42 La Habana (Havana): old town and its fortifications*, Cuba
43 Trinidad and Valley de los Ingenios, Cuba
44 Santiago de Cuba: San Pedro de la Roca castle, Cuba
45 First coffee plantations in southeast Cuba: archaeological landscape
46 La Citadelle, Sans Souci and Ramiers: National Historic Park, Haiti
47 Santo Domingo: colonial city, Dominican Republic
48 La Fortaleza and San Juan: historic sites, Puerto Rico
49 Brimstone Hill Fortress National Park, St Kitts and Nevis
50 Willemstad: historic area, inner city and harbour, Curaçao
51 Caracas: university campus, Venezuela
52 Coro: town and its port, La Vela, Venezuela
53 Cartagena: port, fortress and monuments, Colombia
54 Mompós: historic centre, Colombia
55 Parque Arqueológico Nacional Tierradentro, Colombia
56 Parque Arqueológico San Agustín, Colombia
57 Quito: old city, Ecuador
58 Cuenca: historic centre, Ecuador
59 Parque Nacional Río Abiseo, Peru
60 **Chan Chan: archaeological area**, Peru

61 Chavín: archaeological site, Peru
62 Lima: historic centre, Peru
63 Santuario Histórico Machu Picchu*, Peru
64 Cuzco: old city, Peru
65 Nazca: geoglyphs and Pampas de Juma, Peru
66 Arequipa: historic centre, Peru
67 Tiwanaku: pre-Hispanic city, Bolivia
68 Potosí, Bolivia
69 Sucre: historic city, Bolivia
70 El Fuerte de Samaipata, Bolivia
71 Chiquitos Jesuit missions, Bolivia
72 Jesús and Trinidad: Jesuit missions, Paraguay
73 Brasília, Brazil
74 Parque Nacional Serra da Capivara, Brazil
75 São Luis: historic centre, Brazil
76 Olinda: historic centre, Brazil
77 Salvador de Bahia: historic centre, Brazil
78 Diamantina: historic centre, Brazil
79 Ouro Prêto: historic town, Brazil
80 Congonhas: Sanctuary of Bom Jesus, Brazil
81 São Miguel: Jesuit mission ruins, Brazil; Loreto, San Ignacio Miní, Santa Ana & Santa Maria Mayor: Guaraní Jesuit missions, Argentina
82 Colonia del Sacramento: historic quarter, Uruguay
83 Córdoba: Jesuit Block and estancias, Argentina
84 Cueva de las Manos, Río Pinturas, Argentina
85 Isla de Chiloé, Chile
86 Parque Nacional Rapa Nui, Easter Island

EUROPE† (including Atlantic islands)
87 Angra do Heroísmo: central area, Terceira, Azores
88 San Cristóbal de la Laguna, Tenerife, Canary Is.
89 Urnes: stave church, Norway
90 Røros: mining town, Norway
91 Alta: rock drawings, Norway
92 Lapponian area, Sweden
93 Luleå: Gammelstad church town, Sweden
94 Rauma: old town, Finland
95 Sammallahdenmäki: Bronze Age burial site, Finland
96 Petäjävesi: old church, Finland
97 Verla: groundwood and board mill, Finland

RUSSIAN FEDERATION†
98 Solovetskiye Ostrova: cultural and historic ensemble
99 Khizi Pogost
100 Kazan: Kremlin

AFRICA†
101 Thebes: ancient city and necropolis (incl. Hatshepsut's Temple*, Karnak*, Luxor, Valley of the Kings*, Valley of the Queens*), Egypt
102 Abu Simbel* to Philae: Nubian monuments, Egypt
103 Aksum: archaeological site, Ethiopia
104 Fasil Ghebbi & Gonder monuments, Ethiopia
105 Lalibela: rock-hewn churches, Ethiopia
106 Awash lower valley, Ethiopia
107 Tiya: carved steles, Ethiopia
108 Omo lower valley, Ethiopia
109 Tadrart Acacus: rock-art sites, Libya
110 Tassili n'Ajjer, Algeria
111 Chinguetti, Ouadane, Oualata and Tichitt: trading and religious centres, Mauritania
112 **Tombouctou (Timbuktu)**, Mali
113 Djenné: old towns, Mali
114 Île de St Louis, Senegal
115 Île de Gorée, Senegal
116 Ashante traditional buildings, Ghana
117 Accra and Volta areas: forts and castles, Ghana
118 **Abomey: royal palaces**, Benin
119 Sukur: cultural landscape, Nigeria
120 Zanzibar: stone town*, Tanzania
121 Kilwa Kisiwani and Songo Mnara: ruins, Tanzania
122 Ilha de Moçambique, Mozambique
123 Great Zimbabwe National Monument*, Zimbabwe
124 Khami Ruins National Monument, Zimbabwe
125 Sterkfontein, Swartkrans, Kromdraai and environs: fossil hominid sites, South Africa

Map labels (North & South America):

LINCOLN SEA · AXEL HEIBURG I. · PARRY ISLANDS · DEVON I. · ELLESMERE I. · BANKS I. · VICTORIA I. · QIKIQTALUK (BAFFIN I.) · BAFFIN BAY · Greenland (Den.) · BEAUFORT SEA · SOUTHAMPTON I. · DAVIS STRAIT · Cape Farewell · L. Winnipeg · Great Bear Lake · Great Slave Lake · HUDSON BAY · CANADA · LABRADOR SEA · Alaska (US) · BERING SEA · GULF OF ALASKA · ALEUTIAN ISLANDS · VANCOUVER I. · L. Superior · Québec · L. Huron · NEWFOUNDLAND · St-Pierre et Miquelon (Fr.) · Lunenburg · L. Michigan · UNITED STATES OF AMERICA · L. Ontario · L. Erie · LONG I. · NO ATLA OC · Angr. Heroi. · Tropic of Cancer · BAJA CALIFORNIA · Bermuda (UK) · St George · MONDAY INTERNATIONAL DATE LINE · SUNDAY · Hawaiian Is. (US) · Zacatecas · La Habana (Havana) · GULF OF MEXICO · BAHAMAS · Turks & Caicos Is. (UK) · CUBA · DOMINICAN REPUBLIC · San Juan · MEXICO · Cayman Is. (UK) · HAITI · JAMAICA · Sto. Domingo · Willemstad · GUATEMALA · HONDURAS · EL SALVADOR · NICARAGUA · Cartagena · BARBADOS · GRENADA · TRINIDAD & TOBAGO · PACIFIC OCEAN · KIRIBATI · Tokelau (NZ) · American Samoa (US) · SAMOA · Cook Is. (NZ) · Niue (NZ) · French Polynesia (Fr.) · Pitcairn Is. (UK) · Easter I. (Chile) · COSTA RICA · PANAMA · Ciudad de Panamá (Panama City) · Mompós · Coro & La Vela · VENEZUELA · GUYANA · SURINAM · French Guiana (Fr.) · COLOMBIA · Galápagos Is. (Ec.) · Quito · ECUADOR · Cuenca · São Luís · PERU · Lima · Cuzco · BRAZIL · Salv. de E · BOLIVIA · Brasília · Diamantina · Arequipa · Sucre · Ouro Prêt · Potosí · PARAGUAY · Tropic of Capricorn · Islas Juan Fernández (Chile) · CHILE · URUGUAY · Colonia del Sacramento · ARGENTINA · Cape Horn · TIERRA DEL FUEGO · Falkland Is. (UK) · South Georgia (UK) · DRAKE PASSAGE · SCOTIA SEA

Caribbean island key:
1 Puerto Rico (US)
2 Virgin Is. (US, UK)
3 Anguilla (UK)
4 St Maarten (Neths.) & St-M
ST KITTS & NEVIS
6 Montserrat (UK)
7 ANTIGUA & BARBUDA
8 Guadeloupe (Fr.)
9 DOMINICA
10 Martinique (Fr.)
11 ST LUCIA
12 ST VINCENT & THE GRENA
13 Bonaire (Neths.)
14 Curaçao (Neths.)
15 Aruba (Neths.)

Mexico / Central America inset:
Guanajuato · Querétaro · BAHÍA DE CAMPECHE · Morelia · MEXICO · Campeche · YUCATÁN PEN. · Cd. de México (Mexico City) · Puebla · Tlacotalpan · Oaxaca · BELIZE · GUATEMALA · Antigua · HONDURAS · EL SALVADOR · NICARAG. · PACIFIC OCEAN · 1000 km · 500 miles · Equator

UNESCO: Cultural Heritage

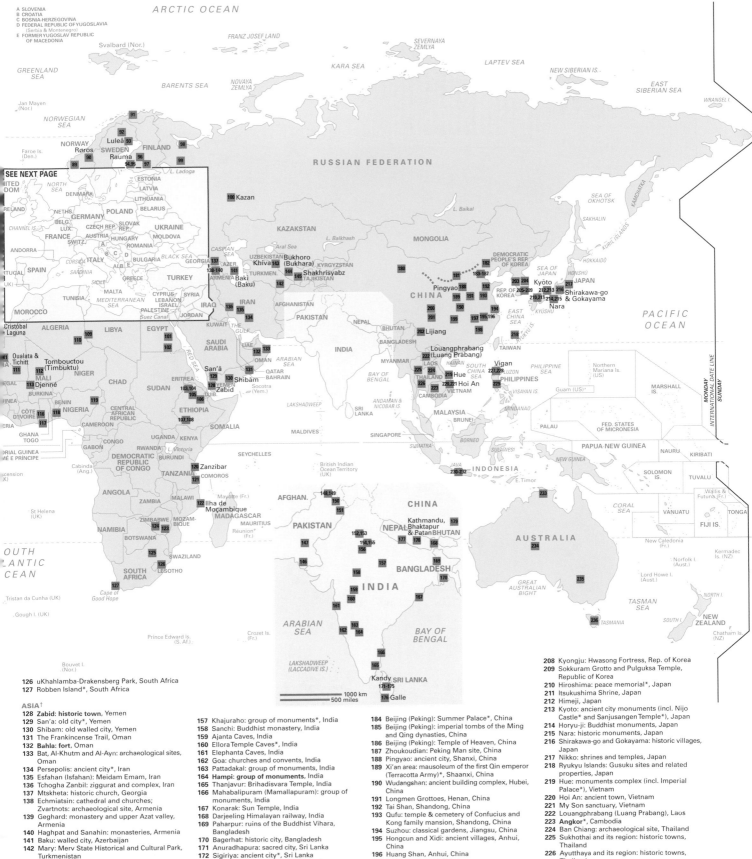

A SLOVENIA
B CROATIA
C BOSNIA-HERZEGOVINA
D FEDERAL REPUBLIC OF YUGOSLAVIA
   (Serbia & Montenegro)
E FORMER YUGOSLAV REPUBLIC
   OF MACEDONIA

126 uKhahlamba-Drakensberg Park, South Africa
127 Robben Island*, South Africa

ASIA†
128 **Zabid: historic town**, Yemen
129 San'a: old city*, Yemen
130 Shibam: old walled city, Yemen
131 The Frankincense Trail, Oman
132 **Bahla: fort**, Oman
133 Bat, Al-Khutm and Al-Ayn: archaeological sites, Oman
134 Persepolis: ancient city*, Iran
135 Esfahan (Isfahan): Meidam Emam, Iran
136 Tchogha Zanbil: ziggurat and complex, Iran
137 Mtskheta: historic church, Georgia
138 Echmiatsin: cathedral and churches; Zvartnots: archaeological site, Armenia
139 Geghard: monastery and upper Azat valley, Armenia
140 Haghpat and Sanahin: monasteries, Armenia
141 Baku: walled city, Azerbaijan
142 Mary: Merv State Historical and Cultural Park, Turkmenistan
143 Itchan Kala, Uzbekistan
144 Bukhoro (Bukhara): historic centre, Uzbekistan
145 Shakhrisyabz: historic centre, Uzbekistan
146 Thatta: historical monuments, Pakistan
147 Mohenjodaro: archaeological site, Pakistan
148 Takht-i-Bakhi: Buddhist ruins; Sahr-i-Bahlol: remains of city, Pakistan
149 Taxila: archaeological site, Pakistan
150 Rohtas: fort, Pakistan
151 **Lahore: fort and Shalimar gardens**, Pakistan
152 Delhi: Humayun's tomb, India
153 Delhi: Qutb Minar and its monuments, India
154 Agra Fort, India
155 Taj Mahal*, Agra, India
156 Fatehpur Sikri: Mongol city, India

157 Khajuraho: group of monuments*, India
158 Sanchi: Buddhist monastery, India
159 Ajanta Caves, India
160 Ellora Temple Caves*, India
161 Elephanta Caves, India
162 Goa: churches and convents, India
163 Pattadakal: group of monuments, India
164 **Hampi: group of monuments**, India
165 Thanjavur: Brihadisvara Temple, India
166 Mahabalipuram (Mamallapuram): group of monuments, India
167 Konarak: Sun Temple, India
168 Darjeeling Himalayan railway, India
169 Paharpur: ruins of the Buddhist Vihara, Bangladesh
170 Bagerhat: historic city, Bangladesh
171 Anuradhapura: sacred city, Sri Lanka
172 Sigiriya: ancient city*, Sri Lanka
173 Polonnaruwa: ancient city, Sri Lanka
174 Dambulla Golden Rock Temple, Sri Lanka
175 Kandy: sacred city (incl. Temple of the Sacred Tooth*), Sri Lanka
176 Galle: old town and its fortifications, Sri Lanka
177 Lumbini: birthplace of Lord Buddha, Nepal
178 Kathmandu valley, Nepal
179 Lhasa: Potala Palace* and Jokhang Temple Monastery, Tibet, China
180 Mogao Caves, Gansu, China
181 Great Wall of China*
182 Chengde: mountain resort and outlying temples, Hebei, China
183 Beijing (Peking): imperial palace of the Ming and Qing dynasties (Forbidden City)*, China

184 Beijing (Peking): Summer Palace*, China
185 Beijing (Peking): imperial tombs of the Ming and Qing dynasties, China
186 Beijing (Peking): Temple of Heaven, China
187 Zhoukoudian: Peking Man site, China
188 Pingyao: ancient city, Shanxi, China
189 Xi'an area: mausoleum of the first Qin emperor (Terracotta Army)*, Shaanxi, China
190 Wudangshan: ancient building complex, Hubei, China
191 Longmen Grottoes, Henan, China
192 Tai Shan, Shandong, China
193 Qufu: temple & cemetery of Confucius and Kong family mansion, Shandong, China
194 Suzhou: classical gardens, Jiangsu, China
195 Hongcun and Xidi: ancient villages, Anhui, China
196 Huang Shan, Anhui, China
197 Lu Shan, Jiangxi, China
198 Wuyi Shan, Fujian, China
199 Dazu rock carvings, Chongqing, China
200 Qincheng Shan and Dujiangyan irrigation system, Sichuan, China
201 Emei Shan and Leshan giant buddha, Sichuan, China
202 Lijiang: old town, Yunnan, China
203 Soul (Seoul): Ch'angdokkung Palace complex, Republic of Korea
204 Chongmyo Shrine, Republic of Korea
205 Haeinsa Temple*, Republic of Korea
206 Hwasun, Kanghwa and Koch'ang: Megalithic cemeteries, Republic of Korea
207 Kyongju: historic areas*, Republic of Korea

208 Kyongju: Hwasong Fortress, Rep. of Korea
209 Sokkuram Grotto and Pulguksa Temple, Republic of Korea
210 Hiroshima: peace memorial*, Japan
211 Itsukushima Shrine, Japan
212 Himeji, Japan
213 Kyoto: ancient city monuments (incl. Nijo Castle* and Sanjusangen Temple*), Japan
214 Horyu-ji: Buddhist monuments, Japan
215 Nara: historic monuments, Japan
216 Shirakawa-go and Gokayama: historic villages, Japan
217 Nikko: shrines and temples, Japan
218 Ryukyu Islands: Gusuku sites and related properties, Japan
219 Hue: monuments complex (incl. Imperial Palace*), Vietnam
220 Hoi An: ancient town, Vietnam
221 My Son sanctuary, Vietnam
222 Louangphrabang (Luang Prabang), Laos
223 **Angkor***, Cambodia
224 Ban Chiang: archaeological site, Thailand
225 Sukhothai and its region: historic towns, Thailand
226 Ayutthaya and its region: historic towns, Thailand
227 Vigan: historic town, the Philippines
228 Cordillera Central: rice terraces*, the Philippines
229 Manila: Baroque churches, the Philippines
230 Borobudur: temple compound, Indonesia
231 Prambanan: temple compound*, Indonesia
232 Sangiran: early man site, Indonesia

AUSTRALASIA & OCEANIA
233 Kakadu National Park*, Australia
234 Uluru-Kata Tjuta National Park*, Australia
235 Willandra Lakes region, Australia
236 Tasmanian wilderness, Australia

†See next page for other sites in these areas

UNESCO: Cultural Heritage

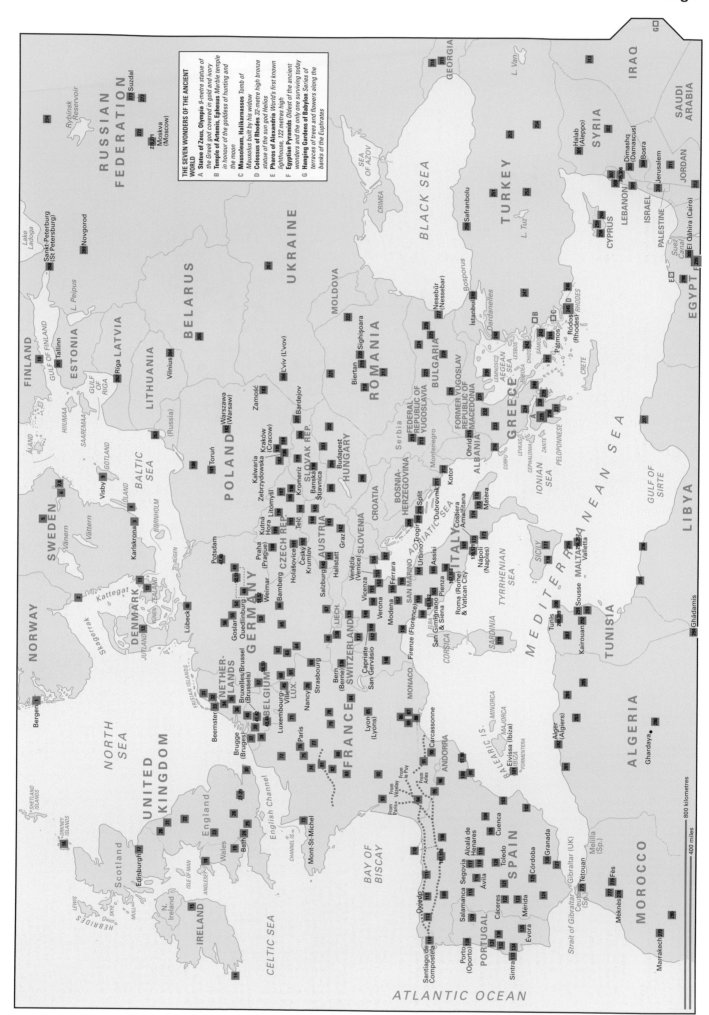

THE SEVEN WONDERS OF THE ANCIENT WORLD

A **Statue of Zeus, Olympia** 9-metre statue of the Greek god covered in gold and ivory

B **Temple of Artemis, Ephesus** Marble temple in honour of the goddess of hunting and the moon

C **Mausoleum, Halikarnassos** Tomb of Mausolus built by his widow

D **Colossus of Rhodes** 32-metre high bronze statue of the sun god Helios

E **Pharos of Alexandria** World's first known lighthouse, 122 metres high

F **Egyptian Pyramids** Oldest of the ancient wonders and the only one surviving today

G **Hanging Gardens of Babylon** Series of terraces of trees and flowers along the banks of the Euphrates

UNESCO: Cultural Heritage

Properties named in red are included on the list of World Heritage in Danger. Cities named on the map are members of the Organisation of World Heritage Cities (OWHC) - see previous page for explanation.

Sites marked with an asterisk (*) are featured in Columbus Travel Guides' *Tourist Attractions and Events of the World*, 2nd edition. For more information, call +44 (0)20 7608 6666.

EUROPE (including Turkey)

1 Bergen: Bryggen*, Norway
2 Tanum: rock carvings, Sweden
3 Karlskrona: naval city, Sweden
4 Öland: agricultural landscape of the southern part of the island, Sweden
5 Engelsberg: ironworks, Sweden
6 Birka and Hovgården: archaeological sites, Sweden
7 Drottningholms Slot (Drottningholm Royal Palace)*, Sweden
8 Stockholm: Skogskyrkogarden, Sweden
9 Visby: Hanseatic town and former Viking site, Sweden
10 Helsinki (Helsingfors): Suomenlinna Sea Fortress*, Finland
11 Helsingør (Elsinore): Kronborg Slot (Kronborg Castle)*, Denmark
12 Roskilde: cathedral, Denmark
13 Jelling: mounds, runic stones and church, Denmark
14 Skellig Michael: monastic complex, Ireland
15 Brú Na Bóinne: archaeological ensemble at the bend of the Boyne, Ireland
16 Neolithic Orkney, Scotland
17 Edinburgh: old and new towns (incl. Castle*, Royal Botanic Garden*, Royal Museum & Museum of Scotland*, Scotch Whisky Heritage Centre & Royal Mile*), Scotland
18 Castles and town walls of King Edward (incl. Caernarfon Castle*), northwest Wales
19 Blaenavon: industrial landscape, Wales
20 Hadrian's Wall*, England
21 Durham: castle and cathedral*, England
22 Studley Royal Park and Fountains Abbey ruins, England
23 Ironbridge Gorge, England
24 Bath (incl. Roman baths and pumproom*), England
25 Stonehenge*, Avebury and associated Megalithic sites, England
26 Blenheim Palace, England
27 London: Tower of London*, England
28 London: Westminster Palace (Big Ben and the Houses of Parliament)*, Westminster Abbey* and St Margaret's Church, England
29 London: Maritime Greenwich*, England
30 Canterbury: cathedral*, St Augustine's Abbey and St Martin's Church, England
31 D.F. Wouda steam pumping station, The Netherlands
32 Schokland: prehistoric settlements, The Netherlands
33 Droogmakerij de Beemster (Beemster Polder), The Netherlands
34 Amsterdam: defence line, The Netherlands
35 Utrecht: Rietveld Schröderhuis, The Netherlands
36 Kinderdijk-Elshout: mill network, The Netherlands
37 Brugge (Bruges): historic centre, Belgium
38 Tournai: Cáthedrale Notre-Dame, Belgium
39 Belfries of Flanders and Wallonia (incl. Onze Lieve Vrouwekathedraal, Antwerpen (Antwerp)*), Belgium
40 Flemish Béguinages, Belgium
41 Bruxelles/Brussel (Brussels): Grand-Place*, Belgium
42 Bruxelles/Brussel (Brussels): four town houses of architect Victor Horta, Belgium
43 Canal du Centre: four boat-lifts and environs, La Louvière and Le Rœulx, Belgium
44 Mons: Spiennes Neolithic flint mines, Belgium
45 Luxembourg-Ville: old quarters and fortifications
46 Lübeck: Hanseatic city, Germany
47 Berlin: Museumsinsel (incl. Pergamonmuseum*), Germany
48 Potsdam and SW Berlin: palaces and parks (incl. Schloss Sanssouci*), Germany
49 Eisleben and Wittenberg: Luther memorials, Germany
50 Dessau-Wörlitz: Garden Kingdom, Germany
51 Dessau and Weimar: Bauhaus buildings, Germany
52 Weimar: classical city, Germany
53 Wartburg: castle, Germany
54 Quedlinburg: collegiate church, castle and old town, Germany
55 Goslar: historic town and Rammelsberg mines, Germany
56 Hildesheim: cathedral and St Michaeliskirche, Germany
57 Aachen (Aix-la-Chapelle): cathedral, Germany
58 Köln (Cologne): cathedral*, Germany
59 Brühl: Schloss Augustusburg and Jagdschloss Falkenlust, Germany
60 Trier: Roman monuments, cathedral and Liebfrauenkirche, Germany
61 Völklingen: ironworks, Germany
62 Lorsch: abbey and Altenmünster, Germany
63 Speyer: cathedral, Germany
64 Maulbronn: Cistercian monastery complex, Germany
65 Würzburg: Residenz with the court gardens and square, Germany
66 Bamberg, Germany
67 Wies: pilgrimage church, Germany
68 Reichenau: Benedictine monastery remains, Germany
69 Strasbourg: Grand Île, France
70 Nancy: Place Stanislas, Place de la Carrière and Place d'Alliance, France
71 Reims: Cáthedrale Notre-Dame, Abbaye St Remi and Palais du Tau, France
72 Amiens: cathedral, France
73 Mont St-Michel* and its bay, France
74 Chartres: cathedral*, France
75 Versailles: palace and park*, France
76 Paris: banks of the Seine (incl. Tour Eiffel*, Musée du Louvre*, Musée d'Orsay*, Cathédrale de Notre-Dame*), France
77 Fontainebleau: palace and park, France
78 Fontenay: Cistercian abbey, France
79 Vézelay: basilica and hill, France
80 Bourges: cathedral, France
81 Loire Valley between Chalonnes and Sully-sur-Loire
82 Chambord: château and estate, France
83 St-Savin-sur-Gartempe: church, France
84 Arc-et-Senans: royal saltworks, France
85 Lyon (Lyons): historic city, France
86 Orange: Roman theatre and its surroundings and the triumphal arch, France
87 Avignon: historic centre (incl. Palais des Papes*, Pont St-Bénézet*), France
88 Arles: Roman and Romanesque monuments (incl. Roman amphitheatre*), France
89 Remoulins: Pont du Gard Roman aqueduct*, France
90 Carcassonne: historic fortified city*, France
91 Canal du Midi, France
92 Vallée du Vézère: Lascaux* and other decorated grottoes, France
93 St-Émilion: vineyard landscape, France
94 The Way of St James pilgrimage route: four routes through France
95 Mont Perdu/Monte Perdido, France/Spain
96 Vall de Boí: Catalan Romanesque churches, Spain
97 Barcelona: Parque and Palacio Güell* and Casa Milá, Spain
98 Barcelona: Palau de la Música Catalaña and the Hospital de Sant Pau, Spain
99 Tarragona: Roman city of Tárraco, Spain
100 Poblet: monastery, Spain
101 Ibiza: biodiversity and culture, Spain
102 Elx (Elche): Palmeral date palm landscape, Spain
103 Valencia: La Lonja de la Sada, Spain
104 Teruel: Mujedar architecture, Spain
105 Cuenca: historic walled town, Spain
106 San Millán and Suso: monasteries, Spain
107 Burgos: cathedral, Spain
108 Cuevas de Atapuerca: archaeological site, Spain
109 Las Médulas, Spain
110 Camino de Santiago: the Way of St James pilgrimage route, Spain
111 Cuevas de Altamira: archaeological site, Spain
112 Oviedo: churches of the Asturias Kingdom, Spain
113 Lugo: Roman walls, Spain
114 Santiago de Compostela: old town (incl. cathedral*), Spain
115 Salamanca: old city, Spain
116 Ávila: old town with extra-muros churches, Spain
117 Segovia: old town and aqueduct*, Spain
118 El Escorial: monastery*, Spain
119 Alcalá de Henares: university and historic precinct, Spain
120 Toledo: historic city, Spain
121 Guadalupe: Real Monasterio de Santa Maria, Spain
122 Cáceres: old town, Spain
123 Mérida: archaeological ensemble, Spain
124 Sevilla (Seville): cathedral*, Alcazar and Archivo de Indias, Spain
125 Córdoba: mosque and historic centre, Spain
126 Granada: Alhambra*, Generalife & Albaicín quarter, Spain
127 Mediterranean seaboard prehistoric rock-art sites, Spain
128 Porto (Oporto): historic centre, Portugal
129 Vale do Côa: prehistoric rock-art sites, Portugal
130 Tomar: Convent of Christ, Portugal
131 Batalha: monastery, Portugal
132 Alcobaça: monastery, Portugal
133 Sintra: historic city, Portugal
134 Lisboa (Lisbon): Mosteiro dos Jerónimos* and Torre de Belém*, Portugal
135 Évora: historic centre, Portugal
136 Bern (Berne): old city, Switzerland
137 Bellinzona: group of fortifications, Switzerland
138 St Gallen (St Gall): convent, Switzerland
139 Müstair: Benedictine convent of St John, Switzerland
140 Salzburg: historic centre (incl. Mozart's birthplace and residence*), Austria
141 Hallstatt-Dachstein-Salzkammergut: cultural landscape, Austria
142 Graz: historic centre, Austria
143 Semmering Railway, Austria
144 Wachau: cultural landscape, Austria
145 Wien (Vienna): Schloss Schönbrunn and gardens*, Austria
146 Torino (Turin): Residences of the Royal House of Savoy, Italy
147 Milano (Milan): church and Dominican convent of Santa Maria delle Grazie with 'The Last Supper' by Leonardo da Vinci, Italy
148 Crespi d'Adda: industrial workers' town, Italy
149 Val Camónica: rock drawings, Italy
150 Verona: historic city, Italy
151 Vicenza: city and the Palladian villas of the Veneto, Italy
152 Pádova (Padua): botanical garden, Italy
153 Venézia (Venice) and lagoon (incl. Basilica di San Marco*, Palazzo Ducale*), Italy
154 Aquileia: archaeological site including Patriarchal Basilica, Italy
155 Ferrara: Renaissance city, Italy
156 Ravenna: early Christian monuments and mosaics, Italy
157 Modena: cathedral, Torre Civica and Piazza Grande, Italy
158 Portovénere, Cinque Terre, Ísola Palmária, Í. del Tino and Í. del Tinetto, Italy
159 Firenze (Florence): historic centre (incl. Duomo Santa Maria del Fiore*, Galleria degli Uffizi*, Ponte Vecchio*), Italy
160 Pisa: Piazza del Duomo (incl. Torre Pendente*), Italy
161 San Gimignano: historic centre, Italy
162 Siena: historic centre (incl. Piazza del Campo*), Italy
163 Pienza: historic centre, Italy
164 Urbino: historic centre, Italy
165 Assisi: Basilica di San Francesco and other Franciscan sites, Italy
166 Villa Adriana (Hadrian's Villa), Italy
167 Vatican City (incl. Basilica di San Pietro*, Musei Vaticani & Capella Sistina*)
168 Roma (Rome): historic centre and extraterritorial properties of the Holy See & San Paolo fuori le Mura (incl. Colosseo*, Fontana di Trevi*, Foro Romano*, Pantheon*, Spanish Steps & Keats-Shelley Memorial House*), Italy
169 Caserta: Palazzo Reale & gardens, Vanvitelli aqueduct & San Leucio complex, Italy
170 Nápoli (Naples): historic centre, Italy
171 Herculaneum, Pompeii* and Torre Annunziata: archaeological areas, Italy
172 Costiera Amalfitana, Italy
173 Cilento area: cultural landscape including Parco Nazionale del Cilento e Vallo di Diano, Certosa di San Lorenzo in Padula and the archaeological sites of Paestum and Vélia, Italy
174 Castel del Monte: medieval castle, Italy
175 Matera: I Sassi di Matera troglodyte settlement, Italy
176 Alberobello: Trulli houses, Italy
177 Villa Romana del Casale, Sicily, Italy
178 Agrigento: archaeological area, Sicily, Italy
179 Su Nuraxi di Barúmini, Sardinia, Italy
180 Malbork: Teutonic castle, Poland
181 Torun: medieval town, Poland
182 Warszawa (Warsaw): historic centre (incl. Warsaw Royal Castle*), Poland
183 Zamosc: old city, Poland
184 Wieliczka: salt mines, Poland
185 Kraków (Cracow): historic centre (incl. Market Sq.*, Wawel Royal Castle*), Poland
186 Kalwaria Zebrzydowska: Mannerist architectural and park landscape complex and pilgrimage park, Poland
187 Oswiecim (Auschwitz): Auschwitz-Birkenau concentration camp*, Poland
188 Praha (Prague): historic centre (incl. Charles Bridge*, Castle & St Vitus Cathedral*, Old Town Square*), Czech Republic
189 Kutná Hora*: historical centre, Church of Santa Barbara and Cathedral of Our Lady at Sedlec, Czech Republic
190 Litomysl Castle, Czech Republic
191 Holasovice: historical village reservation, Czech Republic
192 Cesky Krumlov: historic centre, Czech Republic
193 Telc: historic centre, Czech Republic
194 Lednice-Valtice: cultural landscape, Czech Republic
195 Zelená Hora: St John of Nepomuk, Czech Republic
196 Kromeriz: castle and gardens, Czech Republic
197 Olomouc: Holy Trinity column, Czech Republic
198 Banská Stiavnica, Slovak Republic
199 Vlkolinec, Slovak Republic
200 Spisské Pohradie: Spissky Hrad* and associated monuments, Slovak Republic
201 Bardejov: fortified medieval town, Slovak Republic
202 Hortobágyi national park, Hungary
203 Hollokö: traditional village, Hungary
204 Budapest: banks of the Danube and Buda Castle* area (incl. Fisherman's Bastion*), Hungary
205 Pannonhalma: millenary Benedictine abbey and its natural environment, Hungary
206 Pécs: early Christian cemetery, Hungary
207 Porec: Episcopal complex, Croatia
208 Sibenik: St James cathedral, Croatia
209 Trogir: historic city, Croatia
210 Split: historic centre with Diocletian palace, Croatia
211 Dubrovnik: old city*, Croatia
212 **Kotor and its gulf**, Federal Republic of Yugoslavia
213 Studenica: monastery, Federal Republic of Yugoslavia
214 Stari Ras: medieval buildings and monuments; Sopocani Monastery, Federal Republic of Yugoslavia
215 Ohrid Lake and its region, Former Yugoslav Republic of Macedonia
216 **Butrint (Buthrotum): archaeological site**, Albania
217 Horezu: monastery, Romania
218 Orastie mountains: Dacian fortresses, Romania
219 Biertan: town and fortified church, Romania
220 Sighisoara: historic centre, Romania
221 Maramures: wooden churches, Romania
222 Moldavian churches, Romania
223 Boyana: church, Bulgaria
224 Sveshtari: Thracian tomb, Bulgaria
225 Ivanovo: rock chapels, Bulgaria
226 Madara: horseman stone relief, Bulgaria
227 Nesebur (Nessebar): ancient city, Bulgaria
228 Kazanluk: Thracian tomb, Bulgaria
229 Rila: monastery*, Bulgaria
230 Áthos, Greece
231 Thessaloníki: Palaeochristian and Byzantine monuments, Greece
232 Vergina: archaeological site, Greece
233 Metéora, Greece
234 Delfí (Delphi): archaeological site*, Greece
235 Olimbía (Olympia): archaeological site*, Greece
236 Bassae: Temple of Apollo Epicurius, Greece
237 Mistrás, Greece
238 Mycenae* and Tiryns; archaeological sites, Greece
239 Epidavros (Epidaurus): archaeological site*, Greece
240 Athina (Athens): Acropolis*, Greece
241 Dilos, Greece
242 Hios (Chios): Daphni, Hossios, Luckas and Néa Moni monasteries, Greece
243 Sámos: Pythagoreion and Heraion, Greece
244 Pátmos: historic centre (chorá) with the monastery of St John the Theologian and the Cave of the Apocalypse, Greece
245 Ródos (Rhodes): medieval city, Greece
246 Xanthos-Letoon, Turkey
247 Hierapolis-Pamukkale, Turkey
248 Truva (Troy): archaeological site*, Turkey
249 Istanbul: historic areas (incl. Blue Mosque*, Hagia Sophia*, Topkapi Palace*), Turkey
250 Safranbolu, Turkey
251 Hattusha: Hittite city, Turkey
252 Göreme National Park* and Cappadocia rock sites, Turkey
253 Divrigi: Great Mosque and hospital, Turkey
254 Nemrut Dagi: archaeological site, Turkey
255 Ggantija: Megalithic temples, Malta
256 Hal Saflieni Hypogeum, Malta
257 Valletta: old city, Malta
258 Pafos (Paphos): archaeological site*, Cyprus
259 Troodos region: painted churches, Cyprus
260 Choirokoitia: archaeological site, Cyprus
261 Tallinn: historic centre (incl. Town Hall Square*), Estonia
262 Riga: historic centre, Latvia
263 Curonian Spit, Lithuania/Russian Federation
264 Vilnius: old city, Lithuania
265 Mir: castle complex, Belarus
266 L'viv (L'vov): historic centre, Ukraine
267 Kyiv (Kiev): St Sophia Cathedral, related monastic buildings and Lavra of Kyiv-Pechersk, Ukraine

RUSSIAN FEDERATION

268 Sankt-Peterburg (St Petersburg): historic centre (incl. State Hermitage Museum*)
269 Novgorod: historic monuments and surroundings
270 Moskva (Moscow): Kremlin*, Red Square* and St Basil's Cathedral*
271 Moskva (Moscow): Church of the Ascension at Kolomenskoye
272 Sergiyev Posad: architectural ensemble of the Trinity Sergius Lavra
273 Vladimir and Suzdal: White Monuments
274 Ferapontov Monastery

AFRICA

275 Tétouan: medina, Morocco
276 Fès: medina*, Morocco
277 Volubilis: archaeological site, Morocco
278 Meknès: historic city, Morocco
279 Marrakech (Marrakesh): medina, Morocco
280 Aït Benhaddou: fortified village, Morocco
281 Tipasa: archaeological park, Algeria
282 Alger (Algiers): kasbah, Algeria
283 Benî Hammâd: Al Qal'a, Algeria
284 Djemila: Roman ruins, Algeria
285 Timgad: Roman ruins, Algeria
286 M'Zab Valley, Algeria
287 Dougga, Tunisia
288 Tunis: medina*, Tunisia
289 Carthage: archaeological site*, Tunisia
290 Kerkouane: Punic town and its necropolis, Tunisia
291 Sousse: medina, Tunisia
292 Kairouan, Tunisia
293 El Jem: amphitheatre, Tunisia
294 Ghadamis: old town, Libya
295 Sabratha: archaeological site, Libya
296 Leptis Magna: archaeological site, Libya
297 Cyrene: archaeological site, Libya
298 Abu Mena: Christian ruins, Egypt
299 Memphis: Pyramid fields from Giza to Dahshur and its necropolis*, Egypt
300 El Qâhira (Cairo): Islamic city (incl. Egyptian Antiquities Museum*), Egypt

ASIA

301 Halab: ancient city of Aleppo*, Syria
302 Tadmur: archaeological site of Palmyra*, Syria
303 Dimashq (Damascus): ancient city, Syria
304 Bosra: ancient city, Syria
305 Anjar: archaeological site, Lebanon
306 Baalbek, Lebanon
307 Holy Valley and Forest of the Cedars of God, Lebanon
308 Byblos, Lebanon
309 Soûr: archaeological site of Tyre*, Lebanon
310 **Jerusalem: old city and walls** (incl. Temple Mount*, Wailing Wall*) *site proposed by Jordan*
311 Qasr Amra, Jordan
312 Petra*, Jordan
313 Hatra, Iraq
314 Upper Svaneti area, Georgia
315 Kutaisi: Bagrati Cathedral and Gelati Monastery, Georgia

Europe

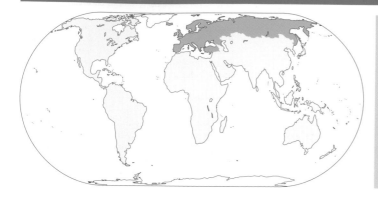

Key facts	Europe	World	Europe %
Number of Countries	48	226	21.2%
Area ('000 sq km)	8,738	135,463	6.5%
Population (000)	707,166	5,973,801	11.8%
Population Density (/sq km)	81	44	–
Gross Nat. Income (US$m)	9,374,515	29,986,364	31.3%
Visitor Arrivals ('000)	378,344	649,223	58.3%
Visitor Receipts (US$m)	230,800	456,402	50.6%
Travel Departures ('000)	379,787	594,797	63.9%
Travel Expenditure (US$m)	215,625	397,040	54.3%

GNI figures relate to 1999. Population figures are taken from the most recent census or reliable estimate. Travel figures (from the WTO) are generally for 1999, but where these are unavailable or unreliable, figures from earlier years have been used. All travel figures are based on overnight stays, not same-day visitors. Where data for certain countries was not available, this has been regarded as zero. Global totals for Visitor Arrivals/Travel Departures and Visitor Receipts/Travel Expenditure do not equal each other due to differing methods of reporting inbound and outbound data. For more information on what is regarded as a country for the purposes of this book, and for more detailed statistical information, please see the Countries A-Z section from page 181.

EUROPE IS easily the world's most visited continent. Its extensive and varied natural and man-made attractions, generally excellent transport network, wide range of climates and widespread political stability all contributed to the arrival of nearly 380 million international visitors in 1999, almost 60% of the world's total and an increase of 2.7% over 1998. The twin threats of global recession and the ongoing struggle against terrorism may, in the short term at least, have severe consequences on the continent's highly competitive travel and tourist industries, particularly (as was shown within a month of the attacks) its airlines. None the less, many European travel patterns – several of which are intra-European and thus less reliant on air travel – are well established and probably impervious to all but the worst catastrophes. More vulnerable may be the countries, such as the UK, which attract a significant number of visitors from North America.

Of all the well-established European holiday patterns, perhaps the most enduring is the movement from Northern to Southern Europe, traditionally in the high summer, but increasingly at other times of the year. Amongst both Britons and Germans, for instance, over 50% of foreign trips are to the same five European countries.

■ Heading south

Top five visited countries by Britons and Germans during 1999
Source: WTO

	by Britons	by Germans
to Italy	2,076	8,849
to France	11,747	15,180
to Greece	2,433	2,450
to Spain	12,181	11,586
to Portugal	1,847	889
TOTAL	**30,284**	**38,954**
% of total outbound trips	56%	53%

With so many diverse attractions in such close proximity, it is not surprising that so many Europeans holiday in their own continent. This, coupled with the increase in business travel, has led to the situation of 17 out of 20 journeys which start in Europe also finishing there.

Package holidays with flights and accommodation to beach locations are the biggest category of family

■ European breaks

Percentage of trips taken within Europe from selected countries, 1999
Source: WTO

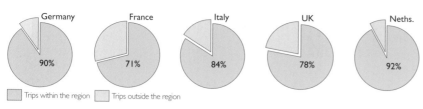

| Germany 90% | France 71% | Italy 84% | UK 78% | Neths. 92% |

□ Trips within the region □ Trips outside the region

summer holidays. Those on smaller budgets opt for camping and mobile homes on organised sites. The rush to the sun has not diminished because, although Spain and Portugal have long been the established favourites, there is constant demand for new destinations. This has over three decades precipitated the development of the whole northern coast of the Mediterranean Sea as a package holiday area, including southern France, Italy, Greece and Turkey. Croatia has made a tentative return into the package holiday sector following its involvement in the Yugoslavian civil war. With so many countries with different attractions, histories and cultures in such close proximity, touring holidays by car, caravan and campervan remain a popular holiday choice. Drivers from all starting points can cover huge swathes of Europe by utilising the continent's integrated motorway network.

Before the break up of the Eastern Bloc driving tours were concentrated into the western half of Europe and, to a lesser extent, Scandinavia. About as far east as the touring market stretched was Austria and Italy but the emergence of a free east brought Hungary, Poland, the Czech Republic and Slovakia into the touring equation, although the numbers remain small in comparison to western Europe.

The winter holiday migration pattern reverses into a north-easterly dash to the Alps for skiing and associated sports. As the biggest single activity holidays, skiing and snowboarding continue to grow. Alpine France, Switzerland and Austria are the most popular destinations but on the eastern side of the Alps, Slovenia, Romania and Bulgaria are emerging winter sports options: growth, however, has been slow. Sweden and Norway, traditionally home to cross-country skiing, are making in-roads into the European ski market.

■ Big spenders

Visitor expenditure by Europeans on foreign travel, 1999 (US$ millions – excl. international transport)
Source: WTO

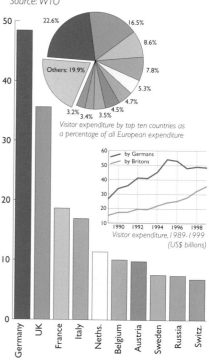

Visitor expenditure by top ten countries as a percentage of all European expenditure

Visitor expenditure, 1989–1999 (US$ billions)

Growth areas

The demands of the cash-rich, time-poor society have given birth to city breaks. Flying visits to sample the splendour, history, architecture and ambience of the great cities of Europe is now a strong area. Paris, Amsterdam and Rome are acknowledged as top short-break cities. This sector is a better growth area than touring or skiing holidays for eastern Europe. The mystique of cities formerly hidden behind the Iron Curtain – Moscow and St Petersburg in Russia; Prague in the Czech Republic; Cracow in Poland; and Budapest in Hungary – have made them sought-after for tour operators' specialist programmes.

A sub-plot to city breaks are sunshine short breaks to beach resorts. Leading this still-emerging trend are Palma, Cannes and Valletta.

Eastern Europe is also at the forefront of another emerging niche – spa holidays. The spa resorts of Hungary and the Czech Republic have been well-kept secrets but with the new interest in fitness and pampering breaks, they are playing a significant part in dedicated programmes currently being developed.

Europe: Introduction

- Europe occupies 6.4% of the world's land area and is home to nearly 12% of the world's population.
- Europe's combined GDI is US$9,374,515 million, just over 31% of the world's total.
- Europe accounts for 64% of global travel departures and 58% of arrivals.
- International travel and tourism contributed over US$230 billion to Europe's economy in 1999, an increase of 0.9% over 1998.
- Ten countries in Europe received more than US$5 billion from travel and tourism in 1999.
- Of the 15 most visited travel destinations in the world, 11 are in Europe.
- Of the top five tourism earners in the world, four are in Europe (Spain, France, Italy and the UK).
- Of the top five tourism spenders in the world, three are in Europe (Germany, the UK and France).
- Germans continue to spend more money on foreign travel than any other nationality.
- 12 European countries received more than 10 million visitors in 1999.
- The most popular destination, France, on its own received almost one in nine of the world's international travellers.
- There were 378 million international tourist arrivals in Europe in 1999, an increase of 2.7% over 1998, slightly below the world average.
- The most significant growth in tourist arrivals was in Southern Europe (including Italy, Iberia and Greece) which showed a rise of 5.5%.
- Albania showed the largest growth in tourist arrivals compared to 1998 (39.3%), followed by Armenia (28.1%) and Ukraine (20.8%).
- Of the major European destinations (more than 10 million visitors), the country with the largest growth in tourist arrivals compared to 1998 was Russia (17%). The country with the largest decrease was Hungary (-13.8%).
- Of these destinations, Russia also recorded the largest growth in international travel receipts in 1999 – 19.5% compared to 1998.
- Between 1987 and 1999, Poland's receipts from international travel and tourism have increased from US$185 million to US$6.1 billion.
- Tourism employs more people in Scotland than do the whisky, gas and oil industries combined.
- Tourism provided over 6% of Ireland's export earnings in 1999.
- Visitors to Denmark in 1999 each spent an average of US$1,820, the highest expenditure per head in Europe. Belgium, Slovenia and Sweden were the only other European countries where 1999 visitor expenditure per head was over US$1,000.

Bright lights

Top 10 European city breaks ex-UK, 1999 (1998 ratings in brackets)
Source: Travelscene

	Most popular	Emerging destinations
1.	Paris (1)	Palma
2.	Amsterdam (2)	Helsinki
3.	Bruges (3)	Warsaw
4.	Rome (5)	Naples
5.	Brussels (4)	Oslo
6.	Barcelona (6)	Cannes
7.	Dublin (8)	Zurich
8.	Venice (7)	Valletta
9.	Madrid (10)	Cracow
10.	Prague (9)	Innsbruck

The growth in golf holidays has fluctuated over the past three years but remains on the up. After two years of 12 per cent growth, 2000 saw it rise by just six – still good for a sport in which 80 per cent of people who try it do not become regular players. The climates of Spain and Portugal maintain them as European market leaders with France's uncrowded courses making it a strengthening force in the market.

Away from it all

European regions generating the most tourists, 1998
Source: IPK International

1. North Rhine-Westphalia (incl. Cologne & Düsseldorf)
2. South-East England, UK (incl. London)
3. Bavaria, Germany (incl. Munich & Nuremberg)
4. Baden-Württemberg, Germany (incl. Stuttgart)
5. North England, UK (incl. Manchester & Newcastle)
6. Randstad, Neth. (incl. Amsterdam & Rotterdam)
7. Central Sweden (incl. Stockholm)
8. East Austria (incl. Vienna)

Business travel

The business travel market – from where many airlines derive much of their profits – is closely linked to the health of the economy: and across Europe, corporate belts are tightening. Many travellers have downgraded from four and five-star hotels, and fly with the new breed of low-fare airlines. Similarly, no-frills hotels are now competing with the more deluxe hotel brands for the attention of the business traveller.

External factors

The terrorist attacks on the USA in September 2001 have cast a long shadow over many sectors of the world's economy, travel and tourism not least. One inevitable result will be a considerable tightening of airline security procedures (although Europe already has very high standards in this respect). If this leads to increased costs and check-in times (as appears likely) then the continent's high-speed rail operators could stand to benefit. The threat of global recession – always more likely when being openly discussed – would affect many airlines and operators, particularly in such a competitive market where margins are already very tight. The long-term prognosis is impossible to predict: what is certain is that the struggle for profits and market share will be conducted in global circumstances far more challenging than during what are already being seen as the halcyon days of the late 1990s.

January 2002 saw 12 EU states adopt the Euro currency: the UK, Sweden and Denmark are so far

Big earners

Receipts from foreign travel, 1999
(US$ millions – excluding international transport)
Source: WTO

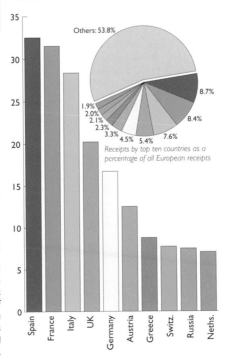

Receipts by top ten countries as a percentage of all European receipts

holding back. There are clear benefits for travellers in being able to cross most of the EU without changing currencies. The impact that this move will have on travel to, and from, the UK, the only major EU economy not to have joined the Euro, remains uncertain.

During 2001, foot and mouth disease severely damaged the tourism of the UK and Ireland. It remains to be seen whether the disease will affect other European states, and with what results for their tourist industries.

New developments

Low-cost airlines continue to make an impact on European travel but not just for cheap fares. No-frills airlines such as Buzz, Ryanair, EasyJet and Go are being credited with boosting holidays in France, Spain and Italy by more than 10 per cent. Their strategy of using the secondary airports has assisted new regions into the tourism limelight.

Visitors

International arrivals and average receipts, 1999
Source: WTO

	Visitors (thousands)	Av. receipts per visitor
France	73,042	$431
Spain	46,776	$695
Italy	36,516	$777
UK	25,394	$796
Russia	18,493	$406
Poland	17,950	$340
Austria	17,467	$718
Hungary	17,248	$197
Germany	17,116	$977
Greece	12,164	$722
Portugal	11,632	$441
Switzerland	10,700	$723
Netherlands	9,881	$718
Turkey	6,893	$755
Ireland	6,403	$530
Belgium	6,369	$1,105
Czech Rep.	5,610	$541
Norway	4,481	$497
Ukraine	4,232	$756
Croatia	3,443	$724
Romania	3,209	$79
San Marino	3,148	n/a
Sweden	2,595	$1,501
Bulgaria	2,472	$377
Finland	2,454	$618
Cyprus	2,434	$772
Denmark	2,023	$1,820
Lithuania	1,422	$387
Malta	1,214	$556
Slovak Rep.	975	$473
Estonia	950	$589
Slovenia	884	$1,078
Luxembourg	833	n/a
Latvia	490	$241
Belarus	355	$37
Monaco	278	n/a
Iceland	263	$863
Macedonia, FYR	181	$204
Yugoslavia, Fed. Rep.	152	$112
Bosnia-Herzegovina	89	$236
Liechtenstein	60	n/a
Albania	39	n/a
Moldova	14	$143

(Visitor arrival figures not available for Andorra, Channel Islands, Faroe Islands, Greenland or Gibraltar)

Maps, charts and statistics on Europe follow on pages 48 to 101. See also the Countries A-Z section from page 181, and the Index from page 190.

Thanks to: Travelscene.

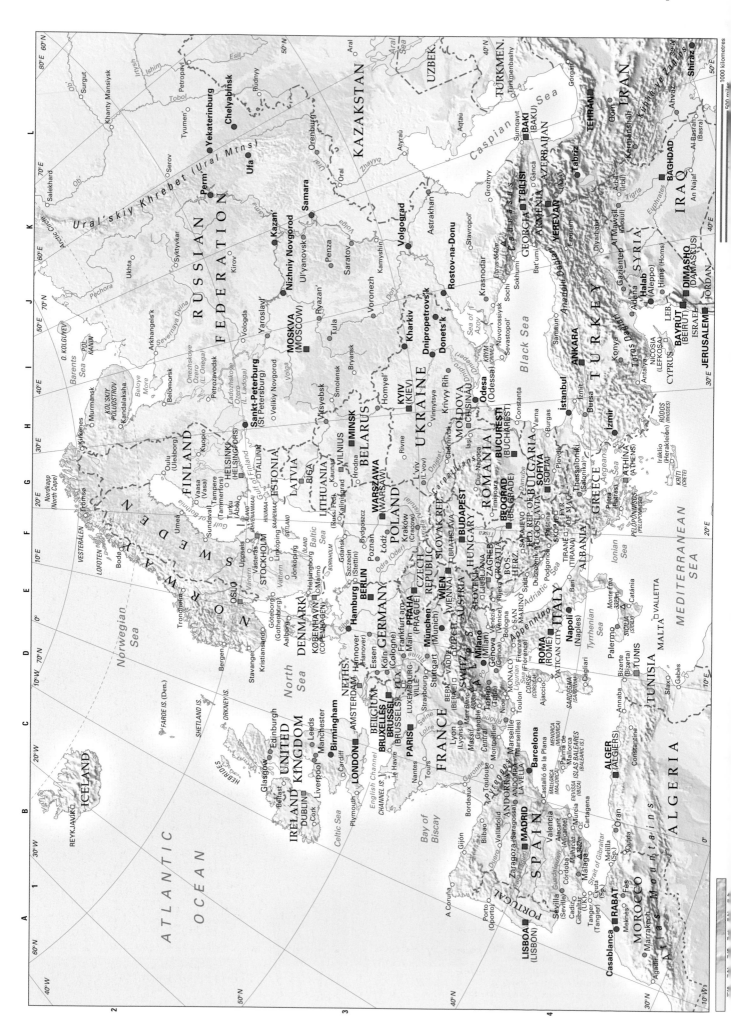

Climate

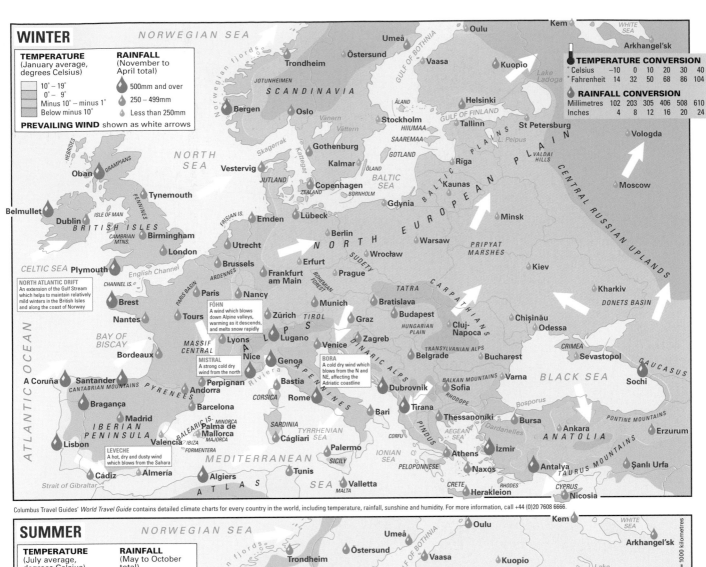

WINTER

TEMPERATURE
(January average, degrees Celsius)
- 10° – 19°
- 0° – 9°
- Minus 10° – minus 1°
- Below minus 10°

RAINFALL
(November to April total)
- 500mm and over
- 250 – 499mm
- Less than 250mm

PREVAILING WIND shown as white arrows

TEMPERATURE CONVERSION

°Celsius	−10	0	10	20	30	40
°Fahrenheit	14	32	50	68	86	104

RAINFALL CONVERSION

Millimetres	102	203	305	406	508	610
Inches	4	8	12	16	20	24

NORTH ATLANTIC DRIFT
An extension of the Gulf Stream which helps to maintain relatively mild winters in the British Isles and along the coast of Norway

FÖHN
A wind which blows down Alpine valleys, warming as it descends, and melts snow rapidly

MISTRAL
A strong cold dry wind from the north

BORA
A cold dry wind which blows from the N and NE, affecting the Adriatic coastline

LEVECHE
A hot, dry and dusty wind which blows from the Sahara

Columbus Travel Guides' *World Travel Guide* contains detailed climate charts for every country in the world, including temperature, rainfall, sunshine and humidity. For more information, call +44 (0)20 7608 6666.

SUMMER

TEMPERATURE
(July average, degrees Celsius)
- 30° and over
- 20° – 29°
- 10° – 19°
- 0° – 9°

RAINFALL
(May to October total)
- 500mm and over
- 250 – 499mm
- Less than 250mm

PREVAILING WIND shown as white arrows

SIROCCO
A hot dusty wind which blows from north Africa; after crossing the Mediterranean the wind is often very humid

ETESIAN WIND / MELTEMI
A wind blowing from the N and NW, often creating rough seas

This map shows selected aspects of European history between the end of the Roman Empire in the 5th century and the Peace of Westphalia in 1648. Modern equivalents of important cities are included in parentheses. No historical boundaries are indicated apart from the maximum extent of Roman and Islamic conquests. The present-day coastline is shown and current international boundaries are marked in grey.

Northern limit of the Roman Empire at its greatest extent

Northern limit of Islamic conquests in Europe between the 7th and 11th centuries

Trieste Cities and regions which came under Venetian influence in any period prior to 1648. Venice acquired many trading posts at various times during its period of commercial expansion in the late Middle Ages

X Sites of major battles in the period 476–1648, with date. In general, battles have only been marked which had important political consequences

The Hanseatic League
A commercial union of northern European cities, designed to create economic security in an age of political chaos, which flourished in the 14th and 15th centuries

● Principal cities

◆ Principal foreign trading posts (kontore)

● Principal cities of the Lombard League
A shifting political alliance of northern Italian cities designed to combat the territorial ambitions of the Holy Roman Emperors (principally Frederick I and Frederick II) between 1153 and 1288

The Cinque Ports
A loose confederation of towns in southern England whose defensive obligations were first established in the 11th century and subsequently redefined by many royal charters, principally that of 1278. At one time there were over 30 towns and villages in the Cinque Ports Confederation; the original five are shown here

○ Universities founded prior to 1600, with year of foundation. In some cases, particularly for the oldest universities, precise dates are open to debate

Major ecclesiastical centres, 16th century:

Roman Catholic (Patriarchal and Archiepiscopal Sees)

Orthodox (Patriarchal Sees and other major centres)

Camino de Santiago (the Way of St James)
A medieval pilgrimage route which developed after the discovery of the tomb of St James the Apostle in Galicia in about 812; the pilgrimage's popularity was at its height in the 11th and 12th centuries, resulting in the legacy of many churches and chapels along its various routes

Historical

VIKING AND ISLAMIC CONQUESTS AND THE CAROLINGIAN EMPIRE

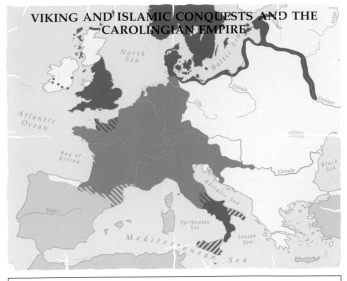

▢	Maximum extent of Islamic conquests, 7th – 11th centuries	▨	Areas ruled by the Vikings or Normans, 9th – 12th centuries	▨ Carolingian Empire at the death of Charlemagne in 814

THE ANGEVIN AND HOHENSTAUFEN EMPIRES

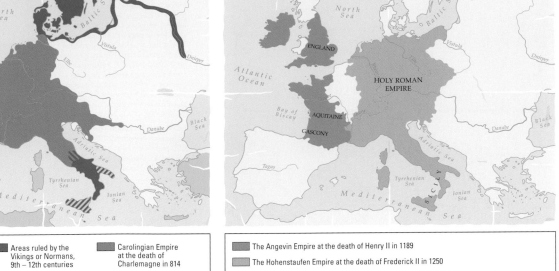

- ▨ The Angevin Empire at the death of Henry II in 1189
- ▨ The Hohenstaufen Empire at the death of Frederick II in 1250

THE EMPIRE OF CHARLES V

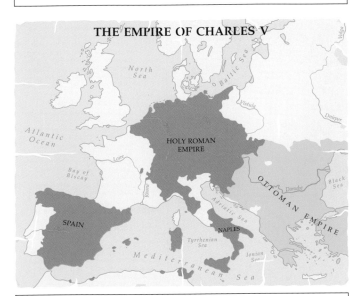

- ▨ The European Habsburg Empire at the abdication of Charles V in 1556
- ▢ The Ottoman Empire, c1560

THE EMPIRE OF NAPOLEON

- ▨ Area under direct rule of Napoleon in 1812
- ▢ Dependent states in 1812

EVE OF WORLD WAR ONE

- ▨ Triple Alliance, 1914 (Austria-Hungary, Germany, Italy)
- ▨ Triple Entente, 1914 (France, Russia, United Kingdom)

THE COLD WAR

- ▨ North Atlantic Treaty Organisation (NATO), 1962 *[other members: Iceland, Canada, USA]*
- ▨ Warsaw Pact, 1962

European Union

Greenland exercised its autonomy under the Danish Crown and withdrew from the EEC in 1985. The territory now has an Association Agreement with the EU.

The European Union has its origin in the European Coal and Steel Community, established in 1951 with the signing of the Treaty of Paris. It aimed to ensure continued peace in Europe by combining the essential interests of the six member countries. Moves towards closer integration culminated in the signing of the Treaty of Rome on 25 March 1957, and these six countries became the founder members of both the European Economic Community (EEC) and the European Atomic Energy Community (EAEC or Euratom).

The European Union came into being on 1 November 1993 after EEC member states ratifed the Maastricht Treaty, in which moves towards a common currency were set out.

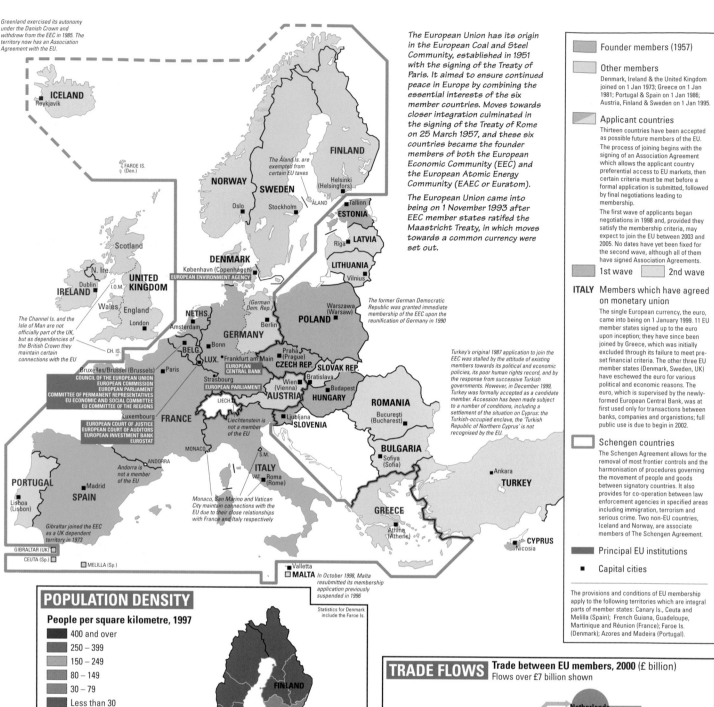

The Åland Is. are exempted from certain EU taxes

The former German Democratic Republic was granted immediate membership of the EEC upon the reunification of Germany in 1990

Turkey's original 1987 application to join the EEC was stalled by the attitude of existing members towards its political and economic policies, its poor human rights record, and by the response from successive Turkish governments. However, in December 1999, Turkey was formally accepted as a candidate member. Accession has been made subject to a number of conditions, including a settlement of the situation on Cyprus: the Turkish-occupied enclave, the 'Turkish Republic of Northern Cyprus' is not recognised by the EU.

The Channel Is. and the Isle of Man are not officially part of the UK, but as dependencies of the British Crown they maintain certain connections with the EU

Liechtenstein is not a member of the EU

Andorra is not a member of the EU

Monaco, San Marino and Vatican City maintain connections with the EU due to their close relationships with France and Italy respectively

Gibraltar joined the EEC as a UK dependent territory in 1973

In October 1998, Malta resubmitted its membership application previously suspended in 1996

COUNCIL OF THE EUROPEAN UNION
EUROPEAN COMMISSION
EUROPEAN PARLIAMENT
COMMITTEE OF PERMANENT REPRESENTATIVES
EU ECONOMIC AND SOCIAL COMMITTEE
EU COMMITTEE OF THE REGIONS

EUROPEAN COURT OF JUSTICE
EUROPEAN COURT OF AUDITORS
EUROPEAN INVESTMENT BANK
EUROSTAT

EUROPEAN ENVIRONMENT AGENCY
EUROPEAN CENTRAL BANK
EUROPEAN PARLIAMENT

Legend

Founder members (1957)

Other members
Denmark, Ireland & the United Kingdom joined on 1 Jan 1973; Greece on 1 Jan 1981; Portugal & Spain on 1 Jan 1986; Austria, Finland & Sweden on 1 Jan 1995.

Applicant countries
Thirteen countries have been accepted as possible future members of the EU.
The process of joining begins with the signing of an Association Agreement which allows the applicant country preferential access to EU markets, then certain criteria must be met before a formal application is submitted, followed by final negotiations leading to membership.
The first wave of applicants began negotiations in 1998 and, provided they satisfy the membership criteria, may expect to join the EU between 2003 and 2005. No dates have yet been fixed for the second wave, although all of them have signed Association Agreements.

1st wave   2nd wave

ITALY Members which have agreed on monetary union
The single European currency, the euro, came into being on 1 January 1999. 11 EU member states signed up to the euro upon inception; they have since been joined by Greece, which was initially excluded through its failure to meet pre-set financial criteria. The other three EU member states (Denmark, Sweden, UK) have eschewed the euro for various political and economic reasons. The euro, which is supervised by the newly-formed European Central Bank, was at first used only for transactions between banks, companies and organistions; full public use is due to begin in 2002.

Schengen countries
The Schengen Agreement allows for the removal of most frontier controls and the harmonisation of procedures governing the movement of people and goods between signatory countries. It also provides for co-operation between law enforcement agencies in specified areas including immigration, terrorism and serious crime. Two non-EU countries, Iceland and Norway, are associate members of The Schengen Agreement.

Principal EU institutions

■ **Capital cities**

The provisions and conditions of EU membership apply to the following territories which are integral parts of member states: Canary Is., Ceuta and Melilla (Spain); French Guiana, Guadeloupe, Martinique and Réunion (France); Faroe Is. (Denmark); Azores and Madeira (Portugal).

POPULATION DENSITY

People per square kilometre, 1997

- 400 and over
- 250 – 399
- 150 – 249
- 80 – 149
- 30 – 79
- Less than 30

Statistics for Denmark include the Faroe Is.

The EU's largest urban agglomerations
(Estimated population in 2000)

1. Paris 9.64 million
2. Greater London 7.64m
3. Essen 6.56m *[incl. Bochum, Dortmund, Duisburg]*
4. Milano (Milan) 4.25m
5. Madrid 4.07m
6. Frankfurt am Main 3.70m *[incl. Darmstadt, Offenbach a.M, Wiesbaden]*
7. Berlin 3.34m
8. Düsseldorf 3.25m *[incl. Mönchengladbach, Solingen, Wuppertal]*
9. Athina (Athens) 3.10m
10. Köln (Cologne) 3.07m *[incl. Bonn, Leverkusen]*
11. Nápoli (Naples) 3.01m
12. Barcelona 2.82m
13. Roma (Rome) 2.69m
14. Stuttgart 2.69m
15. Hamburg 2.68m
16. München (Munich) 2.31m
17. West Midlands 2.27m *[Birmingham area]*
18. Greater Manchester 2.25m
19. Wien (Vienna) 2.07m

The UN defines the term 'urban agglomeration' as a contiguous area inhabited at a density regarded as urban, ignoring administrative boundaries.
Source: United Nations

French Guiana (Fr.)*
Guadeloupe (Fr.)*
Martinique (Fr.)*
Réunion (Fr.)*

Azores (Port.)
Madeira (Port.)
Canary Is. (Sp.)
Ceuta & Melilla (Sp.)

Source: Eurostat   *1999 figures

TRADE FLOWS Trade between EU members, 2000 (£ billion)
Flows over £7 billion shown

Netherlands

Ireland 11.18 / 8.86 United Kingdom 9.43 / 11.80 Belgium Sweden

8.88 / 15.12   14.07 / 15.30   14.96 / 18.16   22.39 / 37.56

26.24 / 29.83

22.02 / 16.98   10.72 / 8.89

France 14.62 / 20.98 Germany 7.10 Greece

8.15 / 8.51

30.40 / 40.88

13.75 / 19.40   18.58 / 18.52   23.49 / 27.10   13.69 / 19.00

Spain 9.63 Italy Austria

8.84 / 16.31

Denmark, Finland, Luxembourg and Portugal are not shown here as their trade with any one single EU country did not exceed £7bn in 2000

Source: The Economist Diary 2002 edition   *Estimate

European Union

TRADE

EU countries' external trade, 2000
(billion euros)

◄ Total trade

Trade with other EU countries
(for details of principal trade flows between EU states, see diagram on previous page)

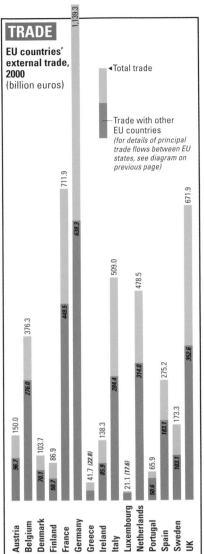

Austria — 150.0 / 96.7
Belgium — 376.3 / 276.0
Denmark — 103.7 / 70.1
Finland — 86.9 / 50.7
France — 711.9 / 449.5
Germany — 1,139.3 / 638.3
Greece — 41.7 (22.8)
Ireland — 138.3 / 85.9
Italy — 509.0 / 294.4
Luxembourg — 21.1 (17.6)
Netherlands — 478.5 / 314.0
Portugal — 65.9 / 50.6
Spain — 275.2 / 183.1
Sweden — 173.3 / 103.1
UK — 671.9 / 352.6

Source: Eurostat   *Estimate

THE EU BUDGET

Contributions by member states to the EU, 1999
(Total: 82,531 million euros)

- Germany **21,069m euros** (25.5%)
- France **13,994m** (17.0%)
- UK **11,084m** (13.4%)
- Italy **10,766m** (13.0%)
- Spain **6,231m** (7.6%)
- Netherlands **5,091m** (6.2%)
- Belgium **3,196m** (3.9%)
- Sweden **2,349m** (2.8%)
- Austria **2,054m** (2.5%)
- Denmark **1,656m** (2.0%)
- Greece **1,349m** (1.6%)
- Portugal **1,227m** (1.5%)
- Finland **1,211m** (1.5%)
- Ireland **1,060m** (1.3%)
- Luxembourg **194m** (0.2%)

Source: EU

EU budget allocations, 1999
(Total: 92,417 million euros)

- *Agriculture* **40,973m euros** (44.3%) including Common Agricultural Policy
- *Structural operations* **32,678m** (35.4%) Regional operations, fisheries and other structural operations
- *External action* **7,992m** (8.7%) Aid and co-operation with developing countries **4,778m** (5.2%) Pre-accession aid **3,167m** (3.4%) Common security and foreign policy **47m** (0.05%)
- *Internal policies* **6,051m** (6.5%) Research & dev'mt **3,630m** (3.9%) Training, culture, media and information **843m** (0.9%) Transport and trans-European networks **709m** (0.8%) Consumer protection, internal market and industry **522m** (0.6%) Energy and environment **211m** (0.2%) Other **135m** (0.1%)
- *Administration* **4,724m** (5.1%)

SUMMARY TABLE

Country	Exchange rate, 1 Apr 2000 One euro equals:	Central Bank interest rate, 1 Apr 2000 (%)	Normal VAT rate (%)	Inflation, 2000 (%)	Unemployment, March 2001 (% of workforce)	Balance of payments, 2000 (m euros)	Budget surplus/ deficit, 2000 (% of GDP)	Government debt, 2000 (% of GDP)
Austria	*Schilling* 13.76	4.68	20 [1]	2.0	3.7	−6,384	−1.10	63.8
Belgium	*Belgian franc* 40.34	4.68	21	2.7	6.8	+11,562	−0.30	113.0
Denmark	*Krone* 7.44	5.04	25 [2]	2.7	4.7	+6,514	+2.60	47.3
Finland	*Markka* 5.95	4.68	22 [3]	3.0	9.0	+9,639	+4.50	42.2
France	*French franc* 6.56	4.68	19.6 [4]	1.8	8.6	+25,286	−1.30	63.3
Germany	*Deutschmark* 1.96	4.68	16 [5]	2.1	7.7	−22,362	−1.40	58.1
Greece	*Drachma* 340.75	4.68	18 [6]	2.9	11.1	−4,981	−0.80	102.0
Ireland	*Punt* 0.79	4.68	20	5.3	3.8	+309	+4.70	41.0
Italy	*Lira* 1,936.3	4.68	20 [7]	2.6	9.9	−6,994	−1.54	110.2
Luxembourg	*Lux. franc* 40.34	4.68	15	3.8	2.3	n/a	+3.60	6.6
Netherlands	*Guilder* 2.20	4.68	19	2.3	2.5	+14,821	+1.80	55.8
Portugal	*Escudo* 200.48	4.68	17 [8]	2.8	4.6	−12,201	−1.40	53.8
Spain	*Peseta* 166.39	4.68	16 [9]	3.5	13.5	−19,400	−0.34	67.8
Sweden	*Krona* 9.13	3.94	25	1.3	5.4	+9,372	+2.90	56.7
UK	*Pound Sterling (£)* 0.62	5.33	17.5 [10]	0.8	5.2	−26,064	+2.10	46.9

Countries in red have agreed to monetary union. Their currency rates were set with the creation of the euro on 1st Jan 1999 (except Greece, which joined on 1st Jan 2001). Interest rates in the eurozone are set by the European Central Bank [1] 16% in Jungholz & Mittelberg. [2] Not applicable in Faroe Is. or Greenland. [3] Excl. Åland Is. [4] 8.5% in Guadeloupe, Martinique & Réunion. [5] Not applicable in Helgoland. [6] 13% on many of the Greek islands. No VAT applies to Mt Athos. [7] Excl. Livigno, the Italian enclave of Campione d'Italia & territorial waters of Lake Lugano. [8] 12% in the Azores & Madeira. [9] Excl. Canary Is., Ceuta & Melilla. [10] Excl. Channel Is.

Sources: EU; Eurostat; The Economist

INCOME

Statistics for Denmark include the Faroe Is.

Gross domestic product per person, 1998

- ECU 25,000 and over
- ECU 20,000 – 24,999
- ECU 15,000 – 19,999
- ECU 12,000 – 14,999
- ECU 10,000 – 11,999
- Less than ECU 10,000

Prior to the introduction of the euro, the European Currency Unit (ECU) was used as a common financial instrument within the EU. The value of the ECU was calculated as a weighted average of participating national currencies. Sterling equivalents since 1991 are shown below:

1 Jan,	One ECU equals:
1991	£0.71
1992	£0.72
1993	£0.80
1994	£0.75
1995	£0.78
1996	£0.83
1997	£0.73
1998	£0.67

1 Jan,	One euro equals:
1999	£0.71
2000	£0.62
2001	£0.63

French Guiana (Fr.)
Guadeloupe (Fr.)
Martinique (Fr.)
Réunion (Fr.)

Canary Is. (Sp.)
Ceuta & Melilla (Sp.)

Azores (Port.)
Madeira (Port.)

Source: Eurostat

UNEMPLOYMENT

Statistics for Denmark include the Faroe Is.

Unemployed as a percentage of the workforce, April 2000

- 20% and over
- 15.0% – 19.9%
- 11.0% – 14.9%
- 8.0% – 10.9%
- 5.0% – 7.9%
- Less than 5.0%

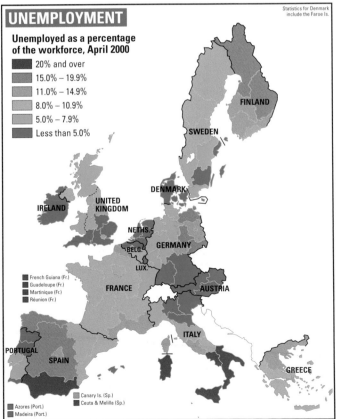

French Guiana (Fr.)
Guadeloupe (Fr.)
Martinique (Fr.)
Réunion (Fr.)

Canary Is. (Sp.)
Ceuta & Melilla (Sp.)

Azores (Port.)
Madeira (Port.)

Source: Eurostat

Airports & High-Speed Rail

Faced with stern competition from the ever-increasing high-speed rail services and the need to utilise precious runway slots for the more lucrative long-haul routes, several European airlines have been forced into co-operation with rail companies. As a result, many previously prestigious air routes, such as Air France's Paris–Brussels and Lufthansa's Stuttgart–Frankfurt, are now run by, or in conjunction with, high-speed rail operators offering city-centre to city-centre services. As the European rail network expands, as its standards of safety, speed and comfort improve and as the continent's airports become more overcrowded, this development is likely to become more widespread. Increasingly, a consideration of Europe's air routes thus also requires an appreciation of these complementary high-speed rail services.

Note: the airports shown are selected, on the basic of international passenger movements, from those which report to Airports Council International (ACI). Some airports in some countries (including Greece) are therefore not shown.

Airports & High-Speed Rail

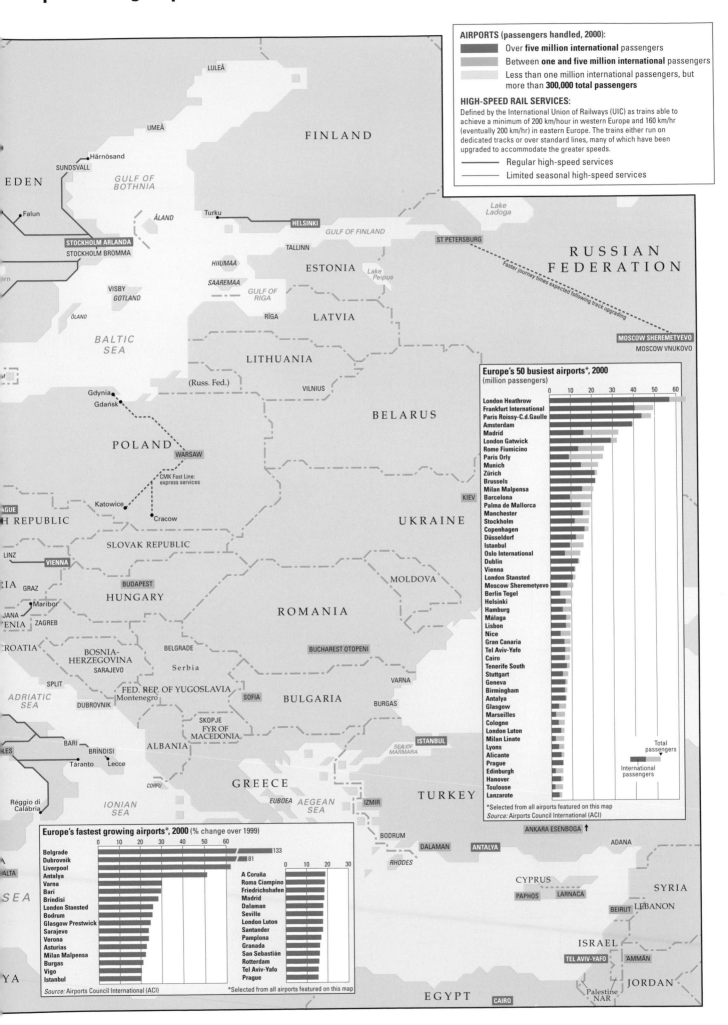

AIRPORTS (passengers handled, 2000):

Over **five million international** passengers
Between **one and five million international** passengers
Less than one million international passengers, but more than **300,000 total passengers**

HIGH-SPEED RAIL SERVICES:
Defined by the International Union of Railways (UIC) as trains able to achieve a minimum of 200 km/hour in western Europe and 160 km/hr (eventually 200 km/hr) in eastern Europe. The trains either run on dedicated tracks or over standard lines, many of which have been upgraded to accommodate the greater speeds.

Regular high-speed services
Limited seasonal high-speed services

Europe's 50 busiest airports*, 2000
(million passengers)

0 10 20 30 40 50 60

London Heathrow
Frankfurt International
Paris Roissy-C.d.Gaulle
Amsterdam
Madrid
London Gatwick
Rome Fiumicino
Paris Orly
Munich
Zürich
Brussels
Milan Malpensa
Barcelona
Palma de Mallorca
Manchester
Stockholm
Copenhagen
Düsseldorf
Istanbul
Oslo International
Dublin
Vienna
London Stansted
Moscow Sheremetyevo
Berlin Tegel
Helsinki
Hamburg
Málaga
Lisbon
Nice
Gran Canaria
Tel Aviv-Yafo
Cairo
Tenerife South
Stuttgart
Geneva
Birmingham
Antalya
Glasgow
Marseilles
Cologne
London Luton
Milan Linate
Lyons
Alicante
Prague
Edinburgh
Hanover
Toulouse
Lanzarote

Total passengers ▼
International passengers

*Selected from all airports featured on this map
Source: Airports Council International (ACI)

Europe's fastest growing airports*, 2000 (% change over 1999)

0 10 20 30 40 50 60

Belgrade — 133
Dubrovnik — 81
Liverpool
Antalya
Varna
Bari
Bríndisi
London Stansted
Bodrum
Glasgow Prestwick
Sarajevo
Verona
Asturias
Milan Malpensa
Burgas
Vigo
Istanbul

0 10 20 30

A Coruña
Roma Ciampino
Friedrichshafen
Madrid
Dalaman
Seville
London Luton
Santander
Pamplona
Granada
San Sebastián
Rotterdam
Tel Aviv-Yafo
Prague

Source: Airports Council International (ACI)   *Selected from all airports featured on this map

This map shows principal passenger rail and shipping routes in Europe. Some of the railways marked have limited services but are included because of their significance (such as connection to resort or international crossing).

A number of European rail passes are available, offering free travel on many rail and ferry services.

The Eurail pass is valid for first-class rail travel in the countries shown on the map.
For those under 26, the Eurail Youthpass is valid in the same countries for second-class rail travel. The pass is not available to European residents or to visitors from Algeria, Morocco, Tunisia, Turkey or the former Soviet Union.

European residents are eligible for the Inter-Rail pass, offering train travel in the area shown on the map, excluding the country of purchase. Passes are available for one or more zones within the validity area.

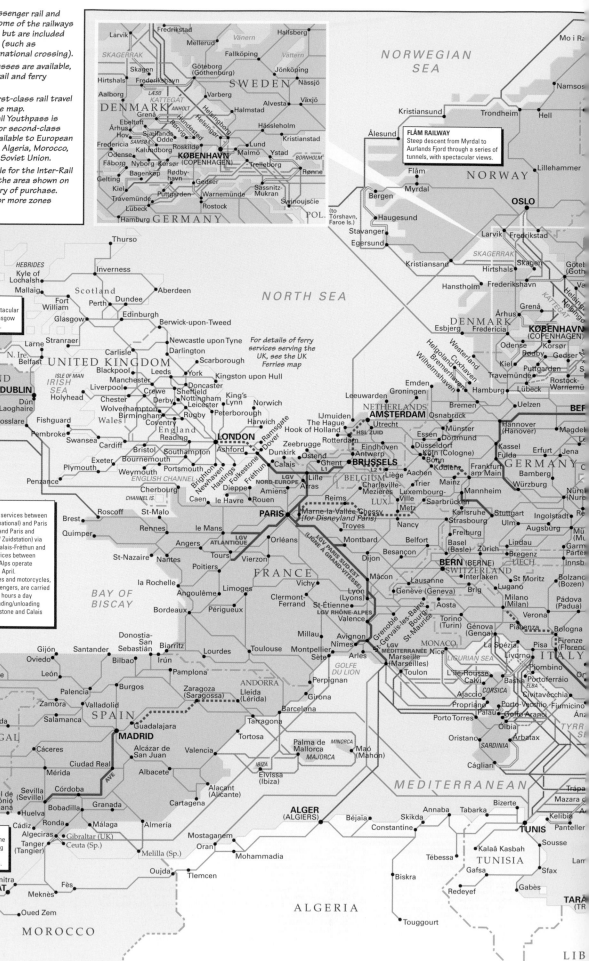

FLÅM RAILWAY
Steep descent from Myrdal to Aurlands Fjord through a series of tunnels, with spectacular views.

WEST HIGHLAND LINE
One of Britain's most spectacular railways, running from Glasgow to Mallaig via Fort William.

For details of ferry services serving the UK, see the UK Ferries map

CHANNEL TUNNEL
Eurostar: Direct railway services between London (Waterloo International) and Paris (Gare du Nord), Disneyland Paris and Brussels (Gare du Midi / Zuidstation) via Ashford International, Calais-Fréthun and Lille-Europe. Direct services between London and the French Alps operate between December and April.
Le Shuttle: Cars, coaches and motorcycles, together with their passengers, are carried on shuttles operating 24 hours a day throughout the year. Loading/unloading takes place at the Folkestone and Calais Coquelles terminals.

AL ANDALUS
A luxury train service through the Andalusian countryside. Starting and ending at Seville, visiting Antequera, Granada and Ronda.

Railways & Ferries

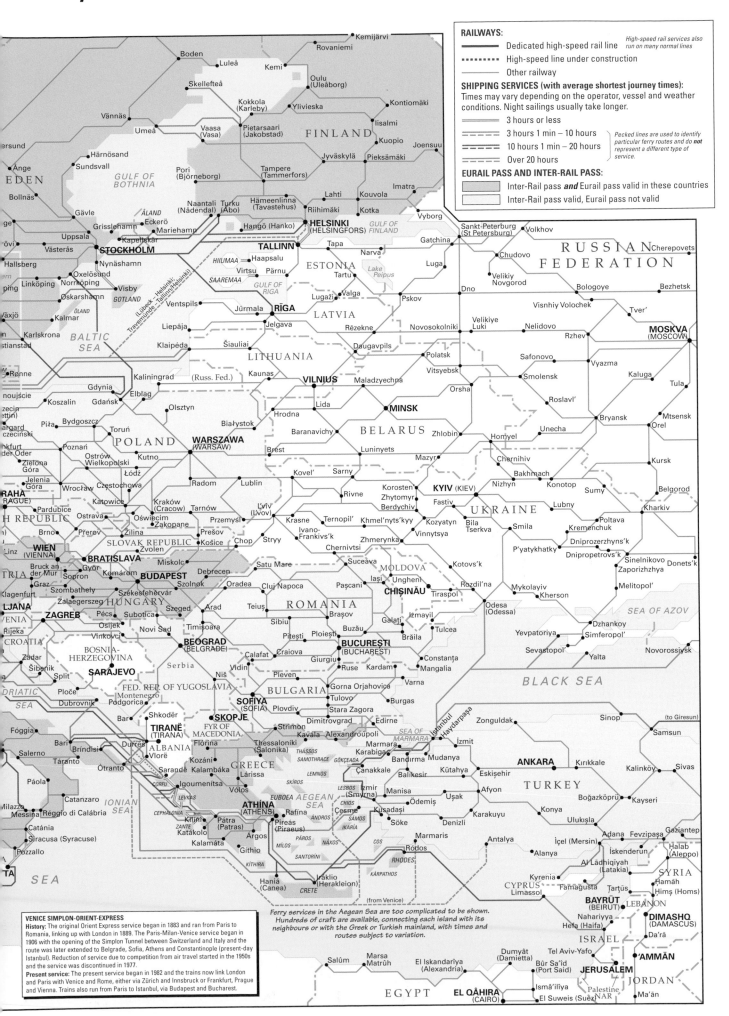

RAILWAYS:

———— Dedicated high-speed rail line — *High-speed rail services also run on many normal lines*

---- High-speed line under construction

———— Other railway

SHIPPING SERVICES (with average shortest journey times):
Times may vary depending on the operator, vessel and weather conditions. Night sailings usually take longer.

═══ 3 hours or less
═══ 3 hours 1 min – 10 hours
═══ 10 hours 1 min – 20 hours
--- Over 20 hours

*Pecked lines are used to identify particular ferry routes and do **not** represent a different type of service.*

EURAIL PASS AND INTER-RAIL PASS:

Inter-Rail pass **and** Eurail pass valid in these countries

Inter-Rail pass valid, Eurail pass not valid

VENICE SIMPLON-ORIENT-EXPRESS
History: The original Orient Express service began in 1883 and ran from Paris to Romania, linking up with London in 1889. The Paris-Milan-Venice service began in 1906 with the opening of the Simplon Tunnel between Switzerland and Italy and the route was later extended to Belgrade, Sofia, Athens and Constantinople (present-day Istanbul). Reduction of service due to competition from air travel started in the 1950s and the service was discontinued in 1977.
Present service: The present service began in 1982 and the trains now link London and Paris with Venice and Rome, either via Zürich and Innsbruck or Frankfurt, Prague and Vienna. Trains also run from Paris to Istanbul, via Budapest and Bucharest.

Ferry services in the Aegean Sea are too complicated to be shown. Hundreds of craft are available, connecting each island with its neighbours or with the Greek or Turkish mainland, with times and routes subject to variation.

National Parks

This map shows the most important areas that have been designated as National Parks throughout Western and Central Europe. The best period for visiting each park is shown in blue (no date: all year or information not available).

Sites marked with an asterisk (*) are featured in Columbus Travel Guides' *Tourist Attractions and Events of the World*, 2nd edition. For more information, call +44 (0)20 7608 6666.

Iceland
1 Jökulsárgljúfur
Spectacular glacial canyon landscape
2 Skaftafell
Glacial country with icecap & sand plain

Norway
3 Øvre Pasvik May-Sep
Forest & tundra
4 Stabbursdalen May-Oct
Arctic landscape with tundra, lakes, gravel plains & forest
5 Øvre Anarjokka
May-Sep Undulating tundra with woodland & lakes
6 Reisa May-Oct
Mixed mountain country
7 Øvre Dividal May-Sep
Mountainous country with tundra & woodland
8 Ånderdalen May-Oct
Mixed mountain country
9 Saltfjellet-Svartisen
May-Sep Varied landscape; fjords, mountains & glacier
10 Børgefjell May-Oct
Remote mountain area with varied habitats
11 Gressåmoen May-Oct
Mountainous country & spruce forest
12 Dovrefjell May-Aug
Mountainous tundra & permanent snowfields; famous for its flora
13 Rondane May-Sep
Mountain country with varied landscapes
14 Jotunheimen May-Sep
Mountainous area with tundra, bogs & forest
15 Hardangervidda
May-Oct Large mountain plateau, a popular walking area

Sweden
16 Vadvetjåkka May-Sep
Mountainous country
17 Abisko May-Sep
Mountain & forest with tundra, lakes & rivers
18 Muddus May-Sep
Forest, tundra & bog
19 Padjelanta, Sarek and Stora Sjöfallet May-Sep
3 parks protect Europe's largest wilderness area; mixed landscape
20 Pieljekaise May-Sep
Wooded mountainous country with tundra, open water & bogs
21 Skuleskogen Apr-Oct
Forested hill country
22 Töfsingdalen May-Oct
Woodland, tundra & bog
23 Sånfjället May-Oct
Woodland, tundra & bog
24 Hamra May-Oct
Woodland, tundra & bog, noted for its insects
25 Garphyttan Apr-Oct
Forest & meadows
26 Tiveden May-Oct
Hilly forest, lakes & bogs
27 Store Mosse May-Oct
Predominantly boggy, with lakes & forest

Finland
28 Pallas-Ounastunturi
May-Sep Upland plateau & taiga, with lakes, tundra, gorges & forest
29 Lemmenjoki May-Sep
Wilderness mountain area; gold rush in 1940's
30 Urho Kekkonen May-Sep Large wilderness area with fells & pine moors
31 Pyhätunturi May-Sep
Mountainous area with tundra, bogs & forest
32 Oulanka May-Sep
Varied tundra landscape
33 Petkeljärvi May-Oct
Typical Finnish lakeland scenery, with lakes, bogs, forest & moorland
34 Linnansaari May-Oct
Mainly lake with some islands
35 Pyhä-Häkki May-Sep
Mainly forest & bog
36 Liesjärvi May-Oct
Lakes, previously cultivated land & forest
37 Saaristomeri May-Sep
Extensive island group with mixed habitats

Ireland
38 Glenveagh Apr-Jul
Mixed upland area
39 Connemara Apr-Sep
Typical western Ireland mountain area
40 Killarney* May-Oct
Ancient woodland with moorland, lakes, bogs, wetland & mountains
41 Wicklow Mountains
May-Aug Partly wooded mountains with upland moorland & grassland

United Kingdom
42 Loch Lomond & the Trossachs
Lakeland and wooded valley with literary associations
43 Northumberland Apr-Oct
Mainly upland grassy moorland; Hadrian's Wall in the south
44 Lake District Apr-Nov
Mountain & lakeland; very popular all year
45 Yorkshire Dales May-Jul
Varied upland country
46 North York Moors
Apr-Sep Hilly uplands with heather moorland
47 Peak District May-Jul
Limestone in the south, with many caves; high peat moors in the north
48 Snowdonia* May-Aug
Mountain country with lakes, moorland, grassland & woodland
49 Pembrokeshire Coast
Apr-Jul Scenic coastline; varied seabird habitats
50 Brecon Beacons*
May-Oct Mainly grass-covered mountain area
51 Exmoor May-Jul
High heather moorland & wooded valley, with dramatic coastline
52 Dartmoor May-Jul
Granite uplands with heather & grassland

Netherlands
53 Dwingelderveld
May-Sep Heathland, fen & woodland with lakes
54 De Hoge Veluwe Apr-Oct
Variety of habitats: heathland, saltmarsh, wet heath & woodland
55 Veluwezoom Apr-Oct
Heath & mixed woodland

Germany
56 Niedersächsisches Wattenmeer
East Frisian Islands; mudflats & saltmarsh
57 Hamburgisches W'meer
Mudflats & saltmarsh
58 Schleswig-Holsteinisches W'meer
Mudflats & saltmarsh
59 Vorpommersche Boddenlandschaft
Mudflats & saltmarsh with dunes, lagoons, lakes & woodland
60 Jasmund May-Nov
Varied landscape with cliffs, lakes & woodland
61 Müritz Apr-Nov
Woodland & lakes with heath, marsh & pasture
62 Unteres Odertal
Apr-Jun, Sep-Nov
Floodplain of the Oder; park shared with Poland
63 Sächsische Schweiz
Apr-Oct Numerous rock towers; lower slopes wooded; deep valleys
64 Hoch Harz May-Oct
Wooded mountains with moorland, bogs & lakes; affected by acid rain
65 Bayerischer Wald
May-Aug
Wooded mountain area
66 Berchtesgaden
May-Sep Mountain landscape with Alpine pastures, small glaciers, cliffs, lakes & varied woodland

France
67 Vanoise Jun-Sep
High mountain scenery
68 Écrins May-Jul
High mountain scenery with many glaciers
69 Mercantour Apr-Sep
Some of the best parts of the Maritime Alps
70 Port-Cros Mar-Sep
Small wooded island
71 Cévennes May-Sep
Varied mountain & forest
72 Pyrénées Occidentales
May-Oct Diverse mountain landscape; snowfields, pastures & woodland

Spain
73 Ordesa May-Jul
Spectacular mountain & gorge scenery; forests & Alpine pastures
74 Covadonga May-Sep
Mountain area with mixed woodlands, pasture & glacial lakes
75 Tablas de Daimiel
Apr-Jul Small wetland
76 Doñana Feb-Jun
Guadalquivir delta; important wildlife site
77 Caldera de Taburiente
Volcanic landscape
78 Garajonay
Heavily wooded area
79 Cañadas del Teide
Volcanic landscapes
80 Timanfaya
Volcanic landscapes

Portugal
81 Peneda-Gerês Apr-Oct
Mountain & forest area; cliffs & rock formations

Switzerland
82 The Swiss National Park
May-Oct Strictly controlled mountainous area; forests, pastures, lakes, cliffs & snowfields

Austria
83 Hohe Tauern May-Sep
High Alpine scenery; forests in lower areas

84 Nockberge Apr-Oct
Forested mountain area with bogs & moors

Italy
85 Stelvio Apr-Oct
Typical Alpine scenery & Italy's largest glacier
86 Gran Paradiso Apr-Oct
High Alpine country; famous for the Ibex
87 Abruzzo Apr-Oct
Wooded mountain area
88 Circeo Mar-Jun
Coastal marsh & rocky promontory near Rome
89 Calábria Apr-Jul
Three areas of wooded mountainous landscape

Poland
90 Wolinski Apr-Oct
Woodland, lakes and sea cliffs; white-tailed sea eagle the main attraction
91 Slowinski May-Oct
Coastal landscape with shifting sand dunes
92 Kampinoski May-Oct
Varied landscape close to Warsaw
93 Mazurski & Wigierski
Numerous lakes and extensive forests
94 Biebrzanski Apr-Jul
Central Europe's largest area of natural peat bogs
95 Bialowieski Apr-Jul
Europe's largest original lowland forest; principal attraction the European bison
96 Bieszczadzki May-Sep
Remote wooded mountain area in Eastern Carpathians
97 Babiogórski, Tatrzanski, Gorczanski & Pieninski
May-Oct Four parks in the spectacular High Tatra mountains
98 Ojcówski May-Sep
Hilly landscape with many rock pinnacles
99 Gory Stolowe & Karkonoski May-Sep
Dramatic mountain scenery of the Sudety Mountains

Czech Republic
100 Krkonose May-Oct
Wooded mountain area with Alpine pastures, meadows, bogs & lakes

Slovak Republic
101 Vysoké Tatry* May-Oct
(High Tatras)
Nízke Tatry* Apr-Jul
(Low Tatras)
Spectacular mountain area with forests, lakes, grassland & bogs
102 Pieninsky May-Oct
Limestone mountains with mixed forests

Hungary
103 Aggtelek Apr-Oct
Important karst scenery
104 Bukk Apr-Jul
Hilly forested region
105 Hortobágy
Varied steppe landscape good for birdwatching
106 Kiskunság Apr-Jul
Wide range of lowland habitats

Slovenia
107 Triglav
Limestone mountain scenery & mixed forest

108 Krka
Park follows the route of the Krka river; lakes, dams, gorges, falls & woodland

Croatia
109 Risnjak
Limestone mountain scenery & mixed forest
110 Plitvice Lakes*
Scenic lakes linked by waterfalls formed by limestone deposition
111 Paklenica
Limestone peaks, gorges & mixed forest
112 Kornati
Limestone islands with karst scenery
113 Mljet
Western part of island

Bosnia-Herzegovina
114 Sutjeska
Wooded mountainous area; mixed landscape & reserve of virgin forest

Federal Republic of Yugoslavia
115 Fruska Gora
Wooded hilly valley
116 Djerdap
Gorge of the Danube; dam has created a long thin lake
117 Tara
Mixed upland scenery
118 Durmitor
Mountain area in the west, Tara Gorge in east; mixed landscape & karst
119 Biogradska Gora
Mountain area with high grasslands & five lakes
120 Lovcen
Wooded limestone mountains
121 Skadarsko jezero
Yugoslav part of Lake Scutari

Former Yugoslav Rep. of Macedonia
122 Mavrovo
Mountain area, partly wooded
123 Galicica
S. end of Dinaric Alps; mostly natural forest
124 Pelister
Wooded mountain area with Alpine pastures

Albania
125 Dajtit, Lura & Thethi
Three separate parks; forested mountain areas
126 Divjaka
Dunes & coastal woodland
127 Tomorri
Mountainous landscape with forests & pastures
128 Llogara
Woodland & pastures

Romania
129 Retezat May-Sep
Mountain country with extensive forests

Bulgaria
130 Rusenski Lom May-Oct
Deciduous woodland
131 Vitosa May-Oct
Varied mountain area
132 Pirin Apr-Oct
High mountains; forest & mixed landscape

Greece
133 Préspa Apr-Jul
Shallow lakes with reed- & sedge-beds
134 Olimbos (Olympus)
Apr-Oct Mountain area with maquis & forest; home of the gods in ancient Greek mythology
135 Pindos May-Oct
Wooded mountain area
136 Vikos-Aóos May-Jun
Wooded mountain area; Vikos & Aóos gorges
137 Aínos Mar-Jul
Area around Mt Aínos
138 Iti Óros May-Oct
Wooded mountain area
139 Parnassós Apr-Nov
Wilderness mountain area; mixed habitats
140 Párnitha Apr-Jul
Limestone area; maquis
141 Soúnion Mar-May
Typical Greek coast

Turkey
142 Manyas-Kuscenneti
Part of large lake

Estonia
143 Lahemaa
Wooded area & scenic coast

Latvia
144 Gauja
River & gorge scenery; the 'Switzerland of Latvia'

Lithuania
145 Zemaitija
Lakeland area
146 Aukstaitija (Ignalina)
Forest & lakes; great diversity of wildlife
147 Trakai
Five lakes with Trakai Castle as centrepiece
148 Dzukija
Confluence of Nemunas & Merkys rivers

Leisure Parks

This map shows major theme parks and amusement parks in Europe. Most of those shown are members of either the International Association of Amusement Parks and Attractions (IAAPA) or the European Federation of Amusement and Leisure Parks (Europark). Most parks which primarily attract visitors from the local area have been excluded.

Sites marked with an asterisk (*) are featured in Columbus Travel Guides' *Tourist Attractions and Events of the World*, 2nd edition. For more information, call +44 (0)20 7608 6666.

Norway
1 **Kristiansand Dyrepark**
Combined animal park and entertainment park
2 **Telemark Sommerland**, Bø
Combined theme park and waterpark
3 **Lunds Tivoli**, Oslo
Amusement park
4 **TusenFryd & VikingLandet**, Vinterbru
Theme park with many rides and large Viking Land

Sweden
5 **Liseberg**, Gothenburg
Large theme park with convention facilities, exhibition hall and sports stadium
6 **Parken Zoo i Eskilstuna**
Theme park, waterpark and zoo
7 **Gröna Lunds Tivoli**, Stockholm
Amusement park in the centre of Stockholm
8 **Furuviksparken**, Gavle
Amusement park and zoo
9 **Jamtli Historieland**, Östersund
Historical theme park

Finland
10 **Wasalandia**, Vaasa
Amusement park; Tropical Spa Tropiclandia nearby
11 **Tampereen Sarkanniemi Oy**, Tampere
City-centre amusement park and entertainment centre; also includes an art museum
12 **Linnanmäki**, Helsinki
Finland's most popular amusement park

Denmark
13 **Jesperhus Blomsterpark**, Nykøbing, Mors
Amusement park, family entertainment centre and zoo
14 **Fårup Aquapark & Sommerland**, Saltum
Amusement park with more than 30 activities and Scandinavia's largest waterpark
15 **Djurs Sommerland**, Nimtofte
Amusement park with more than 50 activities in six attractions: *Summerland*, *Waterland*, *Africa Land*, *Mexico Land*, *Cowboy Village* and *Lillensland*; plus *Grand Prix Land* and *Laredo Theatre*
16 **LEGOLAND***, Billund
Theme park based on LEGO toy products; 22 family rides plus 75,000 square metres of LEGO brick replicas of world monuments; *DUPLO Land* for the younger children; *Port of Copenhagen* with electronically-controlled trains, cranes and ships
17 **Dyrehavsbakken** ('Bakken'), Klampenborg
The world's oldest amusement park, with 24 rides
18 **Tivoli***, Copenhagen
Large amusement park in the centre of Copenhagen, opened in 1843; rides include *Golden Tower*, *Valhalla Castle*, *The Monsoon*, a ferris wheel and a rollercoaster which zooms through the treetops; the famous Copenhagen Christmas Market is held here in Nov & Dec

Ireland
19 **Perks Pleasure Park**, Youghal
Major rides include *Vampire Ghost Train*, *Trabant* and a giant big wheel supported by Perkie Bear
20 **Clara Lara Fun Park**, Wicklow
Park and amusement centre including *Aqua Shuttle* and *Pirate Galleon* plus a junior playground

United Kingdom
21 **Barry's Amusement Park**, Portrush
Star rides include *Looping Dipper* and *Music Express*
22 **Blackpool Pleasure Beach***
Opened in 1896, with rides classified according to their 'terror factor'; A class rides include *Pepsi Max Big One*, *Big Dipper* and *Log Flume*; B class rides include *Ghost Train* and *Black Hole*; C class rides, more suitable for children include *Noah's Ark* and *Flying Machines*; *Valhalla* is the world's biggest ride in the dark
23 **Camelot Theme Park**, Chorley, Lancashire
A medieval world with over 100 attractions and rides including *Excalibur*, a 360˚ rotation swing ride
24 **Lightwater Valley**, Ripon
Theme park with unique attractions including the world's first suspended hang-glider ride and the world's longest rollercoaster
25 **Flamingo Land**, Malton
Popular holiday village and zoo with many rides
26 **Alton Towers***, near Stoke-on-Trent
One of the UK's most popular theme parks with 125 rides and attractions including *Black Hole*, *Submission*, *Nemesis* and *Corkscrew* rollercoasters and a number of different kingdoms: *Ugland*, *Forbidden Valley*, *Towers Street* and *Cred Street*
27 **Gullivers Kingdom**, Matlock Bath
Family theme park with over 40 rides, hot-air balloon flights and chair lift
28 **American Adventure World**, Ilkeston
Theme park with *Nightmare Niagara* log flume
29 **Magical World of Fantasy Island**, Ingoldmells
Themed indoor family resort; based on Jules Verne
30 **Drayton Manor Park**, Tamworth
Theme park and zoo; over 100 rides and attractions including *Paratower*, *Jungle Cruise*, *Pirate's Adventure*, *Splash Canyon* and *The Haunting*
31 **Pleasurewood Hills**, Lowestoft
50 rides including *Pirate Ship*, *Cannonball Express* rollercoaster and the *Log Flume*
32 **Oakwood Adventure**, Narberth
Amusement park with over 40 attractions including *Megafobia* rollercoaster, *The Bounce*, *Snake River Falls* flume and a bobsleigh run
33 **LEGOLAND Windsor***
Children's theme park divided into eight areas: *The Beginning*, *Imagination Centre*, *Miniland*, the park's founding feature and one of its biggest attractions, *DUPLO Gardens*, *LEGO Traffic*, *My Town*, *Wild Woods* and *Castleland*
34 **Thorpe Park**, Chertsey
Theme park with many rides including *Canada Creek*, *Carousel Kingdom*, *A Drive in the Country*, *Flying Fish*, *Depth Charge* and *No Way Out*, a backwards dark ride

35 **Chessington World of Adventures***
Zoo and amusement park with rides including *Samurai*, *Dragons Falls* and *Rameses Revenge*; *Beanoland* celebrates Dennis the Menace cartoon character; zoo includes *Trail of the Kings* animal enclosure, with gorillas and large cats
36 **Fun Acres**, Southsea
Seaside park with boat trips and 10 major rides
37 **Harbour Park**, Littlehampton
Seaside amusement park

The Netherlands
38 **Attractiepark Slagharen**, Slagharen
Theme park with Wild West shows and over 40 rides
39 **Avonturenpark Hellendoorn**
Amusement park with many rides and animal attractions
40 **Six Flags**, Dronten
Family amusement park with *El Condor* rollercoaster and *Crazy River* water flume
41 **Dolfinarium Harderwijk**
Europe's largest marine park, with a research department; six different shows with animals and an open-air dolphin lagoon
42 **Duinrell**, Wassenaar
Theme park close to the beach with over 50 rides and attractions, including *Splash* and *Waterspin*
43 **Drievliet**, Rijswijk
More than 20 major attractions, including *Coppermine* rollercoaster
44 **De Efteling**, Kaatsheuvel
Family leisure park with a full range of attractions including a golf course, *Dreamflight* dark ride, *Fata Morgana*, *Inca City* and two rollercoasters

Belgium
45 **Meli Park**, De Panne
Attractions and rides plus a bird and animal park
46 **Bellewaerde Park**, Ypres
Exotic animals on display; six areas: *Canada*, *Far West*, *India*, *Jungle*, *Mexico* and *Pepinoland*; over 30 rides
47 **Action Planet**, Antwerp
Indoor adventure sports park
48 **Bobbejaanland**, Lichtaart
Amusement and theme park with 45 major rides, including *The Revolution* and *Arcade 2000*; also includes *Kinderland*, a covered children's play area with 20 rides
49 **Walibi**, Wavre
Amusement park and waterpark with 40 rides including *Rapid River*, *Shuttle Loop*, *Corkscrew* and *Jumbo Jet*

Germany
50 **Familien-Freizeitpark Tolk-Schau**, Tolk
Amusement park situated in a scenic landscape
51 **Hansapark**, Neustadt in Holstein
Theme park with rides and attractions including an *Aqua Stadium*, a water circus and *Adventureland*
52 **Ferienzentrum Schloss Dankern**, Haren
Family entertainment centre with many water facilities
53 **Heide-Park**, Soltau
Amusement park with 36 major rides including a rapids ride, two monorails, a looping rollercoaster with four 360˚ turns and a bobsleigh ride
54 **Serengeti Safaripark**, Hodenhagen
Animal park with leisure attractions
55 **Dinosaurier Park Münchehagen**, Rehburg-Loccum
Dinosaur park
56 **Warner Brothers Movie World**, Bottrop
A unique movie theme park
57 **Hollywood-Park**, Schloss Holte-Stukenbrock
Combined safari park and amusement park, with attractions including *Hollywood Theatre*, a circus and a western show, a monkey area, *Disco Round*, *Flying Carpet*, a steam carousel and rollercoasters
58 **Fort Fun Abenteuerland**, Bestwig
Amusement park with a Western town
59 **Panoramapark Sauerland**, Kirchhundem
Wild animal park and amusement park with its own 500-kilowatt windpower station
60 **Phantasialand**, Brühl
Theme park divided into five areas: *China Town*, *Old Berlin*, *Mexico*, *Petite Paris* and *Future World*; many rides including *Mystery Castle*, *Colorado Adventure-The Michael Jackson Thrill Ride* and *Galaxy*
61 **Eifelpark**, Gondorf bei Bitburg
Wild animal park and amusement park, includes the *Eifel Express*
62 **Holiday-Park**, Hassloch
Theme park with many attractions including *Thunder River*, *The Barrels of the Devil*, *Lilliput-Express*, *Aquascope*, *Stormship*, a 180˚ cinema, *Falkenstein Castle*, *Pfalz Village* and a looping rollercoaster
63 **Erlebnispark Tripsdrill**, Cleebronn
Germany's oldest amusement park
64 **Freizeit-Land**, Geiselwind
Theme park with many attractions including *Cinema 2000*, a Viking ship, a space adventure area, prehistoric world; *Enterprise ride*, *Shuttle ride* and a rollercoaster
65 **Freizeit- und Miniaturpark Allgäu**, Weitnau
Adventure park with many miniature buildings and trains; includes a large children's park with *Nautic Jet*, *Luna Loop* and *Butterfly*
66 **Europa-Park**, Rust
Large theme park with many rides

France
67 **Mirapolis**, Cergy-Pontoise
Large amusement park with activities related to legends and epics, includes *Gargantua* statue
68 **Jardin d'Acclimation**, Paris
Amusement park with family rides and a zoo
69 **Parc Floral**, Paris
Amusement park set within a large garden area
70 **La Mer de Sable**, Ermenonville
Amusement park developed into themed areas: *China*, *Wild West* and *Morocco*; includes *Babagattau Village*
71 **Parc Astérix***, Plailly
Theme park based on comic strip hero Astérix with over 30 rides including *Tonnere de Zeus* rollercoaster, and *la Trace du Hourra* giant slide; shows and displays include *Théâtre du Poséidon* sea lion and dolphin display and *Main Basse sur la Joconde* suspense show to steal the Mona Lisa

72 **Disneyland Paris***, Marne-la-Vallée
Europe's most popular park; divided into five 'lands': *Main Street USA*, *Frontierland*, *Adventureland*, *Fantasyland* and *Discoveryland*; attractions include *Space Mountain*, *Raiders of The Lost Ark* and *Honey I Shrunk The Audience*
73 **Futuroscope***, Poitiers
Space-age park with futuristic architecture and advanced visual-image technology; *le Tapis Magique* (flying carpet) giant audiovisual display; nightly *Lac aux Images* and *Son et Lumière* laser and light show; *Cyber Avenue* highlights multimedia and virtual technology

Spain
74 **Parc d'Atraccions Tibidabo**, Barcelona
Urban amusement park, founded 1899, renovated 1988
75 **Universal Studios Port Aventura***, Salou
Spain's largest theme park with five areas: *Mediterránia*, *Polynesia*, *China*, *Mexico* and *Far West*; attractions include *Templo del Fuego*, with fire and water effects, *Sea Odyssey* underwater adventure, *Stampida* rollercoaster, *Grand Canyon Rapids* and *Tutuki Splash* water rides
76 **Terra Mítica***, Benidorm
Five different areas, all related to the Mediterranean Sea: *Egypt*, *Iberia*, *Greece*, *Rome* and *The Islands*; rides include *Bravo Train*, *Phoenix Flight*, *Cheops' Mystery*, *Minotaur's Labyrinth* and *Ulysee's Rescue*.
77 **Txiki Park**, Pamplona
Family entertainment centre designed for children
78 **Parque de Atracciones Casa de Campo**, Madrid
Urban amusement park, Madrid's main entertainment centre
79 **Sioux City**, San Agustín
Theme park with stage shows and concerts

Portugal
80 **Zoomarine**, Albufeira
Zoo and marine theme park

Switzerland
81 **Conny-Land**, Lipperswil
Amusement park with underwater and animal shows

Austria
82 **Safari- und Abenteuerpark**, Gänserndorf
Adventure park and drive-through safari park

Italy
83 **Gardaland**, Castelnuovo del Garda
Large amusement park with 25 different attractions, eleven entertainments and four themed villages
84 **Mirabilandia**, Savio
30 attractions including two 60m twin towers called the *Turbo Drop*, plus *River Rapid* water ride
85 **Fiabilandia**, Rimini
Amusement park and funfair
86 **Luneur**, Rome
Amusement park and funfair
87 **Edenlandia**, Naples
Amusement/theme park

Turkey
88 **Tatilya Turizm**, Avcilar, Istanbul
World's fourth largest indoor entertainment centre
89 **Aqua Fantasy***, Selçuk
Turkey's largest water park, with *Treasure Island* area for younger children

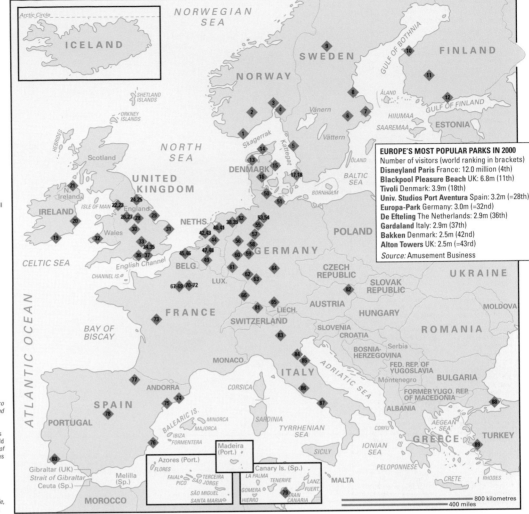

EUROPE'S MOST POPULAR PARKS IN 2000
Number of visitors (world ranking in brackets)
Disneyland Paris France: 12.0 million (4th)
Blackpool Pleasure Beach UK: 6.8m (11th)
Tivoli Denmark: 3.9m (18th)
Univ. Studios Port Aventura Spain: 3.2m (=28th)
Europa-Park Germany: 3.0m (=32nd)
De Efteling The Netherlands: 2.9m (36th)
Gardaland Italy: 2.9m (37th)
Bakken Denmark: 2.5m (42nd)
Alton Towers UK: 2.5m (=43rd)
Source: Amusement Business

Museums & Art Galleries

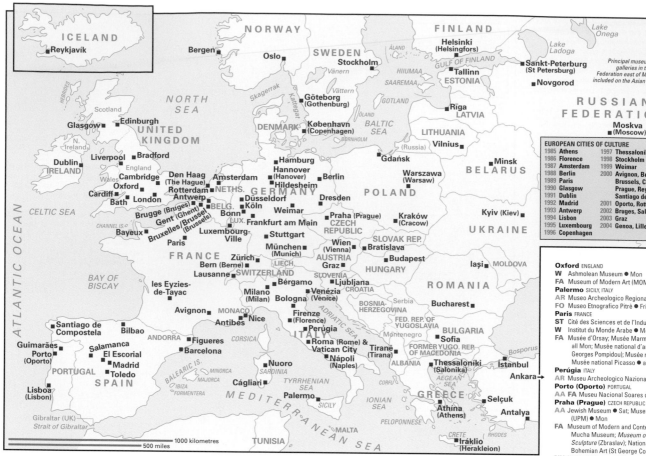

EUROPEAN CITIES OF CULTURE

1985	Athens	1997	Thessaloniki
1986	Florence	1998	Stockholm
1987	Amsterdam	1999	Weimar
1988	Berlin	2000	Avignon, Bergen, Bologna,
1989	Paris		Brussels, Cracow, Helsinki,
1990	Glasgow		Prague, Reykjavik,
1991	Dublin		Santiago de Compostela
1992	Madrid	2001	Oporto, Rotterdam
1993	Antwerp	2002	Bruges, Salamanca
1994	Lisbon	2003	Graz
1995	Luxembourg	2004	Genoa, Lille
1996	Copenhagen		

Principal museums and art galleries in the Russian Federation east of Moscow are included on the Asian map, p.119

Europe's most important museums and art galleries are listed here. Selection is based on importance and depth of the collection and its cultural diversity within a geographic spread.

Most cities named will also offer the visitor a number of smaller museums of specialist interest. Many single great works of art may also be housed in local cathedrals and churches.

Data compiled by Jon A. Gillaspie
email: info@sarastro.com

Principal contents of institution:

AA Applied & decorative art
AR Archaeology / ancient art
FA Fine art (paintings, sculpture)
FO Folk art & culture / ethnology
H History / historical site / reconstruction
NH Natural history
ST Science / technology
W Wide range of subjects

Opening times:
Days or months preceded by a red circle (●) indicate when the institution is closed.
Many close on national holidays and other special days. Some museums and galleries have shorter opening hours at certain days of the week or in certain months.

Admission charges:
All charge for admission except those shown in *italics*, where entry is free (although charges for special exhibitions may apply).
Some institutions allow free entry or reduce their admission charges on certain days.

Amsterdam THE NETHERLANDS
W *Rijksmuseum*
FA Stedelijk Museum; Van Gogh Museum
Ankara TURKEY
AR Museum of Anatolian Civilizations ● Mon
Antalya TURKEY
AR Archaeological Museum ● Mon
Antibes FRANCE
FA Musée Picasso ● Mon
Antwerpen (Antwerp) BELGIUM
FA Museum voor Schone Kunsten ● Mon
Athína (Athens) GREECE
AR Acropolis Museum; Nat. Archaeological Mus.
W Benáki Museum ● Tue

AR Museum of Cycladic and Ancient Greek Art ● Tue & Sun
Avignon FRANCE
W Musée Calvet ● Tue
FA Musée du Petit Palais ● Tue
Barcelona SPAIN
AR Museu Arqueològic ● Mon
FA Museu d'Art Contemporani; Museu Nac. d'Art de Catalunya; Museu Picasso ● all Mon
Bath ENGLAND
AA Museum of Costume
AR Roman Baths and Museum
Bayeux FRANCE
AA Bayeux Tapestry
Bérgamo ITALY
FA Accademia Carrara ● Mon
Bergen NORWAY
AR Bryggens Museum
FA Rasmus Meyer Collection ● Mon (Sep-May)
Berlin GERMANY
AR Ägyptisches Museum ● Mon; Antiken Museum ● Fri
W Dahlem museums ● Mon
ST Deutsches Teknikmuseum ● Mon
W Kulturforum ● Mon includes:
FA Gemäldegalerie
AA Kunstgewerbemuseum
NH Museum für Naturkunde ● Mon
W Museumsinsel ● Mon includes:
FA Alte Nationalgalerie
AR Bodemuseum; Pergamonmuseum
Bern (Berne) SWITZERLAND
AR Kunstmuseum ● Mon
Bilbao SPAIN
FA Mus. de Bellas Arte; Mus. Guggenheim ● Mon
Bologna ITALY
AR Museo Civico Archeologico ● Mon
Bonn GERMANY
NH Alexander-Koenig-Museum ● Mon
FA Kunstmuseum ● Mon
Bradford UNITED KINGDOM
ST Nat. Mus. of Photography, Film & TV ● Mon
Bratislava SLOVAK REPUBLIC
FA National Gallery ● Mon
W National Museum ● Mon
Brugge (Bruges) BELGIUM
FA Groeningemuseum ● Tue (Oct-Mar)
Bruxelles/Brussel (Brussels) BELGIUM
FA Musées Royaux des Beaux-Arts ● Mon
Bucharest ROMANIA
FA National Art Museum ● Mon & Tue
AR H National History Museum ● Mon & Tue
Budapest HUNGARY
FA National Gall.; Mus. of Fine Arts ● both Mon
AA National Jewish Museum ● Sat
W National Museum ● Mon
Cágliari SARDINIA, ITALY
AR Museo Nazionale Archeologico
Cambridge ENGLAND
FA Fitzwilliam Museum ● Mon
Cardiff WALES
FO Museum of Welsh Life, St Fagans
W National Museum and Gallery ● Mon
Den Haag (The Hague) THE NETHERLANDS
W Gemeentemuseum ● Mon

FA *Mauritshuis* ● Mon
Dresden GERMANY
AA Gemäldegalerie Alte Meister ● Mon
Dublin IRELAND
FA *National Gallery*
W *National Museum* ● Mon
Düsseldorf GERMANY
W Kunstmuseum ● Mon
FA Kunstsammlung Nordrhein-Westfalen ● Mon
Edinburgh SCOTLAND
W *Royal Museum & Museum of Scotland*
FA *National Gallery of Scotland; Gall. of Modern Art (GOMA); Scottish National Portrait Gall.*
El Escorial SPAIN
FA Monasterio de El Escorial ● Mon
Les Eyzies-de-Tayac FRANCE
AR Musée National de Préhistoire ● Tue
Figueres SPAIN
FA Teatre-Museu Dalí ● Mon (Oct-Jun)
Firenze (Florence) ITALY
FA Uffizi ● Mon; Bargello ● Mon (& 1st+3rd Sun)
AR Museo Archeologico ● Mon
Frankfurt am Main GERMANY
FA Museum für Moderne Kunst ● Mon
W Museumsufer ● Mon & Thu includes:
AA FA Städel; Museum für Kunsthandwerk
Gdansk POLAND
W National Art Museum ● Mon
Gent (Ghent) BELGIUM
FA *Museum voor Schone Kunsten*
Glasgow SCOTLAND
FA *Kelvingrove Art Gallery and Museum*
W *Burrell Collection*
FA Hunterian Art Gallery and Museum ● Sun
Göteborg (Gothenburg) SWEDEN
FA Konstmuseet ● Mon (Sep-Apr)
AA Röhsska Konstlöjdmuseet ● Mon (Sep-Apr)
Graz AUSTRIA
FA Alte Galerie ● Sun; Neue Galerie ● Mon
W Landesmuseum Joanneum
H Landeszeughaus (Provincial Arsenal) ● Mon; Stadtmuseum ● Sun & Mon
NH Naturhistorisches Museum ● Mon
Guimarães PORTUGAL
AA Museu Alberto Sampaio ● Mon
AA Museu Martins Sarmiento ● Mon
AA Sé (Cathedral museum), Braga
Hamburg GERMANY
FA Kunsthalle ● Mon
AA Museum für Kunst und Gewerbe ● Mon
Hannover (Hanover) GERMANY
FA Sprengel Museum ● Mon
Hildesheim GERMANY
AR Roemer-Pelizaeus Museum ● Mon
Helsinki (Helsingfors) FINLAND
FA Helsinki kaupingin museo ● Mon & Tue
W Kansallismuseo; Kiasma
Iasi ROMANIA
W Palace of Culture ● Mon
Iráklio (Herakleion) CRETE, GREECE
AR Archaeological Museum
Istanbul TURKEY
W Museum of Turkish and Islamic Art ● Mon
København (Copenhagen) DENMARK
FO Norsk Folkemuseum
AR Nationalmuseet ● Mon

W Ny Carlsberg Glyptotek ● Mon
FA Statens Museum for Kunst ● Mon
Köln (Cologne) GERMANY
AR Römisch-Germanisches Museum ● Mon
FA Wallraf-Richartz/Ludwig Museum ● Mon
Kraków (Cracow) POLAND
W Czartoryski Museum ● Mon
FO Museum of Ethnography ● Tue
Kyiv (Kiev) UKRAINE
W Historical Treasures Museum
FA Russian Art Museum ● Thu
Lausanne SWITZERLAND
H Musée Olympique ● Mon (Oct-Apr)
Lisboa (Lisbon) PORTUGAL
FA Museu Nacional de Arte Antiga ● Mon
W Museu Calouste Gulbenkian ● Mon
Liverpool ENGLAND
FA *Walker Art Gallery*
Ljubljana SLOVENIA
FA National Gallery ● Sun & Mon
W National Museum ● Sun & Mon
London ENGLAND
W *British Museum; Museum of London*
FA *National Gallery; National Portrait Gallery; Tate Britain; Tate Modern*
NH *Natural History Museum*
ST *Science Museum*
AA *Victoria and Albert Museum*
Luxembourg-Ville LUXEMBOURG
W *Musée national* ● Mon
Madrid SPAIN
FA Centro de Arte Reina Sofia ● Tue; Museo del Prado; Mus. Thyssen-Bornemisza ● both Mon
AR Museo Arqueológico Nacional ● Mon
W Museo de América ● Mon
Minsk BELARUS
FA Belarusian State Art Museum ● Tue
W National Mus. of History and Culture ● Wed
Milano (Milan) ITALY
FA *Civico Museo di Arte Contemporanea;* Pinacoteca Ambrosiana; Pinacoteca di Brera ● Mon
AR Museo Civico di Archeologia ● Mon
Moskva (Moscow) RUSSIAN FEDERATION
AA Kremlin ● Thu
FA Museum of Private Collections ● Mon & Tue; Tretyakov Gallery ● Mon
W Pushkin Museum of Fine Arts ● Mon
München (Munich) GERMANY
FA Alte Pinakothek, Neue Pinakothek ● both Mon
AA Bayerisches Nationalmuseum ● Mon
ST Deutsches Museum
AR Glyptothek und Antikensammlungen ● Mon
Nápoli (Naples) ITALY
AR Museo Archeologico Nazionale
Nice FRANCE
FA Musée Marc-Chagall; Mus. Matisse ● both Tue
Novgorod RUSSIAN FEDERATION
AA Museum of History, Architecture and Art ● Tue
Nuoro SARDINIA, ITALY
FO Museo Etnografico ● Mon (Oct-Easter)
Oslo NORWAY
FA Nasjonalgalleriet ● Mon
FO Norsk Folkemuseum
AR Vikingskiphuset ● Mon (Sep-May)

Oxford ENGLAND
W Ashmolean Museum ● Mon
FA Museum of Modern Art (MOMA) ● Mon
Palermo SICILY, ITALY
AR Museo Archeologico Regionale
FO Museo Etnografico Pitrè ● Fri
Paris FRANCE
ST Cité des Sciences et de l'Industrie ● Mon
W Institut du Monde Arabe ● Mon; Louvre ● Tue
FA Musée d'Orsay; Musée Marmottan; Musée Rodin all Mon; Musée national d'art moderne (Centre Georges Pompidou); Musée national du Moyen-Âge; Musée national Picasso ● all Tue
Perúgia ITALY
AR Museo Archeologico Nazionale dell'Umbria ● Mo
Porto (Oporto) PORTUGAL
AA FA Museu Nacional Soares dos Reis ● Mon
Praha (Prague) CZECH REPUBLIC
AA Jewish Museum ● Sat; Museum of Decorative Art (UPM) ● Mon
FA Museum of Modern and Contemporary Czech Art; Mucha Museum; *Museum of Modern Czech Sculpture* (Zbraslav); National Gallery of Old Bohemian Art (St George Convent) ● all Mon
NH National Museum ● Tue
ST National Museum of Technology ● Mon
Reykjavik ICELAND
W *Thjódminjasafn Íslands (National Museum)*
Riga LATVIA
AA Museum of Decorative and Applied Arts ● Mon
Roma (Rome) ITALY & Vatican City
W Capitoline museums ● Mon includes:
AR Museo Capitolino
W Museo del Palazzo del Conservatori
AR Museo Nazionale di Villa Giulia; Museo Nazionale Romano ● Mon
FA Galleria Borghese; Palazzo Barberini ● both Mon; Galleria Doria Pamphilj ● Thu
W Musei Vaticani ● Sun
Rotterdam THE NETHERLANDS
FA Museum Boymans-van Beuningen ● Mon
Salamanca SPAIN
AA Museo Art Nouveau y Art Deco ● Mon
Sankt-Peterburg (St Petersburg) RUSSIAN FED.
W Hermitage ● Mon
FO Museum of Anthropology and Ethnography ● Mon
FA Russian Museum ● Mon
Santiago de Compostela SPAIN
AA Catedral
Selçuk TURKEY
AR Archaeological Museum
Sofia BULGARIA
FO Ethnographic Museum ● Mon & Tue
FA National Art Gallery ● Mon & Tue
AR H National Historical Museum ● Mon
Stockholm SWEDEN
FA Modernmuséet ● Mon
AA Nationalmuseum ● Mon
AR Vasamuseet
Stuttgart GERMANY
FA Staatsgalerie ● Mon
Tallinn ESTONIA
FA National Art Museum ● Tue
Thessaloníki (Salonika) GREECE
AR Archaeological Museum
FO Folklore Museum ● Tue (summer), Thu (winter)
Tiranë (Tirana) ALBANIA
AR National Archaeology Museum
FA National Art Gallery
W National Historical Museum
Toledo SPAIN
AR Museo de Arte Visigótico ● Mon
FA Museo de Santa Cruz
Venézia (Venice) ITALY
FA Coll. Guggenheim ● Tue; Galleria dell'Accademia
W Musei Correr
AA Museo Vitario di Murano ● Wed
Vilnius LITHUANIA
AA Lith. History and Ethnographic Mus. ● Mon & Tue
Warszawa (Warsaw) POLAND
W National Museum ● Mon
Weimar GERMANY
FA Schlossmuseum ● Mon
Wien (Vienna) AUSTRIA
FA Albertina; Kunsthistorisches Museum ● both Mon; Österreichische Galerie, Belvedere ● Tue
W MuseumsQuartier, includes:
FA MUMOK (Mus. mod. Kunst); Leopold Mus. ● both Mon
Zürich SWITZERLAND
FA Kunsthaus ● Mon
W Schweizerisches Landesmuseum ● Mon

Skiing & Snowboarding

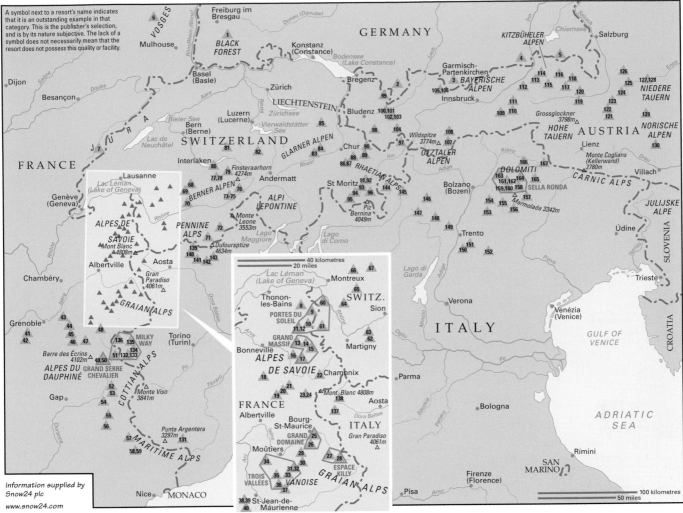

A symbol next to a resort's name indicates that it is an outstanding example in that category. This is the publisher's selection, and is by its nature subjective. The lack of a symbol does not necessarily mean that the resort does not possess this quality or facility.

Information supplied by
Snow24 plc
www.snow24.com

Legend

▲ **THE MOST BEAUTIFUL RESORTS**
Ski areas with spectacular scenery

❄ **SNOWSURE**
The best reputations for season-long snow cover

▲ **SUMMER SKIING DESTINATIONS**
Resorts where lifts stay open for skiing or boarding during the summer

◆ **EXPERT**
Best of the black diamond destinations

■ **BEGINNER SKI AREAS**
Best choices for first timers

◆ **FAMILY FRIENDLY**
Ideal choices for family ski holidays

● **PARTY TOWNS**
Après ski centres

▼ **SNOWBOARDER HEAVEN**
Best bets for boarders

★ **NOT JUST SKIING**
Plenty to do if you don't want to slide

THE LARGEST SKI AREAS △

Portes du Soleil France/Switzerland
9 Châtel
10 Avoriaz
11 Morzine
12 les Gets
60 Torgon
61 Champéry-Planachaux / Val-d'Illiez / Les Crosets

Grand Massif France
13 Morillon les Essert
14 Samoëns
15 Sixt
17 Flaine

Grand Domaine France
25 les Arcs
26 Peisey / Nancroix-Vallandry

Espace Killy France
27 Tignes
28 Val d'Isère

Trois Vallées France
31 la Tania
32 Courchevel
33 Méribel

35 St-Martin-de-Belleville
36 les Menuires
37 Val Thorens

Grand Serre-Chevalier France
49 Serre-Chevalier
50 Briançon

Milky Way France/Italy
51 Montgenèvre
132 San Sicário / Cesana
133 Clavière
134 Sestriere
135 Sàuze d'Oulx

Sella Ronda Italy
158 Arabba
159 Campitello di Fassa
160 Canazei
161 Santa Cristina / Pranauron
162 Selva Gardena (Wolkenstein)
163 Ortisei (St Ulrich)
164 Alta Badia [Colfosco / Corvara / La Villa (Stern) / San Cassiano (St Kassian) / Pedráces / San Leonardo (St Leonhard)]

Germany
1 Feldberg ■▼★
2 Oberstdorf ▲❄■■
3 Garmisch-Partenkirchen ▲❄■▲●◆★
4 Bayrischzell ▲■
5 Reit im Winkl ▲■★

France
6 la Bresse-Hohneck ■▼
7 Métabief / le Mont d'Or ❄★
8 Abondance / la Chapelle d'Abóndance ▲■❄
9 Châtel ▲
10 Avoriaz ❄◆■▲●▼
11 Morzine ▲◆❄●★
12 les Gets ▲■❄
13 Morillon les Essert ▲■
14 Samoëns ▲■
16 les Carroz ▲■
17 Flaine ❄■▲▼
18 la Clusaz ●▼
19 Notre-Dame-de-Bellecombe ■
20 Praz-sur-Arly ◆
21 Megève ▲●★
22 Chamonix-Mont Blanc ▲❄◆▼

23 St-Nicolas-de-Véroce ▲■
24 les Contamines-Montjoie ▲❄◆■
25 les Arcs ❄◆■▲●▼
27 Tignes ❄▲◆▼
28 Val d'Isère ❄▲◆●▼
29 la Plagne / les Coches / Montchavin / Plagne Montalbert ❄▲●▼★
30 Champagny-Vanoise ▲❄▼
31 la Tania ❄▲❄
32 Courchevel ◆◆●▼
33 Méribel ▲◆●▼★
34 Valmorel ■▼
35 St-Martin-de-Belleville ▲❄
36 les Menuires ◆■▲▼
37 Val Thorens ❄▲◆▼
38 la Toussuire ▲❄
39 le Corbier ▲
40 St-Jean d'Arves ▲
41 Villard-de-Lans / Cote 2000 ●
42 Corrençon-en-Vercors ▲
43 les Sept Laux (le Pleiney / Prapoutel) ▲
44 Vaujany / Oz-en-Oisans ▲◆
45 Alpe d'Huez / Auris-en-Oisans / Villard-Reculas ▲❄▲◆●▼
46 les Deux Alpes ▲❄▲■▲●▼★
47 la Grave ❄▲◆
48 Valloire ❄★
49 Serre-Chevalier ▲■▲▼★
50 Briançon ▲❄
51 Montgenèvre ❄■●▼
52 Risoul ❄■▲
53 Vars ❄
54 les Orres ▲❄▼
55 Pra-Loup ■★●★
56 Val d'Allos-La Foux ▲❄
57 Auron / St-Étienne-de-Tinée ●
58,59 Valberg ▲
59 Beuil-les-Launes ▲

Switzerland
61 Champéry-Planachaux / Val-d'Illiez / Les Crosets ▲■❄▲★
62 Verbier ▲❄◆■▲●▼★
63 La Tzoumas (Mayens-de-Riddes) ❄❄
64 Villars-sur-Ollon / Gryon ▲❄▲●▼
65 Les Diablerets ▲❄◆●▲★
66 Château-d'Oex ▲■▼
67 Gstaad-Saanenland ▲❄▲●▼★
68 Adelboden ▲❄◆●▼
69 Lenk ▲❄●▼
70 Crans-Montana ▲❄▼★
71 Zermatt ▲❄▲◆●▼★

72 Saas Fee ▲❄▲◆■▲▼★
73 Bettmeralp ▲❄
74 Mörel-Breiten ■
75 Fiesch ★
76 Sörenberg ▲
77 Wengen ▲❄●▼
78 Mürren / Stechelberg ■▲
79 Riederalp ▲
80 Interlaken / Wilderswil bei Interlaken ■●★
81 Grindelwald ▲❄▼
82 Engelberg ▲❄▲●▼★
83 Laax ▲❄◆▲▼
84 Flims ❄■❄
85 Flumserberg ■▲
86 Lenzerheide-Valbella ❄◆▲●
87 Parpan ▲
88 Arosa ▲❄▲●★
89 Davos ▲❄■▲●▼
90 Klosters / Fideris ▲❄◆●▼
91 Celerina ❄
92 Samedan ❄
93 St Moritz ❄◆▲●▼★
94 Sils-Maria ▲❄
95 Maloja ❄
96 Pontresina ❄▼
97 Samnaun ▲❄●★

Austria
98 St Gallenkirch ■▼
99 Kleinwalsertal [Hirschegg / Mittelberg / Riezlern] ▲■
100 Lech / Oberlech ❄◆■●▼
101 Zürs ❄
102 St Anton am Arlberg / St Jakob am Arlberg ▲❄◆●▼
103 St Christoph am Arlberg ❄◆
104 Ischgl / Silvretta ❄◆●▼★
105 Lermoos ▲❄
106 Ehrwald ❄▲■
107 Obergurgl / Hochgurgl ▲❄❄
108 Sölden ❄▲■▲●▼
109 Hintertux ▲❄▼
110 Mayrhofen ▲■❄●▼★
111 Zell am Ziller ▲■❄●
112 Alpbach ▲■❄
113 Hopfgarten im Brixental ■❄▼
114 Söll ▲❄■▼
115 Kitzbühel ▲❄◆●▼★
116 Fieberbrunn ❄●▼
117 Saalbach Hinterglemm ◆■●▼
118 Leogang ▲■▼
119 Kaprun ▲❄▲■▼

120 Zell am See ▲●★
121 Badgastein ■▲★
122 Bad Hofgastein ●★
123 Grossarl ▼
124 Flachau ◆▼
125 Altenmarkt-Zauchensee ★
126 Annaberg im Lammertal ▲
127 Ramsau am Dachstein ▲
128 Schladming ▲❄▲◆●▼★
129 St Michael im Lungau ▲★
130 Bad Kleinkirchheim ▲▼★

Italy
131 Limone Piemonte ■●
133 Clavière ■●
134 Sestriere ❄◆●▼
135 Sàuze d'Oulx ❄■●
136 Bardonécchia ❄■●
137 la Thuile ❄■▲
138 Courmayeur ●★
139 Breuil-Cervínia ❄▲
140 Valtournenche ▲
141 Champoluc / Antagnod ❄❄
142 Gressoney-la-Trinité / Gressoney-St Jean
143 Alagna-Valsésia ❄▲◆
144 Livigno ■❄●■
145 Bormio ▲●★
146 Folgárida ●▼
147 Passo Tonale ❄▲■★
148 Madonna di Campíglio ▲❄●▼★
149 Andalo ▲
150 Folgaria ★
151 Lavarone / Luserna ▲
152 Asiago / Canove ★
153 Cavalese ▲
154 Obereggen ▼
155 Bellamonte ■●
156 San Martino di Castrozza ▲★
157 Alleghe ■
158 Arabba ▲▲■❄
159 Campitello di Fassa ▲
160 Canazei ■
161 Santa Cristina / Pranauron ▲●
162 Selva Gardena (Wolkenstein) ▲●
164 Alta Badia [Colfosco / Corvara / La Villa (Stern) / San Cassiano (St Kassian) / Pedráces / San Leonardo (St Leonhard)] ▲❄■
165 Cortina ■▲❄●★
166 San Vigilio di Marebbe ■
167 Versciaco (Vierschach) ❄▲

ATLANTIC OCEAN

NORTH SEA

SHETLAND ISLANDS

UNST
YELL
FETLAR
WHALSAY
MAINLAND
FOULA
Lerwick
BRESSAY
60° N

FAIR ISLE

WESTRAY
N. RONALDSAY
ROUSAY
MAINLAND
Stromness
SHAPINSAY
STRONSAY
Kirkwall
HOY
S. RONALDSAY
ORKNEY ISLANDS
Thurso

ORKNEY ISLANDS
FAIR ISLE
WESTRAY
N. RONALDSAY
ROUSAY
MAINLAND
Stromness
Kirkwall
SHAPINSAY
STRONSAY
HOY
S. RONALDSAY

Cape Wrath
Duncansby Head
John o'Groats
Thurso
Wick

LEWIS
Stornoway
The Minch

OUTER HEBRIDES
NORTH UIST
Ullapool
Northwest Highlands
ST KILDA
HARRIS
Little Minch
BENBECULA
SOUTH UIST
BARRA
SKYE
Portree
Kyle of Lochalsh
RUM
Mallaig
COLL
TIREE
Ben Nevis 1344m
Fort William
MULL
Oban
COLONSAY
JURA
ISLAY
INNER HEBRIDES

Inverness
Loch Ness
Aviemore
Grampian Mountains
Spey
Elgin
Moray Firth
Fraserburgh
Peterhead
Aberdeen
Montrose
Dundee

SCOTLAND
Crianlarich
L. Lomond
Perth
Forth
St Andrews
Stirling
Dunfermline
Firth of Forth
Greenock
Hamilton
Edinburgh
Berwick-upon-Tweed
Glasgow
East Kilbride
Kilmarnock
Ayr
ARRAN
KINTYRE
Tweed

UNITED
North Channel
Malin Head
Londonderry
Coleraine
Larne

NORTHERN
Ballymena
Newtownabbey
Donegal
Omagh
Lough Neagh
Bangor
IRELAND
Belfast
Donegal Bay
Ballina
Sligo
Enniskillen
Newry
Dundalk (Dún Dealgan)

Stranraer
Dumfries
Kirkcudbright
Solway Firth
Carlisle
Penrith
Lake District
Scafell Pike 977m
Kendal

KINGDOM
Tyne
Newcastle upon Tyne
Gateshead
Sunderland
Durham
Darlington
Middlesbrough
Whitby
Scarborough
Flamborough Head

DOM
Pennines
Wharfe
York
Kingston upon Hull
Spurn Head
Grimsby

ISLE OF MAN
Douglas
Barrow-in-Furness

Irish Sea

Westport
Castlebar
Connemara
L. Corrib
Roscommon
Longford
Athlone
IRELAND
Galway (Gaillimh)
Galway Bay
ARAN IS.
L. Derg
Shannon
Portlaoise
Roscrea
Ennis (Inis)
Limerick (Luimneach)
Tralee (Trálí)
DINGLE
Killarney
IVERAGH PEN.
Carrauntoohill 1041m
Mizen Head

ARAN I.
Drogheda (Droichead Átha)
Swords
Lucan
DUBLIN (BAILE ÁTHA CLIATH)
Dún Laoghaire
Barrow
Wicklow Mtns
Carlow
Kilkenny
Tipperary
Clonmel
Waterford (Port Láirge)
Wexford
Rosslare
Cork (Corcaigh)
Cobh

Blackpool
Preston
Bolton
Bradford
Leeds
Huddersfield
Manchester
Doncaster
Liverpool
Sheffield
Birkenhead
Lincoln
ENGLAND
Rhyl
Chester
Crewe
Nottingham
Stoke-on-Trent
Derby
The Wash
King's Lynn
Cromer

ANGLESEY
Holyhead
Bangor
Caernarfon
Snowdon 1085m
Porthmadog
Dolgellau
Cardigan Bay
Aberystwyth
WALES
Cambrian Mountains
Shrewsbury
Wolverhampton
Walsall
Leicester
Peterborough
Norwich
Great Yarmouth
Lowestoft
East Anglia
Ipswich
Birmingham
Coventry
Northampton
Cambridge
Worcester
Stratford-upon-Avon
Harwich
Hereford
Gloucester
Oxford
Luton
Colchester
Abergavenny
Severn
Watford
LONDON
Southend-on-Sea
Newport
Bristol
Swindon
Slough
Thames
Maidstone
Fishguard
Carmarthen
Cardiff
Reading
Guildford
Croydon
Dover
St David's
Swansea
Bath
Basingstoke
Winchester
Brighton
Hastings
Folkestone
Milford Haven
Pembroke
Weston-super-Mare
Salisbury
Southampton
Portsmouth
Calais
Boulogne
Strait of Dover

Celtic Sea
St George's Channel
Bristol Channel
LUNDY
Ilfracombe
Exmoor
Barnstaple
Taunton
Bournemouth
Poole
ISLE OF WIGHT
Newquay
Dartmoor
Weymouth
I. OF PORTLAND
Exeter
Torquay
Plymouth
Penzance
Truro
Start Point
ISLES OF SCILLY
Land's End
Lizard Point
English Channel (La Manche)

ATLANTIC OCEAN

CHANNEL ISLANDS
ALDERNEY
GUERNSEY
St Peter Port
SARK
St Helier
JERSEY
Golfe de St-Malo
Cherbourg
Baie de la Seine
le Havre
Rouen
Dieppe
Caen
Seine
Roscoff
St-Malo
ÎLE D'OUESSANT
Brest

FRANCE

Blue boxes indicate focus map coverage

Lambert Equal Area Projection

200 kilometres
100 miles

UK: Beaches & National Parks

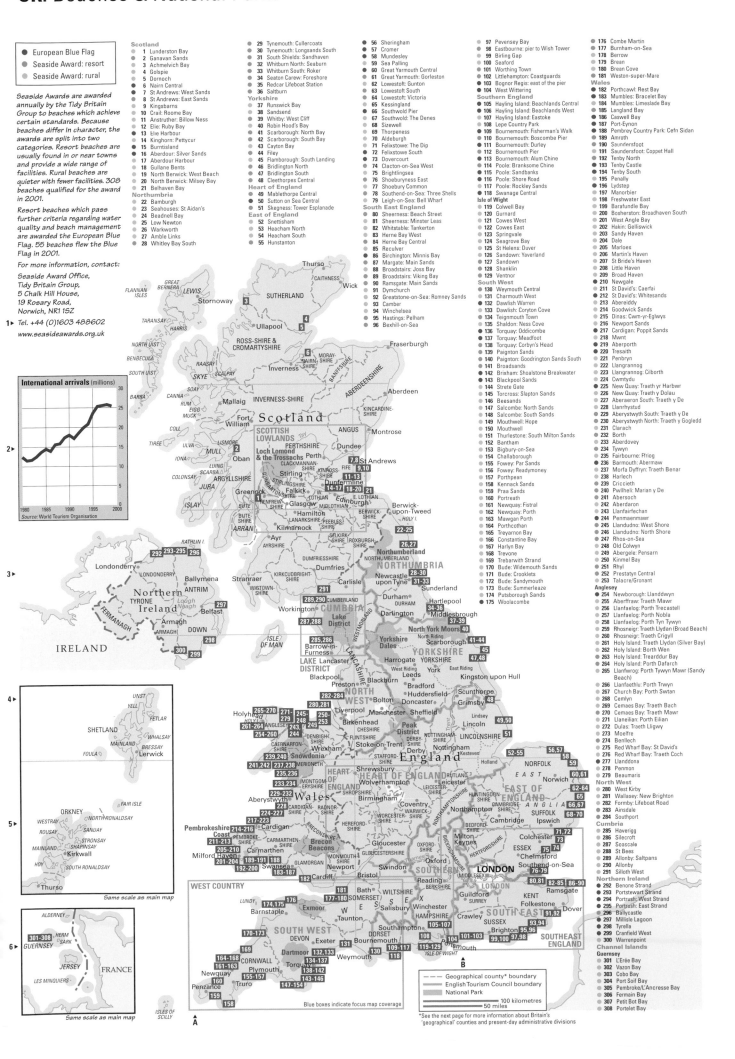

Legend:
- ● European Blue Flag
- ● Seaside Award: resort
- ○ Seaside Award: rural

Seaside Awards are awarded annually by the Tidy Britain Group to beaches which achieve certain standards. Because beaches differ in character, the awards are split into two categories. Resort beaches are usually found in or near towns and provide a wide range of facilities. Rural beaches are quieter with fewer facilities. 308 beaches qualified for the award in 2001.

Resort beaches which pass further criteria regarding water quality and beach management are awarded the European Blue Flag. 55 beaches flew the Blue Flag in 2001.

For more information, contact:

Seaside Award Office,
Tidy Britain Group,
5 Chalk Hill House,
19 Rosary Road,
Norwich, NR1 1SZ
Tel. +44 (0)1603 488602
www.seasideawards.org.uk

International arrivals (millions)
Source: World Tourism Organisation

Scotland
1 Lunderston Bay
2 Ganavan Sands
3 Achmelvich Bay
4 Golspie
5 Dornoch
6 Nairn Central
7 St Andrews: West Sands
8 St Andrews: East Sands
9 Kingsbarns
10 Crail: Roome Bay
11 Anstruther: Billow Ness
12 Elie: Ruby Bay
13 Elie Harbour
14 Kinghorn: Pettycur
15 Burntisland
16 Aberdour: Silver Sands
17 Aberdour Harbour
18 Gullane Bents
19 North Berwick: West Beach
20 North Berwick: Milsey Bay
21 Belhaven Bay

Northumbria
22 Bamburgh
23 Seahouses: St Aidan's
24 Beadnell Bay
25 Low Newton
26 Warkworth
27 Amble Links
28 Whitley Bay South
29 Tynemouth: Cullercoats
30 Tynemouth: Longsands South
31 South Shields: Sandhaven
32 Whitburn North: Seaburn
33 Whitburn South: Roker
34 Seaton Carew: Foreshore
35 Redcar Lifeboat Station
36 Saltburn

Yorkshire
37 Runswick Bay
38 Sandsend
39 Whitby: West Cliff
40 Robin Hood's Bay
41 Scarborough: North Bay
42 Scarborough: South Bay
43 Cayton Bay
44 Filey
45 Flamborough: South Landing
46 Bridlington North
47 Bridlington South
48 Cleethorpes Central

Heart of England
49 Mablethorpe Central
50 Sutton on Sea Central
51 Skegness: Tower Esplanade

East of England
52 Snettisham
53 Heacham North
54 Heacham South
55 Hunstanton
56 Sheringham
57 Cromer
58 Mundesley
59 Sea Palling
60 Great Yarmouth Central
61 Great Yarmouth: Gorleston
62 Lowestoft: Gunton
63 Lowestoft South
64 Lowestoft: Victoria
65 Kessingland
66 Southwold Pier
67 Southwold: The Denes
68 Sizewell
69 Thorpeness
70 Aldeburgh
71 Felixstowe: The Dip
72 Felixstowe South
73 Dovercourt
74 Clacton-on-Sea West
75 Brightlingsea
76 Shoeburyness East
77 Shoebury Common
78 Southend-on-Sea: Three Shells
79 Leigh-on-Sea: Bell Wharf

South East England
80 Sheerness: Beach Street
81 Sheerness: Minster Leas
82 Whitstable: Tankerton
83 Herne Bay West
84 Herne Bay Central
85 Reculver
86 Birchington: Minnis Bay
87 Margate: Main Sands
88 Broadstairs: Joss Bay
89 Broadstairs: Viking Bay
90 Ramsgate: Main Sands
91 Dymchurch
92 Greatstone-on-Sea: Romney Sands
93 Camber
94 Winchelsea
95 Hastings: Pelham
96 Bexhill-on-Sea
97 Pevensey Bay
98 Eastbourne: pier to Wish Tower
99 Birling Gap
100 Seaford
101 Worthing Town
102 Littlehampton: Coastguards
103 Bognor Regis: east of the pier
104 West Wittering

Southern England
105 Hayling Island: Beachlands Central
106 Hayling Island: Beachlands West
107 Hayling Island: Eastoke
108 Lepe Country Park
109 Bournemouth: Fisherman's Walk
110 Bournemouth: Boscombe Pier
111 Bournemouth: Durley
112 Bournemouth Pier
113 Bournemouth: Alum Chine
114 Poole: Branksome Chine
115 Poole: Sandbanks
116 Poole: Shore Road
117 Poole: Rockley Sands
118 Swanage Central

Isle of Wight
119 Colwell Bay
120 Gurnard
121 Cowes West
122 Cowes East
123 Springvale
124 Seagrove Bay
125 St Helens: Duver
126 Sandown: Yaverland
127 Sandown
128 Shanklin
129 Ventnor

South West
130 Weymouth Central
131 Charmouth West
132 Dawlish Warren
133 Dawlish: Coryton Cove
134 Teignmouth Town
135 Shaldon: Ness Cove
136 Torquay: Oddicombe
137 Torquay: Meadfoot
138 Torquay: Corbyn's Head
139 Paignton Sands
140 Paignton: Goodrington Sands South
141 Broadsands
142 Brixham: Shoalstone Breakwater
143 Blackpool Sands
144 Strete Gate
145 Torcross: Slapton Sands
146 Beesands
147 Salcombe: North Sands
148 Salcombe: South Sands
149 Mouthwell: Hope
150 Mouthwell
151 Thurlestone: South Milton Sands
152 Bantham
153 Bigbury-on-Sea
154 Challaborough
155 Fowey: Par Sands
156 Fowey: Readymoney
157 Porthpean
158 Kennack Sands
159 Praa Sands
160 Portreath
161 Newquay: Fistral
162 Newquay: Porth
163 Mawgan Porth
164 Porthcothan
165 Treyarnon Bay
166 Constantine Bay
167 Harlyn Bay
168 Trevone
169 Trebarwith Strand
170 Bude: Widemouth Sands
171 Bude: Crooklets
172 Bude: Sandymouth
173 Bude: Summerleaze
174 Putsborough Sands
175 Woolacombe
176 Combe Martin
177 Burnham-on-Sea
178 Berrow
179 Brean
180 Brean Cove
181 Weston-super-Mare

Wales
182 Porthcawl: Rest Bay
183 Mumbles: Bracelet Bay
184 Mumbles: Limeslade Bay
185 Langland Bay
186 Caswell Bay
187 Port-Eynon
188 Pembrey Country Park: Cefn Sidan
189 Amroth
190 Saundersfoot
191 Saundersfoot: Coppet Hall
192 Tenby North
193 Tenby Castle
194 Tenby South
195 Penally
196 Lydstep
197 Manorbier
198 Freshwater East
199 Barafundle Bay
200 Bosherston: Broadhaven South
201 West Angle Bay
202 Hakin: Gelliswick
203 Sandy Haven
204 Dale
205 Marloes
206 Martin's Haven
207 St Bride's Haven
208 Little Haven
209 Broad Haven
210 Newgale
211 St David's: Caerfai
212 St David's: Whitesands
213 Abereiddy
214 Goodwick Sands
215 Dinas: Cwm-yr-Eglwys
216 Newport Sands
217 Cardigan: Poppit Sands
218 Mwnt
219 Aberporth
220 Tresaith
221 Penbryn
222 Llangrannog
223 Llangrannog: Cilborth
224 Cwmtydu
225 New Quay: Traeth yr Harbwr
226 New Quay: Traeth y Dolau
227 Aberaeron South: Traeth y De
228 Llanrhystud
229 Aberystwyth South: Traeth y De
230 Aberystwyth North: Traeth y Gogledd
231 Clarach
232 Borth
233 Aberdovey
234 Tywyn
235 Fairbourne: Ffriog
236 Barmouth: Abermaw
237 Morfa Dyffryn: Traeth Benar
238 Harlech
239 Criccieth
240 Pwllheli: Marian y De
241 Abersoch
242 Aberdaron
243 Llanfairfechan
244 Penmaenmawr
245 Llandudno: West Shore
246 Llandudno: North Shore
247 Rhos-on-Sea
248 Old Colwyn
249 Abergele: Pensarn
250 Kinmel Bay
251 Rhyl
252 Prestatyn Central
253 Talacre/Gronant

Anglesey
254 Newborough: Llanddwyn
255 Aberffraw: Traeth Mawr
256 Llanfaelog: Porth Trecastell
257 Llanfaelog: Porth Nobla
258 Llanfaelog: Porth Tyn Tywyn
259 Rhosneigr: Traeth Llydan (Broad Beach)
260 Rhosneigr: Traeth Crigyll
261 Holy Island: Traeth Llydan (Silver Bay)
262 Holy Island: North Beach
263 Holy Island: Trearddur Bay
264 Holy Island: Porth Dafarch
265 Llanfwrog: Porth Tywyn Mawr (Sandy Beach)
266 Llanfaethlu: Porth Trwyn
267 Church Bay: Porth Swtan
268 Cemlyn
269 Cemaes Bay: Traeth Bach
270 Cemaes Bay: Traeth Mawr
271 Llaneilian: Porth Eilian
272 Dulas: Traeth Lligwy
273 Moelfre
274 Benllech
275 Red Wharf Bay: St David's
276 Red Wharf Bay: Traeth Coch
277 Llanddona
278 Penmon
279 Beaumaris

North West
280 West Kirby
281 Wallasey: New Brighton
282 Formby: Lifeboat Road
283 Ainsdale
284 Southport

Cumbria
285 Haverigg
286 Silecroft
287 Seascale
288 St Bees
289 Allonby: Saltpans
290 Allonby
291 Silloth West

Northern Ireland
292 Benone Strand
293 Portstewart Strand
294 Portrush: West Strand
295 Portrush: East Strand
296 Ballycastle
297 Millisle Lagoon
298 Tyrella
299 Cranfield West
300 Warrenpoint

Channel Islands
Guernsey
301 L'Erée Bay
302 Vazon Bay
303 Cobo Bay
304 Port Soif Bay
305 Pembroke/L'Ancresse Bay
306 Fermain Bay
307 Petit Bot Bay
308 Portelet Bay

- – – Geographical county* boundary
- ——— English Tourism Council boundary
- National Park
- Blue boxes indicate focus map coverage
- 100 kilometres
- 50 miles

*See the next page for more information about Britain's 'geographical' counties and present-day administrative divisions

UK: Geographical & Administrative Divisions

The next major change was the Local Government Act of 1972. Its most dramatic provision was the creation of six Metropolitan Counties and Greater London; more insidious was the abolition of the terms 'County Borough' and 'Administrative Counties' in favour of the simpler, but ambiguous, 'County' as the top tier of all the non-Metropolitan administrative units. Subsequent reorganisations have led to the situation displayed on the map – 46 'Unitary Authorities' with control over all aspects of local government, with the rest of the country divided into 'Administrative Counties' with some functions handled by a second tier of Borough or District Councils. Many of these Counties have the same names as their Geographical forebears, although rarely exactly the same borders. Ironically, one of the few which does is Rutland, which became a potent symbol of this issue after its administrative demise in 1972 – a reaction against the successive waves of new administrative names which were often short-lived, generally unloved and at times virtually impossible to locate.

The original, 'geographical', counties of England were mostly established in Saxon times; all but six pre-date the Norman Conquest. Those of Wales and Scotland are almost equally ancient. For centuries they provided a well-understood and efficient basis for the local administration of an agrarian country.

The first serious reorganisation of Britain's local government, prompted by the demographic shifts of industrialisation, took place in 1888 and '89. This created a new tier of 'Administrative Counties' and 'County Boroughs' in England and Wales, with similar terms used in Scotland. Most borrowed the names – and in many cases the actual borders – of the geographical counties which, for administrative purposes only, they replaced. This solution, which must have seemed simple and logical at the time, contained the seeds of the later confusion about the nature of counties; for henceforward each county name, as well as the very word 'county' itself, would refer to more than one entity.

The names and borders of the 'Geographical Counties' were never altered by any local government reforms; partly because, never having been created by statute in the first place it would have been difficult to abolish or even change them by this method; and partly because, as a direct result of these changes, the geographical counties were becoming less and less important as administrative units. As a result they began to disappear from many maps, although they remained, and remain, potent symbols of local identity.

Because of its distinct legal system, acts pertaining to Scotland were passed separately and so some different terms were used. In Wales, the position was rendered, to non-Welsh speakers, wholly opaque by the bilingualism of the newly created names. The confusions caused by these overlapping and shifting tiers are, however, broadly common to the whole of Great Britain.

Several other points are worthy of note. In 1997, 'Ceremonial Counties' were established, dividing up Britain roughly (but by no means exactly) according to the 'Geographical Counties'. Although based on no exact historical, or useful administrative, logic, they perhaps correspond closely with most people's mental map of Britain; for they include the Metropolitan Authorities, abolished as units in 1986 but still alive as useful descriptions of large urban areas. Secondly, many other structures such as parliamentary constituencies, health authorities, police forces and sporting organisations have borrowed names from all kinds of local divisions – including some, such as Mercia and Wessex, which pre-date even the 'Geographical Counties' – thus creating new and specific regional associations. Thirdly, there are the so-called 'Postal Counties' of the Royal Mail and as post-codes have overtaken county names of whatever kind as the key ingredient of an address, so the distinction between the various kinds of counties have blurred yet further. Fourthly, there are the regions of Britain as defined by the EU, as well as possible changes resulting from regional devolution, the long-term impact of which is still uncertain. Finally, in this as in other aspects of British tradition, old usages survive in cricket. Here one will still find Middlesex and Huntingdonshire and the undivided Sussex, Yorkshire and Glamorgan.

For further information on Britain's Geographical Counties, see:
http://www.abcounties.co.uk/index.htm

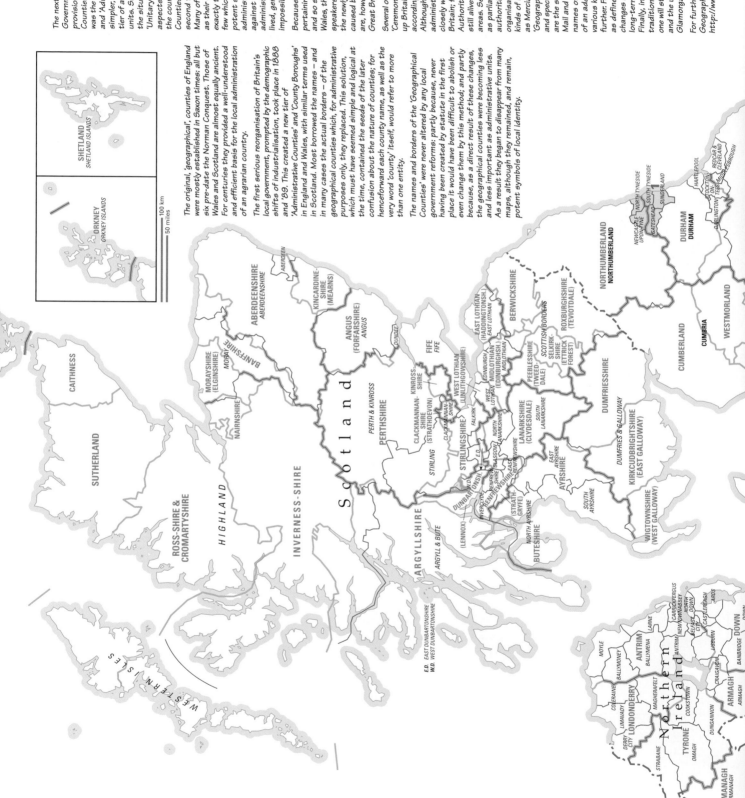

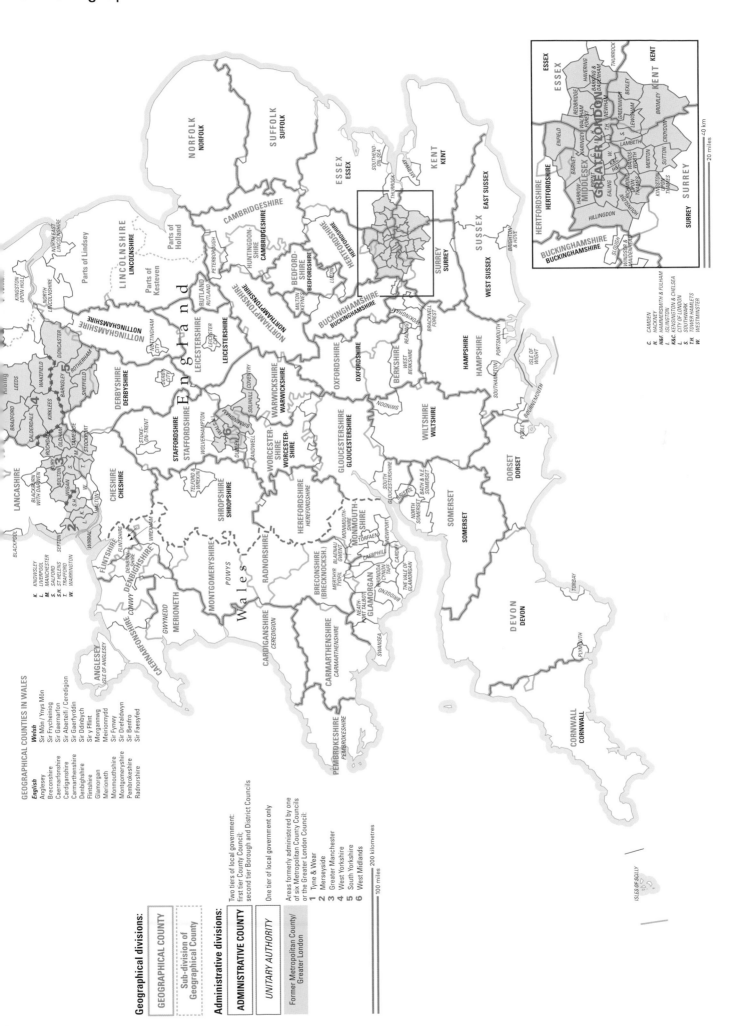

Geographical divisions:

GEOGRAPHICAL COUNTY

Sub-division of Geographical County

Administrative divisions:

ADMINISTRATIVE COUNTY

UNITARY AUTHORITY — One tier of local government only

Two tiers of local government: first tier County Council; second tier Borough and District Councils

Areas formerly administered by one of six Metropolitan County Councils or the Greater London Council:

Former Metropolitan County/ Greater London

1 Tyne & Wear
2 Merseyside
3 Greater Manchester
4 West Yorkshire
5 South Yorkshire
6 West Midlands

GEOGRAPHICAL COUNTIES IN WALES

English	Welsh
Anglesey	Sir Môn / Ynys Môn
Breconshire	Sir Frycheiniog
Caernarfonshire	Sir Gaernarfon
Cardiganshire	Sir Aberteifi / Ceredigion
Carmarthenshire	Sir Gaerfyrddin
Denbighshire	Sir Ddinbych
Flintshire	Sir y Fflint
Glamorgan	Morgannwg
Merioneth	Meirionnydd
Monmouthshire	Sir Fynwy
Montgomeryshire	Sir Drefaldwyn
Pembrokeshire	Sir Benfro
Radnorshire	Sir Faesyfed

K. KNOWSLEY
L. LIVERPOOL
M. MANCHESTER
S. SALFORD
S.H. ST HELENS
T. TRAFFORD
W. WARRINGTON

C. CAMDEN
H. HACKNEY
H&F. HAMMERSMITH & FULHAM
I. ISLINGTON
K&C. KENSINGTON & CHELSEA
L. CITY OF LONDON
S. SOUTHWARK
T.H. TOWER HAMLETS
W. WESTMINSTER

100 miles   200 kilometres

20 miles   40 km

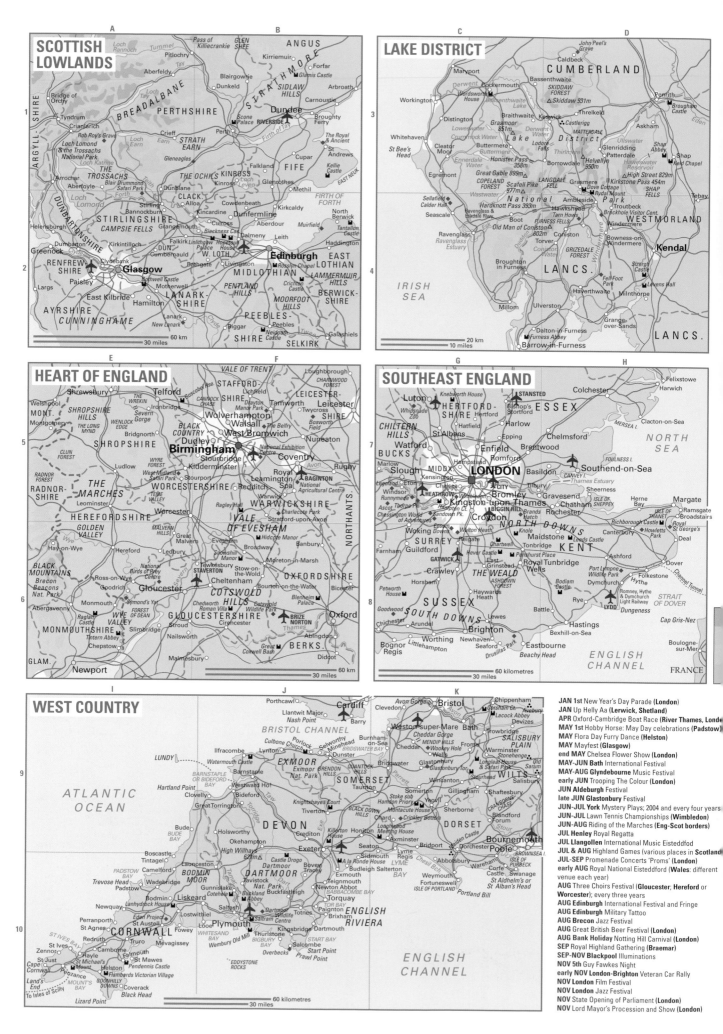

UK: Rail Operators

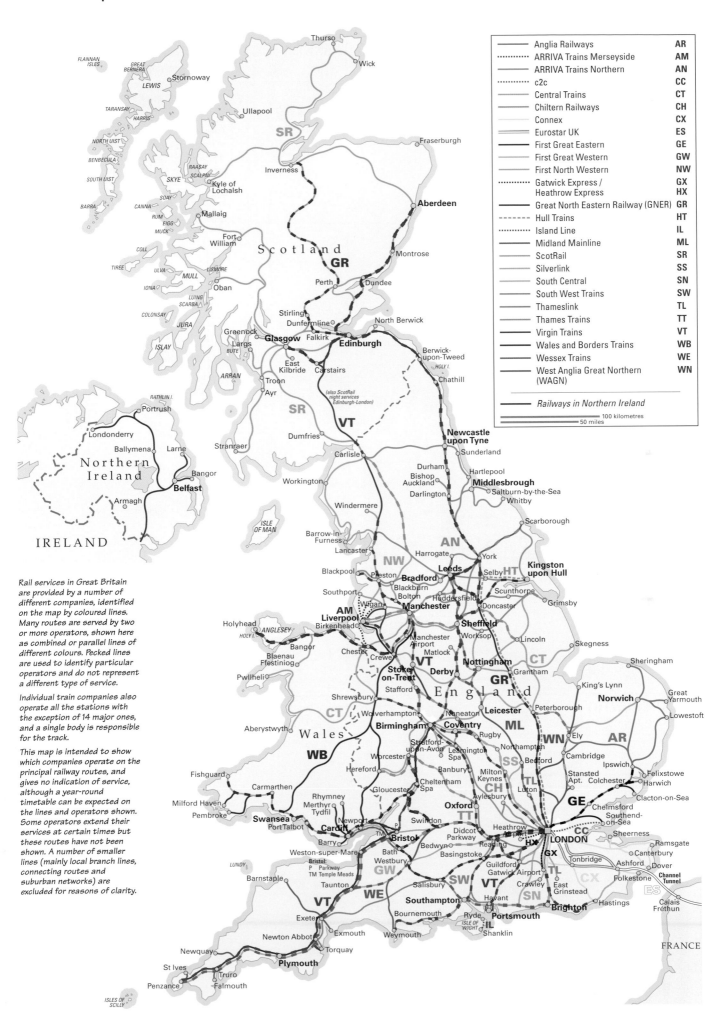

Legend:

Anglia Railways	AR
ARRIVA Trains Merseyside	AM
ARRIVA Trains Northern	AN
c2c	CC
Central Trains	CT
Chiltern Railways	CH
Connex	CX
Eurostar UK	ES
First Great Eastern	GE
First Great Western	GW
First North Western	NW
Gatwick Express /	GX
Heathrow Express	HX
Great North Eastern Railway (GNER)	GR
Hull Trains	HT
Island Line	IL
Midland Mainline	ML
ScotRail	SR
Silverlink	SS
South Central	SN
South West Trains	SW
Thameslink	TL
Thames Trains	TT
Virgin Trains	VT
Wales and Borders Trains	WB
Wessex Trains	WE
West Anglia Great Northern (WAGN)	WN

Railways in Northern Ireland

100 kilometres
50 miles

Rail services in Great Britain are provided by a number of different companies, identified on the map by coloured lines. Many routes are served by two or more operators, shown here as combined or parallel lines of different colours. Pecked lines are used to identify particular operators and do not represent a different type of service.

Individual train companies also operate all the stations with the exception of 14 major ones, and a single body is responsible for the track.

This map is intended to show which companies operate on the principal railway routes, and gives no indication of service, although a year-round timetable can be expected on the lines and operators shown. Some operators extend their services at certain times but these routes have not been shown. A number of smaller lines (mainly local branch lines, connecting routes and suburban networks) are excluded for reasons of clarity.

UK: Airports, Motorways & Ferries

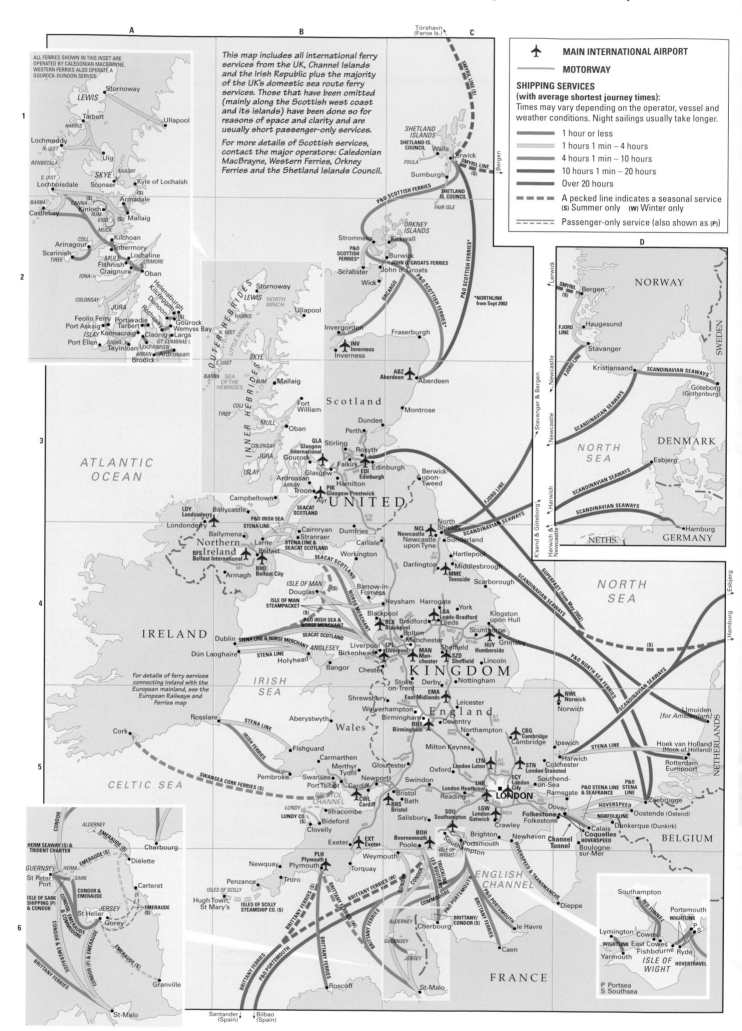

This map includes all international ferry services from the UK, Channel Islands and the Irish Republic plus the majority of the UK's domestic sea route ferry services. Those that have been omitted (mainly along the Scottish west coast and its islands) have been done so for reasons of space and clarity and are usually short passenger-only services.

For more details of Scottish services, contact the major operators: Caledonian MacBrayne, Western Ferries, Orkney Ferries and the Shetland Islands Council.

✈ MAIN INTERNATIONAL AIRPORT
—— MOTORWAY

SHIPPING SERVICES
(with average shortest journey times):
Times may vary depending on the operator, vessel and weather conditions. Night sailings usually take longer.

— 1 hour or less
— 1 hours 1 min – 4 hours
— 4 hours 1 min – 10 hours
— 10 hours 1 min – 20 hours
— Over 20 hours
- - - A pecked line indicates a seasonal service
(S) Summer only (W) Winter only
- - - Passenger-only service (also shown as (P))

ALL FERRIES SHOWN IN THIS INSET ARE OPERATED BY CALEDONIAN MACBRAYNE. WESTERN FERRIES ALSO OPERATE A GOUROCK-DUNOON SERVICE.

UK: London Airport Connections

This diagram shows principal public transport connections to London's airports from central London and links between airports.

It is not drawn to scale. Connections are shown as simple lines to improve legibility.

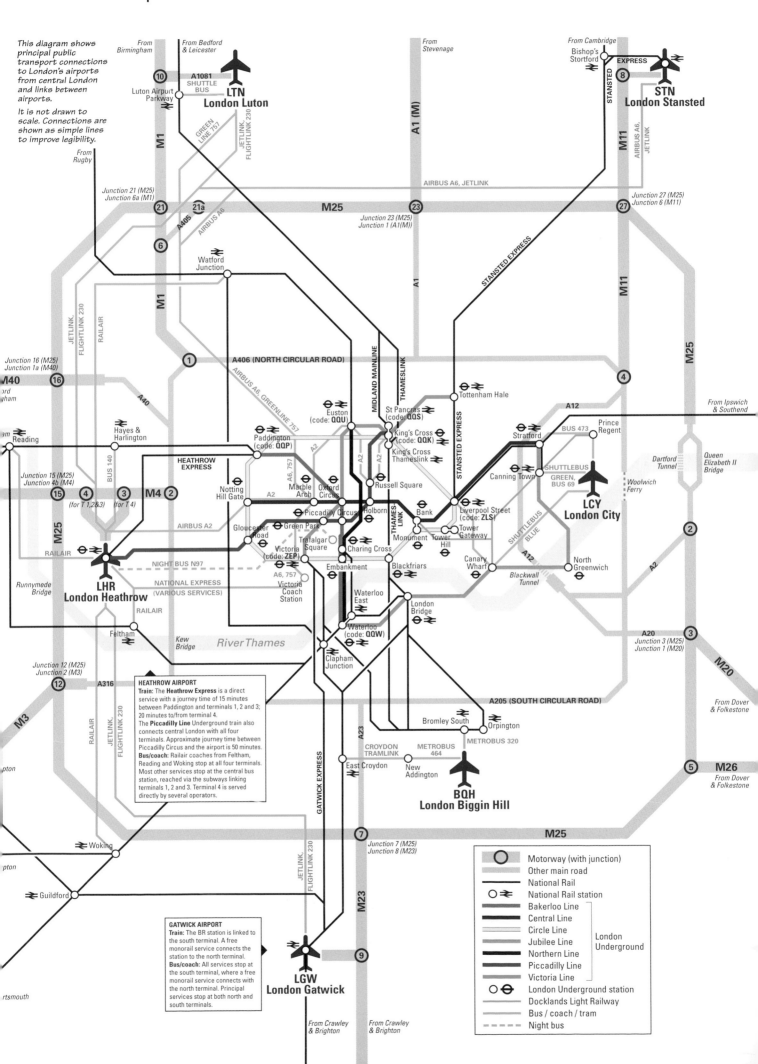

HEATHROW AIRPORT
Train: The **Heathrow Express** is a direct service with a journey time of 15 minutes between Paddington and terminals 1, 2 and 3; 20 minutes to/from terminal 4.
The **Piccadilly Line** Underground train also connects central London with all four terminals. Approximate journey time between Piccadilly Circus and the airport is 50 minutes.
Bus/coach: Railair coaches from Feltham, Reading and Woking stop at all four terminals. Most other services stop at the central bus station, reached via the subways linking terminals 1, 2 and 3. Terminal 4 is served directly by several operators.

GATWICK AIRPORT
Train: The BR station is linked to the south terminal. A free monorail service connects the station to the north terminal.
Bus/coach: All services stop at the south terminal, where a free monorail service connects with the north terminal. Principal services stop at both north and south terminals.

Legend

⬤	Motorway (with junction)
	Other main road
	National Rail
O≠	National Rail station
	Bakerloo Line
	Central Line
	Circle Line
	Jubilee Line · London Underground
	Northern Line
	Piccadilly Line
	Victoria Line
O⬤	London Underground station
	Docklands Light Railway
	Bus / coach / tram
- - -	Night bus

Ireland

Legend
- – – – County boundary
- ● County capital
- Province boundary

200 km
100 miles

A   B

TORY I.
Inishowen Peninsula
ARAN I.
ULSTER
Letterkenny
Lifford
DONEGAL
Donegal
Northern Ireland (UK)
Lough Neagh
Lower Lough Erne

MULLET PENINSULA
Sligo
ACHILL I.
Ballina
SLIGO
CLARE I.
MAYO
NOC Knock
Castlebar
Carrick-on-Shannon
LEITRIM
Upper Lough Erne
Monaghan
MONAGHAN
CAVAN
ULSTER
Dundalk (Dún Dealgan)
LOUTH
INISHBOFIN
Westport
CONNACHT (CONNAUGHT)
ROSCOMMON
Longford
LONGFORD
MEATH
Drogheda (Droichead Átha)
DUBLIN & EAST COAST
MURRISK
Roscommon
Mullingar
WESTMEATH
Trim
DUB Dublin
CONNEMARA
GALWAY
Athlone
Royal Canal
DUBLIN (BAILE ÁTHA CLIATH)
ARAN ISLANDS
Galway (Gaillimh)
Ballinasloe
OFFALY
BOG OF ALLEN
Grand Canal
DUBLIN Dún Laoghaire
Tullamore
THE BURREN
Lough Derg
Portlaoise
LAOIS
Naas
KILDARE
WICKLOW MTNS
Wicklow
CLARE
Ennis
SNN Shannon
Roscrea
LEINSTER
WICKLOW
Carlow
MOUTH OF THE SHANNON
Limerick (Luimneach)
TIPPERARY
North Riding
Kilkenny
CARLOW
Arklow
Dingle Peninsula
Tralee (Traighli)
KERRY
LIMERICK
Cashel
South Riding
KILKENNY
WEXFORD
GREAT BLASKET I.
Clonmel
Wexford
VALENTIA I.
MUNSTER
Tipperary
Rosslare
IVERAGH PENINSULA
Killarney
CORK
WATERFORD
Waterford (Port Láirge)
Beara Peninsula
Cork (Corcaigh)
Dungarvan
BEAR I.
Bantry
ORK Cork
WEST COAST

WEST COAST

International arrivals (millions)

Source: World Tourism Organisation

(chart: 1980 1985 1990 1995 2000; values 0–7)

MAR 17th St Patrick's Day
APR-MAY Cork International Choral Festival
JUL Galway Arts Festival
JUL Fleadh Cheoil na Éireann (different venue each year)
AUG Rose of **Tralee** International Festival
AUG Puck Fair **(Killorglin)**
AUG Royal **Dublin** Society's Horse Show
AUG Kilkenny International Arts Week
SEP Lisdoonvarna Matchmaking Festival
OCT Cork Film Festival
OCT Cork Jazz Festival
OCT-NOV Wexford Opera Festival

WEST COAST

E   F

INISHMURRAY
Bundoran
Benwee Head
Céide Fields
Ballycastle
Lissadell House
Drumcliff
Benbulbin 525m
LEITRIM
MULLET PENINSULA
Belmullet
KILLALA BAY
Killala
Inishcrone
SLIGO BAY
Rosses Pt.
Bangor
INISHKEA NORTH / INISHKEA SOUTH
Crossmolina
Moyne Abbey
Ballina
SLIEVE GAMPH (OX MTNS)
Tobercurry
Sligo
L. Gill
Creerlea
Colloney
BLACKSOD BAY
Achill Head
Keel
ACHILL ISLAND
CORRAUN PEN.
Mulranny
NEPHIN BEG RANGE
Nephin
Lough Conn
Foxford
Achonry
Ballymote
L. Arrow
Key
Newport
MAYO
Castlebar
KNOCK
Charlestown
Ballaghaderreen
Tulsk
CLARE I.
CLEW BAY
Westport House
Westport
Ballintober
PLAINS OF MAYO
Knock
Ballyhaunis
ROSCOMMON
Castlerea
Louisburgh
Croagh Patrick 765m
MURRISK
Claremorris
Dunmore
Roscommon
INISHTURK
Mweelrea 819m
PARTRY MTNS
Ballinrobe
L. Carra
Suck
INISHBOFIN / INISHARK
Letterfrack
JOYCE'S COUNTRY
Lough Mask
PLAINS OF ELLERTRIN
Cong
Connemara Nat. Park
Clifden
MAAM TURK MTNS
Ross Abbey
Tuam
Athenry
Ballinasloe
Slyne Head
THE TWELVE BENS
CONNEMARA
Oughterard
Claregalway Abbey
GALWAY
Kilconnell Friary
Roundstone
IAR-CHONNACHT
Lough Corrib
Loughrea
LETTERMORE
Carraroe
Spiddal
GALWAY BAY
Galway (Gaillimh)
SLIEVE AUGHTY MTNS
GORUMNA I.
INISHMORE
Dún Aengus
Kilronan
Ballyvaughan
Kinvarra
Portumna
Lough Derg
ARAN ISLANDS
INISHMAAN
INISHEER
Lisdoonvarna
THE BURREN
Gort
Kilmacduagh
Cliffs of Moher
Doolin
Kilfenora
Mountshannon
ATLANTIC OCEAN
Lehinch
Ennistymon
Corofin
Milltown Malbay
Ennis (Inis)
Tulla
Nenagh
CLARE
Killaloe
TIPP.
Kilkee
Clare Abbey
Newmarket on Fergus
Bunratty Castle & Folk Park
Castleconnell
CLARE GLENS
Falls of Doonass
Loop Head
SHANNON
Kilrush
Limerick (Luimneach)
MOUTH OF THE SHANNON
Tarbert
Foynes
LIMERICK
Ballybunion
Castle Matrix
Rathkeale
Adare
Lough Gur
Kerry Head
Listowel
Newcastle West
Tipperary
Ballyheige
Abbeyfeale
Kilmallock
Moor Abbey
TRALEE BAY
Ardfert
Fenit
Castlegregory
Cloghane
SLIEVE MISH MTNS
Tralee (Traighli)
MULLAGHAREIRK MOUNTAINS
Rath Luirc
GALTY MTNS
Brandon Mountain 953m
Castleisland
Buttevant
DINGLE PENINSULA
Gallarus Oratory
Dunquin
Dingle
KERRY
Castlemaine
Newmarket
Kanturk Castle
Mitchelstown
GREAT BLASKET I.
DINGLE BAY
Anascaul
Ventry
Glenbeigh
Killorglin
Mallow
Fermoy
Gap of Dunloe
Blackwater
VALENTIA I.
Lakes of Killarney
Muckross Abbey
Millstreet
BOGGERAGH MTNS
Ring of Kerry
Cahirciveen
Carrauntoohil 1041m
MACGILLICUDDY'S REEKS
Killarney Nat. Park
DERRYNASAGGART MOUNTAINS
Carrigadrohid Reservoir
Blarney
IVERAGH PENINSULA
Kenmare
Macroom
Cork (Corcaigh)
Midleton
Waterville
Staigue Fort
Sneem
Lee
CORK
LITTLE SKELLIG
Caherdaniel
KENMARE R.
Cobh
SKELLIG MICHAEL (GREAT SKELLIG)
SCARIFF I.
Crosshaven
Glengarriff
Kilcrea Abbey
BEARA PENINSULA
Castletownbere
Dunmanway
Bandon
Kinsale
Allihies
BEAR I.
WHIDDY I.
Bantry
Clonakilty
Courtmacsherry
DURSEY I.
BANTRY BAY
Ballydehob
Leap
Ross Carbery
Old Head of Kinsale
Sheep's Head
CLONAKILTY BAY
DUNMANUS BAY
Schull
Skibbereen
Baltimore
SHERKIN I.
Mizen Head
CLEAR I.
Cape Clear

60 km
30 miles

DUBLIN & EAST COAST

C   D

Sliabh Na Caillighe 276m
Kells (Ceanannas Mór)
Mellifont Abbey
Slane
Clogher Head
Fore Abbey
Knowth
Dowth
Drogheda (Droichead Átha)
IRISH SEA
Delvin
Clonmellon
Newgrange
Brú Na Bóinne
Donore
Duleek
WESTMEATH
Ballivor
Bective Abbey
Navan (An Uaimh)
Blackwater
Balbriggan
Delvin
Athboy
Boyne
Tara
Skerries
Ballinor
Trim
MEATH
Naul
Rush
Kinnegad
Dunshaughlin
Ashbourne
DUBLIN
Donabate
LAMBAY I.
Royal Canal
Innfield
Maynooth
Swords
IRELAND'S EYE
Carbury
Kilcock
Dunboyne
Malahide
Portmarnock
Edenderry
Leixlip
Lucan
Phoenix Park
Howth
BOG OF ALLEN
Castletown House
DUBLIN (BAILE ÁTHA CLIATH)
OFFALY
Rathcoole
Grand Canal
Robertstown
Sallins
DUBLIN BAY
Peatland World
Naas
Dún Laoghaire
DALKEY I.
Portarlington
Kildare
Droichead Nua
Punchestown
Leopardstown
Seapoint
Dalkey
Killiney
The Curragh
Rathangan
Enniskerry
Powerscourt House
GLENCREE
Bray
Monasterevin
Kilcullen
Russborough House
Blessington
Bray Head
Vicarstown
Old Kilcullen
Ballymore Eustace
Lacken Reservoir
Greystones
KILDARE
Dunlavin
WICKLOW MOUNTAINS
Stradbally
Athy
Ballitore
Moone
Glendalough
LAOIS
Ballylynan
Dunboyne
Baltinglass
Lugnaquillia 926m
GLENMALURE
WICKLOW
Wicklow
Wicklow Head
Rathdrum
VALE OF AVOCA
Castledermot
Rathvilly
Aughrim
Avoca
BRITTAS BAY
CARLOW
Carlow
Tinahely
Mizen Head
KILKENNY
Tullow
Arklow
WEXFORD
Kilmichael Point

40 kilometres / 20 miles

Benelux

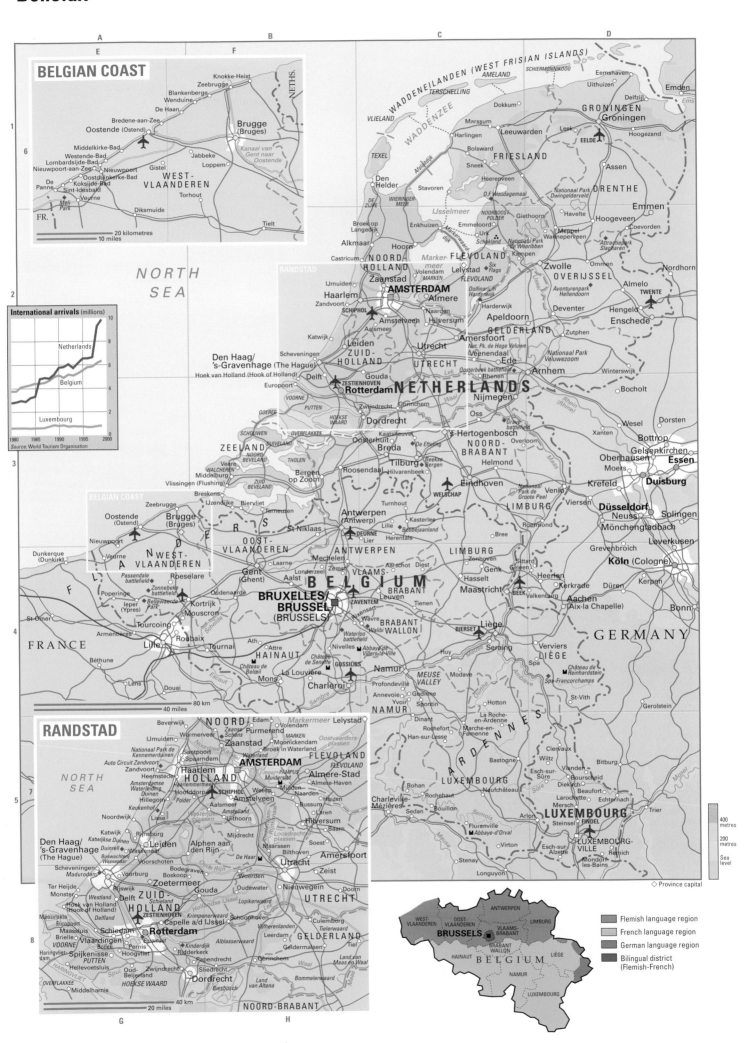

Netherlands: Attractions

Legend:
- Theme park, leisure park
- Museum, gallery
- Religious building
- Park, flowers, zoo
- Historic building
- Water-related attraction (canal, dam, lake, windmill)
- Other place of interest

Attractions in cities marked in **red** are listed on the left of the map

Amsterdam
MUSEUM AMSTELKRING
AMSTERDAMS HISTORISCH MUSEUM
ANNE FRANKHUIS
JOODS HISTORISCH MUSEUM
MADAME TUSSAUD SCENERAMA
MUSEUM HET REMBRANDTHUIS
NEDERLANDS SCHEEPVAART MUSEUM
NEW METROPLIS
RIJKSMUSEUM
STEDELIJK MUSEUM
TROPENMUSEUM
VAN GOGH MUSEUM
NIEUWE KERK
WESTERKERK
ARTIS
BLOEMENMARKT
BEGIJNHOF
KONINKLIJK PALEIS
Amsterdam canals (grachten)

Haarlem
FRANS HALSMUSEUM
TEYLERS MUSEUM
ST BAVOKERK
VLEESHAL
GROTE MARKT

Leiden
MUSEUM BOERHAAVE
NATURALIS
STEDELIJK MUSEUM DE LAKENHAL
RIJKSMUSEUM VAN OUDHEDEN
RIJKSMUSEUM VOOR VOLKENKUNDE
DE BURCHT

Den Haag (The Hague)
MADURODAM
MUSEUM VOOR COMMUNICATIE
GEMEENTEMUSEUM
MAURITSHUIS
MUSEUM & PANORAMA MESDAG
MUSEON
SCHILDERIJENGALERIJ PRINS WILLEM V
BINNENHOF

Gouda
STEDELIJK MUS. HET CATHARINA GASTHUIS
ST JANSKERK
STADHUIS

Delft
KONINKLIJK NEDERLANDS
LEGER- EN WAPENMUSEUM
PRINSENHOF
NIEUWE KERK

Rotterdam
MUSEUM BOYMANS-VAN BEUNINGEN
MUSEUM DE DUBBELDE PALMBOOM
HISTORISCH MUSEUM
HET SCHIELANDSHUIS
NEDERLANDS ARCHITECTUURINSTITUUT
DIERGAARDE BLIJDORP
Boat trips to the port
ERASMUSBRUG
EUROMAST

Utrecht
CENTRAAL MUSEUM
MUSEUM HET CATHARIJNECONVENT
NATIONAAL MUSEUM VAN
SPEELKLOK TOT PIEREMENT
NEDERLANDS SPOORWEGMUSEUM
DOMKERK & DOMTOREN
PIETERSKERK
RIETVELD SCHRÖDERHUIS

Festivals:
FEB/MAR Carnaval (**Breda, Maastricht** & **'s-Hertogenbosch**)
MAR Stille Ommegang: silent procession (**Amsterdam**)
MAR-MAY National Floral Exhibition (**Keukenhof**)
APR Floral Procession (**Haarlem to Noordwijk**)
APR 30th Koninginnedag: Queen's Birthday
MAY-SEP Passion Plays (**Tegelen**); 2005 and every five years
JUN Holland Festival (**Amsterdam**)
JUL North Sea Jazz Festival (**The Hague**)
AUG International Fireworks Festival (**Scheveningen**)
AUG-SEP Festival of Ancient Music (**Utrecht**)
SEP Bloemen Corso: floral procession (**Aalsmeer to Amsterdam**)
SEP Jordaan Festival (**Amsterdam**)
OCT 3rd Leidens Ontzet: historical procession (**Leiden**)
mid NOV St Nicholas' official entrance (**Amsterdam**)
DEC Candle Festival (**Gouda**)

Germany

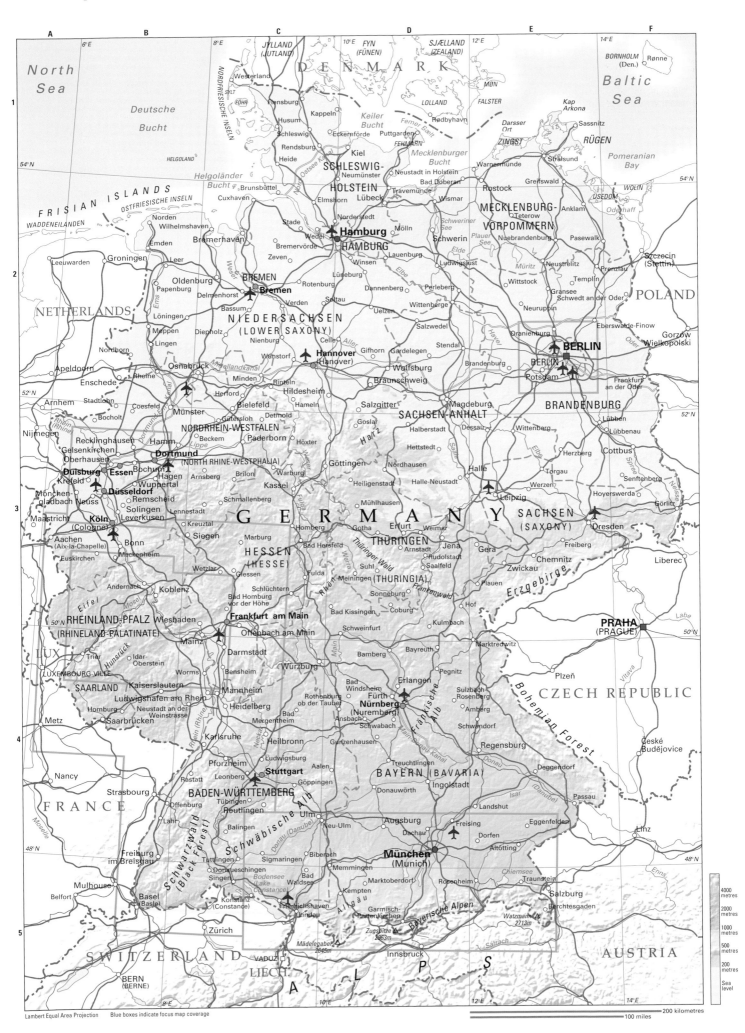

North Sea
Deutsche Bucht
Baltic Sea
DENMARK
JYLLAND (JUTLAND)
FYN (FÜNEN)
SJÆLLAND (ZEALAND)
BORNHOLM (Den.)
Rønne
MØN
LOLLAND
FALSTER
Darsser Ort
ZINGST
Kap Arkona
RÜGEN
Sassnitz
Pomeranian Bay
WOLIN
USEDOM
Oderhaff
POLAND
Szczecin (Stettin)
Gorzów Wielkopolski
Eberswalde-Finow
BERLIN
BRANDENBURG
Frankfurt an der Oder
SACHSEN (SAXONY)
Dresden
Görlitz
Liberec
PRAHA (PRAGUE)
CZECH REPUBLIC
Bohemian Forest
Plzeň
České Budějovice
Linz
AUSTRIA
Salzburg
Berchtesgaden

HELGOLAND
FRISIAN ISLANDS
OSTFRIESISCHE INSELN
WADDENEILANDEN
NORDFRIESISCHE INSELN
SYLT
FÖHR

NETHERLANDS
Leeuwarden
Groningen
Enschede
Arnhem
Nijmegen
Maastricht
Aachen (Aix-la-Chapelle)

SCHLESWIG-HOLSTEIN
HAMBURG
BREMEN
NIEDERSACHSEN (LOWER SAXONY)
MECKLENBURG-VORPOMMERN
NORDRHEIN-WESTFALEN (NORTH RHINE-WESTPHALIA)
SACHSEN-ANHALT
HESSEN (HESSE)
THÜRINGEN (THURINGIA)
RHEINLAND-PFALZ (RHINELAND-PALATINATE)
SAARLAND
BADEN-WÜRTTEMBERG
BAYERN (BAVARIA)

GERMANY

FRANCE
SWITZERLAND
ALPS
LIECH.
LUX.

Hamburg
HAMBURG
Bremen
BREMEN
Hannover (Hanover)
BERLIN
Dortmund
Duisburg
Essen
Düsseldorf
Köln (Cologne)
Frankfurt am Main
Nürnberg (Nuremberg)
Stuttgart
München (Munich)

4000 metres
2000 metres
1000 metres
500 metres
200 metres
Sea level

Lambert Equal Area Projection   Blue boxes indicate focus map coverage

200 kilometres
100 miles

Germany

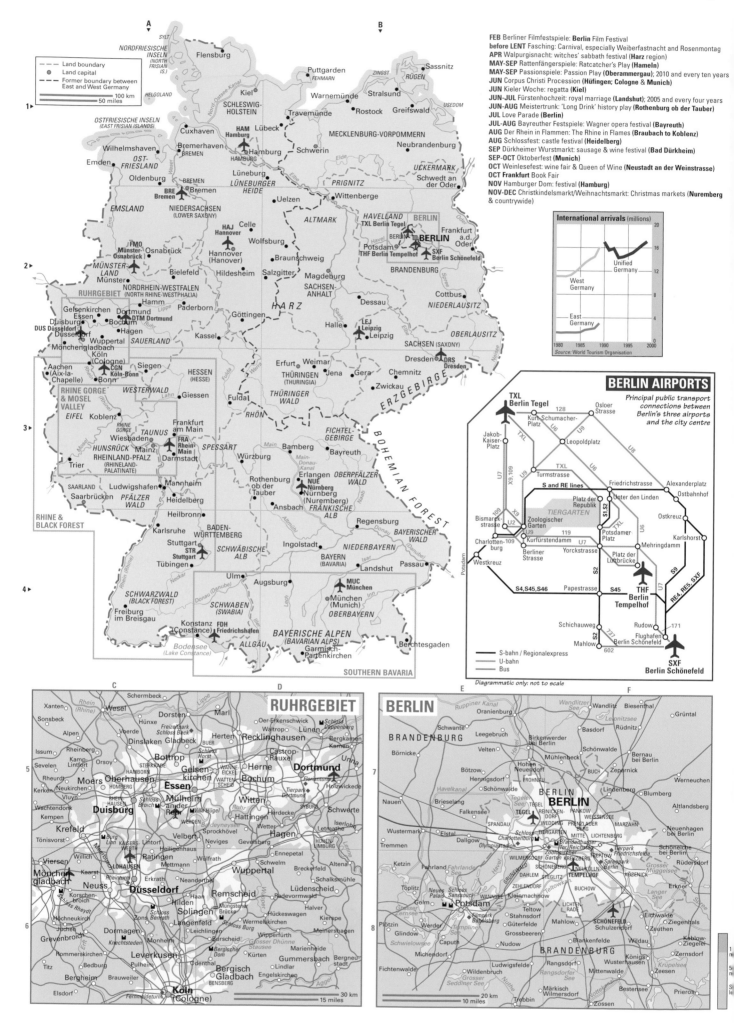

Germany

Germany has a well-developed network of tourist routes passing through areas of scenic or historic interest. Some of the most well-known are:

Romantische Strasse (Romantic Road). Established in 1950, the route runs for 350 kilometres from northern Bavaria to the Austrian border. See panel for the route.

Strasse der Kaiser und Könige (Route of Emperors and Kings). One of Germany's oldest transit routes, running from Frankfurt am Main in the west, following the Main and Danube rivers to Passau and then continuing to Vienna.

Weinstrasse (Wine Road). Germany's oldest designated tourist route, passing through the vineyards of the Pfalz.

Mosel Weinstrasse (Mosel Wine Road). Follows the Mosel from Trier to Koblenz. Boat cruises are popular along this stretch of river.

Deutsche Märchenstrasse (German Fairy-Tale Road). This route runs from Bremen to the River Main through many places connected with fairy tales.

Burgenstrasse (Castle Road). Passes many fortifications in the Neckar valley between Mannheim and Heilbronn, then continues east to Nuremberg.

Schwarzwald-Hochstrasse (Black Forest Scenic Route). One of Germany's most famous roads, linking Baden-Baden with Freudenstadt.

ROMANTIC ROAD

- **Würzburg**
- Tauberbischofsheim
- Bad Morgentheim
- Weikersheim
- Röttingen
- Creglingen
- **Rothenburg ob der Tauber**
- Schillingsfürst
- Feuchtwangen
- Dinkelsbühl
- Wallerstein
- **Nördlingen im Ries**
- Harburg
- **Donauwörth**
- **Augsburg**
- Friedberg
- **Landsberg am Lech**
- Hohenfurch
- Schongau
- Peiting
- Rottenbuch
- Wildsteig
- Wieskirche
- Steingaden
- Schwangau
- **Füssen**

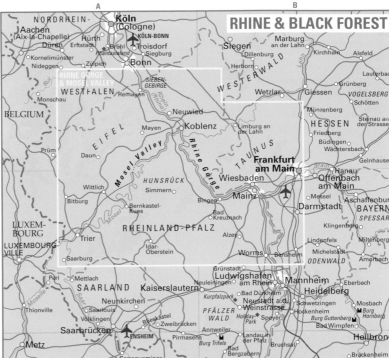

RHINE & BLACK FOREST

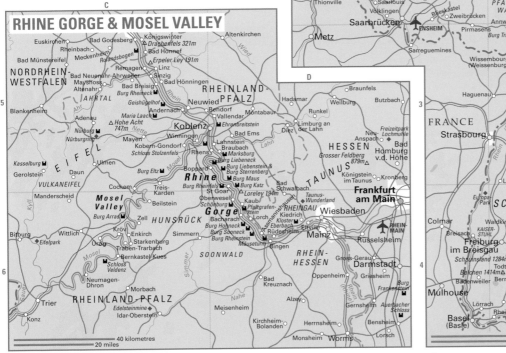

RHINE GORGE & MOSEL VALLEY

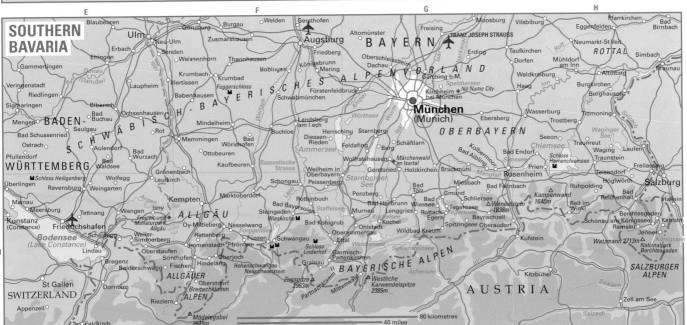

SOUTHERN BAVARIA

1000 metres
500 metres
Sea level

Germany: Attractions

Theme park, leisure park
Museum, gallery
Religious building
Park, reserve, zoo, etc.
Historic building
Water-related attraction
Other place of interest

Attractions in cities marked in **red**
are listed around the edge of the map

100 kilometres
50 miles

SYLT
NORDFRIESISCHE INSELN
Westerland
Flensburg
NORDFRIESISCHE
Schleswig
NATIONALPARK
SCHLESWIG-
HOLSTEINISCHES
WATTENMEER
NYDAM-BOOT
Husum
Puttgarden
FEHMARN
Kiel
FREILICHTMUSEUM
HINDENBURGUFER
KIELER FÖRDE
FAMILIEN-FREIZEITPARK
TOLK-SCHAU
NATIONALPARK
JASMUND
Sassnitz
NATIONALPARK
VORPOMMERSCHE
BODDENLANDSCHAFT
RÜGEN
ZINGST
Stralsund
USEDOM

SCHLESWIG-
HOLSTEIN
HELGOLAND
Itzehoe
HANSAPARK
Travemünde
Lübeck
ALTSTADT
Schwerin
SCHLOSS
Schweriner
See
Warnemünde
Rostock
Greifswald
MECKLENBURG-VORPOMMERN
Neubrandenburg
TOWN FORTIFICATIONS
Neustrelitz

NATIONALPARK
HAMBURGISCHES
WATTENMEER
Cuxhaven
NATIONALPARK
NIEDERSÄCHSISCHES
WATTENMEER
Norden
Wilhelmshaven
Emden
Hamburg
HAMBURG
Ludwigslust
SCHLOSS
Elde
Wittenberge
Müritz
MÜRITZ-
NATIONALPARK
Schwedt an
der Oder
NATIONALPARK
UNTERES ODERTAL

BREMEN
Bremerhaven
DEUTSCHES SCHIFFFAHRTSMUSEUM
Oldenburg
BREMEN
Bremen
FOCKE-MUSEUM
MARKTPLATZ
Delmenhorst
Lüneburg
RATHAUS
Eberswalde-
Finow
Wittstock
SCHLOSS RHEINSBERG
Oder

FERIENZENTRUM
SCHLOSS DANKERN
Lingen
Nordhorn
Diepholz
NIEDERSACHSEN
(LOWER SAXONY)
HEIDE-PARK
Uelzen
SERENGETI SAFARIPARK
Celle
KLOSTER WIENHAUSEN
ALTSTADT
Stendal
BRANDENBURG
BERLIN
BERLIN
Frankfurt an
der Oder

Recklinghausen
IKONENMUSEUM
DINOSAURIER PARK
MÜNCHEHAGEN
Minden
SCHACHTSCHLEUSE
Hannover
(Hanover)
SPRENGEL MUSEUM
HERRENHÄUSER GÄRTEN
Wolfsburg
SACHSEN-
ANHALT
Brandenburg
Potsdam
FILMPARK BABELSBERG
NIKOLAIKIRCHE
SCHLOSS SANSSOUCI
NEUES PALAIS
Spree

Bochum
DEUTSCHES BERGBAU MUSEUM
Herford
Hameln
Braunschweig
Hildesheim
ROEMER-PELIZAEUS MUSEUM
Magdeburg
DOM
KLOSTER UNSER LIEBEN FRAUEN
Lübben

Essen
MUSEUM FOLKWANG
VILLA HÜGEL
Münster
DOM
Bielefeld
Salzgitter
ALTE LATEINSCHULE
Goslar
DOM ST STEPHANUS
DOMSCHATZ
Bad Gandersheim
Halberstadt
Lübbenau
Cottbus

SCHLOSS VISCHERING
SCHLOSS NORDKIRCHEN
HOLLYWOOD-PARK
Paderborn
Einbeck
MARKTPLATZ
TIEDEXERSTRASSE
NATIONALPARK
HOCHHARZ
Quedlinburg
STIFTSKIRCHE ST SERVATIUS
ALTSTADT
Dessau

WARNER BROS. MOVIE WORLD
Hamm
NORDRHEIN-WESTFALEN
(NORTH RHINE-WESTPHALIA)
Göttingen
Wernigerode
RATHAUS
FACHWERKHÄUSER
Halle
STAATLICHE GALERIE MORITZBURG
Torgau
Hoyerswerda

Oberhausen
Dortmund
SCHLOSS WILHELMSTHAL
Nordhausen
Merseburg
DOM
Leipzig
MUSEUM DER BILDENEN KUNST
Görlitz

Duisburg
Krefeld
Wuppertal
Hagen
Arnsberg
WESTFÄLISCHES
FREILICHTMUSEUM
FORT FUN ABENTEUERLAND
Kassel
WILHELMSHÖHE
THÜRINGEN
(THURINGIA)
Naumburg
DOM
Meissen
ALBRECHTSBURG
SCHLOSS MORITZBURG
Dresden
NATIONALPARK
SÄCHSISCHE
SCHWEIZ

Düsseldorf
Mönchengladbach
Neuss
Remscheid
Solingen
Leverkusen
PANORAMA SAUERLAND
Erfurt
DOM
Gotha
Weimar
SCHLOSSMUSEUM
GOETHEHAUS
GOETHES GARTENHAUS
SCHILLERHAUS
Jena
LINDENAU-MUSEUM
Altenburg
SACHSEN
(SAXONY)

SCHLOSS AUGUSTUSBURG &
JAGDSCHLOSS FALKENLUST
PHANTASIALAND
Köln
(Cologne)
Siegen
Marburg
ELISABETHKIRCHE
ALTSTADT
WARTBURG
Gera
Chemnitz
Annaberg-Buchholtz
ST ANNENKIRCHE

Aachen
(Aix-la-Chapelle)
DOM
Bonn
Monschau
FACHWERKHÄUSER
HESSEN
(HESSE)
Giessen
Fulda
Suhl
Zwickau
Plauen

Koblenz
EHRENBREITSTEIN
MARKSBURG
BURG ELTZ
BURG RHEINFELS
LORELEY
Wetzlar
BURG MÜNZENBERG
BURG KAISERPFALZ
Bad Homburg
vor der Höhe
WALLFAHRTSKIRCHE
VIERZEHNHEILIGEN
Hof

RHEINLAND-PFALZ
(RHINELAND-
PALATINATE)
EIFELPARK
MOSELTAL
RHEINTAL
Wiesbaden
Frankfurt am Main
Offenbach am Main
Schweinfurt
Main
PLASSENBURG
Bamberg
DOM
ALTES RATHAUS
Bayreuth
MARKGRÄFLICHES OPERNHAUS

Trier
DOM
PORTA NIGRA
HAUPTMARKT
Mosel
Rüdesheim
KLOSTER EBERBACH
BURG RHEINSTEIN
Mainz
GUTENBERG MUS.
DOM
Darmstadt
Aschaffenburg
Würzburg
RESIDENZ
SCHLOSS WEISSENSTEIN
Main-Donau
Kanal
Erlangen

Worms
STÄDTISCHE KUNSTHALLE
SCHLOSS
Mannheim
FREIZEIT-LAND
Rothenburg
ob der Tauber
ALTSTADT
Fürth
Nürnberg
(Nuremberg)

Ludwigshafen
am Rhein
Heidelberg
SCHLOSSGARTEN
SCHLOSS
SCHLOSS WEIKERSHEIM
Ansbach
SCHLOSS
GERMANISCHES NATIONALMUSEUM
SEBALDUSKIRCHE
Cham

Kaiserslautern
SAARLAND
Speyer
DOM
Bad Wimpfen
BAD WIMPFEN AM BERG
Schwäbisch Hall
MARKTPLATZ
Regensburg
DOM

Saarbrücken
ALTSTADT
HOLIDAY-PARK
Heilbronn
Eichstätt
BISCHÖFLICHER RESIDENZBEZIRK
Altmühl
Naab

BURG TRIFELS
SCHLOSS SCHWETZINGEN
Rastatt
SCHLOSS BRUCHSAL
ERLEBNISPARK TRIPSDRILL
Karlsruhe
MÄRCHENGARTEN
SCHLOSS
Ludwigsburg
Donauwörth
NATIONALPARK
BAYERISCHER WALD

SCHLOSS FAVORITE
Baden-Baden
LICHTENTALER ALLEE
Pforzheim
Stuttgart
LINDEN MUSEUM
STAATSGALERIE
Göppingen
Ingolstadt
Deggendorf

Offenburg
Tübingen
PLATANENALLEE
BADEN-
WÜRTTEMBERG
Reutlingen
Neckar
BAYERN
(BAVARIA)
Landshut
Passau
GLASMUSEUM
VESTE OBERHAUS

EUROPA-PARK
SCHWARZWALD
(BLACK FOREST)
SCHLOSS HOHENZOLLERN
Ulm
MÜNSTER
KONZENTRATIONSLAGER
DACHAU
Augsburg
FUGGEREI
Oberschleissheim
NEUES SCHLOSS
Eggenfelden
Burghausen

Freiburg im Breisgau
AUGUSTINERMUSEUM
MÜNSTER
Donaueschingen
ZWIEFALTENKIRCHE
Donau (Danube)
Memmingen
Ammersee
STARNBERGER SEE
München
(Munich)
BURG
Inn

Badenweiler
KURPARK
Konstanz
(Constance)
INSEL MAINAU
Friedrichshafen
Ottobeuren
KLOSTERKIRCHE
WIESKIRCHE
Chiemsee
Rosenheim
SCHLOSS HERRENCHIEMSEE

St Blasien
DOM
BODENSEE
(LAKE CONSTANCE)
LINDAU
Kempten
FREIZEIT- UND
MINIATURPARK PARK
KÖNIGSCHLÖSSER VON
HOHENSCHWANGAU
& NEUSCHWANSTEIN
SCHLOSS LINDERHOF
Oberammergau
Garmisch-Partenkirchen
PARTNACHKLAMM
WANK
ZUGSPTIZE
Berchtesgaden
KEHLSTEIN
NATIONALPARK
BERCHTESGADEN

Oberstdorf
BREITACHKLAMM
NEBELHORN

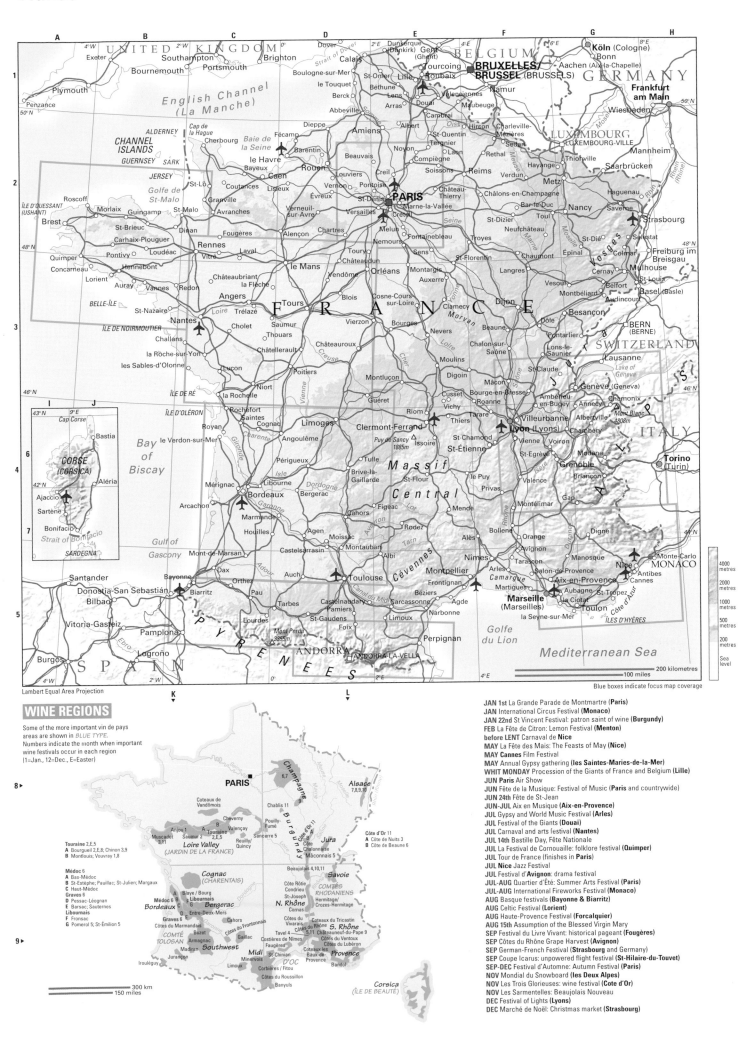

WINE REGIONS

Some of the more important vin de pays areas are shown in BLUE TYPE. Numbers indicate the month when important wine festivals occur in each region (1=Jan., 12=Dec., E=Easter)

Touraine 2,E,5
A Bourgueil 2,E,8; Chinon 3,9
B Montlouis; Vouvray 1,8

Médoc 6
A Bas-Médoc
B St-Estèphe; Pauillac; St-Julien; Margaux
C Haut-Médoc
Graves 6
D Pessac-Léognan
E Barsac; Sauternes
Libournais
F Fronsac
G Pomerol 5; St-Émilion 5

A Côte de Nuits 3
B Côte de Beaune 6

JAN 1st La Grande Parade de Montmartre (**Paris**)
JAN International Circus Festival (**Monaco**)
JAN 22nd St Vincent Festival: patron saint of wine (**Burgundy**)
FEB La Fête de Citron: Lemon Festival (**Menton**)
before LENT Carnaval de Nice
MAY La Fête des Mais: The Feasts of May (**Nice**)
MAY Cannes Film Festival
MAY Annual Gypsy gathering (**les Saintes-Maries-de-la-Mer**)
WHIT MONDAY Procession of the Giants of France and Belgium (**Lille**)
JUN Paris Air Show
JUN Fête de la Musique: Festival of Music (**Paris** and countrywide)
JUN 24th Fête de St-Jean
JUN-JUL Aix en Musique (**Aix-en-Provence**)
JUL Gypsy and World Music Festival (**Arles**)
JUL Festival of the Giants (**Douai**)
JUL Carnaval and arts festival (**Nantes**)
JUL 14th Bastille Day, Fête Nationale
JUL La Festival de Cornouaille: folklore festival (**Quimper**)
JUL Tour de France (finishes in **Paris**)
JUL Nice Jazz Festival
JUL Festival d'Avignon: drama festival
JUL-AUG Quartier d'Été: Summer Arts Festival (**Paris**)
JUL-AUG International Fireworks Festival (**Monaco**)
AUG Basque festivals (**Bayonne & Biarritz**)
AUG Celtic Festival (**Lorient**)
AUG Haute-Provence Festival (**Forcalquier**)
AUG 15th Assumption of the Blessed Virgin Mary
SEP Festival du Livre Vivant: historical pageant (**Fougères**)
SEP Côtes du Rhône Grape Harvest (**Avignon**)
SEP German-French Festival (**Strasbourg** and Germany)
SEP Coupe Icarus: unpowered flight festival (**St-Hilaire-du-Touvet**)
SEP-DEC Festival d'Automne: Autumn Festival (**Paris**)
NOV Mondial du Snowboard (**les Deux Alpes**)
NOV Les Trois Glorieuses: wine festival (**Cote d'Or**)
NOV Les Sarmentelles: Beaujolais Nouveau
DEC Festival of Lights (**Lyons**)
DEC Marché de Noël: Christmas market (**Strasbourg**)

France

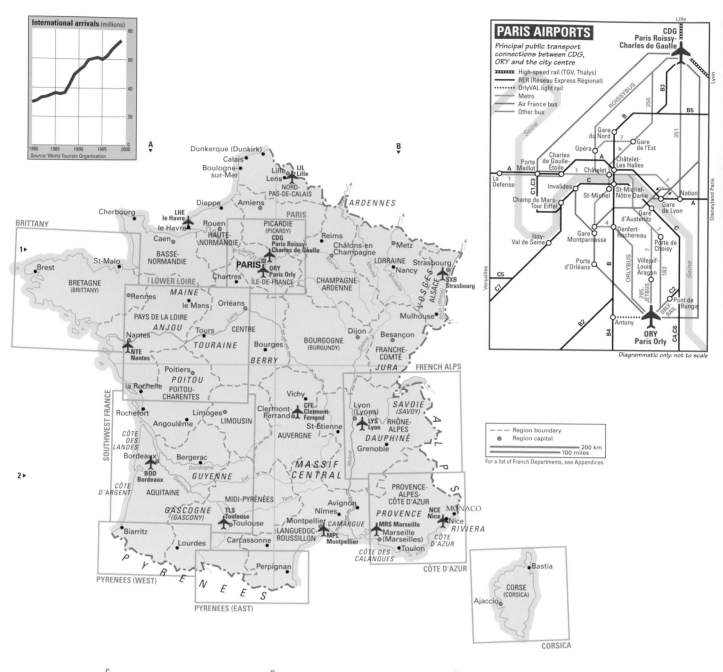

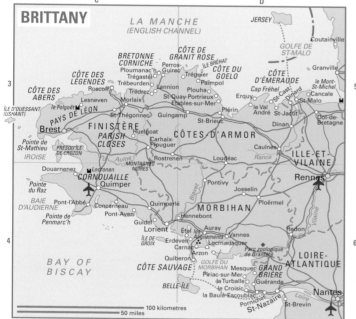

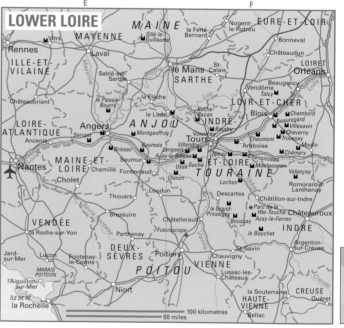

France

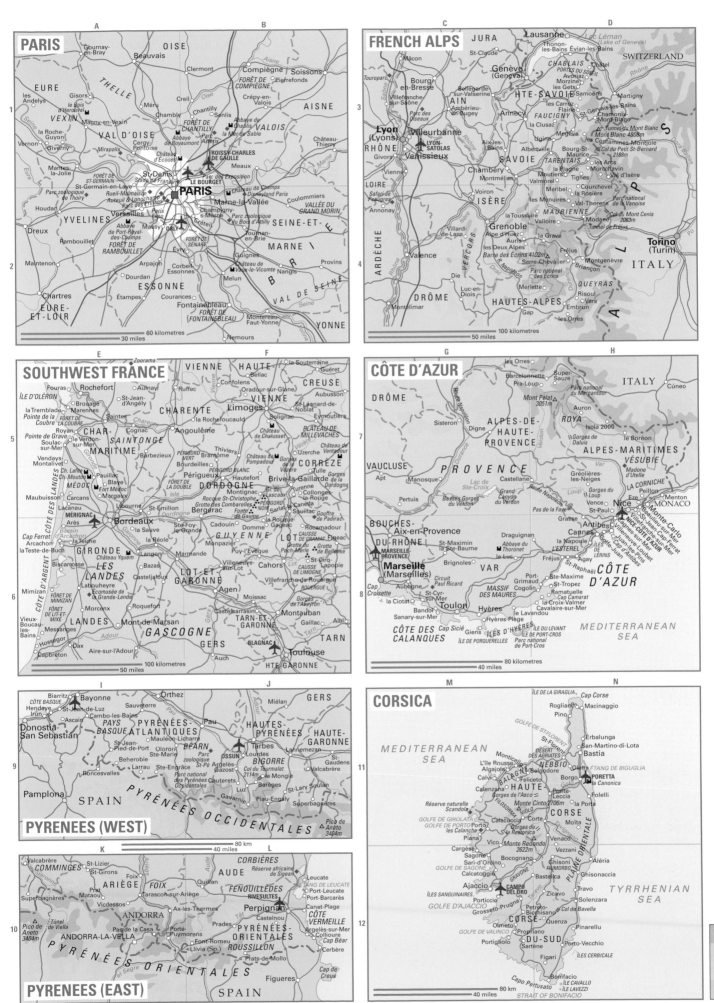

France: Attractions

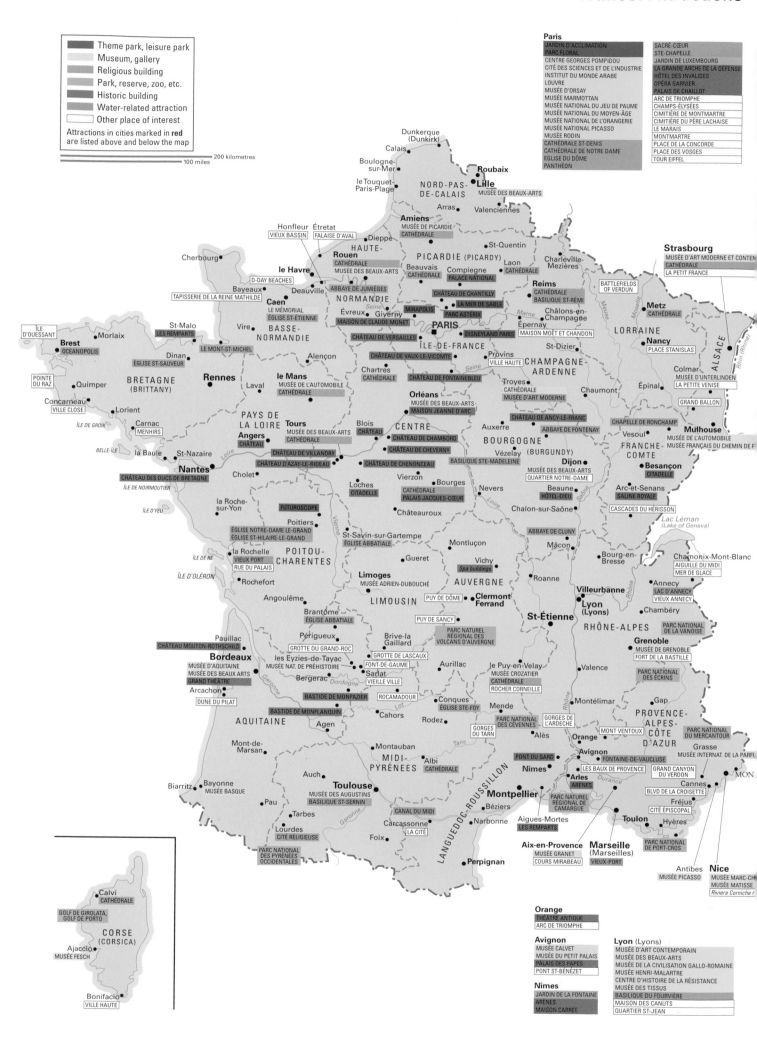

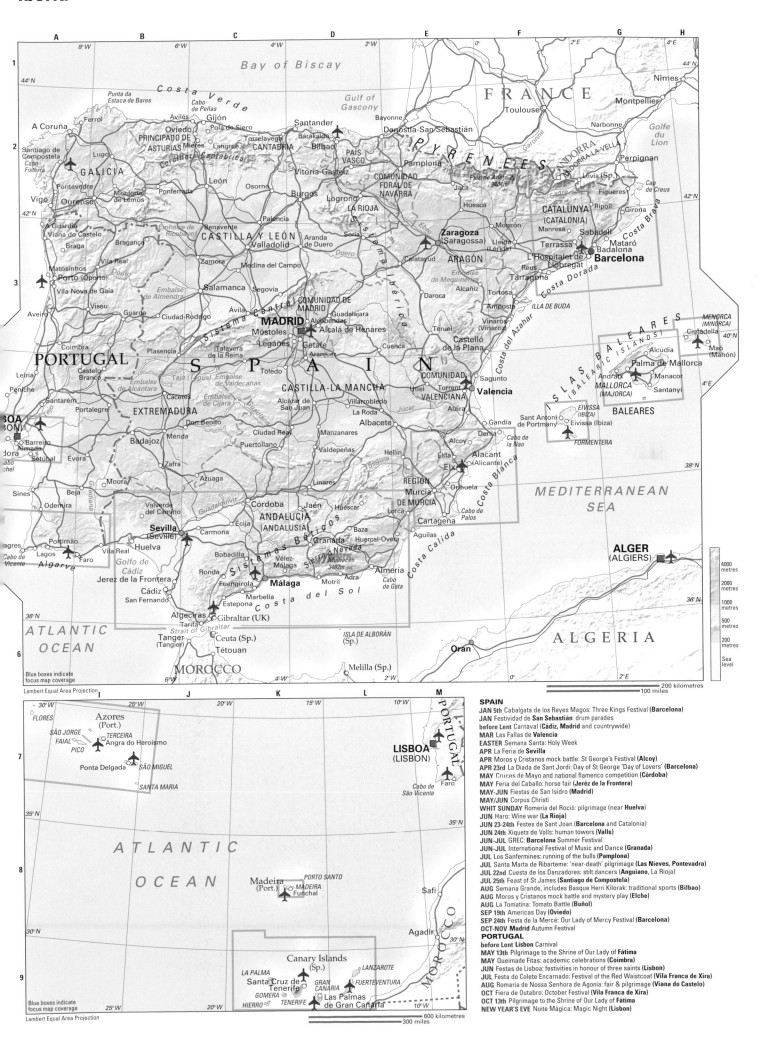

200 kilometres
100 miles

600 kilometres
300 miles

SPAIN
JAN 5th Cabalgata de los Reyes Magos: Three Kings Festival **(Barcelona)**
JAN Festividad de **San Sebastián**: drum parades
before Lent Carnaval **(Cádiz, Madrid** and countrywide)
MAR Las Fallas de **Valencia**
EASTER Semana Santa: Holy Week
APR La Feria de **Sevilla**
APR Moros y Cristianos mock battle: St George's Festival **(Alcoy)**
APR 23rd La Diada de Sant Jordi: Day of St George 'Day of Lovers' **(Barcelona)**
MAY Cruces de Mayo and national flamenco competition **(Córdoba)**
MAY Feria del Caballo: horse fair **(Jeréz de la Frontera)**
MAY-JUN Fiestas de San Isidro **(Madrid)**
MAY/JUN Corpus Christi
WHIT SUNDAY Romería del Rocío: pilgrimage (near **Huelva)**
JUN Haro: Wine war **(La Rioja)**
JUN 23-24th Festes de Sant Joan **(Barcelona** and Catalonia)
JUN 24th Xiquets de Valls: human towers **(Valls)**
JUN-JUL GREC: **Barcelona** Summer Festival
JUN-JUL International Festival of Music and Dance **(Granada)**
JUL Los Sanfermines: running of the bulls **(Pamplona)**
JUL Santa Marta de Ribarteme: 'near-death' pilgrimage **(Las Nieves, Pontevedra)**
JUL 22nd Cuesta de los Danzadores: stilt dancers **(Anguiano,** La Rioja)
JUL 25th Feast of St James **(Santiago de Compostela)**
AUG Semana Grande, includes Basque Herri Kilorak: traditional sports **(Bilbao)**
AUG Moros y Cristianos mock battle and mystery play **(Elche)**
AUG La Tomatina: Tomato Battle **(Buñol)**
SEP 19th Americas Day **(Oviedo)**
SEP 24th Festa de la Mercé: Our Lady of Mercy Festival **(Barcelona)**
OCT-NOV **Madrid** Autumn Festival
PORTUGAL
before Lent **Lisbon** Carnival
MAY 13th Pilgrimage to the Shrine of Our Lady of **Fátima**
MAY Queimade Fitas: academic celebrations **(Coimbra)**
JUN Festas de Lisboa: festivities in honour of three saints **(Lisbon)**
JUL Festa do Colete Encarnado: Festival of the Red Waistcoat **(Vila Franca de Xira)**
AUG Romaria de Nossa Senhora de Agonia: fair & pilgrimage **(Viana do Castelo)**
OCT Fiera de Outabro: October Festival **(Vila Franca de Xira)**
OCT 13th Pilgrimage to the Shrine of Our Lady of **Fátima**
NEW YEAR'S EVE Noite Mágica: Magic Night **(Lisbon)**

Spain

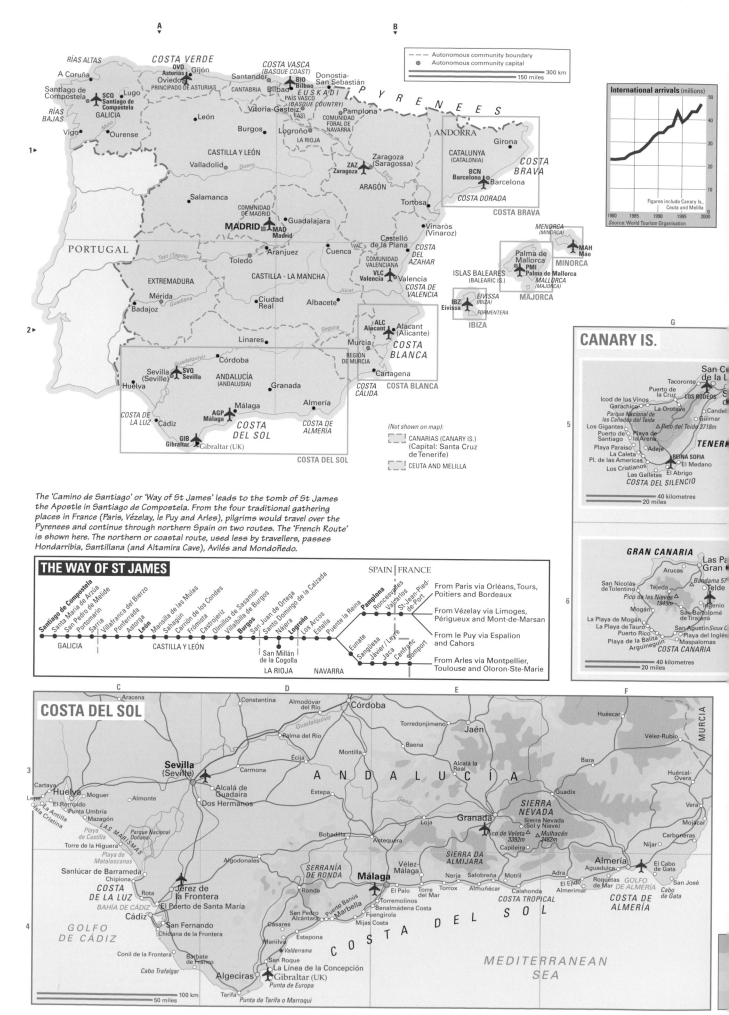

The 'Camino de Santiago' or 'Way of St James' leads to the tomb of St James the Apostle in Santiago de Compostela. From the four traditional gathering places in France (Paris, Vézelay, le Puy and Arles), pilgrims would travel over the Pyrenees and continue through northern Spain on two routes. The 'French Route' is shown here. The northern or coastal route, used less by travellers, passes Hondarribia, Santillana (and Altamira Cave), Avilés and Mondoñedo.

Spain

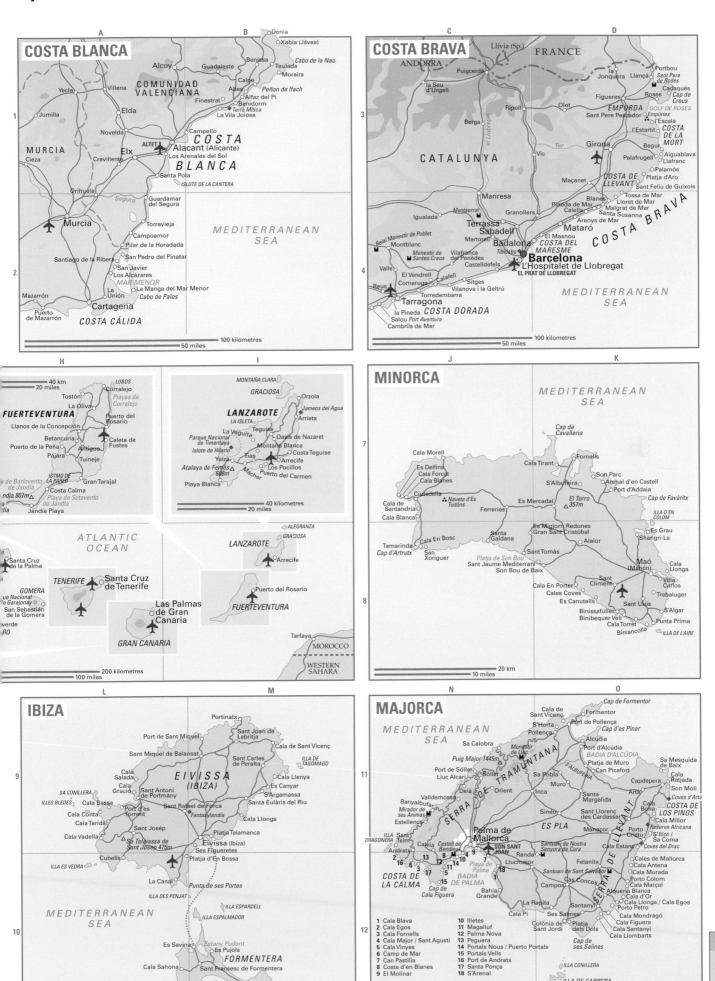

Portugal

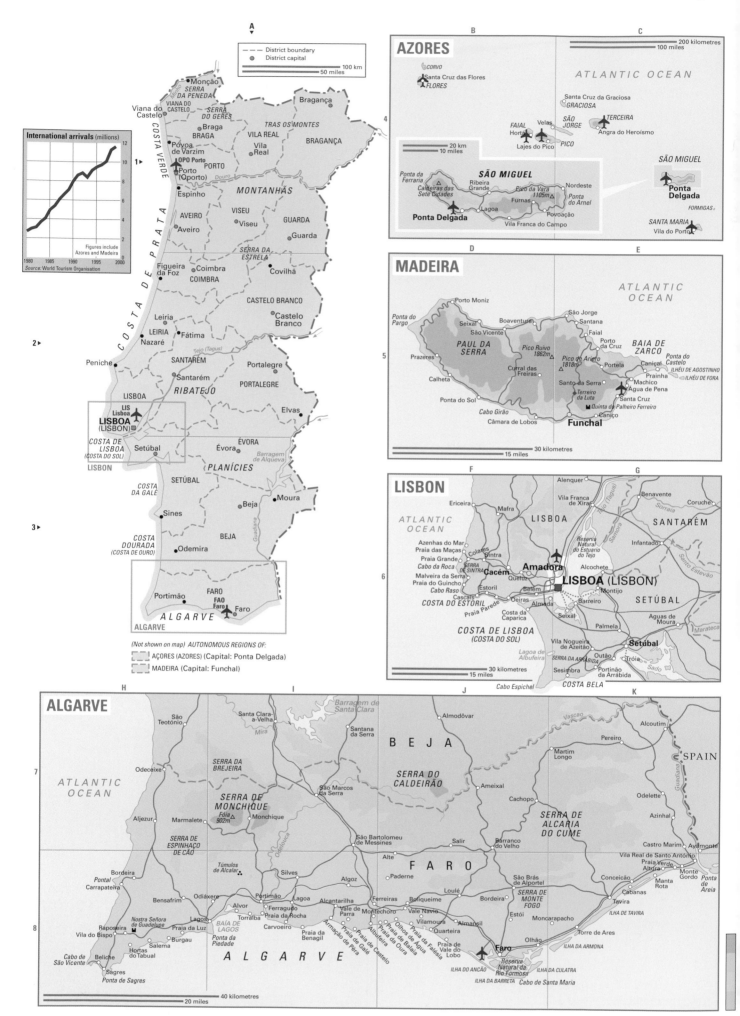

Italy

Lambert Equal Area Projection   Blue boxes indicate focus map coverage

200 kilometres
100 miles

4000 metres
2000 metres
1000 metres
500 metres
200 metres
Sea level

Italy

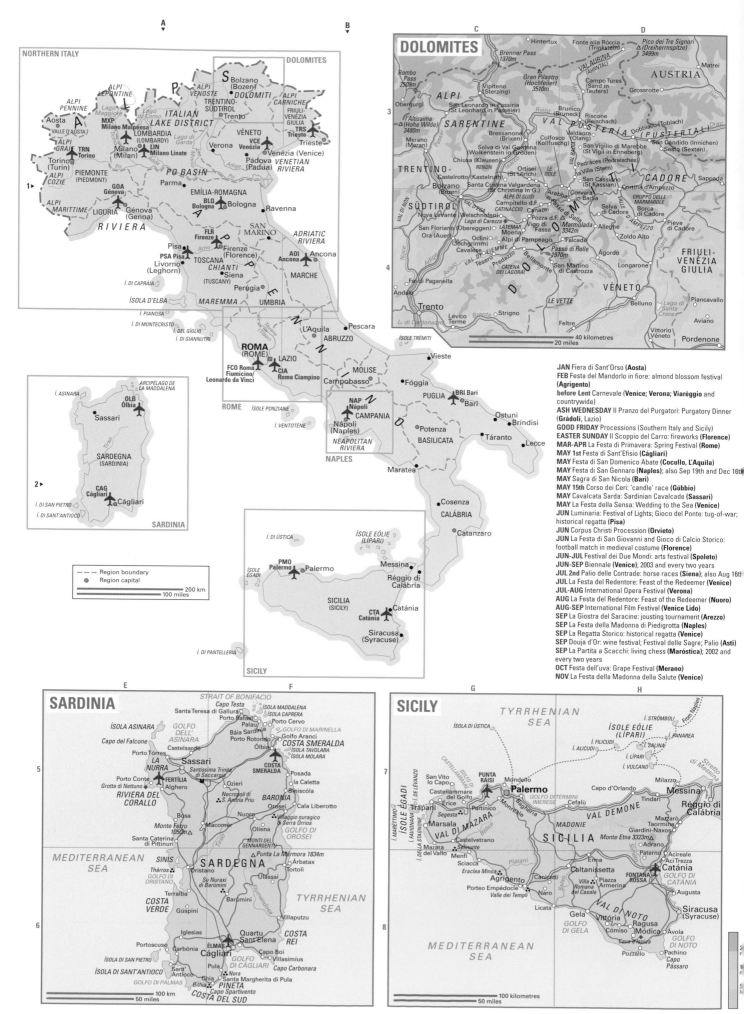

JAN Fiera di Sant'Orso (**Aosta**)
FEB Festa del Mandorlo in fiore: almond blossom festival (**Agrigento**)
before Lent Carnevale (**Venice; Verona; Viaréggio** and countrywide)
ASH WEDNESDAY Il Pranzo del Purgatori: Purgatory Dinner (**Grádoli**, Lazio)
GOOD FRIDAY Processions (Southern Italy and Sicily)
EASTER SUNDAY Il Scoppio del Carro: fireworks (**Florence**)
MAR-APR La Festa di Primavera: Spring Festival (**Rome**)
MAY 1st Festa di Sant'Efisio (**Cágliari**)
MAY Festa di San Domenico Abate (**Cocullo, L'Aquila**)
MAY Festa di San Gennaro (**Naples**); also Sep 19th and Dec 16th
MAY Sagra di San Nicola (**Bari**)
MAY 15th Corso dei Ceri: 'candle' race (**Gúbbio**)
MAY Cavalcata Sarda: Sardinian Cavalcade (**Sassari**)
MAY La Festa della Sensa: Wedding to the Sea (**Venice**)
JUN Luminaria: Festival of Lights; Gioco del Ponte: tug-of-war; historical regatta (**Pisa**)
JUN Corpus Christi Procession (**Orvieto**)
JUN La Festa di San Giovanni and Gioco di Calcio Storico: football match in medieval costume (**Florence**)
JUN-JUL Festival dei Due Mondi: arts festival (**Spoleto**)
JUN-SEP Biennale (**Venice**); 2003 and every two years
JUL 2nd Palio delle Contrade: horse races (**Siena**); also Aug 16th
JUL La Festa del Redentore: Feast of the Redeemer (**Venice**)
JUL-AUG International Opera Festival (**Verona**)
AUG La Festa del Redentore: Feast of the Redeemer (**Nuoro**)
AUG-SEP International Film Festival (**Venice Lido**)
SEP La Giostra del Saracine: jousting tournament (**Arezzo**)
SEP La Festa della Madonna di Piedigrotta (**Naples**)
SEP La Regatta Storico: historical regatta (**Venice**)
SEP Douja d'Or: wine festival; Festival delle Sagre; Palio (**Asti**)
SEP La Partita a Scacchi: living chess (**Maróstica**); 2002 and every two years
OCT Festa dell'uva: Grape Festival (**Merano**)
NOV La Festa della Madonna della Salute (**Venice**)

Italy

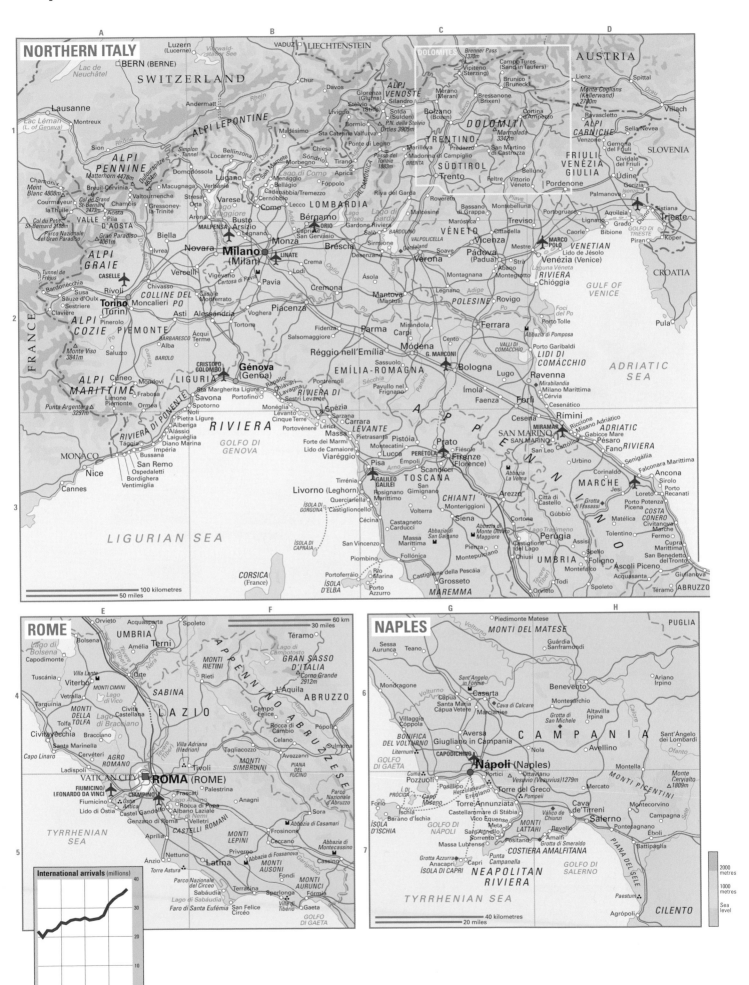

Italy: Attractions

Legend:
- Theme park, leisure park
- Museum, gallery
- Religious building
- Park, garden, zoo, etc.
- Historic building
- Water-related attraction
- Other place of interest

Attractions in cities marked in **red** are listed around the map

200 km / 100 miles

Torino (Turin)
GALLERIA SABAUDA
MUSEO DELL'AUTOMOBILE
MUSEO EGIZIO
PALAZZO REALE
BASILICA DI SUPERGA
PIAZZA SAN CARLO

Milano (Milan)
IL CENACOLO (Last Supper)
CIVICO MUSEO DI ARTE CONTEMPORANEA
MUSEO CIVICO DI ARCHEOLOGICO
PINACOTECA AMBROSIANA
PINACOTECA BI BRERA
DUOMO
CASTELLO SFORZESCO
TEATRO ALLA SCALA

Verona
ARCHE SCALIGERI
CHIESA DI SAN ZENO MAGGIORE
ARENA
CASA DI GIULIETTA
CASTELVECCHIO
PIAZZA DELLE ERBE
PIAZZA DEI SIGNORI

Bologna
MUSEO CIVICO ARCHEOLOGICO
PINACOTECA NAZIONALE
BASILICA DI SAN PETRONIO
PIAZZALE MAGGIORE E DEL NETTUNO
TORRE PENDENTI

Venézia (Venice)
COLLEZIONE GUGGENHEIM
GALLERIA DELL'ACCADEMIA
MUSEO CORRER
MUSEO VITRARIO DI MURANO
CHIESA DI SANTA MARIA DELLA SALUTE
CHIESA DI SANTA MARIA GLORIOSA DEI FRARI
CHIESA DI SAN ZACCARIA
PALAZZO DUCALE
SCUOLA DI SAN GIORGIO DEGLI SCHIAVONI
SCUOLA DI SAN ROCCO
CANAL GRANDE
GHETTO
MURANO
PIAZZA SAN MARCO
PONTE DEI SOSPIRI (Bridge of Sighs)

Firenze (Florence)
GALLERIA DEGLI UFFIZI
GALLERIA DELL'ACCADEMIA
MUSEO ARCHEOLOGICO
MUSEO DELL'OPERA DEL DUOMO
MUSEO DI SAN MARCO
PALAZZO E MUSEO NAZIONALE DEL BARGELLO
PALAZZO MEDICI-RICCARDI
PALAZZO PITTI
CHIESA DI SAN LORENZO
CHIESA DI SANTA CROCE
CHIESA DI SANTA MARIA NOVELLA
PIAZZA DEL DUOMO
GIARDINO DI BOBOLI
PALAZZO VECCHIO
PONTE VECCHIO

Roma (Rome) & Vatican City
LUNEUR
GALLERIA BORGHESE
GALLERIA DORIA PAMPHILI
MUSEO CAPITOLINO
MUSEO DEL PALAZZO DEL CONSERVATORI
MUSEO NAZIONALE DI VILLA GIULIA
MUSEO NAZIONALE ROMANO
MUSEI VATICANI E CAPPELLA SISTINA
PALAZZO BARBERINI
BASILICA DI SAN GIOVANNI IN LATERANO
BASILICA DI SAN PAOLO FUORI LE MURA
BASILICA DI SAN PIETRO
CHIESA DEL GESÙ
CHIESA DI SANTA MARIA MAGGIORE
CHIESA DI SANTA MARIA DELLA VITTORIA
GIARDINI VATICANI
CASTEL SANT'ANGELO
COLOSSEO
KEATS-SHELLEY MEMORIAL HOUSE
PANTHEON
CAMPIDOGLIO
CATACOMBE
FONTANA DI TREVI
FORI IMPERIALI
FORO ROMANI
PALATINO
PIAZZA NAVONA
PIAZZA DEL POPOLO
PIAZZA DI SAN PIETRO
PIAZZA DEL SPAGNA & Spanish Steps
TERME DI CARACALLA

Nápoli (Naples)
EDENLANDIA
MUSEO ARCHEOLOGICO NAZIONALE
PALAZZO E GALLERIA NAZIONALE DI CAPODIMONTE
CERTOSA DI SAN MARTINO
CASTEL NUOVO
CATACOMBE DI SAN GENNARO
PORTO DI SANTA LUCIA

Map labels

Tremezzo — VILLA CARLOTTA
Bellágio — VILLA SERBELLONI / VILLA MELZI
Merano (Meran) — PASSEGGIATE
Bressanone (Brixen) — ABBAZIA DI NOVACELLA / PLOSE
Bolzano (Bozen)
Cortina — TOFANA DI MEZZO / TONDI DI MEZZO
Cividale del Friuli — MUSEO ARCHEOLOGICO NAZIONALE / TEMPIETTO
PARCO NAZIONALE DELLO STELVIO
VAL CAMÓNICA
TRENTINO-SÜDTIROL
Trento
Sondrio
FRIULI-VENÉZIA GIULIA
Údine — PIAZZA DELLA LIBERTÀ
Pordenone
Aquiléia — BASILICA
Trieste — COLLE DI SAN GIUSTO
LAGO MAGGIORE
VILLA TÁRANTO
ÍSOLE BORROMEE
Aosta
VALLE D'AOSTA
PARCO NAZIONALE DEL GRAN PARADISO
PIEMONTE (PIEDMONT)
LOMBARDIA (LOMBARDY)
Como — DUOMO
LAGO DI COMO
Lago d'Iseo
Monza
Bérgamo — ACCADEMIA CARRARA / CITTÀ ALTA
LAGO DI GARDA
Vicenza — LA ROTONDA / PIAZZA DEI SIGNORI
VÉNETO
Novara
Milano (Milan)
CERTOSA DI PAVIA
Pavia
Alessándria
Torino (Turin)
SACRA DI SAN MICHELE
Cuneo
Piacenza — PALAZZO DEL COMUNE
Cremona — PIAZZA DEL COMUNE
Mantova (Mantua) — PALAZZO DUCALE / PALAZZO DEL TE
GARDALAND
Verona
RIVIERA DEL BRENTA
Venézia (Venice)
Pádova (Padua) — BASILICA DEL SANTO / CAPPELLA DEGLI SCROVEGNI / CHIESA DEGLI EREMITANI / ORTO BOTANICO
Parma — GALLERIA NAZIONALE / CENTRO EPISCOPALE
Réggio nell'Emília
Modena — GALERIA ESTENSE / DUOMO
Ferrara — DUOMO / PALAZZO DEI DIAMANTI
ABBAZIA DI POMPOSA
EMÍLIA-ROMAGNA
Génova (Genoa) — PORTO VECCHIO
LIGURIA
PARCO NATURALE DI PORTOFINO
Savona
San Remo
La Spézia — CINQUE TERRE
Bologna
Ravenna — BASILICA DI SAN VITALE / MAUSOLEO DI GALLA PLACIDIA
MIRABILANDIA
Forlì
Rímini — FIABILANDIA
SAN MARINO — ROCCA GUALTA
Úrbino — PALAZZO DUCALE / GALLERIA NAZIONALE DELLE MARCHE
Pistóia — PIAZZA DEL DUOMO
Prato — DUOMO
Firenze (Florence)
Lucca — MUSEO NAZIONALE GUINIGI / CHIESA DI SAN FREDIANO / DUOMO
Pisa — MUSEO NAZIONALE DI SAN MATTEO / PIAZZA DEL DUOMO
Livorno (Leghorn)
TOSCANA (TUSCANY)
Arezzo — CHIESA DI SAN FRANCISCO
MARCHE
Ancona
Loreto — SANTUARIO DELLA SANTA CASA
Volterra — PIAZZA DEI PRIORI
San Gimignano — PIAZZA DEL DUOMO / PIAZZA DELLA CISTERNA
Cortona — PIAZZA DEL DUOMO
Tolentino — BASILICA DI SAN NICOLA
Gúbbio — PALAZZO DEI CONSOLI / CITTÀ VECCHIA
Pienza
Montepulciano — MADONNA DI SAN BIAGIO / PIAZZA GRANDE
Siena — PINACOTECA / DUOMO / PIAZZA DEL CAMPO
Massa Maríttima — PZA. GARIBALDI
Grosseto
ABBAZIA DI MONTE OLIVETO MAGGIORE
UMBRIA
Orviéto — DUOMO
Todi — PIAZZA DEL POPOLO
Perúgia — MUSEO ARCHEOLOGICO NAZIONALE DELL'UMBRIA / CHIESA DI SAN PIETRO / PIAZZA 4 NOVEMBRE
Áscoli Piceno — PIAZZA DEL POPOLO
Assisi — BASILICA DI SAN FRANCISCO / CHIESA DI SANTA CHIARA / EREMO DELLE CARCERI / ROCCA MAGGIORE
L'Áquila — MUSEO NAZIONALE D'ABRUZZO / BASILICA DI SAN BERNARDINO
Tarquínia — NECROPOLI ETRUSCA
Cervéteri — NECROPOLI DELLA BANDITACCACCIA
Civitavécchia
ABBAZIA DI SAN CLEMENTE A CASAURIA
ÍSOLE TRÉMITI
Vieste
LAZIO
ABRUZZO
PARCO NAZIONALE DEL GARGANO
VATICAN CITY / ROMA (ROME)
Tívoli — VILLA D'ESTE / VILLA ADRIANA
OSTIA ANTICA
CASTELLI ROMANI
PARCO NAZIONALE D'ABRUZZO
MOLISE
Campobasso
Fóggia
ABBAZIA DI CASAMARI
ABBAZIA DI FOSSANOVA
ABBAZIA DI MONTECASSINO
PARCO NAZIONALE DEL CIRCEO
Caserta — LA REGGIA
Benevento — ARCO DI TRAIANO
CAMPANIA
Bari — BASILICA DI SAN NICOLA
PUGLIA
GROTTE DI CASTELLANA
Alberobello — TRULLI
Bríndisi
Nápoli (Naples)
VESUVIO
ÍSOLA D'ISCHIA
POMPEII
Erculano — HERCULANEUM
Sorrento
Salerno — DUOMO
ÍSOLA DI CAPRI
PAESTUM
Potenza
Matera — SASSI
BASILICATA
Táranto — MUSEO NAZIONALE
Lecce
BASILICA DI SANTA CROCE / PIAZZA DEL DUOMO
Amalfi — COSTIERA AMALFITANA / GROTTA DELLO SMERALDO
Ravello — VILLA CIMBRONE / VILLA RUFOLO
Maratea
CALÁBRIA
Cosenza
PARCO NAZIONALE DELLA CALABRIA
Crotone
Lamézia
Catanzaro
Réggio di Calábria — MUSEO NAZIONALE
Messina
Taormina — TEATRO GRECO
Palermo — MUSEO ARCHEOLOGICO REGIONALE / MUSEO ETNOGRAFICO PITRÈ / LA MARTORANA / PALAZZO DEI NORMANNI
Monreale — DUOMO
Cefalù — CATTEDRALE
Segesta
Trápani
ÍSOLE EGADI
ÍSOLE EÓLIE E LÍPARI
ÍSOLE PONZIANE
MONTE ETNA
SICILIA (SICILY)
Caltanissetta
Catánia
Agrigento — VALLI DEI TEMPLI
Siracusa (Syracuse) — MUSEO ARCHEOLOGICO REGIONALE / ZONA ARCHEOLOGICA
Ragusa
Í. DI ÚSTICA
Í. DI PANTELLERIA

Sardegna:
ARCIPÉLAGO DE LA MADDALENA
Í. ASINARA
COSTA SMERALDA
Porto Tórres — GROTTA DI NETTUNO
Ólbia
Sassari
Alghero
Nuoro
SARDEGNA (SÁRDINIA)
Oristano
SU NURAXI DU BARÚMINI
Cágliari — MUSEO NAZIONALE ACHEOLOGICO
Í. DI SAN PIETRO
Í. DI SANT'ANTIOCO

Central Europe: North

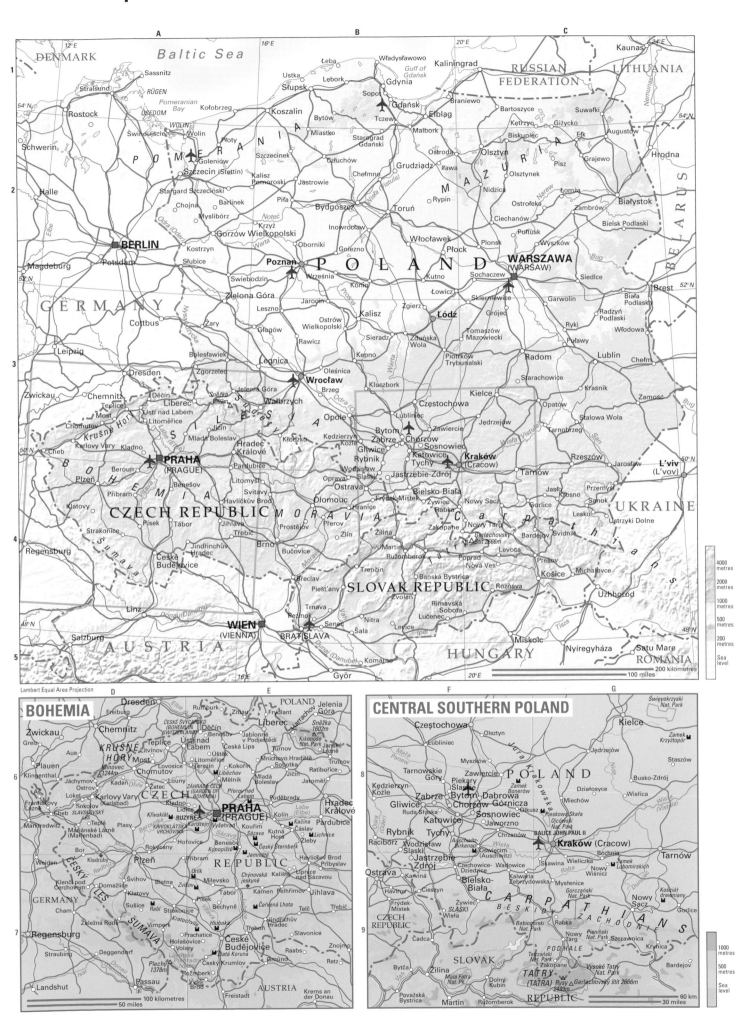

BOHEMIA

CENTRAL SOUTHERN POLAND

Lambert Equal Area Projection

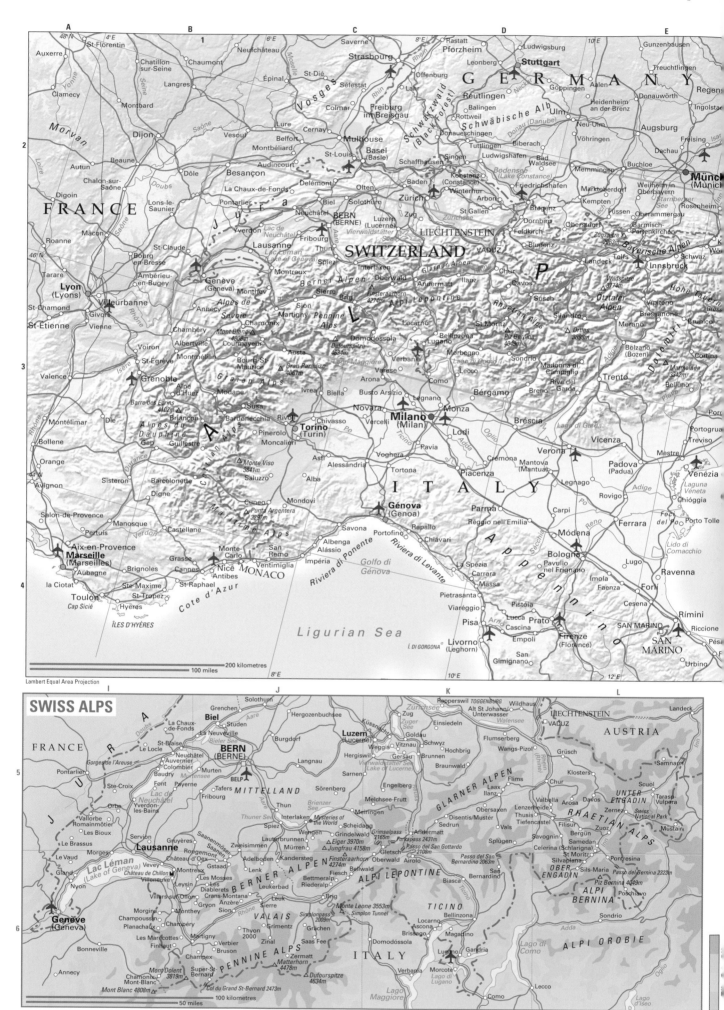

The Alps

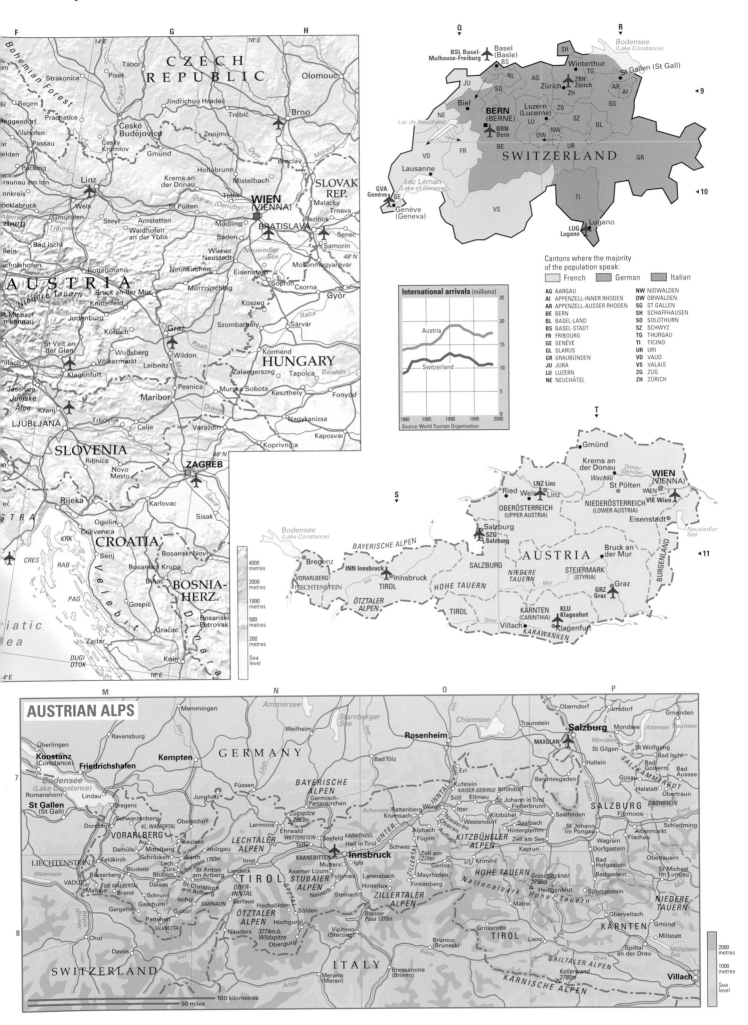

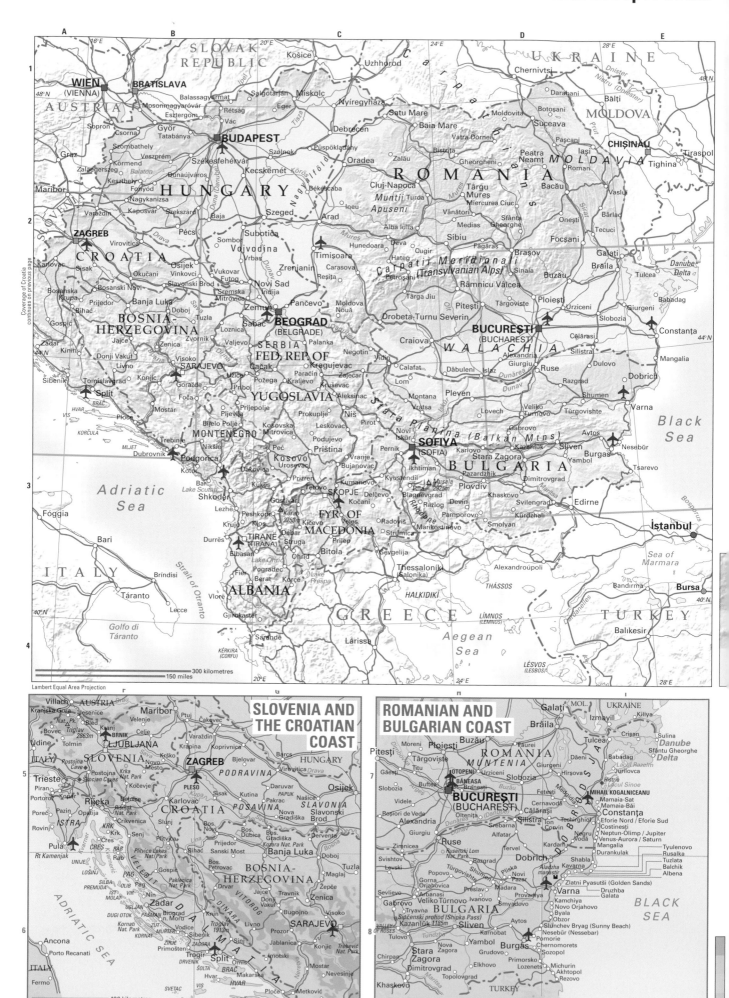

SLOVENIA AND THE CROATIAN COAST

ROMANIAN AND BULGARIAN COAST

Greece

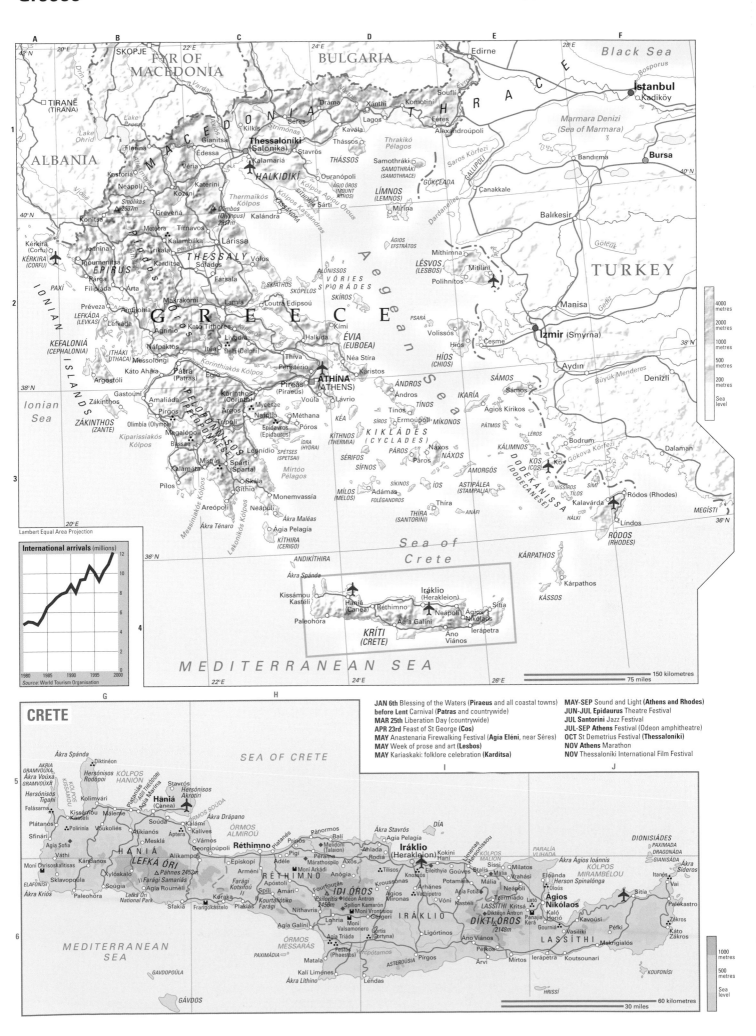

Greece

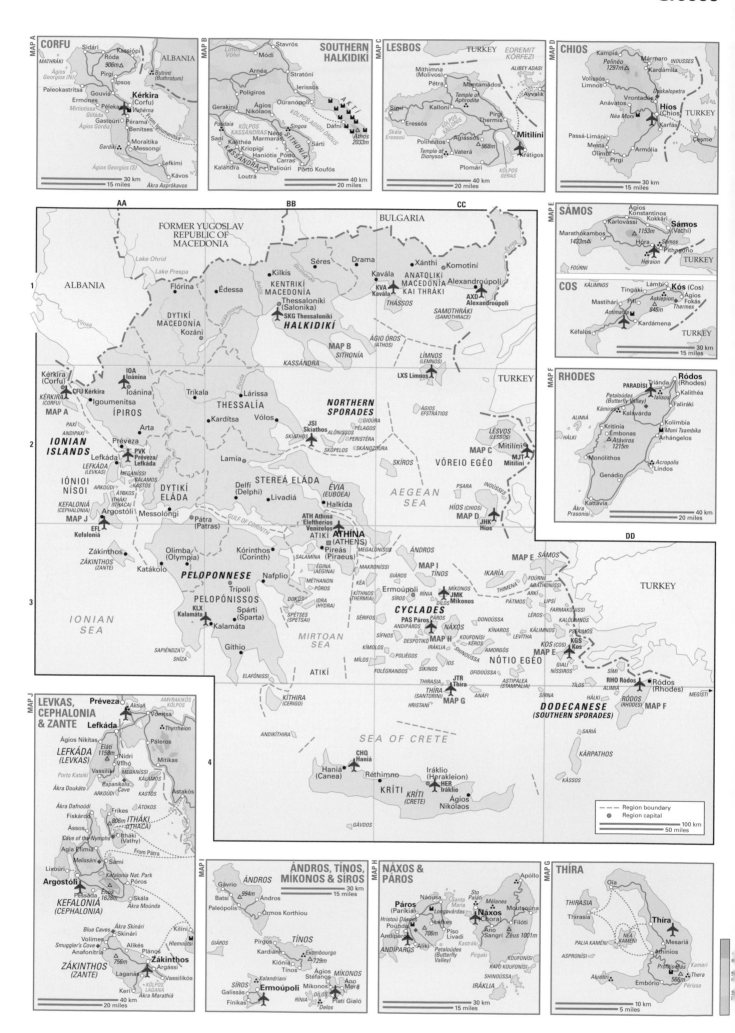

Turkey

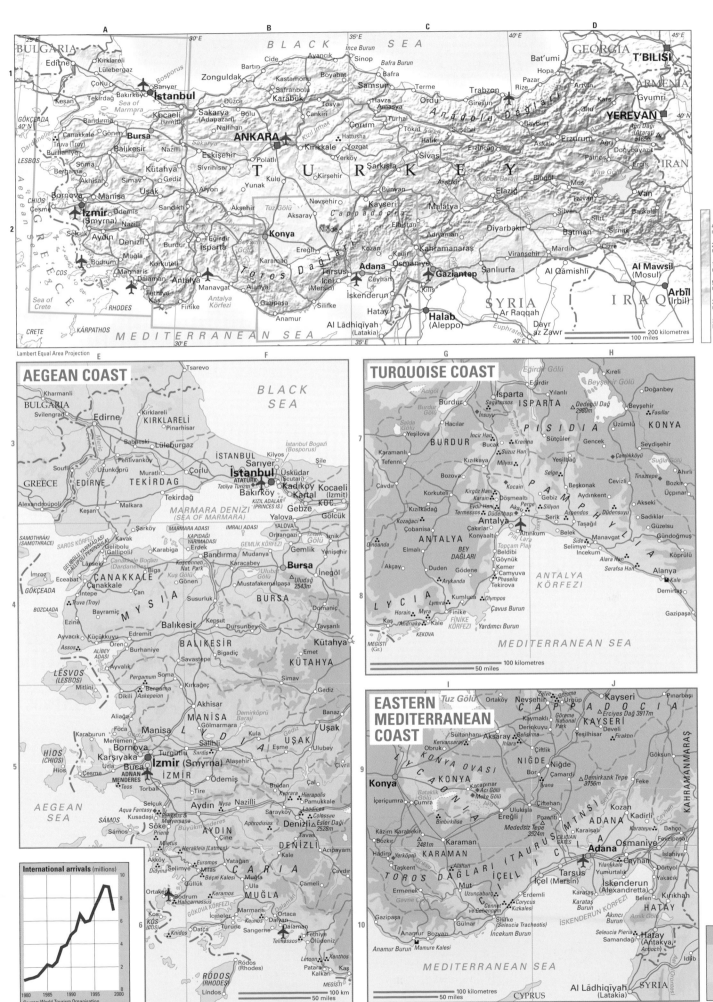

The Mediterranean

This map shows the principal diving destinations in the Mediterranean Sea and the main underwater attractions including the existence of soft corals or sea fans, cliffs and caves and shipwrecks (including submerged aircraft). The diver may encounter turtle and dolphin at any time, shark and rays less often, but only those places where regular sightings occur are indicated here. Whales are now exceedingly rare.

Diving facilities for each destination, including availability of scuba diving equipment and related support services, are graded as limited, good or excellent. It must be emphasised that these grades are a general reflection on the overall availability of everything required by the visiting scuba diver and are not an interpretation of the standards found within any one facility or organisation.

Each diving destination provides every level of depth from the very shallow to the extremely deep.

FRANCE: SOUTH COAST
1 2 3 4 D S T W ★

Dive sites all along the coast; main facilities in Marseilles, Nice and Toulon

Shipwreck 'Liban' off Cap Croisette and submarine 'Rubis' off Cap Camarat are outstanding; the diving infrastructure on mainland France is rather limited, largely because French divers favour the club system for diving; PADI is, however, opening up new shops and facilities all the time and it is worth requesting a PADI Centre List before departure

FRANCE: CORSICA
1 2 3 4 D S T W ★

Dive sites all along the island; main facilities in Ajaccio, Calvi and Sagone

British Vickers Viking, Canadian CL215 and US B17 bomber provide three very unusual aircraft wrecks off the west coast

ITALY: MAINLAND
1 2 3 4 D S T W ★★★

Dive sites all along the coast; facilities in all major towns, especially Genoa and Portofino

Diving is very popular in Italy; there are numerous shipwrecks, both ancient and modern, although many lie in very deep waters; cave systems on the Adriatic coast and steep underwater cliffs everywhere; away from the busy industrial ports, water clarity is very good

ITALY: SARDINIA
1 2 3 4 D S T W ★✔

Dive sites all around the island; facilities centred on Bosa, Cágliari, Orosei and Palau

Several shipwrecks including 'Romagna'; at least one aircraft plus several cave systems including the Nereo Caves off Cape Caccia

ITALY: WESTERN ISLANDS
(Capráia, Elba, Giannutri, Giglio, Montecristo)
1 2 3 4 D S T W ★

Dive sites all around the islands; some facilities on Elba but generally very limited on the islands – best nearby mainland facilities at Portofino

Spectacular vertical cliffs with outstanding seafans, red coral and large shoals of tuna; a few very exciting shipwrecks, such as the vehicle ferry 'Nasim II' off Giannutri

ITALY: SICILY
1 2 3 4 D S T W ★★

Dive sites all around the island; facilities centred on Catánia, Messina and Palermo

Shipwreck 'Amerique' on the northern tip of the island; Sicily attracts large pelagics and large shoals of tuna at certain times of the year

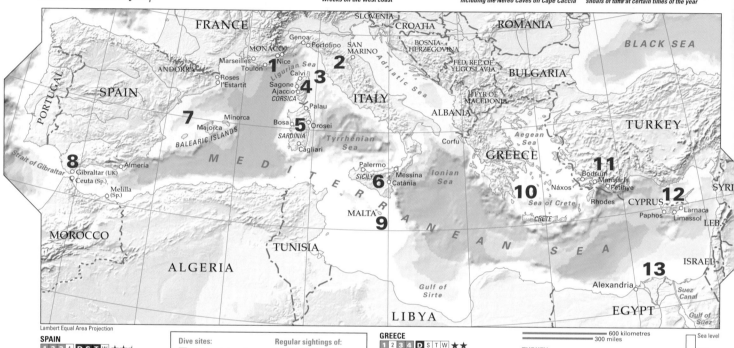

Lambert Equal Area Projection

SPAIN
1 2 3 4 D S T W ★★★✔

Main dive areas Balearic Islands and Costa Brava; best facilities at l'Estartit and Roses (Costa Brava), Almería, Majorca, Minorca

Submarine cave system 'Pont en Gill' holds outstanding examples of submerged stalactites and stalagmites; the Medes Islands (off l'Estartit) are a protected marine reserve where the flora and fauna is quite prolific

GIBRALTAR
1 2 3 4 D S T W ★★★

Main dive sites off the western and southern coastlines; facilities in Gibraltar town

Shipwrecks 'Excellent' and 'Rosslyn' just outside Gibraltar Harbour are outstanding; there is also ongoing artificial reef programme which involves the sinking of small vessels near Rosia Bay

Dive sites:
1 Soft corals / sea fans
2 Steep underwater cliffs
3 Cave diving
4 Shipwrecks

White square: not present

Regular sightings of:
D Dolphins
S Sharks / rays / pelagics
T Turtles
W Whales

White square: not regularly seen

Facilities for the diver:
★ Limited ★★ Good ★★★ Excellent

MALTA
1 2 3 4 D S T W ★★★

Dive sites all around the islands; facilities in all resort towns

Diving is very popular here although a valid medical certificate and proof of diving experience/qualifications are required; outstanding submarine arches, walls, reefs, tunnels and caves plus some new and very exciting shipwrecks deliberately sunk for divers

GREECE
1 2 3 4 D S T W ★★

Main dive areas Corfu, Crete, Náxos and Rhodes; best facilities on Crete

Until recently, Greece frowned upon scuba divers; today, however, new centres are opening all the time and there are several sites of ancient amphora where the diver is allowed to look but not touch; there are also spectacular submarine cave systems

CYPRUS
1 2 3 4 D S T W ★★★

Main dive sites off the southern and western coastlines; facilities centred on Larnaca, Limassol and Paphos

12,000 tonne ro-ro ferry 'Zenobia' sank off Larnaca in 1980 and is the largest shipwreck in the Mediterranean; the seas are very warm but Cyprus suffers from severe over-fishing

The Turkish Republic of Northern Cyprus has less opportunities for divers and limited facilities

TURKEY
1 2 3 4 D S T W ★★★✔

Dive sites all along the coast; facilities centred on the southwest coast, in particular at Bodrum, Fetihye and Marmaris

Many ancient amphora wrecks available for inspection and new diving areas are being explored all the time before being opened to visitors

EGYPT: NORTH COAST
1 2 3 4 D S T W ★

Main dive sites and facilities at Alexandria

Not as popular as Egypt's Red Sea coast and often overlooked; the remains of Cleopatra's Palace were recently found in Alexandria Harbour
For Egypt's Red Sea dive sites, see page 109

Data compiled by Ned Middleton, all rights reserved
email: ned.middleton@which.net

600 kilometres
300 miles

Sea level
-200 metres
-1000 metres
-2000 metres

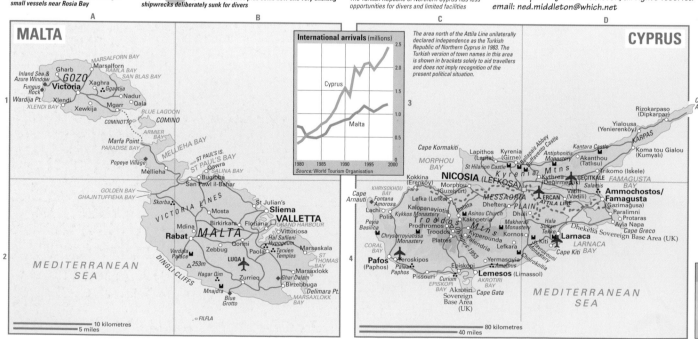

MALTA

International arrivals (millions)
Cyprus
Malta
1980 1985 1990 1995 2000
Source: World Tourism Organisation

The area north of the Attila Line unilaterally declared independence as the Turkish Republic of Northern Cyprus in 1983. The Turkish version of town names in this area is shown in brackets solely to aid travellers and does not imply recognition of the present political situation.

CYPRUS

10 kilometres
5 miles

80 kilometres
40 miles

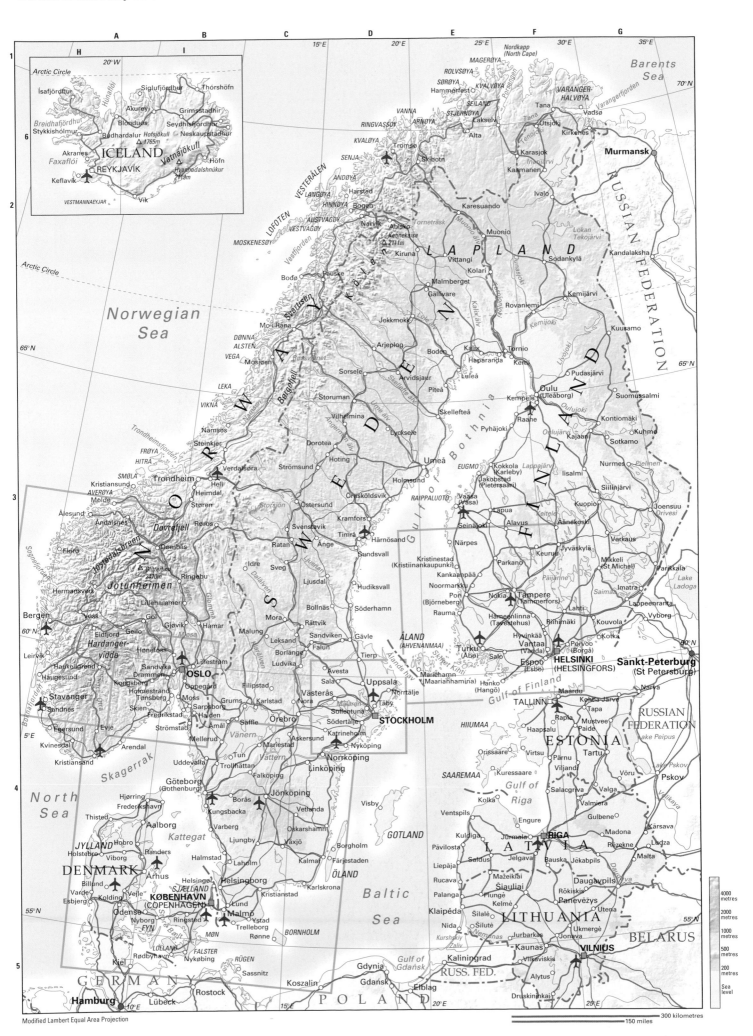

Modified Lambert Equal Area Projection

300 kilometres

150 miles

4000 metres
2000 metres
1000 metres
500 metres
200 metres
Sea level

Scandinavia

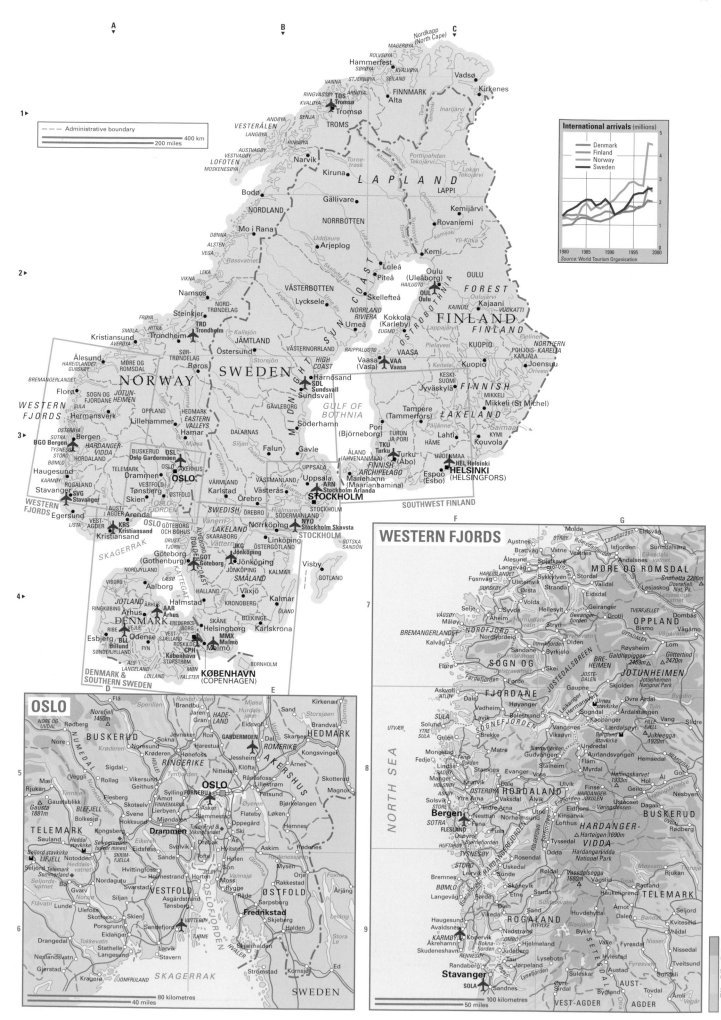

A B C

Nordkapp
(North Cape)
MAGERØYA
ROLVSØYA
Hammerfest
SØRØYA KVALØYA
Vadsø
STJERNØYA SEILAND
Kirkenes
VANNA Alta FINNMARK
ARNØYA
RINGVASSØY TOS
KVALØYA Tromsø FINNMARK
Tromsø
ANDØYA TROMS
VESTERÅLEN SENJA
LANGØYA
HINNØYA
AUSTVÅGØY Narvik
VESTVÅGØY
LOFOTEN Kiruna
MOSKENESØYA
LAPLAND
LAPPI
Bodø
Gällivare
NORDLAND
Kemijärvi
DØNNA Mo i Rana Rovaniemi
ALSTEN
VEGA Arjeplog Kemi
Rössvatnet OULU
Oulu
VIKNA (Uleåborg) OULU
LEKA HAILUOTO Oulu
Namsos Skellefteå FINLAND
Steinkjer VÄSTERBOTTEN Kajaani
FRØYA NORD- FINLAND VUOKATTI
SMØLA HITRA TRØNDELAG KAINUU
Kristiansund TRD Lycksele
AVERØYA Trondheim JÄMTLAND Kokkola NORTHERN
Trondheim (Karleby) POHJOIS-KARJALA
Ålesund SØR- Östersund EUGMO KARELIA
HAREIDLANDET TRØNDELAG Umeå Joensuu
GURSKØY NORRLAND KUOPIO
BREMANGERLANDET SWEDEN RIVIERA Kuopio Orivesi
Florø NORWAY Vaasa VAASA FINNISH
SULA JOTUN- (Vasa) Vaasa Jyväskylä
HEIMEN Härnösand KESKI- LAKELAND
WESTERN Hermansverk SDL SUOMI Mikkeli (St Michel)
FJORDS OPPLAND Sundsvall MIKKELI
HEDMARK Sundsvall
OSTERØYA EASTERN Tampere
SOTRA Bergen Lillehammer VALLEYS (Tammerfors) Lahti
BGO Bergen HARDANGER- Hamar Pori KYMI
TYSNESØY VIDDA DALARNAS (Björneborg) TURUN Kouvola
STORD Mjøsa GÄVLEBORG JA PORI
BØMLO HORDALAND Falun Gävle ÅLAND TKU HÄME UUDENMAA
Haugesund OSL Söderhamn (ÅHVENANMAA) Turku HEL Helsinki
KARMØY Oslo Gardermoen Turku (Åbo) HELSINKI
Stavanger ROGALAND OSLO AKERHUS UPPSALA FINNISH Espoo (HELSINGFORS)
SVG TELEMARK ARCHIPELAGO (Esbo)
Stavanger Drammen Uppsala Mariehamn
VESTFOLD VÄRMLAND VÄSTMANLAND Uppsala (Maarianhamina)
WESTERN Tønsberg ARN SOUTHWEST FINLAND
FJORDS AUST- Skien ØSTFOLD Västerås Stockholm Arlanda
Egersund AGDER Karlstad NYO
LISTA Arendal OSLO- Örebro STOCKHOLM
VEST- KRS FJORDEN SWEDISH Norrköping STOCKHOLM
AGDER Kristiansand LAKELAND Stockholm Skavsta
Kristiansand OSLO GÖTEBORG SKARABORG ÖREBRO STOCKHOLM
OCH BOHUS Linköping GOTSKA
SKAGERRAK ORUST ÖSTERGÖTLAND SANDÖN
GÖLDEN Jönköping
NORDJYLLAND COAST GOT Göteborg UKG
VIBORG LÆSØ Göteborg (Gothenburg) Jönköping SMÅLAND Visby
Aalborg JÖNKÖPING Kalmar GOTLAND
JÜTLAND HALLAND Växjö
Halmstad KRONOBERG ÖLAND
RINGKØBING AAR BLEKINGE
Århus SKÅNE Kalmar
DENMARK Århus FREDERIKS- Helsingborg Karlskrona
EJLE BORG Helsingborg
RIBE Esbjerg BLL FYN VEST- MMX
Billund Odense SJÆLLAND Malmö
SØNDERJYLLAND ROSKILDE Malmö
ALS København CPH
LANGELAND STORSTRØM København
DENMARK & LOLLAND MØN BORNHOLM
SOUTHERN SWEDEN FALSTER KØBENHAVN
(COPENHAGEN)

International arrivals (millions)

Denmark
Finland
Norway
Sweden

1980 1985 1990 1995 2000

Source: World Tourism Organisation

WESTERN FJORDS

F G

Molde
Austnes ØTRØY Eidsvåg
OTRØY Langfjorden
Sunndalsøra
Brattvåg Vatne Isfjorden Eikesdals-
Spjelkavik Vestnes vatn
Ålesund Storfjord Andalsnes
HAREIDLANDET Skodje MØRE OG ROMSDAL
Langevåg Sykkylven Stordal Snøhetta 2286m △
Fosnvåg Ulsteinvik Ørsta Stranda Validal Dovrefjell
GURSKØY Volda Eidsdal Lesjaskog Nat.Pk.
Åheim Hellesylt TVERFJELLET Dombås
VÅGSØY Selje Syvde Geiranger-
Måløy fjord Grotli OPPLAND
BREMANGERLANDET NORDFJORD Stryn Bismo Vågåmo
Kalvåg Nordfjordeid OTTADALEN
Sandane Olden Lom
Eloro Byrkjelo Røyheim Glittertind
SOGN OG Skei JOSTEDALSBREEN BRE- Galdhøpiggen △2470m
HEIMEN 2469m △
Førde JOSTE- JOTUNHEIMEN
FJORDANE DALEN Jotunheimen
Askvoll Dale National Park
ATLØY Vadheim Høyanger Gaupne
Solund Lavik Leikanger Øvre Årdal
SULA Vangsnes Hermansvik Sogndal Årdalstangen
YTRE Gulen Brekke Kaupanger FILLE-
UTVÆR SULA SOGNEFJORDEN Viksøyri Urnes FJELL Vang
stavkirke Slidre
Undredal Borgund Jukleegga
Mongstad Matre Nærøyfjorden stavkirke △1920m
Fedje Fensfjorden Gudvangen Lærdalsøyri
NORTH SEA Lindås Stamnes Evanger Flåm
RADØY Manger Dale Stalheim Aurlandsvangen
HOLSNØY Knarvik Voss Hemsedal
ASKØY Ytre Arna Ulvik Hallingskarvet Myrdal
Solvik STORE Indre Arna Ål △1933m
Sotra Nesttun Vaksdal Ålvik Geilo
Bergen Osøyro Norheimsund HARDANGER- Dagali BUSKERUD
FLESLAND Fusa Eidfjord JØKULEN Varingstassen
SOTRA Harteigen △1690m
HUFTARØY Bjørnafjorden Lofthus Kinsarvik Hol
TYSNESØY Tyssedal HARDANGER- Rødberg
STORD Rosendal Odda VIDDA
BØMLO Leirvik Sunde Hardangervidda
Bremnes Skånevik Røldal National Park Måbøen
Langevåg Etne Sauda Vassdalsegga Rjukan
Førde Ølen △1680m Vågslid
Vikedal Åmot TELEMARK
ROGALAND Hovdehytta
Haugesund Nedstrand Hjelmeland Dalen Seljord
Avaldsnes RYFYLKE Bykle
KARMØY Kopervik COMBO Suldal Valle Fyresdal Nissedal
Åkrehamn Bokna- Lyseboth AUST-
Skudeneshavn fjord Tau Jørpeland Suleskar Åmli AGDER
RENNESØY Øvre VEST-AGDER AGDER
Stavanger Sirdal Bygland
SOLA Sandnes Tovdal
Vikebygd

OSLO

D E

Flå Randsfjorden Kirkenær
NORE OG Brandbu Sand
UVDAL Norefjell Jevnaker Storsjøen
1460m Rødberg HADE- Eidsvoll
Nore Jaren LAND
Gran Brandval
Sokna HEDMARK
BUSKERUD GARDERMOEN
Sigdal Harestua Dal Skarnes
Noresund Hønefoss ROMERIKE
Veggli Rollag Sylling Jessheim Kongsvinger
Vikersund RINGERIKE Kløfta
Mæl FORNEBU
Rjukan Geithus Nittedal OSLO Årnes
Tinnsjø Flesberg HOLEÅ Asker Rånåsfoss
Gausta Gaustablikk Skotselv Lierbyen Oppegård Skotterud
1881m BLEFJELL Mjøndalen FINNEMARKA Ski Magnor
Bolkesjø Drammen Tusenfryd & Fetsund
Hokksund Vikinglandet
TELEMARK Kongsberg Svelvik Drøbak Hvitsten Askim Rødenes
Sauland Eidsfoss Sande Hølen Rakkestad
Heddal Hvittingfoss Holmestrand Son AKERSHUS
stavkirke Notodden Horten Moss
Seljord Telemark Gvarv ØSTFOLD
stavkirke LIFJELL Heddals- Tønsberg Rygge Årjäng
vatnet Nordagutu Åsgårdstrand Vannsjø
Summerland Bø Siljan Svarstad VESTFOLD Sarpsborg
Seljords- Lunde VÅTTERØY Sandefjord Fredrikstad
vatnet Ulefoss TJØME Skjeberg
Flåvatn Skien Larvik Halden
Porsgrunn Eidanger Stavern HVALER
Drangedal Stathelle
Neslandsvatn Langesund SKAGERRAK
Gjerstad Kragerø JOMFRULAND
SWEDEN
Ed
Kornsjø
Strömstad

--- Administrative boundary
400 km
200 miles

80 kilometres
40 miles

100 kilometres
50 miles

Scandinavia

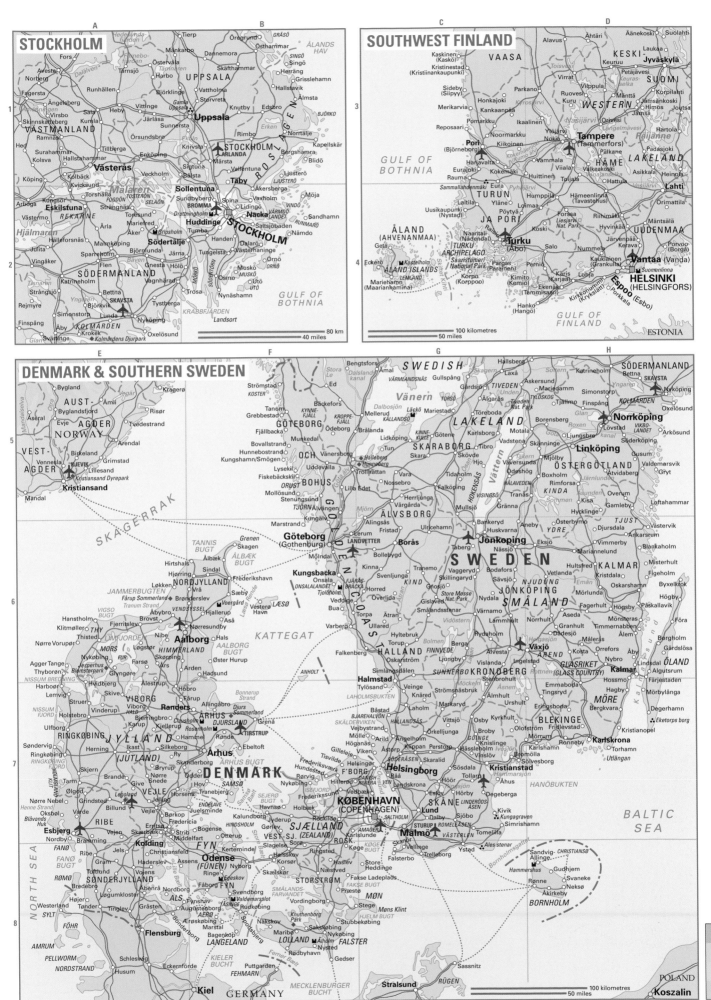

STOCKHOLM

Fors, Örregrund, Mönkarbo, Dannemora, Östhammar, SINGÖ, GRÄSÖ, ÅLANDS HAV, Avesta, Norberg, Österväla, Harbo, Herräng, Grisslehamn, Fagersta, Ängelsberg, Runhällen, UPPSALA, Björkling, Hallstavik, Älmsta, Skinnskatteberg, Virsbo, Sala, Heby, Vittinge, Knutby, Edsbro, VÄSTMANLAND, Ramnäs, Kumla, Järlåsa, Uppsala, Rimbo, Norrtälje, Kapellskär, Hed, Surahammar, Hallstahammar, Örsundsbro, Ekolsund, BJÖRKÖ, Kolsva, Kvicksund, Sigtuna, Märsta, Bergshamra, Blidö, Köping, Kölbäck, Torshälla, Veckholm, STOCKHOLM, ARLANDA, Vallentuna, Åkersberga, Arboga, Kungsör, VÄSTERÅS, Strängnäs, Mariefred, Åker, Enköping, Sundbyberg, BROMMA, Spånga, Lidingö, Vaxholm, Möja, Sollentuna, Sandhamn, Eskilstuna, Huddinge, Drottningholm, Nacka, VÄRMDÖ, RUNMARÖ, Västermo, REKARNE, Ärla, STOCKHOLM, Saltsjöbaden, Hjälmaren, Hälleforsnäs, Malmköping, Järna, Handen, Örnö, Köping, Tumba, Västerhaninge, Julita, Sparreholm, Björnlunda, Gnesta, Hölö, Osmo, Musko, MUSKÖ, Vingåker, Flen, Vagnhärad, UTÖ, SÖDERMANLAND, Katrineholm, Bettna, Trosa, Nynäshamn, Strängsjö, Rejmyre, Björkvik, Tystberga, KRABBFJÄRDEN, Simonstorp, SKAVSTA, Lunda, Landsort, Finspång, Åby, KOLMÅRDEN, Nyköping, Glan, Svärtinge, Krokek, Oxelösund, Kolmårdens Djurpark

80 km / 40 miles

SOUTHWEST FINLAND

Ähtäri, Äänekoski, Suolahti, Alavus, VAASA, Keuruu, Laukaa, KESKI-, Jyväskylä, Kaskinen, (Kaskö), Keuruu, Petäjävesi, SUOMI, Kristinestad, (Kristiinankaupunki), Parkano, Virrat, Vilppula, Mänttä, Jämsänkoski, Sideby, (Siipyy), Ruovesi, Kuru, WESTERN, Himos, Joutsa, Merikarvia, Honkajoki, Kankaanpää, Ikaalinen, Nokia, Tampere, (Tammerfors), Pälkäne, Padasjoki, GULF OF BOTHNIA, Reposaari, Noormarkku, Pomarkku, Hämeenlinna, HÄME, Heinola, Pori, (Björneborg), Harjavalta, Vammala, Viiala, Valkeakoski, Asikkala, Lahti, Eurajoki, Kokemäki, Huittinen, Toijala, Hattula, Rauma, Euta, TURUN, Humppila, Hämeenlinna, (Tavastehus), Riihimäki, Hyvinkää, Mäntsälä, Uusikaupunki, (Nystad), Yläne, Loimaa, Forssa, Orimattila, ÅLAND, (AHVENANMAA), Geta, JA PORI, Pöytyä, Koski, Liesjärvi Nat. Park, Järvenpää, Kerava, Porvoo, (Borgå), Naantali, (Nådendal), Turku, (Åbo), Salo, Nummela, UUDENMAA, ÅLAND ISLANDS, Eckerö, Kastelholm, Saaristomeri, Pargas, (Parainen), Perniö, Kaukola, (Grankulla), Vantaa, (Vanda), Mariehamn, (Maarianhamina), Korpo, (Korppoo), Kimito, (Kemiö), Karis, Karjaa, Lohja, Espoo, (Esbo), HELSINKI, (HELSINGFORS), Hanko, (Hangö), Ekenäs, (Tammisaari), Kirkkonummi, (Kyrkslätt), Porkkala, GULF OF FINLAND, ESTONIA

100 kilometres / 50 miles

DENMARK & SOUTHERN SWEDEN

Bygland, Kragerø, Strömstad, Bengtsfors, SWEDISH, Hallsberg, Katrineholm, SÖDERMANLAND, AUST-, Åmli, KOSTER, Stora Le, Dalslands kanal, Åmål, VÄRMLANDSNÄS, Gullspång, Laxå, Bettna, SKAVSTA, AGDER, Bygglandsfjord, Risør, Tanum, Grebbestad, Ed, Dalbosjön, Mellerud, TIVEDEN, Tiveden, Simonstorp, Nyköping, NORWAY, Evje, Tvedestrand, KYNNE-, FJÄLL, Bäckefors, Läckö, Mariestad, Nat. Park, Tjällmo, TJÅLMO, Finspång, KOLMÅRDEN, VEST-, Birkeland, Arendal, GÖTEBORG, Fjällbacka, Ödeborg, Brålanda, KALLANDSÖ, Götene, Borensberg, Ljungsbro, Lövstad, VIKBO-, Oxelösund, AGDER, Vennesla, Grimstad, Bovallstrand, Munkedal, Vänersborg, Lidköping, SKARABORG, Tibro, Vadstena, Skänninge, LANDET, Arkösund, Kristiansand Dyrepark, Kungshamn/Smögen, Uddevalla, Trollhättan, Vara, Skara, Skövde, Hjo, Väversunda, Ödeshög, Mjölby, Linköping, HIEVIK, Lillesand, OCH, Hällebergget, Hunneberg, Tidaholm, Nossebro, Falköping, Gränna, Boxholm, ÖSTERGÖTLAND, Kristiansand, Fiskebäckskil, BOHUS, Lilla Edet, Herrljunga, VISINGSÖ, ÅLEVEDEN, Tranås, Rimforsa, Gusum, Valdemarsvik, Mandal, Mollösund, Stenungsund, Älvängen, Vårgårda, Ulricehamn, Bankeryd, Österbymo, Kisa, Gamleby, Gryt, Marstrand, Kungälv, Alingsås, Fristad, Huskvarna, Aneby, YDRE, Djursdala, Loftahammar, SKÄGERRAK, TANNIS BUGT, Grenen, Skagen, Göteborg, (Gothenburg), LANDVETTER, Borås, Taberg, Jönköping, Eksjö, Vimmerby, Blankaholm, Grenå, Ålbæk, Mölndal, Kinna, Bollebygd, Nässjö, Vaggeryd, SWEDEN, Hultsfred, KALMAR, Misterhult, Hirtshals, ÄLBÆK BUGT, Svenljunga, Tranemo, Bodafors, Vetlanda, Kristdala, Högsby, Figeholm, Hjørring, Sindal, Frederikshavn, Gnosjö, Sävsjö, JÖNKÖPING, Oskarshamn, Byxelkrok, Løkken, Vrå, NORDJYLLAND, FJÅRÅS, BRÄCKA, Horred, Överlida, Gislaved, SMÅLAND, NJUDUNG, Nydala, Mörlunda, Byxelkrok, Fårup Sommerland, Brønderslev, Voergård, Onsala, ONSALAALANDET, Tjolöholm, Veddige, Bua, Smålandsstenar, Värnamo, Norrhult, Granhult, Fagerhult, Timmernabben, Föra, Sæby, Vestero Havn, Torpa, Åtran, Vidöstern, Rydaholm, Dädesjö, Målerås, ÖLAND, Hanstholm, Åbybro, Hjallerup, Hals, LÆSØ, Varberg, Hyltebruk, Torup, Bolmen, Berga, Nässjö, Bergkvara, Gärdslösa, Klitmøller, THY, Thisted, Fjerritslev, Brovst, Nørresundby, Falkenberg, Oskarström, Ljungby, Alvesta, Ingelstad, Växjö, AREND, Orrefors, Nybro, Nørre Vorupør, AALBORG, Simlångsdalen, Veinge, Strömsnäsbruk, Älmhult, Urshult, GLASRIKET, (GLASS COUNTRY), Kalmar, Agger Tange, Nykøbing, FUR, Skørping, Års, ØSTER HURUP, ANHOLT, Halmstad, Knäred, Laholm, Markaryd, Eringsboda, Rödeby, MÖRE, Algutsrum, Thyborøn, Jesperhus, Blomsterpark, Glyngøre, Farsø, Arden, Hadsund, Tylösand, LAHOLMSBUKTEN, Laholm, Osby, Kyrkhult, Ronneby, Degerhamn, Möckeln, Åsnen, Tingsryd, Mörbylånga, NISSUM BREDNING, Harboøre, Hvidbjerg, Skive, HIMMERLAND, Hobro, Bonnerup Strand, Båstad, Åstorp, Klippan, Perstorp, Broby, Olofström, Fridlevstad, Eketorps borg, Lemvig, Struer, VIBORG, Randers, DJURSLAND, Grenå, Viken, Höganäs, Angelholm, BLEKINGE, Karlskrona, Ulfborg, Holstebro, Vinderup, Viborg, HALD, Allingåbro, Bjerringbro, Rosenholm, Djurs Sommerland, Ålborg, Simrishamn, Arild, Mölle, Örkelljunga, Hässleholm, Karlshamn, Torhamn, RINGKØBING, JYLLAND, Ikast, Silkeborg, Kjellerup, Hammel, Rønde, TIRSTRUP, ÅRHUS, Ebeltoft, Tisvilde, Frederiksværk, Helsinge, Mörarp, SÖDERÅSEN, Höör, Vinslöv, Björnlöv, Sölvesborg, Utlängan, Ringkøbing, Herning, Bryrup, Skanderborg, Ebeltoft, ÅRHUS BUGT, Gilleleje, DANISH RIVIERA, Helsingør, Klippan, Hässleholm, Kristianstad, Åhus, HANÖBUKTEN, RINGKØBING FJORD, Skjern, Tarm, Brande, Give, Hov, Snede, Hundested, Rørvig, Helsingborg, Råå, Sösdala, Tollarp, Skjern, LEGOLAND, VEJLE, Jelling, Horsens, SAMSØ, ENDELAVE, Juelsminde, Nykøbing, Hillerød, Frederiksund, F'BORG, Landskrona, Eslöv, Hörby, Degeberga, Kivik, BALTIC SEA, Nørre Nebel, Varde, Billund, Vejle, Børkop, ISEFJORD, Holbæk, Roskilde, KØBENHAVN, (COPENHAGEN), SKÅNE, LINDERÖDS, ÅSEN, Kungagraven, Esbjerg, Nordby, RIBE, Fredericia, Kalundborg, Gørlev, SJÆLLAND, (ZEALAND), Lund, Dalby, Simrishamn, FANØ, Bramming, Vejen, Skærbæk, Strib, Middelfart, Bogense, Otterup, VEST-SJ., ROSK., SALTHOLM, Sturup, ROMELEÅSEN, Ales stenar, Kolding, Christiansfeld, Jels, Assens, Ringsted, AMAGER, Malmö, VÅSTERLEN, Tomelilla, FANØ BUGT, FYN, Odense, (FUNEN), Kerteminde, Nyborg, Slagelse, Sorø, Karlslunde, Køge, Vellinge, Trelleborg, Ystad, SØNDERJYLLAND, Haderslev, Gram, Vejen, Ringe, Svendborg, Fåborg, Korsør, Skælskør, Næstved, Store Heddinge, KØGE BUGT, Falsterbo, RØMØ, Bredebro, Augustenborg, ALS, FYN, Svendborg, Rudkøbing, Rudkøbing, STORSTRØM, MØN, Stege, Møns Klint, Sandvig, CHRISTIANSØ, Allinge, Gudhjem, Løgumkloster, Tinglev, Gråsten, TÅSINGE, Valdemarsslot, Ærøskøbing, Marstal, Bagenkop, Nakskov, Maribo, LOLLAND, Ålholm, FALSTER, Nykøbing, Stubbekøbing, Hammershus, Svaneke, Neksø, Åkirkeby, BORNHOLM, Rønne, Flensburg, Schleswig, Husum, Kiel, GERMANY, Eckernförde, KIELER BUCHT, Femer Bælt, Gedser, Rødbyhavn, Puttgarden, FEHMARN, Stralsund, RÜGEN, Sassnitz, MECKLENBURGER BUCHT, POLAND, Koszalin

100 kilometres / 50 miles

1000 metres / 500 metres / Sea level

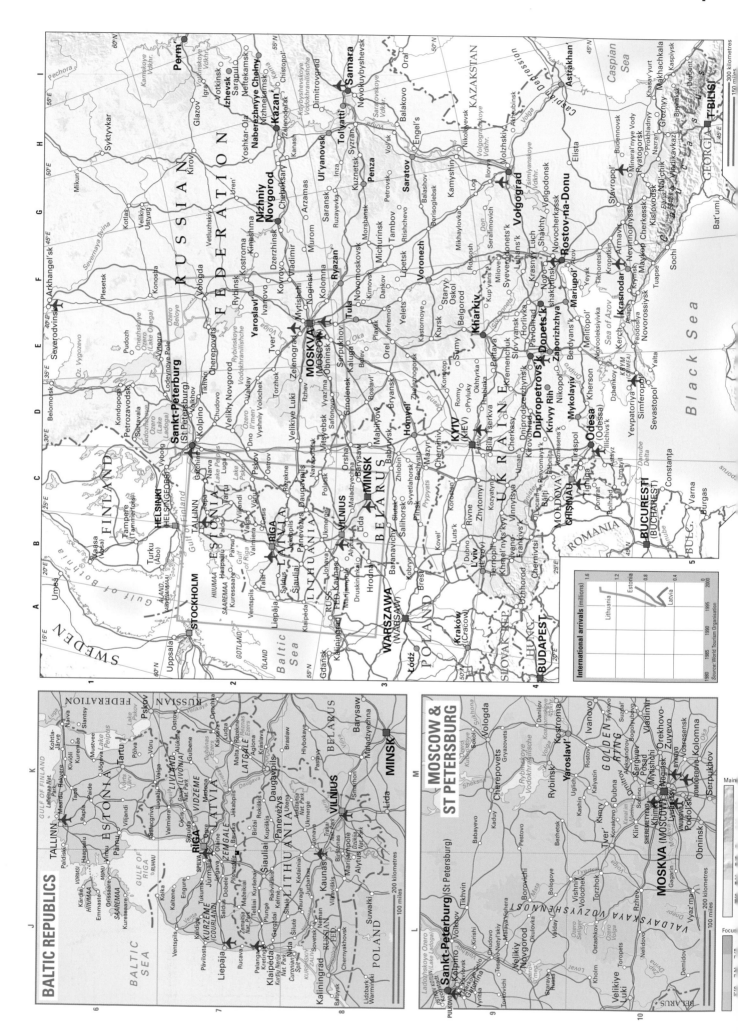

BALTIC REPUBLICS

MOSCOW & ST PETERSBURG

International arrivals (millions)

Source: World Tourism Organisation

The Russian Federation

International arrivals (millions)

Russian Federation

Soviet Union

Source: World Tourism Organisation

Africa

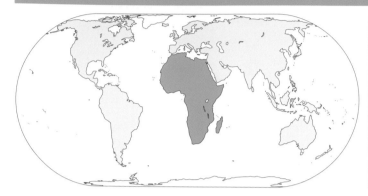

Key facts	Africa	World	Africa %
Number of Countries	57	226	25.2%
Area ('000 sq km)	46,502	135,463	34.3%
Population ('000)	806,968	5,973,801	13.5%
Population Density (/sq km)	17	44	–
Gross Nat. Income (US$m)	843,594	29,986,364	2.8%
Visitor Arrivals ('000)	30,566	649,223	4.7%
Visitor Receipts (US$m)	14,116	456,402	3.1%
Travel Departures ('000)	12,136	594,797	2.0%
Travel Expenditure (US$m)	8,151	397,040	2.1%

GNI figures relate to 1999. Population figures are taken from the most recent census or reliable estimate. Travel figures (from the WTO) are generally for 1999, but where these are unavailable or unreliable, figures from earlier years have been used. All travel figures are based on overnight stays, not same-day visitors. Where data for certain countries was not available, this has been regarded as zero. Global totals for Visitor Arrivals/Travel Departures and Visitor Receipts/Travel Expenditure do not equal each other due to differing methods of reporting inbound and outbound data. For more information on what is regarded as a country for the purposes of this book, and for more detailed statistical information, please see the Countries A-Z section from page 181.

HALF A CENTURY after the first bricks of colonialism began to be dislodged, Africa remains the major enigma of travel. Huge tracts of this awesomely diverse yet often impenetrable continent remain untouched by travellers. While Africa occupies over one third of the world's landmass (a fact often obscured by map projections), is home to over one seventh of the world's population and possesses staggering natural resources, it accounts for under 3% of the world's GNI and under 5% of the world's visitor arrivals. Investment in travel and tourism infrastructure is not a high priority for many African states. These statistics speak of a vast potential that a variety of political and economic problems have failed to see translated into reality. Only certain countries – almost all of which have coastlines – have sustained a tourism product, and then often against a background of negative elements.

Holiday trends

Adventure is the key feature of African holidays: but, in general, tourism involves only a handful of countries. Adventure carries a premium here and, unlike many other areas of the world, is not a budget option.

South Africa and Kenya have well-administered game parks which enable them to count safari holidays as a major foreign currency earner. These offer a sanitised version of adventure and danger, in which the only shooting done in this environmentally-friendly age is with camera and camcorder. Slightly closer brushes with danger can be sampled on Africa's rivers, where canoeing and rafting offer close-ups of nature.

Coach touring is a more relaxing way of seeing South Africa. This appeals to those unsure of taking on a self-drive tour and the older age groups to whom escorted touring is the 'safe' option.

Luxury holidays are a growing niche in the African tourism make-up. The options range from luxury lodges in the game parks, to secure country club accommodation and the now-famous Blue Train of South Africa where the quality of food, service and accommodation are high and even baths are available on board. Beach holidays, often combined with remarkable diving opportunities and, south of the Sahara, with safaris, also remain high on this agenda.

Established favourites

At the centre of the leisure holiday market is South

■ African adventures

Game parks in Sub-Saharan Africa, 2000
Source: Safari Consultants Ltd

Most visited...

1 Kruger, S.A.
2 Hluhluwe, S.A.
3 Tsavo. Ken.
4 Masai Mara, Ken.
5 Samburu, Ken.
6 Serengeti, Tanz.
7 Ngorogoro, Tanz.
8 Etosha, Nam.
9 Hwange, Zim.
10 Luangwe, Zam.

Up-and-coming...

1 Selous, Tanz.
2 Ruaha, Tanz.
3 Kafue, Zam.
4 Limpopo Valley, Bots.
5 Meru, Ken.

Africa, which despite its problems since the ending of apartheid, has the excellent infrastructure of big cites such as Cape Town, Johannesburg and Durban to support a thriving travel industry.

The North African states of Egypt, Morocco and Tunisia – which between them account for over 40% of Africa's travel arrivals – have the advantage of being able to market themselves as Mediterranean destinations.

With the impending collapse of Zimbabwe's market, Kenya is the only other sub-Saharan mainland African country with a major claim to a tourism industry. In terms of arrival figures, Botswana, Algeria and Nigeria run Kenya close, although these three rely far more heavily than does Kenya on arrivals from neighbouring countries rather than from outside Africa.

The major selling points of the big five are, apart from their year-round sunshine:

■ Big spenders

Expenditure by Africans on foreign travel, 1999 (US$ billions – excluding international transport)
Source: WTO

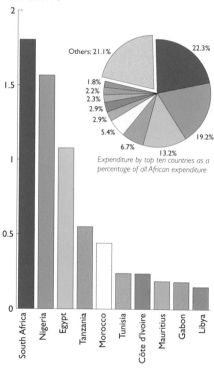

Expenditure by top ten countries as a percentage of all African expenditure

• South Africa – A modern infrastructure by African standards with a range of products including safaris, luxury train journeys, touring and golf.

• Kenya – Safaris and beach holidays are the dominant travel themes here with, respectively, Nairobi and Mombassa being principally gateways for these activities.

• Egypt – Thousands of years of history to explore, with modern hotels in many cities and the chance to cruise the River Nile in luxury. Cairo is also a popular short-break destination from Europe.

• Morocco – In close proximity to Europe, golf, the Sahara desert, fine beaches on its Atlantic coast and enough exotic and historic Imperial cities to make a whole tour itinerary.

• Tunisia – A number of developed resorts to suit European tastes and a growing inventory of excellent golf courses. 65% of international visitors are from Europe.

■ African breaks

The five biggest travellers: percentage of trips taken within Africa.
Source: WTO

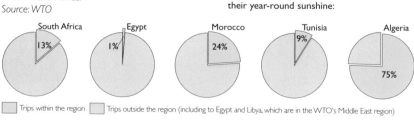

Trips within the region

Trips outside the region (including to Egypt and Libya, which are in the WTO's Middle East region)

Africa: Introduction

- Africa occupies 34% of the world's land area and is home to over 13% of the world's population.
- Africa's combined GDI is US$843,594 million, just under 3% of the world's total.
- Africa accounts for less than 5% of global travel departures and 2% of arrivals.
- International travel and tourism contributed over US$14 billion to Africa's economy in 1999, an increase of 14% over 1998.
- The eight most visited countries in Africa are in the north (Tunisia, Egypt, Morocco and Algeria) and the south (South Africa, Zimbabwe, Kenya and Botswana). Between them, these countries attracted over 77% of the continent's foreign visitors.
- Five African countries – South Africa, Tunisia, Egypt Morocco and Zimababwe – received nearly 70% of all visitor arrivals to Africa in 1999.
- The most-visited country in Africa, South Africa, ranked 25th in the world in 1999. Tunisia is 29th and Egypt 32nd.
- Four African countries – Egypt, South Africa, Morocco and Tunisia – accounted for nearly 70% of Africa's earnings from international travel and tourism in 1999.
- There were 31 million international tourist arrivals in Africa in 1999, an increase of 11.2% over 1998, nearly three times the world average. Only Asia showed a larger increase.
- The most significant growth in tourist arrivals was in North Africa (Algeria, Morocco, Tunisia, Sudan, Egypt and Libya) which showed a rise of 17.2%.
- All regions of Africa showed a growth in tourist arrivals in 1999 over 1998 of at least 6%.
- Of the countries with arrivals in excess of 500,000 in 1999, the greatest increase compared to 1998 was shown by Morocco (18%).
- Only 10% of the guests in international-standard hotels in West Africa in 1999 were tourists: the remainder were business travellers.
- Africa has a total of around 425,000 hotel rooms.
- South Africans are Africa's biggest travellers, accounting for over 27% of all Africa's recorded international departures.
- Lest anyone doubt the economic, as well as environmental, importance of the species, the research institute Panos Media has calculated that a Kenyan elephant is worth £560,000 in tourism revenue if it is allowed to realise its full lifespan.
- The Indian Ocean Islands of the Seychelles and Mauritius receive respectively 13.1% and 21.5% of their GNIs from travel and tourism.

The Indian Ocean islands of the Seychelles, Réunion and Mauritius have, partly because of their physical isolation, avoided the worst of the continent's problems. All are in different ways exceedingly beautiful and ecologically unique, and have – generally successfully – used these advantages to create a viable tourism industry. Travel receipts from these three states combined is exceeded only by South Africa, Morocco, Tunisia and Egypt. The economies here are in general heavily dependent on travel and tourism: in the Seychelles, this sector contributes nearly 70% of hard currency earnings and is responsible for around 30% of jobs.

Developing areas
Africa is still developing in tourism, and even the countries leading the way still have much to do to realise their ambitions. The challenges of geography, politics and economics are vast.

Many countries, including Namibia, Zambia, Côte d'Ivoire, Tanzania, Ghana and (perhaps surprisingly) Libya offer, in different ways and for different reasons, hopes for future travel and tourism growth. Political stability and international perceptions will remain key to progress here, and elsewhere in the continent.

Despite all its problems, Africa remains a uniquely fascinating and rewarding continent for all kinds of travellers, particularly those seeking adventure. It is to be hoped that responsible tourism policies, both by suppliers and consumers, can assist the continent in breaking the vicious cycle of poverty and perception which has haunted it for so long.

Business travel
Business travel has always been strong to Africa because colonialism left French, British, Belgian and German interests involved in mining, oil, diamonds, gold and minerals. None the less, the current slow-down in global economic activity is likely to affect Africa at least as much as other regions of the world. Intra-African business travel continues to be hampered by a poor transport infrastructure.

Problem areas
Political instability stalks the continent, in part due to the colonial legacy. Strife in one country can ignite whole regions in ethnic and tribal conflict. Rwanda is a case in point: once famous for its gorilla colonies, today it is a travel pariah because of genocide and atrocities committed during the 1990s.

Civil wars in many states, including the Democratic Republic of Congo, Angola, Sierra Leone, Sudan, Guinea Bissau, Algeria and Eritrea, show no immediate signs of cessation.

Zimbabwe, home to a number of major game parks and (with Zambia) the Victoria Falls, had a strong tourism profile in the late 1990s after developing safari and adventure products. Its markets have, however, since been lost as a result of continuing political uncertainty, civil unrest and economic deterioration.

There are personal safety fears in visiting many parts of Africa. The climate is often extreme, the maladies unfamiliar and the medical services uncertain. Visitors to the game parks are protected by armed wardens from the obvious dangers from wild animals. The cities also provide their hazards. Western government departments have constant advisories posted about a range of dangers; although urban crime is of course not a uniquely African problem.

Well-being concerns of a different nature centre on a number of diseases. These include malaria, yellow fever, polio and typhoid. (For more information, see pages 30-31.)

The real scourge of Africa's health is the rampant spread of AIDS. Poverty, drugs, tribal superstition and lack of sex education have all played their parts in its spread through much of central and southern Africa.

Visitors
Visitor arrivals and average receipts per visitor, 1999
Source: WTO

	Visitors (thousands)	Receipts per visitor
South Africa	6,026	$419
Tunisia	4,832	$323
Egypt	4,490	$869
Morocco	3,817	$493
Zimbabwe	2,101	$96
Kenya	857	$355
Botswana	750	$233
Algeria	749	$32
Nigeria	739	$192
Mauritius	578	$943
Namibia	560	$514
Zambia	456	$186
Tanzania	450	n/a
Réunion	394	$685
Ghana	373	$815
Senegal	369	$450
Swaziland	319	$110
Côte d'Ivoire	301	$359
Malawi	254	$79
Uganda	205	$727
Lesotho	186	$102
Gabon	178	$62
Burkina	160	$263
Benin	152	$217
Madagascar	138	$725
Cameroon	133	$301
Seychelles	125	$896
Ethiopia	92	$174
Gambia, The	91	$352
Mali	87	$575
Togo	70	$86
Cape Verde	67	$343
Eritrea	57	$491
Congo, Dem. Rep.	53	$38
Chad	47	$213
Angola	45	$289
Niger	43	$558
Libya	40	$700
Sudan	39	$51
Guinea	27	$259
Burundi	26	$38
Comoros	24	$792
Mauritania	24	n/a
Djibouti	21	$190
Central African Rep.	10	$600
Sierra Leone	6	$1,333
Congo	5	n/a

(Visitor arrival figures not available for Equatorial Guinea, Guinea-Bissau, Liberia, Mayotte, Mozambique, Rwanda, St Helena, São Tomé e Príncipe, Somalia or Western Sahara.)

Big earners
Receipts from foreign travel, 1999
(US$ billions – excluding international transport)
Source: WTO

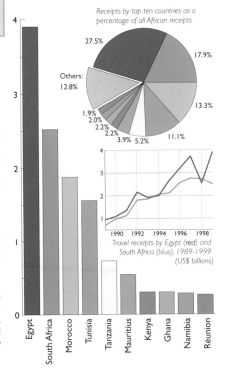

Receipts by top ten countries as a percentage of all African receipts

27.5%
17.9%
Others: 12.8%
13.3%
1.9%
2.0%
2.2%
2.2%
3.9% 5.2% 11.1%

Egypt
South Africa
Morocco
Tunisia
Tanzania
Mauritius
Kenya
Ghana
Namibia
Réunion

1990 1992 1994 1996 1998
Travel receipts by Egypt (red) and South Africa (blue), 1989-1999
(US$ billions)

Maps, charts and statistics on Africa follow on pages 104 to 113. See also the Countries A-Z section from page 184, and the Index from page 193.

Thanks to: James Hewlett of Somak; Jonathan Vernon-Powell of Nomadic Thoughts; Bill Adams of Safari Consultants Ltd.

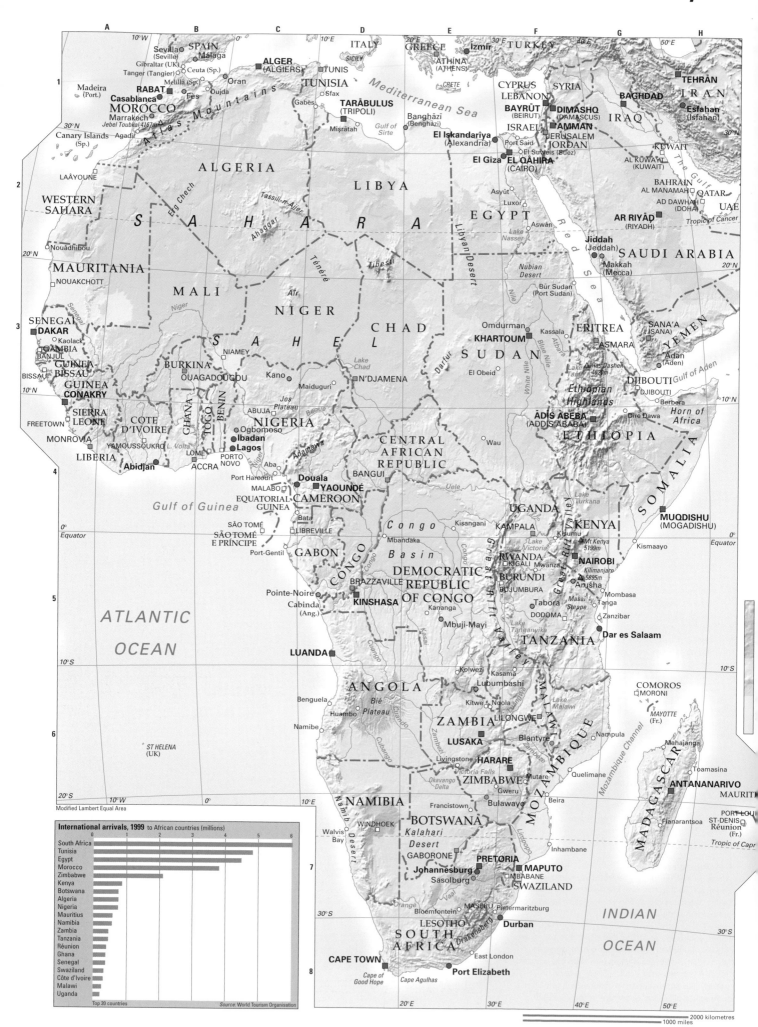

International arrivals, 1999 to African countries (millions)

South Africa
Tunisia
Egypt
Morocco
Zimbabwe
Kenya
Botswana
Algeria
Nigeria
Mauritius
Namibia
Zambia
Tanzania
Réunion
Ghana
Senegal
Swaziland
Côte d'Ivoire
Malawi
Uganda

Top 20 countries   Source: World Tourism Organisation

Modified Lambert Equal Area

2000 kilometres
1000 miles

Climate

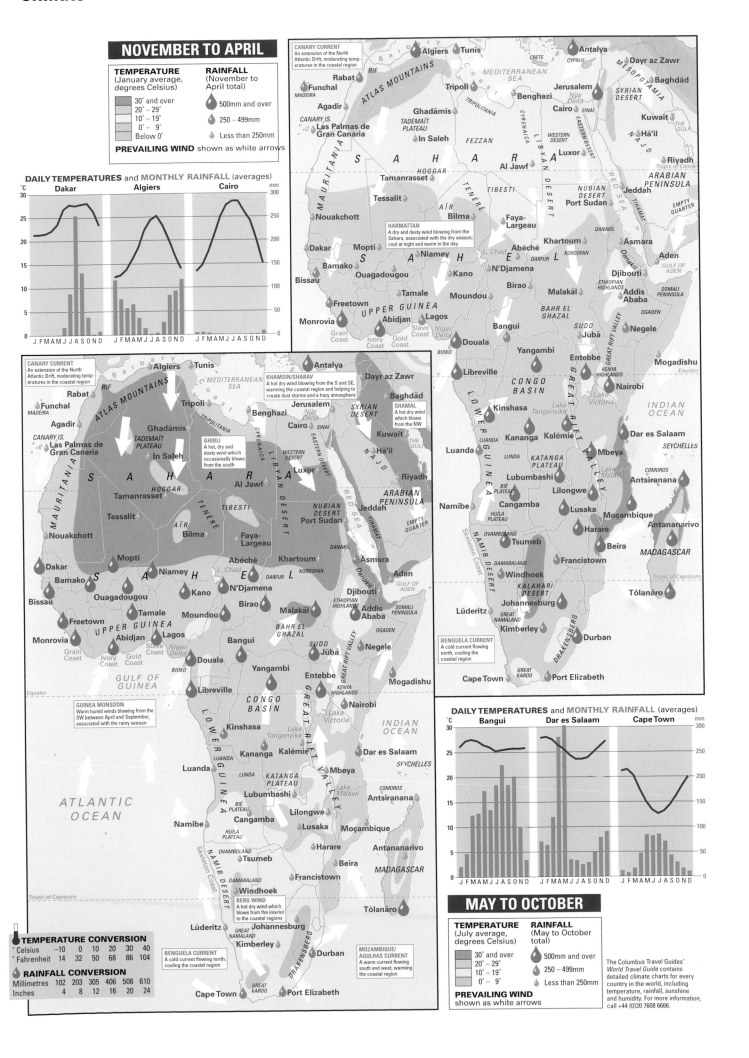

Africa: Northwest & West

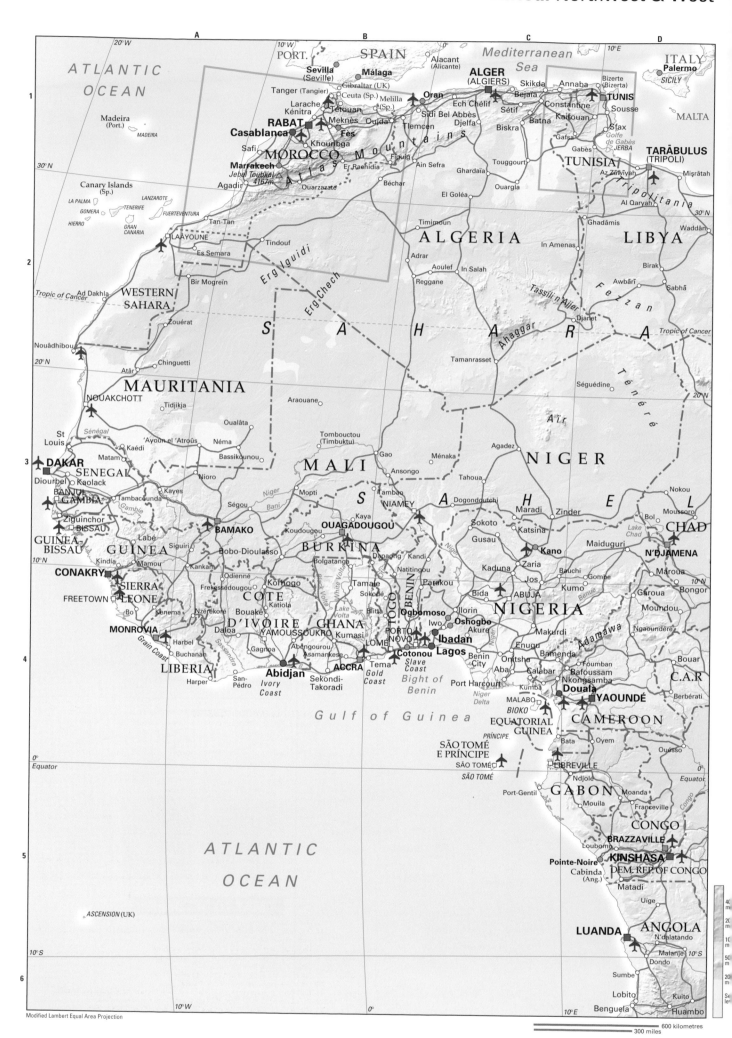

ATLANTIC OCEAN

PORT.

SPAIN

Mediterranean Sea

ITALY

Palermo

SICILY

Madeira (Port.)

MADEIRA

Sevilla (Seville)

Málaga

Tanger (Tangier)

Gibraltar (UK)

Ceuta (Sp.)

Melilla (Sp.)

Alacant (Alicante)

ALGER (ALGIERS)

Skikda

Annaba

Bizerte (Bizerta)

TUNIS

MALTA

Larache

Tétouan

Oran

Ech Chélif

Bejaia

Constantine

Sousse

Kénitra

Meknès

Oujda

Sidi Bel Abbès

Sétif

Kaïfouan

Sfax

RABAT

Fès

Tlemcen

Djelfa

Biskra

Batna

Golfe de Gabès

JERBA

Casablanca

Khouribga

Figuig

Ain Sefra

Ghardaïa

Touggourt

Gafsa

Gabès

TARÂBULUS (TRIPOLI)

Safi

MOROCCO

Er Rachidia

Ouargla

TUNISIA

Mişrātah

Marrakech

Jebel Toubkal 4167m

Ouarzazate

Béchar

El Goléa

Az Zāwiyah

Al Qaryah

LIBYA

Agadir

Tan-Tan

Timimoun

Ghadāmis

Waddān

Canary Islands (Sp.)

LA PALMA

LANZAROTE

Tropic of Cancer

LAAYOUNE

Es Semara

Tindouf

Adrar

Aoulef

In Salah

In Amenas

Birak

Awbārī

Sabhā

GOMERA

TENERIFE

FUERTEVENTURA

ALGERIA

HIERRO

GRAN CANARIA

Ad Dakhla

WESTERN SAHARA

Bir Mogreïn

Reggane

Tassili n'Ajjer

Felzan

Nouâdhibou

Zouérat

Ahaggar

Djanet

Tropic of Cancer

Chinguetti

Atâr

Tamanrasset

Ténéré

MAURITANIA

NOUAKCHOTT

Tidjikja

Araouane

Aïr

Séguédine

St Louis

Kaédi

Oualâta

Séléda

Agadez

NIGER

DAKAR

Matam

Néma

Tombouctou (Timbuktu)

Ménaka

Nokou

SENEGAL

Diourbel

Kaolack

Bassikounou

Gao

NIAMEY

Maradi

Zinder

Moussoro

BANJUL

Tambacounda

Kayes

Nioro

Ségou

Ansongo

Tahoua

Sokoto

Lake Chad

Bol

GAMBIA

Gambie

MALI

Mopti

Bani

Niger

Tambao

Dogondoutchi

Gusau

Katsina

Maiduguri

CHAD

Ziguinchor

Labé

Siguiri

Koudougou

OUAGADOUGOU

Kaya

Zaria

N'DJAMENA

BISSAU

GUINEA BISSAU

Kindia

Mamou

Bobo-Dioulasso

BURKINA

Kandi

Kano

Bauchi

Gombe

Mâroua

CONAKRY

SIERRA LEONE

FREETOWN

Kankan

Odienné

Frekessédougou

Korhogo

Katiola

Bolgatanga

Dapaong

Natitingou

Parakou

Kaduna

Jos

Kumo

Bongor

Garoua

NIGERIA

ABUJA

Ilorin

Bida

Makurdi

Enugu

Bamenda

Foumban

Ngaoundéré

Bouar

Bo

Kenema

Nzérékoré

Bouaké

Tamale

Sokodé

Blitta

Ogbomoso

Oshogbo

Akure

C.A.R

MONROVIA

Harbel

Daloa

COTE D'IVOIRE

GHANA

Lake Volta

Iwo

Ibadan

Benin City

Onitsha

Aba

Calabar

Bafoussam

Bouar

Berbérati

LIBERIA

Buchanan

Gagnoa

YAMOUSSOUKRO

Kumasi

LOMÉ

Lagos

Port Harcourt

Kumba

Nkongsamba

Douala

YAOUNDÉ

Harper

San-Pédro

Abéngourou

Asamankese

Tema

Cotonou

Slave Coast

Niger Delta

MALABO

CAMEROON

Grain Coast

Sassandra

Abidjan

Ivory Coast

Sekondi-Takoradi

Gold Coast

ACCRA

Bight of Benin

BIOKO

EQUATORIAL GUINEA

Bata

Oyem

Quésso

ATLANTIC OCEAN

Gulf of Guinea

SÃO TOMÉ E PRÍNCIPE

SÃO TOMÉ

PRÍNCIPE

SÃO TOMÉ

LIBREVILLE

Ndjolé

Moanda

GABON

Equator

Port-Gentil

Mouila

Francevile

Congo

CONGO

BRAZZAVILLE

ASCENSION (UK)

Pointe-Noire

KINSHASA

Cabinda (Ang.)

DEM. REP. OF CONGO

Matadi

Uíge

ANGOLA

LUANDA

N'dalatando

Malanje

Dondo

Sumbe

Lobito

Kuito

Benguela

Huambo

SAHARA

SAHEL

Erg Iguidi

Erg Chech

Sénégal

PORTO-NOVO

TOGO

BENIN

Modified Lambert Equal Area Projection

600 kilometres

300 miles

Languages, Morocco & Tunisia

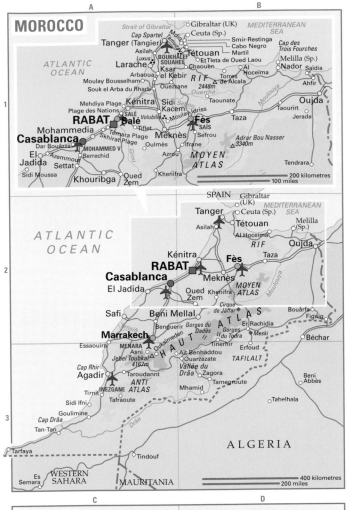

MOROCCO

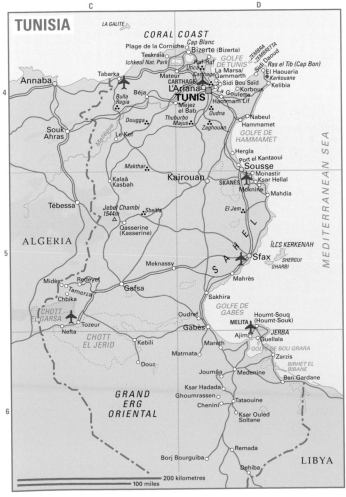

TUNISIA

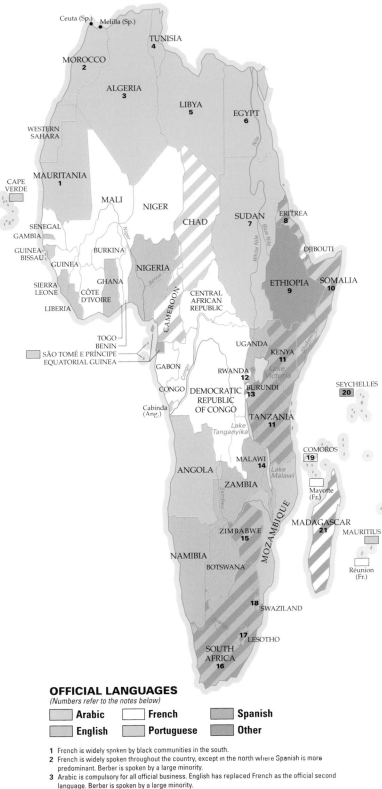

OFFICIAL LANGUAGES
(Numbers refer to the notes below)

Arabic	French	Spanish
English	Portuguese	Other

1 French is widely spoken by black communities in the south.
2 French is widely spoken throughout the country, except in the north where Spanish is more predominant. Berber is spoken by a large minority.
3 Arabic is compulsory for all official business. English has replaced French as the official second language. Berber is spoken by a large minority.
4 French is used for most business transactions. English is spoken in major cities and resorts. Berber is spoken by a large minority.
5 English is normally understood in hotels, restaurants and shops.
6 English and French are widely spoken in urban centres.
7 English is widely spoken throughout the country.
8 The official languages are Arabic and Tigrinya. English and Italian are the most common foreign languages.
9 The official language is Ahmaric, and English is widely understood. Italian and French are still widely spoken.
10 The official languages are Arabic and Somali. Some English and Italian are also spoken.
11 The official languages are English and Swahili.
12 The official languages are English, French and Kinyarwanda.
13 The official languages are French and Kirundi.
14 Chichewa is widely spoken and is regarded as the national language by Malawi's largest ethnic group, the Chewa.
15 The official languages are English, Ndebele and Shona.
16 The official languages are Afrikaans, English, Ndebele, Pedi, Sesotho, Siswati, Tsonga, Tswana, Venda, Xhosa and Zulu.
17 The official languages are English and Sesotho.
18 The official languages are English and Siswati.
19 The official languages are English, French and Comorian (a blend of Arabic and Swahili).
20 The official language is Creole, but English and French are widely spoken.
21 The official languages are French and Malagasy. Very little English is spoken.

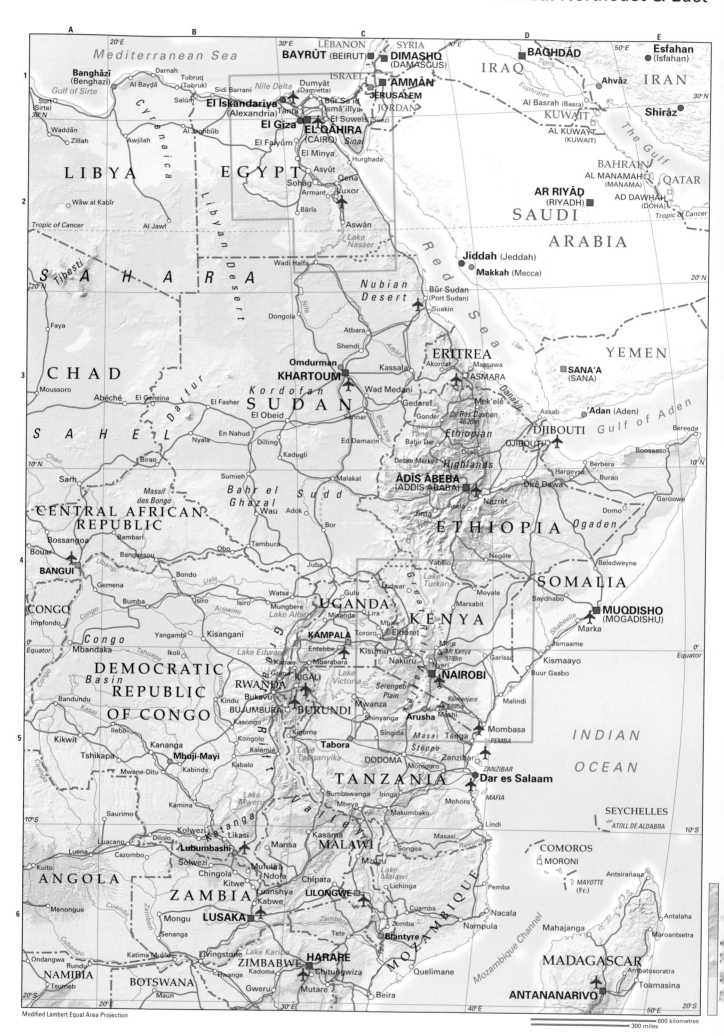

600 kilometres

300 miles

Egypt, Kenya & Red Sea Diving

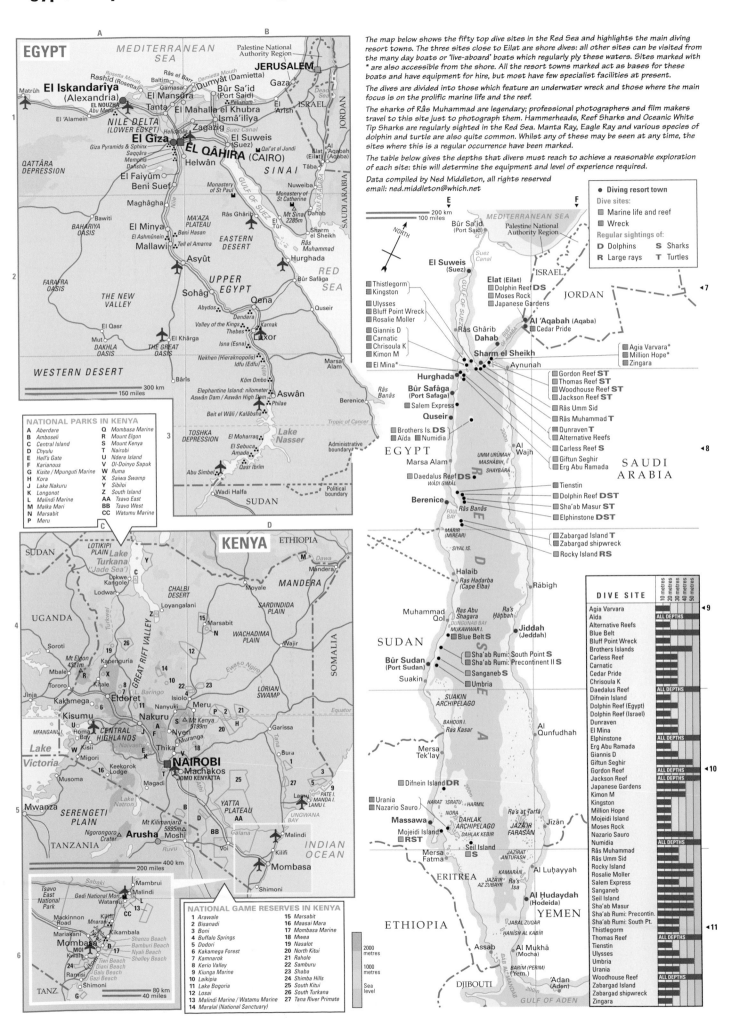

Southern Africa

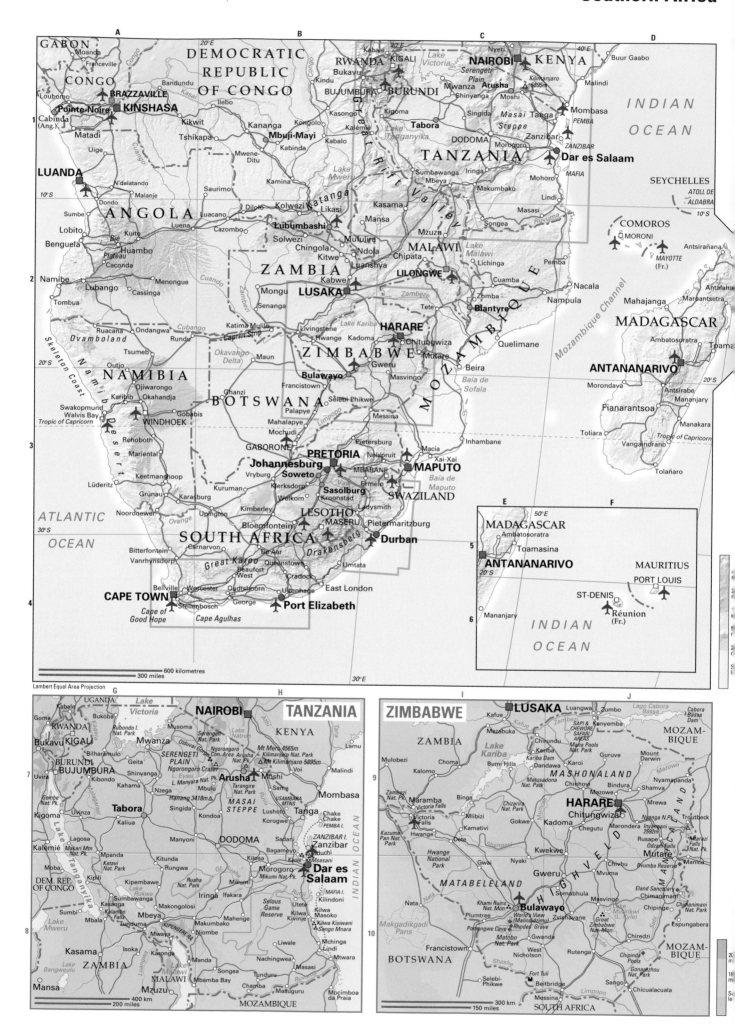

South Africa

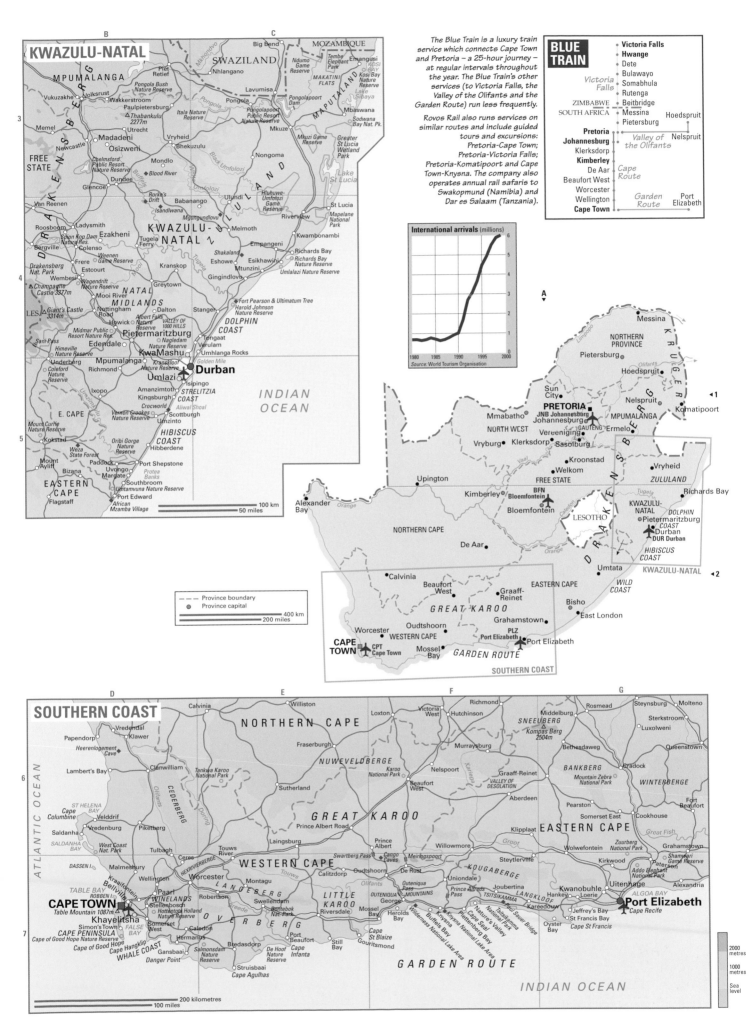

Wildlife Parks & Reserves

Africa is a prime destination for wildlife holidays: its national parks, game reserves and wildlife sanctuaries feature prominently in package holidays and tourist itineraries. Many parks, such as the Masai Mara, Serengeti and Kruger, are well-known throughout the world and a number of them have been recognised by both UNESCO and the WWF for their unique and important character.

The area of Africa south of the Sahara is featured here. Although there are areas of wildlife interest in northern Africa, particularly on the Mediterranean coast, these are generally on a much smaller scale and do not usually provide the primary motivation for travel to these countries.

The map and table features the major parks and reserves used by tour operators and visited by overseas tourists. Some lesser-known parks are also included to give a broader geographical spread; access to many of these may be difficult due to poor infrastructure or political problems.

The table lists the major species most likely to be seen while visiting each park or those animals for which the park is famous, according to government literature and independent reports. Quality of information varies considerably from country to country and the following table should be regarded as a rough guide only; in some cases no species information is currently available. Poaching is a serious problem in some countries, particularly where wildlife tourism is less developed.

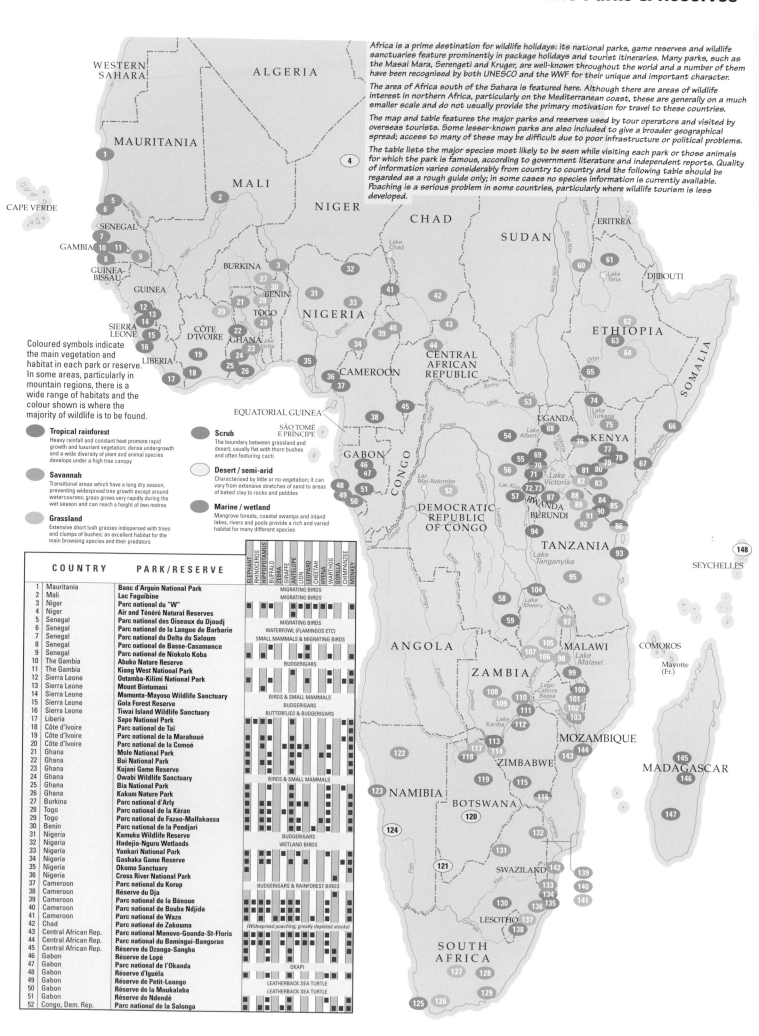

Coloured symbols indicate the main vegetation and habitat in each park or reserve. In some areas, particularly in mountain regions, there is a wide range of habitats and the colour shown is where the majority of wildlife is to be found.

Tropical rainforest
Heavy rainfall and constant heat promote rapid growth and luxuriant vegetation; dense undergrowth and a wide diversity of plant and animal species develops under a high tree canopy

Savannah
Transitional areas which have a long dry season, preventing widespread tree growth except around watercourses; grass grows very rapidly during the wet season and can reach a height of two metres

Grassland
Extensive short lush grasses indispersed with trees and clumps of bushes; an excellent habitat for the main browsing species and their predators

Scrub
The boundary between grassland and desert; usually flat with thorn bushes and often featuring cacti

Desert / semi-arid
Characterised by little or no vegetation; it can vary from extensive stretches of sand to areas of baked clay to rocks and pebbles

Marine / wetland
Mangrove forests, coastal swamps and inland lakes, rivers and pools provide a rich and varied habitat for many different species

	COUNTRY	PARK/RESERVE
1	Mauritania	Banc d'Arguin National Park
2	Mali	Lac Faguibine
3	Niger	Parc national du "W"
4	Niger	Aïr and Ténéré Natural Reserves
5	Senegal	Parc national des Oiseaux du Djoudj
6	Senegal	Parc national de la Langue de Barbarie
7	Senegal	Parc national du Delta du Saloum
8	Senegal	Parc national de Basse-Casamance
9	Senegal	Parc national de Niokolo Koba
10	The Gambia	Abuko Nature Reserve
11	The Gambia	Kiang West National Park
12	Sierra Leone	Outamba-Kilimi National Park
13	Sierra Leone	Mount Bintumani
14	Sierra Leone	Mamunta-Mayoso Wildlife Sanctuary
15	Sierra Leone	Gola Forest Reserve
16	Sierra Leone	Tiwai Island Wildlife Sanctuary
17	Liberia	Sapo National Park
18	Côte d'Ivoire	Parc national de Taï
19	Côte d'Ivoire	Parc national de la Marahoué
20	Côte d'Ivoire	Parc national de la Comoé
21	Ghana	Mole National Park
22	Ghana	Bui National Park
23	Ghana	Kujani Game Reserve
24	Ghana	Owabi Wildlife Sanctuary
25	Ghana	Bia National Park
26	Ghana	Kakum Nature Park
27	Burkina	Parc national d'Arly
28	Togo	Parc national de la Kéran
29	Togo	Parc national de Fazao-Malfakassa
30	Benin	Parc national de la Pendjari
31	Nigeria	Kamuku Wildlife Reserve
32	Nigeria	Hadejia-Nguru Wetlands
33	Nigeria	Yankari National Park
34	Nigeria	Gashaka Game Reserve
35	Nigeria	Okomo Sanctuary
36	Nigeria	Cross River National Park
37	Cameroon	Parc national du Korup
38	Cameroon	Réserve du Dja
39	Cameroon	Parc national de la Bénoue
40	Cameroon	Parc national de Bouba Ndjida
41	Cameroon	Parc national de Waza
42	Chad	Parc national de Zakouma
43	Central African Rep.	Parc national Manovo-Gounda-St-Floris
44	Central African Rep.	Parc national du Bamingui-Bangoran
45	Central African Rep.	Réserve du Dzanga-Sangha
46	Gabon	Réserve de Lopé
47	Gabon	Parc national de l'Okanda
48	Gabon	Réserve d'Iguéla
49	Gabon	Réserve de Petit-Loango
50	Gabon	Réserve de la Moukalaba
51	Gabon	Réserve de Ndendé
52	Congo, Dem. Rep.	Parc national de la Salonga

Table species column headers: ELEPHANT, RHINOCEROS, HIPPOPOTAMUS, BUFFALO, ZEBRA, GIRAFFE, ANTELOPE, LION, LEOPARD, CHEETAH, HYENA, WARTHOG, GORILLA, CHIMPANZEE, MONKEY

Table annotations: MIGRATING BIRDS; WATERFOWL (FLAMINGOS ETC); SMALL MAMMALS & MIGRATING BIRDS; BUDGERIGARS; BIRDS & SMALL MAMMALS; BUTTERFLIES & BUDGERIGARS; WETLAND BIRDS; BUDGERIGARS & RAINFOREST BIRDS; (Widespread poaching; greatly depleted stocks); OKAPI; LEATHERBACK SEA TURTLE

SEYCHELLES
COMOROS
Mayotte (Fr.)

Wildlife Parks & Reserves; Indian Ocean Islands

	COUNTRY	PARK/RESERVE
53	Congo, Dem. Rep.	Parc national de la Garamba
54	Congo, Dem. Rep.	Réserve du Okapi
55	Congo, Dem. Rep.	Parc national des Virunga
56	Congo, Dem. Rep.	Parc national de la Maiko
57	Congo, Dem. Rep.	Parc national du Kahuzi-Biega
58	Congo, Dem. Rep.	Parc national de l'Upemba
59	Congo, Dem. Rep.	Parc national de Kundelungu
60	Sudan	Dinder National Park
61	Ethiopia	Simien National Park
62	Ethiopia	Awash National Park
63	Ethiopia	Langano & Shala-Abiyata Lakes Nat. Park
64	Ethiopia	Bale Mountains National Park
65	Ethiopia	Omo and Mago National Parks
66	Somalia	Hargeysa National Park
67	Somalia	Kismayo National Park
68	Uganda	Murchison Falls National Park
69	Uganda	Ruwenzori National Park
70	Uganda	Queen Elizabeth National Park
71	Uganda	Bwindi Impenetrable Forest National Park*
72	Rwanda	Parc des Volcans
73	Rwanda	Parc national de l'Akagera
74	Kenya	Sibiloi National Park
75	Kenya	Marsabit National Park
76	Kenya	Mount Elgon National Park
77	Kenya	Samburu National Reserve
78	Kenya	Meru National Park
79	Kenya	Mount Kenya National Park*
80	Kenya	Aberdare National Park
81	Kenya	Lake Nakuru National Park
82	Kenya	Maasai Mara National Reserve*
83	Kenya	Nairobi National Park
84	Kenya	Amboseli National Park*
85	Kenya	Tsavo National Park
86	Kenya	Shimba Hills National Reserve
87	Tanzania	Rubondo Island National Park
88	Tanzania	Serengeti National Park*
89	Tanzania	Ngorongoro Conservation Area
90	Tanzania	Kilimanjaro National Park*
91	Tanzania	Arusha National Park
92	Tanzania	Tarangire National Park
93	Tanzania	Jozani Reserve, Zanzibar
94	Tanzania	Gombe National Park
95	Tanzania	Ruaha National Park
96	Tanzania	Selous Game Reserve
97	Malawi	Nyika National Park
98	Malawi	Kasungu National Park
99	Malawi	Lake Malawi National Park*
100	Malawi	Liwonde National Park*
101	Malawi	Majete Game Reserve
102	Malawi	Lengwe National Park
103	Malawi	Mwabvi National Park
104	Zambia	Sumbu National Park
105	Zambia	North Luangwa National Park
106	Zambia	South Luangwa National Park
107	Zambia	Kasanka National Park
108	Zambia	Kafue National Park
109	Zambia	Lochinvar National Park
110	Zambia	Lower Zambezi National Park
111	Zimbabwe	Mana Pools National Park
112	Zimbabwe	Matsudona National Park
113	Zimbabwe	Zambezi National Park
114	Zimbabwe	Hwange National Park
115	Zimbabwe	Matobo National Park
116	Zimbabwe	Gonarezhou National Park
117	Botswana	Chobe National Park
118	Botswana	Moremi Wildlife Reserve*
119	Botswana	Makgadikgadi Pans Game Reserve
120	Botswana	Central Kalahari Game Reserve
121	Botswana / S. Africa	Kgalagadi Transfrontier Park
122	Namibia	Etosha National Park*
123	Namibia	Cape Cross Reserve
124	Namibia	Namib-Naukluft National Park
125	South Africa	Cape of Good Hope Nature Reserve
126	South Africa	Bontebok National Park
127	South Africa	Karoo National Park
128	South Africa	Mountain Zebra National Park
129	South Africa	Addo Elephant National Park
130	South Africa	Willem Pretorius Game Reserve
131	South Africa	Pilanesberg National Park
132	South Africa	Kruger National Park*
133	South Africa	Ndumo Game Reserve
134	South Africa	Mkuzi Game Reserve
135	South Africa	Greater St Lucia Wetland Park
136	South Africa	Hluhluwe-Umfolozi Game Reserve
137	South Africa	Giant's Castle Game Reserve
138	Lesotho	Sehlabathebe National Park
139	Swaziland	Hlane Game Sanctuary
140	Swaziland	Malolotja Nature Reserve
141	Swaziland	Mkhaya Nature Reserve
142	Mozambique	Maputo Elephant Reserve
143	Mozambique	Parque Nacional da Gorongosa
144	Mozambique	Reserve de Marromeu
145	Madagascar	Réserve de Perinet
146	Madagascar	Parc national de Ranomafana
147	Madagascar	Parc national de l'Isalo
148	Seychelles	Cousin Island Nature Reserve

Column headings (left to right): ELEPHANT, RHINOCEROS, HIPPOPOTAMUS, BUFFALO, ZEBRA, GIRAFFE, ANTELOPE, LION, LEOPARD, CHEETAH, HYENA, WARTHOG, GORILLA, CHIMPANZEE, MONKEY

Notes appearing within the table: OKAPI; (Data unavailable); BIRDS; FLAMINGOS; SABLE ANTELOPE; WETLAND BIRDS; RED COLOBUS MONKEY; BUTTERFLIES & BIRDS; Heavily poached in 1980's; lodges re-opened 1997; FLAMINGOS; SEALS; BONTEBOK; MOUNTAIN ZEBRA; BABOONS & BIRDS; (Wide range of habitats; small mammals most likely to be seen but larger game being reintroduced into the country); (Data unavailable); BIRDS

Parks and reserves marked with an asterisk (*) are featured in Columbus Travel Guides' *Tourist Attractions and Events of the World*, 2nd edition.
For more information, call +44 (0)20 7608 6666.

International arrivals (millions)

Lines labelled: Mauritius, Réunion, Seychelles
Years: 1980, 1985, 1990, 1995, 2000
Source: World Tourism Organisation

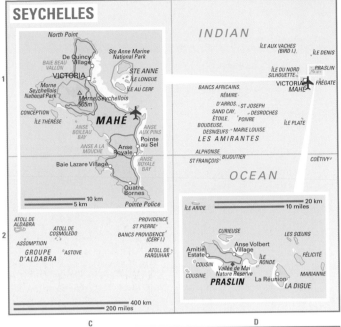

SEYCHELLES

RÉUNION

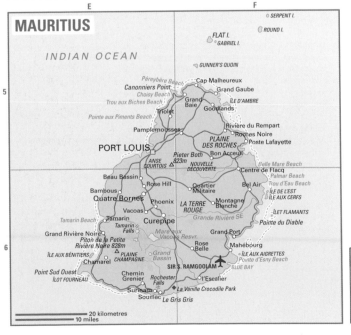

MAURITIUS

1000 metres
500 metres
Sea level

Asia

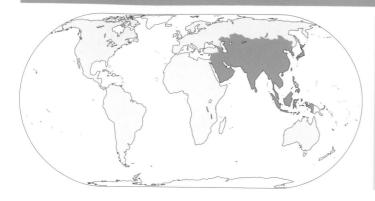

Key facts	Asia	World	Asia %
Number of Countries	48	226	21.2%
Area ('000 sq km)	31,415	135,463	23.2%
Population (000)	3,377,482	5,973,801	56.5%
Population Density (/sq km)	107	44	–
Gross Nat. Income (US$m)	7,716,804	29,986,364	25.7%
Visitor Arrivals ('000)	109,225	649,223	16.8%
Visitor Receipts (US$m)	75,971	456,402	16.6%
Travel Departures ('000)	93,106	594,797	15.7%
Travel Expenditure (US$m)	74,740	397,040	18.8%

GNI figures relate to 1999. Population figures are taken from the most recent census or reliable estimate. Travel figures (from the WTO) are generally for 1999, but where these are unavailable or unreliable, figures from earlier years have been used. All travel figures are based on overnight stays, not same-day visitors. Where data for certain countries was not available, this has been regarded as zero. Global totals for Visitor Arrivals/Travel Departures and Visitor Receipts/Travel Expenditure do not equal each other due to differing methods of reporting inbound and outbound data. For more information on what is regarded as a country for the purposes of this book, and for more detailed statistical information, please see the Countries A-Z section from page 184.

ASIA OFFERS probably more variety for the traveller than any other region. It stretches from the Mediterranean to the Pacific, from the exotic cultures of the Middle East to the mysteries of China, and from the arid expanse of the Gobi Desert to the rain forests of New Guinea. It has over half the world's population and six of the world's ten largest cities. After two years of sluggish growth, 1999 saw travel visitors to Asia rise by over 13%. The continent has both the potential for further growth and the financial means to accomplish it. Many of the wealthier countries are investing heavily in construction and, where necessary, modernisation – China, for example, is currently engaged in a US$750 billion infrastructure programme. The increasing liberalisation of China's economy is likely to be the most significant long-term feature of Asia's travel industry: with one fifth of the world's population now openly engaged in the pursuit of material wealth, other countries – both inside and outside Asia – will be considering how they can secure their share of the increase in business and leisure travel from China that is likely to ensue.

Travel trends

From older generations with savings and disposable incomes to back-packers on a budget, Asia has been holding a particular appeal, with its diverse histories and cultures being primary reasons for choosing the region.

With so many more people maintaining active lifestyles, adventure is also playing a big part in the future of tourism across Asia. Jungle hiking, cycling and canoeing feature in many specialist tour programmes.

Asia's cities, such as Hong Kong, Singapore, Tokyo and Mumbai (Bombay), have long offered a fascinating blend of the familiar and the exotic. Many are also well-established stop-off points en route to and from Europe, Australia and the Americas.

Established favourites

The stars of Asian tourism include:

* Singapore, often described as clinical in its cleanliness, has long been a popular city-breaks choice. It is looking to attract a younger clientele and to increase lengths of stay. Dual-centre packages with neighbouring and trouble-hit Indonesia have been in decline recently.

* Thailand has sustained dramatic growth since the Asian financial crisis. Its exceptional beaches and resorts such as Pattaya have enjoyed an environmental clean-up. Steps have also been taken

to eradicate the sex tourism that has scarred Thailand's image.

* Hong Kong, a popular and bustling destination, is recovering from three years in the doldrums following return of sovereignty to China.

* The Maldives' tourism industry is based on fabulous beaches, blue seas and good hotels. Together with the Seychelles and Mauritius, they are world leaders for weddings and honeymoons.

■ Asian leaders

Top 10 Asian destinations (Kuoni holidays, ex-UK)
Source: Kuoni

	'99	'00	'01	World
Thailand	1	1	1	1
Maldives	2	2	2	2
Sri Lanka	4	3	3	3
Hong Kong	3	4	4	6
Dubai (UAE)	8	5	6	7
Singapore	5	6	5	8
Malaysia	7	7	7	9
Indonesia	6	8	8	10

(2001 figures are estimates)

Developing areas

* China – retains great mystique but the 'Bamboo Curtain' is parting and a discernible dilution of communism offers greater access.

* Malaysia – beach holidays to Penang and Langkawi dominate. Sarawak, Tioman and Redang are being developed as resorts of the future.

■ Asian breaks

■ Asian breaks

The five biggest travellers: percentage of trips taken within the Asia/Pacific region.
Source: WTO, 1999

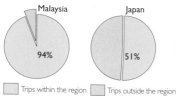

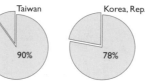

Malaysia	Japan	China	Taiwan	Korea, Rep.
94%	51%	83%	90%	78%

☐ Trips within the region   ☐ Trips outside the region

■ Big spenders

Expenditure by Asians on foreign travel, 1999
(US$ millions – excluding international transport)
Source: WTO

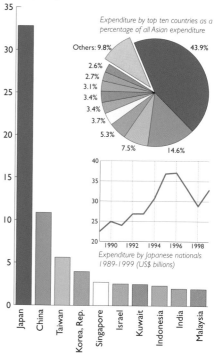

Expenditure by top ten countries as a percentage of all Asian expenditure

Others: 9.8%
2.6%
2.7%
3.1%
3.4%
3.4%
3.7%
5.3%
7.5%
14.6%
43.9%

Expenditure by Japanese nationals 1989-1999 (US$ billions)

Japan / China / Taiwan / Korea, Rep. / Singapore / Israel / Kuwait / Indonesia / India / Malaysia

* Cambodia – working with neighbouring Thailand on the *Two Kingdoms, One Destination* campaign which recognises Bangkok as the gateway to Cambodia and Vietnam.

* Dubai – billions of dollars have been invested in landmark hotels, golf courses and shopping facilities to make it the Middle East's most popular short-break destination.

* India – with Nepal, it attracts the adventurous and the backpackers. Goa and the Golden Triangle are ever-popular. The north-eastern states are now being promoted to foreign visitors.

Issues

The so-called Tiger Economy dominated by Japan, South Korea, Taiwan, Thailand, Singapore and Hong Kong was cowed by a crash four years ago, but has been showing signs of recovery.

The 2002 football World Cup is not only thrusting joint hosts Japan and South Korea into the world tourism shop window, but also Asia as a whole. While

Asia: Introduction

- Asia occupies 23% of the world's land area and is home to over 56% of the world's population.
- Asia's combined GDI is US$7,716,804 million, just over a quarter of the world's total.
- Asia accounts for just under 16% of global travel departures and just under 19% of arrivals.
- International travel and tourism contributed nearly US$75 billion to Asia's economy in 1999.
- The most visited country in Asia in 1999 was China (not including Hong Kong or Macau), which received over 27 million visitors: worldwide, only France, the USA, Spain and Italy received more. More than two thirds of these arrivals were ethnic Chinese, mainly coming from Hong Kong, Macau and Taiwan.
- Four countries – China (including Hong Kong and Macau), Thailand, Malaysia and Singapore – received over 60% of all visitors to Asia in 1999.
- 14 other Asian countries received more than 1 million visitors in 1999.
- There were 109 million international tourist arrivals in Asia in 1999, an increase of 13.5% over 1998, three and a half times the world's average.
- The largest growth in tourist arrivals was in Southeast Asia (including Malaysia, Singapore, Thailand and Vietnam) which showed a rise of 15.3%.
- The country with the largest growth in tourist arrivals compared to 1998 was Malaysia (49.2%), followed by Laos (35%) and Cambodia (28.7%).
- Of the countries for which WTO figures are available, only two – Mongolia and Myanmar – showed a decrease in 1999 visitor arrivals compared to 1998: but these two countries accounted for less than 0.5% of Asia's total.
- 15 countries (including Hong Kong and Macau) received in excess of US$1 billion from travel and tourism receipts in 1999.
- Macau's casinos contributed around 50% of the territory's revenue in 1999.
- Of these 15 countries, the largest increases compared to 1998 were all in Southeast Asia: Malaysia (14.9%); Cambodia (14.5%); Thailand (12.8%); and Singapore (10.6%).
- China (including Hong Kong and Macau) received nearly US$24 billion from travel and tourism in 1999, over 30% of Asia's total.
- Malaysians are Asia's biggest travellers, recording over 26 million overseas journeys in 1999, 28% of Asia's total. Worldwide, only five nationalities travelled more.
- Between 1995 and 1999, the number of hotel rooms in South Asia (including the Indian sub-continent) increased by over 17%.
- Despite a recent slowdown, the Japanese continue comfortably to top the Asian big spenders' league: their expenditure on travel and tourism in 1999 was nearly US$33 billion, 44% of Asia's total. Worldwide, only the Americans, the Germans and the British spent more.

Japan, with its higher profile as a tourist destination, was welcoming the increased exposure, Korea was looking to shake off a 'business travel only' tag and inject a greater leisure element into its tourism.

The thawing of relations between South and North Korea, if successful, is likely to lead both to the opening up of what is in many ways the travel industry's last frontier, and – in the longer term – to there being an additional 21 million people in the world who can afford to travel.

Gulf States such as Qatar and Bahrain are developing a tourism product as insurance for when the oil runs out. With attractions such as golf and historic sites, they have ambitions to be more than shopping stopovers en route from Europe to the east, and are more liberal about alcohol than other Islamic states.

On the western boundaries of Asia, Syria, Lebanon, and Jordan find their tourism fortunes inextricably linked with that of their neighbours Israel and the Palestinian Authority. The new Syrian regime is moving towards a more liberal economy which will encourage tourism. Lebanon, with Beirut one of the region's highlights before it was destroyed by its own long civil war, has seen attempts to lure back visitors thwarted by tensions among its southern neighbours. Jordan has a sufficiently-established tourism business thanks to Petra, the rose-red city carved out of rock, and other historical sites, to withstand most of the effects of regional problems.

Business travel
The once-strong economies of the east made Japan, South Korea, Taiwan, Singapore and Hong Kong some of the most visited business travel destinations in the world. Video-conferencing and e-mail communication have contributed to reduced demand, as has the Asian recession and the generally depressed global business travel sector. The consequences of the economic liberalisation in China might help to reverse this trend.

Problem areas
Political problems have not dampened Asia's overall tourism success. Indonesia has been high on the instability list with unrest and violence in non-tourist regions and the violent suppression of East Timor. Political and ethnic violence in Sumatra, Java, Sulawesi, and Kalimantan prompted western government warnings about visiting.

Once viewed as one of the most idyllic of destinations, Bali stood immune from Indonesia's troubles until its own political unrest erupted in 2000.

Although thousands of miles away from the scene of the crime, the shockwaves of the terrorist attacks on the USA impacted on much of the Asia region. Afghanistan became the target for American reprisals and the large centres of Islam such as Indonesia, Malaysia, Pakistan and the Middle East led the protests.

The Philippines' trouble spots have hitherto been well away from the popular beach resorts of Cebu and Boracay and the capital Manila.

Myanmar, formerly Burma, remains accused of widespread human rights abuses and attracts little in international tourism.

China continues to attract unfavourable attention because of its human rights record.

Sri Lanka has several times tried to reintroduce tourism, efforts consistently undermined by the activities of Tamil separatists who have been waging a terror campaign over several decades.

In the Middle East, the continuing Israeli/Palestinian conflict has resulted in severe damage to Israel's tourism industry of beach and scuba diving holidays in the Red Sea resort of Eilat and pilgrimages and coach touring around Biblical locations.

Asia is one of the world's major sources of illegal drugs. In some parts of the region, the circumstances which contribute to and result from this do not tend towards the political and economic stability upon which a successful travel industry depends.

■ Visitors
Visitor arrivals and average receipts per visitor, 1999
Source: WTO

	Visitors (thousands)	Receipts per visitor
China	27,047	$521
China: Hong Kong	11,328	$636
Thailand	8,651	$774
Malaysia	7,931	$446
Singapore	6,258	$955
China: Macau	5,050	$488
Indonesia	4,728	$996
Korea, Rep. (South)	4,660	$1,460
Japan	4,438	$772
India	2,482	$1,223
United Arab Emirates	2,481	$245
Taiwan	2,411	$1,481
Israel	2,312	$1,286
Philippines	2,171	$1,167
Bahrain	1,991	$205
Kuwait	1,884	$129
Vietnam	1,782	$48
Syria	1,386	$981
Jordan	1,358	$585
Iran	1,321	$501
Brunei	964	$38
Lebanon	673	$999
Azerbaijan	602	$135
Oman	502	$207
Nepal	492	$341
Sri Lanka	436	$631
Qatar	435	n/a
Pakistan	432	$176
Maldives	430	$777
Georgia	384	$1,042
Cambodia	368	$516
Turkmenistan	300	$640
Uzbekistan	272	$70
Palestine NAR	271	$487
Laos	259	$375
Myanmar	198	$177
Bangladesh	173	$289
Mongolia	159	$226
Yemen	88	$727
Kyrgyzstan	69	$116
Armenia	41	$659
Bhutan	7	$1,286

(Visitor arrival figures not available for Afghanistan, Iraq, Kazakstan, Korea, DPR, Saudi Arabia or Tajikistan.)

Maps, charts and statistics on Asia follow on pages 116 to 131. See also the Countries A-Z section from page 184, and the Index from page 193.

Thanks to: Anne-Marie Hansen, Kuoni Travel

■ Big earners
Receipts from foreign travel, 1999
(US$ millions – excluding international transport)
Source: WTO

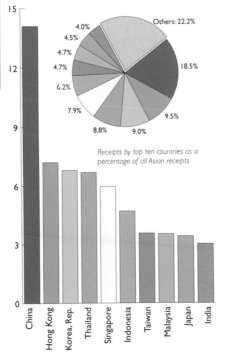

Others: 22.2%
18.5%
9.5%
9.0%
8.8%
7.9%
6.2%
4.7%
4.7%
4.5%
4.0%

Receipts by top ten countries as a percentage of all Asian receipts

China | Hong Kong | Korea, Rep. | Thailand | Singapore | Indonesia | Taiwan | Malaysia | Japan | India

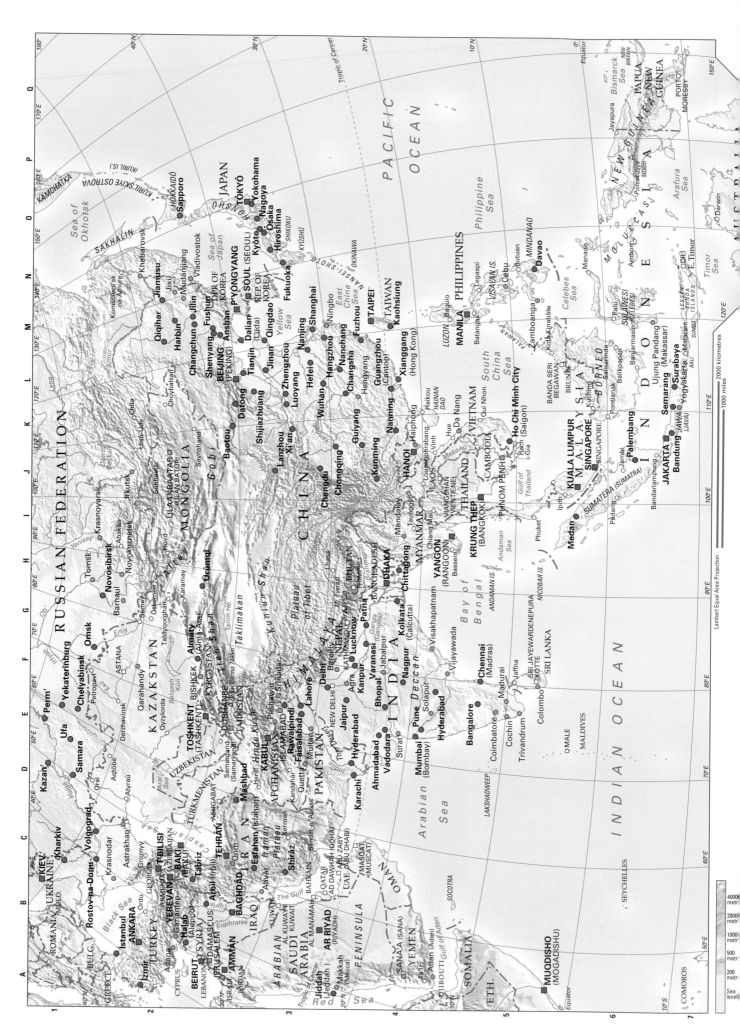

Climate

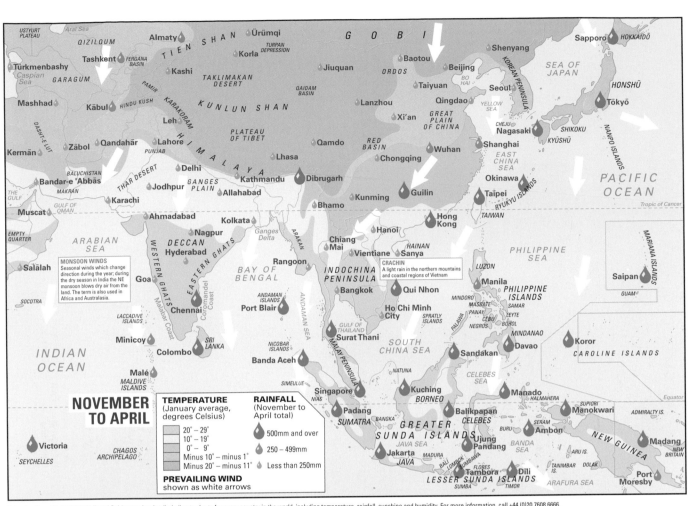

NOVEMBER TO APRIL

TEMPERATURE
(January average, degrees Celsius)

20° – 29°
10° – 19°
0° – 9°
Minus 10° – minus 1°
Minus 20° – minus 11°

RAINFALL
(November to April total)

500mm and over
250 – 499mm
Less than 250mm

PREVAILING WIND
shown as white arrows

MONSOON WINDS
Seasonal winds which change direction during the year; during the dry season in India the NE monsoon blows dry air from the land. The term is also used in Africa and Australasia.

CRACHIN
A light rain in the northern mountains and coastal regions of Vietnam

Columbus Travel Guides' *World Travel Guide* contains detailed climate charts for every country in the world, including temperature, rainfall, sunshine and humidity. For more information, call +44 (0)20 7608 6666.

MAY TO OCTOBER

TEMPERATURE
(July average, degrees Celsius)

30° and over
20° – 29°
10° – 19°
0° – 9°
Minus 10° – minus 1°

RAINFALL
(May to October total)

500mm and over
250 – 499mm
Less than 250mm

PREVAILING WIND
shown as white arrows

MONSOON WINDS
Seasonal winds which change direction during the year; during the wet season in India the SW monsoon blows humid air from the ocean. The term is also used in Africa and Australasia.

KHARIF
The rainy season in northern India and Arab countries

TEMPERATURE CONVERSION						
°Celsius	−10	0	10	20	30	40
°Fahrenheit	14	32	50	68	86	104

RAINFALL CONVERSION						
Millimetres	102	203	305	406	508	610
Inches	4	8	12	16	20	24

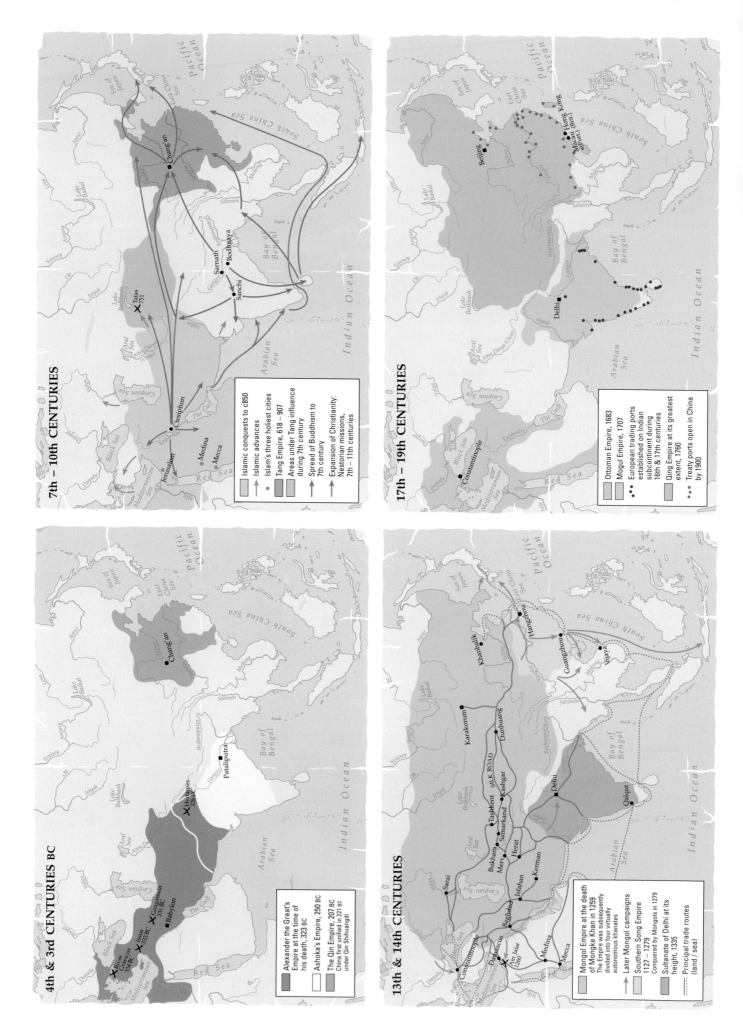

7th – 10th CENTURIES

Talas 751
Chang'an
Sarnath
Bodhgaya
Sanchi
Ctesiphon
Jerusalem
Medina
Mecca

- Islamic conquests to c850
- Islamic advances
- Islam's three holiest cities
- Tang Empire, 618 – 907
- Areas under Tang influence during 7th century
- Spread of Buddhism to 7th century
- Expansion of Christianity: Nestorian missions, 7th – 11th centuries

17th – 19th CENTURIES

Beijing
Hong Kong
Macau (Port.)
Delhi
Constantinople

- Ottoman Empire, 1683
- Mogul Empire, 1707
- European trading ports established on Indian subcontinent during 16th & 17th centuries
- Qing Empire at its greatest extent, 1760
- Treaty ports open in China by 1900

4th & 3rd CENTURIES BC

Chang'an
Pataliputra
Hydaspes 326 BC
Gaugamela 331 BC
Babylon
Issus 333 BC
River Granicus 334 BC

- Alexander the Great's Empire at the time of his death, 323 BC
- Ashoka's Empire, 250 BC
- The Qin Empire, 207 BC China first unified in 221 BC under Qin Shihuangdi

13th & 14th CENTURIES

Hangzhou
Karakorum
Kharbalik
Guangzhou
Vijaya
Dunhuang
SILK ROAD
Kashgar
Delhi
Tashkent
Samarkand
Bukhara
Herat
Merv
Kerman
Isfahan
Calicut
Sarai
Baghdad
Damascus
Ain Jalut 1260
Constantinople
Medina
Mecca

- Mongol Empire at the death of Mongke Khan in 1259 The Empire was subsequently divided into four virtually autonomous khanates
- Later Mongol campaigns
- Southern Song Empire 1127 – 1279 Conquered by Mongols in 1279
- Sultanate of Delhi at its height, 1335
- Principal trade routes (land / sea)

Museums and Art Galleries

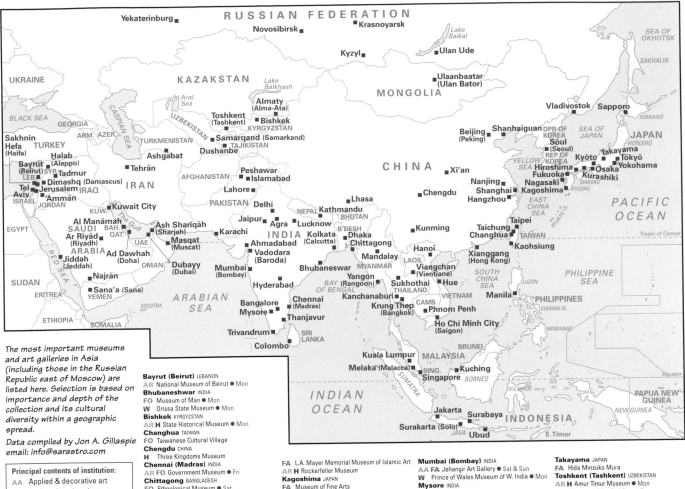

The most important museums and art galleries in Asia (including those in the Russian Republic east of Moscow) are listed here. Selection is based on importance and depth of the collection and its cultural diversity within a geographic spread.

Data compiled by Jon A. Gillaspie
email: info@sarastro.com

Principal contents of institution:

AA Applied & decorative art
AR Archaeology / ancient art
FA Fine art (paintings, sculpture)
FO Folk art & culture / ethnology
H History / historical site / reconstruction
NH Natural history
ST Science / technology
W Wide range of subjects

Opening times:

Days or months preceded by a red circle (●) indicate when the institution is closed.
Many close on national holidays and other special days. Some museums and galleries have shorter opening hours at certain days of the week or in certain months.

Admission charges:

All charge for admission except those shown in *italics*, where entry is free (although charges for special exhibitions may apply).
Some institutions allow free entry or reduce their admission charges on certain days.

Ad Dawhah (Doha) QATAR
FO *Ethnographic Museum* ● Sat
W *Qatar National Museum* ● Sat
Agra INDIA
H Taj Mahal Museum
Ahmadabad INDIA
FA NC Mehta Gallery (Indology Institute) ● Mon
FO *Tribal Art Museum* ● Sun
Al Manamah BAHRAIN
W National Museum ● Fri
Almaty KAZAKHSTAN
AR H Central State Museum ● Tue
FA Kasteyev Museum of Fine Arts ● Mon
Amman JORDAN
FO Jordanian Mus. of Popular Traditions ● Tue
AR National Archaeology Museum ● Tue
FA National Gallery of Fine Art
Ar Riyad (Riyadh) SAUDI ARABIA
AR FO Riyadh Museum ● Thu & Fri
Ashgabat TURKMENISTAN
FO NH Brunei Museum ● Mon
FO Malay Technology Museum ● Mon
Ash Shariqah (Sharjah) UNITED ARAB EM.
AR Archaeological Museum
FA Sharjah Art Museum ● Fri
ST Sharjah Science Museum ● Sun
Bangalore INDIA
W Government Museum ● Wed
Beijing (Peking) CHINA
FA China Art Gall.; Xu Beihong Mus. ● both Mon
FO Cultural Palace of National Minorities ● Mon
AR FO Museum of Chinese History ● Mon
NH Natural History Museum

Bayrut (Beirut) LEBANON
AR National Museum of Beirut ● Mon
Bhubaneshwar INDIA
FO Museum of Man ● Mon
W Orissa State Museum ● Mon
Bishkek KYRGYZSTAN
AR H State Historical Museum ● Mon
Changhua TAIWAN
FO Taiwanese Cultural Village
Chengdu CHINA
H Three Kingdoms Museum
Chennai (Madras) INDIA
AR FO Government Museum ● Fri
Chittagong BANGLADESH
FO Ethnological Museum ● Sat
Colombo SRI LANKA
H Dutch Period Museum ● Fri
FA National Art Gallery
AR H National Museum ● Fri
Delhi INDIA
FA National Gallery of Modern Art
W National Museum ● Mon
Dhaka BANGLADESH
W National Museum ● Thu
Dimashq (Damascus) SYRIA
W National Museum ● Tue
Dubayy (Dubai) UNITED ARAB EMIRATES
W Dubai Museum
Dushanbe TAJIKISTAN
AA Museum of Ethnography ● Sun
W Tajikistan Unified Museum ● Sun
Fukuoka JAPAN
FA Fukuoka Art Museum
Hangzhou CHINA
AR Zhejiang Provincial Museum ● Mon
Halab (Aleppo) SYRIA
FO Museum of Popular Tradition ● Tue
W National Museum of Aleppo ● Tue
Hanoi VIETNAM
AR H History Museum ● Mon
H Ho Chi Minh Museum; Museum of the Vietnamese Revolution ● both Mon
FA FO National Fine Arts Museum ● Mon
Hefa (Haifa) ISRAEL
FA Haifa Museum of Art
ST National Museum of Science & Technology
Hiroshima JAPAN
H Hiroshima Peace Memorial Museum
Ho Chi Minh City (Saigon) VIETNAM
W History Museum ● Mon
H Revolut. Mus.; War Crimes Mus. ● both Mon
Hue VIETNAM
AA AR Hue Museum of Antique Objects
Hyderabad INDIA
AR Archaeology Museum ● Mon
W Salar Jung Museum ● Fri
Islamabad PAKISTAN
AR Lok Virsa Museum ● Fri
FO Islamabad Museum ● Wed
Jaipur INDIA
W Central Museum ● Fri; Museum of Indology
Jakarta INDONESIA
AA FA Adam Malik Museum; Balai Seni Rupa ● both Mon
W National Museum ● Mon
W Taman Mini Indonesia Indah, includes: Asmat Museum; Museum Indonesia; Komodo Museum; Science Museum
Jiddah (Jeddah) SAUDI ARABIA
AR FO Reg. Mus. of Archaeol. & Ethnology ● Thu
Jerusalem ISRAEL/PALESTINE NAR
ST Bloomfield Science Museum
AR Islamic Museum ● Fri; Museum of the History of Jerusalem; Wohl Archaeology Museum (& Burnt House) ● Sat
W Israel Museum ● Sun

FA L.A. Mayer Memorial Museum of Islamic Art
AR H Rockerfeller Museum
Kagoshima JAPAN
FA Museum of Fine Arts
W Reimeikan – Prefectural Museum of Culture
Kanchanaburi THAILAND
H JEATH War Museum (River Kwai Bridge)
Kaohsiung TAIWAN
FA Fine Arts Museum ● Mon
ST Science & Technology Museum ● Mon
Karachi PAKISTAN
W National Museum
Kathmandu NEPAL
W Biheswari – National Museum ● Tue
Kolkata (Calcutta) INDIA
FA Academy of Fine Arts ● Mon
H Ashutosh Museum of Indian History ● Sun
FA FO Birla Academy of Art & Culture ● Mon
ST Birla Industrial & Technological Mus. ● Mon
AR H Indian Museum ● Mon
Krasnoyarsk RUSSIAN FEDERATION
FA Surikov Art Museum ● Mon
Krung Thep (Bangkok) THAILAND
AR National Museum ● Mon & Tue
AA FA Thai Houses of Jim Thompson ● Sun
Kuala Lumpur MALAYSIA
AR FA Muzium Negara
FA National Art Gallery
W National Museum of Islamic Arts ● Mon
Kuching MALAYSIA
W Islamic Museum; Sarawak Museum
Kunming CHINA
W Kunming City Museum ● Mon
Kurashiki JAPAN
FA Ohara New Art Museum ● Mon
Kuwait City KUWAIT
FA Tareq Rajab Museum ● Fri
Kyoto JAPAN
AR Archaeological Museum ● Mon
AA FA Kyoto Municipal Museum of Art ● Mon
FA Kyoto National Museum; National Museum of Modern Art ● both Mon
Kyzyl RUSSIAN FEDERATION
W Tuva National Museum ● Mon
Lahore PAKISTAN
W Lahore Central Museum ● Sat & 1st Wed
Lhasa CHINA
AR H Potala Palace
Lucknow INDIA
FO Kaisarbagh's Folk Art Museum ● Sat & Sun
FA Muhammad Ali Shah Art Gallery
AR State Museum ● Mon
Mandalay MYANMAR
W National Museum & Library
Manila THE PHILIPPINES
AR FA Metropolitan Museum ● Mon
ST Museo Pambata ● Mon
FA Museum of the Filipino People ● Mon
W Nayong Pilipino, includes: Museum of Ethnology; Museo ng Buhag; Torogan House
Masqat (Muscat) OMAN
W Oman Museum ● Fri
Melaka (Malacca) MALAYSIA
W Istana Ke Sultanan
FO Museum of Ethnology ● Tue

Mumbai (Bombay) INDIA
AA FA Jehangir Art Gallery ● Sat & Sun
W Prince of Wales Museum of W. India ● Mon
Mysore INDIA
FA Jayachamarahendra Art Gallery
Nagasaki JAPAN
H Atomic Bomb Museum
Najran SAUDI ARABIA
W Najran Museum ● Thu & Fri
Nanjing CHINA
AR H Municipal Museum; Nanjing Mus. ● Mon; Taiping Heavenly Kingdom History Museum
Novosibirsk RUSSIAN FEDERATION
AR FO Russian Inst. of Archaeology & Ethnography
Osaka JAPAN
FO Japanese Folk Art Museum; National Ethnology Museum ● both Wed
FA National International Art Museum ● Wed
AR FA Osaka Municipal Art Museum ● Mon
Pengosekan INDONESIA
FA Agung Rai Museum of Art (ARRIA)
Peshawar PAKISTAN
AR FO Peshawar Museum ● Wed
Phnom Penh CAMBODIA
W National Museum ● Mon
Sakhnin ISRAEL
FO Museum of Palestinian Folk Heritage
Samarqand (Samarkand) UZBEKISTAN
AR Historical Mus. of Uzbek Culture & Art ● Wed
Sana'a (Sana) YEMEN
AA FA Museum of Arts & Crafts ● Fri
W National Museum ● Fri
Sapporo JAPAN
FA Hokkaido Museum of Modern Art; National Migishi Kotaro Museum of Art ● both Mon
Shanghai CHINA
FA Art Museum
W Shanghai Museum ● Sun
Shanhaiguan CHINA
AR H Great Wall Museum
Singapore
AR H Asian Civilization Museum ● Mon
H Changi Prison Museum ● Sun
FA Singapore Art Museum ● Mon
ST Singapore Science Centre ● Mon
Soul (Seoul) REP. OF KOREA
FO National Folk Museum ● Tue
W National Museum ● Mon
FA National Museum of Contemporary Art ● Mon
Sukhothai THAILAND
AR Ramkhamhaeng Museum ● Mon & Tue
Surabaya INDONESIA
FO H Museum Negeri Propinsi Jawa Timur ● Mon
Surakarta (Solo) INDONESIA
W Radya Pustaka Museum
Tadmur SYRIA
AR Palmyra Archaeological Museum ● Tue
Taichung TAIWAN
FA Taiwan Museum of Art ● Mon
ST National Science Museum ● Mon
Taipei TAIWAN
AA Chang Foundation Museum ● Mon
FA Fine Arts Museum ● Mon
W National Palace Museum ● Mon
FO Taiwan Folk Arts Museum

Takayama JAPAN
FA Hida Minzuko Mura
Toshkent (Tashkent) UZBEKISTAN
AR H Amur Timur Museum ● Mon
AA Museum of Applied Arts ● Tue
AA AR Museum of the History of the People of Uzbekistan ● Sun
FA State Fine Arts Museum ● Tue
Tehran IRAN
AA FA Islamic Arts Museum ● Mon
AR National Museum ● Mon
FA Tehran Mus. of Contemporary Art ● Fri am
Tel Aviv ISRAEL
AR Eretz Yisra'el Museum (HaAretz Museum)
FA Tel Aviv Museum of Art
Thanjavur INDIA
FA Nayak Durbar Hall Art Museum
AR Rajaraja Cholan Museum
Tokyo JAPAN
FA National Museum of Modern Art; National Museum of Western Art; Tokyo Central Museum of Art; Tokyo Metropolitan Fine Art Museum ● all Mon
NH Natural Science Museum ● Mon
ST Science & Technology Museum ● Mon
H Shitamachi History Museum ● Mon
AA FA Suntory Bijutsukan ● Mon
AR FA Tokyo National Museum ● Mon
Trivandrum INDIA
FO Government (Napier) Museum ● Mon
FA Shri Chitra Art Gallery ● Mon
Ubud BALI, INDONESIA
FA Neka Museum
Ulaanbaatar (Ulan Bator) MONGOLIA
FA Mongolian National Modern Art Gallery; Zanabazar Museum of Fine Arts
AR H Museum of Mongolian History
Ulan Ude RUSSIAN FEDERATION
AR FO Ethnographical Museum ● Mon
FA Fine Arts Museum ● Mon
AR Mus. of Oriental Art & Buryat History ● Mon
Vadodara (Baroda) INDIA
W Baroda Museum & Picture Gallery
Viangchan (Vientiane) LAOS
AR FA Haw Pha Kaew ● Mon
Vladivostok RUSSIAN FEDERATION
W Arsenev Regional Museum ● Mon
FA Primorsky Art Museum ● Sun & Mon
Xi'an CHINA
AR Shaanxi History Museum
W Tang Dynasty Arts Museum
Xianggang (Hong Kong) CHINA
ST Hong Kong Space Museum ● Tue
FA Museum of Art ● Thu
H Museum of History ● Fri
AR H Sam Tung Uk Museum ● Tue
AR University Museum ● Mon
Yangon (Rangoon) MYANMAR
AR FO National Museum ● Fri
Yekaterinburg RUSSIAN FEDERATION
AA FA Fine Arts Museum
AR H History & Local Studies Museum
Yokohama JAPAN
W Kanagawa Kenritsu Hakubutsukan ● Mon
AA Silk Centre Museum

West Asia & the Holy Land

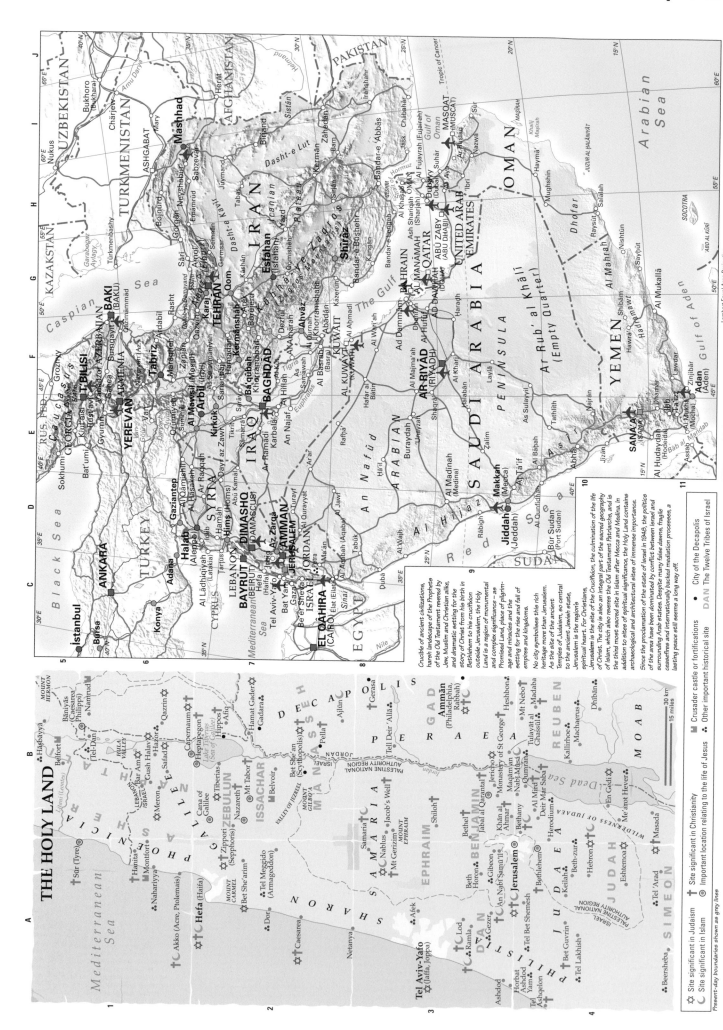

Central Asia & the Silk Road

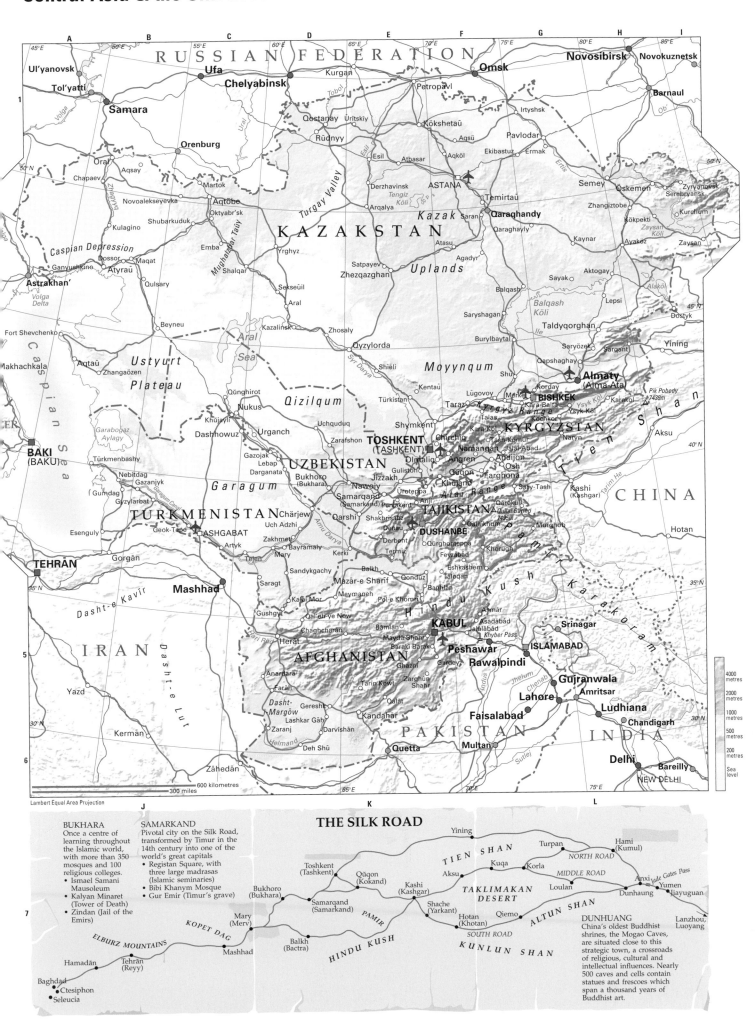

South Asia

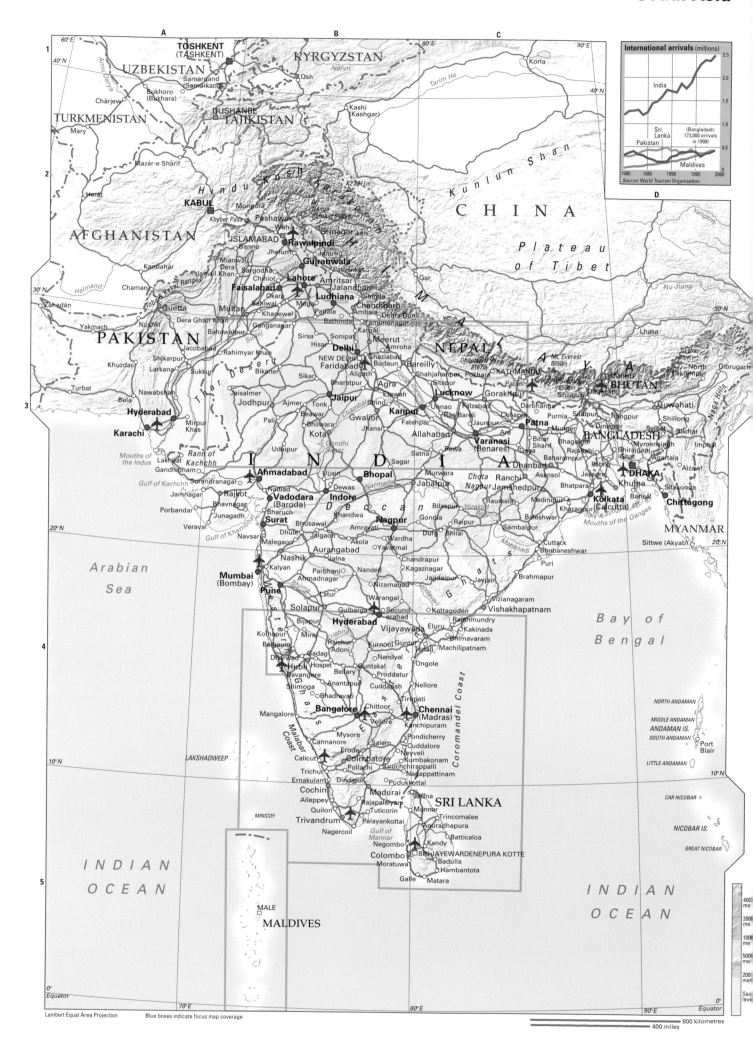

International arrivals (millions)

India

Sri Lanka

Pakistan

(Bangladesh: 173,000 arrivals in 1999)

Maldives

1980 1985 1990 1995 2000

Source: World Tourism Organisation

UZBEKISTAN

TOSHKENT (TASHKENT)

KYRGYZSTAN

TURKMENISTAN

TAJIKISTAN

DUSHANBE

CHINA

Plateau of Tibet

AFGHANISTAN

KABUL

Khyber Pass

Hindu Kush

Karakoram

K2 8611m

Kunlun Shan

Yangtze

ISLAMABAD

Rawalpindi

Gujranwala

Lahore

Faisalabad

Ludhiana

Amritsar

Chandigarh

HIMALAYA

NEPAL

KATHMANDU

Mt. Everest 8850m

THIMPHU

BHUTAN

Darjeeling

PAKISTAN

Quetta

Multan

Thar Desert

Delhi

NEW DELHI

Faridabad

Agra

Lucknow

Kanpur

Patna

Varanasi (Benares)

BANGLADESH

DHAKA

Khulna

Chittagong

Hyderabad

Karachi

Rann of Kachchh

Gulf of Kachchh

Ahmadabad

Bhopal

INDIA

Jabalpur

Deccan

Chota Nagpur

Ranchi

Jamshedpur

Kolkata (Calcutta)

Mouths of the Ganges

MYANMAR

Vadodara (Baroda)

Indore

Narmada

Surat

Gulf of Khambhat

Nagpur

Western Ghats

Mumbai (Bombay)

Pune

Hyderabad

Eastern Ghats

Bay of Bengal

Arabian Sea

Solapur

Secunderabad

Vijayawada

Vishakhapatnam

NORTH ANDAMAN

MIDDLE ANDAMAN

ANDAMAN IS.

SOUTH ANDAMAN

Port Blair

LITTLE ANDAMAN

Bangalore

Chennai (Madras)

Coromandel Coast

Malabar Coast

Mangalore

Mysore

LAKSHADWEEP

Coimbatore

Cochin

Madurai

Jaffna

SRI LANKA

CAR NICOBAR

NICOBAR IS.

GREAT NICOBAR

Trivandrum

MINICOY

Colombo

SRI JAYEWARDENEPURA KOTTE

Galle

INDIAN OCEAN

MALE

MALDIVES

INDIAN OCEAN

Lambert Equal Area Projection

Blue boxes indicate focus map coverage

800 kilometres

400 miles

India

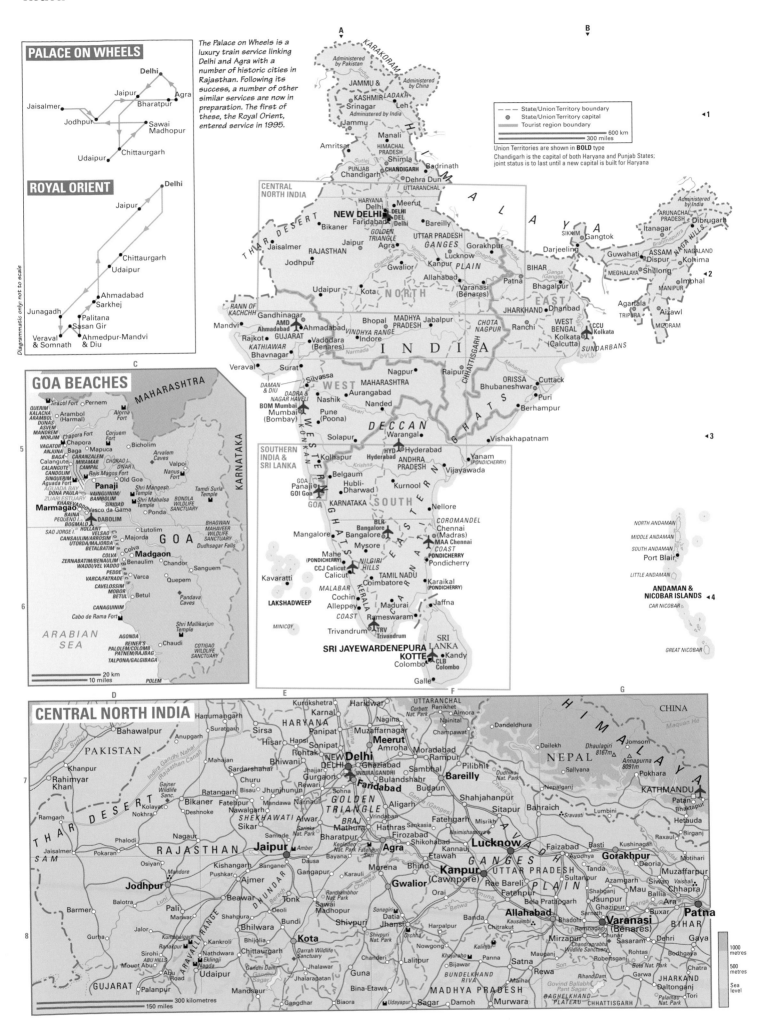

India, Sri Lanka & The Maldives

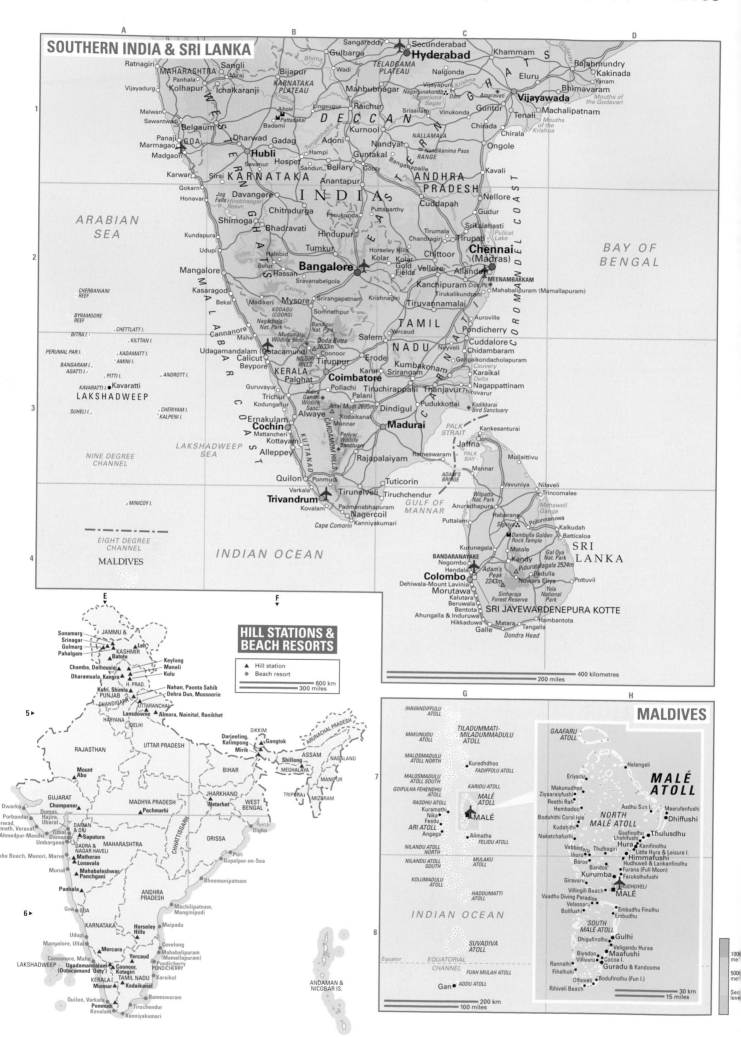

China, Mongolia & Korea

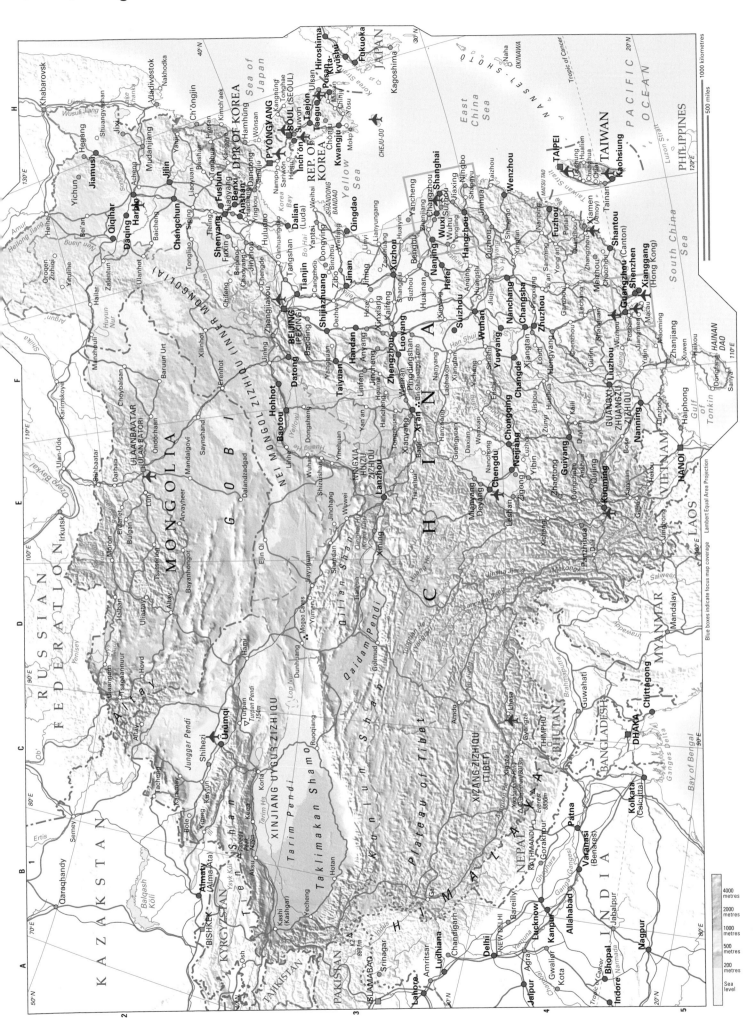

China

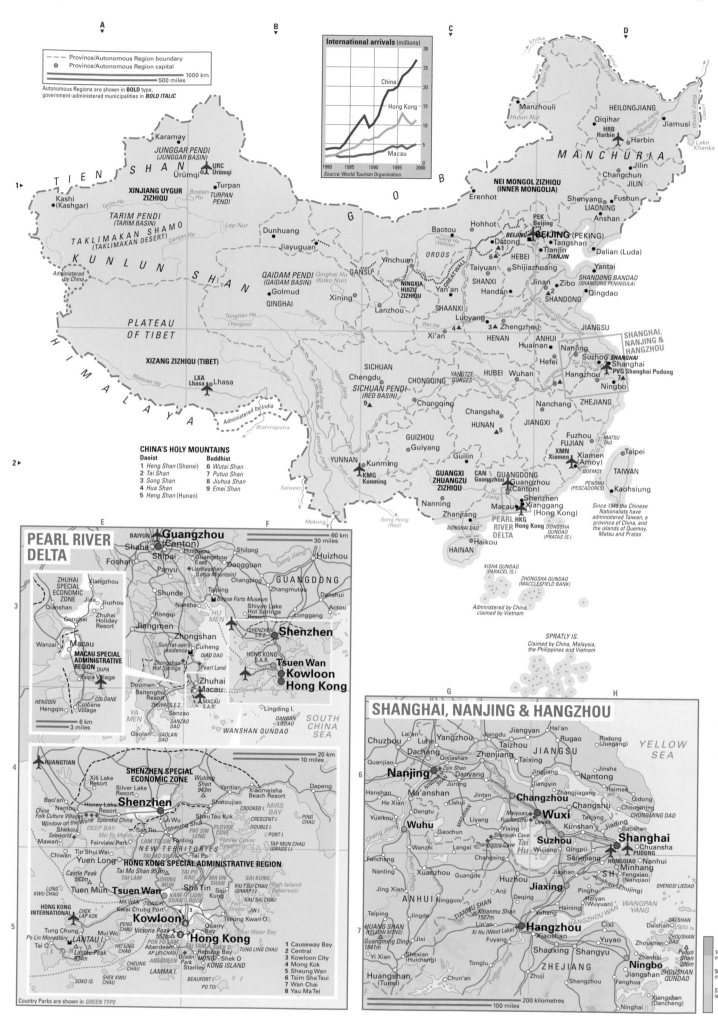

Japan

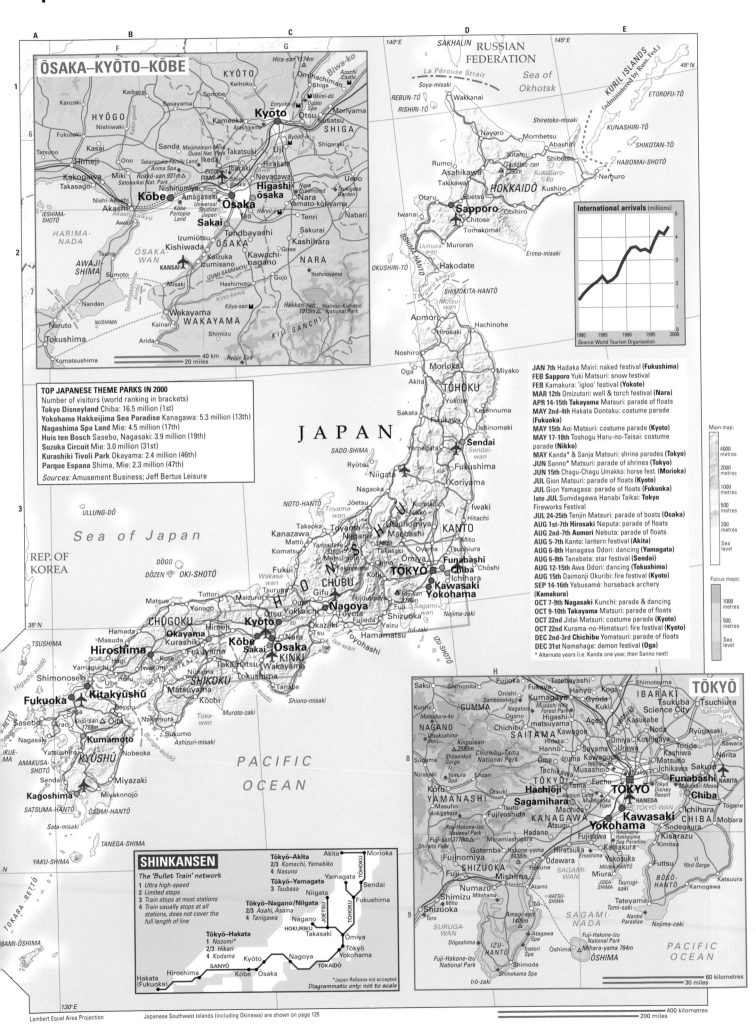

South-East Asia

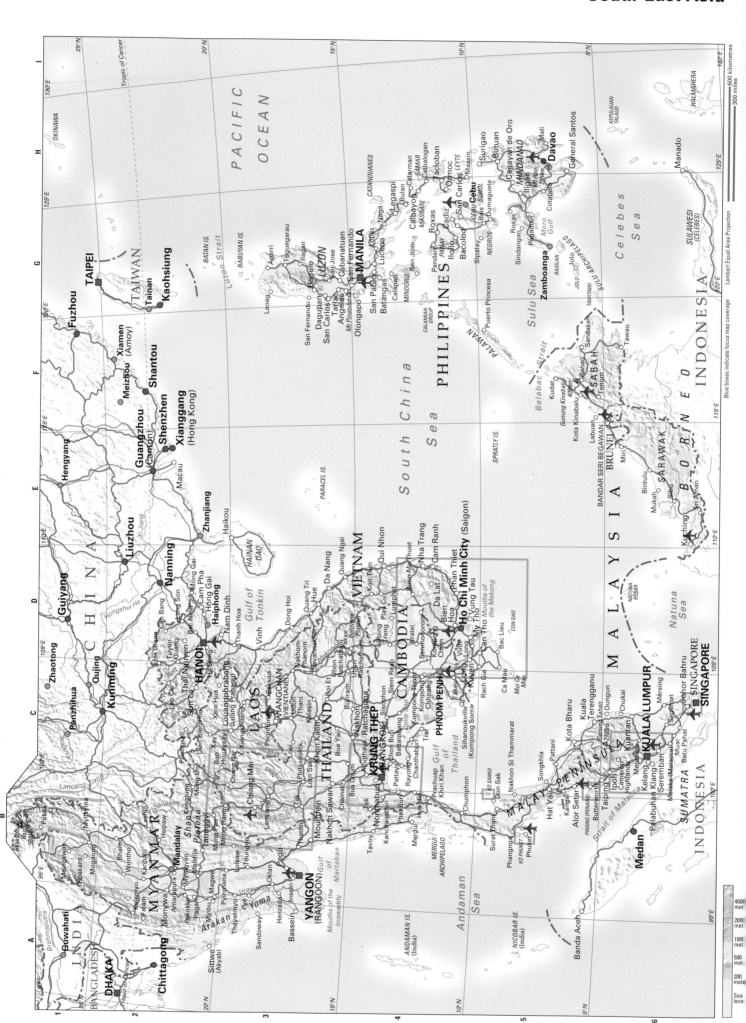

Indochina

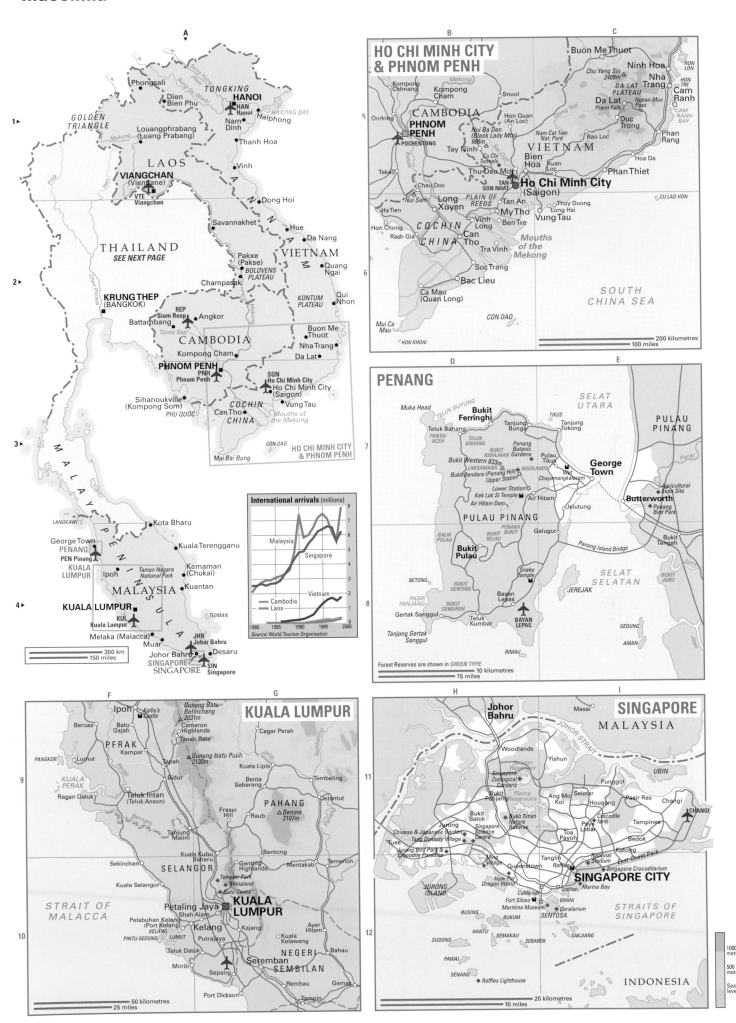

Thailand

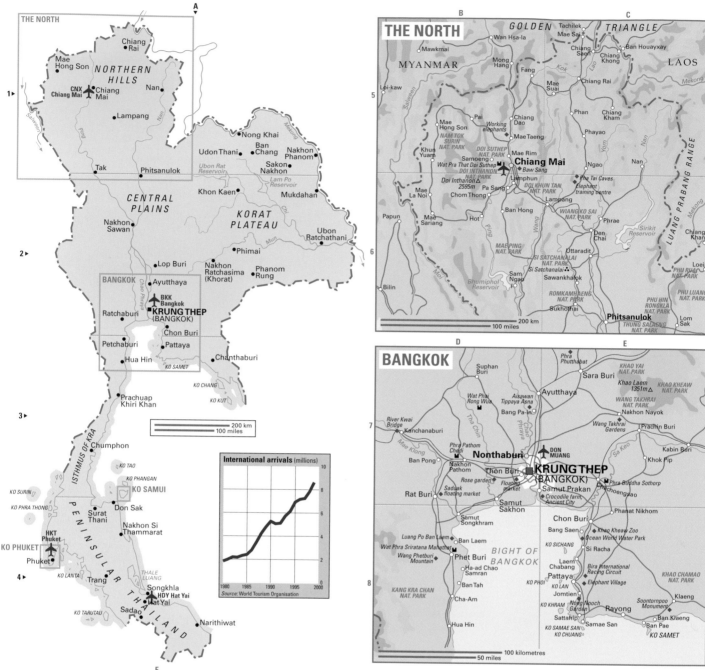

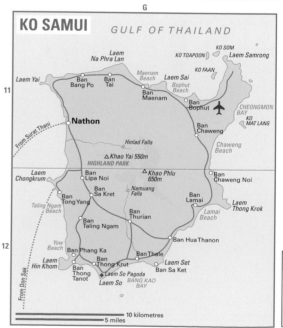

EASTERN & ORIENTAL EXPRESS

	Distance from Bangkok	
	Kilometres	Miles
Chiang Mai	751	467
Lampang	642	390
Phitsanulok	389	242
Ayutthaya	71	44
Bangkok	0	0
Kanchanaburi	(138)	(86)
Hua Hin	229	142
Hat Yai	945	587
Butterworth	1161	721
Kuala Lumpur	1552	964
Singapore	1946	1209

The Eastern & Oriental Express is a luxury train service operating on two routes: an overnight service between Bangkok and Chiang Mai and a service between Bangkok to Singapore which takes three days and includes guided tours of Kanchanaburi, River Kwai and Penang.

Indonesia

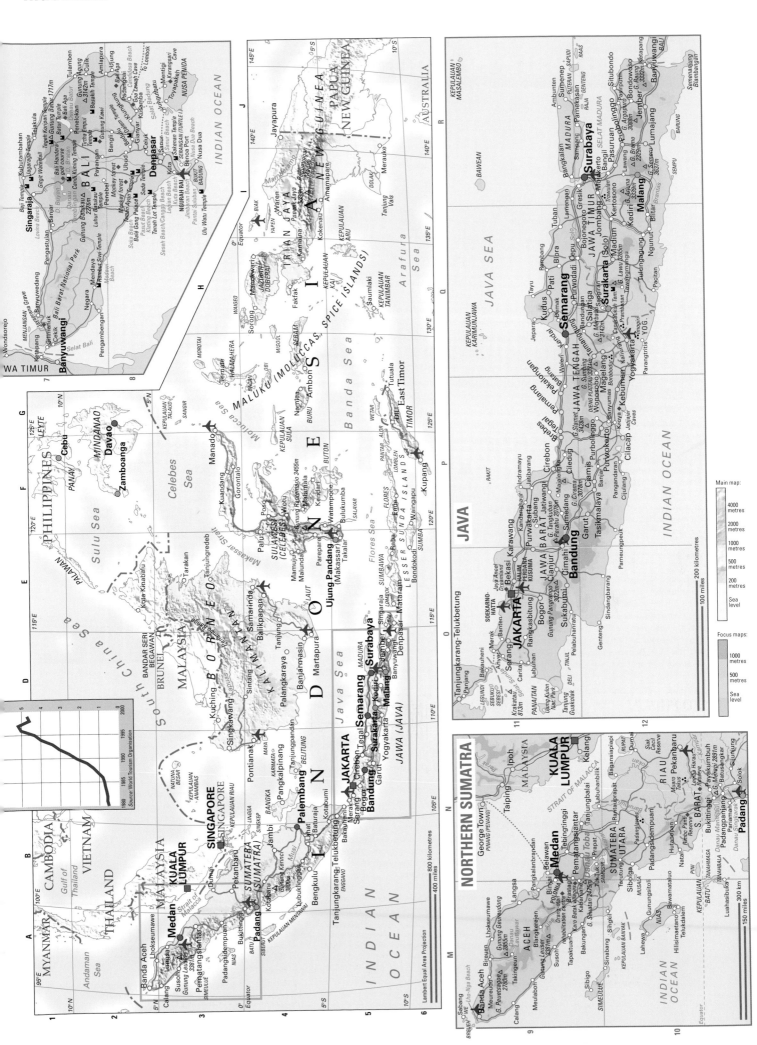

Australasia & Oceania

Key facts	A&O	World	A&O %
Number of Countries	22	226	9.7%
Area ('000 sq km)	9,567	135,463	7.1%
Population ('000)	279,132	5,973,801	4.7%
Population Density (/sq km)	29	44	–
Gross Nat. Income (US$m)	516,258	29,986,364	1.7%
Visitor Arrivals ('000)	8,821	649,223	1.4%
Visitor Receipts (US$m)	13,140	456,402	2.9%
Travel Departures ('000)	4,709	594,797	0.8%
Travel Expenditure (US$m)	7,430	397,040	1.9%

GNI figures relate to 1999. Population figures are taken from the most recent census or reliable estimate. Travel figures (from the WTO) are generally for 1999, but where these are unavailable or unreliable, figures from earlier years have been used. All travel figures are based on overnight stays, not same-day visitors. Where data for certain countries was not available, this has been regarded as zero. Global totals for Visitor Arrivals/Travel Departures and Visitor Receipts/Travel Expenditure do not equal each other due to differing methods of reporting inbound and outbound data. For more information on what is regarded as a country for the purposes of this book, and for more detailed statistical information, please see the Countries A-Z section from page 184.

Note that information on Hawaii may be found in the USA & Canada section of the book.

AUSTRALASIA & OCEANIA possesses to a high degree both the advantages and the disadvantages of its comparative isolation. On the positive side, it has generally avoided being drawn into global political conflicts; its landscapes and coastlines are some of the most unsullied on earth; and it can market itself with justification as being truly 'away from it all.' Its economies, especially Australia, have come to be linked with those of East Asia during the last 25 years, although many of the Pacific islands remain chronically underdeveloped and dependent on foreign aid. Distances both to and within the region are vast, so deterring many would-be visitors. All these factors have shaped Australasia's travel characteristics: it receives a comparatively small number of visitors, each spending a comparatively large amount of money, the majority coming from within the region or from Asia. All come in search of Australasia's unique blend of the exotic, the untamed and the familiar.

Holiday trends

These currently 'hot' destinations satisfy the full range of holiday types. The 'grey' market is strong with Australia being high among the must-sees for retirees taking the long-awaited trip of a lifetime. The region is similarly high on young backpackers' itineraries and Australia and New Zealand retain strong VFR (visiting friends and relations) markets as a result of their former assisted emigration policies of the 1950s and 1960s.

Both Australia and New Zealand see themselves as being of the Asian region – albeit on the fringe – as well as part of a more far-flung and historical global English-speaking world community; two groupings whose interests are not always identical. The resulting balancing act is not dissimilar to Britain's in its dealings with Europe and the USA. Both Australia and New Zealand have been quick to spot the ever-increasing importance of the Chinese market, and in May 1999 finalised 'approved destination status' with Beijing to stimulate Sino-Antipodean travel. The results are already bearing fruit: Chinese visits to Australia rose by over 32% in 1999, while 2000 first-quarter figures for New Zealand showed an increase of nearly 80%.

Adventure holidays of all kinds have long been popular in Australia and New Zealand. There is a wide range of landscapes, many comparatively close (by Australasian standards) to major centres.

Australia's cities are among the most cosmopolitan in the world, each with its unique blend of Asian,

■ Australasian breaks

Percentage of trips taken within East Asia and the Pacific by Australians and New Zealanders
Source: WTO

Australia

New Zealand

☐ Trips within the region   ☐ Trips outside the region

■ On the up down-under

Fastest-growing holiday types, 2000
Source: Travel 2

1. Independent self-drive touring in Australia and New Zealand
2. In-depth, authentic South Pacific experiences.
3. Gourmet food and wine experiences, especially in New Zealand.
4. Rail travel, including great journeys like the Great South Pacific Express in Australia and numerous scenic routes in New Zealand.
5. Multi-country itineraries taking in an increasing number of regional destinations.

European, American and native qualities.

Touring is also a major growth area in the form of self-drive car itineraries, coach tours and, increasingly, motorhomes.

Australia also has the world-famous Great Barrier Reef, offering probably the most spectacular scuba diving opportunities in the world.

The Pacific islands have traditionally been stopover points, but are increasingly popular as single- or multi-centre destinations, with people increasingly seeking out the more out-of-the-way locations. The advent of air fares which allow for a number of stops en route has meant that even more visitors are combining both Australia and New Zealand with one of the South Pacific destinations.

Established favourites – Australia

- New South Wales – Australia's most visited state; Sydney is Australia's main gateway. The state has superb surfing conditions as well as skiing in the Blue Mountains.

- Queensland – the main city is Brisbane. Beach lovers have hundreds of miles of choice, including the Gold Coast resort area. Few miss out on a boat or helicopter trip out to the Great Barrier Reef.

■ Aussie rules

International visitor arrivals, 1999
Source: WTO/Australian Bureau of Tourism Research

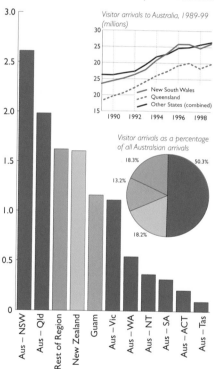

- Western Australia – taking up the whole western third of the country, with Perth as its capital. Famed for the unique Wave Rock and Pinnacles geological formations.

- Victoria – home to Australia's second largest city, Melbourne, and several national parks and reserves for seals, koala bears and penguins.

- Northern Territory – made famous by the Crocodile Dundee films. Top attractions are the Outback, the town of Alice Springs and Australia's greatest icon, Ayers Rock.

Established favourites – New Zealand

The scenery of the two islands of New Zealand is exceptional.

It is home to some of the most celebrated wilderness walking itineraries in the world.

The North Island city of Auckland attracts the sailing fraternity. Its Sky Tower is the southern hemisphere's tallest.

- Australasia & Oceania (A&O) occupies just over 7% of the world's land area and is home to just under 5% of the world's population.
- A&O's combined GDI is US$516,258 million, under 2% of the world's total.
- A&O accounts for nearly 5% of global travel departures and over 8% of arrivals.
- International travel and tourism contributed over US$13 billion to A&O's economy in 1999, an increase of 6.5% over 1998.
- Australia dominates the travel economy of the region. It receives 51% of all international visitors and 57% of all international travel receipts, and provides 68% of all international departures and 78% of all international expenditure.
- If the UK had the same population density as Australia it would have around 600,000 people, roughly the population of Glasgow.
- Travel and tourism is Australia's largest single earner of foreign exchange and accounts for about 11.5% of the country's jobs.
- Sydney spent over A$3.3 billion of public and private money on infrastructure and facilities prior to hosting the 2000 Olympics. Over 35 new hotels opened in the run-up to the event.
- An estimated 700,000 people visited the Sydney Olympics, 111,000 of whom were from overseas. Projections for 2001-4 indicate that the country will receive an additional 1 million visitors due to interest generated by the Olympic coverage, which attracted an estimated 3.7 billion television viewers worldwide. In the period 1997-2004, it is estimated that the event will have contributed over A$6 billion to the national economy and created 150,000 jobs.
- Visitor arrivals in 1999 showed an increase in A&O's three major destinations: Australia (7.0%); New Zealand (8.2%); and Guam (2.2%).
- The most significant growth in tourist arrivals was in Tonga (14.8%) and the Cook Islands (14.3%). The largest decrease was to Palau (-14.1%). These three countries, however, received less than 150,000 visitors between them.
- Australia supplied 32% of New Zealand's international visitors in 1999, and New Zealand supplied 16% of Australia's.
- Australia and New Zealand between them were responsible for over 98% of all A&O's foreign travel expenditure in 1999.
- An estimated 3.5 million British nationals were living in Australia in 2001, an increase of some 300,000 compared to 1997.
- The region's third most visited country, Guam, received over 85% of its 1997 visitors from Japan. Since then, visitors from Taiwan and Korea Rep. have increased dramatically: arrivals from each country more than doubled in 1999 compared to 1998.
- The 1,000-odd visitors to Kiribati each spent an average of US$2,000 in 1999: only the Turks & Caicos Islands enjoyed higher per capita receipts. For the majority of countries in Australasia, receipts per capita were in excess of US$1,000.
- Distances in the Pacific are vast. The islands of French Polynesia, for example, are spread over an area of ocean about the size of Europe; yet, put together, they would comfortably fit inside the US state of Connecticut.

Hot springs and spectacular geysers are found throughout the country

Pacific islands
The islands north and west of Australia and New Zealand offer the rare ability to step into yesterday by crossing the International Date Line. Technically, the furthest west of Greenwich Mean Time are French Polynesia, the Kiribati, Cook and Pitcairn Islands and Easter Island. Scattered the other side of the line are Vanuatu, Tuvalu and the Marshall, Solomon and Micronesia groups.

Top Pacific island holiday spots include:

- Fiji – The islands have excellent beaches for resort holidays and mountains for trekking, although it has been hard hit by recent political unrest. Remoter islands such as Treasure Island and Castaway Island are increasing in popularity.

- Guam – Particularly popular with the Asian market, the island is making significant investment in its tourism infrastructure.

- French Polynesia – A tropical taste of France, although in 1999 American visitors US exceeded French ones for the first time. A French-backed plan is in place to diversify the economy.

Issues
Praised as being the best ever Olympics, the 2000 Sydney Olympiad left the region basking in the afterglow of success. Many of Australia's travel projections for the coming years rely upon the 'Olympic effect' as people decide to see the place first-hand. The government predicts that positive effects in terms of visitor numbers will be being felt into 2004. New Zealand also hopes to benefit from this development.

The biggest challenge for the Pacific island states is that of developing sustainable and diverse economies, all against the sombre backdrop of the threat of rising sea levels faced by these generally low-lying countries.

Business travel
Adding to the depressed state of global business travel has been corporate realisation that time and money on long-haul flights to the region can be reduced by relying more on email and video-conferencing.

Drawbacks
From most of the world, the flying times to the region are considerable – up to 21 hours, for instance, to reach Adelaide in South Australia from Western Europe. Much of the controversy over Deep Vein Thrombosis (DVT) has centred on ultra-long haul flights as experienced by travellers to the Antipodes.

■ Big earners
Receipts from foreign travel, 1999
(US$ billions – excluding international transport)
Source: WTO

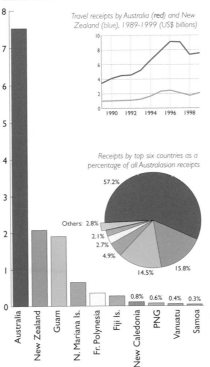

Travel receipts by Australia (red) and New Zealand (blue), 1989-1999 (US$ billions)

Receipts by top six countries as a percentage of all Australasian receipts

■ Comings and goings
Inbound and outbound travel to and from Australia and New Zealand by region
Source: WTO

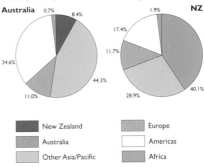

Visitor arrivals to Australia and NZ by region of origin

Travel departures from Australia and NZ by region of destination

Legend:
- New Zealand
- Australia
- Other Asia/Pacific
- Europe
- Americas
- Africa

Australia has many species of highly venomous plant, reptile, insect and marine life.

For water sports enthusiasts and divers, sea rescue facilities in some of the Pacific islands may not be comprehensive. Medical facilities may also be basic.

Fiji has a chequered recent political history of army takeovers and Commonwealth expulsion and re-admittance. The ramifications of the 2000 attempted coup have been a sharp decline in holiday bookings with signs of recovery taking time to emerge. Sporadic unrest, often due to ethnic conflicts, is also a risk in the Solomon Islands.

■ Visitors
Visitor arrivals and average receipts per visitor, 1999
Source: WTO

	Visitors (thousands)	Receipts per visitor
Australia	4,459	$1,688
New Zealand	1,607	$1,296
Guam	1,162	$1,642
Northern Mariana Is.	498	$1,299
Fiji Is.	410	$671
French Polynesia	211	$1,678
New Caledonia	100	$1,110
Samoa	85	$494
Papua New Guinea	67	$1,134
Cook Is.	56	$696
Palau	55	n/a
Vanuatu	50	$1,120
Tonga	31	$290
Solomon Is.	21	$286
Marshall Is.	5	$800
Niue	2	$500
Tuvalu	1	$1,000
Kiribati	1	$2,000

(Visitor arrival figures not available for the Federated States of Micronesia, Nauru, Wallis & Futuna or American Samoa.)

Maps, charts and statistics on Australasia & Oceania follow on pages 134 to 139. See also the *Countries A-Z* section from page 184, and the *Index* from page 193.

Thanks to: David Ezra of Saltmarsh PR; Travel 2; Alasdair McIntyre; Ben Janeczko and Kate Kenward of the ATC; Patrick Fitzgerald; the Foreign & Commonwealth Office.

Oceania

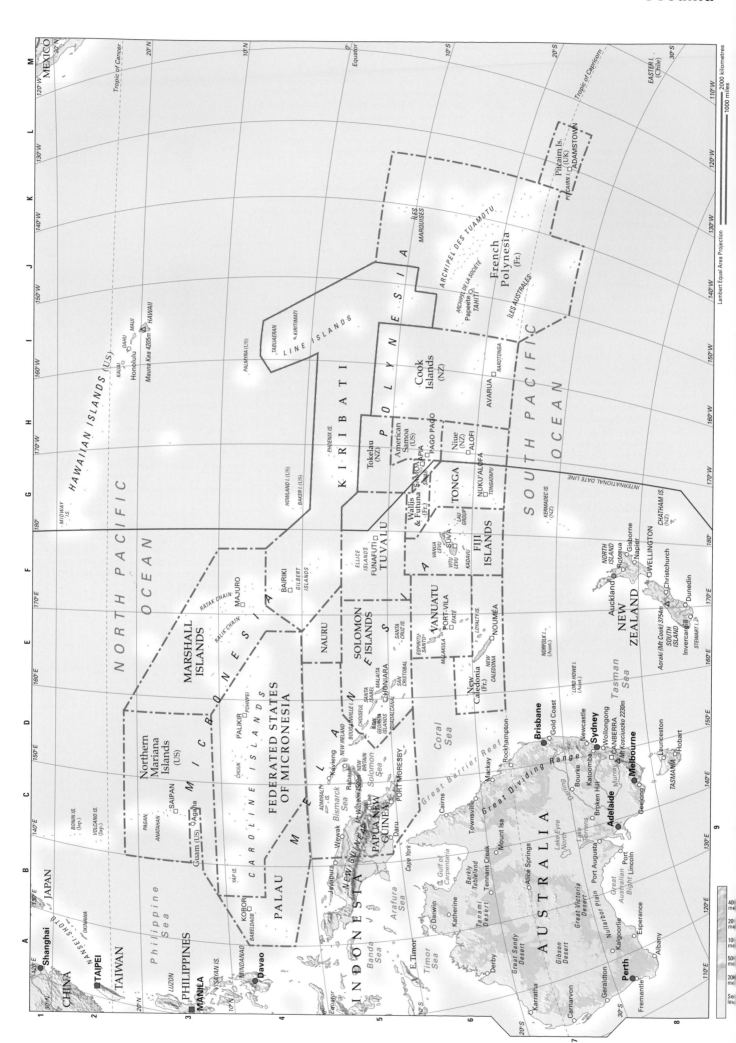

Australia

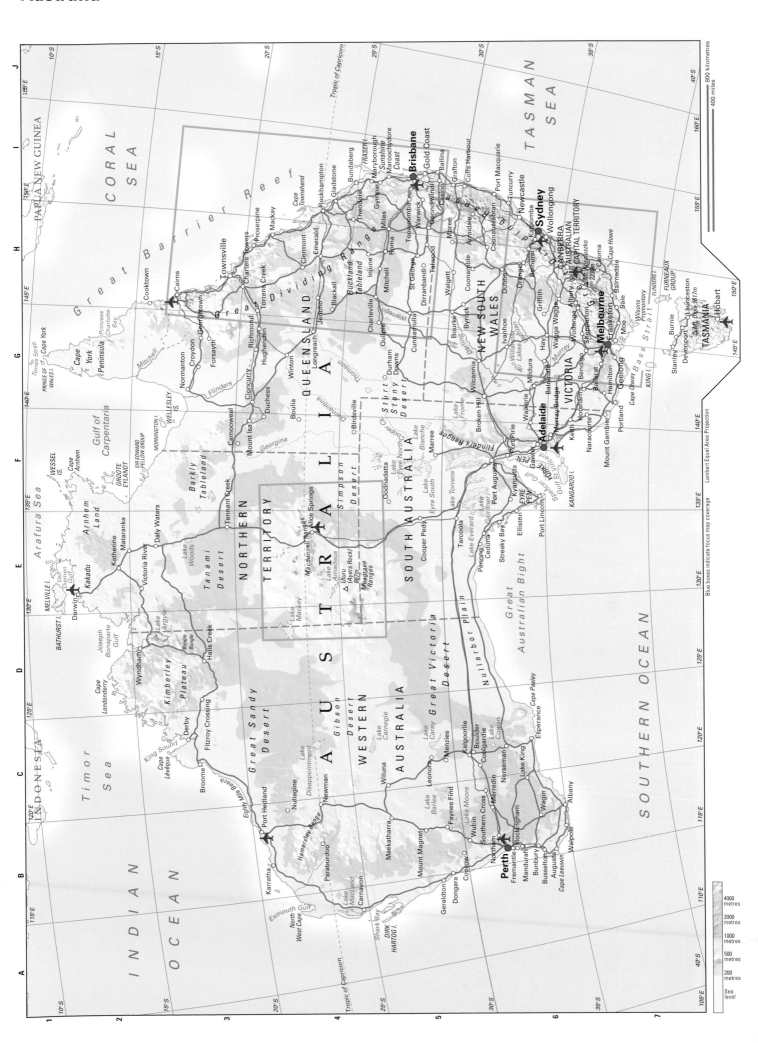

Australia

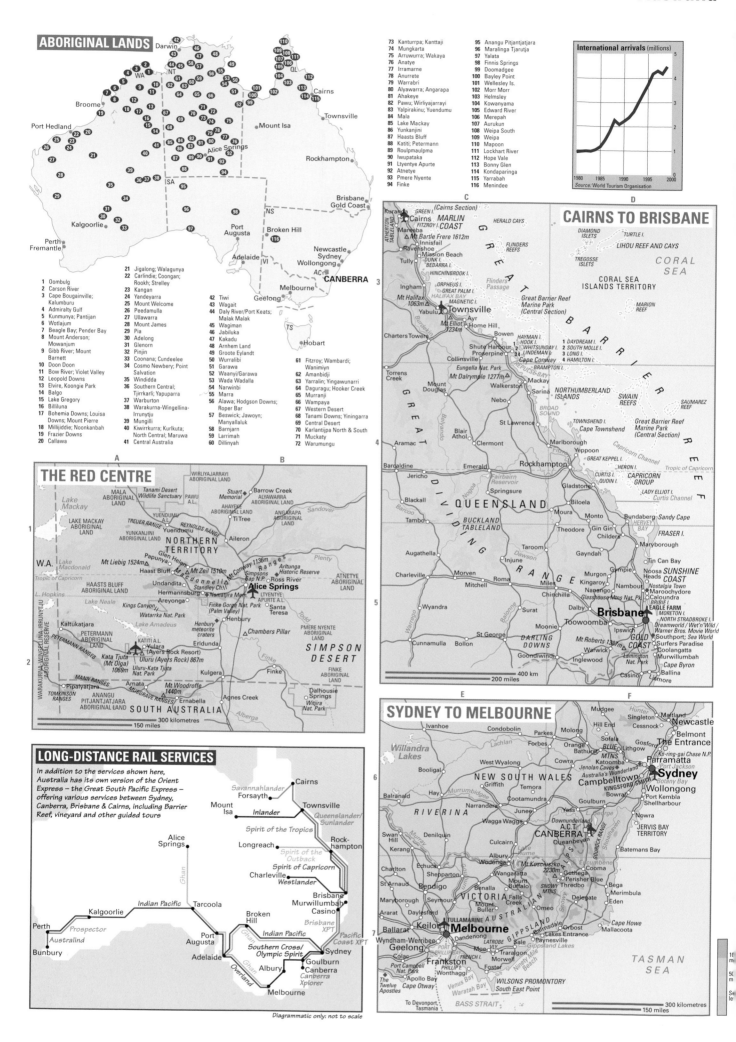

New Zealand

The Pacific

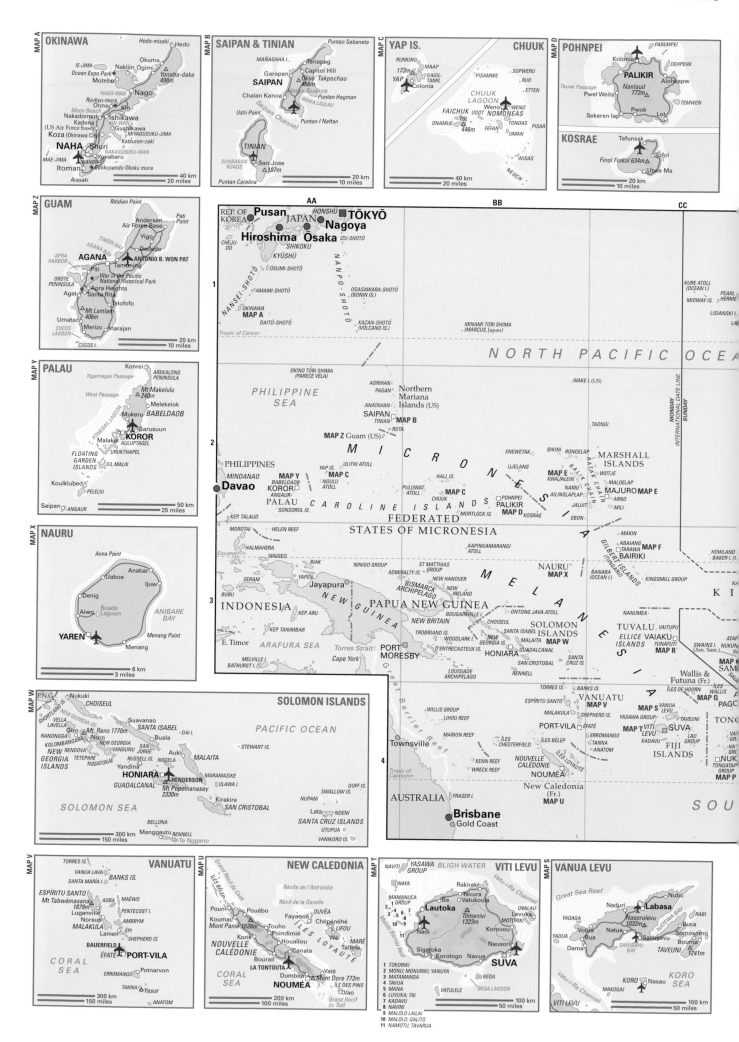

MAP A OKINAWA

Hedo-misaki · Hedo
Okuma
IE-JIMA · Nakijin · Ogimi · Yonaha-dake 498m
Ocean Expo Park · Onna
Motobu
NAGO-WAN · Nago
Ryukyu-mura · Kin
Moon Beach
Nakadomari · Ishikawa
Kadena (US Air Force base) · Gushikawa
Koza (Okinawa City) · MIYAGUSUKU-JIMA
Katsuren-zaki
NAKAGUSUKU-WAN
NAHA · Shuri · Yonabaru
MAE-JIMA · WANBU
Itoman · Gyokusendo Okoku mura
Arasaki

40 km
20 miles

MAP B SAIPAN & TINIAN

Puntan Sabaneta
MAÑAGAHA I. · Tanapag
Garapan · Capitol Hill
Okso' Takpochao 466m
SAIPAN
Chalan Kanoa · Hagoi Susupe · Puntan Hagman
Ushi Point · BAHIA LAULAU
Puntan I Naftan
TINIAN
SUNBARAN ROADS
San Jose 187m
Puntan Carolina

20 km
10 miles

MAP C YAP IS. CHUUK

RUMUNG
173m · MAAP
YAP · GAGIL-TAMIL
Colonia · PISAMWE
SOPWERU
RUO
WENO
CHUUK LAGOON · Weno
FAICHUK · NOMONEAS · ETTEN
ONANUE · TOL · UDOT · FEFAN · TONOAS · PISAR
446m · UMAN
WISAS
NE-OCH

40 km
20 miles

MAP D POHNPEI

PAREMPEI
Kolonia · DEHPEHK
PALIKIR · Alohkapw
Nanlaud 772m
Tauak Passage · Pwel Weite
Sekeren Iap · Pwok · Lot · TEMWEN

KOSRAE
Tafunsak
Tofol
Finol Finkol 634m · Utwa Ma

20 km
10 miles

MAP Z GUAM

Ritidian Point
Pati Point
Andersen Air Force Base
TIMON BAY · Yigo
AGANA BAY · Dededo
Apra · ANTÓNIO B. WON PAT
HARBOR · AGANA · Tamoning
Piti
OROTE · War in the Pacific National Historical Park
PENINSULA · Apra Heights · Santa Rita
Agat
Mt Lamlam 406m · Talofofo
Umatac · Merizo · Inarajan
COCOS LAGOON
COCOS I.

20 km
10 miles

MAP Y PALAU

Konrei
AREKALONG PENINSULA
Ngamegei Passage · Mt Makelulu 240m
West Passage · Melekeiok
Mukeru · BABELDAOB
Garusuun
Malakal · KOROR · AULUPTAGEL
URUKTHAPEL
FLOATING GARDEN ISLANDS · EIL MALK
Koulklubed · PELELIU
Saipan · ANGAUR

50 km
25 miles

MAP X NAURU

Anna Point
Anabar
Uaboe · Ijuw
Denig
Buada Lagoon
Aiwo · ANIBARE BAY
YAREN
Menang Point
Menang

6 km
3 miles

AA   BB   CC

REP. OF KOREA · **Pusan**
HONSHŪ · **TŌKYŌ**
JAPAN · **Nagoya**
CHEJU-DO · **Hiroshima** · **Ōsaka** · IZU-SHOTŌ
SHIKOKU
KYŪSHŪ · NANPO-SHOTŌ
ŌSUMI-SHOTŌ

1

AMAMI-SHOTŌ · OGASAWARA-SHOTŌ (BONIN IS.)
KAZAN-SHOTŌ (VOLCANO IS.)
DAITŌ-SHOTŌ
Tropic of Cancer

OKINAWA
MAP A

KURE ATOLL (OCEAN I.)
MIDWAY IS. · PEARL & HERME
LISIANSKI I.

MINAMI TORI SHIMA (MARCUS, Japan)

NORTH PACIFIC OCEAN

Okino Tori Shima (PARECE VELA)
WAKE I. (US)

PHILIPPINE SEA
AGRIHAN
PAGAN · Northern Mariana Islands (US)
ANATAHAN
SAIPAN · **MAP B**
TINIAN
ROTA

2

PHILIPPINES
MINDANAO · **MAP Y** · YAP IS. · **MAP C**
Davao · KOROR · NGULU ATOLL
ANGAUR · ULITHI ATOLL
PALAU · SONSOROL IS.
KEP. TALAUD

TAONGI

ENEWETAK · BIKINI · RONGELAP
UJELANG · **MAP E**
KWAJALEIN · WOTJE
MARSHALL ISLANDS
NAMU
AILINGLAPLAP · ARNO
MAJURO **MAP E**
JALUIT · MILI
EBON

M I C R O N E S I A

HALL IS.
PULUWAT ATOLL
CHUUK · **MAP C**
POHNPEI · PALIKIR **MAP D** · KOSRAE
MORTLOCK IS.
CAROLINE ISLANDS

MONDAY SUNDAY
INTERNATIONAL DATE LINE

FEDERATED STATES OF MICRONESIA

MOROTAI · HELEN REEF
HALMAHERA
Equator · WAIGEO
BURU · BIAK · YAPEN
KEP. ARU
KEP. TANIMBAR

MAKIN
ABAIANG · **MAP F**
TARAWA · BAIRIKI
GILBERT ISLANDS (TUNGARU)
BANABA (OCEAN I.)

HOWLAND BAKER I. (U

KAPINGAMARANGI ATOLL

3

INDONESIA
E. Timor
ARAFURA SEA
MELVILLE I.
BATHURST I.

NINIGO GROUP
Jayapura
NEW GUINEA
PAPUA NEW GUINEA
SERAM

ST MATTHIAS GROUP
ADMIRALTY IS. · NEW HANOVER
BISMARCK ARCHIPELAGO · NEW IRELAND
NEW BRITAIN
BOUGAINVILLE I. · CHOISEUL
TROBRIAND IS. · ONTONG JAVA ATOLL
WOODLARK I. · SANTA ISABEL
PORT MORESBY · D'ENTRECASTEAUX IS. · NEW GEORGIA IS. · MALAITA **MAP W**
Torres Strait · HONIARA · GUADALCANAL
Cape York · LOUISIADE ARCHIPELAGO · SAN CRISTOBAL
RENNELL

NAURU **MAP X**

M E L A N E S I A

SOLOMON ISLANDS

SANTA CRUZ IS.

NANUMEA
TUVALU · VAITUPU
ELLICE VAIAKU ISLANDS · FUNAFUTI **MAP R**
SWAINS I. (Am. Sam.)

KI

MAP
SAM

4

Townsville
AUSTRALIA
FRASER I.
Brisbane
Gold Coast

Great Barrier Reef
Tropic of Capricorn

WILLIS GROUP
LIHOU REEF
MARION REEF
KENN REEF
WRECK REEF
ÎLES CHESTERFIELD

NOUVELLE CALÉDONIE
NOUMÉA
New Caledonia (Fr.)
MAP U

ESPÍRITU SANTO
MALAKULA · SHEPHERD IS.
PORT-VILA · ÉFATÉ
ERROMANGO
TANNA · ANATOM
VANUATU **MAP V**
YASAWA GROUP
VANUA LEVU **MAP S**
ÎLES BÉLEP · ÎLES DE HOORN
ÎLES LOYAUTÉ

Wallis & Futuna (Fr.)
ÎLES WALLIS · **MAP Q**

PAG

TONG

SUVA
LAU GROUP
KADAVU
FIJI ISLANDS
VITI LEVU **MAP T**

NUK
TONGATAP
MAP P

SOU

MAP W SOLOMON ISLANDS

P.N.G. · Nukuki · CHOISEUL
SHORTLAND IS.
NEW GEORGIA SD
VELLA LAVELLA · Gizo · Mt Rano 1770m · SANTA ISABEL · DAI I.
RANONGGA · KOLOMBANGARA · Noro · Buala
NEW GEORGIA · SAN JORGE · Auki
Suavanao
RENDOVA · VANGUNU · RUSSELL IS. · NGGELA · MALAITA
NEW GEORGIA ISLANDS · TETEPARE · Yandina · MARAMASIKE
NGGATOKAE
HONIARA · ULAWA I.
GUADALCANAL · Mt Popomanasey 2330m · Kirakira
HENDERSON · SAN CRISTOBAL
SOLOMON SEA · BELLONA
Manggautu · RENNELL · Te Nggano

PACIFIC OCEAN
STEWART IS.
DUFF IS.
SWALLOW IS.
NUPANI
Lata · NDENI
SANTA CRUZ ISLANDS · UTUPUA
VANIKORO IS.

300 km
150 miles

MAP V VANUATU

TORRES IS.
VANUA LAVA
SANTA MARÍA I. · BANKS IS.
ESPÍRITU SANTO
Mt Tabwémasana 1879m · MAÊWO
Luganville · PENTECOST I.
Norsup · AMBRYM
MALAKULA · ÉPI
Lamen · SHEPHERD IS.
BAUERFIELD · ÉFATÉ · **PORT-VILA**
CORAL SEA
ERROMANGO · Potnarvon
TANNA · Yasur
ANATOM

300 km
150 miles

MAP U NEW CALEDONIA

NAVITI · YASAWA GROUP · BLIGH WATER
Grand Récif de Cook
ÎLES BÉLEP · Récifs de l'Astrolabe
Récif de la Gazelle
Poum · Pouébo · OUVÉA
Koumac · Fayaoué
Mont Panié 1628m · Touho · Chépénéhé
Kone · Poindimié · LIFOU
Houailou · Wé
Bourail · Canala · MARÉ · Tadine
NOUVELLE CALÉDONIE
LA TONTOUTA · ÎLES LOYAUTÉ
Dumbea · Yaté
NOUMÉA · Mont Dore 772m · ÎLE DES PINS
CORAL SEA · Vao
Grand Récif du Sud

200 km
100 miles

MAP T VITI LEVU

MAMANUCA GROUP
WAYA
Rakiraki
Tavura · Vatukoula
Lautoka · OVALAU
Tomanivi 1323m · MOTURIKI
Nadi · Levuka
Korovou
Sigatoka · Nausori
Korotogo · Navua
BEQA · **SUVA**
Malolo Barrier Reef
VATULELE · BEQA LAGOON

1 TOKORIKI
2 MONU; MONURIKI; YANUYA
3 MATAMANOA
4 TAVUA
5 MANA
6 LUVUKA; TAI
7 NAVINI
8 MALOLO LAILAI
9 MALOLO LAILAI
10 MALOLO; QALITO
11 NAMOTU; TAVARUA

100 km
50 miles

MAP S VANUA LEVU

Great Sea Reef
Nubu
Naduri · **Labasa** · RABI
Nasorolevu 1032m · Buca
YAQAGA · Natua · Somosomo
Votua · Bua · Dama · Bouma
YADUA · SAVUSAVU BAY · TAVEUNI 1241m
KORO
MAKOGAI · Nasau
VITI LEVU · KORO SEA
Vatu-i-Ra Channel

100 km
50 miles

The Pacific

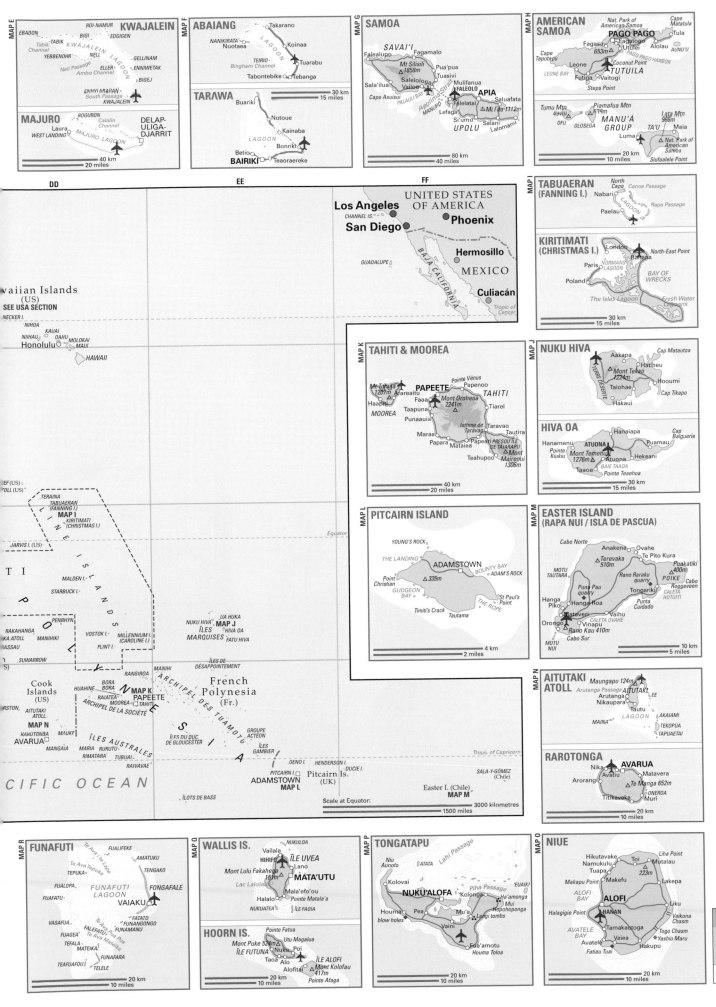

USA & Canada

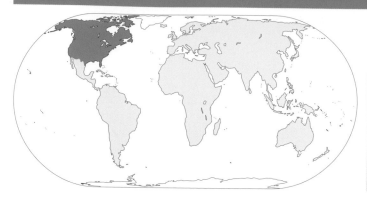

Key Facts	USA&C	World	USA&C %
Number of Countries	2	226	0.9%
Area ('000 sq km)	19,343	135,463	14.3%
Population ('000)	308,728	5,973,801	5.2%
Population Density (/sq km)	16	44	–
Gross Nat. Income (US$m)	9,493,573	29,986,364	31.6%
Visitor Arrivals ('000)	67,902	649,223	10.5%
Visitor Receipts (US$m)	85,052	456,402	18.6%
Travel Departures ('000)	76,754	594,797	12.9%
Travel Expenditure (US$m)	70,696	397,040	17.8%

GNI figures relate to 1999. Population figures are taken from the most recent census or reliable estimate. Travel figures (from the WTO) are generally for 1999, but where these are unavailable or unreliable, figures from earlier years have been used. All travel figures are based on overnight stays, not same-day visitors. Where data for certain countries was not available, this has been regarded as zero. Global totals for Visitor Arrivals/Travel Departures and Visitor Receipts/Travel Expenditure do not equal each other due to differing methods of reporting inbound and outbound data. For more information on what is regarded as a country for the purposes of this book, and for more detailed statistical information, please see the Countries A-Z section from page 184.

US statistical convention employs three gradations of territorial definition: (a) Domestic (the 50 states and DC, including Alaska and Hawaii); (b) Overseas (all other countries of the world except Canada and Mexico); and (c) International (all other countries of the world including Canada and Mexico). Dependencies and territories such as Guam, Puerto Rico and the USVI are generally regarded as 'international'.

WHAT MIGHT be termed the American way of life – its popular culture, free-market economics and libertarianism – exerts a massive influence, both amongst those who aspire to it and those who reject it utterly. The architect of this global influence is essentially the USA, but neighbouring Canada, the world's second largest country, has mirrored it. The USA is comfortably the world's richest nation, accounting for a staggering 29.6% of the world's GNI: with only 0.5% of the world's population, a further 2% is contributed by Canada. The continent is rich in other ways, and from mountains to beaches, cities to wildernesses, theme parks to museums, America can match anything the planet has to offer. It has been said that the whole world can be found within the boundaries of North America. The events of September 2001 showed this remark also to be true in a darker way. How the USA reconciles its zestful, open society with the new demands of internal security will be crucial to the health of the travel business in America; and hence – as with so many other industries – in the rest of the world as well.

Holiday trends

Almost all US travel and tourism promotion is conducted at state, rather than national, level, creating the sometimes confusing illusion of 50 separate destinations. To a slightly lesser extent, the same is true of Canada. Whatever the marketing hype, it is true that virtually all tastes are catered for in North America. Once arrived, long-distance internal travel of all kinds is the norm, by both air and land, and touring has always been a major American attraction: 15% of US visitors take in three or more states.

Long-haul city breaks were pioneered in North America starting with shopping and theatre weekends in New York, but other US and Canadian cities have since muscled in and developed a strong market from Europe, even to cities with a flying time in excess of 10 hours.

Over 30% of international travellers to the USA in 2000 made a visit to a theme park, and this trend is set to increase. In 1999, four of the top five and seven of the top 10 theme parks in the USA in terms of visitor numbers were in Florida. These top ten attracted a total of some 82 million visitors, equivalent to the population of Germany.

Major beach destinations are Florida and California, although every state with a coastline has something to offer in this respect. One quarter of all overseas visi-

■ North American breaks

Percentage of foreign trips taken within North America by US and Canadian residents
Source: WTO

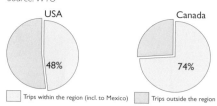

■ Comings & goings

Inbound and outbound travel to and from the USA and Canada by region
Source: WTO

Visitor arrivals to USA and Canada, by region of origin

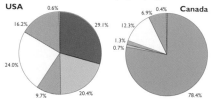

Travel departures from USA and Canada, by region of destination

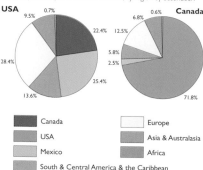

tors to the USA spent at least part of their holiday sunbathing or engaging in watersports. 'Soft adventure' opportunities include skiing, white-water rafting, canoeing and national parks trekking in many of the wilderness areas that both the USA and Canada have diligently preserved. There were over 64 million domestic and international visitors to US national parks in 1999: one in five overseas visitors went to at least one.

Winter sports have long been popular in both countries, and US and Canadian resorts are becoming increasingly

■ Top states

Top 10 US US states by overseas (not from Canada or Mexico) visitors, 1999 (millions)
Source: ITA Tourism Industries/CIC Research, California

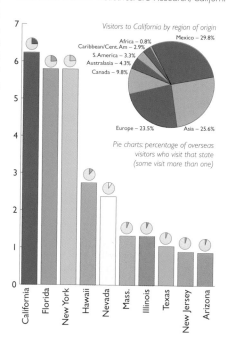

popular with foreign visitors. Top winter sports areas in Canada include: Banff, Alberta; Lake Louise, Alberta; Whistler, British Columbia; and Mont Tremblant, Quebec. Top winter sports areas in the USA include: Aspen, Colorado; Breckenridge, Colorado; Park City/Deer Valley, Utah; Stowe, Vermont; Mammoth Mountain, California; Heavenly, California; and Vail, Colorado.

USA established favourites

California, Florida and New York dominate the US inbound travel market. Over 70% of all overseas visitors spend time in at least one, and the USA's five most-visited cities are all in these three states.

California, the USA's most populous state, is also the most visited. Its myriad attractions include not only beaches and theme parks but also city visits and touring.

Florida's image is almost exclusively one of sun-drenched pleasure. Its beaches, hotels and theme parks cater for all the family. Another strength is golf: the state has over 1,000 courses.

New York offers probably the world's most intense urban experience, as well as spectacular up-state coun-

- The USA and Canada (USA&C) occupies over 14% of the world's land area and is home to over 5% of the world's population.
- USA&C's combined GDI is US$9,493,573 million, nearly 32% of the world's total.
- USA&C accounts for nearly 13% of global travel departures and over 10% of arrivals.
- International travel and tourism contributed over US$85 billion to USA&C's economy in 1999, an increase of 4.6% over 1998.
- Just under half of international visitors to the USA in 1999 were from Canada (14.1 million) and Mexico (9.9 million). 23% of the rest came from Europe: 38% of these visitors – 17.4% of non-Canadian/Mexican visitors and 8.7% of all international arrivals – were from the UK.
- California's tourism receipts in 2000 were US$75.4 billion, the most of any state. Of this, some 85% was generated by US residents.
- Britons spent US$7.8 billion in the USA in 1999 (not including international transport), out of a total for Western Europeans of US$23.7.
- Just over 78% of all international visitors to Canada in 1999 were from the USA (15.2 million). Nearly half of these visitors were residents of New York, Michigan, Washington State, California or Ohio.
- Of the non-US visitors to Canada in 1999, 18.8% were from the UK. Visitors from the UK, Japan, France and Germany accounted for over 50% of all non-US visitors to Canada in 1999.
- The USA spends more on, and receives more from, international travel than any other country. Only France received more foreign visitors in 1999, and only the Germans made more foreign trips.
- 14% of all US travel receipts in 2000 were from nationals of Japan. The two countries which supplied the most visitors, Canada and Mexico, contributed 8% and 5% respectively.
- Travel and tourism is the USA's fourth largest export, contributing 37% of service sector exports.
- In 1999, the USA received US$13 billion more from international travel and tourism than it spent: it has recorded a surplus every year since 1989. In 1999, Canada recorded a deficit of US$1.3 billion.
- Overseas visitors (excluding those from Canada and Mexico) spend on average six times as much per head on travel as do their US counterparts.
- 14 of the world's 20 most visited theme parks in 1998 are in the USA.
- 38% of overseas visitors to the USA arrived at either New York, Miami or Los Angeles.
- 1.1 million Britons visited New York City in 2000, 16.6% of all international visitors to the city. In all, New York City received 37.4 million visitors (domestic, overseas and international) in 2000, an increase of 1.9% over 1999.
- According to the UN's Human Development Index, Canada enjoys the highest quality of life in the world. The USA was 3rd= (with Australia).
- 72% of overseas leisure arrivals and 80% of business arrivals to the USA in 2000 were repeat visitors.
- 79% of overseas visitors to the USA in 2000 were independent travellers.
- The average length of stay by overseas visitors to the USA in 1999 was 15.2 days.
- Over five times as many US and Canadian residents went on a cruise in 2000 compared to 1980: 6.88 million as against 1.43 million.
- 15% of overseas trips by US nationals involve visits to two countries, and 8% to three or more.
- The US states with the largest increase in 1999 overseas visitors compared to 1998 were Minnesota (65%), North Carolina (42%), Georgia (32%) and Tennessee (30%). The largest decreases were shown by Maine, Alaska and Missouri (all -29%).
- Over 48,000 Cubans visited the USA in 1999, an increase of a massive 766% over 1998, the largest for any country of origin. Cuban travel to Canada was also up 93% over the same period.
- Ontario accounted for 37% of Canada's foreign tourism revenues in 1999 and 44% of its visitors.
- The UK received 17% of all US overseas (non-Canadian and Mexican) visitors in 1999, an increase of 13% over 1998.

tryside stretching to the Canadian border. Neighbouring New Jersey has also long been popular. Major redevelopment plans are afoot in the famous, but now somewhat faded, gaming resort of Atlantic City.

Hawaii is a firm favourite with the USA's Far East market. Tourism is the state's main industry: its 1999 tourism budget was US$60 million, the highest in the country.

Nevada, where tourism accounts for over 35% of all state employment, is home to the comparison-defying city of Las Vegas.

The US capital, Washington DC, and its surrounding states of Virginia and Maryland, are strongly associated with some of the country's most historic events and have a strong 'heritage' appeal.

The New England states of Vermont, Connecticut, Rhode Island, New Hampshire, Massachusetts and Maine are among the most popular for family touring and skiing.

Leading soft adventure destinations are California, Washington and Arizona, for activities that range from rafting and trekking to mountain climbing and cycling.

Canada established favourites
The geography of Canada has dictated its holiday patterns. Vast prairies take up its central region which means visitors fly into Toronto in the east or Vancouver in the west. Many tours take in both wings of the country but skip the middle.

Eastern Canada's highlights include Ontario and Québec, large provinces with excellent variety for touring and city visiting. In the west, Vancouver is the gateway to Vancouver Island and the Rocky Mountains. Many visitors combine a self-drive tour of British Columbia with Alberta on the eastern side of the Rockies, or with the Pacific US States to the south.

Up and coming in the USA
The Deep South is attracting ever-increasing international interest, particularly New Orleans for its Cajun

■ Top cities
Top ten US cities by overseas (not ex Canada or Mexico) visitors, 1999 (millions)
Source: ITA Tourism Industries/NYC & Co

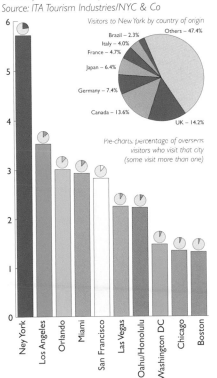

Visitors to New York by country of origin

- Others – 47.4%
- Brazil – 2.3%
- Italy – 4.0%
- France – 4.7%
- Japan – 6.4%
- Germany – 7.4%
- Canada – 13.6%
- UK – 14.2%

Pie-charts: percentage of overseas visitors who visit that city (some visit more than one)

(Bar chart cities: New York, Los Angeles, Orlando, Miami, San Francisco, Las Vegas, Oahu/Honolulu, Washington DC, Chicago, Boston)

■ Airline decline
Performance of ATA US-member airlines* between January 2000 and September 2001.
Source: Air Transport Association

* Alaska, America West, American, American Trans-Air, Continental, Delta, Northwest, Southwest, Trans World, United, US Airways, Aloha, Continental Micronesia, Hawaiian and Midwest Express.

- Revenue passenger miles (billions)
- Passenger enplanements (millions)

culture and jazz; and Georgia, one of the country's fastest growing economies, whose capital, Atlanta, was host to the 1996 Olympics. Only Las Vegas, Orlando and Los Angeles have more hotel rooms than Atlanta.

The Rocky Mountain states of Montana, Wyoming and Idaho are cashing in on the lifestyles sector and offering adventure activities.

Texas has recently been targeting overseas markets to draw attention to its diversity. In 1999, only Hawaii, Florida and Illinois spent more on tourist promotion.

Up and coming in Canada
The Atlantic coast provinces such as Labrador, Nova Scotia, Prince Edward Island and New Brunswick offer Canada at its rugged and bracing best. Historic fishing villages offer the quiet life and cities such as Halifax, Nova Scotia are bidding for a slice of the short-breaks' pie.

Issues
The events of September 2001 have led to a tightening of airline security, likely to be paid for by consumers in the form of longer check-in times and higher fares. The word 'crisis' is being avoided, but the entire aviation industry, both in North America and globally, is facing the stiffest of challenges to rebuild consumer confidence. Many smaller airlines may not survive.

■ Business before pleasure
Top 10 domestic business travel destinations (1998 ranking in brackets)
Source: Runzheimer International

1. Chicago (1)
2. Dallas (5)
3. Atlanta (3)
4. Los Angeles (4)
5. New York (2)
6. Washington DC (7)
7. San Francisco (8)
8. Boston (6)
9. Phoenix (-)
10. Denver (10)

Business travel has always been one of North America's strengths given its corporate links that spread across the world: over seven million such visits were made to the USA in 1999 (not including those from Canada or Mexico). A slowdown in the general economic climate had sparked global downturn in business travel in 2001 before the terrorist attacks further exacerbated the problem.

■ Visitors
Visitor arrivals and average receipts per visitor, 1999
Source: WTO

	Visitors (thousands)	Receipts per visitor
USA	48,491	$1,544
Canada	19,411	$524

Maps, charts and statistics on the USA and Canada follow on pages 142 to 161. See also the *Countries A-Z* section from page 184, and the *Index* from page 193.

Thanks to: Eileen Hook of California Tourism; Patrick Thorne of Ski24; Tom Bridges of the *Travel Industry World Yearbook*; NYC & Co; Andrea Stueve of the Travel Industry Association of America; Tony Peisley.

Physical

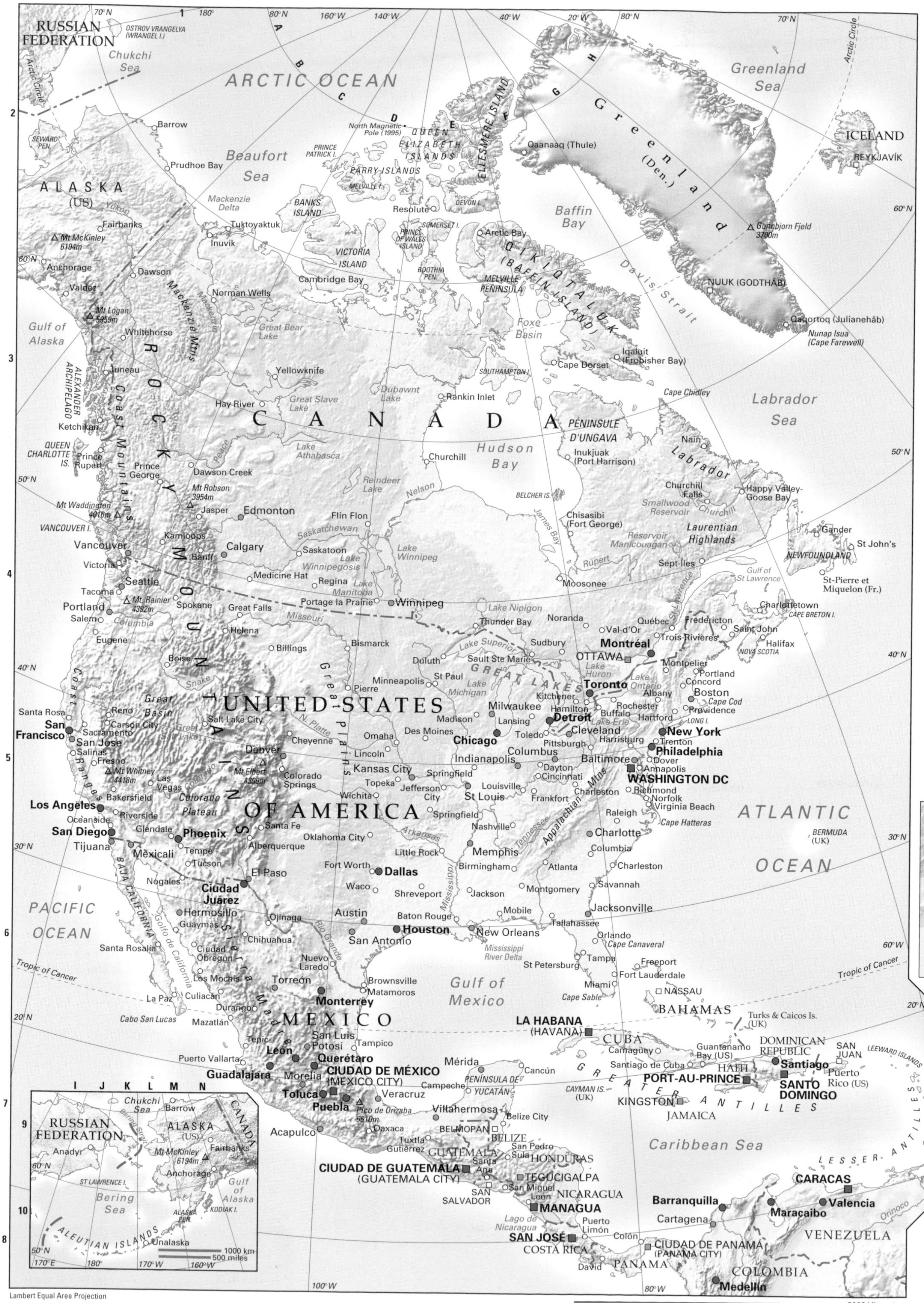
RUSSIAN FEDERATION
OSTROV VRANGELYA (WRANGEL I.)
Chukchi Sea
Arctic Circle
ARCTIC OCEAN
Greenland Sea
ICELAND
REYKJAVÍK
Barrow
SEWARD PEN.
Prudhoe Bay
Beaufort Sea
PRINCE PATRICK I.
North Magnetic Pole (1995)
QUEEN ELIZABETH ISLANDS
PARRY ISLANDS
MELVILLE I.
ELLESMERE ISLAND
Qaanaaq (Thule)
Greenland (Den.)
ALASKA (US)
Yukon
Mackenzie Delta
BANKS ISLAND
Resolute
DEVON I.
Baffin Bay
Fairbanks
Tuktoyaktuk
Inuvik
SOMERSET I.
PRINCE OF WALES ISLAND
Arctic Bay
Gunnbjorn Fjeld 3700m
Mt McKinley 6194m
VICTORIA ISLAND
Anchorage
Dawson
Cambridge Bay
BOOTHIA PEN.
MELVILLE PENINSULA
QIKIQTALUK (BAFFIN ISLAND)
Davis Strait
NUUK (GODTHÅB)
Valdez
Mackenzie Mtns
Norman Wells
Mt Logan 5959m
Great Bear Lake
Foxe Basin
Qaqortoq (Julianehåb)
Nunap Isua (Cape Farewell)
Gulf of Alaska
Whitehorse
Iqaluit (Frobisher Bay)
Cape Dorset
ALEXANDER ARCHIPELAGO
Juneau
Yellowknife
SOUTHAMPTON I.
Cape Chidley
Labrador Sea
Dubawnt Lake
Rankin Inlet
Hay River
Great Slave Lake
CANADA
PÉNINSULE D'UNGAVA
Ketchikan
Coast Mountains
ROCKY MOUNTAINS
Nain
Labrador
QUEEN CHARLOTTE IS.
Prince Rupert
Prince George
Lake Athabasca
Churchill
Hudson Bay
Inukjuak (Port Harrison)
Peace
Dawson Creek
Mt Robson 3954m
Reindeer Lake
Nelson
BELCHER IS.
Churchill Falls
Smallwood Reservoir
Happy Valley-Goose Bay
Mt Waddington 4016m
Jasper
Edmonton
Flin Flon
James Bay
Chisasibi (Fort George)
Laurentian Highlands
VANCOUVER I.
Kamloops
Saskatchewan
Réservoir Manicouagan
Gander
St John's
NEWFOUNDLAND
Vancouver
Calgary
Saskatoon
Lake Winnipeg
Lake Winnipegosis
Rupert
Sept-Îles
Victoria
Banff
Medicine Hat
St-Pierre et Miquelon (Fr.)
Gulf of St Lawrence
Seattle
Regina
Lake Manitoba
Moosonee
Tacoma
Mt Rainier 4392m
Portage la Prairie
Winnipeg
Lake Nipigon
Charlottetown
CAPE BRETON I.
Portland
Spokane
Great Falls
Salem
Columbia
Missouri
Thunder Bay
Noranda
Québec
Fredericton
Val-d'Or
Saint John
Helena
Eugene
Billings
Bismarck
Sudbury
Montréal
Trois-Rivières
Halifax
NOVA SCOTIA
Lake Superior
Sault Ste Marie
OTTAWA
Boise
Duluth
Lake Huron
Montpelier
Portland
Snake
Great Plains
Minneapolis
St Paul
GREAT LAKES
Toronto
Lake Ontario
Concord
Coast Ranges
Great Basin
UNITED STATES OF AMERICA
Pierre
Lake Michigan
Kitchener
Albany
Boston
Cape Cod
Santa Rosa
Reno
Salt Lake City
Milwaukee
Hamilton
Rochester
Providence
San Francisco
Carson City
Great Salt Lake
N. Platte
Madison
Lansing
Detroit
Buffalo
Lake Erie
Hartford
LONG I.
Sacramento
Cheyenne
Omaha
Des Moines
Chicago
Toledo
Cleveland
New York
San Jose
Harrisburg
Trenton
Salinas
Denver
Lincoln
Pittsburgh
Philadelphia
Fresno
Columbus
Dover
Mt Whitney 4418m
Mt Elbert 4399m
Indianapolis
Baltimore
Annapolis
Las Vegas
Colorado Springs
Kansas City
Springfield
Dayton
WASHINGTON DC
Bakersfield
Colorado
Colorado Plateau
Topeka
Jefferson City
Louisville
Cincinnati
Charleston
Richmond
Norfolk
Los Angeles
Wichita
St Louis
Frankfort
Virginia Beach
Oceanside
Riverside
Santa Fe
Springfield
Raleigh
Cape Hatteras
ATLANTIC OCEAN
San Diego
Glendale
Phoenix
Nashville
Tennessee
Appalachian Mtns
Charlotte
BERMUDA (UK)
Tijuana
Mexicali
Tempe
Oklahoma City
Arkansas
Memphis
Columbia
Albuquerque
Little Rock
Tucson
Fort Worth
Dallas
Birmingham
Atlanta
Charleston
BAJA CALIFORNIA
Nogales
El Paso
Ciudad Juárez
Waco
Mississippi
Shreveport
Jackson
Montgomery
Savannah
PACIFIC OCEAN
Hermosillo
Golfo de California
Ojinaga
Austin
Baton Rouge
Mobile
Jacksonville
Guaymas
Rio Grande
Houston
New Orleans
Tallahassee
Santa Rosalia
Chihuahua
San Antonio
Orlando
Cape Canaveral
Ciudad Obregón
Nuevo Laredo
Mississippi River Delta
St Petersburg
Tampa
Freeport
Tropic of Cancer
Los Mochis
Sierra Madre
Torreón
Brownsville
Gulf of Mexico
Fort Lauderdale
La Paz
Culiacán
Monterrey
Matamoros
Miami
Cape Sable
NASSAU
BAHAMAS
Durango
Cabo San Lucas
Mazatlán
MEXICO
LA HABANA (HAVANA)
Turks & Caicos Is. (UK)
Tepic
San Luis Potosí
Tampico
CUBA
Camagüey
Guantánamo Bay (US)
DOMINICAN REPUBLIC
SAN JUAN
LEEWARD ISLANDS
León
Querétaro
Puerto Vallarta
Mérida
Santiago de Cuba
HAITI
Santiago
Guadalajara
Morelia
CIUDAD DE MÉXICO (MEXICO CITY)
Cancún
PENÍNSULA DE YUCATÁN
PORT-AU-PRINCE
Puerto Rico (US)
Campeche
CAYMAN IS. (UK)
GREATER ANTILLES
SANTO DOMINGO
Toluca
Veracruz
Puebla
KINGSTON
JAMAICA
Pico de Orizaba 5610m
Villahermosa
Belize City
Oaxaca
BELMOPAN
BELIZE
WINDWARD ISLANDS
Acapulco
Tuxtla Gutiérrez
GUATEMALA
San Pedro Sula
Caribbean Sea
HONDURAS
LESSER ANTILLES
CIUDAD DE GUATEMALA (GUATEMALA CITY)
Santa Ana
TEGUCIGALPA
CARACAS
SAN SALVADOR
San Miguel
León
NICARAGUA
Barranquilla
Valencia
Maracaibo
Orinoco
MANAGUA
Cartagena
Lago de Nicaragua
Puerto Limón
SAN JOSÉ
COSTA RICA
Colón
CIUDAD DE PANAMÁ (PANAMA CITY)
VENEZUELA
David
PANAMA
COLOMBIA
Medellín
RUSSIAN FEDERATION
Chukchi Sea
Bering Strait
ALASKA (US)
CANADA
Barrow
Anadyr
Fairbanks
Mt McKinley 6194m
Anchorage
ST LAWRENCE I.
Bering Sea
Gulf of Alaska
ALASKA PEN.
KODIAK I.
ALEUTIAN ISLANDS
Unalaska
1000 km
500 miles
70° N
80° N
160° W
140° W
40° W
20° W
180°
60° N
50° N
40° N
30° N
20° N
100° W
80° W
60° W
170° E
170° W
A B C D E F G H
I J K L M N
1 2 3 4 5 6 7 8 9 10

Lambert Equal Area Projection

2000 kilometres
1000 miles

Climate

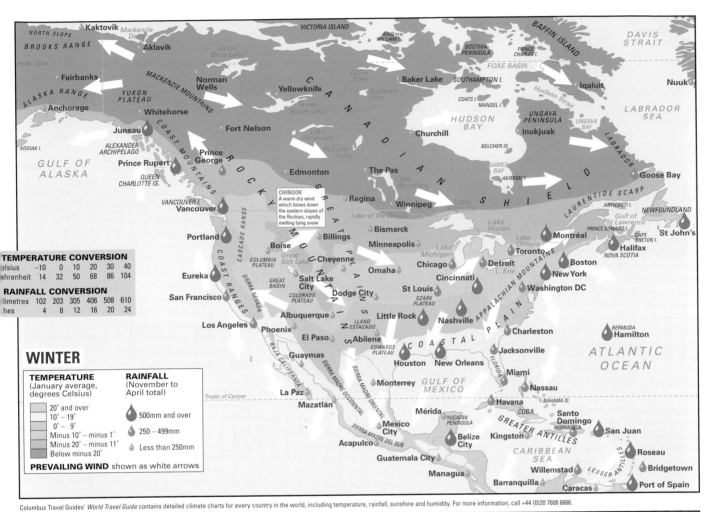

TEMPERATURE CONVERSION

Celsius	−10	0	10	20	30	40
Fahrenheit	14	32	50	68	86	104

RAINFALL CONVERSION

Millimetres	102	203	305	406	508	610
Inches	4	8	12	16	20	24

WINTER

TEMPERATURE
(January average, degrees Celsius)

- 20° and over
- 10° – 19°
- 0° – 9°
- Minus 10° – minus 1°
- Minus 20° – minus 11°
- Below minus 20°

RAINFALL
(November to April total)

- 500mm and over
- 250 – 499mm
- Less than 250mm

PREVAILING WIND shown as white arrows

CHINOOK
A warm dry wind which blows down the eastern slopes of the Rockies, rapidly melting lying snow

Columbus Travel Guides' *World Travel Guide* contains detailed climate charts for every country in the world, including temperature, rainfall, sunshine and humidity. For more information, call +44 (0)20 7608 6666.

LABRADOR CURRENT
A cold current flowing south, carrying icebergs and keeping the coastal region relatively cool during the summer; fogs are caused off the Newfoundland coast where the current meets the warmer Gulf Stream flowing NE from the Gulf of Mexico

CALIFORNIA CURRENT
A cold current which flows south, cooling the coastal region, and responsible for the frequent sea fogs particularly during the summer

SUMMER

TEMPERATURE
(July average, degrees Celsius)

- 30° and over
- 20° – 29°
- 10° – 19°
- 0° – 9°
- Minus 10° – minus 1°

RAINFALL
(May to October total)

- 500mm and over
- 250 – 499mm
- Less than 250mm

PREVAILING WIND shown as white arrows

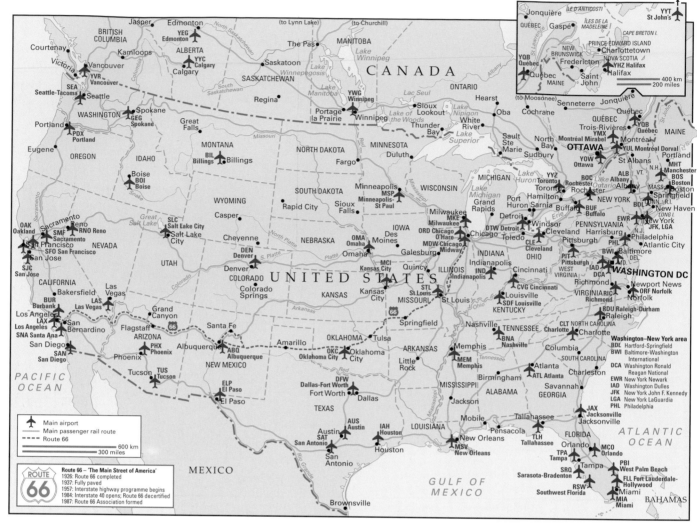

The 50 busiest airports in the USA & Canada, 2000 (million passengers)

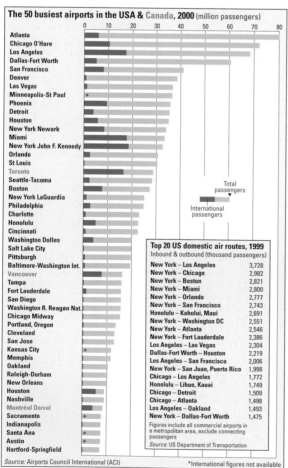

Atlanta
Chicago O'Hare
Los Angeles
Dallas-Fort Worth
San Francisco
Denver
Las Vegas
Minneapolis-St Paul
Phoenix
Detroit
Houston
New York Newark
Miami
New York John F. Kennedy
Orlando
St Louis
Toronto
Seattle-Tacoma
Boston
New York LaGuardia
Philadelphia
Charlotte
Honolulu
Cincinnati
Washington Dulles
Salt Lake City
Pittsburgh
Baltimore-Washington Int.
Vancouver
Tampa
Fort Lauderdale
San Diego
Washington R. Reagan Nat.
Chicago Midway
Portland, Oregon
Cleveland
San Jose
Kansas City
Memphis
Oakland
Raleigh-Durham
New Orleans
Houston
Nashville
Montréal Dorval
Sacramento
Indianapolis
Santa Ana
Austin
Hartford-Springfield

Total passengers
International passengers

*International figures not available

Source: Airports Council International (ACI)

Top 20 US domestic air routes, 1999
Inbound & outbound (thousand passengers)

New York – Los Angeles	3,728
New York – Chicago	2,982
New York – Boston	2,821
New York – Miami	2,800
New York – Orlando	2,777
New York – San Francisco	2,743
Honolulu – Kahului, Maui	2,691
New York – Washington DC	2,551
New York – Atlanta	2,546
New York – Fort Lauderdale	2,386
Los Angeles – Las Vegas	2,304
Dallas-Fort Worth – Houston	2,219
Los Angeles – San Francisco	2,006
New York – San Juan, Puerto Rico	1,998
Chicago – Los Angeles	1,772
Honolulu – Lihue, Kauai	1,749
Chicago – Detroit	1,509
Chicago – Atlanta	1,498
Los Angeles – Oakland	1,493
New York – Dallas-Fort Worth	1,475

Figures include all commercial airports in a metropolitan area, exclude connecting passengers

Source: US Department of Transportation

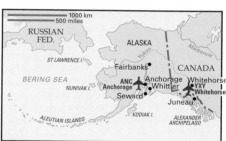

LONG-DISTANCE RAIL SERVICES

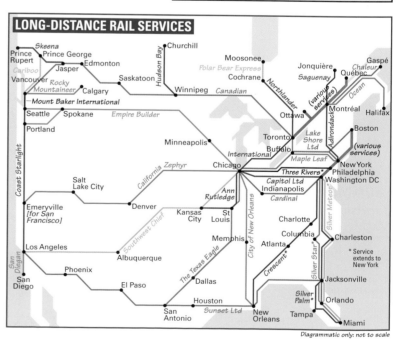

Diagrammatic only: not to scale

Museums & Art Galleries

The most important museums and art galleries in the United States and Canada are listed here. Selection is based on importance and depth of the collection and its cultural diversity within a geographic spread.

Data compiled by Jon A. Gillaspie email: info@sarastro.com

Principal contents of institution:

- **AA** Applied & decorative art
- **AR** Archaeology / ancient art
- **FA** Fine art (paintings, sculpture)
- **FO** Folk art & culture / ethnology
- **H** History / historical site / reconstruction
- **NH** Natural history
- **ST** Science / technology
- **W** Wide range of subjects

Opening times:

Days or months preceded by a red circle (●) indicate when the institution is closed.
Many close on national holidays and other special days. Some museums and galleries have shorter opening hours at certain days of the week or in certain months.

Admission charges:

All charge for admission except those shown in *italics*, where entry is free (although charges for special exhibitions may apply).
Some institutions allow free entry or reduce their admission charges on certain days.

Albuquerque NEW MEXICO
W Indian Pueblo Cultural Center
Atlanta GEORGIA
FA High Museum of Art ● Mon
W Michael C. Carlos Museum (Emory Univ.)
Baltimore MARYLAND
FA Baltimore Museum of Art ● Mon & Tue
W Walters Art Gallery ● Mon
Banff ALBERTA
NH Whyte Museum of Rockies ● Mon (Oct-May)
Baraboo WISCONSIN
H Circus World Museum ● no shows Oct-Apr
Baton Rouge LOUISIANA
W LSU Rural Life Museum
Boston MASSACHUSETTS
FA Isabella Stewart Gardner Museum ● Mon
W Museum of Fine Arts
Bozeman MONTANA
W Museum of the Rockies
Buffalo NEW YORK
FA Albright-Knox Art Gallery ● Mon
Burlington VERMONT
W Shelburne Museum ● tours only Nov-May
Calgary ALBERTA
W Glenbow Museum ● Mon (Sep-May)
Cedar Rapids IOWA
FA Museum of Art ● Mon

Charlotte NORTH CAROLINA
ST Discovery Place
W Mint Museum of Art ● Mon
Chicago ILLINOIS
FA Art Institute of Chicago; Museum of Contemporary Art ● Mon
W Field Museum of Chicago
ST Museum of Science and Technology
Cincinnati OHIO
FA Cincinnati Art Museum ● Mon; Contemporary Arts Center ● Sun; Taft Museum
Cleveland OHIO
ST Great Lakes Science Center
FA Museum of Art ● Mon
NH Museum of Natural History
H Rock and Roll Hall of Fame
Cody WYOMING
H Buffalo Bill Hist. Center ● Tue & Wed (Nov-Apr) includes: Plains Ind. Mus., Witney Gall.
Columbus OHIO
FA Columbus Museum of Art ● Mon
Corpus Christi TEXAS
FA Art Museum of South Texas ● Mon
Dallas TEXAS
FO African-American Museum ● Mon
AR FA *Dallas Museum of Art* ● Mon
NH Dallas Museum of Natural History
H Sixth Floor Museum (School Book Depository)
Denver COLORADO
H Black Amer. West Mus. ● Mon & Tue (winter)
W Art Museum ● Mon; Mus. of Natural History
Des Moines IOWA
FA Des Moines Art Center ● Mon
Detroit OHIO
W Detroit Institute of Art ● Mon & Tue
H Museum of Afro-American History ● Mon
Drumheller ALBERTA
NH Royal Tyrrell Museum of Paleontology ● Mon (Oct-May)
Durham NORTH CAROLINA
W Duke University Museum of Art ● Mon
Edmonton ALBERTA
ST Edmonton Space and Science Center ● Mon
Flagstaff ARIZONA
FO Museum of Northern Arizona
Fort Steele BRITISH COLUMBIA
H Fort Steele Heritage Town
Fort Worth TEXAS
FA Amon Carter Museum; Kimbell Art Museum; Modern Art Museum; Sid Richardson Collection of Western Art ● Mon
W *Museum of Science and History* ● Mon
Fredericton NEW BRUNSWICK
FA Beaverbrook Art Gallery ● Mon (winter)
Halifax NOVA SCOTIA
H Atlantic Maritime Museum ● Mon (Oct-May)
NH NS Natural History Museum ● Mon (Oct-May)
Houston TEXAS
FA Museum of Fine Arts ● Mon
NH Museum of Natural Science
ST Space Center Houston
Huntsville ALABAMA
ST Space and Rocket Center
Indianapolis INDIANA
FO Eiteljorg Museum ● Mon (Sep-Jun)
FA Indianapolis Museum of Art ● Sun & Mon
W Children's Mus. of Indianap. ● Mon (winter)
Kansas City MISSOURI
W Nelson-Atkins Mus. of Art ● Mon
Kingston ONTARIO
W Agnes Etherington Art Center ● Mon
Los Angeles CALIFORNIA
AA FA *Getty Center* ● Mon
FA Armand Hammer Museum of Art; Museum of Contemporary Art (MOCA) ● Mon

AR FA LA County Museum of Art (LACMA)
W Natural History Museum of LA County ● Mon
H Simon Weisenthal Center (Beit Hashoa Mus.)
Louisville KENTUCKY
FA *J.B. Speed Art Museum* ● Mon
Macon GEORGIA
W Tubman African-American Museum
Manchester NEW HAMPSHIRE
AA FA Currier Gallery of Art ● Tue
Memphis TENNESSEE
W National Civil Rights Museum ● Tue
Merritt Island FLORIDA
ST *Kennedy Space Center*
Mesa Verde National Park COLORADO
AR Archaeological Museum
Miami FLORIDA
FA Bass Mus.; Center for Fine Arts ● both Mon
W Lowe Art Museum (Univ. of Miami) ● Mon
AA Wolfsonian Museum ● Mon
Milwaukee WISCONSIN
FA Milwaukee Art Gallery ● Mon
W Museum Center
Minneapolis and St Paul MINNESOTA
W *Minneapolis Institute of Arts* ● Mon; Minnesota Children's Museum ● Mon (winter)
ST Science Museum of Minnesota
FA Walker Art Cent. and Sculpture Gdn. ● Mon
Montréal QUÉBEC
NH Biodôme
AA Canadian Cent. for Architecture ● Mon & Tue (Oct-May); Chât. Ramezay ● Mon (Oct-May)
AR Mont. Mus. of Archaeology & History ● Mon
FA Montréal Museum of Fine Arts; Montréal Contemporary Art Museum ● both Mon
H McCord Museum of Canadian History
Montgomery ALABAMA
FA Montgomery Museum of Fine Art ● Mon
Morrisburg ONTARIO
H Upper Canada Village ● Oct-May
Mystic CONNECTICUT
H Mystic Seaport
Nashville TENNESSEE
H Country Music Hall of Fame
W Tennessee State Museum ● Mon
New Haven CONNECTICUT
FA *Center for British Art* ● Mon; *Yale University Library* ● Mon (Jul-Aug)
NH Peabody Museum of Natural History
New Orleans LOUISIANA
W Louisiana State Museum ● Mon includes: Cabildo; Presbytere; 1850 House; Jazz Mus.
FA New Orleans Museum of Art ● Mon
New York NEW YORK
W American Mus. of Natural History; Brooklyn Mus. ● Mon & Tue; Metropolitan Mus. of Art; NY Historical Society ● Mon
AA Cooper-Hewitt National Design Mus. ● Mon
FA Guggenheim Mus. ● Thu; Whitney Museum of American Art ● Mon & Tue
AA FA Museum of Modern Art (MoMA) ● Wed
FO National Museum of the American Indian
Norfolk VIRGINIA
FA Chrysler Museum ● Mon
Oberlin OHIO
W Allen Memorial Art Museum ● Mon

Oklahoma City OKLAHOMA
FA FO National Cowboy Hall of Fame
Omaha NEBRASKA
H Great Plains Black Museum ● Sat & Sun
Orlando FLORIDA
ST EPCOT Center
Ottawa QUÉBEC
NH Canadian Museum of Nature
W Can. Museum of Civilization ● Mon (Oct-Apr)
FA FO National Gallery ● Mon & Tue (Sep-Apr)
ST National Aviation Museum ● Mon (Sep-Apr)
ST National Museum of Science ● Mon (Sep-Apr)
Pasadena CALIFORNIA
FA Huntington Museum and Library ● Mon; Norton Simon Museum ● Mon, Tue & Wed
Philadelphia PENNSYLVANIA
H Afro-American Hist. & Cultural Mus. ● Mon
AR FO Museum of Archaeology and Anthro-pology (University of Pennsylvania) ● Mon
FA Philadelphia Museum of Art; Rodin Museum ● both Mon
Phoenix ARIZONA
FO Heard Museum
Pittsburgh PENNSYLVANIA
FA Andy Warhol Museum ● Mon; Museum of Art (Carnegie Center) ● Mon (Sep-Jun)
AA FA Frick Art Museum ● Mon
Portland OREGON
ST Oregon Museum of Science and Industry ● Mon (winter)
W Portland Art Museum ● Mon
Princeton NEW JERSEY
ST Carnegie Science Center
NH Natural History Museum ● Mon (Sep-Jun)
W University Art Museum ● Mon
Québec QUÉBEC
W Museum of Civilization ● Mon (Sep-Jun)
FA Québec Museum ● Mon (Sep-May)
Raleigh NORTH CAROLINA
FA North Carolina Museum of Art ● Mon
ST North Carolina Museum of Natural Sciences
Rapid City SOUTH DAKOTA
H Sioux Indian Museum ● Mon
Richmond VIRGINIA
W Virginia Museum of Fine Arts ● Mon
Rochester NEW YORK
AA International Museum of Photography ● Mon
Saint John NEW BRUNSWICK
W New Brunswick Museum
St Louis MISSOURI
H Museum of Western Expansion
W St Louis Art Museum ● Mon
St Petersburg FLORIDA
W Museum of Fine Arts ● Mon
FA Salvador Dali Museum
Salem MASSACHUSETTS
W Peabody Essex Museum
H Plimoth Plantation
San Diego CALIFORNIA
FA Museum of Contemporary Art, La Jolla ● Mon
San Francisco CALIFORNIA
FA California Palace of the Legion of Honor; Yerba Buena Gardens; San Francisco Art Institute ● all Mon; San Francisco Museum of Modern Art ● Wed

Santa Fe NEW MEXICO
W Museum of New Mexico ● Mon includes:
FA Georgia O'Keeffe Mus.; Mus. of Fine Arts
FO Mus. of Indian Arts; Mus. of Internat. Folk Art
Sarasota FLORIDA
FA Ringling Museum Complex
Saskatoon SASKATCHEWAN
FA Mendel Art Gallery
Seattle WASHINGTON
FA Henry Art Gallery ● Mon
ST Museum of Flight; Pacific Science Center
FO Thomas Burke Memorial Museum
Sudbury ONTARIO
ST Science North
Tallahassee FLORIDA
W Black Archives Research Center ● Sat & Sun
Tampa FLORIDA
ST Museum of Science and Industry ● varies
W Tampa Museum of Art ● Fri
Toronto ONTARIO
FA Art Gallery of Ontario (AGO) ● Mon, ● Tue (Oct-May); McMichael Canadian Art Collection ● Mon (Oct-May); Thomson Gallery ● Sun
FO *Gallery of Inuit Art*
ST Ontario Science Centre
W Royal Ontario Museum (ROM)
Tucson ARIZONA
NH Arizona-Sonora Desert Museum
FO Arizona State Museum
AR FA Tucson Museum of Art ● Mon (Jun-Aug)
Vancouver BRITISH COLUMBIA
FO UBC Museum of Anthropology ● Mon (Sep-May)
Victoria BRITISH COLUMBIA
W Royal British Columbia Museum
Virginia Beach VIRGINIA
ST Virginia Marine Museum
Washington DC
FA *Corcoran Gallery* ● Tue; *National Gall. of Art*, *National Mus. of Women in the Arts*; *Phillips Coll.*
H *US Holocaust Memorial Museum*
W *Smithsonian Institution* includes:
AA FA *Freer Gallery of Art*
FA *Hirshhorn Museum; National Museum of American Art; National Portrait Gallery*
ST *National Air and Space Museum*
FO *National Museum of African Art; Sackler Gallery*
FA *National Museum of American History*
NH *National Museum of Natural History*
Wichita KANSAS
FA *Wichita Art Museum* ● Mon
Williamsburg VIRGINIA
H *Colonial Williamsburg; Jamestown Settlement*
Wilmington DELAWARE
AA Nemours Mansion
AA FO Winterthur Museum, Winterthur
Windsor ONTARIO
FA Art Gallery of Windsor ● Mon
Winnipeg MANITOBA
NH Manit. Museum of Man & Nature ● Mon (Sep-Jun)
FA Winnipeg Art Gallery ● Mon (Sep-May)
Winston-Salem NORTH CAROLINA
FA Reynolda House Museum of American Art ● Mon

Skiing & Snowboarding

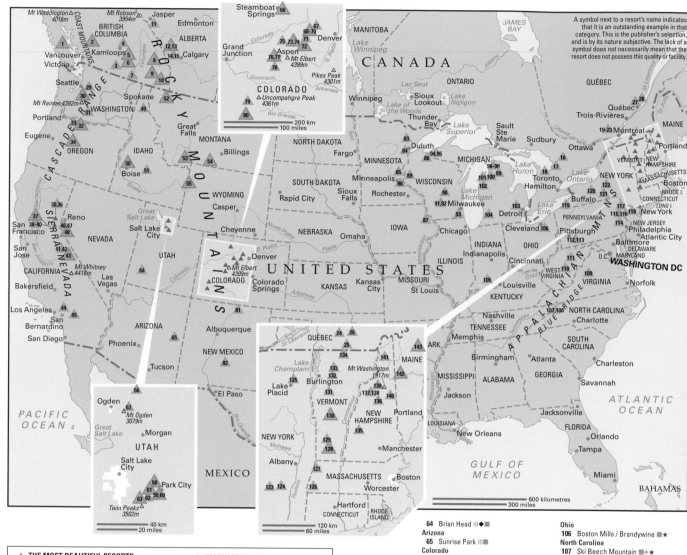

A symbol next to a resort's name indicates that it is an outstanding example in that category. This is the publisher's selection, and is by its nature subjective. The lack of a symbol does not necessarily mean that the resort does not possess this quality or facility.

THE MOST BEAUTIFUL RESORTS
Ski areas with spectacular scenery

❄ SNOWSURE
The best reputations for season-long snow cover

◆ EXPERT
Best of the black diamond destinations

■ BEGINNER SKI AREAS
Best choices for first timers

♠ FAMILY FRIENDLY
Ideal choices for family ski holidays

● PARTY TOWNS
Après ski centres

★ SNOWBOARDER HEAVEN
Best bets for boarders

★ NOT JUST SKIING
Plenty to do if you don't want to slide

THE LARGEST SKI AREAS △
1 Mount Washington, BC
2 Whistler & Blackcomb, BC
5 Silver Star, BC
6 Big White, BC
8 Panorama, BC
9 Kimberley, BC
10 Fernie Snow Valley, BC
12 Lake Louise (Banff), AL
13 Sunshine Village (Banff), AL
30 Crystal Mountain, WA
32 Mount Hood Meadows, OR
34 Mount Bachelor, OR
37 Squaw Valley, CA
43 Mammoth Mountain, CA
48 Heavenly, NV
50 Bogus Basin, ID
52 Big Mountain, MT
53 Big Sky, MT
54 Red Lodge Mountain, MT
55 Jackson Hole, Teton, WY
58 The Canyons, UT
59 Deer Valley, UT
60 Park City, UT
61 Solitude, UT
63 Snowbird, UT
66 Steamboat, CO
68 Winter Park (Mary Jane), CO
69 Loveland, CO
70 Keystone, CO
72 Breckenridge, CO
73 Copper Mountain, CO
74 Vail, CO
76 Snowmass, CO
77 Aspen, CO
80 Durango Mountain Resort, CO
128 Mount Snow (Haystack / Carinthia), VT
130 Killington, VT
142 Sunday River, ME
143 Sugarloaf USA, ME

Canada
British Columbia
1 Mount Washington ❄▼
2 Whistler & Blackcomb ❄◆♠●▼★
3 Apex ◆■♠▼
4 Sun Peaks ❄◆■♠▼
5 Silver Star ❄■♠▼
6 Big White ❄■♠▼
7 Red Mountain ❄◆♠▼
8 Panorama ▲❄◆■♠▼
9 Kimberley ❄■♠♥▼
10 Fernie Snow Valley ❄▼

Alberta
11 Marmot Basin (Jasper) ▲❄■♠●▼★
12 Lake Louise (Banff) ▲❄◆♠
13 Sunshine Village (Banff) ❄■♠●▼★
14 Fortress Mountain ▲❄■
15 Nakiska ❄❄▼

Ontario
16 Sir Sam's ■♠★
17 Mount St Louis / Moonstone ■♠▼
18 Blue Mountain ■♠▼▼

Québec
19 Mont Gabriel ❄❄
20 Mont Ste-Sauveur ■♠▼★
21 Ski Morin Heights ■
22 Mont Blanc ■♠▼★
23 Tremblant ❄■♠●▼★
24 Bromont ■♠▼
25 Owl's Head ■♠▼
26 Mont Orford ❄■♠▼
27 Mont Ste-Anne ▲❄■♠●▼★
28 Stoneham ❄■♠▼★

United States
Washington
29 Stevens Pass ♠
30 Crystal Mountain ▲◆♠▼
31 White Pass Village ❄■♠

Oregon
32 Mount Hood Meadows ▲❄◆▼
33 Timberline ▲❄■♠▼
34 Mount Bachelor ▲❄◆▼

California
35 Donner Ski Ranch ▲▼
36 Boreal ■▼
37 Squaw Valley ❄◆■♠▼★
38 Alpine Meadows ▲❄◆▼
39 Sierra-at-Tahoe ▲❄■♠▼
40 Kirkwood ▲❄◆▼
41 Dodge Ridge ▼
42 June Mountain ▲■♠▼
43 Mammoth Mountain ▲❄◆♠●▼★
44 Mountain High ❄❄▼
45 Snow Summit ■▼

Nevada
46 Diamond Peak ▲▲
47 Mount Rose ◆▼
48 Heavenly ▲❄◆■♠●▼★

Idaho
49 Silver Mountain ❄■♠▼
51 Sun Valley ▲❄◆■▼★

Montana
52 Big Mountain ◆■♠▼★
53 Big Sky ▲◆■♠●
54 Red Lodge Mountain ▲❄♠●▼

Wyoming
55 Jackson Hole, Teton ▲❄◆■♠●▼★

Utah
56 Powder Mountain ❄◆■
57 Snowbasin ❄◆▼
58 The Canyons ❄◆■♠▼★
59 Deer Valley ❄■♠●★
60 Park City ❄■♠●▼★
61 Solitude ▲■♠▼
62 Alta ◆❄■♠★
63 Snowbird ▲❄■◆▼●

Colorado
64 Brian Head ❄◆■
Arizona
65 Sunrise Park ❄■
Colorado
66 Steamboat ▲❄■♠●▼★
67 Eldora Mountain ▼
68 Winter Park (Mary Jane)
69 Loveland ▲❄◆
70 Keystone ▲❄■♠●▼
71 Arapahoe Basin ❄◆
72 Breckenridge ❄◆■♠●▼★
73 Copper Mountain ▲❄◆■♠●▼★
74 Vail ◆❄♠●★
75 Beaver Creek ▲❄■♠▼★
76 Snowmass ❄■♠●▼★
77 Aspen ▲❄◆■♠●▼★
78 Crested Butte ▲❄■◆♠●▼
79 Telluride ▲❄◆■♠●▼★
80 Durango Mountain Resort ❄◆♠▼★

New Mexico
81 Taos ▲❄◆▼
82 Ski Apache ◆●▼★

Minnesota
83 Giants Ridge ■★
84 Spirit Mountain ■♠▼
85 Afton Alps ■▼
86 Buck Hill ■▼

Iowa
87 Sundown Mountain ▼★

Wisconsin
88 Whitecap Mountains ■▼★
89 Trollhaugen ❄❄▼
90 Nordic Mountain ■■▼
91 Cascade Mountain ●■▼
92 Devils Head ■■◆
93 Wilmot Mountain ■▼

Michigan
94 Big Powderhorn Mountain ❄❄▼
95 Indianhead Mountain & Bear Creek ◆★
96 Boyne Mountain ■♠★
97 Boyne Highlands ■♠▼★
99 Nub's Nob ■▼
99 Treetops / Sylvan ■▼
100 Shanty Creek / Schuss Mountain ■
101 Caberfae Peaks ■★
102 Sugar Loaf ▼
103 Alpine Valley ■
104 Timber Ridge ■

Indiana
105 Paoli Peaks ■♠▼

Ohio
106 Boston Mills / Brandywine ■★
North Carolina
107 Ski Beech Mountain ■♠★
108 Sugar Mountain ■♠▼
Virginia
109 Wintergreen ▲■★
West Virginia
110 Snowshoe ▲■♠▼★
111 Canaan Valley ▲■♠★
Pennsylvania
112 Hidden Valley ▲■♠★
113 Seven Springs ▲■♠▼
114 Doe Mountain ■▼
115 Big Boulder ❄■♠▼
116 Camelback ❄■▼
117 Shawnee Mountain ■▼
New Jersey
118 Mountain Creek ■♠▼★
New York
119 Holiday Valley ■♠◆
120 Bristol Mountain ★
121 Greek Peak ■
122 Labrador Mountain ■▼
123 Belleayre ▲
124 Hunter Mountain ■♠▼
125 Whiteface Mountain ▼★
Massachusetts
126 Butternut Basin ♠
127 Jiminy Peak ■♠
Vermont
128 Mount Snow (Haystack / Carinthia)
129 Stratton ▲❄■♠▼★
130 Killington ❄◆■♠●▼
131 Sugarbush ■♠▼
132 Stowe (Mount Mansfield) ▲◆●▼♠★
133 Smugglers' Notch ▲❄■♠●★
134 Jay Peak ❄❄★
New Hampshire
135 Mount Sunapee ▲
136 Waterville Valley ▲▼★
137 Loon ▲♠
138 Cannon ▲▼
139 Bretton Woods ♠
140 Attitash-Bear Peak ▼★
141 The Balsams ▲■♠★
Maine
142 Sunday River ❄◆■♠▼★
143 Sugarloaf USA ▲❄◆■♠▼★

Information supplied by Snow24 plc
www.snow24.com

United States of America

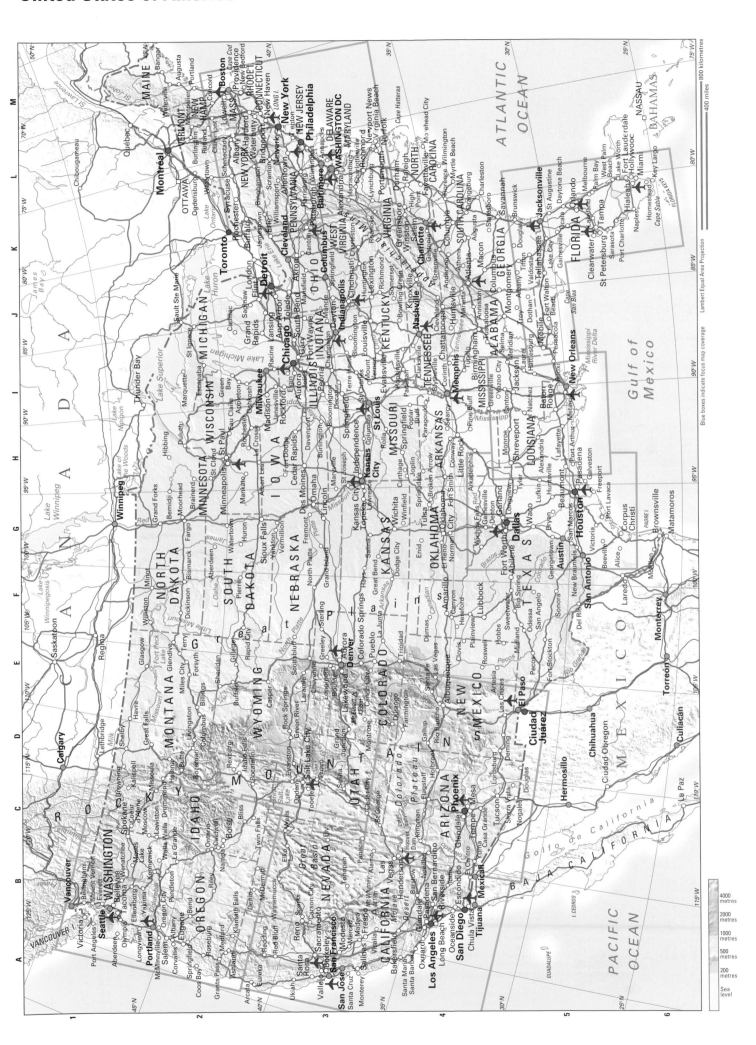

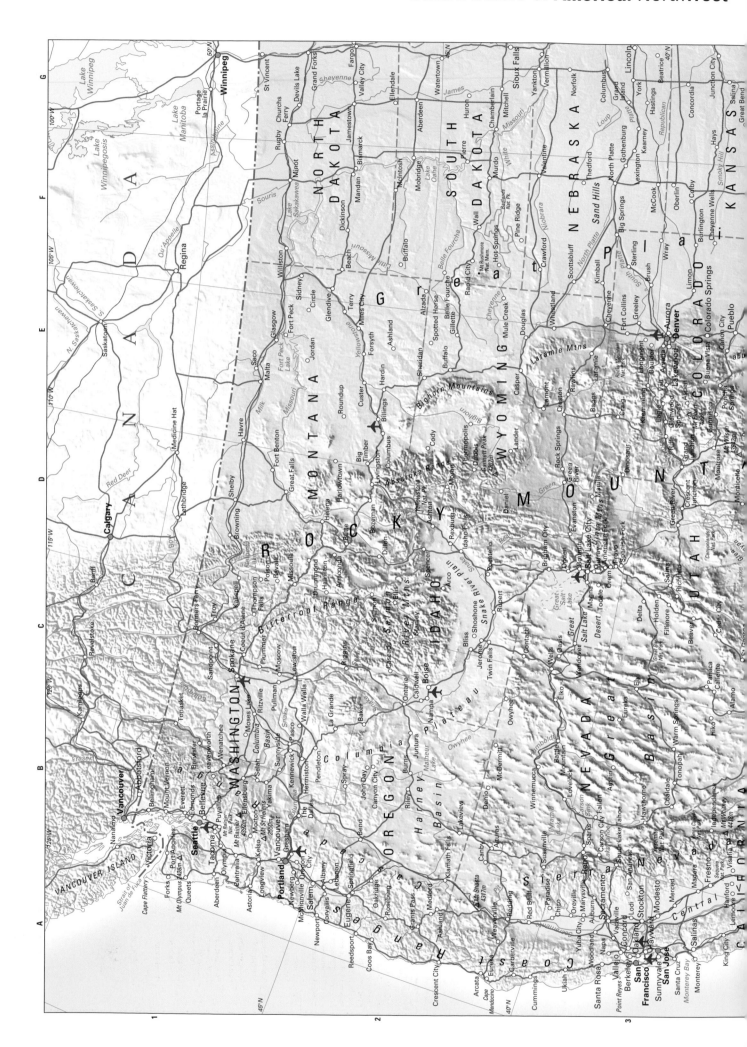

United States of America: Southwest

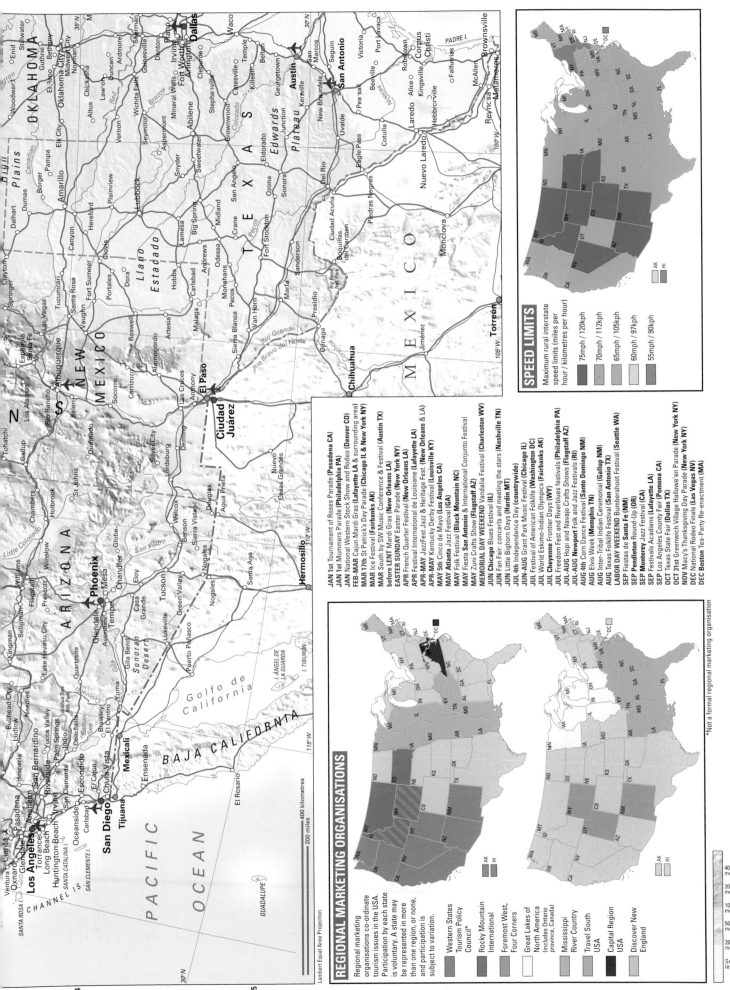

SPEED LIMITS

Maximum rural interstate speed limits (miles per hour / kilometres per hour)

- 75mph / 120kph
- 70mph / 112kph
- 65mph / 105kph
- 60mph / 97kph
- 55mph / 90kph

Festivals

- JAN 1st Tournament of Roses Parade (Pasadena CA)
- JAN 1st Mummers Parade (Philadelphia PA)
- JAN National Western Stock Show and Rodeo (Denver CO)
- FEB-MAR Cajun Mardi Gras (Lafayette LA & surrounding area)
- MAR 17th St Patrick's Day Parade (Chicago IL & New York NY)
- MAR Ice Festival (Fairbanks AK)
- MAR South by SW Music Conference & Festival (Austin TX)
- before LENT Mardi Gras (New Orleans LA)
- EASTER SUNDAY Easter Parade (New York NY)
- APR French Quarter Festival (New Orleans LA)
- APR Festival International de Louisiane (Lafayette LA)
- APR-MAY JazzFest Jazz & Heritage Fest. (New Orleans & LA)
- APR-MAY Kentucky Derby Festival (Louisville KY)
- MAY 5th Cinco de Mayo (Los Angeles CA)
- MAY Atlanta Jazz Festival (GA)
- MAY Folk Festival (Black Mountain NC)
- MAY Fiesta San Antonio & International Conjunto Festival
- MAY Zuni Crafts Show (Flagstaff AZ)
- MEMORIAL DAY WEEKEND Vandalia Festival (Charleston WV)
- JUN Chicago Blues Festival (IL)
- JUN Fan Fair: concerts and meeting the stars (Nashville TN)
- JUN Little Bighorn Days (Hardin MT)
- JUL 4th Independence Day (countrywide)
- JUN-AUG Grant Park Music Festival (Chicago IL)
- JUL Festival of American Folklife (Washington DC)
- JUL World Eskimo-Indian Olympics (Fairbanks AK)
- JUL Cheyenne Frontier Days (WY)
- JUL Freedom Fest and Riverblues festivals (Philadelphia PA)
- JUL-AUG Hopi and Navajo Crafts Shows (Flagstaff AZ)
- JUL-AUG Newport Folk and Jazz Festivals (RI)
- AUG 4th Corn Dance Festival (Santo Domingo NM)
- AUG Elvis Week (Memphis TN)
- AUG Inter-Tribal Indian Ceremonial (Gallup NM)
- AUG Texas Folklife Festival (San Antonio TX)
- LABOR DAY WEEKEND Bumbershoot Festival (Seattle WA)
- SEP Fiestas de Santa Fe (NM)
- SEP Pendleton Round-Up (OR)
- SEP Monterey Jazz Festival (CA)
- SEP Festivals Acadiens (Lafayette LA)
- SEP Los Angeles County Fair (Pomona CA)
- OCT Texas State Fair (Dallas TX)
- OCT 31st Greenwich Village Hallowe'en Parade (New York NY)
- NOV Macy's Thanksgiving Day Parade (New York NY)
- DEC National Rodeo Finals (Las Vegas NV)
- DEC Boston Tea-Party Re-enactment (MA)

REGIONAL MARKETING ORGANISATIONS

Regional marketing organisations co-ordinate tourism issues in the USA. Participation by each state is voluntary. A state may be represented in more than one region, or none, and participation is subject to variation.

- Western States Tourism Policy Council*
- Rocky Mountain International
- Foremost West, Four Corners
- Great Lakes of North America (includes Ontario province, Canada)
- Mississippi River Country
- Travel South USA
- Capital Region USA
- Discover New England

*Not a formal regional marketing organisation

Lambert Equal Area Projection

0   200   400 miles
0   200   400 kilometres

- 4000 metres
- 2000 metres
- 1000 metres
- 500 metres
- 200 metres
- Sea level

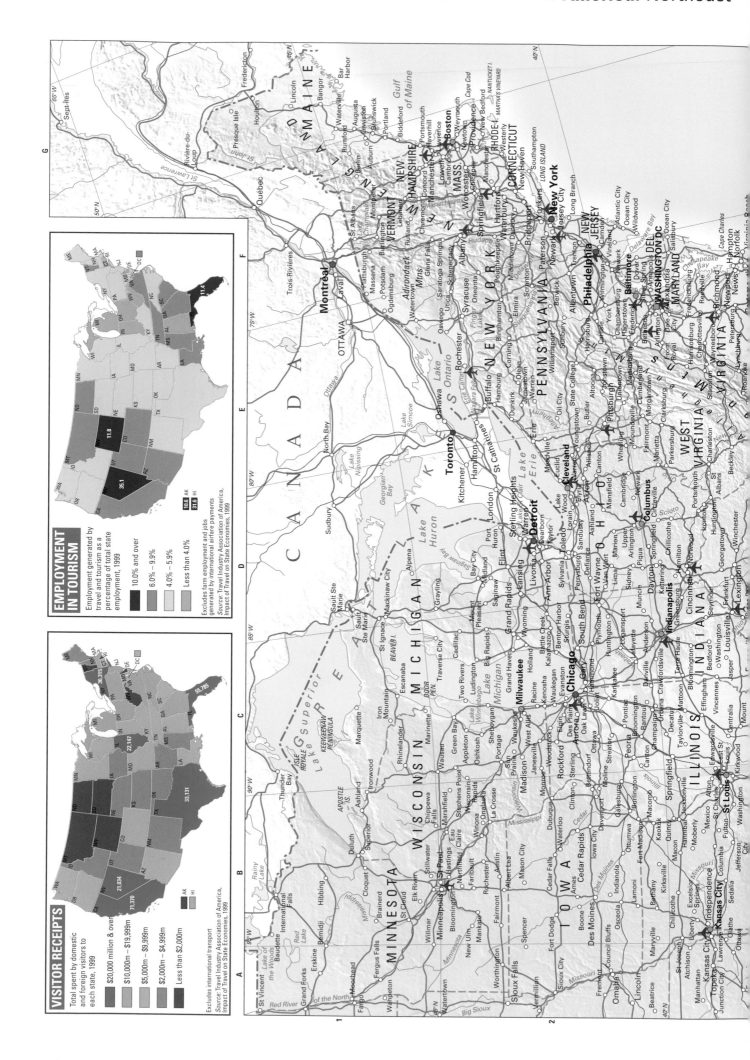

VISITOR RECEIPTS

Total spent by domestic and foreign visitors to each state, 1999

- $20,000 million & over
- $10,000m – $19,999m
- $5,000m – $9,999m
- $2,000m – $4,999m
- Less than $2,000m

Excludes international transport

Source: Travel Industry Association of America, Impact of Travel on State Economies, 1999

EMPLOYMENT IN TOURISM

Employment generated by travel and tourism as a percentage of total state employment, 1999

- 10.0% and over
- 6.0% – 9.9%
- 4.0% – 5.9%
- Less than 4.0%

Excludes farm employment and jobs generated by international airfare payments

Source: Travel Industry Association of America, Impact of Travel on State Economies, 1999

United States of America: Southeast

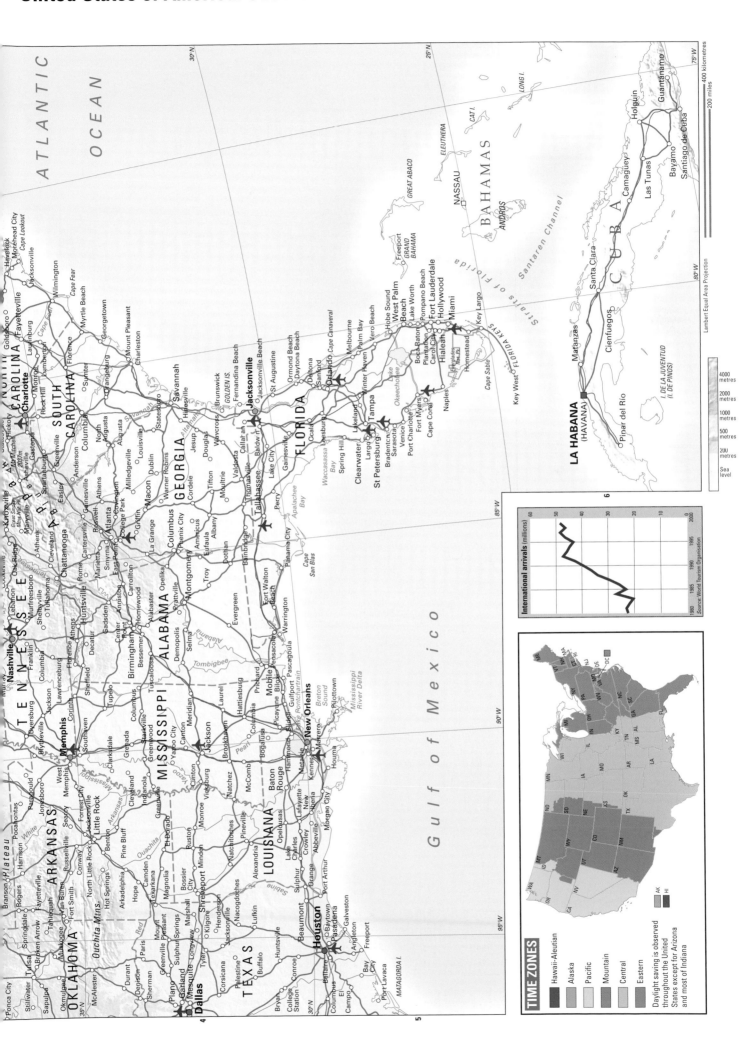

US National Parks

■ **National Park / Preserve**
National Parks contain a variety of resources protected by large areas of land or water; National Preserves permit activities not permitted in National Parks, such as hunting, fishing and mineral extraction

▲ **National Memorial**
Commemorate a historical subject or person

● **National Monument**
National Monuments administered by the US National Parks Service tend to focus on one site or on a feature of national significance; those shown in *italics* are managed by the Bureau of Land Management's National Landscape Conservation System (NLCS), established to focus attention on some of the nation's most remarkable and rugged landscapes in the West

▲ **National Recreation Area / Seashore / Lakeshore**
National Recreation Areas are set aside for purely recreational use and are often near major cities; National Seashores and Lakeshores provide water-oriented recreation whilst preserving shorelines and islands

◆ **National Battlefield / Battlefield Park / Battlefield Site / Military Park**
All associated with US military history

▼ **National Historic Site / Historical Park**
National Historic Sites preserve locations and commemorate persons or events important in the nation's history; National Historical Parks are similar but larger and more complex

✪ **National Parkways**
Roadways that have been preserved for their scenic value.

Other protected areas managed either by the National Park Service or the National Landscape Conservation System include National Conservation Areas, National Rivers, Wild & Scenic Rivers and National Scenic & Historic Trails. Affiliated areas include National Heritage Areas which are managed by government-private partnerships.

TEN MOST VISITED NATIONAL PARKS IN THE USA IN 1999	Number in list
Number of recreational visitors (total for all National Parks: 64,304,453)	
1 **Great Smoky Mountains** Tenn/N Car: 10,282,453 (www.nps.gov/grsm)	233
2 **Grand Canyon** Arizona: 4,575,124 (www.nps.gov/grca)	102
3 **Yosemite** California: 3,493,607 (www.nps.gov/yose)	50
4 **Olympic** Washington: 3,364,266 (www.nps.gov/olym)	24
5 **Rocky Mountain** Colorado: 3,186,323 (www.nps.gov/romo)	88
6 **Yellowstone** Wyoming/Montana: 3,131,381 (www.nps.gov/yell)	73
7 **Grand Teton** Wyoming: 2,680,025 (www.nps.gov/grte)	75
8 **Acadia** Maine: 2,602,227 (www.nps.gov/acad)	348
9 **Zion** Utah: 2,449,664 (www.nps.gov/zion)	79
10 **Haleakala** Hawaii: 1,963,187 (www.nps.gov/hale)	18

Source: National Parks Service

Sites marked with an asterisk (*) are featured in Columbus Travel Guides' *Tourist Attractions and Events of the World*, 2nd edition. For more information, call +44 (0)20 7608 6666.

Alaska
■ 1 Bering Land Bridge National Preserve
● 2 Cape Krusenstern National Monument
■ 3 Kobuk Valley National Park
■ 4 Noatak National Preserve
■ 5 Gates of the Arctic National Park and Preserve
■ 6 Yukon-Charley Rivers National Preserve
■ 7 Denali National Park and Preserve
■ 8 Lake Clark National Park and Preserve
■ 9 Katmai National Park and Preserve
● 10 Aniakchak National Monument and Preserve
■ 11 Kenai Fjords National Park
■ 12 Wrangell-St Elias National Park and Preserve
▼ 13 Klondike Gold Rush National Historical Park
■ 14 Glacier Bay National Park and Preserve
▼ 15 Sitka National Historical Park

Hawaii
▲ 16 USS Arizona Memorial
▼ 17 Kalaupapa National Historical Park
■ 18 Haleakala National Park
▼ 19 Puukohola Heiau National Historic Site
▼ 20 Kaloko-Honokohau National Historical Park
▼ 21 Pu'uhonua o Honaunau National Historical Park
■ 22 Hawaii Volcanoes National Park*

Washington
▼ 23 San Juan Island National Historical Park
■ 24 Olympic National Park
▼ 25 Ebey's Landing National Historical Reserve
■ 26 North Cascades National Park
▲ 27 Ross Lake National Recreation Area
▲ 28 Lake Chelan National Recreation Area
▲ 29 Lake Roosevelt National Recreation Area
▼ 30 Whitman Mission National Historic Site
■ 31 Mount Rainier National Park
▼ 32 Fort Vancouver National Historic Site

Oregon
▲ 33 Fort Clatsop National Memorial
● 34 John Day Fossil Beds National Monument
■ 35 Crater Lake National Park
● 36 Oregon Caves National Monument

California
■ 37 Redwood National Park
● 38 Lava Beds National Monument
▲ 39 Whiskeytown-Shasta-Trinity National Recreation Area
■ 40 Lassen Volcanic National Park
▲ 41 Point Reyes National Seashore
● 42 Muir Woods National Monument
▼ 43 Fort Point National Historic Site
▲ 44 Golden Gate National Recreation Area (incl. Alcatraz*)
▼ 45 San Francisco Maritime National Historical Park
▼ 46 John Muir National Historic Site
▼ 47 Eugene O'Neill National Historic Site
● 48 Pinnacles National Monument

● 49 *California Coastal National Monument* (runs the entire length of the California coast)
● 50 Yosemite National Park*
● 51 Devils Postpile National Monument
■ 52 Sequoia and Kings Canyon National Parks
▼ 53 Manzanar National Historic Site
■ 54 Death Valley National Park*
■ 55 Channel Islands National Park
▲ 56 Santa Monica Mountains National Recreation Area
● 57 Cabrillo National Monument
■ 58 Joshua Tree National Park
■ 59 Mojave National Preserve

Nevada
▲ 60 Lake Mead National Recreation Area (also in Arizona, includes Hoover Dam*)
■ 61 Great Basin National Park

Idaho
■ 62 City of Rocks National Reserve
● 63 Hagerman Fossil Beds National Monument
● 64 Craters of the Moon National Monument
▼ 65 Nez Perce National Historical Park

Montana
■ 66 Glacier National Park
▼ 67 Grant-Kohrs Ranch National Historic Site
◆ 68 Big Hole National Battlefield
● 69 Bighorn Canyon National Recreation Area
● 70 Little Bighorn Battlefield National Monument

Wyoming
● 71 Devils Tower National Monument
▼ 72 Fort Laramie National Historic Site
■ 73 Yellowstone National Park* (also in Montana)
✪ 74 John D. Rockefeller, Jr. Memorial Parkway
■ 75 Grand Teton National Park
● 76 Fossil Butte National Monument

Utah
▼ 77 Golden Spike National Historic Site
● 78 Timpanogos Cave National Monument
■ 79 Zion National Park
● 80 Cedar Breaks National Monument
■ 81 Bryce Canyon National Park

■ 82 Capitol Reef National Park
● 83 Rainbow Bridge National Monument
● 84 Natural Bridges National Monument
● 85 Canyonlands National Park
■ 86 Arches National Park

Colorado
● 87 Dinosaur National Monument
■ 88 Rocky Mountain National Park
● 89 Colorado National Monument
■ 90 Black Canyon of the Gunnison National Park
▲ 91 Curecanti National Recreation Area
● 92 Hovenweep National Monument (also in Utah)
● 93 *Canyons of the Ancients National Monument*
● 94 Yucca House National Monument
■ 95 Mesa Verde National Park
● 96 Great Sand Dunes National Monument
● 97 Florissant Fossil Beds National Monument
▼ 98 Bent's Old Fort National Historic Site

Arizona
● 99 *Grand Canyon-Parashant National Monument*
● 100 Pipe Spring National Monument
● 101 *Vermilion Cliffs National Monument*
■ 102 Grand Canyon National Park*
▲ 103 Glen Canyon National Recreation Area (also in Utah)
● 104 Navajo National Monument
● 105 Canyon de Chelly National Monument
▼ 106 Hubbell Trading Post National Historic Site
■ 107 Petrified Forest National Park
● 108 Wupatki National Monument
● 109 Sunset Crater Volcano National Monument
● 110 Walnut Canyon National Monument
● 111 Tuzigoot National Monument
● 112 Montezuma Castle National Monument
● 113 *Agua Fria National Monument*
● 114 Tonto National Monument
● 115 Hohokam Pima National Monument
● 116 Casa Grande Ruins National Monument
● 117 *Ironwood Forest National Monument*
● 118 Organ Pipe Cactus National Monument

▼ 119 Tumacacori National Historical Park
▲ 120 Coronado National Memorial
■ 121 Saguaro National Park
▼ 122 Fort Bowie National Historic Site
● 123 Chiricahua National Monument

New Mexico
● 124 Gila Cliff Dwellings National Monument
● 125 White Sands National Monument
■ 126 Carlsbad Caverns National Park
● 127 Salinas Pueblo Missions National Monument
● 128 Aztec Ruins National Monument
▼ 129 Chaco Culture National Historical Park
● 130 El Morro National Monument
● 131 El Malpais National Monument
● 132 Petroglyph National Monument
● 133 Bandelier National Monument
▼ 134 Pecos National Historical Park
● 135 Fort Union National Monument
● 136 Capulin Volcano National Monument

Texas
▲ 137 Lake Meredith National Recreation Area
▲ 138 Alibates Flint Quarries National Monument
▲ 139 Chamizal National Memorial
■ 140 Guadalupe Mountains National Park
▼ 141 Fort Davis National Historic Site
■ 142 Big Bend National Park
▲ 143 Amistad National Recreation Area
▼ 144 Lyndon B. Johnson National Historical Park
▼ 145 San Antonio Missions National Historical Park
▼ 146 Palo Alto Battlefield National Historic Site
▲ 147 Padre Island National Seashore
■ 148 Big Thicket National Preserve

Oklahoma
▲ 149 Chickasaw National Recreation Area
▲ 150 Oklahoma City National Memorial
▼ 151 Washita Battlefield National Historic Site

North Dakota
▼ 152 Fort Union Trading Post National Historic Site
■ 153 Theodore Roosevelt National Park
▼ 154 Knife River Indian Villages National Historic Site

US National Parks

273 Piscataway Park
274 Thomas Stone National Historic Site
275 Assateague Island National Seashore
276 Fort McHenry National Monument and Historic Shrine
277 Greenbelt Park
278 Hampton National Historic Site
279 Catoctin Mountain Park

District of Columbia
280 Constitution Gardens
281 Ford's Theatre National Historic Site
282 Franklin Delano Roosevelt Memorial
283 Frederick Douglass National Historic Site
284 Korean War Veterans Memorial
285 Lincoln Memorial*
286 Lyndon Baines Johnson Memorial Grove on the Potomac
287 Mary McLeod Bethune Council House National Historic Site
288 National Capital parks
289 National Mall
290 Pennsylvania Avenue National Historic Site
291 Rock Creek Park
292 Theodore Roosevelt Island
293 Thomas Jefferson Memorial
294 Vietnam Veterans Memorial
295 Washington Monument
296 The White House*

Pennsylvania
297 Friendship Hill National Historic Site
298 Fort Necessity National Battlefield
299 Johnstown Flood National Memorial
300 Allegheny Portage Railroad National Historic Site
301 Eisenhower National Historic Site
302 Gettysburg National Military Park
303 Hopewell Furnace National Historic Site
304 Valley Forge National Historical Park
305 Edgar Allen Poe National Historic Site
306 Independence National Historical Park*
307 Thaddeus Kosciuszko National Memorial
308 Delaware Water Gap National Recreation Area
309 Steamtown National Historic Site

New York
310 Theodore Roosevelt Inaugural National Historic Site
311 Women's Rights National Historical Park
312 Fort Stanwix National Monument
313 Saratoga National Historical Park
314 Martin Van Buren National Historic Site
315 Eleanor Roosevelt National Historic Site
316 Vanderbilt Mansion National Historic Site
317 Home of Franklin Delano Roosevelt National Historic Site
318 Castle Clinton National Monument
319 Federal Hall National Memorial
320 Gateway National Recreation Area (also in New Jersey)
321 General Grant National Memorial
322 Hamilton Grange National Memorial
323 St Paul's Church National Historic Site
324 Statue of Liberty National Monument*
325 Theodore Roosevelt Birthplace National Historic Site
326 Sagamore Hill National Historic Site
327 Fire Island National Seashore

New Jersey
328 Edison National Historic Site
329 Morristown National Historical Park

Connecticut
330 Weir Farm National Historic Site

Rhode Island
331 Roger Williams National Memorial

Massachusetts
332 Springfield Armory National Historic Site
333 New Bedford Whaling National Historical Park
334 Cape Cod National Seashore
335 Adams National Historic Site
336 Boston African American National Historical Site
337 Boston Harbor Islands National Recreation Area
338 Boston National Historical Park
339 Frederick Law Olmsted National Historic Site
340 John F. Kennedy National Historic Site
341 Longfellow National Historic Site
342 Saugus Iron Works National Historic Site
343 Salem Maritime National Historic Site
344 Lowell National Historical Park
345 Minute Man National Historical Park

Vermont
346 Marsh-Billings National Historical Park

New Hampshire
347 St-Gaudens National Historic Site

Maine
348 Acadia National Park
349 St Croix Island International Historic Site

The following are not shown on the map:

Puerto Rico
San Juan National Historic Site

US Virgin Islands
Buck Island Reef National Monument
Christiansted National Historic Site
Salt River Bay National Historical Park and Ecological Preserve
Virgin Islands National Park

American Samoa
National Park of American Samoa

Northern Mariana Islands
War in the Pacific National Historical Park

South Dakota
155 Jewel Cave National Monument
156 Mount Rushmore National Memorial*
157 Wind Cave National Park
158 Badlands National Park

Minnesota
159 Pipestone National Monument
160 Voyageurs National Park
161 Grand Portage National Monument

Wisconsin
162 Apostle Islands National Lakeshore

Michigan
163 Isle Royale National Park
164 Keweenaw National Historical Park
165 Pictured Rocks National Lakeshore
166 Sleeping Bear Dunes National Lakeshore

Nebraska
167 Agate Fossil Beds National Monument
168 Scotts Bluff National Monument
169 Homestead National Monument of America

Iowa
170 Effigy Mounds National Monument
171 Herbert Hoover National Historic Site

Kansas
172 Nicodemus National Historic Site
173 Fort Larned National Historic Site
174 Tallgrass Prairie National Preserve
175 Brown v. Board of Education National Historic Site
176 Fort Scott National Historic Site

Missouri
177 Harry S. Truman National Historic Site
178 George Washington Carver National Monument
179 Wilson's Creek National Battlefield
180 Ulysses S. Grant National Historic Site
181 Jefferson National Expansion Memorial

Illinois
182 Lincoln Home National Historic Site

Indiana
183 Indiana Dunes National Lakeshore
184 George Rogers Clark National Historical Park

185 Lincoln Boyhood National Memorial

Ohio
186 William Howard Taft National Historic Site
187 Dayton Aviation National Historical Park
188 Hopewell Culture National Historical Park
189 Perry's Victory and International Peace Memorial
190 James A. Garfield National Historic Site
191 Cuyahoga Valley National Recreation Area

Arkansas
192 Pea Ridge National Military Park
193 Fort Smith National Historic Site
194 Hot Springs National Park
195 Arkansas Post National Memorial

Louisiana
196 Poverty Point National Monument
197 Cane River Creole National Historical Park
198 New Orleans Jazz National Historical Park
199 Jean Lafitte National Historical Park and Preserve

Mississippi
200 Natchez National Historical Park
201 Vicksburg National Military Park
202 Natchez Trace Parkway (also in Alabama & Tennessee)
203 Tupelo National Battlefield
204 Brices Cross Roads National Battlefield Site

Alabama
205 Tuskegee Institute National Historic Site
206 Horseshoe Bend National Military Park
207 Little River Canyon National Preserve
208 Russell Cave National Monument

Georgia
209 Chickamauga & Chattanooga National Military Park
210 Kennesaw Mountain National Battlefield Park
211 Chattahoochee River National Recreation Area
212 Martin Luther King Jr. National Historic Site
213 Ocmulgee National Monument
214 Andersonville National Historic Site
215 Jimmy Carter National Historic Site
216 Fort Pulaski National Monument
217 Fort Frederica National Monument

218 Cumberland Island National Seashore

Florida
219 Gulf Islands National Seashore (also in Mississippi)
220 Timucuan Ecological and Historic Preserve
221 Fort Caroline National Memorial
222 Castillo de San Marcos National Monument
223 Fort Matanzas National Monument
224 Canaveral National Seashore
225 De Soto National Memorial
226 Big Cypress National Preserve
227 Everglades National Park*
228 Biscayne National Park
229 Dry Tortugas National Park

Tennessee
230 Shiloh National Military Park
231 Fort Donelson National Battlefield
232 Stones River National Battlefield and Cemetery
233 Great Smoky Mountains National Park (also in North Carolina)
234 Andrew Johnson National Historic Site

Kentucky
235 Cumberland Gap National Historical Park
236 Mammoth Cave National Park
237 Abraham Lincoln Birthplace National Historic Site

South Carolina
238 Fort Sumter National Monument
239 Charles Pinckney National Historic Site
240 Congaree Swamp National Monument
241 Ninety Six National Historic Site
242 Kings Mountain National Military Park
243 Cowpens National Battlefield

North Carolina
244 Carl Sandburg Home National Historic Site
245 Blue Ridge Parkway (also in Virginia)
246 Guilford Courthouse National Military Park
247 Moores Creek National Battlefield
248 Cape Lookout National Seashore
249 Cape Hatteras National Seashore
250 Fort Raleigh National Historic Site
251 Wright Brothers National Memorial

Virginia
252 Booker T. Washington National Monument
253 Appomattox Court House National Historical Park
254 Petersburg National Battlefield
255 Colonial National Historical Park
256 Maggie L. Walker National Historic Site
257 Richmond National Battlefield Park
258 George Washington Birthplace National Monument
259 Shenandoah National Park
260 Fredericksburg and Spotsylvania County Battlefields Memorial National Military Park
261 Prince William Forest Park
262 Manassas National Battlefield Park
263 Wolf Trap Farm Park for the Performing Arts
264 George Washington Memorial Parkway
265 Arlington House, The Robert E. Lee Memorial

West Virginia
266 Gauley River National Recreation Area
267 Harpers Ferry National Historical Park

Maryland
268 Antietam National Battlefield
269 Monocacy National Battlefield
270 Chesapeake and Ohio Canal National Historical Park
271 Clara Barton National Historic Site
272 Fort Washington Park

600 kilometres
300 miles

United States of America

Main map (USA)

A B C D

WASHINGTON & OREGON

Seattle
Olympia
Portland
Salem
Eugene
WASHINGTON
OREGON
CASCADE RANGE
Columbia
Spokane
Great Falls
Helena
MONTANA
Billings
IDAHO
Boise
ROCKY
MISSOURI BREAKS
Missouri
Bismarck
NORTH DAKOTA
Fargo
Duluth
Red
Lake of the Woods
Lake Superior
Great Lakes
MINNESOTA
St Paul
Minneapolis
MICHIGAN
Lake Huron
Lake Michigan
Lake Ontario
MAINE
Augusta
Montpelier
VERMONT
NEW HAMPSHIRE
Portland
Concord
MASSACHUSETTS
Boston
Rochester
NEW YORK
Albany
RHODE ISLAND
Providence
CONNECTICUT
Buffalo
Hartford
LONG I.
New York
PENNSYLVANIA
Trenton
NEW JERSEY
Philadelphia
Atlantic City
HIGH
SIERRA NEVADA
GREAT BASIN
Reno
Carson City
NEVADA
Great Salt Lake
Salt Lake City
UTAH
WYOMING
Casper
Cheyenne
MOUNTAINS
North Platte
South Platte
Platte
NEBRASKA
Omaha
Lincoln
Des Moines
IOWA
Chicago
ILLINOIS
INDIANA
Indianapolis
OHIO
Columbus
Cleveland
Pittsburgh
WEST VIRGINIA
Harrisburg
Baltimore
MARYLAND
Dover
DELAWARE
WASHINGTON DC
Rapid City
SOUTH DAKOTA
Pierre
Sioux Falls
Rochester
WISCONSIN
Madison
Milwaukee
Lansing
Detroit
Lake Erie
Toledo
Sacramento
San Francisco
San Jose
CALIFORNIA
Denver
COLORADO
Colorado Springs
Arkansas
KANSAS
Topeka
Kansas City
MISSOURI
St Louis
Jefferson City
Springfield
Cincinnati
Louisville
KENTUCKY
Frankfort
VIRGINIA
Richmond
Norfolk
Raleigh
Bakersfield
Los Angeles
San Bernardino
CHANNEL IS.
San Diego
Las Vegas
COLORADO PLATEAU
GRAND CANYON
ARIZONA
Phoenix
Santa Fe
Albuquerque
NEW MEXICO
Tucson
LLANO ESTACADO
El Paso
Amarillo
Lubbock
Oklahoma City
OKLAHOMA
Tulsa
Red
ARKANSAS
Little Rock
Memphis
OZARK PLATEAU
Branson
Nashville
TENNESSEE
NORTH CAROLINA
Charlotte
APPALACHIAN MTNS
BLUE RIDGE
Charleston
SOUTH CAROLINA
Columbia
Charleston
Fort Worth
Dallas
TEXAS
Austin
Houston
Galveston
San Antonio
EDWARDS PLATEAU
Rio Grande
Brownsville
LOUISIANA
Baton Rouge
New Orleans
MISSISSIPPI
Jackson
Mississippi
ALABAMA
Montgomery
Birmingham
GEORGIA
Atlanta
Savannah
Jacksonville
Tallahassee
FLORIDA
Orlando
Tampa
Miami
FLORIDA KEYS
MISSISSIPPI RIVER DELTA
EAST TEXAS
WEST OF THE RIO GRANDE
CALIFORNIA & NEVADA
BOSTON–NEW YORK–WASHINGTON

Legend

- – – State boundary
- ● State capital

800 km
400 miles

For an alphabetical list of US states, see Appendices

Inset E — HAWAII

E

NIIHAU KAUAI
OAHU
MOLOKAI
Honolulu
LANAI MAUI
HAWAII
HAWAII

300 km
150 miles

International arrivals (millions)

(line graph)

60
50
40
30
20
10

1980 1985 1990 1995 2000

Source: World Tourism Organisation

Inset F — ALASKA

F

1000 km
500 miles
ALASKA

ST LAWRENCE I.
NUNIVAK I.
Yukon
ALASKA
Anchorage
Juneau
KODIAK I.
ALEUTIAN ISLANDS
ALEXANDER ARCHIPELAGO

CALIFORNIA & NEVADA

I J

OREGON
SNAKE RIVER PLAIN
Snake
IDAHO
Twin Falls
Upper Klamath Lake
Medford
Klamath Falls
Crescent City
Redwood Nat. Park
KLAMATH MOUNTAINS
Mt Shasta 4317m
Lava Beds Nat. Mon.
Alturas
BLACK ROCK DESERT
Granite Peak 2966m
JARBIDGE WILDERNESS AREA
GREAT
Eureka
Punta Gorda
Lassen Volcanic National Park
Susanville
Winnemucca
COWBOY COUNTRY
Elko
Wells
Wendover
BONNEVILLE SALT FLATS
Mackerricher State Park
Redding
Red Bluff
Chico
Quincy
Donner Pass 2160m
Reno
Sparks
Pyramid Lake
Lovelock
Battle Mountain
RUBY MTNS
BASIN
Fort Bragg
Bidwell Manson State Hist. Pk.
CANNON
Carson Sink
Fallon
Austin
Eureka
Ely
PONY EXPRESS
Mendocino
Nevada City
Grass Valley
Virginia City
Carson City
Gabbs
SHOSHONE MOUNTAINS
BIG SMOKY VALLEY
Wheeler Pk. 3982m
Great Basin National Park
Fort Ross State Historic Park
Healdsburg
Napa Valley
Coloma
Auburn
Lake Tahoe
Walker Lake
TERRITORY
NEVADA
Santa Rosa
Sonoma
Sacramento
Stockton
Hawthorne
Lunar Crater
Santa Rosa
Petaluma
Point Reyes
BAY AREA
Berkeley
Oakland
Modesto
Yosemite National Park
Mono Lake
Mammoth Lakes
PIONEER TERRITORY
Tonopah
Caliente
San Francisco
San Mateo
SILICON VALLEY
Paramount's Great America
Sonora
Devils Postpile Nat. Mon.
San Jose
Fremont
Santa Cruz
Merced
Mariposa
Bass Lake
Bishop
Beatty
MONTEREY PENINSULA
Monterey
Carmel
Salinas
San Juan Bautista
Fresno
Mt Whitney 4418m
Kings Canyon National Park
Death Valley National Park
Valley of Fire State Park
Overton
Big Sur
Hanford
Visalia
Porterville
SEQUOIA
Sequoia National Park
Badwater Basin -86m
Las Vegas
McCARRAN
Henderson
Pfeiffer Big Sur State Park
San Simeon
Delano
Hoover Dam
Lake Mead Nat. Rec. Area
Hearst San Simeon State Hist. Mon.
Morro Bay State Park
Bakersfield
MOJAVE DESERT
Mojave National Preserve
Laughlin
San Luis Obispo
Santa Maria
Barstow
Calico Ghost Town
La Purisima Mission State Historic Park
SANTA YNEZ
Santa Barbara
Oxnard
Ventura
Six Flags Magic Mtn
Hollywood
Pasadena
San Bernardino
Big Bear Lake
Needles
Lake Havasu City
Point Conception
SAN MIGUEL I.
SANTA ROSA I.
SANTA CRUZ I.
Channel Islands National Park
Solvang
Marina del Rey
Malibu
DIABLO RANGE
San Joaquin
CALIFORNIA
Los Angeles
Torrance
Long Beach
Disneyland
Santa Ana
Palm Springs
Joshua Tree National Park
PACIFIC OCEAN
SAN NICOLAS I.
CHANNEL ISLANDS
SAN CLEMENTE I.
Huntington Beach
Legoland
Sea World of California
Oceanside
Mission San Luis Rey
San Juan Capistrano
COLORADO DESERT
Anza-Borrego State Park
Salton Sea
Escondido
Vista
San Diego
LINDBERGH FIELD
Chula Vista
Tijuana
Mexicali
Yuma
ARIZ.
MEXICO
Ensenada

300 kilometres
150 miles

WASHINGTON & OREGON

G H

CANADA
VANCOUVER ISLAND
Victoria
Cape Flattery
Port Angeles
Forks
Blaine
Bellingham
Anacortes
San Juan I.
Mt Baker 3285m
Ross Lake Nat. Rec. Area
N. Cascades Nat. Pk.
Waterton Lakes National Park*
Trail
Bonners Ferry
Troy
Glacier National Park
Franklin D. Roosevelt Lake
L. Chelan Nat. Rec. Area
Kalispell
CABINET MTNS
MT
Edmonds
Bremerton
Bellevue
Everett
Seattle
Tacoma
Puyallup
Olympia
Wenatchee
Alpental
Dry Falls
Grand Coulee Dam
Silverwood
Spokane
Coeur d'Alene
Kellogg
Pend Oreille L.
Polson
Flathead Lake
Rattlesnake L.
Missoula
Mt Olympus 2428m
Olympic National Park
Queets
Aberdeen
GRAYS HARBOR
WILLAPA BAY
Centralia
Morton
Ellensburg
WASHINGTON
COLUMBIA BASIN
Yakima
Pullman
Moscow
Nez Perce Nat. Hist. Park
Lewiston
Lolo Pass 1595m
BITTERROOT RANGE
Astoria
Seaside
Fort Clatsop Nat. Mem.
Cannon Beach
Mt Rainier 4392m
Mt Rainier Nat. Pk.
Mt St Helens 2550m
Mt St Helens Nat. Vol. Mon.
Richland
Pasco
Kennewick
Walla Walla
Whitman Mission Nat. Hist. Site
Hells Canyon Nat. Rec. Area
Lost Trail Pass 2138m
Longview
Vancouver
COLUMBIA GORGE
The Dalles
Pendleton
La Grande
WALLOWA MTNS
McMinnville
Portland
Gresham
Mt Hood 3425m
BLUE MTNS
Baker
PACIFIC OCEAN
Lincoln City
Oregon City
Salem
Albany
Deschutes
John Day
John Day Fossil Beds Nat. Mon.
Ontario
McCall
SALMON RIVER MOUNTAINS
Newport
Corvallis
CASCADE RANGE
Bend
Mt Batchelor 2763m
Caldwell
Nampa
Boise
Idaho City
Florence
Springfield
Eugene
Oakridge
Willamette Pass 1563m
OREGON
Riley
Burns
SNAKE RIVER PLAIN
Sun Valley
Shoshone
Oregon Dunes Nat. Rec. Area
Coos Bay
Bandon
Crater Lake National Park
Chemult
GREAT SANDY DESERT
HARNEY BASIN
Hagerman Fossil Beds Nat. Mon.
Salmon Falls
Twin Falls
Bliss
Shoshone
Cape Blanco
Gold Beach
Grants Pass
Medford
FREMONT MTNS
Klamath Falls
Altamont
Malheur Lake
Goose Lake
WARNER VALLEY
Lakeview
City of Rocks Nat. Reserve
Oregon Caves Nat. Mon.
Ashland
Upper Klamath L.
Lake Abert
COLUMBIA PLATEAU
NEVADA

300 kilometres
150 miles

*Combined as the Waterton-Glacier International Peace Park

United States of America

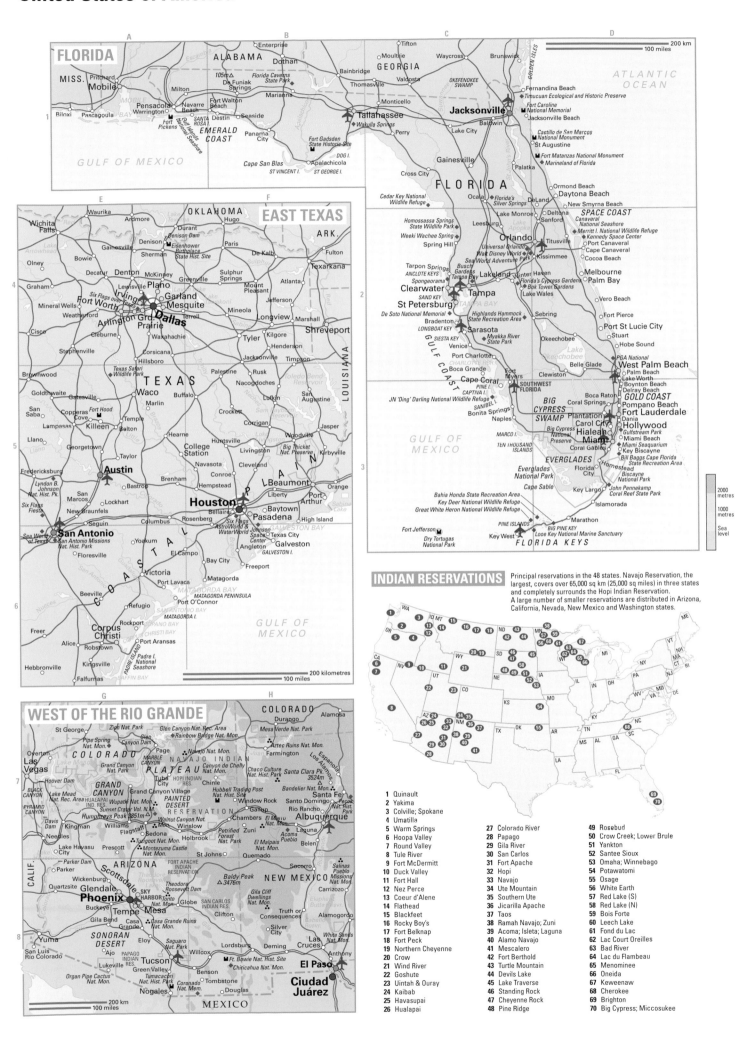

United States of America

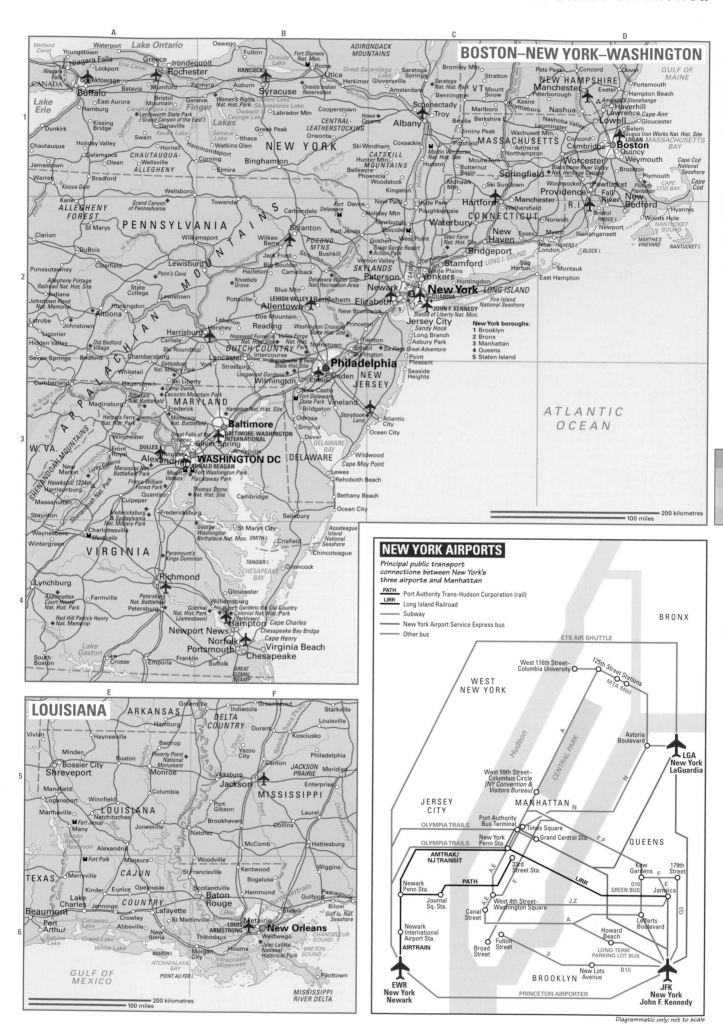

BOSTON–NEW YORK–WASHINGTON

NEW YORK AIRPORTS

Principal public transport connections between New York's three airports and Manhattan

PATH — Port Authority Trans-Hudson Corporation (rail)
LIRR — Long Island Railroad
—— Subway
—— New York Airport Service Express bus
—— Other bus

LOUISIANA

Diagrammatic only: not to scale

United States of America

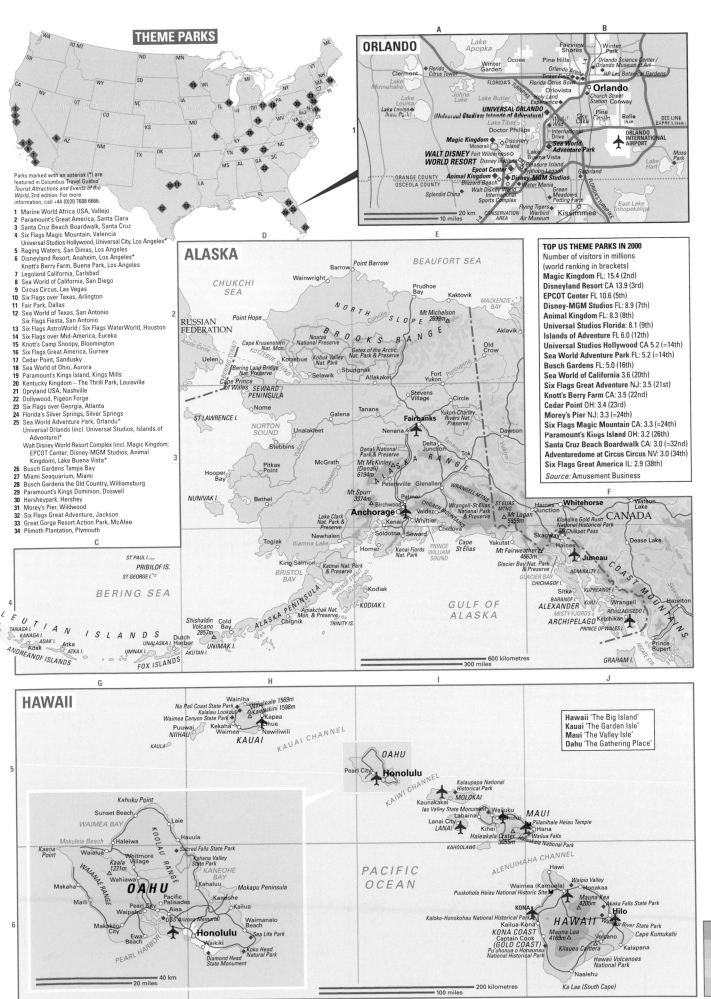

THEME PARKS

Parks marked with an asterisk (*) are featured in Columbus Travel Guides' *Tourist Attractions and Events of the World*, 2nd edition. For more information, call +44 (0)20 7608 6666.

1 Marine World Africa USA, Vallejo
2 Paramount's Great America, Santa Clara
3 Santa Cruz Beach Boardwalk, Santa Cruz
4 Six Flags Magic Mountain, Valencia
   Universal Studios Hollywood, Universal City, Los Angeles*
5 Raging Waters, San Dimas, Los Angeles
6 Disneyland Resort, Anaheim, Los Angeles*
   Knott's Berry Farm, Buena Park, Los Angeles
7 Legoland California, Carlsbad
8 Sea World of California, San Diego
9 Circus Circus, Las Vegas
10 Six Flags over Texas, Arlington
11 Fair Park, Dallas
12 Sea World of Texas, San Antonio
   Six Flags Fiesta, San Antonio
13 Six Flags AstroWorld / Six Flags WaterWorld, Houston
14 Six Flags over Mid-America, Eureka
15 Knott's Camp Snoopy, Bloomington
16 Six Flags Great America, Gurnee
17 Cedar Point, Sandusky
18 Sea World of Ohio, Aurora
19 Paramount's Kings Island, Kings Mills
20 Kentucky Kingdom – The Thrill Park, Louisville
21 Opryland USA, Nashville
22 Dollywood, Pigeon Forge
23 Six Flags over Georgia, Atlanta
24 Florida's Silver Springs, Silver Springs
25 Sea World Adventure Park, Orlando*
   Universal Orlando (incl. Universal Studios; Islands of Adventure)*
   Walt Disney World Resort Complex (incl. Magic Kingdom; EPCOT Center; Disney-MGM Studios; Animal Kingdom), Lake Buena Vista*
26 Busch Gardens Tampa Bay
27 Miami Seaquarium, Miami
28 Busch Gardens the Old Country, Williamsburg
29 Paramount's Kings Dominion, Doswell
30 Hersheypark, Hershey
31 Morey's Pier, Wildwood
32 Six Flags Great Adventure, Jackson
33 Great Gorge Resort Action Park, McAfee
34 Plimoth Plantation, Plymouth

ORLANDO

ALASKA

HAWAII

TOP US THEME PARKS IN 2000

Number of visitors in millions (world ranking in brackets)

Magic Kingdom FL: 15.4 (2nd)
Disneyland Resort CA 13.9 (3rd)
EPCOT Center FL 10.6 (5th)
Disney-MGM Studios FL: 8.9 (7th)
Animal Kingdom FL: 8.3 (8th)
Universal Studios Florida: 8.1 (9th)
Islands of Adventure FL 6.0 (12th)
Universal Studios Hollywood CA 5.2 (=14th)
Sea World Adventure Park FL: 5.2 (=14th)
Busch Gardens FL: 5.0 (16th)
Sea World of California 3.6 (20th)
Six Flags Great Adventure NJ: 3.5 (21st)
Knott's Berry Farm CA: 3.5 (22nd)
Cedar Point OH: 3.4 (23rd)
Morey's Pier NJ: 3.3 (=24th)
Six Flags Magic Mountain CA: 3.3 (=24th)
Paramount's Kings Island OH: 3.2 (26th)
Santa Cruz Beach Boardwalk CA: 3.0 (=32nd)
Adventuredome at Circus Circus NV: 3.0 (34th)
Six Flags Great America IL: 2.9 (38th)

Source: Amusement Business

Hawaii 'The Big Island'
Kauai 'The Garden Isle'
Maui 'The Valley Isle'
Oahu 'The Gathering Place'

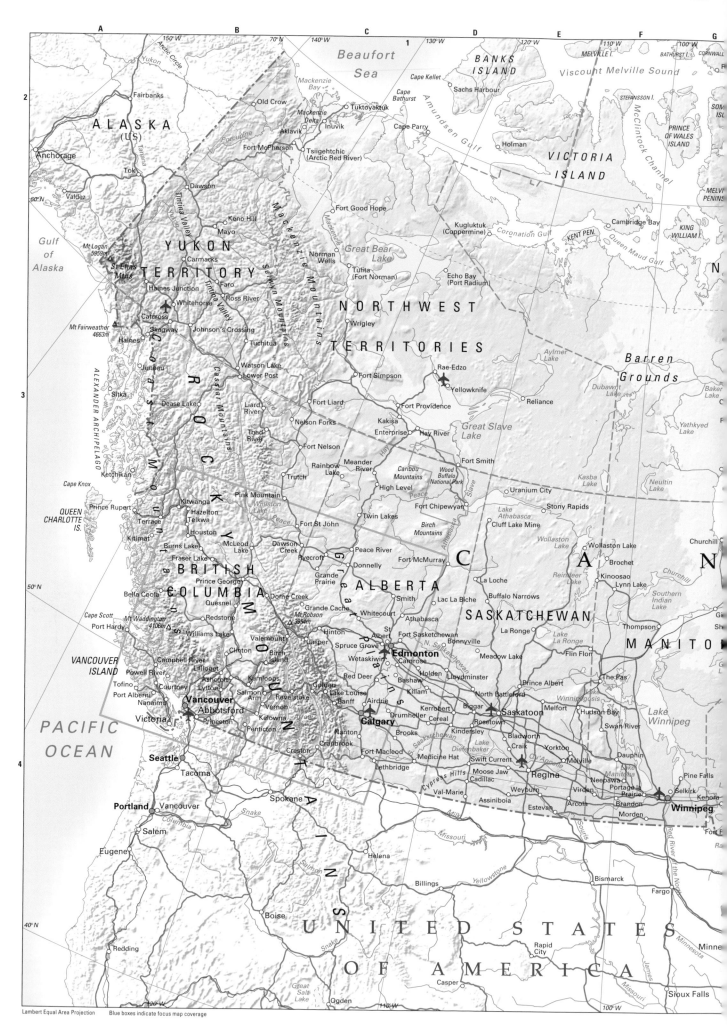

A B 70°N C 1 130°W D 120°W E 110°W F 100°W G

150°W 140°W

Beaufort
Sea

Mackenzie
Bay

Cape Kellet

BANKS
ISLAND

Viscount Melville Sound

MELVILLE I. BATHURST I. CORNWALL

STEFANSSON I.

SOM
ISL

2

Fairbanks

ALASKA
(US)

Old Crow

Tuktoyaktuk

Mackenzie
Delta

Aklavik

Inuvik

Cape
Bathurst

Sachs Harbour

Cape Parry

Amundsen Gulf

Holman

VICTORIA
ISLAND

MCClintock Channel

PRINCE
OF WALES
ISLAND

MELVI
PENINS

Anchorage

Tok

Porcupine

Fort McPherson

Tsiigehtchic
(Arctic Red River)

Yukon

Cambridge Bay

KING
WILLIAM I.

Valdez

60°N

Dawson

Keno Hill

Mayo

Fort Good Hope

Kugluktuk
(Coppermine)

Coronation Gulf

KENT PEN.

Queen Maud Gulf

N

Gulf
of
Alaska

Mt Logan
5959m

St Elias
Mtns

YUKON

Carmacks

Norman
Wells

Great Bear
Lake

Mackenzie

Tulita
(Fort Norman)

Echo Bay
(Port Radium)

Aylmer
Lake

Barren

Dubawnt
Lake

Baker
Lake

TERRITORY

Faro

Selwyn Mountains

NORTHWEST

Grounds

Yathkyed
Lake

Haines Junction

Ross River

Whitehorse

Wrigley

TERRITORIES

Neultin
Lake

Mt Fairweather
4663m

Carcross

Skagway

Johnson's Crossing

Tuchitua

Haines

Juneau

Coast

Watson Lake

Lower Post

Fort Simpson

Rae-Edzo

Yellowknife

Reliance

Sitka

ALEXANDER ARCHIPELAGO

Dease Lake

Cassiar Mountains

Liard
River

Nelson Forks

Fort Liard

Kakisa

Enterprise

Fort Providence

Hay River

Great Slave
Lake

Fort Smith

Kasba
Lake

3

50°N

Cape Knox

QUEEN
CHARLOTTE
IS.

Ketchikan

Prince Rupert

ROCKY

Toad
River

Fort Nelson

Rainbow
Lake

Meander
River

Caribou
Mountains

High Level

Peace

Wood
Buffalo
National Park

Slave

Uranium City

Stony Rapids

Wollaston
Lake

Churchill

Terrace

Kitimat

Kitwanga

Hazelton

Telkwa

Houston

Trutch

Pink Mountain

Williston
Lake

Fort St John

Twin Lakes

Birch
Mountains

Fort Chipewyan

Lake
Athabasca

Cluff Lake Mine

Wollaston Lake

Brochet

Burns Lake

Fraser Lake

McLeod
Lake

Dawson
Creek

Peace River

Fort McMurray

C A

La Loche

Buffalo Narrows

Kinoosao

Lynn Lake

Southern
Indian
Lake

BRITISH

Prince George

Quesnel

Dome Creek

Peace

Ryecroft

Donnelly

Grande
Prairie

ALBERTA

Smith

Lac La Biche

La Ronge

Athabasca

Reindeer
Lake

Thompson

Gi
Sh

COLUMBIA

Bella Coola

Cape Scott

Mt Waddington
4106m

Redstone

Williams Lake

Grande Cache

Mt Robson
3954m

Whitecourt

Athabasca

Fort Sasketchewan

Bonnyville

La Ronge

Meadow Lake

Lake
La Ronge

Prince Albert

Flin Flon

The Pas

Hudson Bay

MANITO

N

Port Hardy

VANCOUVER
ISLAND

Powell River

Courtney

Valemount

Clinton

Campbell River

Lillooet

Ashcroft

Hinton

Jasper

Spruce Grove

St
Albert

Edmonton

Wetaskiwin

Camrose

Holden

Lloydminster

North Battleford

Biggar

Saskatoon

Melfort

Swan River

Lake
Winnipegosis

4

PACIFIC

OCEAN

Tofino

Port Alberni

Nanaimo

Vancouver

Victoria

Abbotsford

Princeton

Lytton

Kamloops

Salmon
Arm

Vernon

Kelowna

Penticton

Birch
Island

Golden

Revelstoke

Lake Louise

Banff

Red Deer

Bashaw

Killam

Airdrie

Drumheller

Cereal

Kerrober

Kindersley

Rosetown

Bladworth

Craik

SASKATCHEWAN

Yorkton

Melville

Neepawa

Dauphin

Lake
Manitoba

Pine Falls

Lake
Winnipeg

Seattle

Tacoma

Creston

Nanton

Cranbrook

Brooks

Fort Macleod

Medicine Hat

Calgary

Lethbridge

Cypress Hills

Swift Current

Moose Jaw

Cadillac

Qu'Appelle

Regina

Weyburn

Virden

Brandon

Portage la
Prairie

Selkirk

Kenora

Winnipeg

Portland

Vancouver

Salem

Eugene

Spokane

Columbia

Snake

Val-Marie

Assiniboia

Estevan

Arcola

Morden

Red River of the No

Fort F

Ra

Helena

Missouri

Souris

Boise

Snake

Salmon

Great
Salt
Lake

Redding

UNITED STATES

Billings

Yellowstone

Rapid
City

Bismarck

Fargo

Minne

40°N

OF AMERICA

Casper

Missouri

Sioux Falls

James

Minnesota

Ogden

120°W 110°W 100°W

Lambert Equal Area Projection   Blue boxes indicate focus map coverage

Canada

Baffin Bay

Greenland (Den.)

Davis Strait

Labrador Sea

ATLANTIC OCEAN

BYLOT I.
Arctic Bay
BORDEN PENINSULA
Pond Inlet
Clyde River

Qeqertarsuaq (Disko)
Qeqertarsuaq (Godhavn)
Kangerlussuaq (Søndre Strømfjord)
Sisimiut

Narsarsuaq
Qaqortoq (Julianehåb)
Nunap Isua (Cape Farewell)

NUUK (GODTHÅB)
Paamiut (Frederikshåb)

MELVILLE PENINSULA
Hall Beach
PRINCE CHARLES I.
CUMBERLAND PENINSULA
Pangnirtung

QIKIQTAALUK (BAFFIN ISLAND)

N U N A V U T

Foxe Basin

Cumberland Sound

Amadjuak Lake
Iqaluit (Frobisher Bay)
HALL PENINSULA

FOXE PENINSULA
Cape Dorset
SALISBURY I.
Frobisher Bay
META INCOGNITA PENINSULA
RESOLUTION I.

SOUTHAMPTON I.
Coral Harbour
Evans Strait
COATS I.
NOTTINGHAM I.
Hudson Strait

Welcome Sound
Fisher Strait
MANSEL I.

Ivujivik
Salluit
Quaqtaq
AKPATOK I.
Cape Chidley
Hebron

Ungava Bay

Mont d'Iberville (Mt Caubvick) 1652m
Nain

Cape Harrison
Makkovik
Rigolet

Aupaluk

PÉNINSULE D'UNGAVA

Koksoak
Kuujjuaq (Fort Chimo)

Port Hope Simpson
Battle Harbour
BELLE ISLE
Cape Bauld
L'Anse aux Meadows

Hudson Bay

Inukjuak (Port Harrison)

C A N A D A

Labrador

NEWFOUNDLAND AND LABRADOR

Smallwood Reservoir

Schefferville
Churchill Falls
Happy Valley-Goose Bay
Blanc-Sablon

Port Saunders
Springdale
Grand Falls
Deer Lake
Corner Brook
Stephenville

Gander
St John's
NEWFOUNDLAND

Cape Race

BELCHER IS.
Cape Henrietta Maria

Réservoir Caniapiscau

Esker
Churchill
Labrador City
Fermont
Laurentian Highlands
Harrington Harbour

Strait of Belle Isle

Channel-Port-aux-Basques
Fortune
St-Pierre et Miquelon (Fr.)
St-Pierre

Winisk

Réservoir La Grande 2
Sakami
Réservoir La Grande 3
Radisson
Chisasibi (Fort George)

Q U É B E C

Natashquan

Eastmain
Réservoir Manicouagan
Gagnon
Havre-St-Pierre
Sept-Îles

ÎLE D'ANTICOSTI

Gulf of St Lawrence

Cabot Strait
Cape North
CAPE BRETON I.
Sydney
Glace Bay

Attawapiskat
AKIMISKI I.
James Bay
Eastmain
Lake Mistassini
Baie-Comeau
Matane
St-Laurent (St Lawrence)
Cap Gaspé
Gaspé
ÎLES DE LA MADELEINE
SABLE I.

Fort Albany
Albany
Moosonee

Chibougamau
Rimouski
Campbellton
Bathurst
PRINCE EDWARD ISLAND
Chatham
Charlottetown
New Glasgow

O N T A R I O

Pickle Lake

Matagami
Miquelon
Roberval
Jonquière
Chicoutimi
Alma
Rivière-du-Loup
Edmundston
NEW BRUNSWICK
Moncton
New Glasgow
Riverview
Truro
Dartmouth
NOVA SCOTIA
Halifax

Armstrong
Nakina
Pagwa River
Hearst
Kapuskasing
Fraserdale
Senneterre
La Tuque
Grand Falls
Fredericton
Saint John
Lunenburg

Lake Nipigon
Red Rock
Terrace Bay
White River
Hearst
Cochrane
Timmins
Noranda
Rouyn
Val-d'Or
Québec
Lévis
Montmagny
St-Georges
Thetford Mines
Bay of Fundy
Shelburne

Thunder Bay
Wawa
Gogama
Kirkland Lake
New Liskeard
Mont-Laurier
Trois-Rivières
Victoriaville
Drummondville
Sherbrooke
Yarmouth
Cape Sable

Lake Superior
Chapleau
Maniwaki
St-Jérôme
Joliette
Sorel
Laval
Lachute

G R E A T
Sudbury
Parry Sound
North Bay
Pembroke
Hull
Gatineau
Montréal
OTTAWA
Nepean
St Albans
Portland
Manchester
ATLANTIC OCEAN

Sault Ste Marie
MANITOULIN I.
Georgian Bay
Huntsville
Bancroft
Brockville
Kingston
Lake Ontario
Hudson
Boston

Owen Sound
Orillia
Lindsay
Trenton
Albany
Providence
Cape Cod

Green Bay
Lake Michigan
Lake Huron
Collingwood
Oshawa
Syracuse
Springfield
LONG I.

Grand Rapids
Lansing
Brampton
Kitchener
Toronto
St Catharines
Hartford
New Haven

Madison
Milwaukee
Detroit
Windsor
Hamilton
Niagara Falls
Buffalo
L A K E S
Lake St Clair
Sarnia
London
Lake Erie

Chicago
Toledo
Cleveland
Lake Erie
New York

4000 metres
2000 metres
1000 metres
500 metres
200 metres
Sea level

600 kilometres
300 miles

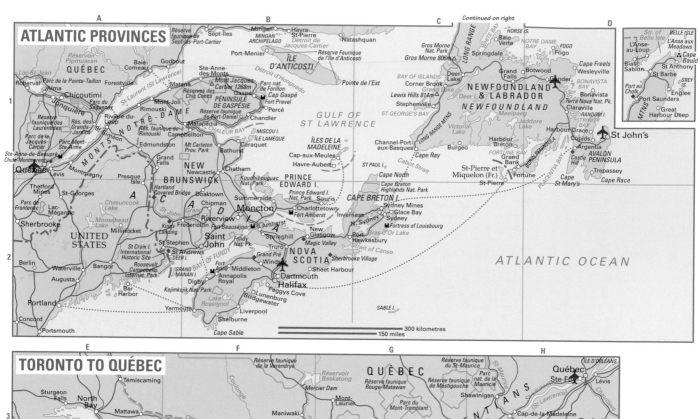

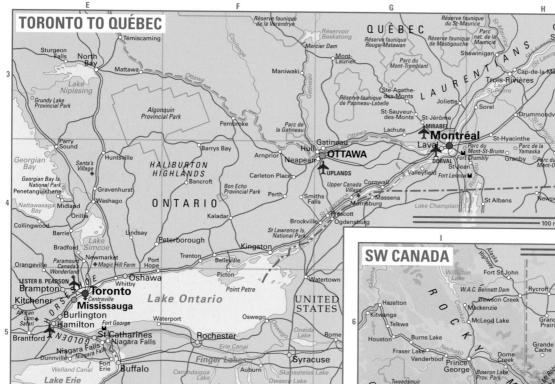

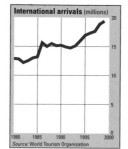

FEB Carnaval de **Québec (QU)**
FEB Winterlude **(Ottawa OT)**
FEB Sourdough Rendezvous **(Whitehorse YT)**
MAY Canadian Tulip Festival **(Ottawa OT)**
MAY-OCT Shakespeare Festival **(Stratford OT)**
JUN Festival d'Été **(Québec City QU)**
JUN Metro International Caravan **(Toronto OT)**
JUN Nova Scotia International Tattoo **(Halifax NS)**
JUN 24th St-Jean Baptiste Day **(Québec City QU)**
JUN-JUL International Jazz Festival **(Montréal OT)**
JUN-SEP Harbourfront Centre Summerfete **(Toronto OT)**
JUL 1st Canada Day **(Ottawa OT** & countrywide)
JUL International Freedom Festival **(Windsor OT)**
JUL Stampede **(Williams Lake BC)**
JUL Sea Festival **(Vancouver BC)**
JUL Loyalist Days Festival **(Saint John NB)**
JUL Klondike Days **(Edmonton AL)**
JUL **Calgary** Exhibition & Stampede **(AL)**
JUL Folklorama **(Winnipeg MN)**
JUL Manitoba Stampede & Exhibition **(Morris MN)**
JUL Manitoba Threshermen's Reunion **(Austin MN)**
JUL New Brunswick Highland Games & Scottish Festival
(Fredericton NB)
JUL-AUG Caribana **(Toronto OT)**
AUG Regatta Day **(St John's NF)**
AUG Abbotsford International Air Show **(BC)**
AUG Folklorama **(Winnipeg MN)**
AUG Gaelic Mod: Scottish festival **(St Ann's NS)**

AUG Fringe Festival **(Edmonton AL)**
AUG Six Nations Native Pageant **(Brantford OT)**
AUG Nova Scotia Fisheries Exhibition & Fishermen's
Reunion **(Lunenburg NS)**
AUG Discovery Day **(Dawson City YT)**
AUG-SEP Canadian National Exhibition **(Toronto OT)**
OCT Oktoberfest **(Kitchener-Waterloo OT)**
NOV Canadian Rodeo Finals **(Edmonton AL)**

International arrivals (millions)

Source: World Tourism Organisation

Canadian National Parks; Central America

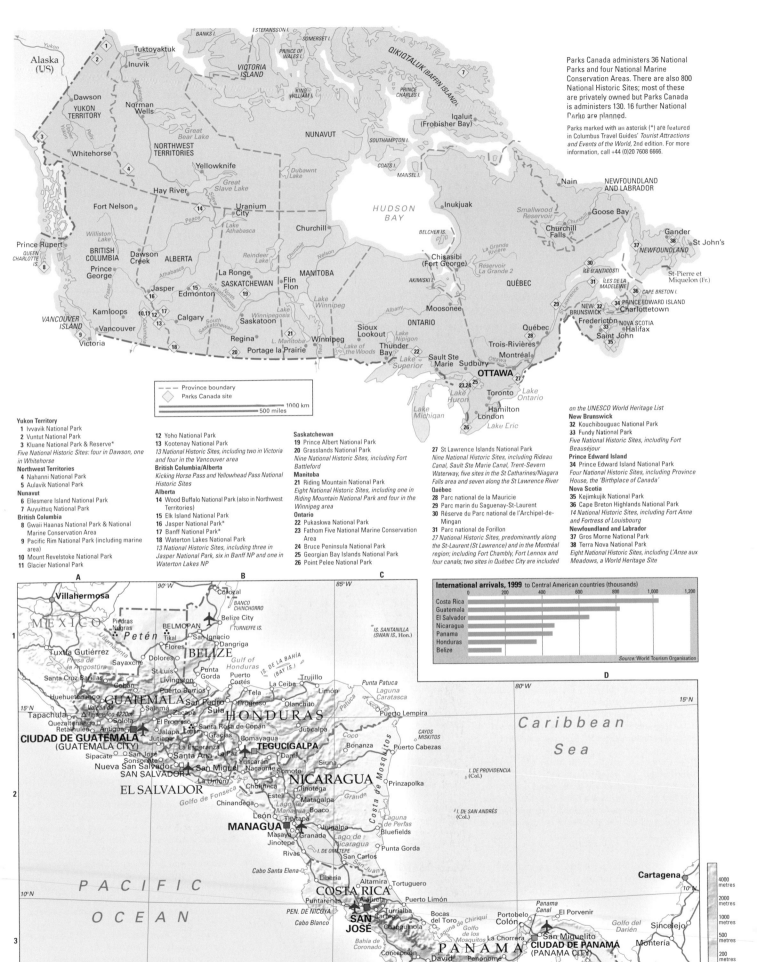

Parks Canada administers 36 National Parks and four National Marine Conservation Areas. There are also 800 National Historic Sites; most of these are privately owned but Parks Canada is administers 130. 16 further National Parks are planned.

Parks marked with an asterisk (*) are featured in Columbus Travel Guides' *Tourist Attractions and Events of the World*, 2nd edition. For more information, call +44 (0)20 7608 6666.

Province boundary
◇ Parks Canada site

1000 km
500 miles

Yukon Territory
1 Ivvavik National Park
2 Vuntut National Park
3 Kluane National Park & Reserve*
Five National Historic Sites: four in Dawson, one in Whitehorse
Northwest Territories
4 Nahanni National Park
5 Aulavik National Park
Nunavut
6 Ellesmere Island National Park
7 Auyuittuq National Park
British Columbia
8 Gwaii Haanas National Park & National Marine Conservation Area
9 Pacific Rim National Park (including marine area)
10 Mount Revelstoke National Park
11 Glacier National Park

12 Yoho National Park
13 Kootenay National Park
13 National Historic Sites, including two in Victoria and four in the Vancouver area
British Columbia/Alberta
Kicking Horse Pass and Yellowhead Pass National Historic Sites
Alberta
14 Wood Buffalo National Park (also in Northwest Territories)
15 Elk Island National Park
16 Jasper National Park*
17 Banff National Park*
18 Waterton Lakes National Park
13 National Historic Sites, including three in Jasper National Park, six in Banff NP and one in Waterton Lakes NP

Saskatchewan
19 Prince Albert National Park
20 Grasslands National Park
Nine National Historic Sites, including Fort Battleford
Manitoba
21 Riding Mountain National Park
Eight National Historic Sites, including one in Riding Mountain National Park and four in the Winnipeg area
Ontario
22 Pukaskwa National Park
23 Fathom Five National Marine Conservation Area
24 Bruce Peninsula National Park
25 Georgian Bay Islands National Park
26 Point Pelee National Park

27 St Lawrence Islands National Park
Nine National Historic Sites, including Rideau Canal, Sault Ste Marie Canal, Trent-Severn Waterway, five sites in the St Catharines/Niagara Falls area and seven along the St Lawrence River
Québec
28 Parc national de la Mauricie
29 Parc marin du Saguenay-St-Laurent
30 Réserve du Parc national de l'Archipel-de-Mingan
31 Parc national de Forillon
27 National Historic Sites, predominantly along the St-Laurent (St Lawrence) and in the Montréal region; including Fort Chambly, Fort Lennox and four canals; two sites in Québec City are included on the UNESCO World Heritage List
New Brunswick
32 Kouchibouguac National Park
33 Fundy National Park
Five National Historic Sites, including Fort Beauséjour
Prince Edward Island
34 Prince Edward Island National Park
Four National Historic Sites, including Province House, the 'Birthplace of Canada'
Nova Scotia
35 Kejimkujik National Park
36 Cape Breton Highlands National Park
14 National Historic Sites, including Fort Anne and Fortress of Louisbourg
Newfoundland and Labrador
37 Gros Morne National Park
38 Terra Nova National Park
Eight National Historic Sites, including L'Anse aux Meadows, a World Heritage Site

International arrivals, 1999 to Central American countries (thousands)

	0	200	400	600	800	1,000	1,200
Costa Rica							
Guatemala							
El Salvador							
Nicaragua							
Panama							
Honduras							
Belize							

Source: World Tourism Organisation

Lambert Equal Area Projection

4000 metres
2000 metres
1000 metres
500 metres
200 metres
Sea level

300 kilometres
150 miles

Latin America & the Caribbean

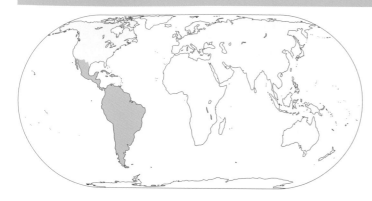

Key facts	LA&C	World	LA&C %
Number of Countries	48	226	21.2%
Area ('000 sq km)	19,897	135,463	14.7%
Population ('000)	494,375	5,973,801	8.2%
Population Density (/sq km)	25	44	–
Gross Nat. Income (US$m)	2,041,620	29,986,364	6.8%
Visitor Arrivals ('000)	54,365	649,223	8.4%
Visitor Receipts (US$m)	37,314	456,402	8.2%
Travel Departures ('000)	28,305	594,797	4.8%
Travel Expenditure (US$m)	20,399	397,040	5.1%

GNI figures relate to 1999. Population figures are taken from the most recent census or reliable estimate. Travel figures (from the WTO) are generally for 1999, but where these are unavailable or unreliable, figures from earlier years have been used. All travel figures are based on overnight stays, not same-day visitors. Where data for certain countries was not available, this has been regarded as zero. Global totals for Visitor Arrivals/Travel Departures and Visitor Receipts/Travel Expenditure do not equal each other due to differing methods of reporting inbound and outbound data. For more information on what is regarded as a country for the purposes of this book, and for more detailed statistical information, please see the Countries A-Z section from page 181.

LATIN AMERICA has experienced a decade of stability during which the twin evils of military dictatorship and hyperinflation have largely been banished. Although the strong economic growth of the early 1990s has recently stalled, there are many sound reasons for optimism. Travel receipts doubled between 1990 and 1999; but even so the boundaries of tourism are still being pushed back. Although many areas have recently become accessible – and not only to the adventurous holidaymaker – much remains unexplored. Despite only occupying 15% of the world's land area, Latin America has a greater latitudinal range than any other continent, reaching from the southern temperate zone of the Northern Hemisphere to the edge of the Antarctic, and offers a commensurate range of attractions and activities. By contrast, the Caribbean islands are firmly established as luxury sunshine holiday destinations. With the exception of the Francophone ones, most are heavily dependent on the United States market.

Holiday trends

South America came relatively late to tourism from the main holidaymaking societies of Europe and the USA. Although visitor numbers have contracted slightly in the last couple of years – Central America excluded – 1998's total was 45% up on 1990's. This rise has been fuelled partly by an increase in family package holidays to beach destinations such as Brazil; partly by an increase in intra-regional travel; and partly by the growth of adventure holidays out of Europe and the USA, a taste which Latin America is well able to satisfy.

Much of the continent has been explored for decades by adventurous backpackers prepared to live rough on a low budget. Many follow the Mayan trail from Mexico to Honduras or the paths of the Aztec through Peru. Most Central American countries have spearheaded a new style in ecological holidays.

The major cities of South America are amongst the largest and most vibrant in the world, with all the attendant advantages and disadvantages. The Carnival in Rio is world-famous, and numerous other local cultural events in the region are celebrated with a verve that draws visitors from all over the world.

The Caribbean islands, with their high average temperatures and warm blue waters of 24°C year-round, are mostly beach and water-sports destinations. The islands are arguably the finest collection of idyllic, palm-fringed beaches in the world. They gave birth to the luxury, all-inclusive concept of holidays where all

■ Latin leapers

Fastest growing destinations and holiday types, 2000
Source: Journey Latin America

Fastest growing destinations...

1. Brazil
2. Chile
3. Cuba
4. Antarctica
5. Guatemala
6. Belize

Fastest growing holiday types...

1. Tailor-made holidays.
2. Active adventures – multi-sport group adventure trips (e.g. rafting, mountain biking, hiking, horse-riding, sea kayaking).
3= Flights only and back-packers.
3= Escorted group tours.

food and services are included in one price. Most of the Caribbean islands rely heavily on tourism, some almost to the exclusion of any other source of income. Around 25% of all jobs depend directly or indirectly on travel and tourism: in some countries, the reliance is closer to 75%. Many Caribbean states are taking urgent steps to diversify their economies.

Caribbean holidays are generally single-destination stay-puts although, with the increased efficiency of intra-island air travel, island hopping is developing. The islands are also a focus for most major cruise lines.

The weather and exotic locations have also enabled the region to achieve top spot for weddings and honeymoons and sailing is also a strong market either with bareboat self-charters or crewed yacht cruising.

Established favourites

- Mexico – This remains one of the world's major holiday destinations, particularly amongst North

■ Big spenders

Expenditure by Latin Americans and Caribbeans on foreign travel, 1999 – top ten countries (US$ billions – excluding international transport)
Source: WTO

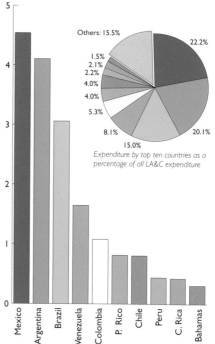

Expenditure by top ten countries as a percentage of all LA&C expenditure

Americans. Mexico City is cleaning up its act by tackling pollution, crime and refurbishing tourist attractions. The top resort areas are Cancun, Acapulco and Puerto Vallarta

- Brazil – Charter flights are opening the country to greater international tourism, mainly for beach holidays at Salvador de Bahia, Recife and Natal. Brazil, measuring more than 2,500 miles north to south, is also home to the majority of the vast Amazon rain forest. Attractions of Rio de Janeiro include Corcovado Mountain with its statue of Christ the Redeemer, and Ipanema and Copacabana beaches.

- Peru – Dramatic mountains and jungles, and Inca cities such as Machu Picchu, have given the country a deserved reputation among adventure-seekers.

- Puerto Rico – Ever popular with the US market, the Commonwealth is engaged in a major hotel construction and refurbishment programme.

- Dominican Republic – Some of the best beaches in the Caribbean are here. The country is re-

■ American breaks

The five biggest travellers: percentage of trips taken within the Americas.
Source: WTO

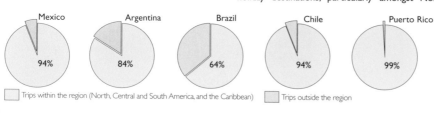

Mexico 94%	Argentina 84%	Brazil 64%	Chile 94%	Puerto Rico 99%

☐ Trips within the region (North, Central and South America, and the Caribbean)   ☐ Trips outside the region

- Latin America and the Caribbean (LA&C) occupies nearly 15% of the world's land area and is home to over 8% of the world's population.
- LA&C's combined GDI is US$2,041,620 million, just under 7% of the world's total.
- LA&C accounts for nearly 5% of global travel departures and over 8% of arrivals.
- International travel and tourism contributed over US$37 billion to LA&C's economy in 1999, an increase of 2.2% over 1998.
- 11 LA&C countries – five in South America, five in the Caribbean and one in Central America – received over 1 million visitors in 1999. Mexico alone accounted for 35% of all regional arrivals.
- The most-visited country in LA&C, Mexico, ranked 8th in the world in 1999 with 19 million visitors: over 90% of these were from the USA.
- Five countries – Mexico, Brazil, Argentina, the Dominican Republic and Puerto Rico – accounted for 50% of LA&C's earnings from international travel and tourism in 1999.
- There were 54.4 million international tourist arrivals in LA&C in 1999, an increase of 0.2% over 1998, considerably below the world average. 38.3 million of these were to the mainland and 16.1 million to the Caribbean.
- The most significant growth in tourist arrivals was in Central America (excluding Mexico) which showed an increase of 16.7%. The Caribbean showed an increase of 1.1%; while Mexico fell by 1.8%, and South America by 0.1%.
- Visitors to the Turks & Caicos Islands in 1999 each spent an average of US$2,033, the highest expenditure per head in the world. In one third of the other countries in LA&C the expenditure per head was in excess of US$1,000.
- The countries which showed the biggest increase in 1999 visitors compared to 1998 were Guatemala (29%) and El Salvador (21%). In South America the biggest increase was shown by Peru (15%); and in the Caribbean by the US Virgin Islands (14.9%) and the Dominican Republic (14.7%).
- Tourism receipts in LA&C showed an increase of 2.2% in 1999 compared to 1998, slightly below the world average. The countries with the largest increases – El Salvador (69%), Guatemala (45%) and Nicaragua (26%) – are all in Central America. The biggest Caribbean increase was the Dominican Republic (19.8%); South America's was Peru (18%).
- Mexicans are LA&C's biggest travellers, accounting for over 27% of all the region's recorded international departures. Nearly 90% of these departures were to the USA.
- The USA accounted for 50% of all arrivals to the region in 1999.

establishing tourism after food standards problems damaged previous promotional efforts.

- Jamaica – golf, beaches, mountains and popular resorts such as Negril, Montego Bay and Ocho Rios are the highlights.

- Cayman Islands – This is a top diving destination that has also pioneered strict rules for reef protection.

- The Bahamas – A country of 700 islands, many of them paradisical. The main resort and cruise liner stops are Grand Bahama and Nassau/Paradise Island.

- Cruising – This remains a vital part of the tourism industry in the Caribbean and the Gulf of Mexico. The Caribbean in particular continues to attract the bulk of the world's new capacity. The industry is undergoing changes resulting from demands for tighter environmental and safety controls.

Growth areas
- Cuba – the last bastion of communism is opening up to tourism. The Varadero resort area is popular internationally and more resorts are planned.

Holidays afloat

Total bed-nights on cruise ships, 2000
Source: Cruise Lines International Association

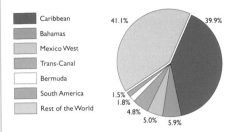

- Caribbean
- Bahamas
- Mexico West
- Trans-Canal
- Bermuda
- South America
- Rest of the World

41.1% 39.9% 1.5% 1.8% 4.8% 5.0% 5.9%

Havana, though a shadow of its former self, seems to be a must for most visitors.

- Tobago – relatively unspoilt by tourism, it has colourful wildlife, good beaches, diving and sailing.

- Central America – has seen the region's biggest visitor growth, and is reaping the rewards of economic and political stability. Lush jungles, ancient monuments and spectacular diving – Belize, for example, has the world's second largest reef – all form part of a successful and varied eco-tourism product.

- Antarctica – although not part of South America, the seasonally accessible parts of this vast, ice-bound continent represent a very specialsied, and fast-growing, eco-tourism and adventure destination.

Problem areas
The Caribbean nations have Dollar-related currencies which link them to the volatility of recession and the money markets: a strengthening US Dollar will reduce the value-for-money element of the Caribbean destinations for European travellers.

Parts of Central America and the Caribbean recently suffered badly at the hands of Hurricanes Mitch and Lenny; other hurricanes will doubtless follow.

Big earners

Receipts from Foreign Travel, 1999
(US$ billions – excluding international transport)
Source: WTO

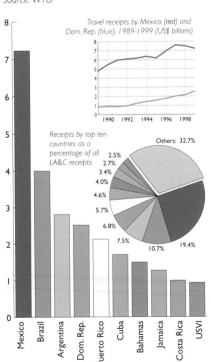

Travel receipts by Mexico (red) and Dom. Rep. (blue), 1989-1999 (US$ billions)

1990 1992 1994 1996 1998

Receipts by top ten countries as a percentage of all LA&C receipts

Others: 32.7%
2.5%
2.7%
3.4%
4.0%
4.6%
5.7%
6.8%
7.5%
10.7%
19.4%

Mexico, Brazil, Argentina, Dom. Rep., Puerto Rico, Cuba, Bahamas, Jamaica, Costa Rica, USVI

The rate of diminution of the rain forests of Central and South America has been cause for concern for more than a decade, yet clearance of vast areas still goes on apace.

Many of the region's coral reefs have suffered considerable degradation in recent years. In some cases the problem is irreversible but active steps are being taken in most countries to prevent further damage.

Colombia, as a source of huge amounts of illegal drugs, remains the pariah of the region. It also has conflicts between rival guerrilla factions.

As with many parts of the world, violent street crime can be rife in some areas.

Visitors

Visitor arrivals and average receipts per visitor, 1999
Source: WTO

	Visitors (thousands)	Receipts per visitor
Mexico	19,043	$379
Brazil	5,107	$782
Puerto Rico	3,024	$707
Argentina	2,898	$970
Dominican Rep.	2,649	$953
Uruguay	2,073	$315
Chile	1,622	$551
Bahamas	1,577	$953
Cuba	1,561	$1,098
Jamaica	1,248	$1,025
Costa Rica	1,032	$971
Peru	944	$943
Guatemala	823	$693
Aruba	683	$1,145
El Salvador	658	$321
Venezuela	587	$1,118
Martinique	564	$716
Guadeloupe (not St Mart.)	561	$668
Panama	555	$969
Colombia	546	$1,700
Barbados	515	$1,315
Ecuador	509	$674
US Virgin Is.	485	$1,938
Nicaragua	468	$229
St Maarten (incl. St Mart.)	454	$1,020
Cayman Is.	395	$1,139
Honduras	371	$526
Bermuda	354	$1,376
Bolivia	342	$523
Trinidad & Tobago	336	$598
British Virgin Is.	286	$1,049
Curaçao & Bonaire	272	$1,143
Paraguay	269	$301
St Lucia	261	$1,192
Antigua & Barbuda	232	$1,254
Belize	181	$619
Haiti	143	$399
Grenada	125	$504
Turks & Caicos Is.	121	$2,033
St Kitts & Nevis	84	$833
Guyana	75	$693
Dominica	74	$662
French Guiana	70	$714
St Vincent & the Gren.	68	$1,132
Surinam	63	$841
Anguilla	47	$1,191
Montserrat	10	$300

(Visitor arrival figures not available for the Falkland Islands.)

Maps, charts and statistics on LA&C follow on pages 164 to 174. See also the *Countries A-Z* section from page 184, and the *Index* from page 193.

Thanks to: Tim Murray-Walker of Journey Latin America; Jonathan Vernon-Powell of Nomadic Thoughts.

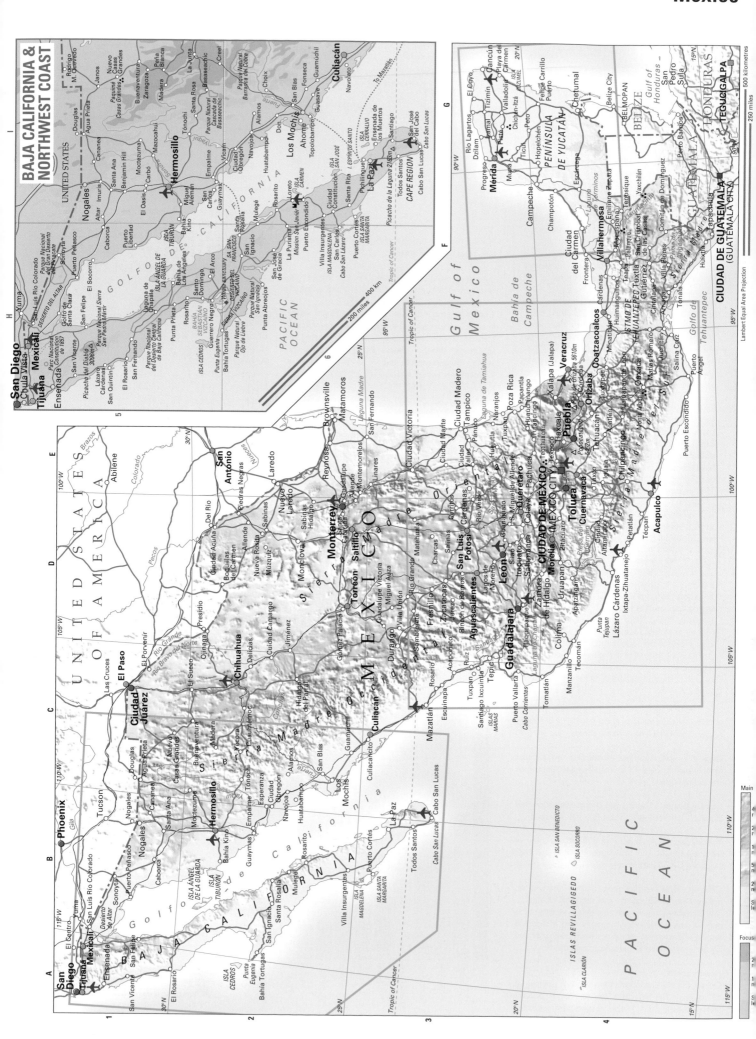

BAJA CALIFORNIA & NORTHWEST COAST

Mexico

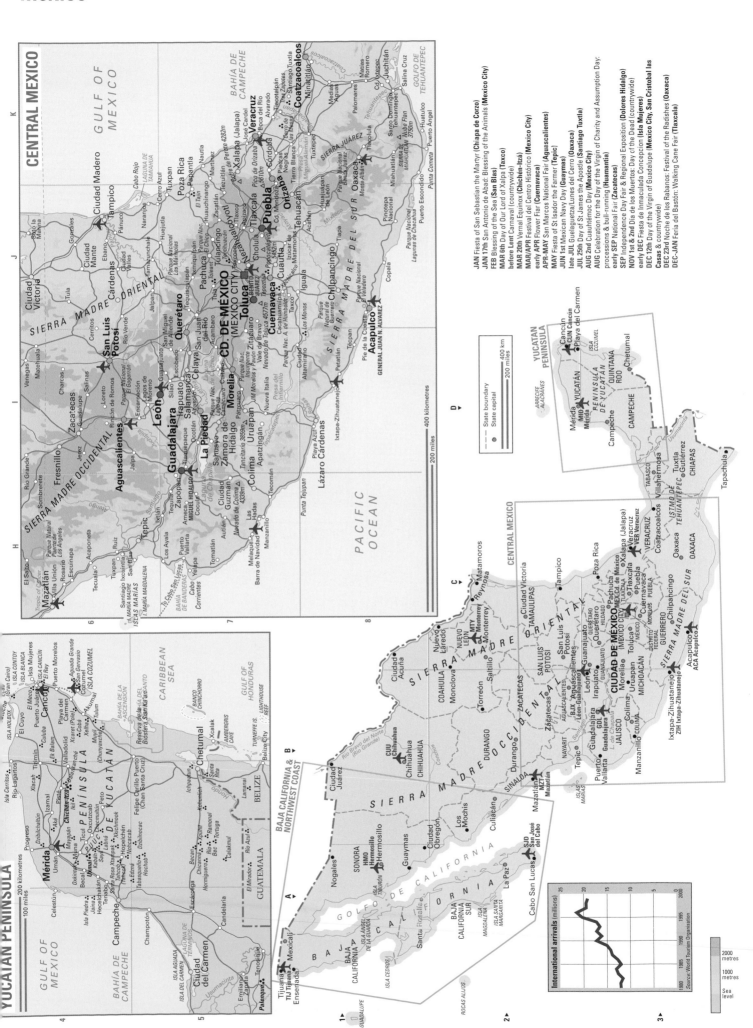

CENTRAL MEXICO

YUCATAN PENINSULA

JAN Fiesta of San Sebastian the Martyr **(Chiapa de Corzo)**
JAN 17th San Antonio de Abad: Blessing of the Animals **(Mexico City)**
FEB Blessing of the Sea **(San Blas)**
MAR 6th Day of Our Lord of Xalpa **(Taxco)**
before Lent Carnaval (countrywide)
MAR 20th Vernal Equinox **(Chichén-Itzá)**
MAR/APR Festival del Centro Histórico **(Mexico City)**
early **APR** Flower Fiar **(Cuernavaca)**
APR-MAY San Marcos National Fair **(Aguascalientes)**
MAY Fiesta of St Isidor the Farmer **(Tepic)**
JUN 1st Mexican Navy Day **(Guaymas)**
late **JUL** Guelaguetza/Lunes del Cerro **(Oaxaca)**
JUL 25th Day of St James the Apostle **(Santiago Tuxtla)**
AUG 2nd Cuauhtémoc Day **(Mexico City)**
AUG Celebration for the Day of the Virgin of Charity and Assumption Day: processions & bull-running **(Huamantla)**
early **SEP** National Fair **(Zacatecas)**
SEP Independence Day Fair & Regional Exposition **(Dolores Hidalgo)**
NOV 1st & 2nd Día de los Muertos: Day of the Dead (countrywide)
early **DEC** Fiesta de Inmaculada Concepción **(Isla Mujeres)**
DEC 12th Day of the Virgin of Guadalupe **(Mexico City, San Cristobal las Casas)** & countrywide
DEC 23rd Noche de los Rabanos: Festival of the Radishes **(Oaxaca)**
DEC-JAN Feria del Bastón: Walking Cane Fair **(Tlaxcala)**

Caribbean Languages & the Greater Antilles

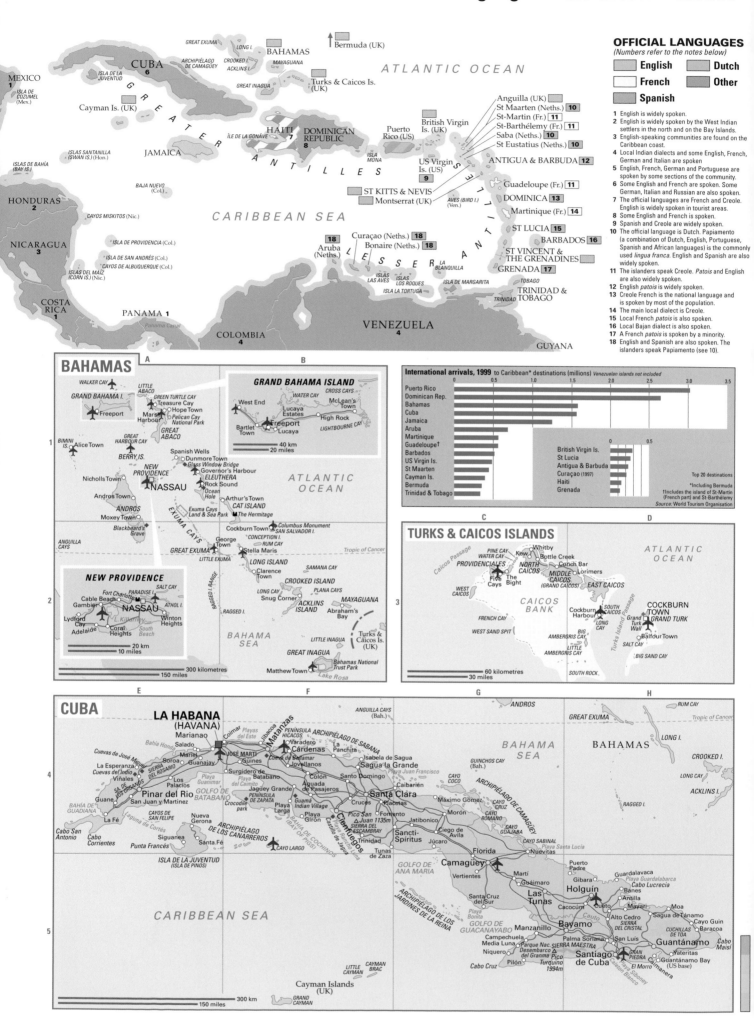

OFFICIAL LANGUAGES
(Numbers refer to the notes below)

- English
- French
- Spanish
- Dutch
- Other

1 English is widely spoken.
2 English is widely spoken by the West Indian settlers in the north and on the Bay Islands.
3 English-speaking communities are found on the Caribbean coast.
4 Local Indian dialects and some English, French, German and Italian are spoken.
5 English, French, German and Portuguese are spoken by some sections of the community.
6 Spanish is widely spoken. Some English and French are spoken. Some German, Italian and Russian are also spoken.
7 The official languages are French and Creole. English is widely spoken in tourist areas.
8 Some English and French is spoken.
9 Spanish and Creole are widely spoken.
10 The official language is Dutch. Papiamento (a combination of Dutch, English, Portuguese, Spanish and African languages) is the commonly used *lingua franca*. English and Spanish are also widely spoken.
11 The islanders speak Creole. Patois and English are also widely spoken.
12 English patois is widely spoken.
13 Creole French is the national language and is spoken by most of the population.
14 The main local dialect is Creole.
15 Local French patois is also spoken.
16 Local Bajan dialect is also spoken.
17 A French patois is spoken by a minority.
18 English and Spanish are also spoken. The islanders speak Papiamento (see 10).

BAHAMAS

GRAND BAHAMA ISLAND

NEW PROVIDENCE

International arrivals, 1999 to Caribbean* destinations (millions) *Venezuelan islands not included*

Top 20 destinations

*Including Bermuda
†Includes the island of St-Martin (French part) and St-Barthélemy
Source: World Tourism Organisation*

TURKS & CAICOS ISLANDS

CUBA

The Greater Antilles

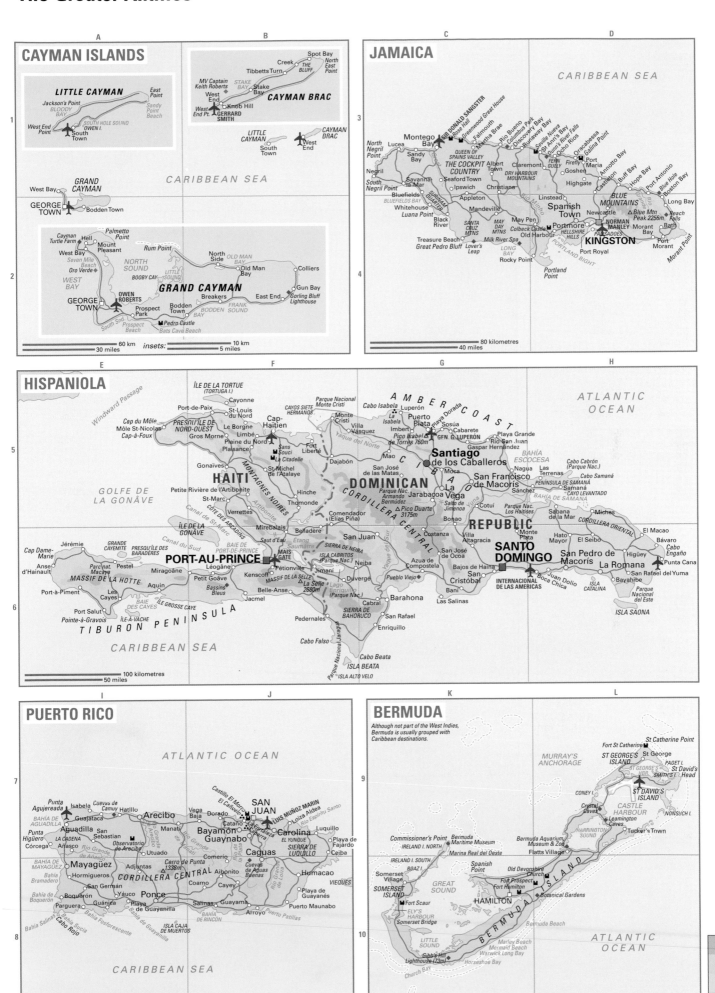

CAYMAN ISLANDS

LITTLE CAYMAN
Jackson's Point
BLOODY BAY
West End Point
SOUTH HOLE SOUND OWEN I.
South Town
East Point
Sandy Point Beach

CAYMAN BRAC
Creek
Spot Bay
North East Point
THE BLUFF
Tibbetts Turn
STAKE BAY
Stake Bay
MV Captain Keith Roberts
West End
Knob Hill
West End Pt.
GERRARD SMITH
LITTLE CAYMAN
South Town
CAYMAN BRAC
West End

West Bay
GRAND CAYMAN
GEORGE TOWN
Bodden Town

CARIBBEAN SEA

Cayman Turtle Farm
Hell
Palmetto Point
Rum Point
West Bay
Mount Pleasant
NORTH SOUND
OLD MAN BAY
North Side
Old Man Bay
Colliers
Seven Mile Beach
Oro Verde
LITTLE SOUND
BOOBY CAY
Gun Bay
WEST BAY
GRAND CAYMAN
East End
Gorling Bluff Lighthouse
GEORGE TOWN
OWEN ROBERTS
Prospect Park
Bodden Town
BODDEN BAY
FRANK SOUND
Prospect Beach
South Snd.
Pedro Castle
Bats Cave Beach

60 km
30 miles
insets:
10 km
5 miles

JAMAICA

CARIBBEAN SEA

SIR DONALD SANGSTER
Montego Bay
Rose Hall
Greenwood Great House
Falmouth
Martha Brae
Rio Bueno
Columbus Park
Discovery Bay
Runaway Bay
Seville Nueva
St Ann's Bay
Dunn's River Falls
Ocho Rios
Oracabessa
Galina Point
North Negril Point
Lucea
Sandy Bay
QUEEN OF SPAINS VALLEY
THE COCKPIT COUNTRY
Albert Town
Claremont
Firefly
Port Maria
Annotto Bay
Negril
South Negril Point
Savanna la-Mar
Seaford Town
Ipswich
Christiana
DRY HARBOUR MOUNTAINS
Goshen
Highgate
Castleton
Buff Bay
Port Antonio
Blue Hole
Boston Bay
Bluefields
SURINAM QUARTER
Appleton
Mandeville
Linstead
Spanish Town
BLUE MOUNTAINS
Newcastle
Blue Mtn Peak 2256m
Long Bay
Whitehouse
BLUEFIELDS BAY
Black River
Luana Point
SANTA CRUZ MTNS
May Pen
MAY DAY MTNS
Portmore
Old Harbour
HELLSHIRE HILLS
NORMAN MANLEY
PALISADOES
Reach Falls
Bath
Treasure Beach
Great Pedro Bluff
Lover's Leap
Colbeck Castle
KINGSTON
Morant Bay
Rocky Point
LONG BAY
Port Royal
Milk River Spa
PORTLAND BIGHT
Portland Point
Port Morant
Morant Point

80 kilometres
40 miles

HISPANIOLA

ÎLE DE LA TORTUE (TORTUGA I.)
Windward Passage
Cayonne
Port-de-Paix
St-Louis du Nord
CAYOS SIETE HERMANOS
Cabo Isabela
Luperón
AMBER COAST
ATLANTIC OCEAN
Cap du Môle
Môle St-Nicolas
Cap-à-Foux
PRESQU'ÎLE DE NORD-OUEST
Le Borgne
Plaine du Nord
Cap-Haïtien
Parque Nacional Monte Cristi
Monte Cristi
La Isabela
Puerto Plata
Imbert
Playa Dorada
Sosúa
Cabarete
Playa Grande
Gros Morne
Limbé
Fort Liberté
Monte Vásquez
Pico Isabel de Torres 760m
GFN G. LUPERÓN
Rio San Juan
Gaspar Hernández
Punta Cana
Gonaïves
Plaisance
Sans Souci
La Citadelle
St-Michel de l'Atalaye
Dajabón
Mao
Santiago de los Caballeros
Moca
San Francisco de Macorís
Las Terrenas
Nagua
PENÍNSULA DE SAMANÁ
Samaná
CAYO LEVANTADO
Cabo Cabrón (Parque Nac.)
Cabo Samaná
GOLFE DE LA GONÂVE
MONTAGNES NOIRES
HAITI
Petite Rivière de l'Artibonite
Hinche
San José de las Matas
DOMINICAN
La Vega
Sánchez
BAHÍA ESCOCESA
BAHÍA DE SAMANÁ
St-Marc
Verrettes
Thomonde
Artibonite
CORDILLERA CENTRAL
Parque Nac. Armando Bermúdez
Jarabacoa
Salto de Jimenoa
Cotuí
Parque Nac. Los Haitises
Sabana de la Mar
Miches
CORDILLERA ORIENTAL
ÎLE DE LA GONÂVE
Canal de la St-Marc
Mirebalais
Belladère
Pico Duarte 3175m
Bonao
El Macao
Cap Dame-Marie
Jérémie
GRANDE CAYEMITE
PRESQU'ÎLE DES BARADERES
Saut d'Eau
Comendador (Elías Piña)
San Juan
Constanza
REPUBLIC
Monte Plata
Hato Mayor
El Seibo
Bávaro
Cabo Engaño
Anse d'Hainault
Parc nat. Macaye
Pestel
Miragoâne
Léogâne
MAIS GATE
Villa Altagracia
SANTO DOMINGO
San Pedro de Macorís
Higüey
Punta Cana
MASSIF DE LA HOTTE
Aquin
Petit Goâve
Bassins Bleus
Kenscoff
PORT-AU-PRINCE
Pétionville
SIERRA DE NEIBA
ISLA CABRITOS (Parque Nac.)
Jimaní
Azua de Compostela
San José de Ocoa
Bajos de Haina
Boca Chica
INTERNACIONAL DE LAS AMERICAS
Juan Dolio
ISLA CATALINA
La Romana
San Rafael del Yuma
Bayahibe
Port-à-Piment
Les Cayes
ÎLE GROSSE CAYE
MASSIF DE LA SELLE
La Selle 2680m
Duvergé
Neiba
Pueblo Viejo
San Cristóbal
Baní
Parque Nacional del Este
Port Salut
Pointe-à-Gravois
ÎLE-À-VACHE
BAIE DES CAYES
Jacmel
Belle-Anse
Étang Saumâtre
Lago Enriquillo (Parque Nac.)
Cabral
Barahona
Las Salinas
ISLA SAONA
TIBURON PENINSULA
Pedernales
SIERRA DE BAHORUCO
San Rafael
Enriquillo
CARIBBEAN SEA
Cabo Falso
Parque Nacional Jaragua
Cabo Beata
ISLA BEATA
ISLA ALTO VELO

CIBAO
La Yuna
Yaque del Sur
Yaque del Norte

100 kilometres
50 miles

PUERTO RICO

ATLANTIC OCEAN
Punta Aguijereada
Isabela
Cuevas de Camuy
Hatillo
Castillo El Morro
El Castillo
SAN JUAN
LUIS MUÑOZ MARÍN
BAHÍA DE AGUADILLA
Aguadilla
Guajataca
Arecibo
Vega Baja
Dorado
Cataño
Bayamón
Carolina
Loíza Aldea
Punta Higüero
Córcega
LA CADENA
Añasco
San Sebastián
Manati
Observatorio de Arecibo
Guaynabo
EL YUNQUE
SIERRA DE LUQUILLO
Luquillo
Playa de Fajardo
Ceiba
BAHÍA DE MAYAGÜEZ
Mayagüez
Utuado
Cerro de Punta 1338m
Comerio
Caguas
Cuevas de Aguas Buenas
Humacao
VIEQUES
Bahía Bramadero
Hormigueros
Adjuntas
Aibonito
Coamo
Cayey
Playa de Guayanés
Bahía de Boquerón
San Germán
Yáuco
Ponce
Salinas
Guayama
Puerto Maunabo
Boquerón
Guánica
Playa de Guayanilla
Arroyo
Parguera
BAHÍA DE GUAYANILLA
Bahía Sucia
Cabo Rojo
Bahía Salinas
Bahía Fosforescente
ISLA CAJA DE MUERTOS
BAHÍA DE RINCÓN
CARIBBEAN SEA

CORDILLERA CENTRAL
Grande de Arecibo
Rio Grande de Añasco
Rio Espíritu Santo
Río Grande de Loíza

80 kilometres
40 miles

BERMUDA

Although not part of the West Indies, Bermuda is usually grouped with Caribbean destinations.

St Catherine Point
Fort St Catherine
MURRAY'S ANCHORAGE
ST GEORGE'S ISLAND
St George
PAGET I.
St David's Head
ST GEORGE'S HBR.
SMITH'S I.
CONEY I.
ST DAVID'S ISLAND
NONSUCH I.
Crystal Caves
CASTLE HARBOUR
Leamington Caves
Tucker's Town
Commissioner's Point
Bermuda Maritime Museum
IRELAND I. NORTH
Marina Real del Oeste
Bermuda Aquarium, Museum & Zoo
HARRINGTON SOUND
Flatts Village
IRELAND I. SOUTH
BOAZ I.
Spanish Point
Old Devonshire Church
Somerset Village
Fort Prospect
Fort Hamilton
SOMERSET ISLAND
GREAT SOUND
Botanical Gardens
Fort Scaur
HAMILTON
BERMUDA ISLAND
ELY'S HARBOUR
Somerset Bridge
LITTLE SOUND
Bermuda Beach
Marley Beach
Mermaid Beach
Gibb's Hill Lighthouse (43m)
Warwick Long Bay
Horseshoe Bay
Church Bay
ATLANTIC OCEAN

10 kilometres
5 miles

1000 metres
500 metres
Sea level

Caribbean Dive Sites & the Lesser Antilles

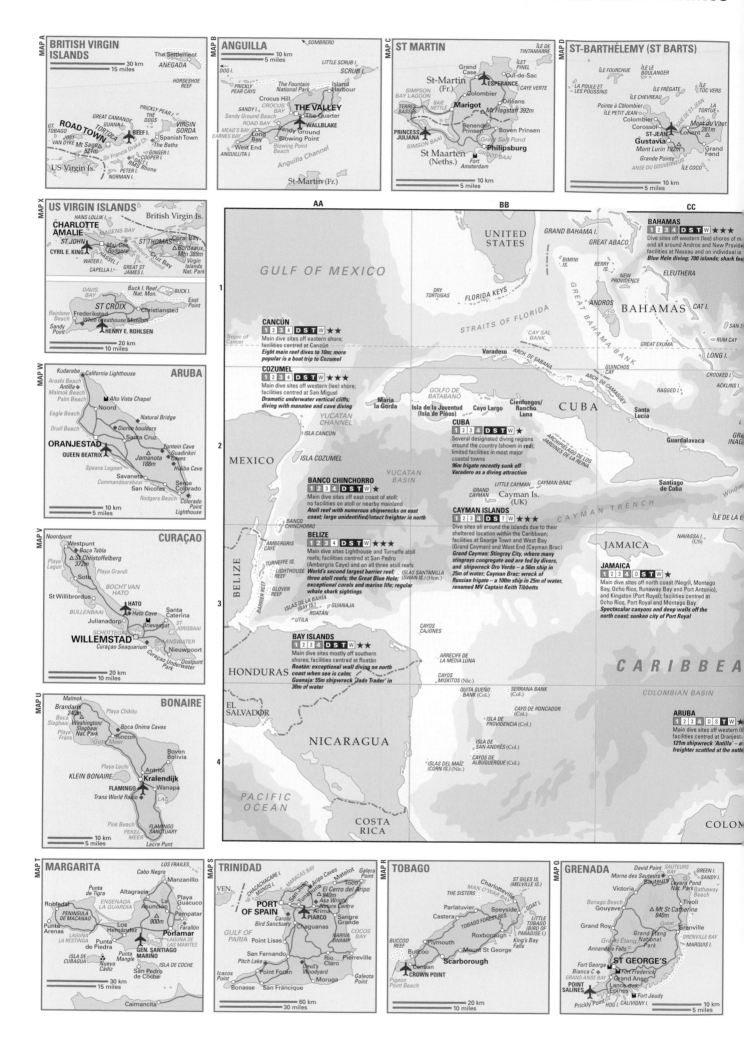

BRITISH VIRGIN ISLANDS (MAP A)

ANGUILLA (MAP B)

ST MARTIN (MAP C)

ST-BARTHÉLEMY (ST BARTS) (MAP D)

US VIRGIN ISLANDS (MAP X)

ARUBA (MAP W)

CURAÇAO (MAP V)

BONAIRE (MAP U)

MARGARITA (MAP T)

TRINIDAD (MAP S)

TOBAGO (MAP R)

GRENADA (MAP Q)

CANCÚN 1 2 3 4 D S T W ★★
Main dive sites off eastern shore; facilities centred at Cancún
Eight main reef dives to 10m; more popular is a boat trip to Cozumel

COZUMEL 1 2 3 4 D S T W ★★★
Main dive sites off western (lee) shore; facilities centred at San Miguel
Dramatic underwater vertical cliffs; diving with manatee and cave diving

BANCO CHINCHORRO 1 2 3 4 D S T W ★
Main dive sites off east coast of atoll; no facilities on atoll or nearby mainland
Atoll reef with numerous shipwrecks on east coast; large unidentified/intact freighter in north

BELIZE 1 2 3 4 D S T W ★★★
Main dive sites Lighthouse and Turneffe atoll reefs; facilities centred at San Pedro (Ambergris Caye) and on all three atoll reefs
World's second largest barrier reef; three atoll reefs; the Great Blue Hole; exceptional corals and marine life; regular whale shark sightings

BAY ISLANDS 1 2 3 4 D S T W ★★
Main dive sites mostly off southern shores; facilities centred at Roatán
Roatán: exceptional wall diving on north coast when sea is calm; Guanaja: 55m shipwreck 'Jado Trader' in 30m of water

BAHAMAS 1 2 3 4 D S T W ★★★
Dive sites off western (lee) shores of m... and all around Andros and New Provid... facilities at Nassau and on individual is...
Blue Hole diving; 700 islands; shark...

CUBA 1 2 3 4 D S T W ★
Several designated diving regions around the country (shown in red); limited facilities in most major coastal towns
96m frigate recently sunk off Varadero as a diving attraction

CAYMAN ISLANDS 1 2 3 4 D S T W ★★★
Dive sites all around the islands due to their sheltered location within the Caribbean; facilities at George Town and West Bay (Grand Cayman) and West End (Cayman Brac)
Grand Cayman: Stingray City, where many stingrays congregate and are fed by divers, and shipwreck Oro Verde – a 50m ship in 25m of water; Cayman Brac: wreck of Russian frigate – a 100m ship in 25m of water, renamed MV Captain Keith Tibbetts

JAMAICA 1 2 3 4 D S T W ★
Main dive sites off north coast (Negril, Montego Bay, Ocho Rios, Runaway Bay and Port Antonio), and Kingston (Port Royal); facilities centred at Ocho Rios, Port Royal and Montego Bay
Spectacular canyons and deep walls off the north coast; sunken city of Port Royal

ARUBA 1 2 3 4 D S T W
Main dive sites off western (l... facilities centred at Oranjest...
121m shipwreck 'Antilla' – a... freighter scuttled at the outb...

Caribbean Dive Sites & the Lesser Antilles

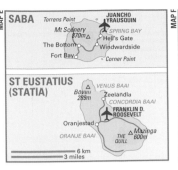

SABA
Torrens Point
Mt Scenery 870m △
Hell's Gate
The Bottom
Fort Bay
Windwardside
Corner Point
JUANCHO YRAUSQUIN ✈
SPRING BAY

ST EUSTATIUS (STATIA)
VENUS BAAI
Boven 289m △
Zeelandia
CONCORDIA BAAI
Oranjestad
FRANKLIN D. ROOSEVELT ✈
ORANJE BAAI
THE QUILL
△ Mazinga 600m

6 km / 3 miles

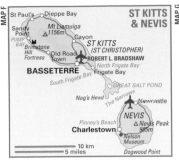

ST KITTS & NEVIS
St Paul's
Dieppe Bay
Sandy Point
PUMP BAY
Brimstone Hill Fortress
Old Road Town
Mt Liamuiga 1156m △
Cayon
ST KITTS (ST CHRISTOPHER)
ROBERT L. BRADSHAW ✈
BASSETERRE
Frigate Bay
North Frigate Bay
South Frigate Bay
GREAT SALT POND
Nag's Head
The Narrows
Newcastle
Pinney's Beach
NEVIS
△ Nevis Peak 985m
Charlestown
Nelson Museum
Dogwood Point
10 km / 5 miles

MONTSERRAT
Recent volcanic activity has destroyed the former capital, Plymouth. The area marked A is an exclusion zone, the area marked B is open during the daytime only.
North West Bluff
△ Silver Hill
Gerald's
St John's
RENDEZVOUS BAY
Katy Hill △
CENTRE HILLS
WILLIAM H. BRAMBLE ✈ (closed)
WOODLANDS BAY
Salem
Olveston
OLD ROAD BAY
FOX'S BAY
Bransby Point
SOUFRIÈRE HILLS
Long Ground
B
Plymouth
Fort Barrington
A
Chances Peak △
Galway's Soufrière
Old Fort Point
Morris
10 km / 5 miles

BARBUDA
Goat Point
Cedar Tree Point
GOAT I.
RABBIT I.
KID I.
CODRINGTON LAGOON
Codrington
THE HIGHLANDS
Palmetto Point
Cocoa Point
Spanish Point
10 km / 5 miles

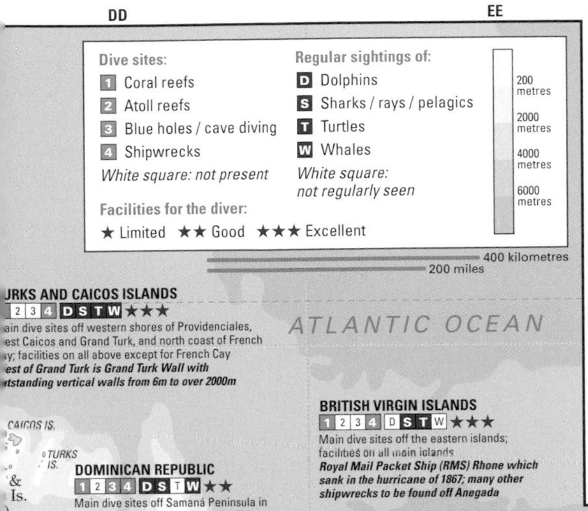

Legend

Dive sites:
1 Coral reefs
2 Atoll reefs
3 Blue holes / cave diving
4 Shipwrecks
White square: not present

Facilities for the diver:
★ Limited ★★ Good ★★★ Excellent

Regular sightings of:
D Dolphins
S Sharks / rays / pelagics
T Turtles
W Whales
White square: not regularly seen

200 metres
2000 metres
4000 metres
6000 metres

400 kilometres / 200 miles

This map shows the Caribbean's principal diving destinations and the main underwater attractions they have to offer. Details include the existence of coral reefs; atoll reefs (of which there are only four in the entire Caribbean); blue hole and cave diving plus the existence of shipwrecks (including wrecked aircraft). Whilst the diver may encounter turtle, shark, large rays and dolphin at any time – and whales occasionally – only those places where these are featured and regular sightings occur are indicated here.

Diving facilities for each destination, including availability of scuba diving equipment and related support services, are graded as limited, good or excellent. It must be emphasised that these grades are a general reflection on the overall availability of everything required by the visiting scuba diver and are not an interpretation of the standards found within any one facility or organisation.

Each diving destination provides every level of depth from the very shallow to the extremely deep.

Data compiled by Ned Middleton, all rights reserved.
email: ned.mIddleton@which.net

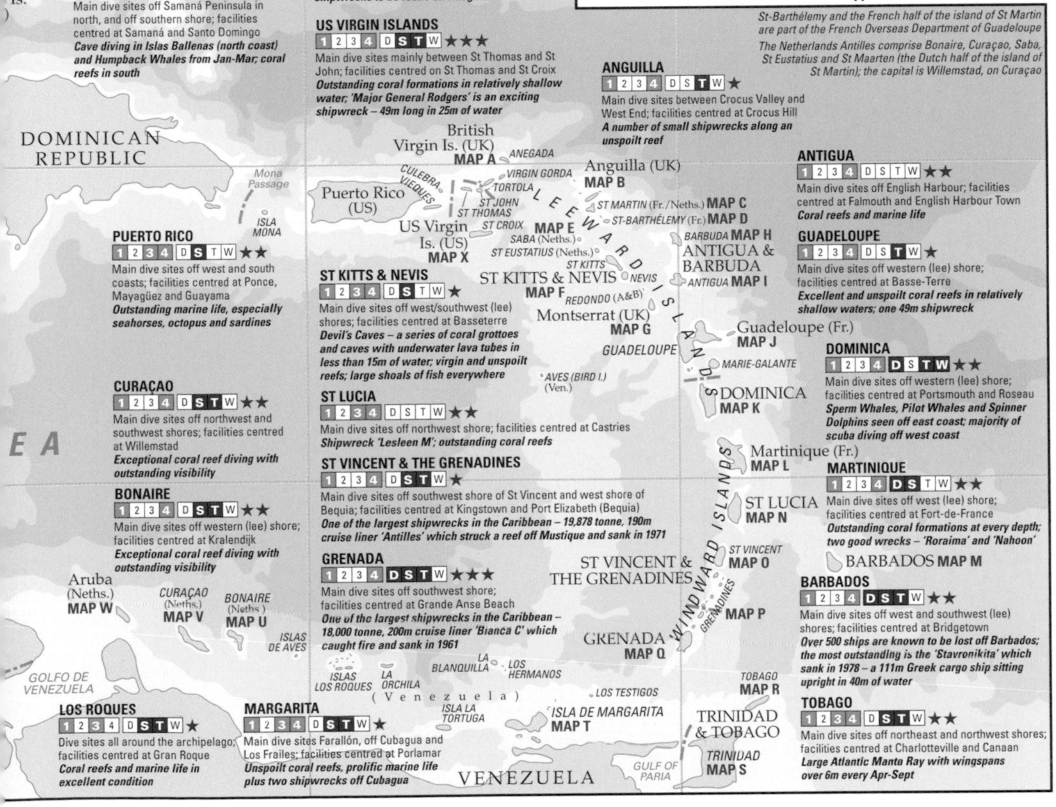

St-Barthélemy and the French half of the island of St Martin are part of the French Overseas Department of Guadeloupe. The Netherlands Antilles comprise Bonaire, Curaçao, Saba, St Eustatius and St Maarten (the Dutch half of the island of St Martin); the capital is Willemstad, on Curaçao.

ANTIGUA
DICKENSON BAY
LONG ISLAND
Cedar Grove
V.C. BIRD ✈
Fort James
PARHAM HARBOUR
GREAT BIRD I.
GUIANA I.
Fort Barrington
ST JOHN'S
Parham
Indian Town Point
FIVE ISLANDS HBR.
All Saints
Devil's Bridge
Bolans
SHEKERLEY MTNS
Freetown
GREEN I.
Boggy Peak 402m △
Potworks Dam
English Harbour Town
Falmouth
HORSE SHOE REEF
Nelson's Dockyard
Shirley Heights
Cape Shirley
CADES REEF
ENGLISH HARBOUR
10 km / 5 miles

GUADELOUPE
Pointe de la Grande Vigie
Anse-Bertrand
Port-Louis
GRANDE-TERRE
Ste-Rose
LE RAIZET ✈
Moule
LA DÉSIRADE
Pointe-à-Pitre
Pointe Noire
St-François
BASSE-TERRE
Gosier
Ste-Anne
Parc naturel
ÎLES DE LA PETITE TERRE
Soufrière 1467m △
St-Claude
Capesterre-Belle-Eau
BASSE-TERRE
Trois-Rivières
MARIE-GALANTE
LES SAINTES
Terre-de-Haut
Grand-Bourg
60 km / 30 miles

DOMINICA
Cape Capucin
Calibishie
Cabrits Nat. Park
Fort Shirley
Portsmouth
MELVILLE HALL ✈
Marigot
PRINCE RUPERT BAY
Morne Diablotins 1447m △
NORTHERN FOREST RESERVE
Carib Reserve
Colihaut
CENT. FOR. RES.
Castle Bruce
St Joseph
Emerald Pool
Mahaut
△ Morne Trois Pitons 1387m
Trafalgar Falls
La Plaine
CANEFIELD ✈
ROSEAU
WOODBRIDGE BAY
Morne Trois Pitons Nat. Park
SOUFRIÈRE BAY
Soufrière
GRAND BAY
Scotts Head
20 km / 10 miles

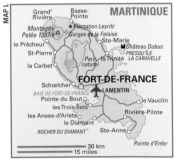

MARTINIQUE
Grand' Rivière
Basse-Pointe
Montagne Pelée 1397m △
Plantation Leyritz
Ste-Marie
le Prêcheur
Gorges de la Falaise
St-Pierre
Château Dubuc
PRESQU'ÎLE LA CARAVELLE
la Carbet
Parc naturel
la Trinité
Schoelcher
BAIE DE FORT-DE-FRANCE
FORT-DE-FRANCE
LAMENTIN ✈
Pointe du Bout
le Vauclin
les Trois-Îlets
les Anses-d'Arlets
le Diamant
ROCHER DU DIAMANT
Rivière-Pilote
Ste-Anne
Pointe d'Enfer
30 km / 15 miles

ATLANTIC OCEAN

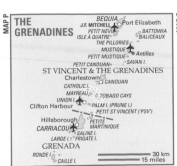

URKS AND CAICOS ISLANDS
1 2 3 4 D S T W ★★★
ain dive sites off western shores of Providenciales, est Caicos and Grand Turk, and north coast of French y; facilities on all above except for French Cay
est of Grand Turk is Grand Turk Wall with utstanding vertical walls from 6m to over 2000m

CAICOS IS.
TURKS IS.

DOMINICAN REPUBLIC
1 2 3 4 D S T W ★★
Main dive sites off Samaná Peninsula in north and off southern shore; facilities centred at Samaná and Santo Domingo
Cave diving in Islas Ballenas (north coast) and Humpback Whales from Jan-Mar; coral reefs in south

DOMINICAN REPUBLIC
Mona Passage
ISLA MONA

PUERTO RICO
1 2 3 4 D S T W ★★
Main dive sites off west and south coasts; facilities centred in Ponce, Mayagüez and Guayama
Outstanding marine life, especially seahorses, octopus and sardines

BRITISH VIRGIN ISLANDS
1 2 3 4 D S T W ★★★
Main dive sites off the eastern islands; facilities on all main islands
Royal Mail Packet Ship (RMS) Rhone which sank in the hurricane of 1867; many other shipwrecks to be found off Anegada

ANEGADA
CULEBRA
VIRGIN GORDA
VIEQUES
TORTOLA
British Virgin Is. (UK) MAP A
Puerto Rico (US)
ST JOHN
ST THOMAS
ST CROIX
US Virgin Is. (US) MAP X
SABA (Neths.)
ST EUSTATIUS (Neths.)

US VIRGIN ISLANDS
1 2 3 4 D S T W ★★
Main dive sites mainly between St Thomas and St John; facilities centred on St Thomas and St Croix
Outstanding coral formations in relatively shallow water; 'Major General Rodgers' is an exciting shipwreck – 49m long in 25m of water

ANGUILLA
1 2 3 4 D S T W ★
Main dive sites between Crocus Valley and West End; facilities centred at Crocus Hill
A number of small shipwrecks along an unspoilt reef

Anguilla (UK) MAP B
ST MARTIN (Fr. /Neths.) MAP C
ST-BARTHÉLEMY (Fr) MAP D
BARBUDA MAP H
ANTIGUA & BARBUDA
ANTIGUA MAP I

ANTIGUA
1 2 3 4 D S T W ★★
Main dive sites off English Harbour; facilities centred at Falmouth and English Harbour Town
Coral reefs and marine life

GUADELOUPE
1 2 3 4 D S T W ★★
Main dive sites off western (lee) shore; facilities centred at Basse-Terre
Excellent and unspoilt coral reefs in relatively shallow waters; one 49m shipwreck

DOMINICA
1 2 3 4 D S T W ★★
Main dive sites off western (lee) shore; facilities centred at Portsmouth and Roseau
Sperm Whales, Pilot Whales and Spinner Dolphins seen off east coast; majority of scuba diving off west coast

DOMINICAN REPUBLIC

ST KITTS & NEVIS
1 2 3 4 D S T W ★★
Main dive sites off west/southwest (lee) shores; facilities centred at Basseterre
Devil's Caves – a series of coral grottoes and caves with underwater lava tubes in less than 15m of water; virgin and unspoilt reefs; large shoals of fish everywhere

ST KITTS & NEVIS
REDONDO (A&B)
NEVIS
MAP F
Montserrat (UK) MAP G
GUADELOUPE
AVES (BIRD I.) (Ven.)
MARIE-GALANTE
Guadeloupe (Fr.) MAP J
DOMINICA MAP K

ST LUCIA
1 2 3 4 D S T W ★★
Main dive sites off northwest shore; facilities centred at Castries
Shipwreck 'Lesleen M'; outstanding coral reefs

ST LUCIA MAP N

ST VINCENT & THE GRENADINES
1 2 3 4 D S T W ★★
Main dive sites off southwest shore of St Vincent and west shore of Bequia; facilities centred at Kingstown and Port Elizabeth (Bequia)
One of the largest shipwrecks in the Caribbean, 190m 'Antilles' which struck a reef off Mustique and sank in 1971

ST VINCENT MAP O

GRENADA
1 2 3 4 D S T W ★★★
Main dive sites off southwest shore; facilities centred at Grande Anse Beach
One of the largest shipwrecks in the Caribbean – 18,000 tonne, 200m cruise liner 'Bianca C' which caught fire and sank in 1961

ST VINCENT & THE GRENADINES
GRENADINES
GRENADA MAP Q

CURAÇAO
1 2 3 4 D S T W ★★
Main dive sites off northwest and southwest shores; facilities centred at Willemstad
Exceptional coral reef diving with outstanding visibility

BONAIRE
1 2 3 4 D S T W ★★
Main dive sites off western (lee) shore; facilities centred at Kralendijk
Exceptional coral reef diving with outstanding visibility

Aruba (Neths.) MAP W
CURAÇAO (Neths.) MAP V
BONAIRE (Neths.) MAP U
ISLAS DE AVES

LOS ROQUES
1 2 3 4 D S T W
Dive sites all around the archipelago; facilities centred at Gran Roque
Coral reefs and marine life in excellent condition

GOLFO DE VENEZUELA
ISLAS LOS ROQUES
LA ORCHILA
LOS HERMANOS
LOS TESTIGOS
ISLA LA TORTUGA
LA BLANQUILLA

MARGARITA
1 2 3 4 D S T W
Main dive sites Farallón, off Cubagua and Los Frailes; facilities centred at Porlamar
Unspoilt coral reefs, prolific marine life plus two shipwrecks off Cubagua

ISLA DE MARGARITA MAP T
VENEZUELA
GULF OF PARIA

MARTINIQUE
1 2 3 4 D S T W ★★
Main dive sites off western (lee) shore; facilities centred at Fort-de-France
Outstanding coral formations at every depth; two good wrecks – 'Roraima' and 'Nahoon'

Martinique (Fr.) MAP L
BARBADOS MAP M

BARBADOS
1 2 3 4 D S T W ★★
Main dive sites off west and southwest (lee) shores; facilities centred at Bridgetown
Over 500 ships are known to be lost off Barbados; the most outstanding is the 'Stavronikita' which sank in 1978 – a 111m Greek cargo ship sitting upright in 40m of water

BARBADOS MAP R

TOBAGO
1 2 3 4 D S T W ★★
Main dive sites off northeast and northwest shores; facilities centred at Charlotteville and Canaan
Large Atlantic Manta Ray with wingspans over 6m every Apr-Sept

TOBAGO MAP R
TRINIDAD & TOBAGO
TRINIDAD MAP S

LEEWARD ISLANDS
WINDWARD ISLANDS
SEA

THE GRENADINES
BEQUIA
J.F. MITCHELL ✈
Port Elizabeth
PETIT NEVIS
ISLE À QUATRE
BATTOWIA
BALICEAUX
THE PILLORIES
PETIT MUSTIQUE
MUSTIQUE
ANTILLES
SAVAN I.
PETIT CANOUAN
ST VINCENT & THE GRENADINES
Charlestown
CANOUAN
CATHOLIC I.
MAYREAU
TOBAGO CAYS
UNION I.
PALM I. (PRUNE I.)
Clifton Harbour
PETIT ST VINCENT ('PSV')
Hillsborough
PETITE MARTINIQUE
CARRIACOU
SALINE I.
LARGE I.
FRIGATE I.
GRENADA
RONDE I.
CAILLE I.
30 km / 15 miles

ST VINCENT
Fancy
Cow and Calves
Falls of Baleine
La Soufrière 1234m △
Sandy Bay
Wallibou Beach
Richmond Beach
CHATEAUBELAIR I.
Crater Lake
MORNE GARU MOUNTAINS
Georgetown
Chateaubelair
Barrouallie
Greggs
Biabou
Layou
Botanic Gardens
Fort Charlotte
KINGSTOWN
Argyle Beach
KINGSTOWN BAY
FT. JOSHUA
Fort Duvernette
YOUNG I.
Stubbs
20 km / 10 miles

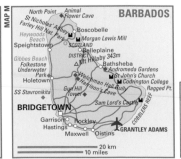 (ST LUCIA)

ST LUCIA
Pigeon I. Nat. Park
Pointe du Cap
Vigie Beach
ANSE LAVOUTTE
RODNEY BAY
Gros Islet
CASTRIES
GEORGE F.L. CHARLES ✈
Lesleen M
Fort Charlotte
Marigot Bay
Anse La Raye
FOND D'OR BAY
Canaries
Dennery
Mt Gimie 950m △
PRASLIN BAY
Soufrière
Diamond Gardens
Micoud
SOUFRIÈRE BAY
Petit Piton 743m △
Sulphur Springs
Gros Piton 798m △
La Pointe Beach
Choiseul
Laborie
Vieux Fort
HEWANORRA ✈
MARIA IS.
Cap Moule à Chique
20 km / 10 miles

BARBADOS
North Point
Animal Flower Cave
St Nicholas' Abbey
Farley Hill Nat. Park
Boscobelle
Heywoods
Morgan Lewis Mill
Speightstown
SCOTLAND DISTRICT
Belleplaine
Gibbes Beach
Mt Hillaby 343m △
Bathsheba
Holetown
Andromeda Gardens
St John's Church
Folkestone Underwater Park
Codrington College
Harrison's Hall Gully
SS Stavronikita
Welchman Hall Gully
Ragged Pt.
Gun Hill Tower
BRIDGETOWN
Sam Lord's Castle
COBBLERS REEF
Garrison
Rockley
GRANTLEY ADAMS ✈
Hastings
Maxwell
Oistins

1000 metres
500 metres
Sea level

20 km / 10 miles

Physical

Caribbean Sea

ATLANTIC OCEAN

PACIFIC OCEAN

NIC.

PANAMA

CIUDAD DE PANAMA (PANAMA CITY)

Colón · David · Colón 5800m △ · Cristóbal
Pico Cristóbal 5800m

Barranquilla · Santa Marta · Ríohacha · PEN. DE GUAJIRA
ARUBA (Neths.) · BONAIRE · CURAÇAO · Neths. Antilles

Cartagena · Maracaibo · Valencia · CARACAS · Petare · Cumaná
Barquisimeto · Maracay · Máturin

GUADELOUPE (Fr.)
DOMINICA
MARTINIQUE (Fr.)
ST LUCIA
ST VINCENT · BARBADOS
GRENADA
PORT OF SPAIN · TOBAGO
TRINIDAD & TOBAGO · TRINIDAD

Sincelejo · Montería · Valera · Mérida · Apure · San Fernando de Apure
Cúcuta · Acarigua · Ciudad Guayana · Ciudad Bolívar
Bucaramanga · San Cristóbal · Orinoco

Quibdó · Medellín · Manizales · Llanos · Puerto Ayacucho
Pereira · BOGOTÁ · Meta · Guaviare

VENEZUELA · GUYANA · SURINAM · French Guiana (Fr.)
GEORGETOWN · PARAMARIBO · CAYENNE

Buenaventura · Ibagué · Villavicencio
Páimira · Cáli · COLOMBIA · Boa Vista
Popayán · Florencia · Río Negro · Branco · Guiana Highlands

ECUADOR · Pasto · Uaupés
QUITO · Chimborazo 6310m △ · AMAZON
Equator 0°

Manta · Ambato · Napo · Amazonas · Amazon
Portoviejo · Guayaquil · Cuenca · Iquitos · Leticia · Santarém
Golfo de Guayaquil · Machala · Marañón · Manaus
Tumbes · Punta Pariñas · Sullana · Piura · BASIN · Selvas
Punta Negra · Chiclayo · Cajamarca · Cruzeiro do Sul · Jurua · Purus · BRAZIL

Mouths of the Amazon
ILHA DE MARAJÓ · Macapá · Bragança
Baía de Marajó · Belém
ILHA DE CAVIANA
Baía de São Marcos · São Luís
Tucuruí
Teresina · Fortaleza (Ceará)
Cabo de São Roque
Natal
Araguaína · Juàzeiro do Norte · João Pessoa
Recife (Pernambuco)
Petrolina · Jaboataó · Maceió
Juàzeiro · Aracaju

Trujillo · Pucallpa · Pôrto Velho · Rio Branco · Ariquemes
Chimbote · Huánuco · La Montaña · Madre de Dios · Vilhena · Telês Pires
Callao · Huancayo · PERU · Beni · Guaporé · Planalto de Mato Grosso
LIMA · Cuzco (Cusco) · Trinidad · Brazilian
Ayacucho · Ica · Juliaca · BOLIVIA · Cuiabá · Highlands
Arequipa · La Paz · Cochabamba · Caceres · Rondónópolis · BRASÍLIA
Nevado Sajama 6542m △ · Oruro · Santa Cruz · Goiânia
Tacna · Altiplano · Sucre · Potosí · Vitória da Conquista
Arica · Atacama · Rio Grande · Araguari · Ilheaus
Iquique · Corumba · Belo Horizonte · Governador Valadares
Calama · Concepción · Campo Grande · Vitória

Antofagasta · Paraguay · Ribeirão Prêto · Campinas · Nova Iguaçu
Ojos del Salado 6900m △ · PARAGUAY · Londrina · São Paulo · São Gonçalo
San Salvador de Jujuy · Pilcomayo · Sorocaba · Rio de Janeiro
Salta · ASUNCIÓN · Ciudad del Este · Santos
San Miguel de Tucumán · Salado · Formosa · Curitiba
Copiapó · Resistencia · Corrientes · Posadas · Uruguai · Florianópolis
Catamarca · Santiago del Estero · Uruguaiana · Santa Maria
La Serena · Laguna Mar Chiquita · Santa Fé · Rivera · Pôrto Alegre
Aconcagua 6960m △ · San Juan · Paraná · Concordia · Lagoa dos Patos
Córdoba · Paraná · Paysandú · Rio Grande
Vina del Mar · Mendoza · Rosario · URUGUAY · Lagoa Mirim
Valparaíso · San Luis · BUENOS AIRES · MONTEVIDEO
SANTIAGO · La Plata · Rio de la Plata · ATLANTIC OCEAN
Talca · ARGENTINA
Concepción · Pampas · Mar del Plata
Neuquén · Bahía Blanca
Temuco · Bahía Blanca
Valdivia · Rio Negro · Punta Rasa
Puerto Montt · Golfo San Matías · PENÍNSULA VALDÉS
ISLA DE CHILOÉ · Rawson
ARCHIPIÉLAGO DE LOS CHONOS · Golfo de San Jorge · Comodoro Rivadavia
Cabo Tres Puntas
Golfo de Penas · ISLA CAMPANA · Patagonia
ISLA WELLINGTON · Bahía Grande · Río Gallegos · FALKLAND ISLANDS (ISLAS MALVINAS) (UK)
ARCHIPIÉLAGO REINA ADELAIDA · Estrecho de Magallanes · Stanley
Punta Arenas · WEST FALKLAND · EAST FALKLAND
ISLA DESOLACIÓN · Tierra del Fuego · ISLA DE LOS ESTADOS
ISLA SANTE INÉS · Ushuaia · ISLA HOSTE · Cabo de Hornos (Cape Horn)

ISLAS DE LOS DESVENTURADOS
ISLAS JUAN FERNÁNDEZ

Tropic of Capricorn

PACIFIC OCEAN

ARCHIPIÉLAGO DE COLÓN (GALAPAGOS IS.) (Ec.)
I. PINTA · I. MARCHENA
I. FERNANDINA · I. SAN SALVADOR · I. SANTA CRUZ
ISLA ISABELA · Puerto Ayora · I. SAN CRISTÓBAL
I. SANTA MARÍA · I. ESPAÑOLA
Equator

QUITO
ECUADOR
Guayaquil
Golfo de Guayaquil
Punta Pariñas
Punta Negra
PERU
Trujillo

Lambert Equal Area Projection

1000 kilometres
500 miles

400 me · 200 me · 100 me · 500 me · 200 me · Sea level

Climate

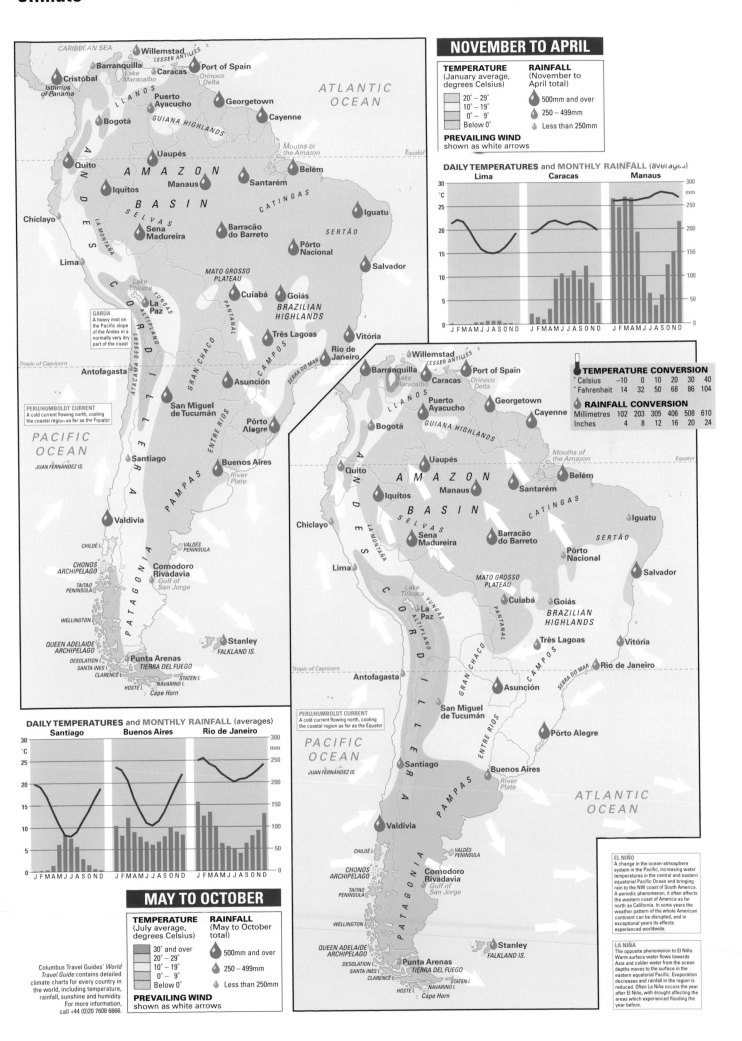

CARIBBEAN SEA
Willemstad
LESSER ANTILLES
Barranquilla
Cristóbal
Isthmus of Panama
Caracas
Port of Spain
Orinoco Delta
ATLANTIC OCEAN
Puerto Ayacucho
Georgetown
Bogotá
LLANOS
GUIANA HIGHLANDS
Cayenne
Uaupés
Mouths of the Amazon
Equator
Quito
Belém
Iquitos
Manaus
Santarém
AMAZON BASIN
Chiclayo
SELVAS
CATINGAS
Sena Madureira
Barracão do Barreto
Iguatu
Lima
SERTÃO
LA MONTAÑA
Pôrto Nacional
Salvador
MATO GROSSO PLATEAU
Lake Titicaca
YUNGAS
Cuiabá
Goiás
La Paz
BRAZILIAN HIGHLANDS
ALTIPLANO
PANTANAL
GARÚA
A heavy mist on the Pacific slope of the Andes in a normally very dry part of the coast
Tropic of Capricorn
Três Lagoas
Vitória
CAMPOS
Antofagasta
GRAN CHACO
Asunción
ENTRE RIOS
SERRA DO MAR
Rio de Janeiro
ATACAMA DESERT
CORDILLERA
San Miguel de Tucumán
PERU/HUMBOLDT CURRENT
A cold current flowing north, cooling the coastal region as far as the Equator
Pôrto Alegre
PACIFIC OCEAN
JUAN FERNÁNDEZ IS.
Santiago
Buenos Aires
River Plate
PAMPAS
Valdivia
CHILOÉ I.
VALDÉS PENINSULA
CHONOS ARCHIPELAGO
Comodoro Rivadavia
Gulf of San Jorge
TAITAO PENINSULA
WELLINGTON I.
PATAGONIA
QUEEN ADELAIDE ARCHIPELAGO
Stanley
FALKLAND IS.
DESOLATION I.
SANTA INÉS I.
CLARENCE I.
Punta Arenas
TIERRA DEL FUEGO
STATEN I.
NAVARINO I.
HOSTE I.
Cape Horn

NOVEMBER TO APRIL

TEMPERATURE
(January average, degrees Celsius)
- 20° – 29°
- 10° – 19°
- 0° – 9°
- Below 0°

PREVAILING WIND
shown as white arrows

RAINFALL
(November to April total)
- 500mm and over
- 250 – 499mm
- Less than 250mm

DAILY TEMPERATURES and MONTHLY RAINFALL (averages)

Lima   Caracas   Manaus

TEMPERATURE CONVERSION
°Celsius	–10	0	10	20	30	40
°Fahrenheit	14	32	50	68	86	104

RAINFALL CONVERSION
Millimetres	102	203	305	406	508	610
Inches	4	8	12	16	20	24

Willemstad
LESSER ANTILLES
Barranquilla
Lake Maracaibo
Caracas
Port of Spain
Orinoco Delta
Puerto Ayacucho
Georgetown
Bogotá
LLANOS
GUIANA HIGHLANDS
Cayenne
Uaupés
Mouths of the Amazon
Equator
Quito
Belém
Iquitos
Manaus
Santarém
AMAZON BASIN
Chiclayo
SELVAS
CATINGAS
Sena Madureira
Barracão do Barreto
LA MONTAÑA
Iguatu
Lima
SERTÃO
Pôrto Nacional
Salvador
MATO GROSSO PLATEAU
Lake Titicaca
YUNGAS
Cuiabá
Goiás
La Paz
BRAZILIAN HIGHLANDS
ALTIPLANO
PANTANAL
Três Lagoas
Vitória
CAMPOS
Tropic of Capricorn
Antofagasta
GRAN CHACO
Asunción
SERRA DO MAR
Rio de Janeiro
PERU/HUMBOLDT CURRENT
A cold current flowing north, cooling the coastal region as far as the Equator
San Miguel de Tucumán
CORDILLERA
ENTRE RIOS
Pôrto Alegre
PACIFIC OCEAN
JUAN FERNÁNDEZ IS.
Santiago
Buenos Aires
River Plate
PAMPAS
ATLANTIC OCEAN
Valdivia
CHILOÉ I.
VALDÉS PENINSULA
CHONOS ARCHIPELAGO
Comodoro Rivadavia
Gulf of San Jorge
TAITAO PENINSULA
PATAGONIA
WELLINGTON I.
QUEEN ADELAIDE ARCHIPELAGO
Stanley
FALKLAND IS.
DESOLATION I.
SANTA INÉS I.
CLARENCE I.
Punta Arenas
TIERRA DEL FUEGO
STATEN I.
NAVARINO I.
HOSTE I.
Cape Horn

EL NIÑO
A change in the ocean-atmosphere system in the Pacific, increasing water temperatures in the central and eastern equatorial Pacific Ocean and bringing rain to the NW coast of South America. A periodic phenomenon, it often affects the western coast of America as far north as California. In some years the weather pattern of the whole American continent can be disrupted, and in exceptional years its effects experienced worldwide.

LA NIÑA
The opposite phenomenon to El Niño. Warm surface water flows towards Asia and colder water from the ocean depths moves to the surface in the eastern equatorial Pacific. Evaporation decreases and rainfall in the region is reduced. Often La Niña occurs the year after El Niño, with drought affecting the areas which experienced flooding the year before.

DAILY TEMPERATURES and MONTHLY RAINFALL (averages)

Santiago   Buenos Aires   Rio de Janeiro

MAY TO OCTOBER

TEMPERATURE
(July average, degrees Celsius)
- 30° and over
- 20° – 29°
- 10° – 19°
- 0° – 9°
- Below 0°

PREVAILING WIND
shown as white arrows

RAINFALL
(May to October total)
- 500mm and over
- 250 – 499mm
- Less than 250mm

Columbus Travel Guides' *World Travel Guide* contains detailed climate charts for every country in the world, including temperature, rainfall, sunshine and humidity. For more information, call +44 (0)20 7608 6666.

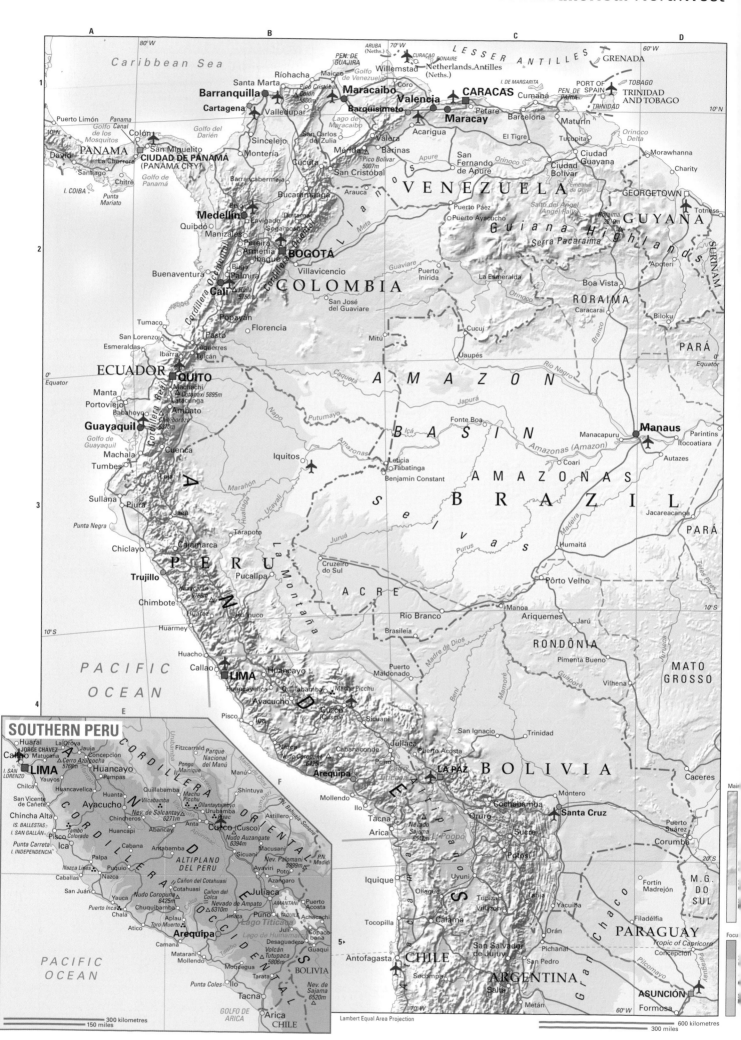

Caribbean Sea

LESSER ANTILLES

GRENADA

PORT OF SPAIN
TRINIDAD AND TOBAGO

PANAMA

Golfo de Panamá

PACIFIC OCEAN

COLOMBIA

VENEZUELA

GUYANA

SURINAM

RORAIMA

PARÁ

ECUADOR

A M A Z O N

B A S I N

BRAZIL

AMAZONAS

PERU

PARÁ

ACRE

RONDÔNIA

MATO GROSSO

BOLIVIA

PARAGUAY

PACIFIC OCEAN

CHILE

ARGENTINA

ASUNCIÓN

SOUTHERN PERU

CORDILLERA OCCIDENTAL

CORDILLERA ORIENTAL

ALTIPLANO DEL PERU

PACIFIC OCEAN

BOLIVIA

CHILE

150 miles
300 kilometres

Lambert Equal Area Projection

300 miles
600 kilometres

South America: East

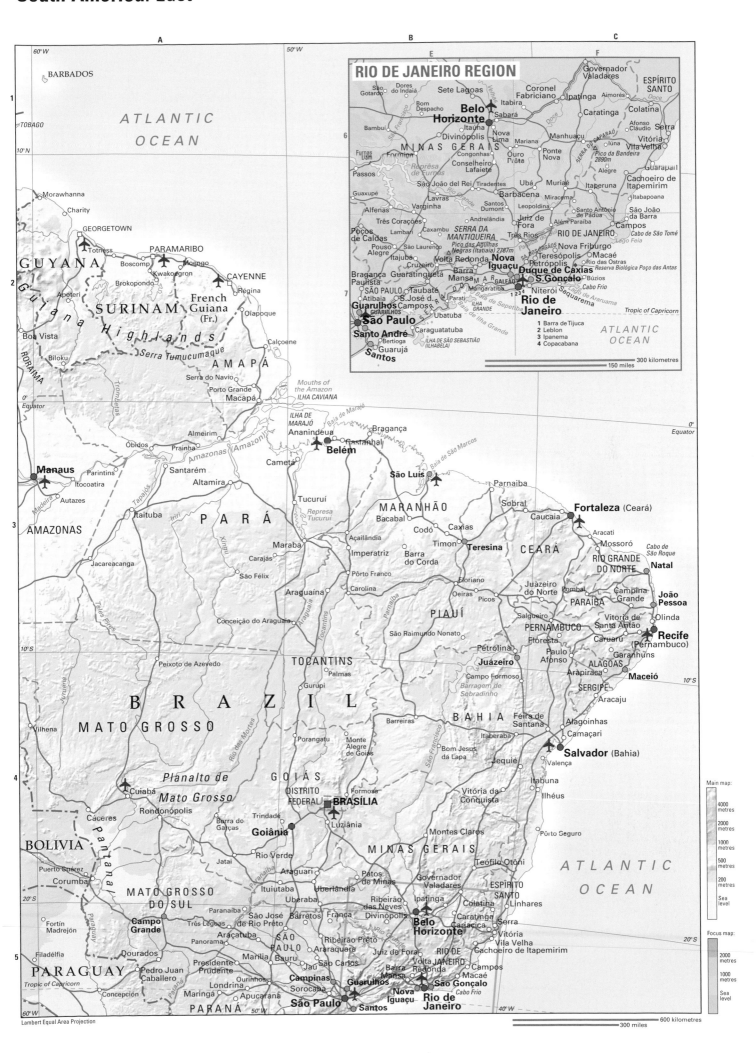

RIO DE JANEIRO REGION

BARBADOS

ATLANTIC OCEAN

TOBAGO

60°W

50°W

40°W

10°N

Morawhanna
Charity
GEORGETOWN
Totness
PARAMARIBO
GUYANA
Boscomp
Moengo
Apoteri
Brokopondo
Kwakoegron
CAYENNE
Régina
SURINAM
French Guiana (Fr.)
Oïapoque
Boa Vista
RORAIMA
Biloku
Serra Tumucumaque
Serra do Navio
Calçoene

Dores do Indaiá
São Gotardo
Sete Lagoas
Coronel Fabriciano
Ipatinga
Aimorés
Governador Valadares
ESPÍRITO SANTO
Bom Despacho
Belo Horizonte
Itabira
Caratinga
Colatina
Sabará
Doce
Bambuí
Nova Lima
Manhuaçu
Afonso Cláudio
Serra
MINAS GERAIS
Itaúna
Mariana
Iúna
Vitória
Divinópolis
Ouro Prêto
Ponte Nova
Pico da Bandeira 2890m
Vila Velha
Furnas
Congonhas
Conselheiro Lafaiete
SERRA DO CAPARAÓ
Guarapari
Formiga
Represa de Furnas
Passos
São João del Rei
Tiradentes
Ubá
Muriaé
Itaperuna
Cachoeiro de Itapemirim
Itabapoana
Guaxupé
Lavras
Barbacena
Miracema
Poços de Caldas
Alfenas
Varginha
Santos Dumont
Leopoldina
Santo Antônio de Pádua
São João da Barra
Três Corações
Andrelândia
Juiz de Fora
Além Paraíba
Campos
Lambari
Caxambu
Três Rios
RIO DE JANEIRO
Cabo de São Tomé
Pouso Alegre
São Lourenço
SERRA DA MANTIQUEIRA
Nova Friburgo
Lago Feia
Itajubá
Pico das Agulhas Negras (Itatiaia) 2787m
Macaé
Cruzeiro
Volta Redonda
Teresópolis
Rio das Ostras
Bragança Paulista
Guaratinguetá
Barra Mansa
Nova Iguaçu
Petrópolis
Reserva Biológica Poço das Antas
Tropic of Capricorn
SÃO PAULO
Taubaté
GALEÃO
Duque de Caxias
Búzios
Atibaia
S.José d.
Mangaratiba
S. Gonçalo
Cabo Frio
Guarulhos
Campos
Niterói
Rio de Janeiro
Saquarema
São Paulo
Parati
Baía de Sepetiba
1234
Lagoa de Araruama
Santo André
Guarujá
Ubatuba
ILHA GRANDE
Baía de Ilha Grande
ATLANTIC OCEAN
Bertioga
Caraguatatuba
Santos
ILHA DE SÃO SEBASTIÃO (ILHABELA)

1 Barra de Tijuca
2 Leblon
3 Ipanema
4 Copacabana

300 kilometres
150 miles

Mouths of the Amazon
ILHA CAVIANA
0° Equator

Almeirim
ILHA DE MARAJÓ
Baía de Marajó
Bragança
Equator 0°

Óbidos
Prainha
Amazonas (Amazon)
Ananindeua
Castanhal
Manaus
Parintins
Santarém
Cametá
Belém
Itacoatiara
Autazes
Altamira
São Luís
Parnaíba
AMAZONAS
Tucuruí
Represa Tucuruí
MARANHÃO
Sobral
Fortaleza (Ceará)
Itaituba
Inri
PARÁ
Açailândia
Bacabal
Caucaia
Aracati
Mossoró
Jacareacanga
Marabá
Imperatriz
Codó
Caxias
Timon
CEARÁ
RIO GRANDE DO NORTE
Cabo de São Roque
Carajás
Barra do Corda
Teresina
Natal
São Félix
Pôrto Franco
Floriano
Juàzeiro do Norte
Pombal
Campina Grande
João Pessoa
Araguaína
Carolina
Oeiras
Picos
PARAÍBA
Salgueiro
Olinda
Conceição do Araguaia
PIAUÍ
São Raimundo Nonato
PERNAMBUCO
Vitória de Santa Antão
Recife (Pernambuco)
Petrolina
Floresta
Caruaru
Peixoto de Azevedo
TOCANTINS
Paulo Afonso
Garanhuns
Palmas
Juàzeiro
ALAGOAS
Arapiraca
Maceió
Gurupi
Campo Formoso
SERGIPE
Barragem de Sobradinho
Aracaju
BRAZIL
Vilhena
MATO GROSSO
BAHIA
Feira de Santana
Alagoinhas
Barreiras
Itaberaba
Camaçari
Rio das Mortes
Bom Jesus da Lapa
Salvador (Bahia)
Porangatu
Monte Alegre de Goiás
Jequié
Valença
Cuiabá
Planalto de Mato Grosso
GOIÁS
Vitória da Conquista
Itabuna
Cáceres
Ilhéus
Rondonópolis
DISTRITO FEDERAL
Formosa
BRASÍLIA
BOLIVIA
Barra do Garças
Trindade
Luziânia
Montes Claros
Pôrto Seguro
Goiânia
MINAS GERAIS
ATLANTIC OCEAN
Rio Verde
Teófilo Otoni
Puerto Suárez
Jataí
Corumbá
Governador Valadares
ESPÍRITO SANTO
Araguari
Patos de Minas
Ipatinga
Fortín Madrejón
MATO GROSSO DO SUL
Ituiutaba
Uberaba
Ribeirão das Neves
Colatina
Linhares
Paranaíba
Uberlândia
Divinópolis
Cariacica
Serra
Campo Grande
Três Lagoas
São José de Rio Prêto
Barretos
Franca
Belo Horizonte
Vitória
Filadélfia
Araçatuba
SÃO PAULO
Ribeirão Prêto
Vila Velha
Fortín Madrejón
Panorama
Juiz de Fora
Cachoeiro de Itapemirim
PARAGUAY
Presidente Prudente
Marília
Bauru
São Carlos
RIO DE JANEIRO
Campos
Tropic of Capricorn
Jaú
Campinas
Guarulhos
São Gonçalo
Macaé
Pedro Juan Caballero
Dourados
Londrina
Apucarana
Sorocaba
Volta Redonda
Cabo Frio
Concepción
Maringá
Ourinhos
Barra Mansa
Nova Iguaçu
São Paulo
Santos
Rio de Janeiro
PARANÁ

600 kilometres
300 miles

Main map:
4000 metres
2000 metres
1000 metres
500 metres
200 metres
Sea level

Focus map:
2000 metres
1000 metres
Sea level

Tacna
Arica
Iquique
Tocopilla
Antofagasta
Copiapó
Vallenar
La Serena
Coquimbo
Ovalle
Viña del Mar
Valparaíso
Rancagua
Pichilemu
Constitución
Talca
Chillán
Talcahuano
Concepción
Lebu
Los Angeles
Temuco
Valdivia
Osorno
Puerto Montt

BOLIVIA
Oruro
Potosí
Uyuni
Villazón
Tupiza
Tarija
Yacuiba
Orán
San Pedro
Pichanal
San Salvador de Jujuy
Socompa
Salta
Metán
Táfi Viejo
San Miguel de Tucumán
Tinogasta
Catamarca
Santiago del Estero
La Rioja
San Juan
Deán Funes
Córdoba
San Francisco
Villa María
Rufino
Las Heras
Mendoza
Los Andes
SANTIAGO
Puente Alto
San Rafael
San Luis
Mercedes
Río Cuarto
Junín
Lomas de Zamora
Malargüe
Santa Rosa
Chos Malal
Neuquén
Zapala
General Roca
Choele Choel
Río Colorado
Punta Alta
San Antonio Oeste
Viedma
San Carlos de Bariloche
Esquel
Nueva Lubecká
Rawson
Sarmiento
Comodoro Rivadavia
Fitz Roy
Cabo Tres Puntas
Puerto Deseado
Gobernador Gregores
San Julián
Puerto Santa Cruz
Calafate
Río Gallegos
Punta Arenas
San Sebastián
Río Grande
Ushuaia

PARAGUAY
ASUNCIÓN
Formosa
Filadélfia
Fortín Madrejón
Concepción
Coronel Oviedo
Villarrica
Presidencia Roque Sáenz Peña
Resistencia
Corrientes
Posadas
Encarnación
Santa Fé
Paraná
Rosario
Buenos Aires
La Plata
Montevideo

BRAZIL
Corumbá
Campo Grande
Dourados
Curitiba
São Paulo
Santos

ATLANTIC OCEAN

RIVER PLATE REGION

FALKLAND ISLANDS (ISLAS MALVINAS) (UK)
WEST FALKLAND
EAST FALKLAND
Stanley

Lambert Equal Area Projection

600 kilometres
300 miles

Arctic & Antarctic

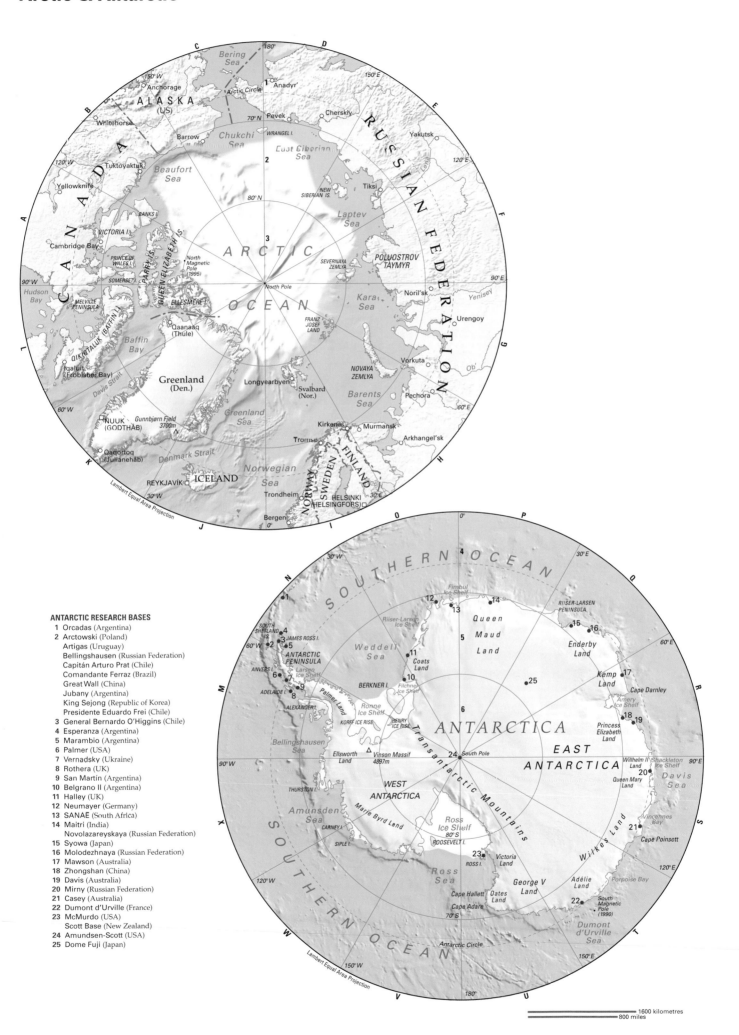

ANTARCTIC RESEARCH BASES

1 Orcadas (Argentina)
2 Arctowski (Poland)
  Artigas (Uruguay)
  Bellingshausen (Russian Federation)
  Capitán Arturo Prat (Chile)
  Comandante Ferraz (Brazil)
  Great Wall (China)
  Jubany (Argentina)
  King Sejong (Republic of Korea)
  Presidente Eduardo Frei (Chile)
3 General Bernardo O'Higgins (Chile)
4 Esperanza (Argentina)
5 Marambio (Argentina)
6 Palmer (USA)
7 Vernadsky (Ukraine)
8 Rothera (UK)
9 San Martín (Argentina)
10 Belgrano II (Argentina)
11 Halley (UK)
12 Neumayer (Germany)
13 SANAE (South Africa)
14 Maitri (India)
  Novolazareyskaya (Russian Federation)
15 Syowa (Japan)
16 Molodezhnaya (Russian Federation)
17 Mawson (Australia)
18 Zhongshan (China)
19 Davis (Australia)
20 Mirny (Russian Federation)
21 Casey (Australia)
22 Dumont d'Urville (France)
23 McMurdo (USA)
  Scott Base (New Zealand)
24 Amundsen-Scott (USA)
25 Dome Fuji (Japan)

1600 kilometres
800 miles

The flags of all the independent states of the world and several dependencies are shown below. Certain states have several different flags – sometimes as many as six – each of which has specific civil, naval, military or governmental usage. In such cases, the most widely used version has generally been shown. Flags for a selection of major international institutions have also been included.

Even in official usage, colours of flags vary considerably, so the tints employed below are not intended to be definitive. Designs are also subject to variation from time to time. Up-to-date information on these and the many flags not shown here, and on vexillological matters generally, may be obtained from The Flag Research Center, Winchester, Mass., USA; or The Flag Institute, Chester, UK.

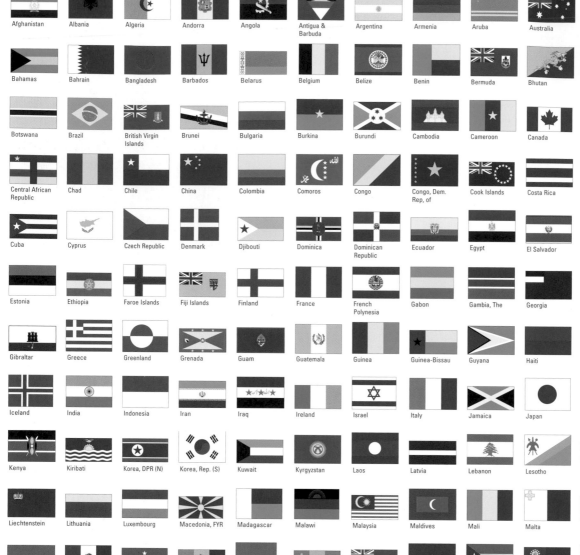

Afghanistan	Albania	Algeria	Andorra	Angola	Antigua & Barbuda	Argentina	Armenia	Aruba	Australia	Austria	Azerbaijan
Bahamas	Bahrain	Bangladesh	Barbados	Belarus	Belgium	Belize	Benin	Bermuda	Bhutan	Bolivia	Bosnia-Herzegovina
Botswana	Brazil	British Virgin Islands	Brunei	Bulgaria	Burkina	Burundi	Cambodia	Cameroon	Canada	Cape Verde	Cayman Islands
Central African Republic	Chad	Chile	China	Colombia	Comoros	Congo	Congo, Dem. Rep, of	Cook Islands	Costa Rica	Côte d'Ivoire	Croatia
Cuba	Cyprus	Czech Republic	Denmark	Djibouti	Dominica	Dominican Republic	Ecuador	Egypt	El Salvador	Equatorial Guinea	Eritrea
Estonia	Ethiopia	Faroe Islands	Fiji Islands	Finland	France	French Polynesia	Gabon	Gambia, The	Georgia	Germany	Ghana
Gibraltar	Greece	Greenland	Grenada	Guam	Guatemala	Guinea	Guinea-Bissau	Guyana	Haiti	Honduras	Hungary
Iceland	India	Indonesia	Iran	Iraq	Ireland	Israel	Italy	Jamaica	Japan	Jordan	Kazakstan
Kenya	Kiribati	Korea, DPR (N)	Korea, Rep. (S)	Kuwait	Kyrgyzstan	Laos	Latvia	Lebanon	Lesotho	Liberia	Libya
Liechtenstein	Lithuania	Luxembourg	Macedonia, FYR	Madagascar	Malawi	Malaysia	Maldives	Mali	Malta	Marshall Islands	Mauritania
Mauritius	Mexico	Micronesia, Fed. States of	Moldova	Monaco	Mongolia	Montserrat	Morocco	Mozambique	Myanmar	Namibia	Nauru
Nepal	Netherlands	New Zealand	Nicaragua	Niger	Nigeria	Niue	Northern Mariana Islands	Norway	Oman	Pakistan	Palau
Palastine NAR	Panama	Papua New Guinea	Paraguay	Peru	Philippines	Poland	Portugal	Puerto Rico	Qatar	Romania	Russia
Rwanda	St Helena	St Kitts & Nevis	St Lucia	St Vincent & the Grenadines	Samoa	San Marino	São Tomé e Príncipe	Saudi Arabia	Senegal	Seychelles	Sierra Leone
Singapore	Slovak Republic	Slovenia	Solomon Islands	Somalia	South Africa	Spain	Sri Lanka	Sudan	Surinam	Swaziland	Sweden
Switzerland	Syria	Taiwan	Tajikistan	Tanzania	Thailand	Togo	Tonga	Trinidad & Tobago	Tunisia	Turkey	Turkmenistan
Turks & Caicos Islands	Tuvalu	Uganda	Ukraine	United Arab Emirates	United Kingdom	United States of America	Uruguay	Uzbekistan	Vanuatu	Vatican City	Venezuela
Vietnam	Western Saraha	Yemen	Yugoslavia	Zambia	Zimbabwe	Antarctica	European Union	United Nations	Red Crescent	Red Cross	Olympic

Appendices 1–4

1: GEOGRAPHICAL DEFINITIONS

The following list includes names and abbreviations which appear in this atlas, together with other terms that are commonly used in the travel industry. Various authorities differ on the exact definitions of some of these entries; the definitions given here are those which are generally understood within the travel trade. For principal world and regional organisations, see pages 24-25.

Arabian Peninsula
Geographical region comprising: Bahrain, Kuwait, Oman, Qatar, Saudi Arabia, United Arab Emirates, Yemen.

Australasia
Geographical region comprising: Australia, New Caledonia, New Zealand, Solomon Islands, Vanuatu and the island of New Guinea including all of Papua New Guinea. Often described as equivalent to all of Oceania between the Equator and 47ûS. The term is not commonly used in Australia and New Zealand because of confusion with Australia itself.

Bahama Islands
Group of islands in the Atlantic Ocean comprising the Commonwealth of The Bahamas and the Turks and Caicos Islands.

Balkans, The
The Balkan Peninsula, which is bordered by the Adriatic and Ionian Seas to the west, the Aegean and Black Seas to the east and the Mediterranean Sea to the south. The countries occupying this peninsula are described as Balkan states: Albania, Bosnia-Herzegovina, Bulgaria, Croatia, Greece, Former Yugoslav Republic of Macedonia, Romania, Slovenia, Federal Republic of Yugoslavia and the European part of Turkey.

Borneo
Island in the Malay Archipelago (qv) divided between Brunei, Indonesia (the provinces of Central, East, South and West Kalimantan) and Malaysia (the states of Sabah and Sarawak).

British Isles
Geographical region comprising: United Kingdom (qv), Republic of Ireland, Isle of Man, Channel Islands.

Caribbean
General tourist destination term used to describe the West Indies (qv).

Caroline Islands
Archipelago in the west Pacific Ocean. Islands comprise the Federated States of Micronesia and Palau.

Celebes
Island in the Malay Archipelago (qv), Sulawesi in Indonesian.

Central America
Geographical region comprising: Belize, Costa Rica, El Salvador, Guatemala, Honduras, Nicaragua, Panama. Usually considered part of the North American (qv) continent.

Ceylon
Island off the southeast coast of India, officially Sri Lanka.

Channel Islands
Group of islands comprising Jersey, Guernsey, Alderney, Sark and Herm, situated off the northwest coast of France. They are possessions of the British Crown and not officially part of the United Kingdom (qv).

East Indies
General geographical term sometimes applied loosely to India, Indochina and the Malay Archipelago (qv). Often used as alternative to the Malay Archipelago or the Republic of Indonesia itself. The term is now rarely used.

Europe
Continent. Northern boundary formed by Arctic Ocean. Eastern boundary formed by Ural Mountains, Ural River and Caspian Sea. Southern boundary formed by Caucasus Mountains, Black Sea, Bosporus, Aegean Sea and Mediterranean Sea. Western boundary formed by Atlantic Ocean. Includes Iceland, Svalbard and area of Turkey west of the Bosporus.

Far East
General geographical term describing east and South-East Asia: Brunei, Cambodia, China, Indonesia, Japan, Democratic People's Republic of Korea (North Korea), Republic of Korea (South Korea), Laos, Malaysia, Myanmar, the Philippines, Singapore, Taiwan, Thailand, Vietnam. Sometimes extended to include Mongolia and the eastern Siberian region of the Russian Federation.

Formosa
Island off the southeast coast of the People's Republic of China, known variously as the Republic of China or Taiwan.

Great Britain
Geographical region comprising: England, Scotland, Wales.

Greater Antilles
Group of Caribbean islands comprising: Cayman Islands, Cuba, Hispaniola, Jamaica, Puerto Rico.

Hispaniola
Island in the Greater Antilles (qv) divided between the Dominican Republic and Haiti.

Iberia
Peninsula in southwest Europe occupied by Spain, Portugal, Andorra and Gibraltar.

Indochina
Geographical region comprising: Cambodia, Laos, Peninsular Malaysia, Myanmar, Singapore, Thailand, Vietnam.

International Air Transport Association (IATA)
An association which acts as a governing body of the major airlines, responsible for establishing fare levels and for rules and regulations concerning international passenger and cargo services. It has over 100 tariff members and a further 100 trade associate airlines.

Latin America
Defined either as: the Spanish- and Portuguese-speaking speaking countries of the Americas (sometimes also including French-speaking Haiti); or all of the Americas south of the United States. This latter, more general, definition is the one used in this atlas.

Lesser Antilles
Group of Caribbean islands comprising: Leeward Islands (qv), Windward Islands (qv), Aruba, Barbados, Bonaire, Cura≤ao, Trinidad and Tobago. Also includes the chain of small Venezuelan islands east of Bonaire.

Leeward Islands
Group of Caribbean islands comprising: Anguilla, Antigua and Barbuda, Dominica, Guadeloupe, Montserrat, Saba, St Eustatius, St Kitts and Nevis, St Maarten/St Martin, Virgin Islands.

Low Countries
Geographical region comprising: Belgium, Luxembourg, The Netherlands.

Maghreb
Arabic name for northwest Africa and, during the Moorish period, Spain. Algeria, Morocco and Tunisia are described as Maghreb countries.

Malay Archipelago
The largest island group in the world, off the southeast coast of Asia and between the Indian and Pacific Oceans. Major islands include Borneo (qv), Sulawesi (Celebes, qv), Jawa (Java), New Guinea and Sumatera (Sumatra). Countries within this archipelago: Brunei, Indonesia, East Malaysia, Papua New Guinea, the Philippines.

Mediterranean
General tourist destination term used to describe the islands of the Mediterranean Sea and the countries bordering it.

Melanesia
Collective name for the islands in the southwest Pacific Ocean, south of the Equator and northeast of Australia. Includes: Fiji Islands, Nauru, New Caledonia, Papua New Guinea (excluding New Guinea mainland), Solomon Islands, Vanuatu.

Micronesia
Collective name for the islands in the west Pacific Ocean, north of the Equator and east of the Philippines. Includes: Guam, Kiribati (west), Marshall Islands, Federated States of Micronesia, Northern Mariana Islands, Palau.

Middle East
General geographical term describing a loosely defined area comprising: countries of the Arabian Peninsula, Egypt, Iran, Iraq, Israel, Jordan, Lebanon, Syria. Sometimes extended to include Algeria, Cyprus, Libya, Morocco, Sudan, Tunisia and Turkey.

Near East
Rarely used general geographical term describing an area of SW Asia: the Arabian Peninsula, Cyprus, Israel, Jordan, Lebanon, Syria, Turkey. Often extended to Egypt and Sudan.

Netherlands Antilles
Islands of the West Indies administered by The Netherlands, comprising: Bonaire, Curaçao, Saba, St Eustatius, St Maarten. Aruba, formerly part of the Netherlands Antilles is now administered from The Netherlands separately.

New Guinea
Island in the Malay Archipelago (qv) divided between Papua New Guinea and the Indonesian province of Irian Jaya.

North America
Continent comprising: USA, Canada, Mexico, Bermuda, West Indies (qv). Usually considered to also include Central America and Greenland.

Oceania
General geographical term describing the islands of the central and south Pacific Ocean, including Melanesia, Micronesia and Polynesia. Sometimes extended to include Australia, New Zealand and the Malay Archipelago (qv).

Polynesia
Collective name for the islands of the central and south Pacific Ocean. Includes: American Samoa, Cook Islands, Easter Island, French Polynesia, Hawaii, Kiribati (east), New Zealand, Niue, Pitcairn Islands, Samoa, Tokelau, Tonga, Tuvalu, Wallis & Futuna.

Scandinavia
Geographical region comprising: Denmark, Norway, Sweden. Often extended to include Finland and Iceland.

South America
Continent comprising: countries on mainland south of Panama, Falkland Islands, Galapagos Islands.

Ulster
Geographical region comprising Northern Ireland plus the counties of Cavan, Donegal and Monaghan in the Republic of Ireland. It is often used (incorrectly) as an unofficial term to describe Northern Ireland.

United Kingdom
Country comprising Great Britain (qv) and Northern Ireland. The Isle of Man and the Channel Islands are Crown dependencies and not officially part of the UK.

West Indies
Islands enclosing the Caribbean Sea, comprising: Bahama Islands (qv), Greater Antilles (qv), Lesser Antilles (qv).

Windward Islands
Group of Caribbean islands comprising: Grenada, Martinique, St Lucia, St Vincent and The Grenadines.

World-Wide Fund For Nature / World Wildlife Fund (WWF)
One of the world's largest private international nature conservation organisations. Its aim is to conserve nature by preserving genetic, species and ecosystem diversity.

2: HIGHEST & LOWEST

Name	*Metres*	*Feet*	*Country*
AFRICA			
Kilimanjaro (Kibo)	5,895	19,340	Tanzania
Lake Assal	–155	–509	Djibouti
ANTARCTICA			
Vinson Massif	4,897	16,066	Antarctica
(ice covered)	–2,538	–8,327	Antarctica
ASIA			
Everest (Qomolangma Feng/ Sagarmatha)	8,850	29,035	China-Nepal
Dead Sea	–411	–1,349	Israel-Jordan-Palestine
AUSTRALASIA & OCEANIA			
Aoraki (Cook)	3,754	12,315	New Zealand
Lake Eyre	–16	–52	Australia
EUROPE & RUSSIAN FEDERATION			
Elbrus	5,642	18,510	Russian Fed.
Caspian Sea	–28	–92	Russia-C. Asia-Caucasus
NORTH AMERICA			
McKinley (Denali)	6,194	20,321	Alaska, USA
Death Valley	–86	–282	California, USA
SOUTH AMERICA			
Aconcagua	6,960	22,834	Argentina
G. Bajo de S. Julián	–105	–344	Argentina

Name	*Metres*	*Feet*	*Country*
SOME OTHER NOTABLE MOUNTAINS			
K2 (Chogori/ Qogir Feng)	8,611	28,250	China-Kashmir
Kangchenjunga	8,586	28,170	India-Nepal
Makalu	8,463	27,766	China-Nepal
Dhaulagiri	8,167	26,795	Nepal
Nanga Parbat	8,126	26,660	Kashmir
Annapurna	8,091	26,545	Nepal
Gosainthan (Xixabangma Feng)	8,013	26,289	China
Qullai Garmo	7,495	24,590	Tajikistan
Ojos del Salado	6,908	22,664	Argentina-Chile
Huascarán	6,768	22,205	Peru
Logan	5,959	19,550	Yukon, Canada
Damavand	5,681	18,638	Iran
Citlaltépetl (Orizaba)	5,610	18,405	Mexico
Kenya (Kirinyaga)	5,199	17,057	Kenya
Ararat	5,165	16,946	Turkey
Mont Blanc	4,808	15,774	France-Italy
Ras Dashen	4,533	14,872	Ethiopia
Whitney	4,418	14,495	California, USA
Kinabalu	4,094	13,432	Malaysia
Fuji	3,776	12,388	Japan

3: THE WORLD'S LONGEST RIVERS

Local names are shown in square brackets: [ ]

River	*Length: (km)*	*(miles)*	*Source(s) and outflow*
Nile Luvironza-Ruvuvu-Kagera-White Nile	6,825	4,240	Lake Victoria region – Mediterranean Sea
Amazon Apurimac-Ene-Tambo-Ucayali	6,516	4,049	Peruvian Andes – Atlantic Ocean
Chang Jiang (Yangtze) [Tuotuo-Tongtian-Jinsha]	6,380	3,964	Tanggula Shan, China – East China Sea
Mississippi-Missouri Red Rock-Beaverhead	5,969	3,709	SW Montana – Gulf of Mexico
Ob-Irtysh [Ertix]	5,568	3,459	Altay Mountains, China – Kara Sea
Yenisey Selenga-Angara	5,550	3,448	Western Mongolia – Kara Sea
Huang He (Yellow)	5,464	3,395	Bayan Har Shan, China – Yellow Sea
Congo Lualaba	4,667	2,900	Katanga Plateau, Congo D.R. – Atlantic Ocean
Paraná Río de la Plata	4,500	2,796	Serra da Mantiquera, Brazil – Atlantic Ocean
Mekong [Za-Lancang]	4,425	2,749	Tanggula Shan, China – South China Sea
Amur Kerulen-Argun	4,416	2,744	Eastern Mongolia – Sea of Japan
Lena Kirenga	4,400	2,734	Baikal Mtns, Russian Fed., – Laptev Sea
Mackenzie Finlay-Peace-Slave	4,241	2,635	Omineca Mtns, BC, Canada– Beaufort Sea
Niger [Joliba/Kworra]	4,184	2,599	Guinea/Sierra Leone border – Gulf of Guinea
Murray-Darling	3,750	2,330	Gt. Dividing Range, Australia – Southern Ocean

4: CONVERSIONS

Kilometres	**10**	**20**	**30**	**40**	**50**	**60**	**70**	**80**	**90**	**100**
Miles	6.2	12.4	18.6	24.9	31.1	37.3	43.5	49.7	55.9	62.1
Metres	**10**	**20**	**30**	**40**	**50**	**60**	**70**	**80**	**90**	**100**
Feet	33	66	98	131	164	197	230	262	295	328

Centimetres	**10**	**20**	**30**	**40**	**50**	**60**	**70**	**80**	**90**	**100**
Inches	3.9	7.9	11.8	15.7	19.7	23.6	27.6	31.5	35.4	39.4
°Centigrade	**-10**	**-5**	**0**	**5**	**10**	**15**	**20**	**25**	**30**	**35**
°Fahrenheit	14	23	32	41	50	59	68	77	86	95

5: GLOSSARY OF FOREIGN GEOGRAPHICAL TERMS

The following list provides the English equivalents for some of the most common foreign geographical terms used in this atlas and other international atlases.

Å, -å	Danish, Norwegian	Stream
Abar, Abyar	Arabic	Wells
Açude	Portuguese	Reservoir
Adalar	Turkish	Islands
Adasi	Turkish	Island
Agía, Ágios	Greek	Saint
Aiguille(s)	French	Peak(s)
Ain, Aïn	Arabic	Spring, well
-air	Indonesian	Stream
Åkra, Akrotírion	Greek	Cape, point
Ala-	Finnish	Lower
A'lá	Arabic	Upper
Alt-	German	Old
Alta, Alto	Italian, Portug., Spanish	Upper
Altiplanicie	Spain	High plain, mesa
Älv, -älven	Swedish	River
am, an	German	On, upon
Ano	Greek	Upper
Anse	French	Bay
Ao	Chinese, Thai	Bay
'Aqabat	Arabic	Pass
Arrecife	Spanish	Reef
Arroio/Arroyo	Portuguese/Spanish	Watercourse
Archipiélago	Spanish	Archipelago
Aust-	Norwegian	East, eastern
Austral	Spanish	Southern
'Ayn	Arabic	Spring, well
Baai	Afrikaans	Bay
Bab	Arabic	Strait
Bach	German	Stream
Bad	German	Spa
Badiyat	Arabic	Desert
Bælt	Danish	Strait
Baharu	Malay	New
Bahía	Spanish	Bay
Bahiret	Arabic	Lagoon
Bahr	Arabic	Bay, canal, lake
Bahra/Bahrat	Arabic	Lagoon/Lake
Baía/Baie	Portuguese/French	Bay
Baixo	Portuguese	Lower
Baja, Bajo	Spanish	Lower
Bala	Persian	Upper
Ban	Cambodian, Laotian, Thai	Village
-bana	Japanese	Cape, point
Bañado	Spanish	Marshy land
Banc/Banco	French/Spanish	Sandbank
Bandao	Chinese	Peninsula
Bandar	Arabian, Malay, Persian	Inlet, port
-bando	Korean	Peninsula
Baraj, Baraji	Turkish	Dam
Barat	Indonesian, Malay	West, western
Barqa	Arabic	Hill
Barra	Portuguese	Sandbank
Barracão	Portuguese	Dam, weir
Barragem	Portuguese	Reservoir
Baruun	Mongolian	Western
Bas, Basse	French	Lower
Bassin	French	Basin
Batin, Batn	Arabic	Depression
Becken	German	Basin
Beek	Flemish	Stream
bei	German	At, near
Bei	Chinese	North, northern
Beinn, Ben	Gaelic	Mountain
Belogor'ye	Russian	Mountain
Bereg	Russian	Bank, shore
-berg	Norwegian, Swedish	Mountain
Berg(e)	German	Mountain(s)
Besar	Indonesian, Malay	Big, great
Bir, Bîr/Bi'ar	Arabic	Well/Wells
Birkat, Birket	Arabic	Pool, well
-bjerg	Danish	Hill
Boca	Portuguese, Spanish	Mouth
Bocche	Italian	Estuary, mouths
Bodden	German	Bay, gulf
Bogazi	Turkish	Strait
Bogen	Norwegian	Bay
Bois	French	Woods
Boloto	Russian	Bog, marsh
Bol'sh-aya, -iye, -oy, -oye	Russian	Big
-bong	Korean	Mountain
Boquerón	Spanish	Pass
Bor	Polish	Forest
-botn/-botten	Norwegian/Swedish	Valley floor
Bouche	French	Estuary, mouth
-bre, -breen	Norwegian	Glacier
Bredning	Danish	Bay
Bron	Afrikaans	Spring, well
-brønn	Norwegian	Spring, well
Bucht/Bugt	German/Danish	Bay
Buhayrat, Buheirat	Arabic	Lake
Bukhta	Russian	Bay
Bukit	Malay	Hill
Bukt, Bukten	Norwegian, Swedish	Bay
Bulag	Mongolian	Spring
Bulak	Russian, Uighur	Spring
Burg	German	Castle
Burun, Burnu	Turkish	Cape, point
Büyük	Turkish	Big
Cabeço	Portuguese	Summit
Cabeza	Spanish	Summit
Cabo	Portuguese, Spanish	Cape, headland
Cachoeira	Portuguese	Waterfall
Cala/Caleta	Catalan/Spanish	Inlet
Cañada	Spanish	Ravine
Cañadón	Spanish	Gorge
Canal	Portuguese, Spanish	Channel
Cañe	Spanish	Stream
Cañon	Spanish	Canyon
Cap/Capo	Catalan, French/Italian	Cape, headland
Catarata	Spanish	Waterfall
Cayo(s)	Spanish	Islet(s), rock(s)
Cerro	Spanish	Hill, peak
Chaco	Spanish	Plain
Chaîne	French	Mountain chain
Chalb	Arabic	Watercourse
Chapada	Portuguese	Hills, uplands
Chebka	Arabic	Hill
-chedo	Korean	Archipelago
Chenal	French	Channel
Chiang	Thai	Town
-ch'on	Korean	River
Chong	Thai	Bay
Chott	Arabic	Marsh, salt lake
Chuluu	Mongolian	Mountain
Chute	French	Waterfall
Ci	Indonesian	Stream
Ciénaga	Spanish	Marshy lake
Cima/Cime	Italian/French	Summit
Città/Ciudad	Italian/Spanish	City, town
Co	Tibetan	Lake
Col	French	High pass
Collado	Spanish	Hill, saddle
Colle	Italian	Pass
Collina	Italian	Hill
Colline(s)	French	Hill(s)
Combe	French	Valley
Conca	Italian	Hollow
Cordillera	Spanish	Mountain chain
Corne/Corno	French/Italian	Peak
Costa	Italian, Portug., Spanish	Coast, shore
Côte	French	Coast, slope
Coteau(x)	French	Hill(s)
Cove	Catalan	Cave
Cuchilla	Spanish	Mountain chain
Cuenca	Spanish	River basin
Cueva	Spanish	Cave
Cun	Chinese	Village
Da	Chinese	Big
Dag/Dagh	Turkish/Persian	Mountain
Daglar	Turkish	Mountain
-dake	Japanese	Peak
-dal	Afrikaans, Danish, Norwegian, Swedish	Valley
Danau	Indonesian	Lake
Dao	Chinese	Island
Darreh	Persian	Valley
Daryacheh	Persian	Lake
Dasht	Persian, Urdu	Desert
Davaa	Mongolian	Pass
Denizi	Turkish	Sea
Dhar	Arabic	Hills, mountain
-diep	Flemish	Channel
Djebel/Djibâl	Arabic	Mountain/Mtns.
-do	Korean	Island
Dolina	Russian	Valley
Dolna/Dolní	Bulgarian/Czech	Lower
Dolny	Polish	Lower
Dong	Chinese	East, eastern
Dong	Thai	Mountain
-dong	Korean	Village
Donja, Donji	Serbo-Croat	Lower
Dorf	German	Village
-dorp	Afrikaans	Village
Dûr	Arabic	Mountains
Dzüün	Mongolian	East, eastern
Eiland(en)	Afrikaans, Flemish	Island(s)
-elv, -elva	Norwegian	River
Embalse	Spanish	Reservoir
Embouchure	French	Estuary
Ensenada	Spanish	Bay
Erg	Arabian	Desert & dunes
Eski	Turkish	Old
Estero	Spanish	Inlet, estuary, swamp
Estrecho	Spanish	Strait
Estreito	Portuguese	Strait
Étang	French	Lake, lagoon
Fajj	Arabic	Watercourse
Fels	German	Rock
Feng	Chinese	Peak
Fiume	Italian	River
-fjäll, -fjället	Swedish	Mountain
-fjärden	Swedish	Fjord
-fjell, -fjellet	Norwegian	Mountain
-fjord, -fjorden	Danish, Norwegian	Fjord, lagoon
Fleuve	French	River
Foce	Italian	River-mouth
-fonn	Norwegian	Glacier
Förde	German	Inlet
Forêt/Forst	French/German	Forest
-foss	Norwegian	Waterfall
Fuente	Spanish	Source, well
-gan	Japanese	Rock
Gang	Chinese	Harbour
Garet	Arabic	Hill
Gardaneh	Persian	Pass
Gat	Flemish	Channel
-gata	Japanese	Inlet, lagoon
Gau	German	District
Gave	French	Torrent
-gawa	Japanese	River
Gebel	Arabic	Mountain
Gebergte	Afrikaans	Mountain range
Gebiet	German	District, region
Gebirge	German	Mountains
Gedigi	Turkish	Pass
Gezîret/Gezâir	Arabic	Island/Islands
Ghadfat	Arabic	Watercourse
Ghadir	Arabic	Well
Ghard	Arabic	Sand dunes
Ghubbat	Arabic	Bay
Gipfel	German	Peak
Gletscher	German	Glacier
Gobi	Mongolian	Desert
Gol	Mongolian	River
Göl, Gölü	Turkish	Lake
Golfe	French	Bay, gulf
Golfete	Spanish	Bay
Golfo	Italian, Spanish	Bay, gulf
Gora	Bulgarian	Forest
Gora/Góra	Russian, Serbo-Croat/Polish	Mountain
Górka	Polish	Hill
Gornja, Gornji	Serbo-Croat	Upper
Gory/Góry	Russian/Polish	Mountains
Goulet	French	Narrow entrance
Grabean	German	Ditch, trench
-grad	Bulgarian, Russian, Serbo-Croat	Town, castle
Grand, Grands	French	Big
Grat	German	Crest, ridge
Greben'	Russian	Ridge
-gród	Polish	Town, castle
Groot	Afrikaans	Big
Gross, -e, -en, -er	German	Big
Grotta/Grotte	Italian/French	Cave, grotto
Grund	German	Ground, valley
Gryada	Russian	Ridge
Guan	Chinese	Pass
Guba	Russian	Bay
Guelta	Arabic	Well
-gunto	Japanese	Island group
Gunung	Indonesian, Malay	Mountain
Hadabat	Arabic	Plain
Hadh, Hadhat	Arabic	Sand dunes
-haehyop	Korean	Strait
Hafar	Arabic	Wells
Hafen	German	Harbour, port
Haff	German	Bay
Hai	Chinese	Sea
Halbinsel	German	Peninsula
-halvøya	Norwegian	Peninsula
Hamad-a, -et	Arabic	Plateau
Hammad-ah, -at	Arabic	Plain, rocky plateau
-hamn	Norwegian, Swedish	Harbour
Hamun	Persian	Marsh
-hanto	Japanese	Peninsula
Hardt	German	Wooded hills
Harrat	Arabic	Lava fields
Hassi, Hasy	Arabic	Well
-haug	Norwegian	Hill
Haut, -e	French	Upper
Hawr	Arabic	Lake
-havn	Danish, Norwegian	Harbour
Hazm	Arabic	Plateau
He	Chinese	River
-hede	Danish, Norwegian	Heath
-hegység	Hungarian	Mountains
-hei/Heide	Norwegian/German	Heath, moor
Hersónisos	Greek	Peninsula
Higashi-	Japanese	East, eastern
-hisar	Turkish	Castle

Hisn	Arabic	Fort
-hø	Norwegian	Peak
Hoch/Hoë	German/Afrikaans	High
Hoek	Flemish	Cape, point
Hög/-høg(d)	Swedish/Norwegian	High, height
Höhe, Hohen-	German	Height
Hoog	Flemish	High
-høoj	Danish	Hill
Hora/Hory	Czech	Mountain/Mtns
Horn	German	Peak, summit
Horní	Czech	Upper
Hot	Mongolian	Town
-høy	Norwegian	Height
-hrad	Czech	Castle
Hu	Chinese	Lake
Hügel	German	Hill
Idd	Arabic	Well
Idhan	Arabic	Sand dunes
'Idwet	Arabic	Mountain
Île(s)/Ilha(s)	French/Portuguese	Island(s)
Illa, Illes	Catalan	Island, islands
im, in	German	In
Inférieur, -e	French	Lower
Insel(n)	German	Island(s)
Irmak	Turkish	Large river
'Irq	Arabic	Sand dunes
Isla(s)/Isle	Spanish/French	Island(s)
Islote	Spanish	Small island
Iso	Finnish	Big
Ísola, Isole	Italian	Island, islands
Istmo	Spanish	Isthmus
Jabal	Arabic	Mountain
-järvi	Finnish	Lake
-jaure, -javrre	Lappish	Lake
Jazirat/Jaza'ir	Arabic	Island/Islands
Jbel, Jebel	Arabic	Mountain
Jezero/Jezioro	Serbo-Croat/Polish	Lake
Jiang	Chinese	River
Jiao	Chinese	Point, reef
Jibal	Arabic	Mountains
-jima	Japanese	Island
-joki/-jokka	Finnish/Lappish	River
-jøkulen	Norwegian	Glacier
-jökull	Icelandic	Glacier
Jun	Arabic	Bay
Kaap	Afrikaans	Cape
-kai	Japanese	Sea, bay, inlet
Kali	Indonesian	River
Kamm	German	Crest, ridge
Kampung	Indonesian, Malay	Village
Kanaal/Kanal	Flemish/German, Russian	Canal
-kapp	Norwegian	Cape
Karif	Arabic	Well
Kathib	Arabic	Sand dunes
Káto	Greek	Lower
-kawa	Japanese	River
Kecil	Indonesian, Malay	Small
Kepulauan	Indonesian	Archipelago
Kereb	Arabic	Hill, ridge
Keski-	Finnish	Central, middle
Khalîg, Khalij	Arabic	Bay, gulf
Khao	Thai	Peak
Khashm	Arabic	Mountain
Khawr, Khor/Khowr	Arabic/Persian	Inlet
Khrebet	Russian	Mountain range
Kis-	Hungarian	Small
Kita-	Japanese	North, northern
Klamm	German	Ravine
Klein	Afrikaans, German	Small
Klint/Klit	Danish	Cliff/Dunes
Klong	Thai	Canal, creek
Kloof	Afrikaans	Gorge
Ko/Koh	Thai/Cambodian	Island
-ko	Japanese	Lake, inlet
Kólpos	Greek	Gulf
Koog	German	Polder
Kop/Kopf	Afrikaans/German	Hill
Körfezi	Turkish	Bay, gulf
Kotlina	Czech, Polish	Basin, depression
Kotlovina	Russian	Depression
-köy	Turkish	Village
Kraj	Czech, Polish, Serbo-Croat	Region
Kray	Russian	Region
Kreis	German	District
Kryazh	Russian	Ridge
Kuala	Malay	Estuary
Küçük	Turkish	Small
Kuduk	Russian	Spring, well
Kuh	Persian	Mountain
Kul'	Russian	Lake
Kület	Arabic	Hill
Kum	Russian	Sandy desert
-kundo	Korean	Island group
-kylä	Finnish	Village
Lac	French	Lake
Laem	Thai	Point
Lago	Italian, Portug., Spanish	Lake
Lagoa	Portuguése	Lagoon
Laguna	Spanish	Lagoon, lake
Lam	Thai	Stream
Län	Swedish	Province
Land	German	Province, area
Lande	French	Heath, sandy moor
Las/Les	Polish/Czech, Russian	Forest, wood
Laut	Indonesia	Sea
Lednik	Russian	Glacier
lès, lez	French	Beside, near
Liedao	Chinese	Island group
Lille	Danish, Norwegian	Small
Liman	Russian	Bay, gulf
Liman, Limani	Turkish	Harbour, port
Límni	Greek	Lake, lagoon
Ling	Chinese	Mountain range
Llano	Spanish	Plain, prairie
Loma	Spanish	Hill
-luoto	Finnish	Rocky island
-lyng	Danish	Heath
Macizo	Spanish	Massif
Madinat	Arabic	City, town
Mae Nam	Thai	River
Mala/Malé	Serbo-Croat/Czech	Small
Malaya, -oye, -yy	Russian	Small
-man	Korean	Bay
Manâqir	Arabic	Hills
Mar	Portuguese, Spanish	Sea
Marais	French	Marsh, swamp
Mare	Italian/Romanian	Sea/Big
Marsá	Arabic	Anchorage, inlet
Marsch	German	Fen, marsh
Masabb	Arabic	Estuary
Mashâsh	Arabic	Well
Massif	French	Mountains, upland
Mayor	Spanish	Higher, larger
Meer	Afrikaans, Flemish, German	Lake, sea
Méga, Megál-a, -i, -o	Greek	Big
Menor	Portuguese, Spanish	Lesser, smaller
Mer	French	Sea
Mersa	Arabic	Anchorage, inlet
Mesa, Meseta	Spanish	Tableland
Mesto	Czech, Serbo-Croat	Town
Mezzo	Italian	Middle, mid-
Miasto	Polish	Town
Mic/Mikr-í, ón	Romanian/Greek	Small
Mina'	Arabic	Harbour, port
Minami-	Japanese	South, southern
Minqâr	Arabic	Hill
-misaki	Japanese	Cape, point
Mishâsh, Mushâsh	Arabic	Well
Miti	Greek	Cape
Mittel-, Mitten-	German	Central, middle
Mjesto	Serbo-Croat	Town
Monasterio/Moni	Spanish/Greek	Monastery
Mont/Monte	French/Italian, Portuguese, Spanish	Mountain
Montagne(s)	French	Mountain(s)
Monti	Italian	Mountains
Moor	German	Bog, moor, swamp
Moos	German	Bog, moss
More	Russian	Sea
Mörön	Mongolian	River
Morro	Portuguese	Hill, mountain
-mose	Danish	Bog, moor
Moyen, -ne	French	Middle, mid-
Muara	Indonesian	Estuary
Mudiriyat	Arabic	Province
Muntii	Romanian	Mountains
-myr	Norwegian, Swedish	Moor, swamp
Mys	Russian	Cape
na	Bulgarian, Russian, Serbo-Croat	On
nad	Czech, Polish, Russian	Above, over
-nada	Japanese	Gulf, sea
Nádrz	Czech	Reservoir
-naes	Danish	Cape, point
Nafud	Arabic	Desert, dune
Nagor'ye	Russian	Highland, uplands
Nagy-	Hungarian	Big, great
Nahr	Arabic	River
Nakhon	Thai	Town
Nam	Korean, Vietnamese	South, southern
Nam	Burmese, Thai, Vietnamese	River
Nan	Chinese	South, southern
Naqb	Arabic	Pass
Nasb	Arabic	Hill, mountain
Né-a, -on, -os	Greek	New
Neder-	Flemish	Lower
Nehri	Turkish	River
Nei	Chinese	Inner
-nes	Icelandic, Norwegian	Cape, point
Neu-/Neuf, Neuve	German/French	New
Nevado	Spanish	Peak
-ni	Korean	Village
Nieder-	German	Lower
Nieu	Afrikaans	New
Nieuw, -e, -en, -er	Flemish	New
Nishi	Japanese	West, western
-nísi	Greek	Island
Nizhn-eye, -iy, -iye, -yaya	Russian	Lower
Nízina/Nízni	Czech	Lowland/Lower
Nizmennost'	Russian	Lowland
Noord-	Flemish	North, northern
Nord	Danish, French, German	North, northern
Nordre, Nørre	Danish	Northern
Norra	Swedish	Northern
Norte	Portuguese, Spanish	North
Nos	Bulgarian, Russian	Point, spit
Nótios	Greek	Southern
Nou	Romanian	New
Nouv-eau, -elle	French	New
Nova	Italian	New
Nova, Novi	Bulgarian, Serbo-Croat	New
Nôvo, Nôvô	Portuguese	New
Nová, Nové, Novy	Czech	New
Nov-aya, -o, -oye, -yy, -yye	Russian	New
Nowa, Nowe, Nowy	Polish	New
Nudo	Spanish	Mountain
Nueva, Nuevo	Spanish	New
Nuruu	Mongolian	Mountains
Nusa	Indonesian	Island
Nuur	Mongolian	Lake
Ny-	Danish, Norweg., Swedish	New
-ö, -ön/-ø	Swedish/Danish	Island
-oaivi, -oaivve	Lappish	Hill, mountain
Ober-	German	Upper
Oblast'	Russian	Province
Occidental	Spanish	Western
-odde	Danish, Norwegian	Cape, point
Ogla, Oglet	Arabic	Well
Okrug	Russian	District
Ömnö-	Mongolian	South, southern
Onder	Flemish	Lower
Öndör-	Mongolian	Upper
-oog	German	Island
Oost, -er, -elijk	Flemish	East, eastern
Orasu	Romanian	Town
Oriental, -e	French, Romanian, Spanish	Eastern
Ormani	Turkish	Forest
Órmos	Greek	Bay
Óros/Ori	Greek	Mountain/Mtns.
Ost-/Øster-	German/Danish, Norweg.	East, eastern
Ostan	Persian	Province
Östra-	Swedish	East, eastern
Ostrov(a)	Russian	Island(s)
Otok/Otoci	Serbo-Croat	Island/Islands
Oud, -e, -en, -er	Flemish	Old
Oued	Arabic	Dry river-bed
Ovasi	Turkish	Plain
Over-	Danish, Flemish	Upper
Över-, Övre-	Norwegian, Swedish	Upper
-øy, -a	Norwegian	Island
Ozero, Ozera	Russian	Lake, lakes
-pää	Finnish	Hill
Palai-á, -ó, Palió	Greek	Old
Parbat	Urdu	Mountain
Parc	French	Park
Pas	French	Low pass, strait
Paso	Spanish	Pass, strait
Pass/Passo	Spanish/Italian	Pass
Pays	French	Region
Pegunungan	Indonesian	Mountain range
Pélagos	Greek	Sea
Peña(s)	Spanish	Cliff(s), rocks(s)
Pendi	Chinese	Basin
Penisola	Italian	Peninsula
Peñon	Spanish	Cliff
Pereval	Russian	Pass
Perv-o, -yy	Russian	First
Peski	Russian	Sands, desert
Petit, -e, -es	French	Little
Pic	French, Spanish	Peak, summit
Pico/Picacho	Portuguese, Spanish	Peak, summit
Pik	Russian	Peak, summit
Pingyuan	Chinese	Plain
Pizzo	Italian	Peak, summit
-plaat	Dutch	Sandbank, shoal
Plage	French	Beach
Plaine/Planicie	French/Spanish	Plain
Plaj(i)	Turkish	Beach(es)
Planalto	Portuguese	Plateau
Planina	Bulgarian, Serbo-Croat	Mountains
Platja/Playa	Catalan/Spanish	Beach
Plato	Afrikaans, Bulg., Russian	Plateau
Platte	German	Plateau, plain
Plosina	Czech	Tableland
Ploskogor'ye	Russian	Plateau
pod	Czech, Russian	Under
Pohor-í, -ie	Czech	Mountain range
Pointe	French	Cape, point
Poluostrov	Russian	Peninsula
Pólwysep	Polish	Peninsula
Pongo	Spanish	Water gap
Ponta, Pontal	Portuguese	Point
Portile	Romanian	Gate
Portillo	Spanish	Gap, pass
Porto	Catalan, Italian, Portug.	Harbour, port
Pradesh	Hindi	State
Praia	Portuguese	Beach, shore

près	French	Near
Presqu'île	French	Peninsula
Pri-	Russian	Near
Proliv	Russian	Strait
Protoka	Russian	Channel
Prusmyk	Czech	Pass
Przelecz	Polish	Pass
Pubu	Chinese	Waterfall
Pueblo	Spanish	Village
Puente	Spanish	Bridge
Puerta	Spanish	Narrow pass
Puerto	Spanish	Harbour, port
Puk-	Korean	North, northern
Pulau	Indonesian, Malay	Island
Puna	Spanish	Desert plateau
Punta	Catalan, Italian, Spanish	Cape, point
Puntjak	Indonesian	Mountain
Puy	French	Peak
Qa	Arabic	Depression
Qalamat, Qalib	Arabic	Well
Qanat	Arabic, Persian	U'ground conduit
Qararat	Arabic	Depression
Qâret	Arabic	Hill
Qiao	Chinese	Bridge
Qiuling	Chinese	Hills
Qoz	Arabic	Hill
Qu	Tibetan	Stream
Quan	Chinese	Spring
Quedas	Portuguese	Rapids
Qulban	Arabic	Wells
Qum	Persian	Sand
Qundao	Chinese	Archipelago
Qûr, Qurayyat	Arabic	Hills
Qurnat	Arabic	Peak
Quwayrat/Qurûn	Arabic	Hill/Hills
Ramlat	Arabic	Sands
Râs/Ra's	Arabic/Arabic, Persian	Cape, point
Raso	Portuguese	Upland
Ravnina/Razlivy	Russian	Plain
Região	Portuguese	Region
Reprêsa	Portuguese	Dam
Reshteh	Persian	Mountain range
-retto	Japanese	Island chain
-rev	Norwegian	Cliff, reef
Ri	Tibetan	Mountain
-ri	Korean	Village
Ria/Ría	Portuguese/Spanish	River-mouth
Ribeirão	Portuguese	River
Ribeiro	Portuguese	Stream
Rio/Río	Portuguese/Spanish	River
Rivier/Rivière	Afrikaans/French	River
Rocher	French	Cliff, rock
Rocque	French	Rock
Rt	Serbo-Croat	Cape, point
Rücken	German	Ridge
Rud, Rudkhaneh	Persian	River
Rudohorie	Czech	Mountains
-saari	Finnish	Island
Sabkhat	Arabic	Salt-flat
Sagar, Sagara	Hindi	Lake
Sahl	Arabic	Plain
Sahra	Arabic	Desert
-saki	Japanese	Cape, point
Salada/Salar, Salina	Spanish	Salt lake/Salt pan
Salto	Portuguese, Spanish	Waterfall
-san	Japanese, Korean	Mountain
-sanchi	Japanese	Mountainous area
Saniyat	Arabic	Well
Sanmaek	Korean	Mountain range
-sanmyaku	Japanese	Mountain range
San	Italian, Portug., Spanish	Saint
Sankt/Sant	German/Catalan	Saint
Santa, Santo	Italian, Portug., Spanish	Saint
São	Portuguese	Saint
Satu	Romanian	Village
Schloss	German	Castle, mansion
Schutzgebiet	German	Reserve
Sebkra	Arabic	Salt-flat
See	German	Lake
-sehir	Turkish	Town
Selat	Indonesian	Channel, strait
Selatan	Indonesian, Malay	South, southern
-selkä	Finnish	Open water, ridge
Selo	Russian, Serbo-Croat	Village
Selva	Spanish	Forest, wood
-sen	Japanese	Mountain
Serra/Serrania	Catalan, Portug. /Span.	Mountain range
-seto	Japanese	Channel, strait
Sever-naya, -noye, -nyy, -o	Russian	North, northern
Sfîntu	Romanian	Saint
Shahr	Persian	Town
Sha'ib, -an	Arabic	Watercourse
Shamo	Chinese	Desert
Shan	Chinese	Mountain(s)
Shandi	Chinese	Mountainous area
Shang	Chinese	Upper
Shankou	Chinese	Pass
Shanmai	Chinese	Mountain range
Sharm	Arabic	Cove, inlet
Shatt	Arabic	River, river-mouth
-shima/-shoto	Japanese	Island/Island group
Shuiku	Chinese	Reservoir
Sierra	Spanish	Mountain range
Silsilesi	Turkish	Mountain range
Sint	Afrikaans, Flemish	Saint
-sjø/sjön	Norwegian/Swedish	Lake
Skala, Skaly	Czech	Cliff, rock
-skog	Norwegian	Woods
-slette	Norwegian	Plain
Sliabh, Slieve	Gaelic	Mountain, upland
Sloboda	Russian	Suburb, large village
Sø	Danish, Norwegian	Lake
Söder-, Södra	Swedish	Southern
Solonchak	Russian	Salt lake
Sommet	French	Peak, summit
Sønder-	Danish	Southern
Søndre	Danish, Norwegian	Southern
Sopka	Russian	Hill
Sør	Norwegian	Southern
sous	French	Under
Spitze	German	Peak
Sredn-a, -i	Bulgarian	Central, middle
Sredn-e, -eye, -iy, -yaya	Russian	Central, middle
-stad	Afrikaans, Norwegian, Swedish	Town
-stadt	German	Town
Stara, Stari	Serbo-Croat	Old
Stará, Staré	Czech	Old
Star-aya, oye, -yy, -yye	Russian	Old
Stausee	German	Reservoir
Stenó	Greek	Pass, strait
Step'	Russian	Steppe
Stít	Czech	Peak
Stor-, Stora/Store	Swedish/Danish	Big
Strand	Gaelic, German	Beach
-strand	Danish, Norweg., Swedish	Beach
Strasse	German	Road
-strede	Norwegian	Passage, strait
Strelka	Russian	Spit
Stretto	Italian	Strait
Sud	French	South
Süd(er)	German	South (southern)
Suhul	Arabic	Plain
Suid	Afrikaans	South
-suido	Japanese	Channel, strait
Sul	Portuguese	South
sul, sull'	Italian	On
Sund	Swedish	Sound, strait
Sungai	Indonesian, Malay	River
-suo	Finnish	Marsh, swamp
Supérieur/Superior	French/Spanish	Upper
Sur	Spanish	South
sur	French	On
Sveti	Serbo-Croat	Saint
Szent-	Hungarian	Saint
-take	Japanese	Peak
Tal	German	Valley
Tall(ât)	Arabic	Hill(s)
Tang	Persian	Pass, strait
Tanjung	Indonesian, Malay	Cape, point
Taraq	Arabic	Hills
Tasek	Malay	Lake
Tau	Russian	Mountain(s)
Tekojärvi	Finnish	Reservoir
Tell	Arabic	Hill
Teluk	Indonesian	Bay
Tengah	Indonesian	Middle
Teniet	Arabic	Pass
Tepe, Tepesi	Turkish	Hill, peak
Tepeler, Tepeleri	Turkish	Hills, peaks
Terre/Tierra	French/Spanish	Land
Thale	Thai	Lake
Tilat	Arabic	Hill
Timur	Indonesian	East, eastern
-tind, -tinderne	Norwegain	Peak, peaks
Tir'at	Arabic	Canal
-tji	Indonesian	Stream
-to	Japanese	Island
-toge	Japanese	Pass
-tong	Korean	Village
Tonle	Cambodian	Lake
-topp	Norwegian	Peak
Torrente	Spanish	Rapids
Travesía	Spanish	Desert
Tulul	Arabic	Hills
Túnel	Spanish	Tunnel
über	German	Above
-udden	Swedish	Cape, point
Új-	Hungarian	New
Ujung	Indonesian	Cape, point
-umi	Japanese	Inlet
Unter-	German	Lower
'Uqlat	Arabic	Well
-ura	Japanese	Inlet
'Urayq	Arabic	Sand ridge
'Uruq	Arabic	Area of dunes
Ust'ye	Russian	Estuary
Utara	Indonesian	North, northern
Uttar	Hindi	Northern
Uul	Mongolian	Mountains
Uval	Russian	Hill
'Uyun	Arabic	Springs
-vaara(t)	Finnish	Hill(s)
-vaart	Flemish	Canal
-våg	Norwegian	Bay
Val, Vall	Italian, Spanish	Valley
Vale	Portuguese, Romanian	Valley
Valle/Vallée	Italian, Spanish/French	Valley
Vallon	French	Small valley
-vann	Norwegian	Lake
-város	Hungarian	Town
-varre	Norwegian	Mountain
Väster, Västra	Swedish	Western
-vatn	Icelandic, Norwegian	Lake
-vatnet	Norwegian	Lake
-vatten, vattnet	Swedish	Lake
Vaux	French	Valleys
Vecchio	Italian	Old
Vechi	Romanian	Old
Velha, Velho	Portuguese	Old
Velik-a, -i	Serbo-Croat	Big
Velik-aya, -iy, -iye	Russian	Big
Vel'k-á, -é, -y	Czech	Big
Verkhn-e, -eye, -iy, -yaya	Russian	Upper
-vesi	Finnish	Lake, water
Vester	Danish	Western
Vest, Vestre	Norwegian	West, western
-vidda	Norwegian	Plateau
Vieja, Viejo/ Vieux	Spanish/French	Old
Vig/-vik	Danish/Norwegian	Bay
Vila	Portuguese	Small town
Ville	French	Town
Víztároló	Hungarian	Reservoir
Vodokhranilishche	Russian	Reservoir
Volcán	Spanish	Volcano
Vorota	Russian	Channel, strait
Vostochn-aya, -oye, -yy	Russian	Eastern
Vozvyshennost'	Russian	Uplands
Vpadina	Russian	Depression
Vrch(y)	Czech	Mountain(s)
Vrchovina	Czech	Mountainous area
Vysocina	Czech	Upland
Vysok-aya, -oye	Russian	Upper
Wad	Flemish	Sand-flat
Wâdi, Wadi	Arabic	Watercourse
Wahat	Arabic	Oasis
Wai	Chinese	Outer
Wald	German	Forest
Wan/-wan	Chinese/Japanese	Bay
Wand	German	Cliff
Wasser	German	Lake, water
Wes-	Afrikaans	West
West, Wester	Flemish, German	West
Wielk-a, -i, -ie, -o	Polish	Big
Wysok-a, -i, -ie	Polish	Upper
Xi	Chinese	Stream, west
Xia	Chinese	Gorge, lower
Xian	Chinese	County
Xiao	Chinese	Small
Xu	Chinese	Islet
-yama	Japanese	Mountain(s)
Yang	Chinese	Ocean
Yarimadasi	Turkish	Peninsula
Yeni	Turkish	New
Yli-	Finnish	Upper
Ytre-	Norwegian	Outer
Ytter-	Norwegian, Swedish	Outer
Yuan	Chinese	Spring
Yugo-	Russian	Southern
Yunhe	Chinese	Canal
Yuzhn-aya, -o, -oye, -yy	Russian	South, southern
-zaki	Japanese	Cape, point
Zalew	Polish	Bay, inlet, lagoon
Zaliv	Russian	Bay
-zan	Japanese	Mountain
Zapadn-aya, -o, -oye, -yy	Russian	West, western
Zatoka	Polish	Gulf
-zee	Flemish	Sea
Zemlya	Russian	Land
-zhen	Chinese	Town
Zhong	Chinese	Middle
Zhou	Chinese	Islet
Zui	Chinese	Point, spit
Zuid	Flemish	South
Zuid-elijk, er	Flemish	Southern

6: GLOSSARY OF CLIMATE TERMS

An alphabetical list of all the terms featured on the regional climate maps.

Benguela Current *Africa maps*
A cold current flowing north along the west coast of South Africa, cooling the coastal region.

Berg Wind *Africa May–October map*
A hot dry wind which blows from the interior to the coastal regions of Namibia and South Africa.

Bora *Europe Winter map*
A cold dry wind which blows from the N and NE, affecting the Adriatic coastlines of Croatia, Italy and Slovenia.

California Current *North America Summer map*
A cold current which flows south along the west coast of California and Mexico, cooling the coastal region, and responsible for the frequent sea fogs particularly during the summer.

Canary Current *Africa maps*
An extension of the North Atlantic Drift (qv), flowing south along the NW Africa coast and moderating temperatures in the coastal region.

Chinook *North America Winter map*
A warm dry wind which blows down the eastern slopes of the Rockies, rapidly melting lying snow.

Crachin *Asia November–April map*
Light rain in the northern mountains and coastal regions of Vietnam.

El Niño *South America maps*
A change in the ocean-atmosphere system in the Pacific, increasing water temperatures in the central and eastern equatorial Pacific Ocean and bringing rain to the NW coast of South America. A periodic phenomenon, it often affects the western coast of America as far north as California. In some years the weather pattern of the whole American continent can be disrupted, and in exceptional years its effects experienced worldwide.

Etesian Wind / Meltemi *Europe Winter map*
A wind blowing from the N and NW in the eastern Mediterranean and the Aegean, often creating rough seas.

Föhn *Europe Winter map*
A wind which blows down Alpine valleys, warming as it descends, and melts snow rapidly.

Garúa *South America November–April map*
A heavy mist on the Pacific slope of the Andes in a normally very dry part of the coast.

Ghibli *Africa May–October map*
Local name for the Sirocco (qv) in Libya.

Guinea Monsoon *Africa May–October map*
Warm humid winds blowing from the SW in West Africa between April and September, associated with the rainy season.

Gulf Stream
North America Summer map (mentioned in 'Labrador current' box)
A warm current which flows NE from the Gulf of Mexico. After passing Newfoundland, it divides and follows three separate routes: 1. northwest towards Europe (the North Atlantic Drift (qv)); 2. southeast; 3. recirculating around an area north of Bermuda.

Harmattan *Africa November–April map*
A dry and dusty NE wind in West Africa blowing from the Sahara, associated with the dry season; cool at night and warm in the day. Opposite of the Guinea Monsoon (qv).

Kharif *Asia May–October map*
The rainy season in northern India and Arab countries.

Khamsin / Sharav *Africa May–October map*
A hot dry wind blowing from the S and SE in the eastern Mediterranean, warming the coastal region and helping to create dust storms and a hazy atmosphere.

Labrador Current *North America Summer map*
A cold current flowing south along the east coast of Canada, carrying icebergs and keeping the coastal region relatively cool druing the summer; fogs are caused off the Newfoundland coast where the current meets the warmer Gulf Stream flowing NE from the Gulf of Mexico.

La Niña *South America maps*
The opposite phenomenon to El Niño. Warm surface water flows towards Asia and colder water from the ocean depths moves to the surface in the eastern equatorial Pacific. Evaporation decreases and rainfall in the region is reduced. Often La Niña occurs the year after El Niño, with drought affecting the areas which experienced flooding the year before.

Leveche *Europe Winter map*
A hot, dry and dusty wind in southern Spain which blows from the Sahara.

Mistral *Europe Winter map*
A strong cold dry wind blowing from the north in southern France; known as Cers in Aude département.

Monsoon Winds *Asia maps*
Seasonal winds which change direction during the year; during the dry season in India the NE monsoon blows dry air from the land and during the wet season the SW monsoon blows wet air from the ocean. The term is also used in Africa and Australasia.

Mozambique Current / Agulhas Current *Africa May–October map*
A warm current flowing south and west along the coast of Mozambique and eastern South Africa, warming the coastal region.

North Atlantic Drift *Europe Winter map*
An extension of the Gulf Stream (qv) which helps to maintain relatively mild winters in the British Isles and along the Norwegian coast.

Peru Current / Humboldt Current *South America maps*
A cold current flowing north along the west coast of South America and cooling the coastal region as far as the Equator.

Shamal *Africa May–October map*
A hot dry wind which blows from the NW in Iraq and The Gulf.

Sirocco *Europe Summer map*
A hot dusty wind blowing towards Europe from north Africa. Known as the Ghibli (qv) in Libya and Leveche (qv) in Spain. Its origins are the same as the Khamsin (qv) or Sharav (qv). On the northern Mediterranean coast, particularly in southern Italy, the wind is moist after crossing the Mediterranean.

7: THE WORLD'S MAJOR URBAN AREAS

The list shows the world's largest urban agglomerations, with UN estimates of their population in 2000. The UN defines the term 'urban agglomeration' as a contiguous area inhabited at a density regarded as urban, ignoring administrative boundaries. Where the agglomeration extends beyond the principal city's metropolitan area to include significant neighbouring towns and cities, these are added below the relevant entry.

The ten biggest cities in 1900 and in 1800 are listed at the foot of the page.

Urban agglomeration & country	Population ('000)
Tokyo, Japan *incl. Chiba, Funabashi, Kawasaki, Yokohama*	28,025
Ciudad de México (Mexico City), Mexico	18,131
Mumbai (Bombay), India	18,042
São Paulo, Brazil	17,711
New York, NY, USA *incl. Jersey City, Newark, Paterson, Yonkers*	16,626
Shanghai, China	14,173
Lagos, Nigeria	13,488
Los Angeles, CA, USA *incl. Anaheim, Long Beach, Santa Ana*	13,129
Kolkata (Calcutta), India	12,900
Buenos Aires, Argentina	12,431
Soul (Seoul), Rep. of Korea	12,215
Beijing (Peking), China	12,033
Karachi, Pakistan	11,774
Delhi, India	11,680
Dhaka, Bangladesh	10,979
Manila, the Philippines *incl. Caloocan, Quezon City*	10,818
El Qâhira (Cairo), Egypt *incl. Giza*	10,772
Osaka, Japan *incl. Amagasaki, Higashiosaka, Sakai*	10,609
Rio de Janeiro, Brazil *incl. Nova Iguaçu*	10,556
Tianjin, China	10,239
Jakarta, Indonesia	9,815
Paris, France	9,638
Istanbul, Turkey *incl. Bakirköy, Kadiköy, Üsküdar*	9,413
Moskva (Moscow), Russian Fed.	9,299
London, United Kingdom	7,640
Lima, Peru *incl. Callao*	7,443
Tehran, Iran	7,380
Krung Thep (Bangkok), Thailand	7,221
Chicago, IL, USA *incl. Gary, Waukegan*	6,945
Bogotá, Colombia	6,834
Hyderabad, India *incl. Secunderabad*	6,833
Chennai (Madras), India	6,639
Essen, Germany *incl. Bochum, Dortmund, Duisburg*	6,559
Hangzhou, China	6,389
Xianggang (Hong Kong), China	6,097
Lahore, Pakistan	6,030
Shenyang, China	5,681
Changchun, China	5,566
Bangalore, India	5,554
Harbin, China	5,475
Chengdu, China	5,293
Santiago, Chile	5,261
Guangzhou (Canton), China	5,162
Sankt-Peterburg (St Petersburg), Russian Fed.	5,132
Kinshasa, Dem. Rep. of Congo	5,068
Baghdad, Iraq	4,796
Jinan, China	4,789
Wuhan, China	4,750
Toronto, OT, Canada	4,657
Yangon (Rangoon), Myanmar	4,458

Urban agglomeration & country	Population ('000)
Alger (Algiers), Algeria	4,447
Philadelphia, PA, USA *incl. Camden*	4,398
Qingdao, China	4,376
Milano (Milan), Italy	4,251
Pusan, Rep. of Korea	4,239
Belo Horizonte, Brazil	4,160
Ahmedabad, India	4,154
Madrid, Spain	4,072
San Francisco, CA, USA *incl. Berkeley, Oakland, Vallejo*	4,051
El Iskandarîya (Alexandria), Egypt	3,995
Washington DC, USA	3,927
Dallas, TX, USA *incl. Arlington, Fort Worth, Irving*	3,912
Guadalajara, Mexico	3,908
Chongqing, China	3,896
Medellín, Colombia	3,831
Detroit, MI, USA *incl. Dearborn, Pontiac*	3,785
Handan, China	3,763
Frankfurt am Main, Germany *incl. Darmstadt, Offenbach a.M., Wiesbaden*	3,700
Pôrto Alegre, Brazil	3,699
Ho Chi Minh City (Saigon), Vietnam	3,678
Sydney, Australia	3,665
Santo Domingo, Dominican Rep.	3,601
Singapore	3,587
Casablanca, Morocco	3,535
Katowice, Poland	3,488
Pune (Poona), India	3,485
Bandung, Indonesia	3,420
Monterrey, Mexico	3,416
Montréal, QU, Canada	3,401
Nagoya, Japan	3,377
Nanjing, China	3,375
Houston, TX, USA *incl. Baytown, Pasadena*	3,365
Abidjan, Côte d'Ivoire	3,359
Xi'an, China	3,352
Berlin, Germany	3,337
Riyadh, Saudi Arabia	3,328
Recife (Pernambuco), Brazil	3,307
Düsseldorf, Germany *incl. Mönchengladbach, Solingen, Wuppertal*	3,251
Ankara, Turkey *incl. Cankaya*	3,190
Melbourne, Australia	3,188
Salvador (Bahia), Brazil	3,180
Dalian (Luda), China	3,153
Caracas, Venezuela	3,153
Adis Abeba (Addis Ababa), Ethiopia	3,112
Athina (Athens), Greece *incl. Pireás (Piraeus)*	3,103
Cape Town, South Africa	3,092
Köln (Cologne), Germany *incl. Bonn, Leverkusen*	3,067
Maputo, Mozambique	3,017
Nápoli (Naples), Italy	3,012
Fortaleza (Ceará), Brazil	3,007
San Diego, CA, USA *incl. Escondido*	2,983
Boston, MA, USA	2,915
Chittagong, Bangladesh	2,906

1900:	('000)
London, United Kingdom	6,500
New York, USA	4,200
Paris, France	3,300
Berlin, Germany	2,700
Chicago, USA	1,700
Vienna, Austro-Hungarian Empire	1,700
Tokyo, Japan	1,500
St Petersburg, Russia	1,400
Manchester, United Kingdom	1,400
Philadelphia, USA	1,400

1800:	('000)
Peking, China	1,100
London, Great Britain	900
Canton, China	800
Tokyo (Edo), Japan	700
Constantinople, Ottoman Empire	600
Paris, France	550
Naples, Kingdom of Naples	450
Hangchow, China	400
Osaka, Japan	380
Kyoto, Japan	380

8: US STATES

ISO* Abbr.	State	Nickname	Date of admission to the Union	State Capital
AL	Alabama	Heart of Dixie	14th Dec 1819	Montgomery
AK	Alaska	The Last Frontier	3rd Jan 1959	Juneau
AZ	Arizona	Grand Canyon State	14th Feb 1912	Phoenix
AR	Arkansas	The Natural State	15th June 1836	Little Rock
CA	California	Golden State	9th Sept 1850	Sacramento
CO	Colorado	Centennial State	1st Aug 1876	Denver
CT	Connecticut	Constitution State	9th Jan 1788 †	Hartford
DE	Delaware	First State / Diamond State	7th Dec 1787 †	Dover
DC	District of Columbia (Federal District, coextensive with the city of Washington)			
FL	Florida	Sunshine State	3rd Mar 1845	Tallahassee
GA	Georgia	Empire State of the South / Peach State	2nd Jan 1788 †	Atlanta
HI	Hawaii	Aloha State	21st Aug 1959	Honolulu
ID	Idaho	Gem State	3rd July 1890	Boise
IL	Illinois	Land of Lincoln	3rd Dec 1818	Springfield
IN	Indiana	Hoosier State	11th Dec 1816	Indianapolis
IA	Iowa	Hawkeye State	28th Dec 1846	Des Moines
KS	Kansas	Sunflower State	29th Jan 1861	Topeka
KY	Kentucky	Bluegrass State	1st June 1792	Frankfort
LA	Louisiana	Pelican State	30th Apr 1812	Baton Rouge
ME	Maine	Pine Tree State	15th Mar 1820	Augusta
MD	Maryland	Old Line State	28th Apr 1788 †	Annapolis
MA	Massachusetts	Bay State	6th Feb 1788 †	Boston
MI	Michigan	Great Lakes State	26th Jan 1837	Lansing
MN	Minnesota	Gopher State / North Star State	11th May 1858	St Paul
MS	Mississippi	Magnolia State	10th Dec 1817	Jackson
MO	Missouri	Show Me State	10th Aug 1821	Jefferson City
MT	Montana	Treasure State	8th Nov 1889	Helena
NE	Nebraska	Cornhusker State	1st Mar 1867	Lincoln
NV	Nevada	Silver State	31st Oct 1864	Carson City
NH	New Hampshire	Granite State	21st June 1788 †	Concord
NJ	New Jersey	Garden State	18th Dec 1787 †	Trenton
NM	New Mexico	Land of Enchantment	6th Jan 1912	Santa Fe
NY	New York	Empire State	26th July 1788 †	Albany
NC	North Carolina	Tar Heel State	21st Nov 1789 †	Raleigh
ND	North Dakota	Flickertail State / Peace Garden State	2nd Nov 1889	Bismarck
OH	Ohio	Buckeye State	1st Mar 1803	Columbus
OK	Oklahoma	Sooner State	16th Nov 1907	Oklahoma City
OR	Oregon	Beaver State	14th Feb 1859	Salem
PA	Pennsylvania	Keystone State	12th Dec 1787 †	Harrisburg
RI	Rhode Island	Ocean State	29th May 1790 †	Providence
SC	South Carolina	Palmetto State	23rd May 1788 †	Columbia
SD	South Dakota	Mount Rushmore State	2nd Nov 1889	Pierre
TN	Tennessee	Volunteer State	1st June 1796	Nashville
TX	Texas	Lone Star State	29th Dec 1845	Austin
UT	Utah	Beehive State	4th Jan 1896	Salt Lake City
VT	Vermont	Green Mountain State	4th Mar 1791	Montpelier
VA	Virginia	Old Dominion State	25th June 1788 †	Richmond
WA	Washington	Evergreen State	11th Nov 1889	Olympia
WV	West Virginia	Mountain State	20th June 1863	Charleston
WI	Wisconsin	Badger State	29th May 1848	Madison
WY	Wyoming	Cowboy State / Equality State	10th July 1890	Cheyenne

International Organisation for Standardisation. † Original 13 states: date of ratification of the Constitution.

9: CANADIAN PROVINCES & TERRITORIES

ISO Abbr.	State	Language*	Date of admission to the Dominion	State Capital
AL	Alberta	English	1st Sept 1905	Edmonton
BC	British Columbia	English	20th July 1871	Victoria
MN	Manitoba	English	15th July 1870	Winnipeg
NB	New Brunswick	English †	1st July 1867	Fredericton
NF	Newfoundland and Labrador	English	31st March 1949	St John's
NT	Northwest Territories	English	1870	Yellowknife
NS	Nova Scotia	English	1st July 1867	Halifax
NU	Nunavut (Territory)	Inuktitut **	1st April 1999	Iqaluit
OT	Ontario	English	1st July 1867	Toronto
PE	Prince Edward Island	English	1st July 1873	Charlottetown
QU	Québec	French	1st July 1867	Québec
SA	Saskatchewan	English	1st Sept 1905	Regina
YT	Yukon Territory	English	13th June 1898	Whitehorse

*Although Canada is officially bilingual (English & French), this column indicates the most commonly-spoken language in each region. † Approx. 35% of the population are French-speaking. ** The language of the Inuit.*

10: AUSTRALIAN STATES & TERRITORIES

ISO Abbr.	State	Nickname	Date of granting of responsible gov't	State Capital
AC	Australian Capital Territory	Nation's Capital	1911	Canberra *
CL	Coral Sea Territory (External Territory bordering the Queensland coast and Gt. Barrier Reef)			
NS	New South Wales	Premier State	1788 †	Sydney
NT	Northern Territory	Outback Australia	1911 **	Darwin
QL	Queensland	Sunshine State	1859	Brisbane
SA	South Australia	Festival State	1856	Adelaide
TS	Tasmania	Holiday Isle	1856	Hobart
VI	Victoria	Garden State	1855	Melbourne
WA	Western Australia	State of Excitement	1890	Perth

*Canberra became the seat of the Australian government on 9th May 1927. † Date of first settlement: New South Wales originally covered the whole island with the exception of Western Australia. ** Transferred to Commonwealth from South Australia in 1911, self-government within the Commonwealth granted 1978.*

11: RUSSIAN REPUBLICS

State	Capital	State	Capital
Adygeya	Maykop	Sakha	Yakutsk
Altay	Gorno-Altaysk	Tatarstan	Kazan'
Bashkortostan	Ufa	Tuva	Kyzyl
Buryatia	Ulan-Ude	Udmurtia	Izhevsk
Chechnya	Groznyy		
Chuvashia	Cheboksary	AUTONOMOUS AREAS & REGIONS:	
Dagestan	Makhachkala	Agin-Buryat	Aginskoye
Ingushetia	Nazran'	Chukot	Anadyr
Kabardino-Balkaria	Nal'chik	Evenki	Tura
Kalmykia	Elitsa	Khanty-Mansi	Khanty-Mansiysk
Karachay-Cherkessia	Cherkessk	Komi-Permyak	Kudymkar
Karelia	Petrozavodsk	Koryak	Palana
Khakassia	Abakan	Nenets	Nar'yan-Mar
Komi	Syktyvkar	Taymyr	Dudinka
Mari-El	Yoshkar-Ola	Ust'-Ordyn-Buryat	Ust'-Ordynskiy
Mordovia	Saransk	Yamalo-Nenets	Salekhard
North Ossetia (Alania)	Vladikavkaz	Jewish Autonomous Region	Birobidzhan

12: BRAZILIAN STATES

State	Capital	State	Capital
North:		**South-East:**	
Acre	Rio Branco	Espírito Santo	Vitória
Amapá	Macapá	Minas Gerais	Belo Horizonte
Amazonas	Manaus	Rio de Janeiro	Rio de Janeiro
Pará	Belém	São Paulo	São Paulo
Rondônia	Pôrto Velho	**South:**	
Roraima	Boa Vista	Paraná	Curitiba
Tocantins	Palmas	Rio Grande do Sul	Pôrto Alegre
North-East:		Santa Catarina	Florianópolis
Alagoas	Maceió	**Central West:**	
Bahia	Salvador	Distrito Federal*	Brasília
Ceará	Fortaleza	Goiás	Goiânia
Maranhão	São Luís	Mato Grosso	Cuiabá
Paraíba	João Pessoa	Mato Grosso do Sul	Campo Grande
Pernambuco	Recife	* Federal District	
Piauí	Teresina		
Rio Grande do Norte	Natal		
Sergipe	Aracaju		

13: FRENCH DEPARTEMENTS

Dept. no.	Département	Capital	Dept. no.	Département	Capital
01	Ain	Bourg-en-Bresse	48	Lozère	Mende
02	Aisne	Laon	49	Maine-et-Loire	Angers
03	Allier	Moulins	50	Manche	St-Lô
04	Alpes-de-Hte-Provence	Digne	51	Marne	Châlons-sur-Marne
05	Hautes-Alpes	Gap	52	Haute-Marne	Chaumont
06	Alpes-Maritimes	Nice	53	Mayenne	Laval
07	Ardèche	Privas	54	Meurthe-et-Moselle	Nancy
08	Ardennes	Charleville-Mézières	55	Meuse	Bar-le-Duc
09	Ariège	Foix	56	Morbihan	Vannes
10	Aube	Troyes	57	Moselle	Metz
11	Aude	Carcassonne	58	Nièvre	Nevers
12	Aveyron	Rodez	59	Nord	Lille
13	Bouches-du-Rhône	Marseille	60	Oise	Beauvais
14	Calvados	Caen	61	Orne	Alençon
15	Cantal	Aurillac	62	Pas-de-Calais	Arras
16	Charente	Angoulême	63	Puy-de-Dôme	Clermont-Ferrand
17	Charente-Maritime	La Rochelle	64	Pyrénées-Atlantiques	Pau
18	Cher	Bourges	65	Hautes-Pyrénées	Tarbes
19	Corrèze	Tulle	66	Pyrénées-Orientales	Perpignan
20	Corse-du-Sud (2A)	Ajaccio	67	Bas-Rhin	Strasbourg
	Haute-Corse (2B)	Bastia	68	Haut-Rhin	Colmar
21	Côte-d'Or	Dijon	69	Rhône	Lyon
22	Côtes-d'Armor	St-Brieuc	70	Haute-Saône	Vesoul
23	Creuse	Guéret	71	Saône-et-Loire	Mâcon
24	Dordogne	Périgueux	72	Sarthe	Le Mans
25	Doubs	Besançon	73	Savoie	Chambéry
26	Drôme	Valence	74	Haute-Savoie	Annecy
27	Eure	Évreux	75	Paris	Paris
28	Eure-et-Loir	Chartres	76	Seine-Maritime	Rouen
29	Finistère	Quimper	77	Seine-et-Marne	Melun
30	Gard	Nîmes	78	Yvelines (canton)	Versailles
31	Haute-Garonne	Toulouse	79	Deux-Sèvres	Niort
32	Gers	Auch	80	Somme	Amiens
33	Gironde	Bordeaux	81	Tarn	Albi
34	Hérault	Montpellier	82	Tarn-et-Garonne	Montauban
35	Ille-et-Vilaine	Rennes	83	Var	Toulon
36	Indre	Châteauroux	84	Vaucluse	Avignon
37	Indre-et-Loire	Tours	85	Vendée	La Roche-sur-Yon
38	Isère	Grenoble	86	Vienne	Poitiers
39	Jura	Lons-le-Saunier	87	Haute-Vienne	Limoges
40	Landes	Mont-de-Marsan	88	Vosges	Épinal
41	Loir-et-Cher	Blois	89	Yonne	Auxerre
42	Loire	St-Étienne	90	Territoire-de-Belfort	Belfort
43	Haute-Loire	Le Puy	91	Essonne (canton)	Évry
44	Loire-Atlantique	Nantes	92	Hauts-de-Seine (canton)	Nanterre
45	Loiret	Orléans	93	Seine-St-Denis (canton)	Bobigny
46	Lot	Cahors	94	Val-de-Marne (canton)	Créteil
47	Lot-et-Garonne	Agen	95	Val-d'Oise (canton)	Cergy

Appendices 14-17

14: THE WORLD'S TALLEST BUILDINGS

Height is measured from the street level of the main entrance to the structural or architectural top of the building, including spires but excluding antennae and flag poles. The list shows the world's tallest traditional buildings (structures intended primarily for human habitation with the great majority of their height divided into occupiable levels). Buildings under construction, TV-tower hybrids and other structures not recognised as traditional buildings are excluded. The world's tallest freestanding structure is Toronto's CN Tower (553m).

Name & location	Height (m)	Date
Petronas Towers I & II, Kuala Lumpur, Malaysia	452	1996
Sears Tower, Chicago, IL, USA	442	1974
Jin Mao Building, Shanghai, China	421	1998
CITIC Plaza, Guangzhou, China	391	1997
Shun Hing Square, Shenzhen, China	384	1996
Empire State Building, New York, NY, USA	381	1931
Central Plaza, Hong Kong, China	374	1992
Bank of China, Hong Kong, China	369	1989
Emirates Towers One, Dubai, UAE	355	2000
The Centre, Hong Kong, China	350	1998
T&C Tower, Kaohsiung, Taiwan	348	1998
Aon Center, Chicago, IL, USA	346	1973
John Hancock Center, Chicago, IL, USA	344	1969
Burj al Arab Hotel, Dubai, UAE	321	1999
Baiyoke Tower II, Bangkok, Thailand	320	1998
Chrysler Building, New York, NY, USA	319	1930
NationsBank Plaza, Atlanta, GA, USA	312	1992
Library Tower, Los Angeles, CA, USA	310	1990
Menara Telekom, Kuala Lumpur, Malaysia	310	2000
AT&T Corporate Center, Chicago, IL, USA	307	1989
Chase Tower, Houston, TX, USA	305	1982
Emirates Towers Two, Dubai, UAE	305	2000
Two Prudential Plaza, Chicago, IL, USA	303	1990
Ryugyong Hotel, Pyongyang, DPR of Korea	300	1995
Commerzbank Tower, Frankfurt, Germany	299	1997
First Canadian Place, Toronto, OT, Canada	298	1975
First Interstate Bank Plaza, Houston, TX, USA	296	1983
Landmark Tower, Yokohama, Japan	296	1993
311 South Wacker Drive, Chicago, IL, USA	293	1990
SEG Plaza, Shenzhen, China	292	2000
Bank of America Center, Seattle, WA, USA	291	1985
American International Building, New York, NY, USA	290	1932
Cheung Kong Centre, Hong Kong, China	290	1999
Key Tower, Cleveland, OH, USA	290	1991
One Liberty Place, Philadelphia, PA, USA	288	1987
Sunjoy Tomorrow Center, Shanghai, China	285	1999
Trump Building (40 Wall Street), New York, NY, USA	283	1930
Bank of America Plaza, Dallas, TX, USA	281	1985
Overseas Union Bank Centre, Singapore	280	1986
United Overseas Bank Plaza One, Singapore	280	1992
Republic Plaza, Singapore	280	1995
Citicorp Center, New York, NY, USA	279	1977
Scotia Plaza, Toronto, OT, Canada	275	1989
Williams Tower, Houston, TX, USA	275	1983
Renaissance Tower, Dallas, TX, USA	270	1974
Al Faisaliah Centre, Riyadh, Saudi Arabia	268	2000
900 North Michigan Avenue, Chicago, IL, USA	265	1989
Bank of America Corporate Center, Charlotte, NC, USA	265	1992
SunTrust Plaza, Atlanta, GA, USA	265	1992
Canada Trust Tower, Toronto, OT, Canada	263	1990
Water Tower Place, Chicago, IL, USA	262	1976
First Interstate Tower, Los Angeles, CA, USA	262	1974
Transamerica Pyramid, San Francisco, CA, USA	260	1972
GE Building, Rockefeller Center, New York, NY, USA	259	1933
Bank One Plaza, Chicago, IL, USA	259	1969
Philippine Bank of Communication, Manila, Philipp.	259	2000
Two Liberty Place, Philadelphia, PA, USA	258	1989

15: THE WORLD'S LONGEST BRIDGES

Name & location	Type	Length (m)	Date
Akashi Kaikyo, Kobe–Akashi Island, Japan	Suspension	1,991	1998
Storebælt East, Fyn (Fünen)–Sjælland (Zealand), Denmark	Suspension	1,624	1998
Humber, England, UK	Suspension	1,410	1981
Jiangyin, Yangtze River, Jiangsu, China	Suspension	1,385	1999
Tsing Ma, Lantau Island–Tsing Yi Island, Hong Kong, China	Suspension	1,377	1997
Verrazano Narrows, Brooklyn–Staten Island NY, USA	Suspension	1,298	1964
Golden Gate, San Francisco Bay, CA, USA	Suspension	1,280	1937
Höga Kusten (High Coast), Ångermanälven River, Sweden	Suspension	1,210	1997
Mackinac Straits, Mackinaw City–St Ignace, MI, USA	Suspension	1,158	1957
Chesapeake Bay 2, VA, USA	Suspension	1,158	1999
Minami Bisan-Seto, Kojima–Sakaide [Honshu–Shikoku], Japan	Suspension	1,100	1988
Bosporus II (Fatih Sultan Mehmet), Turkey	Suspension	1,090	1988
Bosporus I (Atatürk), Turkey	Suspension	1,074	1973
George Washington, Hudson River, NJ-NY, USA	Suspension	1,067	1931
Kurushima Kaikyo III; II, Onomichi–Imabari [Honshu–Shikoku], Japan	Suspension	1,020/1,030	1999
25 de Abril, Tagus River, Lisboa (Lisbon), Portugal	Suspension	1,013	1966
LONGEST BRIDGE SPANS OF OTHER TYPES:			
Tatara, Onomichi – Imabari [Honshu – Shikoku], Japan	Cable-stayed	890	1999
Pont de Normandie, Seine River, Le Havre, France	Cable-stayed	856	1995
Pont de Québec, St Lawrence River, QU, Canada	Cantilever Truss	549	1917
Forth Rail, Scotland, UK	Cantilever Truss	521	1890
New River Gorge, Fayetteville, WV, USA	Steel Arch	518	1977
Bayonne (Kill van Kull), New Jersey – Staten Island NY, USA	Steel Arch	504	1931
Sydney Harbour, Australia	Steel Arch	503	1932

16: THE WORLD'S LONGEST TUNNELS

Name & location	Type	Length (km)	Date
Seikan, Tsugaru Strait [Honshu–Hokkaido], Japan	Rail	53.9 (23.4 subsea)	1988
Channel Tunnel, Strait of Dover [England–France]	Rail	50.5 (38.0 subsea)	1994
Moscow Metro, Belyaevo–Bitsevsky, Moscow, Russian Fed.	Metro	37.9	1979
Northern Line, East Finchley–Morden, London, UK	Metro	27.8	1939
Lærdal, Lærdal–Aurland, Sogn og Fjordane, Norway	Road	24.5	2000
Shimizu, Joetsu Shinkansen, Honshu, Japan	Rail	22.3	1982
Simplon II; I, Brig, Switzerland–Iselle, Italy	Rail	19.8; 19.7	1922; 1906
Vereina, Selfranga–Sagliains, Switzerland	Rail	19.1	1999
Shin-Kanmon, Sanyo Shinkansen [Honshu–Kyushu], Japan	Rail	18.7 (part subsea)	1975
Appennino, 'Direttissima', Bologna–Firenze (Florence), Italy	Rail	18.5	1934
Gotthard (Road), Göschenen–Airolo*, Switzerland	Road	16.9	1980
Rokko, Sanyo Shinkansen [Osaka–Kobe], Honshu, Japan	Rail	16.3	1971
Furka Base, Oberwald–Realp, Switzerland	Rail	15.4	1982
Haruna, Joetsu Shinkansen, Honshu, Japan	Rail	15.4	1982
Severomuysk, Baikal-Amur Line, Russian Federation	Rail	15.3	1984
Monte Santomarco, Páola–Cosenza, Italy	Rail	15.0	1987
Gotthard (Rail), Andermatt–Airolo, Switzerland	Rail	15.0	1882
Nakayama, Joetsu Shinkansen, Japan	Rail	14.8	1982
Lötschberg, Kandersteg–Goppenstein, Switzerland	Rail	14.6	1913
Mount Macdonald, Rogers Pass, BC, Canada	Rail	14.6	1989
Romeriksporten, Oslo–Gardermoen Airport, Norway	Rail	14.6	1999
Dayaoshan, Hengyang–Guangzhou Line, China	Rail	14.3	1987
Arlberg, Langen–St Anton, Austria	Road	14.0	1978

* *Including emergency tunnel*

17: WORLD MONUMENTS WATCH

*The World Monuments Fund is a New York-based non-profit organisation dedicated to the conservation of culturally and historically significant works of art and architecture around the world. WMF's World Monuments Watch, launched in 1995, calls attention to imperiled cultural heritage sites by publishing a list every two years of the world's 100 most endangered sites. The 2002 list is shown below. Following the terrorist attack on New York in September 2001, a 101st site was added**

UNITED STATES & CANADA
Schindler Kings Road House and Studio, West Hollywood, CA
San Luis Capistrano Mission Church, San Luis Capistrano, CA
San Esteban del Ray Mission, Acoma Pueblo, NM
A. Conger Goodyear House, Old Westbury, NY
St Ann and the Holy Trinity Church, Brooklyn, New York, NY
Historic Lower Manhattan, New York, NY*

LATIN AMERICA & THE CARIBBEAN
Immaculada Concepción Chapel, Nurio, Michoacán, Mexico
San Juan de Ulúa Fort, Veracruz, Mexico
Yaxchilán archaeological site, Chiapas, Mexico
Piedras Negras archaeological site, Guatemala
San Lorenzo and San Gerónimo Forts, Colón & Portobelo, Panama
Whylly Plantation, Clifton Point, Bahamas
National Schools of Art, La Habana (Havana), Cuba
Falmouth historic town, Jamaica
Los Pinchudos archaeological site, Parque Nac. Río Abiseo, Peru
Caral archaeological site, Supe, Peru
Oyón Valley Missionary Chapels, near Lima, Peru
Santuario de Nuestra Señora de Cocharcas, Chincheros, Peru
Cuzco historic centre, Peru
San Pedro de Morropé Chapel, Morropé, Peru
Vila de Paranapiacaba, Santo André, Brazil
Ruedas de Agua, Larmahue, Chile

EUROPE (including Turkey)
Sinclair and Girnigoe Castles, near Wick, Scotland
Greenock Sugar Warehouses, Scotland
Selby Abbey, North Yorkshire, England
Stowe House, Buckingham, England
St George's Church, Bloomsbury, London, England
Brading Roman Villa, Isle of Wight, England
Karl-Theodor Brücke, Heidelberg, Germany
Cathédrale St Pierre, Beauvais, France
Château de Chantilly, Chantilly, France
Cinque Terre, Liguria, Italy
Port of Trajan archaeological park, Fiumicino, Italy
Bridge of Chains, Bagni di Lucca, Italy
Wislica archaeological site, Poland
Terezin Fortress, Czech Republic
Vukovar city centre, Croatia
Maritime Quarantine-Lazareti, Dubrovnik, Croatia
Mostor historic centre, Bosnia-Herzegovina
Subotica Synagogue, Vojvodina, Fed. Rep. of Yugoslavia
Pec and Decani Monasteries, Kosovo, Fed. Rep. of Yugoslavia
Prizren historic centre, Kosovo, Fed. Rep. of Yugoslavia
Voskopojë churches, Albania
Palékastro archaeological site, Crete, Greece
Little Hagia Sophia Mosque, Istanbul, Turkey
Temple of Augustus, Ankara, Turkey
Tepebasi district, Gaziantep, Turkey
Ani archaeological site, Ocarli Köyü, Kars, Turkey
Mnajdra prehistoric temples, Malta
Pervomaisk Church, Uzda, Belarus
Church of Our Saviour of Berestove, Kyiv (Kiev), Ukraine
Ancient Chersonesos, Sevastopol', Ukraine
Barbary-Bosia monastery complex, Butuceni, Moldova

RUSSIAN FEDERATION
Karelian petroglyphs, Belomorsk and Pudozh districts
Assumption Church, Kondopoga
Viipuri Library, Vyborg
Resurrection New Jerusalem Monastery, Istra
Arkhangel'skoye State Museum, Moscow
Narcomfin Building, Moscow
Rostov Veliky historic centre and Church of Our Saviour
Oranienbaum State Museum, Lomonosov, Sankt-Peterburg (St Petersburg)

AFRICA
Sultan El-Muayyad Hospital, El Qâhira (Cairo), Egypt
White and Red Monasteries, Sohâg, Egypt
Valley of the Kings, Luxor, Egypt
Temple of Khasekhemwy, Nekhen (Hierakonopolis), Egypt
Médine Fort, Mali
Larabanga Mosque, Ghana
Benin City earthworks, Nigeria
Thimlich Ohinga cultural landscape, Migori, Kenya
Bagamoyo historic town, Tanzania

ASIA
Citadel of Aleppo, Halab (Aleppo), Syria
Old City and Saddle Souk, Dimashq (Damascus), Syria
Enfeh archaeological site, near Tripoli, Lebanon
Bet She'arim archeaological site, Kiryat Tiv'on, Israel
Petra archaeological site, Jordan
Art Nouveau buildings, Bat'umi, K'ut'aisi and T'bilisi, Georgia
T'bilisi historical district, Georgia
Bodbe Cathedral, Qedeli, Georgia
Ninevah and Nimrud Palaces, near Al Mawsil (Mosul), Iraq
Arbil (Erbil) Citadel, Iraq
Tarim historic city, Yemen
Merv archaeological site, Mary, Turkmenistan
Uch monument complex, near Bahawalpur, Pakistan
Maitreya Temples of Basgo, Leh, India
Nako Temples, Himachal Pradesh, India
Lutyens bungalow zone, Delhi, India
Dwarka Dheesh Mandir Temple, Ahmadabad, India
Osmania Women's College, Hyderabad, India
Anagundi historic settlement, Karnataka, India
Itum Baha Monstery, Kathmandu, Nepal
Teku Thapatali Monastery, Kathmandu, Nepal
Da Qin Christian Pagoda and Monastery, Shaanxi, China
Great Wall of China cultural landscape, Beijing (Peking), China
Ohel Rachel Synagogue, Shanghai, China
Shaxi market area, Jianchuan, Yunnan, China
Tomo port town, Fukuyama, Kyushu, Japan
Sri-Ksetra Temples, Hmawa, Myanmar
Banteay Chhmar Temple of Jayavarman VII, Thmar Puok, Cambodia
Kampung Cina river frontage, Kuala Terengganu, Malaysia
George Town historic enclave, Pinang (Penang), Malaysia
Omo Hada, Nias, Indonesia

Countries A-Z: Afghanistan–Benin

This chart provides exact data relevant to many of the thematic maps which appear elsewhere in this atlas: over 8,000 figures in all. Attention is drawn to the notes at the foot of page 192. Various sources have been used in the compilation of these statistics and these are specified on the maps themselves, as are the year/s to which the information relates.

The matter of deciding what is and what is not a country is by no means clear-cut, but no political or other subjective stance has been adopted. Many countries have dependencies, overseas possessions and the like; for various reasons (mainly connected with the availability, reliability or relevance of statistical data) some have been listed separately, some have had their figures amalgamated with those for their mother country and some have been excluded. Again, the notes will give guidance on this point. For more information on countries worldwide, consult the 20th edition of the Columbus *World Travel Guide*.

The data figures have been rounded up or down to either a whole number, or to one or two decimal places. The only exception is Population Density, which has been rounded to the nearest whole number for figures above 9.5 (rounded to 10), and to the nearest single decimal place for those under 9.49 (rounded to 9.5).

The *italic* numbers in the second row for each country (preceded by •) give the country's ranking for that category. These are in descending order (i.e. highest figure ranked number 1) with the exceptions of External Debt and Infant Mortality where ascending order is used. The top 10 countries in each category have their ranking figure in **bold**. Countries whose figures are equal according to whatever rounding has been employed have been ranked equally. As data is not always available for all 225 countries, the figures at the bottom of the chart give the lowest ranking figure in that category: this may be shared by two or more countries.

Throughout, n/a means that, at the time of going to press, data was not available, not reliable or not relevant. For details of other abbreviations used please see the notes on page 192.

Country (Map Ref pp10-11)	Capital	Area 000 sq km	Population 000	Pop. Density people/sq km	Intl Arrivals 000	Visitor Receipts US$m	Intl Departs 000	Visitor Expenditure US$m	Gross Nat'l Income US$m	GNI per Person US$	GDP Growth Av % 1990-99	External Debt US$m	Energy Production m tonnes	Energy Consumption m tonnes	Energy Consumption t/person	Fixed Tel Lines/100	Mobile Tel Lines/100	Internet Subscribers/100	Agricultural Land %	Health Spending % GNI	Military Spending % GNI	Infant Mortality Deaths<5yrs/000	Life Expectancy Years
Afghanistan M4	Kabul	652.10 •41	25,869 •38	40 •146	n/a –	1 •199	n/a –	1 •169	13,529 •79	523 •172	n/a –	n/a –	0.25 •119	0.50 •142	0.02 •206	0.13 •203	nn –	ns –	58 •43	n/a –	n/a –	257 •177	n/a –
Albania J3	Tirana	28.70 •142	3,375 •129	118 •78	39 •180	211 •107	18 •102	12 •144	3,146 •140	930 •153	3.2 •81	821 •55	1.75 •96	2.00 •118	0.59 •128	3.65 •144	0.76 •132	6 •172	41 •97	2.6 •85	1.4 •123	37 •91	72.8 •49
Algeria J4	Algiers	2,381.70 •11	29,950 •34	13 •189	749 •80	24 •164	903 •57	40 •123	46,548 •52	1,550 •133	1.6 •128	30,665 •160	151.50 •16	32.75 •42	1.09 •102	5.20 •133	0.23 •154	7 •171	16 •165	3.4 •65	3.9 •43	40 •95	68.9 •84
American Samoa A6	Pago Pago	0.20 •210	64 •202	320 •30	n/a –	10 •180	n/a –	n/a –	380 •195	6,032 •72	n/a –	n/a –	0.00 –	0.25 •162	3.91 •37	n/a –	n/a –	n/a –	15 •167	n/a –	T	n/a –	n/a –
Andorra J3	Andorra la Vella	0.45 •195	66 •201	147 •66	n/a –	n/a –	n/a –	n/a –	n/a –	14,690 •39	n/a –	n/a –	0.00 –	n/a –	n/a –	44.74 •38	27.43 •42	2558 •21	58 •43	n/a –	T	n/a –	n/a –
Angola J6	Luanda	1,246.70 •23	12,357 D1 •63	10 •196	45 •176	13 •175	3 •109	70 •109	3,276 •135	270 •205	0.4 •146	12,173 •138	41.50 •36	2.50 •110	0.20 •164	0.53 •184	0.20 •160	23 •144	25 •141	7.6 •	20.5 •**3**	292 •179	46.5 •153
Anguilla F5	The Valley	0.16 •214	11 •218	69 •113	47 •174	56 •141	n/a –	6 •157	25 •220	3,125 •98	n/a –	n/a –	0.00 –	0.00 –	n/a –	n/a –	n/a –	n/a –	<0.5 •211	n/a –	T	20 •	77.0 •
Antigua & Barbuda F5	St John's	0.44 •196	67 •200	152 •63	232 •132	291 •97	369 •70	26 •134	606 •185	8,990 •60	4.1 •57	n/a –	0.00 –	0.25 •162	3.73 •40	49.95 •26	28.69 •40	652 •50	27 •136	0.4 •165	M	20 •52	–
Argentina F7	Buenos Aires	2,780.40 •**8**	36,580 •31	13 •189	2,898 •42	2,812 •38	4,786 •25	4,107 •22	276,097 •17	7,550 •65	4.9 •34	144,050 •187	85.75 •25	67.75 •26	1.85 •77	21.53 •81	12.12 •71	243 •81	62 •37	5.1 •41	1.2 •139	22 •58	72.9 •47
Armenia L3	Yerevan	29.80 •141	3,809 •124	128 •73	41 •178	27 •163	34 •128	34 •128	1,878 •154	490 •176	-3.2 •165	800 •54	1.00 •104	2.50 •110	0.66 •124	15.53 •93	0.23 •154	85 •109	44 •82	3.1 •73	3.5 •50	30 •79	70.5 •67
Aruba F5	Oranjestad	0.18 •212	98 •194	544 •17	683 •83	782 •65	n/a –	122 •95	2,973 •142	13,827 •43	n/a –	n/a –	0.00 –	0.25 •162	2.55 •63	37.20 •49	12.21 •69	407 •65	11 •180	n/a –	T	21 •56	73.8 •41
Australia P7	Canberra	7,682.30 •**6**	18,967 •51	2.5 •218	4,459 •34	7,525 •12	3,210 •35	5,792 •15	397,345 •15	20,950 •23	4.1 •57	222,000 •192	219.50 •11	118.50 •16	6.25 •18	52.41 •23	44.63 •27	3497 •**10**	60 •36	5.0 •42	2.2 •81	5 •**4**	78.3 •**7**
Austria J3	Vienna	83.90 •115	8,092 •88	96 •93	17,467 •11	12,533 •**8**	3,954 •30	9,803 •11	205,743 •22	25,430 •13	1.9 •120	31,700 •162	13.75 •60	34.75 •40	4.29 •29	47.36 •32	78.55 •**3**	2558 •	42 •93	6.2 •18	0.9 •151	5 •**4**	77.0 •20
Azerbaijan L3	Baku	86.60 •113	7,983 D2 •89	92 •95	602 •86	81 •132	52 •95	139 •90	3,705 •128	460 •179	-9.6 •176	693 •49	21.00 •53	13.75 •67	1.72 •80	10.36 •104	5.56 •95	16 •152	48 •72	1.3 •140	1.9 •94	46 •103	69.9 •73
Bahamas F4	Nassau	13.90 •158	298 •173	21 •174	1,577 •61	1,503 •53	n/a –	309 •65	3,396 •130	11,395 •51	0.8 •140	349 •43	0.00 –	1.25 •125	4.19 •	37.59 •48	10.36 •75	432 •64	1 •208	2.7 •81	0.7 •162	21 •56	73.8 •41
Bahrain L4	Manama	0.71 •186	666 •159	938 •**8**	1,991 •56	408 •84	n/a –	159 •86	4,900 •115	7,621 •64	4.5 •45	2,000 •78	10.25 •68	9.25 •74	13.89 •**6**	24.97 •69	30.05 •37	584 •54	6 •186	2.8 •80	10.3 •**6**	20 •52	72.9 •47
Bangladesh N4	Dhaka	148.40 •93	127,669 •**10**	860 •**10**	173 •140	50 •145	1,103 •54	212 •78	47,071 •50	370 •189	4.7 •37	16,376 •147	8.25 •71	11.25 •69	0.09 •179	0.34 •192	0.12 •166	4 •182	80 •**6**	1.5 •132	1.4 •123	106 •133	58.1 •121
Barbados F5	Bridgetown	0.43 •197	267 •176	621 •12	515 •94	677 •68	n/a –	82 •104	2,294 •148	8,600 •61	1.1 •138	608 •47	0.25 •119	0.50 •142	1.87 •74	42.71 •42	11.14 •74	223 •83	42 •93	4.6 •47	0.8 •158	15 •42	76.4 •25
Belarus K3	Minsk	207.60 •85	10,032 •77	48 •116	355 •116	13 •175	969 •56	116 •96	26,299 •62	2,620 •106	-3.0 •163	1,120 •63	2.25 •90	27.50 •49	2.74 •57	25.68 •68	0.46 •139	49 •123	45 •78	4.2 •54	1.7 •103	27 •75	68.0 •93
Belgium J3	Brussels	30.50 •139	10,226 •75	335 •27	6,369 •17	7,039 •17	7,773 •18	10,057 •**10**	252,051 •20	24,650 •17	1.7 •125	28,300 •156	12.50 •62	65.25 •27	6.38 •16	49.94 •27	54.89 •23	1968 •27	45 •78	6.7 •14	1.5 •114	6 •17	77.2 •15
Belize E5	Belmopan	23.00 •150	247 •178	11 •194	181 •137	112 •122	n/a –	24 •136	673 •181	2,730 •102	3.5 •73	338 •42	0.00 –	0.10 •185	0.40 •144	15.57 •92	2.63 •111	510 •59	5 •200	2.3 •109	1.6 •105	43 •99	74.7 •36
Benin J5	Porto Novo	112.60 •100	6,114 •99	54 •132	152 •143	33 •158	7 •153	n/a –	2,320 •147	380 •188	4.7 •37	1,647 •72	0.00 –	0.50 •142	0.08 •181	0.66 •178	0.11 •170	17 •150	21 •156	1.6 •125	1.3 •131	165 •158	53.4 •132

•: *Ranking* (top 10 in **bold**).   **n/a**: Not available, not relevant or not reliable.   For more information, see the notes on pages 184 and 192.

ns: No service.   **nn**: No network.   **mn**: No mains.   **M**: See note on page 33.   **T**: See note on page 33.

Countries A-Z: Bermuda–Congo

Country (Map ref)	Capital	Area ('000 sq km)	Population ('000)	Pop. Density (/sq km)	Intl Arrivals ('000)	Visitor Receipts (US$m)	Intl Departs ('000)	Visitor Expenditure (US$m)	Gross Nat'l Income (US$m)	GNI per Person (US$)	GDP Growth (% 1990–99)	External Debt (US$m)	Energy Production (Mt oil equiv.)	Energy Consumption (Mt oil equiv.)	Energy Consumption (t oil/person)	Fixed Tel Lines (/100)	Mobile Tel Lines (/100)	Internet Usage (/10,000)	Agricultural Land (% area)	Health Spending (% GNI)	Military Spending (% GNI)	Infant Mortality (/1000)	Life Expectancy (yrs)
Bermuda (F4)	Hamilton	0.05 (220)	64 (203)	1,280 (6)	354 (117)	487 (81)	n/a	148 (88)	2,474 (146)	38,652 (2)	n/a	n/a	0.00	0.25 (162)	3.91 (37)	85.73 (1)	19.64 (57)	3,901 (8)	<0.5 (211)	n/a	T	n/a	n/a
Bhutan (N4)	Thimphu	46.50 (131)	782 (156)	17 (181)	7 (192)	9 (182)	n/a	n/a	399 (194)	510 (173)	5.1 (28)	120 (200)	0.50 (112)	0.25 (162)	0.32 (151)	1.80 (160)	nn	8 (169)	8 (186)	3.2 (71)	n/a	116 (139)	60.7 (116)
Bolivia (F8)	Note[B1]	1,098.60 (28)	8,138 (87)	7.4 (206)	342 (118)	179 (114)	253 (79)	165 (85)	8,092 (97)	990 (151)	4.2 (52)	6,077 (116)	4.50 (80)	3.00 (106)	0.37 (146)	6.17 (130)	5.16 (97)	96 (105)	26 (139)	1.2 (143)	1.9 (94)	85 (125)	61.4 (115)
Bosnia-Herzegovina (J3)	Sarajevo	51.10 (127)	3,881 (122)	76 (110)	89 (154)	21 (167)	n/a	n/a	4,706 (117)	1,210 (142)	35.2 (1)	4,100 (103)	0.75 (108)	2.25 (116)	0.58 (130)	9.58 (109)	5.53 (96)	9 (166)	39 (103)	5.9 (18)	n/a	17 (44)	n/a
Botswana (K7)	Gaborone	561.70 (47)	1,588 (146)	2.7 (212)	750 (79)	175 (115)	n/a	126 (93)	5,139 (112)	3,240 (96)	4.3 (50)	548 (46)	0.50 (112)	1.25 (125)	0.79 (117)	7.69 (122)	7.45 (87)	74 (112)	47 (73)	2.6 (85)	5.1 (24)	48 (105)	47.4 (149)
Brazil (G6)	Brasília	8,547.40 (5)	167,967 (5)	20 (176)	5,107 (27)	3,994 (25)	2,679 (38)	3,059 (26)	730,424 (8)	4,350 (82)	3.0 (88)	232,004 (193)	152.75 (15)	212.75 (10)	1.27 (95)	14.87 (95)	13.64 (68)	294 (73)	28 (133)	3.6 (62)	1.8 (101)	42 (96)	66.8 (102)
British Virgin Is. (F5)	Road Town	0.13 (216)	19 (214)	146 (67)	286 (123)	300 (95)	n/a	42 (121)	240 (201)	12,000 (48)	n/a	n/a	0.00	0.02 (204)	n/a	n/a	n/a	n/a	60 (36)	n/a	T	n/a	n/a
Brunei (O5)	Bandar Seri Begawan	5.80 (168)	322 (172)	56 (128)	964 (72)	37 (153)	n/a	n/a	6,000 (108)	19,048 (29)	1.2 (137)	0 (1)	20.25 (54)	2.00 (118)	6.21 (19)	24.59 (70)	20.52 (54)	777 (44)	3 (202)	0.7 (159)	4.6 (30)	9 (30)	75.5 (31)
Bulgaria (K3)	Sofia	111.00 (102)	8,208 (86)	74 (111)	2,472 (47)	932 (60)	2,592 (39)	524 (54)	11,572 (88)	1,410 (136)	-2.7 (161)	9,907 (132)	10.75 (67)	21.00 (55)	2.56 (61)	35.43 (55)	8.97 (81)	283 (74)	55 (51)	3.4 (65)	3.0 (55)	17 (44)	71.1 (63)
Burkina (H5)	Ouagadougou	274.10 (74)	10,996 (68)	40 (146)	160 (141)	42 (149)	n/a	32 (129)	2,602 (144)	240 (212)	3.8 (63)	1,399 (70)	0.00	0.25 (162)	0.02 (203)	0.41 (188)	0.04 (180)	3 (184)	35 (114)	1.2 (143)	2.8 (60)	165 (158)	44.4 (158)
Burundi (K6)	Bujumbura	27.80 (145)	6,678 (95)	240 (48)	26 (184)	1 (199)	16 (103)	8 (149)	823 (175)	120 (223)	-2.9 (162)	1,119 (62)	0.00	0.25 (162)	0.04 (196)	0.29 (194)	0.01 (188)	3 (188)	89 (2)	0.7 (159)	6.1 (15)	176 (165)	42.4 (161)
Cambodia (O5)	Phnom Penh	181.00 (89)	11,757 (65)	65 (118)	368 (115)	190 (113)	n/a	n/a	3,023 (141)	260 (207)	4.8 (36)	2,210 (80)	0.00	0.25 (162)	0.02 (204)	0.26 (196)	1.00 (128)	5 (179)	24 (145)	0.6 (162)	4.1 (38)	163 (157)	53.4 (132)
Cameroon (J5)	Yaoundé	475.40 (53)	14,691 (61)	31 (160)	133 (147)	40 (151)	n/a	107 (100)	8,798 (92)	600 (167)	1.3 (134)	9,829 (130)	6.25 (74)	2.25 (116)	0.15 (169)	0.64 (180)	0.03 (184)	14 (155)	19 (160)	1.0 (155)	3.0 (55)	153 (154)	54.7 (128)
Canada (D2)	Ottawa	9,970.60 (2)	30,491 (33)	3.1 (212)	19,411 (7)	10,171 (9)	18,368 (8)	11,345 (8)	614,003 (9)	20,140 (27)	2.7 (97)	253,000 (194)	442.75 (5)	313.00 (6)	10.27 (10)	65.45 (10)	22.55 (49)	4,130 (5)	8 (186)	6.1 (19)	1.3 (131)	6 (17)	79.0 (2)
Cape Verde (H5)	Praia	4.00 (171)	428 (167)	107 (86)	67 (165)	23 (166)	n/a	24 (136)	569 (187)	1,330 (140)	4.7 (37)	244 (37)	0.00	0.05 (194)	0.12 (173)	12.39 (100)	4.62 (100)	187 (89)	17 (161)	2.3 (105)	0.9 (151)	73 (117)	68.9 (84)
Cayman Is. (E5)	George Town	0.26 (204)	39 (208)	150 (64)	395 (109)	450 (83)	n/a	n/a	650 (184)	18,056 (31)	n/a	70 (13)	0.00	0.12 (181)	3.08 (53)	n/a	n/a	n/a	8 (186)	n/a	T	n/a	n/a
Central African Rep. (K5)	Bangui	622.40 (43)	3,540 (128)	5.7 (207)	10 (190)	6 (187)	n/a	39 (124)	1,035 (169)	290 (200)	1.8 (122)	921 (56)	0.00	1.00 (134)	0.28 (157)	0.28 (195)	0.12 (166)	3 (190)	8 (186)	2.0 (115)	3.9 (43)	173 (162)	44.9 (157)
Chad (J5)	Ndjaména	1,284.00 (21)	7,486 (91)	5.8 (207)	47 (174)	10 (180)	n/a	24 (136)	1,555 (160)	210 (216)	2.1 (117)	1,091 (61)	0.00	0.50 (142)	0.06 (190)	0.13 (203)	nn	3 (190)	39 (103)	2.6 (85)	2.7 (65)	198 (169)	47.2 (150)
Channel Is. (I3)	Note[B2]	0.20 (211)	149 (187)	745 (11)	n/a	n/a	n/a	n/a	3,938 (123)	26,790 (10)	n/a	n/a	0.00	n/a	n/a	83.02 (2)	30.94 (36)	n/a	n/a	n/a	T	n/a	n/a
Chile (F7)	Santiago	736.90 (39)	15,018 (59)	20 (176)	1,622 (59)	894 (62)	1,567 (48)	806 (49)	69,602 (45)	4,630 (79)	7.2 (12)	36,302 (151)	6.75 (73)	24.25 (52)	1.61 (81)	22.12 (78)	22.36 (50)	1,155 (35)	23 (151)	2.7 (81)	3.9 (43)	12 (40)	74.9 (33)
China[A1] (O4)	Beijing	9,536.70 (4)	1,253,595 (1)	131 (77)	27047 (5)	14,098 (7)	9,232 (17)	10,864 (9)	979,894 (7)	780 (159)	10.7 (4)	154,599 (189)	771.75 (1)	797.00 (2)	0.64 (125)	8.58 (116)	6.67 (88)	176 (90)	53 (56)	2.0 (115)	2.2 (81)	47 (104)	69.8 (76)
China: Hong Kong (O4)	—	1.10 (179)	6,721 (94)	6,110 (3)	11328 (16)	7,210 (15)	4,175 (28)	n/a	165,122 (25)	24,570 (18)	3.9 (61)	48,100 (176)	0.00	18.50 (59)	2.75 (56)	58.06 (14)	63.61 (16)	3,359 (12)	8 (186)	2.7 (81)	T	n/a	78.5 (6)
China: Macau (O4)	—	0.02 (221)	434 (164)	21,700 (1)	5,050 (28)	2,466 (43)	117 (89)	131 (91)	6,161 (105)	14,200 (41)	4.0 (60)	1,700 (76)	0.00	0.50 (142)	1.15 (98)	39.80 (45)	27.22 (43)	914 (43)	<0.5 (211)	n/a	n/a	n/a	n/a
Colombia (F5)	Bogotá	1,141.70 (26)	41,539 (28)	36 (153)	546 (93)	928 (61)	1,098 (55)	1,078 (45)	90,007 (38)	2,170 (111)	3.3 (75)	33,263 (166)	80.25 (27)	30.50 (46)	0.73 (121)	16.03 (91)	7.53 (85)	160 (94)	44 (82)	1.7 (122)	3.7 (47)	30 (79)	70.4 (68)
Comoros (L6)	Moroni	1.90 (176)	544 (161)	286 (35)	24 (185)	19 (169)	n/a	3 (163)	189 (206)	350 (193)	-0.5 (151)	203 (35)	0.03 (163)	0.03 (189)	0.06 (189)	0.96 (171)	nn	12 (161)	52 (59)	3.3 (68)	1.6 (109)	90 (128)	58.8 (120)
Congo (J6)	Brazzaville	341.80 (63)	2,859 (132)	8.4 (202)	5 (194)	12 (178)	n/a	60 (112)	1,571 (159)	550 (169)	-0.5 (151)	5,119 (112)	14.25 (59)	0.50 (142)	0.17 (167)	0.77 (176)	0.12 (166)	<0.5 (196)	29 (130)	2.3 (105)	4.1 (38)	108 (134)	48.6 (146)

For more information, see the notes on pages 184 and 192.

*: Ranking (top 10 in **bold**).

n/a: Not available, not relevant or not reliable.
ns: No service.
nn: No network.
M: See note on page 33.
T: See note on page 33.

Countries A-Z: Congo, Dem. Rep.–French Polynesia

Key to columns (each cell shows value • ranking figure):

Country (Map Ref)	Capital	Life Expectancy (years)	Infant Mortality (deaths/000)	Military Spending (% GNI)	Health Spending (% GNI)	Agricultural Land (% nat. area)	Internet Usage (subs/10,000)	Mobile Tel. Lines (/100)	Fixed Tel. Lines (/100)	Energy Consumption (t oil equiv/person)	Energy Consumption (m t oil equiv)	Energy Production (m t oil equiv)	External Debt (US$m)	GDP Growth (av. % 1990-99)	GNI per Person (US$)	Gross Nat'l Income (US$m)	Visitor Expenditure (US$m)	International Departs (000)	Visitor Receipts (US$m)	International Arrivals (000)	Population Density (/sq km)	Population (000)	Area (000 sq km)
Congo, Dem. Rep. (K6)	Kinshasa	50.8 •140	207 •174	5.0 •26	1.6 •125	10 •181	<0.5 •196	0.02 •187	0.04 •205	0.06 •188	2.75 •107	2.50 •88	12,919 •140	-5.1 •171	106 •224	5,200 •110	7 •153	50 •96	2 •193	53 •172	21 •174	49,776 •24	2,344.90 •12
Cook Is. (A6)	Avarua	n/a –	n/a –	T –	n/a –	22 •153	n/a –	n/a –	n/a –	1.00 •109	0.02 •203	0.00 –	141 •23	n/a –	2,647 •103	45 •216	n/a –	8 •107	39 •152	56 •170	87 •98	20 •213	0.23 •209
Costa Rica (E5)	San José	76.0 •27	16 •43	0.6 •164	5.5 •30	57 •47	381 •67	3.53 •106	20.41 •84	0.98 •111	3.50 •101	1.75 •96	3,971 •100	5.1 •28	3,570 •88	12,828 •80	428 •59	353 •73	1,002 •57	1,032 •70	70 •112	3,589 •127	51.10 •128
Côte d'Ivoire (I5)	Note B3	46.7 •153	150 •153	1.1 •142	1.5 •132	53 •56	14 •154	1.77 •120	1.81 •159	0.27 •158	4.25 •91	2.25 •90	14,852 •144	3.7 •68	670 •164	10,387 •86	237 •74	n/a –	108 •125	301 •121	48 •139	15,545 •57	320.80 •68
Croatia (J3)	Zagreb	72.6 •52	9 •30	6.3 •14	8.7 •7	43 •88	447 •61	23.09 •48	36.49 •53	2.30 •67	10.25 •70	4.75 •79	8,297 •125	0.2 •149	4,530 •80	20,222 •66	751 •50	n/a –	2,493 •42	3,443 •38	79 •105	4,464 •115	56.50 •126
Cuba (F4)	Havana	75.7 •29	8 •28	2.3 •75	8.2 •**4**	58 •43	54 •120	0.06 •177	4.36 •140	0.87 •114	9.75 •73	3.00 •86	31,200 N1 •161	-5.0 •170	2,150 •112	24,033 •63	n/a –	56 •94	1,714 •50	1,561 •62	101 •90	11,178 •66	110.90 •103
Cyprus A2 (K4)	Nicosia	77.8 •13	9 •29	6.1 •15	4.6 •47	17 •161	1765 •28	32.11 •35	64.72 •11	3.29 •47	2.50 •110	0.00 –	1,270 •68	3.9 •61	11,950 •49	9,086 •91	289 •66	470 •65	1,878 •49	2,434 •49	82 •102	760 •157	9.30 •165
Czech Rep. (J3)	Prague	73.9 •39	6 •17	1.9 •94	7.0 •**9**	54 •54	976 •41	42.18 •28	37.09 •50	3.75 •39	38.50 •37	23.50 •50	25,301 •154	0.8 •140	5,020 •76	51,623 •49	1,474 •41	39,977 •**5**	3,035 •36	5,610 •26	130 •72	10,278 •74	78.90 •117
Denmark (J3)	Copenhagen	76.5 •17	5 •**4**	1.7 •103	6.9 •11	65 •25	3659 •**9**	66.47 •14	70.49 •**6**	4.18 •33	22.25 •54	24.50 •49	44,000 •158	2.4 •105	32,050 •16	170,685 •24	5,084 •23	4,841 •23	3,682 •36	2,023 •55	124 •75	5,326 •105	43.10 •133
Djibouti (L5)	Djibouti	50.4 •142	156 •155	M –	4.1 •38	9 •184	12 •160	0.04 •180	1.40 •163	0.77 •118	0.50 •142	0.00 –	288 •40	-3.5 •166	790 •158	511 •191	5 •159	n/a –	4 •190	21 •187	28 •168	648 •160	23.20 •149
Dominica (F5)	Roseau	n/a –	20 •52	n/a –	6.9 •11	25 •141	261 •80	0.86 •131	27.88 •64	0.55 •131	0.04 •199	0.00 –	109 •17	1.5 •130	3,260 •95	238 •202	7 •153	8 •107	49 •148	74 •160	97 •92	73 •198	0.75 •183
Dominican Rep. (F5)	Santo Domingo	70.6 •66	51 •108	0.55 •131	3.3 •68	73 •13	30 •139	5.02 •98	9.81 •108	0.59 •127	5.00 •88	0.25 •119	4,451 •107	5.8 •21	1,920 •95	16,130 •74	282 •67	364 •71	2,524 •41	2,649 •43	174 •55	8,404 •84	48.40 •130
Ecuador (F6)	Quito	69.5 •78	39 •94	2.7 •81	2.7 •81	29 •130	28 •141	3.09 •107	9.10 •112	0.73 •123	9.00 •75	22.50 •51	15,140 •145	2.2 •113	1,360 •138	16,841 •73	271 •68	386 •68	343 •89	509 •95	45 •142	12,412 D3 •62	275.80 C1 •73
Egypt (K4)	Cairo	66.3 •104	69 •114	2.8 •60	1.7 •122	3 •205	29 •130	2.00 •116	8.08 •120	0.81 •116	50.50 •30	68.00 •30	31,964 •163	4.4 •48	1,380 •137	86,544 •40	1,078 •45	2,886 •37	3,903 •26	4,490 •32	63 •119	62,655 •18	997.70 •30
El Salvador (E5)	San Salvador	69.1 •82	34 •85	0.9 •151	2.6 •85	64 •27	64 •115	6.22 •90	9.08 •113	0.41 •143	2.50 •110	0.75 •108	3,633 •97	5.0 •31	1,920 •119	11,806 •83	80 •105	787 •59	211 •107	658 •85	293 •32	6,154 •98	21.00 •152
Equatorial Guinea (J5)	Malabo	50.0 •144	112 •135	1.5 •190	5.0 •194	13 •173	2 •205	0.07 •175	1.29 •164	0.11 •175	0.05 •194	5.00 •77	306 •41	17.7 •**2**	1,170 •146	516 •190	n/a –	n/a –	16 •174	n/a –	16 •182	443 •163	28.10 •144
Eritrea (K5)	Asmara	50.8 •140	112 •135	2.2 •110	5.0 •42	61 •32	13 •156	nm –	0.79 •175	0.13 •172	0.50 •142	0.00 –	149 •24	5.0 •31	200 •217	779 •178	n/a –	n/a –	28 •160	57 •169	43 •145	3,991 •119	93.70 •109
Estonia (K3)	Tallinn	68.7 •89	22 •58	5.4 •33	5.4 •33	34 •117	1387 •32	38.70 •31	35.74 •54	1.73 •79	2.50 •110	0.50 •112	782 •53	-1.3 •157	3,400 •91	4,906 •114	217 •77	1,780 •43	560 •77	950 •73	32 •159	1,442 •147	45.20 •132
Ethiopia (L5)	Addis Ababa	43.3 •160	173 •162	1.9 •114	1.6 •125	55 •51	2 •205	0.03 •184	0.37 •191	0.02 •205	1.25 •125	0.50 •110	10,352 •134	4.6 •43	100 •225	6,524 •102	55 •114	133 •87	16 •174	92 •152	57 •126	62,782 •17	1,104.30 •27
Falkland Is. (G8)	Stanley	n/a –	n/a –	T –	n/a –	99 •**1**	2 •205	0.03 •184	n/a –	3.33 •45	0.01 •208	0.00 –	n/a –	n/a –	12,500 •44	25 •220	n/a –	n/a –	n/a –	n/a –	0.2 •223	3 •223	12.20 •159
Faroe Is. (I2)	Tórshavn	n/a –	n/a –	T –	n/a –	6 •197	673 •49	24.13 •45	55.72 •20	0.45 •139	0.02 •208	0.00 –	767 •52	n/a –	20,930 •24	900 •173	n/a –	n/a –	n/a –	n/a –	31 •160	44 •206	1.40 •178
Fiji Is. (R6)	Suva	72.7 •50	23 •62	2.4 •72	2.5 •96	24 •145	93 •107	2.90 •110	10.11 •106	0.62 •126	0.50 •142	0.00 –	193 •34	2.4 •140	2,310 •109	1,848 •155	66 •111	89 •90	275 •100	410 •108	44 •143	801 •155	18.30 •155
Finland (K2)	Helsinki	76.8 •22	5 •**4**	1.7 •103	5.5 •30	8 •186	4034 •**6**	72.64 •**5**	55.18 •21	6.34 •17	32.75 •42	11.25 •66	30,000 •158	2.4 •105	24,730 •21	127,764 •30	2,021 •33	5,314 •22	1,517 •52	2,454 •48	15 •184	5,166 •106	338.10 •64
France A3 (J3)	Paris	78.1 •**9**	5 •**4**	3.0 •55	7.0 •**9**	55 •51	1446 •31	49.41 •26	58.02 •15	4.38 •27	256.50 •**8**	123.50 •20	117,600 •184	1.5 •130	24,170 •19	1,453,211 •**4**	18,631 •**5**	16,709 •**9**	31,507 •**3**	73,042 •**1**	107 •86	58,620 •21	549.10 •49
French Guiana A3 (G5)	Cayenne	n/a –	n/a –	T –	1.45 •88	<0.5 •211	115 •102	22.01 •51	28.26 •62	1.45 •88	0.25 •162	0.00 –	1,200 •65	n/a –	9,094 •59	1,573 •158	n/a –	n/a –	50 •145	70 •161	2.0 •218	173 •183	85.50 •114
French Polynesia (B7)	Papeete	n/a –	n/a –	T –	n/a –	12 •176	216 •84	9.49 •80	22.62 •77	1.08 •103	0.25 •162	0.00 –	n/a –	n/a –	16,930 •33	3,908 •124	n/a –	65 •92	354 •88	211 •133	55 •130	231 •179	4.20 •170

*: Ranking (top 10 in **bold**).   n/a: Not available, not relevant or not reliable.   nn: No network.   ns: No service.   M: See note on page 33.   T: See note on page 33.   For more information, see the notes on pages 184 and 192.

Countries A-Z: Gabon–Italy

Country (Map Ref. pp10-11)	Capital	Area '000 sq km	Population '000	Population Density People/sq km	International Arrivals '000	Visitor Receipts US$ million	International Departs '000	Visitor Expenditure US$ million	Gross Nat'l Income US$ million	GNI per Person US$	GDP Growth Av. annual % 1990-99	External Debt US$ million	Energy Production Million tonnes oil equiv.	Energy Consumption Million tonnes oil equiv.	Energy Consumption Tonnes oil equiv./person	Fixed Tel. Lines Lines/100 people	Mobile Tel. Lines Lines/100 people	Internet Usage Subscribers/10,000 people	Agricultural Land % of national area	Health Spending % of GNI	Military Spending % of GNI	Infant Mortality Deaths <5yrs/'000	Life Expectancy Years
Gabon J6	Libreville	267.70 •76	1,208 •150	4.5 •209	178 •139	11 •179	n/a –	183 •82	3,987 •122	3,300 •93	3.2 •81	4,425 •106	18.50 •55	1.25 •125	1.03 •107	3.17 •148	0.74 •133	25 •142	20 •158	0.8 •157	2.0 •90	144 •151	52.4 •136
Gambia, The H5	Banjul	10.70 •163	1,251 •149	117 •79	91 •153	32 •159	n/a –	16 •143	415 •193	330 •194	2.8 •93	477 •45	0.00 –	0.08 •186	0.06 •186	2.30 •155	0.42 •140	24 •143	27 •136	1.3 •140	3.7 •47	82 •122	47.0 •151
Georgia L3	Tbilisi	69.70 •121	5,452 •101	78 •108	384 •111	400 •86	373 •69	270 •70	3,362 •133	620 •166	-11.8 •180	1,674 •75	1.75 •96	4.00 •92	0.73 •122	12.31 •101	1.88 •118	37 •132	38 •107	1.1 •150	1.4 •123	23 •62	72.7 •50
Germany J3	Berlin	357.00 •62	82,100 •12	230 •50	17116 •13	16,730 •6	73,400 •1	48,465 •2	2,103,804 •3	25,620 •12	1.3 •134	399,721 N2 •195	133.50 •19	349.50 •5	4.26 •31	60.12 •13	58.59 •19	2921 •18	49 •70	8.4 •2	1.6 •109	5 •4	77.2 •15
Ghana I5	Accra	238.50 •81	18,785 •52	79 •105	373 •112	304 •93	n/a –	36 •126	7,451 •99	400 •185	4.3 •50	6,884 •120	1.25 •102	2.75 •107	0.15 •170	1.17 •167	0.64 •135	15 •153	41 •97	1.6 •125	0.7 •162	105 •131	60.0 •131
Gibraltar I4	Gibraltar	0.01 •224	27 •211	2,700 •5	n/a –	300 •95	n/a –	n/a –	450 •192	18,000 –	n/a –	n/a –	0.00 –	1.00 •134	37.04 •2	n/a –	n/a –	n/a –	<0.5 •211	n/a –	T –	n/a –	n/a –
Greece K4	Athens	132.00 •96	10,538 •72	80 •103	12164 •14	8,783 •10	n/a –	3,989 •23	127,648 •31	12,110 •46	2.2 •113	41,900 •170	9.75 •69	32.00 •44	3.04 •54	52.81 •22	55.90 •22	939 •42	68 •20	5.3 •42	4.6 •30	7 •25	78.1 •9
Greenland G2	Nuuk	2,166.10 •14	56 •204	0.1 •224	125 •148	63 •139	n/a –	n/a –	700 •180	12,500 •44	2.6 •101	243 •36	0.00 –	0.05 •209	0.00 •208	46.75 •34	28.53 •41	3186 •13	1 •208	2.6 •65	M –	28 •78	n/a –
Grenada F5	St George's	0.34 •201	97 •195	285 •36	n/a –	n/a –	n/a –	5 •159	334 •196	3,440 •90	n/a –	183 •31	0.00 •209	0.05 •194	0.52 •134	33.20 •57	4.55 •101	436 •63	36 •112	n/a –	T –	n/a –	n/a –
Guadeloupe F5	Note B4	1.70 •177	425 •168	250 •44	561 •90	375 •87	n/a –	n/a –	4,501 •120	10,591 •53	n/a –	n/a –	0.00 –	0.50 •142	1.18 •96	44.69 •39	37.25 •32	89 •108	32 •123	n/a –	T –	n/a –	n/a –
Guam Q5	Agaña	0.54 •190	152 •186	281 •39	1,162 •69	1,908 •47	n/a –	22 •139	2,921 •143	19,218 •28	n/a –	n/a –	0.00 –	1.25 •125	8.22 •14	47.20 •33	12.16 •70	35 •133	8 •186	n/a –	M –	n/a –	n/a –
Guatemala E5	Guatemala City	108.90 •104	11,088 •67	102 •89	823 •78	570 •76	391 •67	183 •82	18,625 •70	1,680 •128	4.2 •52	4,565 •108	1.75 •96	3.75 •96	0.34 •150	5.71 •108	3.05 •108	59 •118	41 •123	1.5 •132	1.4 •123	52 •109	64.0 •111
Guinea I5	Conakry	245.90 •78	7,251 •92	29 •166	27 •183	7 •186	n/a –	31 •131	3,556 •130	490 •176	4.2 •52	3,546 •95	0.00 –	0.50 •142	0.07 •184	0.59 •182	0.32 •146	6 •174	24 •145	.7 •143	1.5 •114	197 •168	46.5 •153
Guinea-Bissau I5	Bissau	36.10 •137	1,185 •151	33 •158	n/a –	n/a –	n/a –	n/a –	194 •205	160 •221	0.3 •147	964 •57	0.00 –	0.11 •182	0.09 •178	0.70 •177	0.01 •188	13 •159	50 •69	1.1 •150	3.2 •54	205 •172	45.0 •156
Guyana G5	Georgetown	215.00 •84	856 •154	4.0 •211	75 •159	52 •144	n/a –	22 •139	651 •183	760 •160	9.8 •5	1,653 •73	0.00 –	0.50 •142	0.58 •129	7.49 •124	0.33 •145	35 •133	8 •186	4.8 •46	1.1 •142	79 •121	64.4 •110
Haiti F5	Port-au-Prince	27.80 •146	7,803 •90	281 •39	143 •145	57 •140	n/a –	37 •125	3,584 •129	460 •179	-1.3 •157	1,048 •59	0.00 –	0.50 •142	0.06 •185	0.87 •173	0.31 •147	7 •170	51 •63	1.4 •136	M –	130 •146	53.8 •130
Honduras E5	Tegucigalpa	112.10 •101	6,318 •96	56 •128	371 •113	195 •111	235 •81	94 •101	4,829 •116	760 •160	3.3 •75	5,002 •111	0.50 •112	2.00 •118	0.32 •152	4.61 •139	2.39 •113	62 •117	32 •123	3.0 •77	1.3 •131	44 •101	69.4 •89
Hungary J3	Budapest	93.00 •110	10,068 •76	108 •83	17248 •12	3,394 •32	10,622 •14	1,191 •44	46,751 •51	4,640 •78	1.0 •139	28,580 •157	11.50 •64	26.75 •50	2.66 •59	37.09 •50	29.34 •39	699 •48	66 •21	4.2 •54	1.9 •94	11 •37	70.9 •64
Iceland I2	Reykjavík	103.00 •105	278 •174	2.7 •212	263 •128	227 •108	257 •78	430 •58	8,197 •96	29,540 •9	2.6 •101	2,600 •88	2.00 •93	3.25 •104	11.69 •5	67.74 •4	66.98 •11	5,979 •1	23 •151	6.7 •14	M –	5 •4	79.0 •2
India M4	New Delhi	3,065.00 D2 •7	997,507 D4 •2	325 •29	2,482 •45	3,036 •35	3,811 •31	2,010 •34	441,834 •11	440 •181	6.0 •19	98,232 •182	229.25 •9	304.50 •7	0.31 •154	3.20 •147	0.35 •144	49 •122	61 •32	0.6 •162	2.8 •60	105 •131	62.6 •113
Indonesia O6	Jakarta	1,919.40 •16	207,022 D5 •4	108 •83	4,728 •30	4,710 •24	2,076 •42	2,353 •31	125,043 •32	600 •167	4.7 •37	150,875 •188	190.75 •13	90.00 •22	0.43 •141	3.14 •149	1.73 •121	68 •113	24 •145	0.5 •164	2.3 •75	56 •111	65.1 •108
Iran L4	Tehran	1,648.00 •18	62,977 •16	38 •148	1,321 •66	662 •71	1,450 •51	918 •47	113,729 •34	1,810 •124	3.6 •70	14,391 •143	246.00 •7	116.75 •17	1.85 •76	14.90 •94	1.51 •124	39 •130	38 •107	1.7 •122	3.0 •55	33 •83	69.2 •81
Iraq L4	Baghdad	438.30 •58	22,797 •44	52 •134	n/a –	13 •175	n/a –	430 •58	74,957 •44	3,288 •94	n/a –	130,000 •185	137.00 •18	29.00 •47	1.27 •94	3.01 •153	nn –	ns –	21 •156	n/a –	4.9 •27	125 •145	62.4 •114
Ireland I3	Dublin	70.30 •120	3,752 •125	53 •133	6403 •22	3,392 •33	3,576 •34	2,620 •28	80,559 •41	21,470 •22	6.9 •14	11,000 •135	1.50 •100	14.00 •66	3.73 •40	47.77 •31	59.73 •18	2,102 •26	81 •4	5.0 •42	1.2 •139	7 •25	76.4 •25
Israel K4	Jerusalem	21.90 •151	6,105 D6 •100	279 •41	2,312 •51	2,974 •37	3,203 •36	2,566 •29	99,574 •36	16,310 •34	5.2 •27	18,700 •149	0.00 –	19.50 •58	3.19 •51	46.25 •36	70.18 •8	1,755 •29	28 •133	7.1 •8	9.7 •7	6 •17	77.8 •13
Italy J3	Rome	301.30 •71	57,646 •22	191 •53	36516 •4	28,359 •4	18,962 •7	16,913 •6	1,162,910 •6	20,170 •26	1.4 •133	45,000 •173	35.00 •39	201.00 •11	3.49 •43	46.22 •37	73.73 •4	1,047 •38	56 •48	5.3 •34	2.0 •90	6 •17	78.2 •8

*: Ranking (top 10 in **bold**). n/a: Not available, not relevant or not reliable. nn: No network. ns: No service. M: See note on page 33. T: See note on page 33. For more information, see the notes on pages 184 and 192.

Countries A-Z: Jamaica–Malta

Country (Map Ref. pp.10-11)	Capital	Life Expectancy (years)	Infant Mortality (Deaths <5yrs/'000)	Military Spending (% of GNI)	Health Spending (% of GNI)	Agricultural Land (% of national area)	Internet Usage (Subscribers/10,000)	Mobile Tel. Lines (/100 people)	Fixed Tel. Lines (/100 people)	Energy Consumption (tonnes oil equiv/person)	Energy Consumption (million tonnes oil equiv)	Energy Production (million tonnes oil equiv)	External Debt (US$ million)	GDP Growth (Av. annual % 1990-99)	GNI per Person (US$)	Gross Nat'l Income (US$ million)	Visitor Expenditure (US$ million)	International Departures ('000)	Visitor Receipts (US$ million)	International Arrivals ('000)	Population Density (people/sq km)	Population ('000)	Area ('000 sq km)
Jamaica (F5)	Kingston	74.8 •35	11 •37	0.9 •151	2.3 •105	44 •82	234 •82	14.24 •65	19.86 •87	1.54 •87	4.00 •92	0.25 •119	3,995 •101	0.3 •147	2,430 •107	6,311 •103	227 •75	n/a	1,279 •56	1,248 •67	228 •51	2,598 •136	11.40 •161
Japan (P4)	Tokyo	80.0 •1	4 •1	1.0 •148	5.5 •30	14 •170	3,044 •14	52.62 •25	55.75 •19	4.29 •30	542.75 •4	113.25 •23	0N2 •1	1.3 •134	32,030 •7	4,054,545 •2	32,808 •1	16,358 •10	3,428 •31	4,438 •35	335 •27	126,570 •9	377.80 •61
Jordan (K4)	Amman	70.2 •69	36 •90	9.0 •8	3.5 •64	14 •170	191 •88	5.83 •91	9.29 •110	1.16 •97	5.50 •85	0.25 •119	8,484 •126	5.3 •25	1,630 •131	7,717 •98	355 •61	1,560 •49	795 •64	1,358 •65	52 •134	4,740 •112	91.90 •111
Kazakstan (M3)	Note B5	67.6 •95	43 •99	1.3 •131	2.5 •96	80 •6	43 •126	0.30 •149	10.82 •103	2.45 •65	36.50 •38	58.25 •34	5,714 •114	-5.9 •173	1,250 •141	18,732 •69	445 •55	n/a	289 •98	n/a	5.5 •209	14,927 •60	2,717.30 •9
Kenya (K5)	Nairobi	52.0 •139	117 •141	2.1 •86	2.4 •102	45 •78	65 •114	0.11 •170	1.01 •170	0.13 •171	3.75 •96	1.00 •104	7,010 •121	2.2 •113	360 •191	10,696 •85	115 •97	n/a	304 •93	857 •76	50 •136	29,410 •35	582.60 •46
Kiribati (A6)	Bairiki	n/a	n/a	M	n/a	51 •63	122 •101	0.24 •153	4.26 •141	0.91 •112	0.08 •186	0.00 •–	7 •7	2.0 •118	910 •154	81 •214	2 •167	n/a	2 •193	1 •197	122 •77	88 •196	0.72 •185
Korea, DPR (North) (P3)	Pyongyang	53.2 •135	26 •72	27.5 •1	n/a	16 •165	ns	nn	4.64 •138	1.56 •85	36.50 •38	31.50 •40	12,000 •137	-3.0 •163	440 •181	10,302 •87	n/a	n/a	n/a	n/a	191 •53	23,414 •42	122.80 •98
Korea, Rep. (South) (P4)	Seoul	72.4 •54	5 •4	3.4 •51	2.0 •115	22 •153	4,025 •7	56.69 •21	46.37 •35	3.92 •36	183.75 •12	27.50 •46	139,097 •186	5.7 •22	8,490 •62	397,910 •13	3,975 •24	4,342 •27	6,802 •18	4,660 •31	471 •18	46,858 •25	99.40 •107
Kuwait (L4)	Kuwait City	75.9 •28	13 •41	7.5 •12	2.5 •96	8 •186	527 •56	15.82 •62	24.02 •72	8.84 •11	17.00 •62	114.50P1 •22	9,270 •128	8.0 •8	14,322 •40	29,031 •60	2,510 •30	n/a	243 •105	1,884 •57	108 •83	1,924 •144	17.80 •156
Kyrgyzstan (M3)	Bishkek	67.6 •95	66 •113	1.6 •109	3.1 •73	51 •63	21 •146	0.06 •177	7.62 •123	1.13 •101	5.50 •85	3.50 •82	1,148 •64	-5.4 •172	300 •199	1,465 •164	32 •163	n/a	8 •184	69 •163	24 •171	4,865 •110	199.90 •86
Laos (O5)	Vientiane	53.2 •135	116 •139	3.4 •51	1.1 •150	6 •197	4 •183	0.23 •154	0.66 •178	0.05 •192	0.25 •162	0.25 •119	2,437 •84	6.6 •15	290 •200	1,476 •163	12 •144	n/a	97 •129	259 •130	22 •172	5,097 •107	236.80 •82
Latvia (K3)	Riga	68.4 •90	22 •58	0.9 •151	4.3 •52	40 •101	630 •51	16.86 •61	29.99 •60	1.54 •86	3.75 •96	0.75 •108	756 •118	-4.8 •169	2,430 •107	5,913 •109	288 •71	650 •62	118 •121	490 •99	38 •148	2,431 •138	64.60 •124
Lebanon (K4)	Beirut	69.9 •73	35 •87	3.0 •55	3.3 •68	31 •126	618 •53	19.38 •59	20.09 •85	1.35 •91	5.75 •84	0.25 •119	6,725 •118	7.7 •10	3,700 •86	15,796 •75	341 •62	3,482 •33	673 •70	673 •84	407 •22	4,271 •118	10.50 •164
Lesotho (K7)	Maseru	56.0 •126	136 •148	2.5 •68	2.6 •85	77 •11	5 •178	0.48 •138	1.02 •169	0.08 •183	0.16 •180	0.00 •–	692 •48	4.4 •48	500 •174	1,158 •174	12 •144	n/a	19 •169	186 •136	69 •113	2,105 •141	30.40 •140
Liberia (I5)	Monrovia	n/a	173 •162	4.7 •29	n/a	63 •29	1 •193	n/a	0.23 •199	0.08 •180	0.25 •162	0.00 •–	3,000 •92	n/a	285 •202	868 •184	n/a	n/a	n/a	n/a	31 •160	3,044 •131	99.10 •108
Libya (J4)	Tripoli	70.0 •71	24 •67	6.1 •15	n/a	9 •184	13 •157	0.36 •143	10.05 •107	2.68 •58	14.50 •64	77.50 •29	4,000 •102	-0.5 •151	5,930 •74	32,135 •57	150 •87	650 •62	28 •160	40 •179	3.1 •212	5,419 •102	1,775.50 •17
Liechtenstein (J3)	Vaduz	n/a	n/a	T	n/a	63 •29	n/a	n/a	n/a	n/a	Q1	P2	0 •1	n/a	35,910 •4	1,149 •168	n/a	n/a	n/a	60 •168	200 •52	32 •209	0.16 •215
Lithuania (K3)	Vilnius	69.9 •73	23 •62	0.8 •158	7.9 •5	54 •54	278 •76	14.17 •67	32.11 •58	2.16 •69	8.00 •77	3.00 •86	1,950 •77	-4.0 •167	2,640 •104	9,751 •89	341 •62	n/a	550 •78	1,422 •63	57 •126	3,699 •126	65.30 •123
Luxembourg (J3)	Luxembourg	76.7 •23	5 •4	0.8 •158	6.0 •23	45 •78	2,295 •24	87.22 •4	72.44 •4	11.00 •8	4.75 •89	0.00 •–	n/a	3.3 •75	42,930 •1	18,545 •70	n/a	n/a	309 •92	833 •77	166 •58	432 •165	2.60 •173
Macedonia, FYR (K3)	Skopje	73.1 •44	27 •75	2.5 •27	5.8 •27	51 •63	149 •96	5.72 •92	23.40 •75	1.61 •82	3.25 •104	2.00 •93	2,392 •83	-0.8 •154	1,660 •130	3,348 •134	32 •129	n/a	37 •153	181 •137	79 •105	2,021 •142	25.70 •148
Madagascar (L8)	Antananarivo	57.5 •124	157 •156	1.1 •114	1.1 •150	46 •77	5 •177	0.08 •174	0.32 •193	0.03 •198	0.50 •142	0.25 •119	4,394 •105	1.7 •125	250 •210	3,712 •127	111 •98	n/a	100 •128	138 •146	26 •169	15,051 •58	587.00 •45
Malawi (K6)	Lilongwe	39.3 •165	213 •175	2.4 •102	2.4 •102	38 •107	9 •164	0.21 •158	0.40 •189	0.05 •194	0.50 •142	0.25 •119	2,444 •85	3.6 •70	180 •219	1,961 •153	17 •142	n/a	20 •168	254 •131	91 •96	10,788 •69	118.50 •99
Malaysia (O5)	Kuala Lumpur	72.0 •57	10 •34	2.2 •81	2.4 •102	15 •167	1,505 •30	21.07 •83	21.07 •83	1.87 •75	42.50 •35	79.25 •28	44,773 •172	7.3 •11	3,390 •92	76,944 •43	1,973 •35	26,067 •6	3,540 •20	7,931 •20	69 •113	22,710 •45	329.80 •66
Maldives (M6)	Malé	64.5 •109	87 •126	M	6.3 •17	13 •173	206 •85	2.63 •111	8.40 •118	0.41 •142	0.11 •182	0.00 •–	180 •28	6.5 •16	1,200 •143	322 •197	29 •132	42 •98	334 •90	430 •107	897 •9	269 •175	0.30 •203
Mali (I5)	Bamako	53.3 •134	237 •176	1.7 •103	2.1 •112	27 •136	9 •166	0.04 •180	0.25 •198	0.02 •202	0.25 •162	0.00 •–	3,201 •94	3.6 •70	240 •212	2,577 •145	45 •119	n/a	50 •145	87 •156	8.5 •202	10,584 •71	1,248.60 •22
Malta (J4)	Valletta	77.2 •15	7 •25	0.9 •151	7.4 •7	41 •97	777 •45	29.55 •38	51.23 •38	1.32 •97	0.50 •142	0.00 •–	130 •22	13.0 •3	9,210 •58	3,492 •131	201 •79	179 •83	675 •69	1,214 •68	1,184 •7	379 •171	0.32 •202

•: Ranking (top 10 in *bold*).   **n/a:** Not available, not relevant or not reliable.   **nn:** No network.   **ns:** No service.   **M:** See note on page 33.   **T:** See note on page 33.   For more information, see the notes on pages 184 and 192

Countries A-Z: Marshall Is.–Northern Mariana Is.

Each cell shows the value followed by its ranking (in italics). Top 10 shown in bold.

Country (Map Ref.)	Capital	Area '000 sq km	Population '000	Pop. Density people/sq km	Int'l Arrivals '000	Visitor Receipts US$m	Int'l Depart's '000	Visitor Expenditure US$m	Gross Nat'l Income US$m	GNI per Person US$	GDP Growth Av.% 1990-99	External Debt US$m	Energy Production Mtoe	Energy Consumption Mtoe	Energy Consumption toe/person	Fixed Tel. Lines /100	Mobile Tel. Lines /100	Internet Usage /10,000	Agricultural Land %	Health Spending % GNI	Military Spending % GNI	Infant Mortality /'000	Life Expectancy yrs
Marshall Is. (R5)	Majuro	0.18 /213	51 /205	283 /37	5 /194	4 /190	n/a	n/a	99 /213	1,950 /119	n/a	125 /21	P3	0.11 O2 /182	2.16 /70	6.29 /129	0.70 /134	80 /110	60 /36	n/a	T	n/a	n/a
Martinique (F5)	Fort-de-France	1.10 /180	384 /170	349 /25	564 /89	404 /85	n/a	n/a	4,557 /119	11,866 /50	n/a	180 /28	0.00 /–	0.75 /138	1.95 /71	43.82 /40	41.03 /29	127 /100	33 /120	n/a	T	n/a	n/a
Mauritania (I5)	Nouakchott	1,030.70 /29	2,598 /137	2.5 /212	24 /185	28 /160	55 /114	37 /99	1,001 /170	390 /186	4.2 /52	2,589 /87	0.00 /–	1.25 /125	0.48 /137	0.64 /180	n/a	49 /124	38 /107	1.8 /120	2.3 /75	183 /166	53.5 /131
Mauritius (L7)	Port Louis	2.00 /175	1,174 /152	587 /14	578 /88	545 /79	187 /80	154 /85	4,157 /121	3,540 /89	5.1 /28	2,482 /86	0.00 /–	1.00 /134	0.85 /115	23.71 /73	10.16 /77	734 /46	55 /51	1.9 /118	0.3 /165	23 /62	71.4 /60
Mayotte (L6)	Dzaoudzi	0.37 /199	140 /189	378 /24	n/a	n/a	n/a	n/a	800 /176	5,517 /75	n/a	n/a	0.00 /–	n/a	n/a	7.27 /125	n/a	n/a	52 /59	n/a	T	n/a	n/a
Mexico (D4)	Mexico City	1,967.20 /15	96,566 /11	49 /138	19,043 /8	7,223 /14	4,541 /20	10,352 /16	428,877 /9	4,440 /75	2.7 /97	159,959 /190	225.75 /10	153.50 /14	1.59 /83	12.47 /99	14.23 /66	274 /77	52 /59	2.6 /85	1.1 /142	34 /85	72.2 /56
Micronesia, Fed. States (Q5)	Palikir	0.70 /187	116 /191	166 /58	14 /189	n/a	n/a	n/a	212 /204	1,830 /122	2.0 /118	111 /18	0.00 /–	n/a	n/a	7.99 /121	n/a	172 /91	n/a	n/a	T	n/a	n/a
Moldova (K3)	Chisinău	33.70 /138	4,281 /117	127 /74	n/a	2 /193	n/a	n/a	1,481 /162	410 /183	-11.0 /179	1,035 /58	0.00 /–	3.75 /96	0.88 /113	12.68 /97	3.02 /109	57 /119	80 /6	5.2 /37	1.0 /148	35 /87	67.5 /97
Monaco (J3)	Monaco-Ville	0.00 /225	32 /210	16,000 /2	278 /124	n/a	n/a	n/a	792 /177	24,739 /15	n/a	n/a	0.00 /–	n/a	n/a	n/a	n/a	n/a	<0.5 /211	n/a	T	n/a	n/a
Mongolia (Q3)	Ulan Bator	1,565.00 /19	2,378 /139	1.5 /218	159 /142	36 /155	41 /122	n/a	927 /172	390 /186	0.7 /144	739 /50	1.25 /102	1.75 /121	0.74 /120	4.97 /136	4.04 /103	113 /103	81 /4	4.6 /47	1.9 /94	82 /122	65.9 /106
Montserrat (F5)	Plymouth B6	0.10 /218	11 /219	n/a	10 /190	3 /192	3 /163	n/a	20 /222	1,818 /123	n/a	8 /8	0.00 /–	0.02 /203	n/a	n/a	n/a	n/a	30	n/a	T	n/a	n/a
Morocco (I4)	Rabat	458.70 C3 /55	27,985 D7 /37	61 /121	3,817 /37	1,880 /48	440 /57	1,612 /47	33,715 /55	1,190 /144	2.3 /112	20,687 /150	0.50 /112	10.25 /70	0.37 /147	5.03 /134	8.26 /84	18 /148	69 /19	1.4 /136	4.3 /36	70 /115	66.6 /103
Mozambique (K7)	Maputo	799.40 /35	17,299 /53	22 /172	n/a	n/a	18 /141	n/a	3,804 /126	220 /214	6.2 /18	8,208 /124	0.50 /112	0.50 /142	0.05 /190	0.44 /186	0.11 /170	8 /168	36	2.2 /110	2.8 /60	206 /173	45.2 /155
Myanmar (N4)	Yangon B7	676.60 /40	45,029 /26	67 /117	198 /135	35 /156	88 /102	n/a	12,698 /81	282 /203	6.3 /17	5,680 /113	2.50 /88	3.50 /101	0.08 /182	0.56 /183	0.06 /177	0 /195	17 /161	0.2 /168	7.6 /11	113 /137	60.1 /118
Namibia (J7)	Windhoek	824.30 /34	1,701 /145	2.1 /217	560 /91	288 /99	71 /107	n/a	3,211 /137	1,890 /121	3.4 /74	159 /26	0.50 /112	0.50 /142	0.29 /156	5.94 /131	4.67 /99	171 /92	47 /73	3.7 /61	2.7 /65	74 /118	52.4 /136
Nauru (R6)	Yaren District	0.02 /222	11 /219	550 /15	n/a	n/a	n/a	n/a	32 /218	2,900 /100	n/a	33 /9	0.00 /–	0.06 /190	5.45 /23	n/a	n/a	n/a	<0.5 /211	n/a	M	100 /130	n/a
Nepal (N4)	Kathmandu	140.80 /95	23,384 /43	166 /58	492 /98	168 /116	122 /88	n/a	5,173 /111	220 /214	4.9 /34	2,646 /90	0.25 /119	1.25 /125	0.05 /190	1.16 /168	0.04 /180	22 /145	32 /123	1.2 /143	0.8 /158	117 /141	57.3 /125
Netherlands (J3)	Amsterdam B8	41.50 /134	15,805 /55	381 /23	9,881 /18	7,092 /16	11,366 /7	14,180 /11	397,384 /14	25,140 /14	2.7 /97	n/a	65.25 /31	96.25 /20	6.09 /21	60.67 /12	67.12 /10	2,381 /23	59 /41	5.9 /25	1.9 /94	5 /4	77.9 /12
Netherlands Antilles (F5)	Willemstad	0.80 /182	215 /180	269 /42	726 /82	774 /66	329 /64	n/a	2,100 /149	9,859 /57	n/a	1,350 /69	0.00 /–	4.00 /92	18.60 /4	36.79 /52	7.52 /86	93 /106	10 /181	n/a	T	n/a	n/a
New Caledonia (R7)	Nouméa	18.60 /154	209 /181	11 /194	100 /151	111 /124	69 /91	n/a	3,169 /139	15,160 /36	n/a	79 /14	0.00 /–	0.75 /138	3.59 /42	23.69 /74	23.20 /47	1,115 /36	12 /176	n/a	T	n/a	n/a
New Zealand (R7)	Wellington	270.50 /75	3,811 /123	14 /187	1,607 /60	2,083 /46	1,493 /40	1,185 /52	53,299 /48	13,990 /42	3.1 /86	53,000 /177	17.00 /57	20.25 /56	5.31 /25	49.57 /28	36.61 /34	2,167 /25	64 /27	5.8 /27	1.3 /131	6 /17	76.9 /21
Nicaragua (E5)	Managua	130.70 /97	4,919 /109	38 /148	468 /101	107 /126	74 /106	452 /66	2,012 /151	410 /183	3.2 /81	5,968 /115	0.25 /119	1.50 /123	0.30 /155	3.04 /152	0.90 /130	41 /128	56 /48	4.4 /51	1.5 /114	48 /105	67.9 /94
Niger (J5)	Niamey	1,186.40 /25	10,496 /73	8.8 /199	43 /177	24 /164	26 /134	10 /105	1,974 /152	190 /218	2.4 /105	1,659 /74	0.00 /–	0.50 /142	0.05 /193	0.18 /201	0.01 /188	3 /189	10 /181	1.3 /140	1.1 /142	280 /178	48.5 /147
Nigeria (J5)	Abuja	923.80 /32	**123,897 /10**	134 /69	739 /81	142 /119	n/a	1,567 /39	31,600 /58	260 /207	2.4 /105	30,315 /159	123.00 /21	22.50 /53	0.18 /166	0.43 /187	0.03 /184	9 /165	80 /6	0.3 /167	1.4 /123	187 /167	50.1 /143
Niue (A6)	Alofi	0.26 /205	2 /224	7.7 /202	n/a	1 /199	n/a	n/a	4 /225	2,000 /117	n/a	n/a	0.00 /–	0.00 /209	0.00 /208	n/a	n/a	n/a	31 /126	n/a	T	n/a	n/a
Northern Mariana Is. (Q5)	Saipan	0.46 /193	69 /199	150 /64	498 /97	647 /74	n/a	n/a	105 /212	1,500 /134	n/a	n/a	P4	Q3	n/a	47.97 /30	5.59 /94	n/a	40	n/a	T	n/a	n/a

•: Ranking (top 10 in **bold**). n/a: Not available, not relevant or not reliable. nn: No network. ns: No service. M: See note on page 33. T: See note on page 33. For more information, see the notes on pages 184 and 192.

Countries A-Z: Norway–São Tomé e Príncipe

Country	Map Ref	Capital	Area '000 sq km	Population '000	Pop Density people/sq km	Intl Arrivals '000	Visitor Receipts US$m	Intl Departs '000	Visitor Expenditure US$m	Gross Nat'l Income US$m	GNI per Person US$	GDP Growth Av. % 1990-99	External Debt US$m	Energy Production	Energy Consumption (M tonnes)	Energy Consumption (t/person)	Fixed Tel Lines /100	Mobile Tel Lines /100	Internet Usage /10,000	Agricultural Land %	Health Spending %	Military Spending %	Infant Mortality	Life Expectancy
Norway	J2	Oslo	323.80 •67	4,460 •116	14 •187	4,481 •33	2,229 •44	753 •61	4,751 •19	149,280 •27	33,470 •5	3.8 •63	0 •1	238.75 •8	47.25 •31	10.59 •9	72.91 •3	70.26 •7	4,905 •3	3 •202	6.1 •19	2.1 •86	4 •1	74.4 •38
Oman	L5	Muscat	309.50 •70	2,348 •140	7.6 •202	502 •96	104 •127	n/a •-	47 •118	13,962 •78	5,946 •73	5.9 •20	3,629 •96	53.00 •35	7.50 •35	3.19 •50	8.88 •115	6.48 •89	355 •68	5 •200	2.3 •105	26.1 •2	18 •46	70.9 •64
Pakistan	M4	Islamabad	796.10 C2 •36	130,580 D4 •7	164 •61	432 •106	76 •135	n/a •-	180 •84	62,915 •46	470 •178	3.8 •63	32,229 •164	28.50 •45	45.25 •34	0.35 •149	2.22 •156	0.21 •158	6 •175	34 •117	0.8 •157	5.7 •21	136 •148	64.0 •111
Palau	P5	Koror	0.51 •191	19 •215	37 •151	55 •171	n/a •-	9 •106	n/a •-	123 •210	6,448 •69	n/a •-	100 •15	P4	Q3	n/a •-	7.18 •126	n/a •-	n/a •-	59 •41	n/a •-	T	n/a •-	n/a •-
Palestine NARA4	K4	Jerusalem B9	6.20 •167	2,839 •133	458 •19	271 •126	132 •120	n/a •-	n/a •-	5,063 •113	1,780 •125	3.7 •68	108 •16	0.00 •16	n/a •-	n/a •-	n/a •-	n/a •-	n/a •-	n/a •-	n/a •-	n/a •-	n/a •-	n/a •-
Panama	E5	Panama City	75.50 •118	2,811 •135	37 •151	555 •92	538 •80	221 •82	184 •81	8,657 •93	3,080 •99	4.2 •52	6,689 •117	0.75 •108	4.00 •92	1.42 •90	16.43 •90	8.27 •83	160 •93	29 •130	6.1 •19	1.4 •123	20 •52	73.6 •43
Papua New Guinea	Q6	Port Moresby	462.80 •54	4,705 •113	10 •196	67 •165	76 •135	63 •93	53 •116	3,834 •125	810 •157	4.7 •37	2,692 •125	5.25 •76	1.25 •76	0.27 •159	1.27 •165	0.15 •164	4 •181	1 •208	2.5 •96	1.3 •131	112 •135	57.9 •123
Paraguay	G7	Asunción	406.80 •59	5,359 •104	13 •189	269 •127	81 •132	281 •77	109 •99	8,374 •95	1,560 •132	2.4 •105	2,304 •82	13.50 •61	2.75 •107	0.51 •135	5.00 •135	19.55 •58	37 •131	61 •32	2.7 •81	1.3 •131	33 •83	69.6 •77
Peru	F6	Lima	1,285.20 •20	25,230 •39	20 •176	944 •74	890 •74	616 •63	443 •56	53,705 •47	2,130 •114	5.0 •31	32,397 •165	9.75 •69	13.25 •68	0.53 •133	6.37 •128	4.02 •104	159 •95	24 •145	2.6 •85	2.1 •86	54 •110	68.3 •91
Philippines	P5	Manila	300.00 •72	74,259 •14	248 •45	2,171 •52	2,534 •39	1,755 •44	1,308 •43	77,967 •42	1,050 •150	3.2 •81	47,817 •175	7.00 •72	27.75 •48	0.37 •145	3.98 •143	8.36 •82	266 •79	35 •114	1.4 •136	1.4 •114	44 •101	68.3 •91
Poland	J3	Warsaw	312.70 •69	38,654 •30	124 •75	17950 •10	6,100 •20	55,097 •3	3,600 •25	157,429 •26	4,070 •83	4.5 •45	47,708 •174	81.50 •26	96.00 •21	2.48 •64	26.27 •67	18.13 •60	722 •47	61 •32	4.2 •54	2.3 •75	11 •37	72.5 •53
Portugal A5	I3	Lisbon	91.90 •112	9,989 •78	109 •82	11632 •15	5,131 •23	n/a •-	2,266 •32	110,175 •35	11,030 •52	2.5 •103	13,100 •141	2.25 •90	25.50 •51	2.55 •62	43.05 •41	66.52 •13	5,950 •2	61 •32	4.6 •47	2.4 •72	9 •30	75.3 •32
Puerto Rico	F5	San Juan	8.90 •166	3,890 •121	437 •20	3,024 •41	2,138 •45	1,134 •53	815 •48	30,000 •59	7,874 •63	3.1 •86	n/a •-	0.00 •-	8.75 •76	2.25 •68	33.29 •56	20.92 •53	514 •58	35 •114	n/a •-	T	n/a •-	n/a •-
Qatar	L4	Doha	11.40 •162	565 •161	50 •136	435 •105	n/a •-	n/a •-	n/a •-	10,207 •88	18,065 •30	n/a •-	10,000 •133	61.00 •32	17.50 •60	30.97 •1	26.77 •56	19.96 •56	501 •60	6 •197	2.6 •85	10.5 •5	18 •46	71.7 •58
Réunion	L7	Saint-Denis	2.50 •174	707 •158	283 •37	394 •110	270 •102	319 •76	n/a •-	7,433 •100	10,513 •54	n/a •-	n/a •-	0.25 •119	0.75 •138	1.06 •104	38.86 •46	36.79 •33	145 •97	24 •145	n/a •-	T	n/a •-	n/a •-
Romania	K3	Bucharest	236.40 •83	22,458 •46	95 •94	3,209 •39	254 •103	6,274 •21	395 •60	33,034 •56	1,470 •135	-0.8 •154	9,513 •129	30.75 •41	41.00 •41	1.83 •78	16.70 •89	11.19 •73	268 •78	65 •25	3.4 •65	2.4 •72	24 •67	70.0 •71
Russian Federation	M2	Moscow	17,075.40 •1	146,200 •6	8.6 •199	18493 •9	7,510 •13	12,631 •12	7,434 •13	328,995 •16	2,250 •110	-6.1 •174	183,601 •191	1038.50 •2	650.25 •3	4.45 •26	21.67 •80	1.95 •117	136 •99	66 •21	3.8 •59	4.4 •35	25 •69	66.0 •105
Rwanda	K6	Kigali	26.30 •147	8,310 •85	316 •31	n/a •-	17 •172	n/a •-	71 •107	2,041 •150	250 •210	-1.5 •159	1,226 •66	0.00 •-	0.25 •162	0.03 •199	0.23 •199	0.26 •150	6 •173	66 •21	2.1 •112	n/a •-	170 •160	40.5 •162
St Helena	I7	Jamestown	0.12 •217	7 •221	58 •125	n/a •-	n/a •-	n/a •-	n/a •-	10 •224	1,667 •129	n/a •-	n/a •-	0.00 •209	0.00 •208	n/a •-	nn	n/a •-	n/a •-	12 •176	n/a •-	T	n/a •-	n/a •-
St Kitts & Nevis	F5	Basseterre	0.26 •206	41 •207	158 •62	84 •158	70 •137	n/a •-	6 •157	259 •200	6,330 •70	4.1 •57	115 •19	0.00 •-	0.04 •199	0.98 •110	51.76 •24	1.81 •119	516 •57	42 •93	3.6 •62	M	37 •91	66.0 •105
St Lucia	F5	Castries	0.62 •189	154 •185	248 •45	261 •129	311 •91	n/a •-	29 •132	590 •186	3,820 •84	3.0 •88	184 •32	0.00 •-	0.07 •189	0.45 •139	28.93 •61	1.25 •127	195 •81	34 •117	2.5 •96	M	21 •56	n/a •-
St Pierre et Miquelon	G3	St Pierre	0.24 •207	7 •222	29 •166	n/a •-	13 •173	n/a •-	n/a •-	70 •215	10,000 •55	n/a •-	n/a •-	0.00 •-	0.04 •199	5.71 •22	n/a •-	n/a •-	n/a •-	13 •173	T	M	n/a •-	n/a •-
St Vincent & the Gren.	F5	Kingstown	0.39 •198	114 •192	292 •33	68 •164	77 •134	n/a •-	8 •149	301 •199	2,640 •104	3.3 •75	420 •44	0.00 •-	0.06 •190	0.53 •132	21.96 •79	2.08 •115	309 •70	33 •120	4.2 •54	M	23 •62	n/a •-
Samoa	S6	Apia	2.80 •172	169 •184	60 •123	85 •157	42 •149	n/a •-	4 •161	181 •207	1,070 •149	1.8 •122	180 •28	0.00 •-	0.06 •190	0.36 •148	4.80 •137	1.69 •122	28 •140	43 •88	5.3 •34	M	27 •75	71.4 •60
San Marino	J3	San Marino	0.06 •219	26 •212	433 •21	3,148 •40	2 •193	n/a •-	1 •169	537 •188	20,659 •25	1.5 •130	n/a •-	0.00 •-	0.00 •190	n/a •-	n/a •-	n/a •-	n/a •-	17 •161	T	T	n/a •-	n/a •-
São Tomé e Príncipe	J6	São Tomé	1.00 •181	145 •188	145 •68	2 •193	n/a •-	n/a •-	1 •169	40 •217	270 •205	1.5 •130	246 •38	0.00 •-	0.28 •161	1.93 •72	3.10 •151	n/a •-	n/a •-	39 •103	6.1 •19	0.9 •151	77 •120	n/a •-

•: Ranking (top 10 in **bold**). n/a: Not available, not relevant or not reliable. ns: No service. nn: No network. M: See note on page 33. T: See note on page 33. For more information, see the notes on pages 184 and 192.

Each cell shows the value followed by its ranking in parentheses (top 10 ranks in **bold**).

Country (Map Ref.)	Capital	Area 000 sq km	Population 000	Pop. Density people/sq km	Int'l Arrivals 000	Visitor Receipts US$m	Int'l Departs 000	Visitor Expenditure US$m	Gross Nat'l Income US$m	GNI per Person US$	GDP Growth Av. annual % 1990–99	External Debt US$m	Energy Production Mtoe	Energy Consumption Mtoe	Energy Consumption toe/person	Fixed Tel Lines /100	Mobile Tel Lines /100	Internet Usage /10,000	Agricultural Land %	Health Spending % of GNI	Military Spending % of GNI	Infant Mortality Deaths <3yrs/000	Life Expectancy Years
Saudi Arabia L4	Riyadh	2,200.00 (13)	20,198 (49)	9.2 (199)	n/a (–)	1,462 (54)	n/a (–)	n/a (–)	139,365 (28)	6,900 (66)	-1.6 (160)	28,000 (155)	491.00 P1 (**4**)	108.25 (–)	5.36 (25)	12.95 (96)	4.00 (105)	144 (98)	58 (43)	5.9 (25)	14.5 (**4**)	26 (72)	71.4 (60)
Senegal I5	Dakar	196.20 (87)	9,285 (82)	47 (141)	369 (114)	166 (117)	n/a (–)	53 (116)	4,685 (118)	500 (174)	3.3 (75)	3,861 (98)	0.00 (–)	1.50 (123)	0.16 (168)	2.18 (157)	0.95 (129)	32 (136)	28 (133)	2.6 (85)	1.6 (109)	121 (143)	52.3 (138)
Seychelles L6	Victoria	0.46 (194)	80 (197)	174 (55)	125 (148)	112 (122)	32 (100)	21 (140)	520 (189)	6,500 (68)	2.9 (91)	187 (33)	0.00 (–)	0.25 (162)	3.13 (52)	24.42 (71)	20.29 (55)	622 (52)	15 (167)	5.2 (37)	5.2 (75)	18 (46)	n/a (–)
Sierra Leone I5	Freetown	73.30 (119)	4,949 (108)	68 (116)	6 (193)	8 (184)	n/a (–)	4 (161)	653 (182)	130 (222)	-4.7 (168)	1,243 (67)	0.00 (–)	0.25 (162)	0.05 (191)	0.39 (190)	0.12 (166)	41 (127)	39 (103)	1.6 (125)	5.9 (18)	316 (180)	37.2 (166)
Singapore O5	Singapore	0.65 (188)	3,952 (120)	6,080 (**4**)	6258 (24)	5,974 (21)	3,971 (29)	2,749 (27)	95,429 (37)	24,150 (20)	8.0 (**8**)	n/a (–)	0.00 (–)	34.00 (41)	8.60 (13)	48.45 (29)	68.38 (**9**)	2,987 (16)	8 (186)	1.0 (155)	5.7 (21)	5 (**4**)	77.1 (19)
Slovak Rep. K3	Bratislava	49.00 (129)	5,396 (103)	110 (81)	975 (71)	461 (82)	343 (74)	339 (63)	20,318 (57)	3,770 (85)	1.8 (122)	9,893 (131)	5.00 (77)	17.50 (60)	3.24 (48)	30.67 (59)	23.92 (46)	1,112 (37)	51 (63)	5.2 (37)	2.1 (86)	10 (34)	73.0 (46)
Slovenia J3	Ljubljana	20.30 (153)	1,986 (143)	98 (91)	884 (75)	953 (58)	n/a (–)	539 (53)	19,862 (67)	10,000 (55)	2.4 (105)	4,900 (110)	3.25 (84)	6.75 (82)	3.40 (44)	37.80 (47)	54.66 (24)	1,257 (34)	39 (88)	6.7 (14)	1.7 (103)	5 (**4**)	74.5 (37)
Solomon Is. R6	Honiara	28.40 (143)	429 (166)	15 (184)	21 (187)	6 (187)	n/a (–)	7 (153)	320 (198)	750 (162)	2.8 (93)	152 (25)	0.00 (–)	0.05 (194)	0.12 (174)	1.72 (161)	0.26 (150)	45 (125)	3 (202)	3.9 (58)	M (–)	26 (72)	71.7 (58)
Somalia L5	Mogadishu	637.70 (42)	9,388 (81)	15 (184)	n/a (–)	n/a (–)	n/a (–)	n/a (–)	1,662 (157)	177 (220)	n/a (–)	2,600 (88)	0.00 (–)	0.25 (162)	0.03 (201)	0.16 (202)	n/a (–)	<0.5 (194)	71 (17)	n/a (–)	n/a (–)	204 (171)	n/a (–)
South Africa K7	Note B10	1,224.70 (24)	42,106 (27)	34 (155)	6,026 (25)	2,526 (40)	3,363 (34)	1,806 (37)	133,569 (29)	3,170 (97)	1.9 (120)	24,711 (153)	138.50 (17)	109.75 (18)	2.61 (60)	12.53 (98)	12.01 (72)	549 (55)	78 (**10**)	3.2 (71)	1.8 (101)	83 (124)	54.7 (128)
Spain A6	Madrid	504.80 (51)	39,410 (29)	78 (108)	46,776 (**3**)	32,497 (**2**)	4,794 (24)	5,523 (17)	583,082 (**10**)	14,800 (38)	2.2 (113)	90,000 (181)	29.75 (43)	130.75 (15)	3.32 (46)	42.12 (43)	60.93 (17)	1,327 (33)	60 (36)	5.3 (34)	1.5 (114)	6 (17)	78.0 (11)
Sri Lanka N5	Note B11	65.60 (122)	18,985 (50)	289 (34)	436 (104)	275 (100)	497 (64)	219 (76)	15,578 (76)	820 (156)	5.3 (25)	8,526 (127)	1.00 (104)	4.50 (90)	0.24 (162)	4.06 (142)	2.38 (114)	64 (116)	36 (112)	1.4 (136)	5.1 (24)	19 (50)	73.1 (44)
Sudan K5	Khartoum	2,505.80 (**10**)	28,993 (36)	12 (193)	39 (180)	2 (193)	n/a (–)	35 (127)	9,435 (90)	330 (194)	8.2 (**6**)	16,843 (148)	3.25 (84)	1.75 (121)	0.06 (187)	1.24 (166)	0.07 (175)	3 (186)	51 (63)	2.0 (115)	4.6 (30)	115 (138)	55.0 (127)
Surinam G5	Paramaribo	163.80 (91)	413 (169)	2.5 (212)	63 (167)	53 (143)	n/a (–)	11 (147)	730 (179)	1,763 (126)	0.8 (140)	176 (27)	1.00 (104)	1.00 (134)	2.42 (66)	18.06 (88)	9.84 (78)	281 (75)	<0.5 (211)	2.2 (66)	1.2 (139)	35 (87)	70.1 (70)
Swaziland K7	Mbabane	17.40 (157)	1,019 (153)	59 (124)	319 (120)	35 (156)	n/a (–)	45 (119)	1,379 (166)	1,350 (139)	3.0 (88)	251 (39)	0.25 (119)	0.25 (162)	0.25 (161)	3.12 (150)	1.43 (126)	51 (121)	73 (13)	2.2 (81)	2.5 (68)	90 (128)	60.2 (117)
Sweden J2	Stockholm	450.00 (56)	8,857 (83)	20 (176)	2,595 (44)	3,894 (27)	10,500 (15)	7,557 (12)	236,940 (21)	26,750 (11)	1.6 (128)	66,500 (178)	35.50 (38)	55.00 (29)	6.21 (20)	66.46 (**9**)	70.32 (**6**)	4,558 (**4**)	8 (186)	6.9 (11)	2.2 (81)	4 (**1**)	78.6 (5)
Switzerland J3	Bern	41.10 (135)	7,136 (93)	174 (55)	10,700 (17)	7,739 (11)	12,009 (13)	6,842 (14)	273,856 (18)	38,380 (**3**)	0.6 (145)	n/a (–)	16.75 P5 (58)	30.75 Q4 (45)	4.31 (28)	71.99 (**5**)	64.46 (15)	2,979 (17)	40 (101)	6.8 (13)	1.4 (123)	5 (**4**)	78.7 (**4**)
Syria K4	Damascus	185.20 (88)	15,711 (56)	85 (99)	1,386 (64)	1,360 (55)	2,299 (40)	630 (51)	15,172 (77)	970 (152)	5.7 (22)	22,435 (152)	37.75 (37)	20.25 (56)	1.29 (93)	10.35 (105)	0.17 (162)	19 (147)	75 (12)	n/a (–)	5.6 (23)	32 (81)	68.9 (84)
Taiwan P4	Taipei	36.20 (136)	21,740 (47)	601 (13)	2,411 (50)	3,571 (29)	6,559 (20)	5,635 (16)	261,532 (19)	12,030 (47)	5.5 (24)	35,000 (167)	12.25 (63)	88.00 (23)	4.05 (35)	56.80 (16)	80.31 (**2**)	2,813 (19)	30 (129)	n/a (–)	4.6 (30)	n/a (–)	n/a (–)
Tajikistan M4	Dushanbe	143.10 (94)	6,237 (97)	44 (143)	n/a (–)	n/a (–)	148 (86)	n/a (–)	1,749 (156)	280 (204)	-10.0 (177)	1,070 (60)	4.00 (81)	6.50 (83)	1.04 (106)	3.48 (145)	0.01 (188)	3 (185)	44 (82)	8.3 (**3**)	1.2 (143)	74 (118)	67.2 (101)
Tanzania K6	Dodoma	945.00 (31)	32,923 (35)	35 (154)	450 (103)	733 (67)	n/a (–)	550 (52)	8,515 (94)	260 (207)	2.8 (93)	7,603 (123)	0.50 (112)	1.25 (125)	0.04 (195)	0.49 (185)	0.51 (137)	33 (135)	44 (82)	1.3 (131)	1.3 (131)	142 (150)	47.9 (148)
Thailand O5	Bangkok	513.10 (50)	60,246 (19)	117 (79)	8651 (19)	6,695 (19)	1,686 (45)	1,843 (36)	121,051 (30)	2,010 (116)	4.7 (37)	86,172 (180)	30.00 (42)	61.75 (27)	1.02 (108)	8.57 (117)	4.39 (102)	198 (86)	42 (93)	1.6 (125)	1.6 (125)	37 (91)	68.8 (87)
Togo J5	Lomé	56.80 (125)	4,567 (114)	80 (103)	70 (161)	9 (182)	n/a (–)	3 (163)	1,398 (165)	310 (198)	2.4 (105)	1,448 (71)	0.00 (–)	0.50 (142)	0.11 (176)	0.85 (174)	0.38 (142)	33 (134)	49 (70)	1.2 (143)	2.0 (90)	144 (151)	48.8 (145)
Tonga S6	Nuku'alofa	0.75 (184)	100 (193)	133 (70)	31 (182)	201 (110)	n/a (–)	67 (110)	172 (208)	1,730 (127)	2.7 (97)	62 (–)	0.00 (–)	0.05 (194)	0.50 (136)	9.26 (111)	0.14 (165)	102 (104)	73 (13)	2.0 (90)	M (–)	33 (75)	n/a (–)
Trinidad & Tobago F5	Port of Spain	5.10 (169)	1,293 (148)	254 (43)	336 (119)	201 (110)	248 (80)	67 (110)	6,142 (106)	4,750 (77)	2.7 (97)	2,193 (79)	17.75 (56)	10.00 (72)	7.73 (15)	23.11 (76)	10.29 (76)	330 (69)	26 (139)	2.9 (79)	1.5 (114)	18 (46)	73.8 (41)
Tunisia J4	Tunis	154.50 (92)	9,457 (80)	61 (121)	4,832 (29)	1,560 (51)	1,526 (50)	239 (73)	19,757 (68)	2,090 (115)	4.6 (43)	11,078 (136)	6.25 (74)	7.25 (80)	0.77 (119)	8.99 (114)	0.58 (136)	32 (138)	52 (59)	3.0 (77)	2.0 (77)	32 (81)	69.5 (78)

*: Ranking (top 10 in **bold**). **n/a:** Not available, not relevant or not reliable. **nn:** No network. **ns:** No service. **M:** See note on page 33. **T:** See note on page 33. For more information, see the notes on pages 184 and 192.

Countries A-Z: Turkey–Zimbabwe

Country (Map Ref)	Capital	Area ('000 sq km)	Population ('000)	Pop. Density (/sq km)	Intl Arrivals ('000)	Visitor Receipts ($m)	Intl Departs ('000)	Visitor Expenditure ($m)	Gross Nat'l Income ($m)	GNI per Person ($)	GDP Growth (%)	External Debt ($m)	Energy Production (Mtoe)	Energy Consumption (Mtoe)	Energy Cons. (toe/person)	Fixed Tel. Lines (/100)	Mobile Tel. Lines (/100)	Internet Usage (/10,000)	Agricultural Land (%)	Health Spending (%)	Military Spending (%)	Infant Mortality	Life Expectancy
Turkey *K4*	Ankara	779.50 •37	64,385 •15	83 •100	6,893 •21	5,203 •22	4,758 •26	1,471 •42	186,490 •23	2,900 •100	3.8 •63	102,074 •183	27.25 •47	73.75 •24	1.15 •99	28.00 •63	24.56 •44	304 •71	52 •59	3.1 •73	4.0 •41	42 •96	69.0 •83
Turkmenistan *L4*	Ashgabat	488.10 •52	4,779 •111	10 •196	300 •122	192 •112	357 •72	125 •94	3,205 •138	670 •164	-6.8 •175	2,266 •81	28.75 •44	7.50 •78	1.57 •84	8.19 •119	0.09 •173	5 •180	66 •21	2.6 •85	4.6 •30	72 •116	65.4 •107
Turks & Caicos Is. *F4*	Cockburn Town	0.50 •192	17 •216	34 •155	121 •150	246 •104	n/a	n/a	n/a	6,875 •67	n/a	n/a	0.00 •–	0.00 •209	0.00 •208	n/a	n/a	n/a	2 •205	n/a	T	n/a	n/a
Tuvalu *R6*	Funafuti	0.02 •223	11 •220	550 •15	n/a	1 •199	n/a	n/a	12 •223	1,091 •148	4.5 •45	n/a	0.00 •–	0.00 •209	n/a	n/a	n/a	n/a	<0.5 •211	n/a	T	n/a	n/a
Uganda *K5*	Kampala	241.00 •80	21,479 •48	89 •97	205 •134	149 •118	n/a	141 •89	6,794 •101	320 •197	7.2 •12	3,935 •99	0.25 •119	0.75 •138	0.03 •197	0.26 •196	0.26 •150	12 •162	43 •88	1.8 •120	4.2 •37	134 •147	39.6 •164
Ukraine *K3*	Kyiv (Kiev)	603.70 •44	49,950 •23	83 •100	4,232 •36	3,200 •34	7,399 •19	4,482 •21	41,991 •53	840 •155	-10.7 •178	12,718 •139	87.50 •24	160.75 •13	3.22 •49	19.89 •86	1.62 •123	39 •129	73 •13	4.3 •52	3.7 •47	22 •58	68.8 •87
United Arab Emirates *L4*	Abu Dhabi	83.70 •116	2,815 •134	34 •155	2,481 •46	607 •75	n/a	n/a	41,000 •54	15,051 •37	2.9 •91	15,500 •146	156.25 •14	47.00 •32	16.70 •5	41.79 •44	58.51 •13	3,011 •15	2 •205	5.2 •37	6.9 •13	10 •34	74.9 •33
United Kingdom[A7] *I3*	London	243.50 •79	59,501 •20	244 •47	25,394 •6	20,223 •5	53,881 •4	35,631 •3	1,403,843 •5	23,590 •21	2.5 •103	84,231 [N2] •179	300.25 •6	248.00 •9	4.17 •34	56.72 •17	66.96 •12	2,577 •20	71 •17	5.7 •29	2.7 •65	6 •17	77.2 •15
United States *D3*	Washington DC	9,372.60 •4	278,230 •3	30 •164	48,491 •2	74,881 •1	58,386 •2	59,351 •1	8,879,500 •1	31,910 •14	3.3 •75	862,000 •196	1,807.00 •1	2,426.25 •1	8.72 •12	67.30 •8	40.00 •30	3,466 •11	44 •82	6.0 •23	3.3 •53	8 •28	76.6 •24
US Virgin Is. *F5*	Charlotte Amalie	0.35 •200	120 •190	343	485 •100	940 •59	n/a	n/a	1,500 •161	15,957 •35	n/a	n/a	0.00 •–	7.00 •81	58.33 •1	56.20 •18	n/a	n/a	n/a	n/a	M	n/a	67.4 •99
Uruguay *G7*	Montevideo	176.20 •90	3,313 •130	19 •182	2,073 •54	653 •73	778 •60	280 •68	20,604 •64	6,220 •71	3.8 •63	7,600 •122	1.50 •100	3.75 •96	1.13 •100	27.07 •65	9.54 •79	996 •40	84 •3	1.9 •118	1.4 •123	19 •50	73.9 •39
Uzbekistan *M3*	Tashkent	447.40 •57	24,406 •40	55 •130	272 •125	19 •169	n/a	n/a	17,613 •72	720 •163	-1.2 •156	3,162 •93	59.50 •33	47.00 •33	1.93 •73	6.58 •127	0.22 •157	3 •187	56 •48	3.8 •59	2.5 •68	58 •112	67.5 •97
Vanuatu *R6*	Port Vila	12.20 •160	193 •182	16 •182	50 •173	56 •141	11 •104	9 •148	227 •203	1,180 •145	n/a	63 •12	0.00 •–	0.02 •203	0.10 •177	3.37 •146	0.19 •161	n/a	14 •170	2.5 •96	M	49 •107	67.4 •99
Venezuela *F5*	Caracas	916.50 •33	23,707 •41	26 •169	587 •87	656 •72	891 •58	1,646 •38	87,313 •39	3,680 •87	1.7 •125	37,003 •169	217.25 •12	70.00 •25	2.95 •55	10.91 •102	14.64 •64	393 •66	25 •141	1.1 •150	2.2 •81	25 •69	72.4 •54
Vietnam *O5*	Hanoi	331.70 •65	77,515 •13	234 •49	1,782 •58	86 •130	168 •84	n/a	28,733 •61	370 •189	8.1 •7	22,359 •151	26.25 •48	14.50 •64	0.19 •165	2.68 •154	0.42 •140	13 •158	22 •153	0.4 •165	2.8 •60	42 •96	67.4 •99
Wallis & Futuna *S6*	Matu Utu	0.24 •208	15 •217	63 •119	n/a	n/a	n/a	n/a	30 •219	2,143 •113	n/a	n/a	0.00 •–	0.08 •186	0.32 •153	n/a	n/a	n/a	25 •141	n/a	T	n/a	n/a
Western Sahara *I4*	Laâyoune	252.10 •77	253 •177	1.0 •222	n/a	n/a	n/a	n/a	150 •209	545 •170	n/a	n/a	0.00 •–	n/a	n/a	n/a	n/a	n/a	19	n/a	n/a	n/a	n/a
Yemen *L5*	Sana	555.00 •48	17,048 •54	31 •160	88 •155	64 •138	n/a	83 •103	6,088 •107	360 •191	3.2 •81	4,138 •104	21.25 •52	3.50 •101	0.21 •163	1.67 •162	0.16 •163	6 •176	33 •120	1.5 •132	8.1 •9	121 •143	58.0 •122
Yugoslavia, Fed. Rep. *K3*	Belgrade	102.20 •106	10,616 •70	104 •88	152 •143	17 •172	n/a	n/a	11,932 •82	1,124 •147	n/a	14,100 •142	11.50 •64	15.25 •63	1.44 •89	21.44 •82	5.69 •93	75 •111	56	n/a	4.9 •27	25 •69	72.4 •54
Zambia *K6*	Lusaka	752.60 •38	9,881 •79	13 •189	456 •102	85 •131	n/a	59 •113	3,222 •136	330 •194	0.2 •149	6,865 •119	2.00 •93	2.50 •110	0.25 •160	0.93 •172	0.31 •147	17 •151	47 •73	2.4 •102	1.1 •142	202 •170	40.1 •163
Zimbabwe *K6*	Harare	390.70 •60	11,904 •64	30 •164	2,101 •53	202 •109	331 •75	131 •91	6,302 •104	530 •171	2.8 •104	4,716 •109	3.50 •82	5.50 •85	0.46 •138	2.07 •158	1.51 •124	17 •149	20 •158	3.1 •73	3.8 •46	89 •127	44.1 •159
Lowest rank		**•225**	**•224**	**•224**	**•197**	**•199**	**•109**	**•169**	**•225**	**•224**	**•180**	**•196**	**•119**	**•209**	**•208**	**•205**	**•188**	**•196**	**•211**	**•168**	**•165**	**•180**	**•166**

Some country names have been shortened for reasons of space. For more information on sources and dates, see the pages referred to below. Every attempt has been made to obtain the most recent reliable figures. In some cases, however, these are estimates (official or otherwise). See also the notes below, and at the top of the chart.

Countries & Capitals: pages 10-11.
Area, Population & Population Density: page 16.
Travel: pages 20-1; also the regional introductions (see Contents).
GNI, GDP Growth & External Debt: page 18.
Energy: pages 22-3.

NOTES:

A1 Hong Kong and Macau are Special Administrative Regions of China and are listed separately.
A2 Figures exclude Northern Cyprus
A3 All figures exclude overseas Départements and other dependencies listed separately here.
A4 Palestine National Autonomous Region.
A5 All figures include Madeira and the Azores.
A6 All figures include Balearic and Canary Islands.
A7 All figures exclude Channel Is. and Isle of Man
B1 La Paz (seat of government); Sucre (judicial).
B2 St Peter Port (Guernsey) & St Helier (Jersey).
B3 Yamassoukro (official); Abidjan (administrative & commercial).
B4 Basse-Terre (administrative) & Pointe-à-Pitre (commercial).
B5 Astana (Almaty until December 1998).
B6 Plymouth was largely destroyed in 1997 by volcanic eruption. A temporary administrative centre has been established at Brades.
B7 Formerly called Rangoon
B8 Amsterdam (capital); The Hague (seat of government).
B9 Jerusalem, as declared by Palestinian Authority.
B10 Pretoria (administrative), Cape Town (legislative), Bloemfontein (judicial). This arrangement is currently under review.
B11 Colombo (administrative & commercial); Sri Jayewardenepura Kotte (legislative).
C1 Includes Galápagos.
C2 Excludes the disputed territory of Jammu & Kashmir.
C3 Excludes Western Sahara.
D1 Includes Cabinda.
D2 Includes Naxçivan.
D3 Includes Galápagos.
D4 Excludes the disputed territory of Jammu & Kashmir.
D5 Includes East Timor.
D6 Includes Golan Heights and East Jerusalem.
D7 Excludes Western Sahara.
N1 Includes estimated $20 billion owed to Russia.
N2 Central government only.
P1 Includes production from the Neutral Zone.
P2 Figures included in those for Switzerland.
P3 Figures include Palau and N. Marianas Is.
P4 Figures included in those for Marshall Is.
P5 Figures include those for Liechtenstein.
Q1 Figures included in those for Switzerland.
Q2 Figures include Palau and N. Marianas Is.
Q3 Figures include Palau and N. Marianas Is.
Q4 Figures include those for Marshall Is.

Telecom & Internet: pages 28-9.
Health: page 30.
Agricultural Land: page 33.
Military: page 33.

ABBREVIATIONS:

•: Ranking (top 10 in **bold**).
n/a: Not available, not relevant or not reliable.
nn: No network.
ns: No service.
T: See note on page 33.
M: See note on page 33.

**COMPREHENSIVE INDEX
TO THE COMPLETE ATLAS**
The index lists all locations and features which
appear throughout this atlas, with the exception
of the following special-subject map pages:
- World climate
- World time
- World statistical maps
- World health risks
- World sport
- World airports*
- World flight times
- World cruising
- Europe climate
- Europe empires
- European Union
- Europe airports & high-speed rail
- Europe rail & ferries
- Europe museums & art galleries*
- UK geographical & administrative divisions
- UK railways
- London airports & connections
- The Netherlands attractions
- France attractions
- Italy attractions
- Africa climate
- Asia climate
- Asia empires
- Asia museums & art galleries*
- North America climate
- USA & Canada airports & railways
- USA & Canada museums & art galleries*
- South America climate

Maps marked * include a list of locations on the
page itself

GENERAL ABBREVIATIONS
(for Australian, Canadian and US state/province
abbreviations, see appendices)
Arch.	Archaeological
Hist.	Historic/Historical
I.	Island, Ile and equivalents
Int.	International
Is.	Islands, Iles and equivalents
Mem.	Memorial
Mon.	Monument
Mt	Mount/Mont
Mtn	Mountain/Montagne
Mtns	Mountains/Monts
Nac.	Nacional
Nat.	National
Naz.	Nazionale
Prov.	Provincial
St	Saint/Sankt/Sint

(All 'St' entries are treated as if spelt 'Saint' and
are located in the index accordingly)
Ste	Sainte
Vdkhr.	Vodokhranilishche

Countries and significant dependencies and
possessions are shown in CAPITALS

Hyphens and some accents have been
removed in certain cases for consistency and
ease of viewing. The correct form appears on
the map pages.

The following names, which appear in bold,
indicate the entry is a featured location on one
of the special subject maps:
Aborig	Aboriginal lands map (Australia)
Beach	Beach map
Dive	Diving site map
Hill Sta	Hill station map (India)
Ind Res	Indian Reservation map (USA)
Park L	Leisure/Theme park map
Park N	National Park map
Ski	Ski map
Heritage C	UNESCO cultural heritage map
Heritage N	UNESCO natural heritage map

The following abbreviations appear occasionally
to distinguish features with the same name:
[Adm]	Administrative region
[Apt]	Airport
[Riv]	River

C

W

World

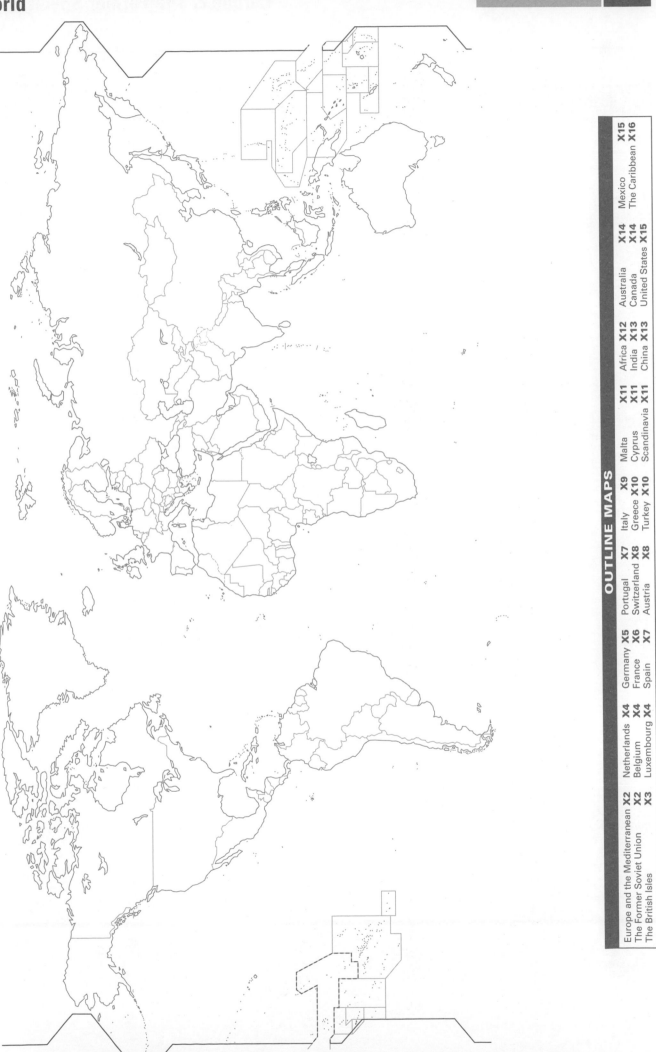

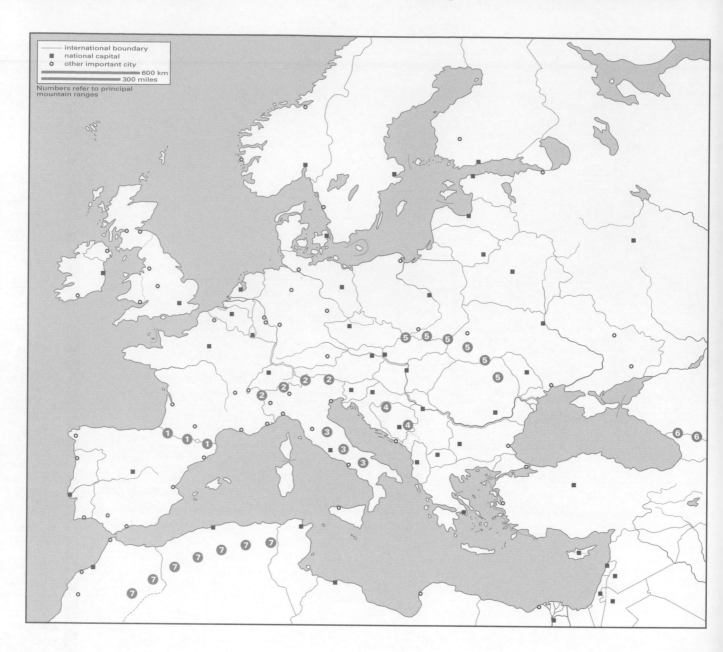

international boundary
■ national capital
○ other important city
600 km
300 miles
Numbers refer to principal
mountain ranges

international boundary
■ national capital
○ other important city

See Europe map

British Isles

- — · — international boundary
- — — — geographical county boundary (UK), regional boundary (Ireland)
- ■ national capital
- ● capital of constituent parts of UK
- ○ other important city/town

100 kilometres
50 miles

Letters refer to English Tourism Council regions

CHANNEL IS.

Benelux

international boundary
provincial boundary
■ national capital
● provincial capital
○ other important city/town
80 km
40 miles

international boundary
provincial boundary
■ national capital
● provincial capital
○ other important city/town
80 km
40 miles

Germany

international boundary
Land boundary
■ national capital
● Land capital
○ other important city/town
100 km
50 miles

France

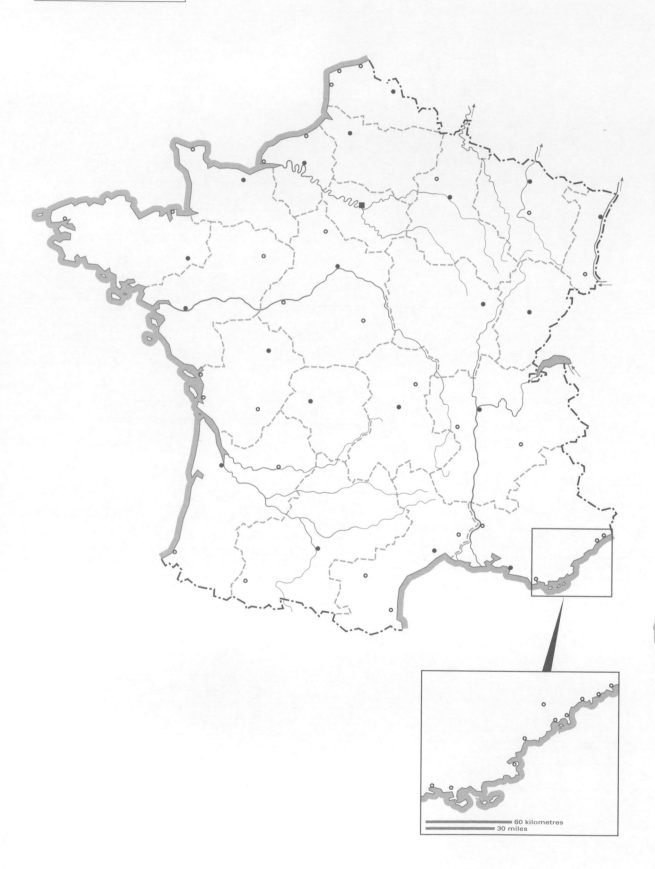

60 kilometres
30 miles

Iberia

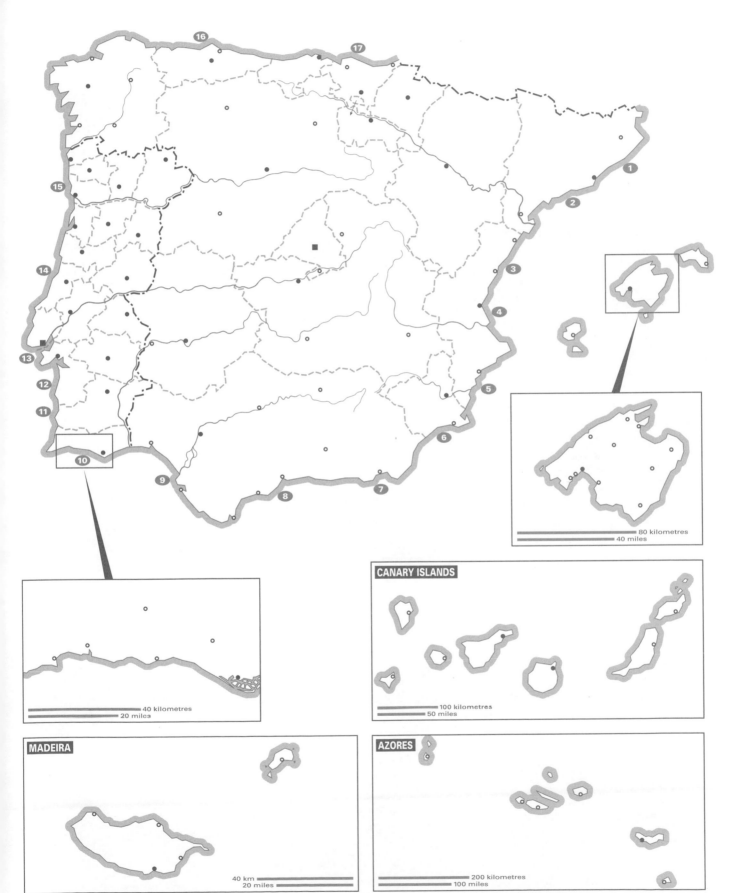

80 kilometres
40 miles

40 kilometres
20 miles

CANARY ISLANDS

100 kilometres
50 miles

MADEIRA

40 km
20 miles

AZORES

200 kilometres
100 miles

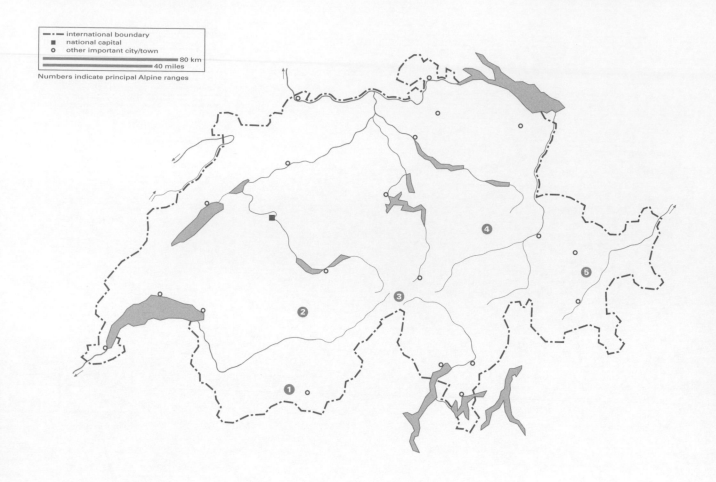

Italy

international boundary
regional boundary
■ national capital
● regional capital
○ other important city/town

200 km
100 miles

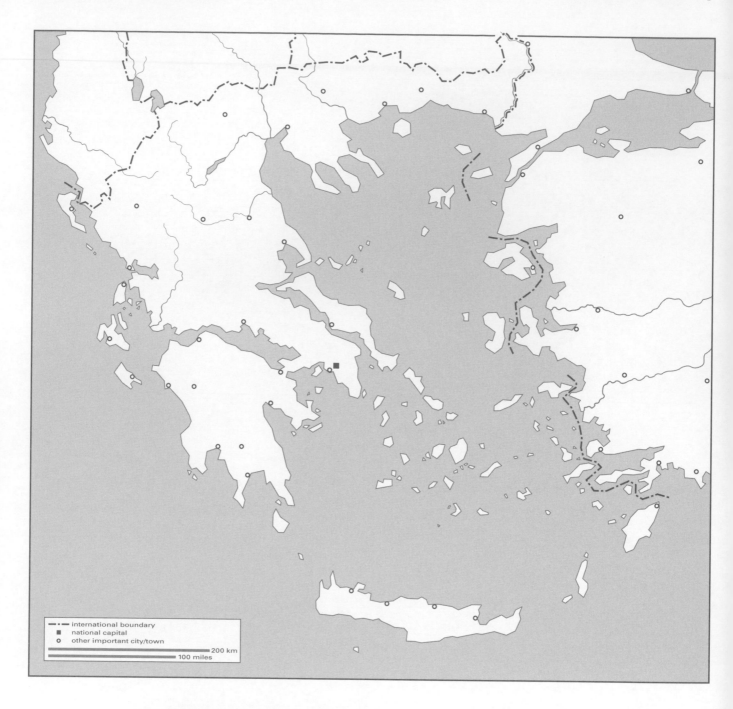

- –·–·– international boundary
- ■ national capital
- ○ other important city/town

200 km
100 miles

- –·–·– international boundary
- ■ national capital
- ○ other important city/town

400 km
200 miles

Scandinavia, Malta & Cyprus

- –·–·– international boundary
- – – – regional boundary
- ■ national capital
- ○ other important city/town

400 km
200 miles

- ■ national capital
- ○ other important town

10 km
5 miles

- ■ national capital
- ○ other important town

60 km
30 miles

Africa

international boundary
■ national capital
○ other important city

-·-·- international boundary
----- provincial boundary
■ national capital
● provincial capital
○ other important city/town
600 km
300 miles

India & China

international boundary
state/union territory boundary
■ national capital
● state capital
○ other important city/town
800 km
400 miles

international boundary
province/autonomous region boundary
■ national capital
● province/autonomous region capital
○ other important city/town
1000 km
500 miles

Canada & Australia

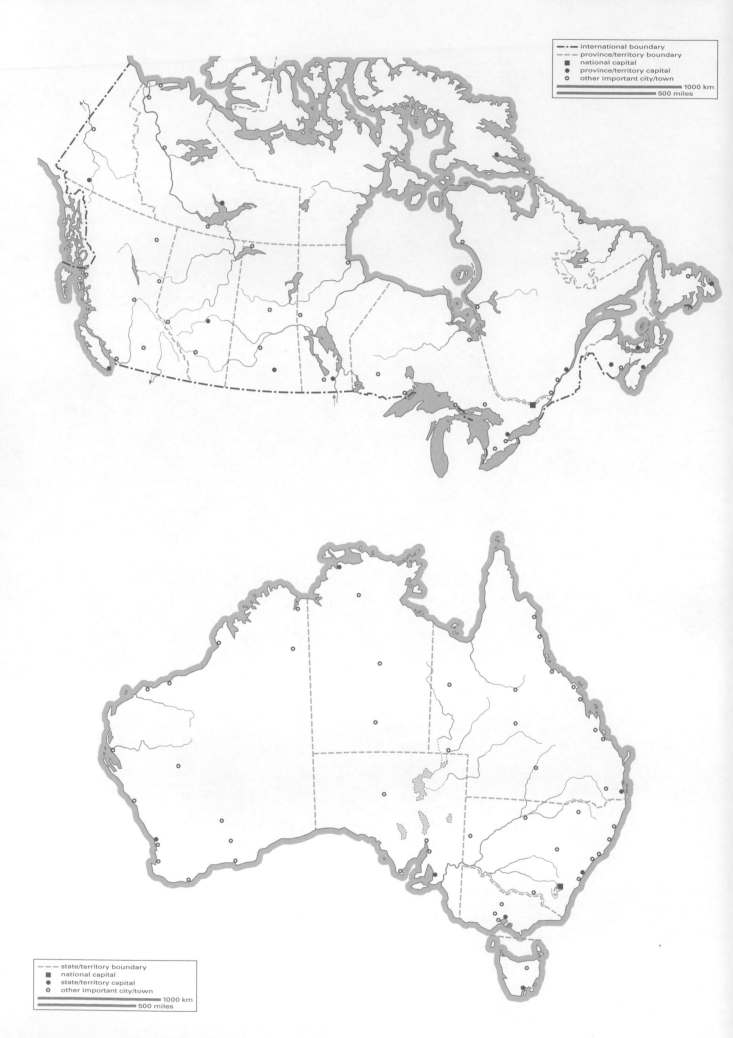

international boundary
province/territory boundary
■ national capital
● province/territory capital
○ other important city/town
1000 km
500 miles

state/territory boundary
■ national capital
● state/territory capital
○ other important city/town
1000 km
500 miles

United States of America & Mexico

international boundary
state boundary
■ national capital
● state capital
○ other important city/town
800 km
400 miles

1000 km
500 miles

300 km
150 miles

international boundary
state boundary
■ national capital
● state capital
○ other important city/town
500 km
250 miles

The Caribbean

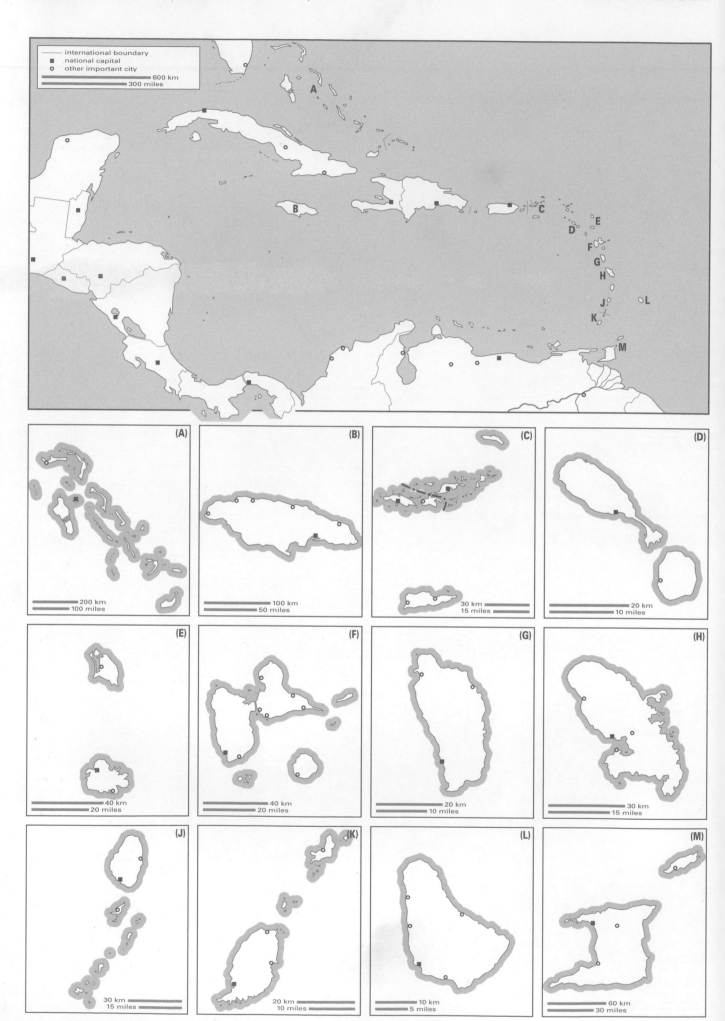

- —— international boundary
- ■ national capital
- ○ other important city

600 km
300 miles

(A) 200 km / 100 miles

(B) 100 km / 50 miles

(C) 30 km / 15 miles

(D) 20 km / 10 miles

(E) 40 km / 20 miles

(F) 40 km / 20 miles

(G) 20 km / 10 miles

(H) 30 km / 15 miles

(J) 30 km / 15 miles

(K) 20 km / 10 miles

(L) 10 km / 5 miles

(M) 60 km / 30 miles